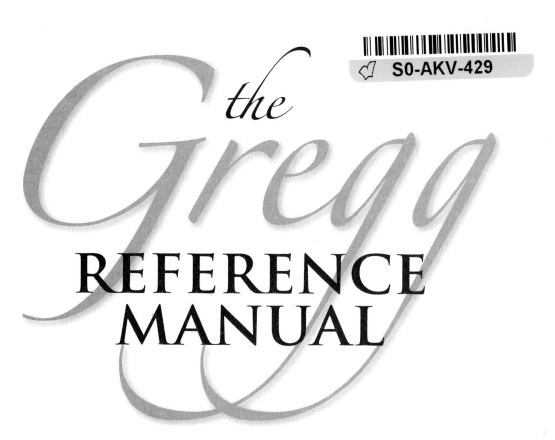

the

REFERENCE MANUAL

SEVENTH CANADIAN EDITION

William A. Sabin

Wilma K. Millar

Sharon L. Sine

G. Wendy Strashok
Southern Alberta Institute of Technology

 **McGraw-Hill
Ryerson**

Toronto Montréal Boston Burr Ridge, IL Dubuque, IA Madison, WI
New York San Francisco St. Louis Bangkok Bogotá Caracas
Kuala Lumpur Lisbon London Madrid Mexico City Milan
New Delhi Santiago Seoul Singapore Sydney Taipei

The Gregg Reference Manual
Seventh Canadian Edition

ISBN-13: 978-0-07-087737-5
ISBN-10: 0-07-087737-8

2 3 4 5 6 7 8 9 10   TRI   0 9 8

Care has been taken to trace ownership of copyright material contained in this text; however, the publisher will welcome any information that enables them to rectify any reference or credit for subsequent editions.

Executive Editor: James Buchanan
Sponsoring Editor: Karen Noxon
Developmental Editor: Christine Gilbert
Marketing Manager: Marc Trudel
Senior Supervising Editor: Margaret Henderson
Copy Editor: Freya Godard
Senior Production Coordinator: Jennifer Wilkie
Composition: Bill Renaud
Cover Design: Dave Murphy/Valid Design & Layout
Printer: Trigraphic

Library and Archives Canada Cataloguing in Publication

The Gregg Reference Manual / William A. Sabin . . . [et al.]. — 7th Canadian ed.

ISBN 0-07-087737-8

1. English language—Business English. 2. English language—Grammar. 3. Commercial correspondence. I. Sabin, William A.

PE1116.S6G3 2006   808'.06665   C2005-907013-7

To the memory of our colleague and friend,
this edition is dedicated to

Sharon Lee Sine
1944–2005

CONTENTS

Part 2   Techniques and Formats

Part 3   References

PREFACE

For some fifty years, *The Gregg Reference Manual* has served as the primary reference for business professionals who are looking for guidance on matters of style, grammar, usage, and formatting. It has gained the reputation of being one of the best style manuals for anyone who writes, edits, and prepares printed material. In these pages the rules of grammar, the correct use of words, and the most attractive style of document formats are all explained from a Canadian perspective.

Why is this reference manual prefixed by the name *Gregg*? John Robert Gregg, inventor of the Gregg shorthand system, founded the Gregg Publishing Company in 1893. By the time McGraw-Hill acquired the publishing company in 1948, the name *Gregg* had come to stand for the highest quality of educational materials, and it is for this reason that *The Gregg Reference Manual* continues to bear the *Gregg* name.

Features of the New Edition

This Seventh Canadian Edition, adapted from William A. Sabin's Tenth U.S. Edition, consists of 20 sections divided into three parts.

Part One (Sections 1–11) continues to highlight the basic rules of grammar and usage, to illustrate the principals with an abundance of varied examples, and to provide comprehensive coverage of punctuation, capitalization, numbers, abbreviations, plurals, possessives, spelling, compound words, and word division.

- With very few exceptions, the spelling of all words referred to is that found in *The Canadian Oxford Dictionary*, published by Oxford University Press.
- An extensive addition to the grammar section now includes details of writing mechanics and business writing styles.
- Examples have been updated and refined where necessary.

Part Two (Sections 12–17) begins by emphasizing the importance of good proofreading and editing in order to produce faultless documents and by offering guidelines for creating and formatting all kinds of written communications—e-mail messages, letters, memos, reports, bibliographies, outlines, tables, minutes, agendas, itineraries, and employment communications, including scannable and traditional résumés as well as one-page résumés suitable for young people entering the workforce.

- Detailed coverage of e-mail is expanded and is now part of the section on letters and memos.
- Procedures to follow for cross-referencing files are discussed and illustrated in the section on alphabetic filing.

- Guidelines for constructing footnotes, endnotes, textnotes, and bibliographic entries have been expanded to include online source materials, such as books, magazines, journals, newspapers, e-mail messages, interviews, speeches, documents from the Internet, and other electronic sources.
- Suggestions are given to help overcome problems with word processing templates and software default settings when more attractive documents are desired.
- Basic guidelines (of particular interest to students) are discussed for avoiding plagiarism and for observing precautions to take in citing electronic materials.

Part Three (Sections 18–20) provides a complete list of model forms of address, a glossary of grammatical terms, and an updated glossary of computer and Internet terms.

Student Supplements

Online Learning Centre (OLC): This powerful electronic learning aid, located at www.mcgrawhill.ca/college/sabin, contains essays of different points of view, Web links, and much more. **Premium Content** is available as an optional package with the text. Those who purchase Premium Content will have access to the **Student Self-Study Workbook** on the OLC.

Self-Study Workbook: Available as Premium Content on the OLC is the self-study *Workbook and Answer Key*, which provides a means of survival for new students of English, for high school graduates with only a minimal knowledge of basic grammar, for educators, and for professionals who still insist on high standards for their documents. The workbook consists of a set of worksheets, which focus mainly on the basic rules covered in Sections 1–11. Each worksheet directs the user to the relevant rules in a section; the answers are found in a key at the back of the workbook. These worksheets help familiarize students with the problems they will encounter in written material and increase their ability to readily find in the manual the solutions to their problems.

Acknowledgments. We would like to acknowledge and extend our thanks to Linda Gardner, Angela McCormick, Joan Newman, Peggy Noble, and Pat Squibb of the Administrative Information Management Program at the Southern Alberta Institute of Technology, and to the Rev. Dr. J.P. Dowling, O.M.I.

We would like to acknowledge the able assistance of the staff at McGraw-Hill Ryerson Limited—Karen Noxon, Sponsoring Editor; Christine Gilbert, Developmental Editor; Margaret Henderson, Senior Supervising Editor; and Freya Godard, Copy Editor.

Our warm thanks as well to our reviewers and colleagues who corrected our copy, offered helpful suggestions and constructive criticism, and authenticated the content of this edition: Margaret MacFarlane, Seneca College; Diane Blaney, Capilano College; Merlyn Gamble, Algonquin College; Ann Korenic, St. Clair College; Jean Mills, Mount Saint Vincent University; Carolyn Whittaker, Centennial College; Nancy Barry, Georgian College; Vivian Lee, Durham College; Cynthia MacDermid, Nova Scotia Community College; and Louise Winterstein, Centennial College.

Wilma Millar
Wendy Strashok

HOW TO LOOK THINGS UP

Suppose you were writing to someone in another department:

> May I please get an advance copy of your confidential report [You hesitate. Should this sentence end with a period or a question mark?]

A common problem in written communication is finding an answer quickly. In this manual there are several ways to proceed.

Using the Index. At the back of this manual is a detailed index. Any of the following entries will solve the problem sentence above:

Period, 101–109	Question mark, 110–118	Request, punctuation
. . .	. . .	of, 103, 127c
with requests, 103	with requests, 103, 113	

In each entry, the **boldface number** refers to the proper rule, ¶103. (If you look up ¶103, you will find that a question mark is the right punctuation for the sentence in question.)

Most index entries show specific rule numbers. In a few cases, however, references may be to page numbers, and these are shown in lightface type. Suppose you were confronted with this problem:

> If you compare the performance records of Catano, Harris, and Williams, you won't find much difference *(between/among)* them.

The index will show the following entries:

> *among-between,* 284   **OR**   *between-among,* 286

(The rule on page 286 indicates that *between* is correct in this situation.)

Using a Fast-Skim Approach. If you have little patience with detailed indexes and would rather skim through the pages to find what you are looking for, then several features of this manual may be helpful:

- The table of contents lists each major subject.
- At the start of each section except the glossaries, you will find a detailed list of all the topics covered in that section. This list will help you quickly find the rule or rules that pertain to your problem. Suppose the following problem came up:

> The point is that new *Federal* [or is it *federal*?] legislation is needed.

The table of contents shows that Section 3 is about capitalization. Skimming the list of topics reveals *Names of Government Bodies* (¶¶325–330). Within that set of rules ¶328 states that *federal* is the proper form.

Cross-references, which could prove helpful, have also been provided throughout the manual. Some take this form: *See* ¶324; others may read *See also* ¶324. The form *See* ¶324 means that ¶324 contains significant information that adds to or qualifies the rule you are currently reading; the word *See* suggests that you really ought to pursue the cross-reference before making a decision. The form *See also* ¶324 carries a good deal less urgency. It means that you will find some additional examples in ¶324 and perhaps a restatement of the rule. It suggests that you don't have to pursue the cross-reference if you don't want to—but it couldn't hurt.

Playing the Numbers. There is still a third way to find the answer to a specific problem. You will observe that each rule number has a section number as a prefix. Section 3 (on capitalization) has a "300" series of rules; Section 4 (on number style) has a "400" series; and so on. Once you become familiar with the section numbers and the section titles, you can find your way around quite easily.

A familiarity with the section numbers and section titles can also save you time when you are using the index. If an index entry lists several different paragraph numbers, you can often guess what the paragraphs will deal with. For example, if you want to know whether to write *5 kg* or *5 kgs* on a purchase order, you might encounter the following entry in the index:

measurements, 4401b, 429–432, 535–538, 620b

If you know that Section 6 deals with plurals, you will try ¶620 first. (The answer you are looking for is *5 kg.*)

Looking Up Specific Words. Many of the problems that arise deal with specific words. For this reason the index has as many entries for such words as space will permit. For example, in the following sentence, should *therefore* be set off by commas or not?

It is(,) *therefore*(,) essential that operations be curtailed.

A check of the index will show the following entry:

therefore, **122, 138–142, 178**

(The rules in ¶141 will tell you that no commas should be used in this sentence.)

If you ask the same question about another specific word and do not find it listed as a separate entry in the index, you should check the index under "Comma" and investigate the most promising references or scan the comma rules in Section 1 until you find the answer you are looking for.

If you are having difficulty with words that look alike and sound alike—*gibe* and *jibe* or *advice* and *advise*—turn directly to ¶719. For other troublesome words and phrases, consult Section 11.

the
Gregg
REFERENCE
MANUAL

PART ONE

Grammar, Usage, and Style

SECTION ONE

Punctuation: Major Marks

THE PERIOD (¶¶101–109)

At the End of a Statement or Command (¶¶101–102)
At the End of a Polite Request or Command (¶103)
At the End of an Indirect Question (¶104)
With Decimal Fractions (¶105)
In Outlines and Displayed Lists (¶¶106–107)
With Headings (¶108)
A Few Don'ts (¶109)

THE QUESTION MARK (¶¶110–118)

To Indicate Direct Questions (¶¶110–113)
To Indicate Questions Within Sentences (¶¶114–117)
To Express Doubt (¶118)

THE EXCLAMATION POINT (¶¶119–121)

To Express Strong Feeling (¶¶119–120)
With *Oh* and *O* (¶121)

THE COMMA (¶¶122–175)

Basic Rules for Commas That Set Off (¶122)
Basic Rules for Commas That Separate (¶¶123–125)
With Clauses in Compound Sentences (¶¶126–129)
With Clauses in Complex Sentences (¶¶130–132)
   Introductory Dependent Clauses (¶130)
   Dependent Clauses Elsewhere in the Sentence (¶¶131–132)
With Clauses in Compound-Complex Sentences (¶¶133–134)
With Participial, Infinitive, and Prepositional Phrases (¶¶135–137)
   Introductory Phrases (¶135)
   Phrases at the Beginning of a Clause (¶136)
   Phrases Elsewhere in the Sentence (¶137)
With Transitional Expressions and Independent Comments (¶¶138–143)
   At the Beginning of a Sentence (¶139)
   At the End of a Sentence (¶140)
   Within the Sentence (¶141)
   At the Beginning of a Clause (¶142)
   With the Adverb *Too* (¶143)

3

Punctuation marks are the mechanical means for making the meaning of a sentence easily understood. They indicate the proper relationships between words, phrases, and clauses when word order alone is not sufficient to make these relationships clear.

One important caution about punctuation. If you find it particularly hard to decide on the right punctuation for a sentence you have written, the chances are that the sentence is improperly constructed. To be on the safe side, recast your thought in a form you can handle with confidence. Do not try to save a badly constructed sentence by means of punctuation.

Section 1 deals with the three marks of terminal punctuation (the period, the question mark, and the exclamation point) plus the three major marks of internal punctuation (the comma, the semicolon, and the colon). All other marks of punctuation are covered in Section 2.

For the number of spaces to leave either before or after a punctuation mark in keyed copy, refer to the chart in ¶298.

THE PERIOD
At the End of a Statement or Command

101 Use a period to mark the end of a sentence that makes a statement or expresses a command.

> Nunavut was established as a new Canadian territory in 1999.
>
> I question the need to cut advertising and promotion expenses at this time.
>
> All monthly expense reports must be in by the 10th of the following month.
>
> Make sure that Kate gets to the airport by 10 a.m. (The period that marks the end of the abbreviation also serves to mark the end of the sentence.)

102 Use a period to mark the end of an *elliptical* (condensed) expression that represents a complete statement or command. Elliptical expressions often occur as answers to questions or as transitional phrases.

> Yes.   No.   Of course.   Indeed.   By all means.
> Enough on that subject.   Now, to proceed to your next point.

NOTE: Do not confuse elliptical expressions with sentence fragments. An elliptical expression *represents* a complete sentence. A sentence fragment is a word, phrase, or clause that is incorrectly treated as a separate sentence when it ought to be incorporated with adjacent words to make up a complete sentence.

> Great news! The laser printer arrived. After we had waited for six weeks. (*Great news* is an elliptical expression; it represents a complete sentence, *I have great news. After we had waited for six weeks* is a sentence fragment, incorrectly treated as a sentence in its own right; this dependent clause should be linked with the main clause that precedes it.)
>
> **REVISED:** Great news! The laser printer arrived after we had waited for six weeks.

At the End of a Polite Request or Command

103 **a.** Requests, suggestions, and commands are often phrased as questions out of politeness. Use a period to end this kind of sentence if you expect your reader to respond *by acting* rather than by giving you a yes-or-no answer.

> Will you please call us at once if we can be of further help.
>
> Would you please send all bills to my bank for payment while I'm away.
>
> May I suggest that you put your request in writing and send it to Mr. Ludwar.
>
> If you can't attend the meeting, could you please send someone else.

NOTE: Use a period only when you are sure that your reader is not likely to consider your request presumptuous.

1

b. If you are asking a favour or making a request that your reader may be unable or unwilling to grant, use a question mark at the end of the sentence. The question mark offers your reader a chance to say no to your request and helps to preserve the politeness of the situation.

May I ask a favour of you? Could you spare fifteen minutes to tell my son about career opportunities in your company?

Will you be able to have someone in your department help me on the Hibernia project?

Will you please handle the production reports for me on Monday?

c. If you are not sure whether to use a question mark or a period, reword the sentence so that it is clearly a question or a statement; then punctuate accordingly. For example, the sentence directly above could be revised as follows:

Would you be willing to handle the production reports for me on Monday?

I would appreciate your handling the production reports for me on Monday.

d. When you are addressing a request to someone who reports to you, you expect that person to comply. Therefore, a period can properly be used to punctuate such requests. However, since most people prefer to be *asked* to do something rather than be *told* to do it, a question mark establishes a nicer tone and often gets better results. Consider using a question mark when your request to a subordinate involves something beyond the routine aspects of the job.

Will you please let me know what your vacation plans are for the month of August. (Routine request to a subordinate.)

May I ask that you avoid scheduling any vacation time during August this year? I will need your help in preparing next year's forecasts and budgets. (Special request to a subordinate. The question mark suggests that the writer is sensitive to the problems this request could cause.)

NOTE: If you are unwilling to give your subordinate the impression that your request allows for a yes-or-no answer, simply drop the attempt at politeness and issue a straightforward command.

I must ask that you not schedule any vacation time during August this year. I will need your help in preparing next year's forecasts and budgets.

At the End of an Indirect Question

104   Use a period to mark the end of an *indirect* question. (See also ¶¶115–116.)

Jean LeBlanc has asked whether an exception can be made for him.

The only question she asked was when the report had to be on your desk.

Why Janet Murray left the company so quickly has never been explained.

I would like to question if migraines are linked to diabetes.

With Decimal Fractions

105 Use a period (without a space before or after it) to separate a whole number from a decimal fraction: for example, *$5.50, 33.33 percent.*

In Outlines and Displayed Lists

106 Use periods after numbers or letters that enumerate items in an outline or a displayed list—unless the numbers or letters are enclosed in parentheses. Set a tab to give an adequate visual break between the numbers or letters and the items that follow on the same line. (See also ¶¶107, 199c, 223, 1344d, 1425e, 1718, 1719 for examples.)

107 **a.** Use periods after independent clauses, dependent clauses, or long phrases that are displayed on separate lines in a list. Also use periods after short phrases that are essential to the grammatical completeness of the statement introducing the list. (In the following example, the three listed items are all objects of the preposition *on* in the introductory statement.)

Please get me year-end figures *on:*   **OR**   Please get me year-end figures *on:*

a. Domestic sales revenues.   • Domestic sales revenues.
b. Total operating costs.   • Total operating costs.
c. Net operating income.   • Net operating income.

NOTE: Avoid the following treatment of displayed lists, which uses semicolons and the words *and* or *or.*

You will profit from inquiries   You will profit from inquiries
through: through:

1. An 800 number;   • An 800 number;
2. A reader service card; and   • A reader service card; or
3. A fax-on-demand service.   • A fax-on-demand service.

b. No periods are needed after short phrases in a list if the introductory statement is grammatically complete (as in the first example below) or if the items are like those on an inventory sheet or a shopping list.

The computers in this price range offer the following features:

• 512-MB DDR RAM
• 80-GB hard drive
• Wireless capability

When you come to take the qualifying examination, please bring three things:

2 HB pencils
1 ballpoint pen

☞ *See ¶1425f for formatting enumerated items in a list.*
See ¶301e for the capitalization of items displayed in a list or an outline.
See ¶¶189 and 191c for the use of a colon in a list.

With Headings

108 **a.** Use a period after a *paragraph* heading (one that begins a paragraph and is immediately followed by text matter on the same line) unless some other mark of punctuation, such as a question mark, is required.

> **Insuring Your Car.** Automobile insurance is actually a package of six different types of coverage. . . .

> **How Much Will It Cost?** How much automobile insurance will cost you depends on your driving record, your age, and how much shopping around you do. . . .

b. Omit the period if the heading is *free-standing* (displayed on a line by itself). However, retain a question mark or an exclamation point with a freestanding head if the wording requires it.

DEBT INVESTMENTS

Traded Debt Investments

> **Advantages and Limitations.** Traded debt investments can be purchased for a variety of fixed-term periods depending upon the specific investment. This allows you to . . .

> **Are They Risky?** These investments are generally fully liquid because you can sell them to another investor . . .

NOTE: A period follows a run-in expression like *Table 6*, even though the heading as a whole is free-standing.

Table 6. SALARY RANGES   Figure 2–4. DEPARTMENTAL STAFF

☞ *For the treatment of headings in reports and manuscripts, see ¶1426.*
For the treatment of headings in tables, see ¶¶1619–1621.
For spacing with periods, see ¶298.

A Few Don'ts

109 Don't use a period:

a. After letters used to designate persons or things (for example, *Manager A, Class B, Grade C, Brand X*). **EXCEPTION:** Use a period when the letter is the initial of a person's name (for example, *Mr. A.* for *Mr. Adams*).

b. After contractions (for example, *cont'd;* see ¶505).

c. After ordinals expressed in figures (*1st, 2nd, 3rd, 4th*).

d. After Roman numerals (for example, *Volume I, Elizabeth II*).

> **EXCEPTION:** Periods follow Roman numerals in an outline. (See ¶¶223, 1718–1719.)

☞ *Periods with abbreviations: see ¶¶506–513, 515.*
Periods with brackets: see ¶296.
Periods with dashes: see ¶¶213, 214a, 215a.
Periods with parentheses: see ¶¶224a, 224b, 226c.
Periods with quotation marks: see ¶¶247, 252, 253, 257, 258, 259.

Three spaced periods (ellipsis marks): see ¶¶274–280, 292.
Spacing with periods: see ¶298.

THE QUESTION MARK
To Indicate Direct Questions

110 **a.** Use a question mark at the end of a direct question. (For guidelines on spacing, see ¶298.)

> Will you be able to meet with us after 5 p.m.?
>
> Either way, how can we lose?

NOTE: Be sure to place the question mark at the *end* of the question.

> How do you account for this entry: "Paid to E. M. Johnson, \$300"?
> (**NOT:** How do you account for this entry? "Paid to E. M. Johnson, \$300.")

☞ *For the punctuation of indirect questions, see ¶¶104, 115, 116.*
For the punctuation of questions with quotations, see ¶249.

  b. Use a question mark (or, for special emphasis, an exclamation point) after a *rhetorical question*, a question to which no reply is expected. (See also ¶119b.)

> Who wouldn't snap up an opportunity like that?
>
> Wouldn't you rather be stuck in the sands of Florida this winter than in the snow-drifts of Manitoba?
>
> Isn't it incredible that people could fall for a scheme like that? (**OR** !)

NOTE: If the first clause of a compound sentence is a rhetorical question and the second clause is a statement, use a period to end the sentence.

> Why don't you look at the attached list of tasks, and then let's discuss which ones you would like to take on.

111 **a.** Use a question mark at the end of an *elliptical* (condensed) *question*, that is, a word or phrase that represents a complete question.

> Marion tells me that you are coming to the Okanagan. When? (The complete question is, "When are you coming?")

NOTE: When a single word like *how*, *when*, or *why* is woven into the flow of a sentence, capitalization and special punctuation are not usually required.

> The questions we need to address at our next board meeting are not *why* or *whether* but *how* and *when*.

  b. Punctuate complete and elliptical questions separately, according to your meaning.

> When will the job be finished? In a week or two?
> (**NOT:** When will the job be finished in a week or two?)
>
> Where shall we meet? At the airport? (With this punctuation, the writer allows for the possibility of meeting elsewhere.)

(Continued on page 10.)

Where shall we meet at the airport? (With this punctuation, the writer simply wants to pinpoint a more precise location within the airport.)

112 Use a question mark at the end of a sentence that is phrased like a statement but spoken with the rising intonation of a question.

You expect me to believe this story?   He still intends to proceed?

113 A request, suggestion, or command phrased as a question out of politeness may not require a question mark. (See ¶103.)

To Indicate Questions Within Sentences

114 When a short direct question falls *within a sentence*, set the question off with commas and put a question mark at the end of the sentence. However, when a short direct question falls *at the end of a sentence*, use a comma before it and a question mark after.

I can alter the terms of my will, *can't I*, whenever I wish?

We aren't obligated to attend the meeting, *are we?*

NOTE: Short questions falling within a sentence may also be set off with dashes or parentheses in place of commas. (See ¶¶214b, 224c.)

115 When a longer direct question comes *at the end of a sentence*, it starts with a capital letter and is preceded by a comma or a colon. If the introductory material is an independent clause, use a colon. The question mark that ends the question also serves to mark the end of the sentence.

NOTE: In the examples below and in ¶116 notice how a simple shift in word order converts a direct question to an indirect question. When the verb precedes the subject (*shall we, can we*), the question is direct. When the verb follows the subject (*we shall, we can*), the question is indirect and requires no punctuation or capitalization.

The key question is, Whom *shall we* nominate for next year's election? election? (A direct question.)

This is the key question: Whom *shall we* nominate for next year's election? (A direct question.)

BUT: We now come to the key question of whom *we shall* nominate for next year's election. (An indirect question.)

OR: We now come to the key question of whom to nominate for next year's election. (An indirect question.)

116 When a longer direct question comes *at the beginning of a sentence*, it should be followed by a question mark (for emphasis) or simply a comma.

How *can we* achieve these goals? is the next question. (A direct question.)

OR: How *can we* achieve these goals, is the next question. (A direct question.)

BUT: How *we can* achieve these goals is the next question. (See ¶115 note.)

117 **a.** A series of brief questions at the end of a sentence may be separated by commas or (for emphasis) by question marks. Do not capitalize the individual questions.

Who will be responsible for drafting the proposal, obtaining comments from all the interested parties, preparing the final version, and coordinating the distribution of copies? (As punctuated, this sentence implies that one person may be asked to perform all these tasks.)

OR: Who will be responsible for drafting the proposal? obtaining comments from all the interested parties? preparing the final version? coordinating the distribution of copies? (As punctuated, this sentence implies that a number of people may be asked to perform one or more of these tasks.)

☞ *See ¶298 for spacing after a question mark within a sentence.*

b. The brief questions in ¶117a are all related to the same subject and predicate (*Who will be responsible for*). Do not confuse this type of sentence pattern with a series of independent questions. Each independent question starts with a capital letter and ends with a question mark.

Before you accept the job offer, think about the following: Will this job give you experience relevant to your real career goal? Will it permit you to keep abreast of the latest technology? Will it pay what you need?

c. Independent questions in a series are often elliptical (condensed) expressions. (See ¶111.)

Has Walter's loan been approved? *When? By whom? For what amount?* (In other words: *When* was the loan approved? *By whom* was the loan approved? *For what amount* was the loan approved?)

(**NOT:** Has Walter's loan been approved, when, by whom, and for what amount?)

To Express Doubt

118 A question mark enclosed in parentheses may be used to express doubt or uncertainty about a word or phrase within a sentence. (See ¶298 for the spacing guidelines of parentheses.)

He joined the firm after his graduation in 2005 (?) from Osgoode Hall.

NOTE: When dates are already enclosed within parentheses, question marks may be inserted as necessary to indicate doubt.

the explorer John Cabot (1455?–1498?)

☞ *Question marks with dashes: see ¶¶214b, 215a.*
Question marks with parentheses: see ¶¶224a, 224c, 226c.
Question marks with quotation marks: see ¶¶249, 252, 254, 257, 258, 259, 261b–c.
Spacing with question marks: see ¶¶298, 1433c.

THE EXCLAMATION POINT

The exclamation point is an emotional mark of punctuation that is most often found in sales and advertising copy. Like the word *very*, it loses its force when overused, so avoid it wherever possible.

To Express Strong Feeling

119 a. Use an exclamation point at the end of a sentence (or an elliptical expression that stands for a sentence) to indicate enthusiasm, surprise, disbelief, urgency, or strong feeling. (Refer to ¶298 and ¶1433c for guidelines on spacing after an exclamation point.)

> Yes! We're selling our entire inventory below cost! Doors open at 9 a.m.!
>
> No! I don't believe it!   What a fantastic achievement!   Incredible!

b. An exclamation point may be used in place of a question mark to express strong feeling. (See also ¶110b.)

> How could you do it! What made you think I'd welcome a call at 2:30 a.m.!

c. The exclamation point may be enclosed in parentheses and placed directly after a word that the writer wants to emphasize.

> We won exclusive(!) distribution rights in the Western Hemisphere.

120 a. A single word may be followed by an exclamation point to express intense feeling. The sentence that follows it is punctuated as usual.

> Congratulations! Your summation at the trial was superb.

b. When such words are repeated for emphasis, an exclamation point follows each repetition.

> Going! Going! Our bargains are almost gone!

c. When exclamations are mild, a comma or a period is sufficient.

> Well, well, things could be worse.   No. I won't accept those conditions.

With *Oh* and *O*

121 The exclamation *oh* may be followed by either an exclamation point or a comma, depending on the emphasis desired. It is capitalized only when it starts a sentence. The capitalized *O*, the sign of direct address, is not usually followed by any punctuation.

> Oh! I didn't expect that!   Oh, what's the use?   O Lord, help me!

☞ *Exclamation point with dashes: see ¶¶214b, 215a.*
Exclamation point with parentheses: see ¶¶224a, 224c, 226c.
Exclamation point with quotation marks: see ¶¶249, 252, 254, 257, 258, 259, 261.
Spacing with exclamation points: see ¶¶298, 1433c.

THE COMMA

The comma has two primary functions: it *sets off* non-essential expressions that interrupt the flow of thought from subject to verb to object or complement, and it *separates* elements within a sentence to clarify their relationship to one another. **Two commas** are needed **to set off**, but only a **single comma** is needed **to separate**.

The following paragraphs (¶¶122–125) present an overview of the rules governing the use of the comma. For a more detailed treatment of the specific rules, see ¶¶126–175.

Basic Rules for Commas That Set Off

122 Use commas to set off *non-essential expressions*—words, phrases, and clauses that are not necessary for the meaning or the structural completeness of the sentence.

> **IMPORTANT NOTE:** In many sentences you can tell whether an expression is non-essential or essential by trying to omit the expression. If you can leave it out without affecting the meaning or the structural completeness of the sentence, the expression is non-essential and should be set off by commas.

> > **NON-ESSENTIAL:** Let's get the advice of Tony Bocale, *who has in-depth experience with all types of personal computers.*
> > **ESSENTIAL:** Let's get the advice of someone *who has in-depth experience with all types of personal computers.* (Without the *who* clause, the meaning of the sentence would be incomplete.)

> > **NON-ESSENTIAL:** There is, *no doubt,* a reasonable explanation for his behaviour at the board meeting.
> > **ESSENTIAL:** There is *no doubt* about her honesty. (Without *no doubt,* the structure of the sentence would be incomplete.)

However, in other sentences the only way you can tell whether an expression is non-essential or essential is by the way you would say it aloud. If your voice tends to *drop* as you utter the expression, it is non-essential; if your voice tends to *rise,* the expression is essential.

> > **NON-ESSENTIAL:** Finch and Chan would prefer, *therefore,* to limit the term of the agreement to two years.
> > **ESSENTIAL:** Finch and Chan would *therefore* prefer to limit the term of the agreement to two years.

☞ *For additional examples, see ¶141, note.*

a. Interrupting Elements. Use commas to set off words, phrases, and clauses when they break the flow of a sentence from subject to verb to object or complement. (See also ¶¶144–147.)

> We can deliver the car on your husband's birthday or, *if you wish,* on the Saturday before. (When this sentence is read aloud, notice how the voice drops on the non-essential expression *if you wish.*)

> They have sufficient assets, *don't they,* to cover these losses?

> Let's take advantage of the special price and order, *say,* 200 reams this quarter instead of our usual quantity of 75.

> Marie LaPierre, *rather than Guy desRosiers,* has been appointed head of the Longueuil office.

> **BUT:** Maria LaPierre has been appointed head of the Longueuil office *rather than Guy desRosiers.* (This phrase is not set off when it does not interrupt.)

b. Afterthoughts. Use commas to set off words, phrases, or clauses loosely added onto the end of a sentence. (See also ¶144.)

(Continued on page 14.)

1

Send us your cheque as soon as you can, *please.*

Grant promised to share expenses with us, *if I remember correctly.*

It is not too late to place an order, *is it?*

c. **Transitional Expressions and Independent Comments.** Use commas to set off transitional expressions (like *however, therefore, on the other hand*) and independent comments (like *obviously, in my opinion, of course*) when they interrupt the flow of the sentence. Do not set these elements off, however, when they are used to emphasize the meaning; the voice goes up in such cases. In the examples that follow, consider how the voice drops when the expression is non-essential and how it rises when the expression is essential. (See also ¶¶138–143.)

NON-ESSENTIAL: We are determined, *nevertheless,* to finish on schedule.
ESSENTIAL: We are *nevertheless* determined to finish on schedule.

NON-ESSENTIAL: It is, *of course,* your prerogative to change your mind. (Here the voice rises on *is* and drops on *of course.*)
ESSENTIAL: It is *of course* your prerogative to change your mind. (Here the voice rises on *of course.*)

d. **Descriptive Expressions.** When descriptive expressions *follow* the words they refer to and provide additional but non-essential information, use commas to set them off. (See also ¶¶148–153.)

NON-ESSENTIAL: His most recent article, "How to Make a Profit With High-Tech Investments," appeared in the June 1 issue of *Forbes.* (*His most recent* indicates which article is meant; the title gives additional but non-essential information.)
ESSENTIAL: The article "How to Make a Profit With High-Tech Investments" appeared in the June 1 issue of *Forbes.* (Here the title is needed to indicate which article is meant.)

NON-ESSENTIAL: Thank you for your letter of April 12, in which you questioned our discount terms. (The date indicates which letter; the *in which* clause gives additional information. See also ¶152.)
ESSENTIAL: Thank you for your letter in which you questioned our discount terms. (Here the *in which* clause is needed to indicate which letter is meant.)

e. **Dates.** Use commas to set off the year in complete dates (for example, Sunday, May 1, 2006, . . .). (See also ¶¶154–155.)

f. **Names.** Use commas to set off abbreviations that follow a person's name (Julie Merkin, *CPS,* announces the opening . . .) and to set off names of provinces or countries following city names (Hull, *Quebec,* will host . . .). In personal and company names, the trend is not to set off elements like *Jr., Sr., III, Inc.,* or *Ltd.* (for example, *Guy Tracy Jr.* and *ATCO Ltd.*); however, individual preferences should be respected when known. (See also ¶¶156–161.)

Basic Rules for Commas That Separate

123 Use a single comma:

a. To separate the two main clauses in a compound sentence when they are joined by *and, but, or,* or *nor,* and occasionally *for, so,* or *yet.* (See also ¶¶126–129.)

We can't accept the marketing restrictions you proposed, *yet* we think there is some basis for a mutually acceptable understanding.

b. To separate three or more items in a series—unless all the items are joined by *and* or *or*. (See also **¶¶**162–167.)

It takes time, effort, *and* a good deal of money.

BUT: It takes time *and* effort *and* a good deal of money.

c. To separate two or more adjectives that both modify the same noun. (See also **¶¶**168–171.)

We need to mount an *exciting, hard-hitting* ad campaign.

d. To separate the digits of numbers into groups of thousands where the readability of numbers in documents is required. (See **¶**413b.)

Sales projections for the Southern Region next year range between $900,000 and $1,000,000.

e. To indicate the omission of key words or to clarify meaning when the word order is unusual. (See also **¶¶**172–175.)

Half the purchase price is due on delivery of the goods; the balance, in three months. (The comma here signifies the omission of *is due*.)

What will happen, we don't know. (The comma here helps the reader cope with the unusual word order; it separates the object, *What will happen*, from the subject, *we*, which follows.)

124 Use a single comma after *introductory elements*—items that begin a sentence and come before the subject and verb of the main clause.

Yes, we can deliver your new printer by Wednesday. (Introductory word.)

Taking all the arguments into consideration, we have decided to modernize these facilities rather than close them down. (Introductory participial phrase.)

To determine the proper mix of ingredients for a particular situation, see the table on page 141. (Introductory infinitive phrase.)

Before we can make a final decision, we will need to run another cost-profit analysis. (Introductory dependent clause.)

a. Use a comma after an *introductory request or command*.

Look, we've been through tougher situations before.

You see, the previous campaigns never did pan out.

Please remember, all expense reports must be on my desk by Friday.

BUT: *Please remember that* all . . . (When *that* is added, *remember* becomes the main verb and is no longer part of an introductory element.)

b. Commas are used after introductory elements and phrases when they function as:

- *Transitional expressions* (such as *well, therefore, however, for example, in the first place*). These express a transition in meaning from the previous sentence.

  In the first place, they don't have sufficient capital.
  Consequently, we will have to cancel the agreement.

(Continued on page 16.)

- *Independent comments* (such as in *my opinion, by all means, obviously, of course*). These express the writer's attitude toward the meaning of the sentence. (See also ¶¶138–143.)

  In my opinion, we ought to look for another candidate.
  Obviously, the request will have to be referred elsewhere.

c. Commas are not needed after *ordinary introductory adverbs* or *introductory prepositional phrases* that answer such questions as:

WHEN:	tomorrow, yesterday, recently, early next week, in the morning, soon, in five years, in 2004
HOW OFTEN:	occasionally, often, frequently, once in a while
WHERE:	here, in this case, at the meeting
WHY:	for that reason, because of this situation

In the morning things may look better. (Short prepositional phrase telling *when*; no comma needed.)

Recently we had a request for school enrolment trends. (Introductory adverb telling *when*; no comma needed.)

125 Separating commas are often improperly used. In the following examples, the diagonals indicate points at which single commas *should not* be used.

a. Do not separate a subject and its verb.

The person she plans to hire for the job/ is Peter Crotty.

Whether profits can be improved this year/ depends on several key variables. (Noun clause as subject.)

b. Do not separate a verb and its object or complement.

The test mailing *has not produced/ the results* we were hoping for. (Verb and object.)

Ms. Lau *will be/ the company's* new director of marketing. (Verb and complement.)

The equipment *is/ easy to operate, inexpensive to maintain, and built to give reliable service for many years.* (Verb and complement.)

Rebecca Hingham *said/ that the research data would be on your desk by Monday morning.* (Noun clause as object.)

c. Do not separate an adjective from a noun that follows it.

The project requires a highly motivated, research-oriented, cost-conscious/manager.

d. Do not separate a noun and a prepositional phrase that follows.

The board of directors/ of the La Flamme Corporation will announce its decision this Friday.

BUT: The board of directors, *of necessity,* must turn down the merger at this time. (Use *two* commas to set off an interrupting expression.)

e. Do not separate a coordinating conjunction (*and, but, or,* or *nor,* and occasionally *for, so,* or *yet*) and the following word.

You can read the draft of the division's medium-range plan now *or/ when* you get home tonight.

1

BUT: You can read the draft of the division's medium-range plan now or, *if you prefer,* when you get home tonight. (Use *two* commas to set off an interrupting expression.)

f. Do not separate *two* words or phrases that are joined by a coordinating conjunction.

The letters on the Gray case/ and *those concerning Mr. Pendleton* should be shown to Mrs. Almquist. (Two subjects.)

I *have read Ms. Popov's capital spending proposal*/ and *find it well done.* (Two predicates. See also ¶127.)

We hope *that you will visit our store soon*/ and *that you will find the styles you like.* (Two noun clauses serving as objects of the verb *hope.*)

The CEO plans *to visit the Western Region*/ and *call personally on the large accounts that have stopped doing business with us.* (Two infinitive phrases serving as objects of the verb *plans.*)

He may go on to graduate school at *McGill*/ or *Dalhousie.* (Two objects of the preposition *at.*)

BUT: *Frank Albano will handle the tickets,* and *Edna Hahn will be responsible for publicity.* (A comma separates two independent clauses joined by a coordinating conjunction. See ¶126.)

NOTE: When the main verb in a sentence is followed by two long phrases or clauses that are joined by a coordinating conjunction, the sentence loses clarity without any punctuation between the two elements. Rather than inserting a comma before the conjunction, convert the second element into a separate sentence.

CONFUSING: We hope you will visit the new store that we plan to open in the Westmount Mall early next month and that you will find styles you like when you browse through our greatly expanded selection of clothes. (Resist the temptation to insert a comma before *and* in an effort to make the sentence clearer.)

BETTER: We hope you will visit the new store that we plan to open in the Westmount Mall early next month. Moreover, we hope you will find styles you like when you browse through our greatly expanded selection of clothes.

The following rules (¶¶126–137) deal with the punctuation of clauses and phrases in sentences.

With Clauses in Compound Sentences

126 a. When a compound sentence consists of *two* independent clauses joined by a coordinating conjunction (*and, but, or,* or *nor,* and sometimes *for, so,* or *yet*), place a separating comma before the conjunction. (See ¶129.)

Mrs. Fenster noticed a small discrepancy in the figures, *and* on that basis she began to reanalyze the data.

BUT: Mrs. Fenster noticed a small discrepancy in the figures *and* on that basis began to reanalyze the data. (See ¶127a–b.)

Show this proposal to Mr. Florio, *and* ask him for his reaction. (See ¶127c.)

Either we step up our promotion efforts, *or* we must be content with our existing share of the market.

(Continued on page 18.)

1

Not only were we the developers of this process, *but* we were the first to apply it to the field of pollution control.

b. For special effect the comma before the coordinating conjunction can be replaced by a period, a question mark, or an exclamation point. The coordinating conjunction is then capitalized, and the second independent clause becomes a separate sentence. However, this treatment, if overused, quickly loses its effectiveness. (See Section 11 for a usage note on *and*.)

Is it self-confidence that makes you successful? Or is it success that makes you self-confident?

I told Callahan that we would not reorder from his company unless he cuts his prices by 20 percent. And he did.

c. When a compound sentence consists of *three* or more independent clauses, punctuate this series like any other series. (See also ¶162.)

Bob can deal with the caterer, Nora can handle publicity, and Bev and I can take care of the rest.

127 Do not confuse a *compound sentence* with a simple sentence containing a *compound predicate*.

a. A *compound sentence* contains at least two independent clauses, and each clause contains a subject and a predicate.

Barbara *just got her master's,* and *she is now looking for a job in sales.*

b. A sentence may contain one subject with a *compound predicate,* that is, two predicates connected by a coordinating conjunction. In such sentences no comma separates the two predicates.

Barbara *just got her master's* and *is now looking for a job in sales.* (When *she* is omitted from the example in *a* above, the sentence becomes a simple sentence with a compound predicate.)

Ogilvey not only *wants a higher discount* but also *demands faster turnarounds on his orders.* (Compound predicate; no comma before *but*.)

BUT: *Ogilvey not only wants a higher discount,* but *he also demands faster turnarounds on his orders.* (Compound sentence; comma before *but*.)

c. When one or both verbs are requests or commands and the subject is not expressed, treat the sentence as a compound sentence and use a comma between the clauses.

Please look at the brochure I have enclosed, and then *get* back to me if you have additional questions.

You may not be able to get away right now, but *do plan* to stay with us whenever you find the time.

Call Ellen Chen sometime next week, and *ask* her whether she will speak at our conference next fall.

BUT: *Call* Ellen Chen and *ask* her whether she will speak at our conference next fall. (Omit the comma if the first clause is short. See ¶129.)

d. When non-essential elements precede the second part of a *compound predicate*, they are treated as interrupting expressions and are set off by two commas. When these same expressions precede the second clause of a *compound sentence*, they are treated as introductory expressions and are followed by one comma.

> We can bill you on our customary terms or, *if you prefer*, offer you our new deferred payment plan. (Interrupting expression requires two commas.)

> We can bill you on our customary terms, or *if you prefer*, we can offer you our new deferred payment plan. (Introductory expression requires one comma.)

> Frank Harrison went into the boardroom and, *without consulting his notes*, proceeded to give the directors precise details about our financial situation. (Interrupting expression.)

> Frank Harrrison went into the boardroom, and *without consulting his notes*, he proceeded to give the directors precise details about our financial situation. (Introductory expression.)

☞ *See also* ¶¶*131c, 136a, 142.*

128 Do not use a comma between two independent clauses that are not joined by a coordinating conjunction (*and, but, or,* or *nor,* and occasionally *for, so,* or *yet*). This error of punctuation is known as a *comma splice* and produces a *run-on sentence*. Use a semicolon, a colon, or a dash (whichever is appropriate), or start a new sentence. (See ¶¶176, 187, 204–205.)

> **WRONG:** Please review these spreadsheets quickly, I need them back tomorrow.

> **RIGHT:** Please review these spreadsheets quickly; I need them back tomorrow.

> **RIGHT:** Please review these spreadsheets quickly. I need them back tomorrow.

129 If either clause of a compound sentence is short, the comma may be omitted before the conjunction.

> *Their prices are low* and *their service is efficient.*

> *Please initial these forms* and *return them by Monday.*

> *Consider leasing* and see whether it costs less in the long run than buying.

> Consider whether leasing costs more than buying and *then decide.*

> **NOTE:** Make sure that the omission of a comma does not lead to confusion.

> **CLEAR:** *Please don't litter,* and *recycle whenever possible.*

> **CONFUSING:** *Please don't litter* and *recycle whenever possible.* (Without a comma after *litter,* the sentence could seem to be saying, ". . . and please don't recycle whenever possible.")

With Clauses in Complex Sentences

A complex sentence contains one independent clause and one or more dependent clauses. *After, although, as, because, before, if, since, unless, when,* and *while* are among the words most frequently used to introduce dependent clauses. (See ¶132 for a longer list.)

(Continued on page 20.)

130 INTRODUCTORY DEPENDENT CLAUSES

a. When a dependent clause *precedes* the independent clause, separate the clauses with a comma.

Before we can make a decision, we must have all the facts.

When you read the Cameron study, look at Appendix 2 first.

If they had invested more carefully, they could have avoided bankruptcy.

After we have studied all aspects of the complaint, <u>we will make</u> a recommendation.

BUT: *Only after we have studied all aspects of the complaint* <u>will we make</u> a recommendation. (No comma follows the introductory clause when the word order in the main clause is abnormal. Compare the abnormal *will we make* with the normal *we will make* in the preceding example.)

b. Be sure you can recognize an introductory dependent clause, even if some of the essential words are omitted from the clause. (Such constructions are known as *elliptical clauses.*)

Whenever possible, he leaves his office by six. (Whenever *it is* possible, . . .)

If so, I will call you tomorrow. (If *that is* so, . . .)

Should you be late, just call to let me know. (*If* you should be late, . . .)

c. Use a comma after an introductory clause when it serves as the *object* of a sentence (but not when it serves as the *subject*).

Whomever you nominate, I will support. (Introductory clause as object.)

Whomever you nominate will have my support. (Introductory clause as subject.)

That the department must be reorganized, I no longer question. (Introductory clause as object.)

That the department must be reorganized is no longer questioned. (Introductory clause as subject.)

d. Sentences with dependent clauses are often introduced by an expression such as *he said that, she believes that,* or *they know that.*

Liz believes that *before we can make a decision,* we must have all the facts. (A separating comma follows the dependent clause, just as if the sentence began with the word *Before.* No comma precedes the dependent clause because it is considered introductory, not interrupting.)

I think that *when you read the Nagano study,* you will gain a new perspective on the situation.

Harry says that *whenever possible,* he leaves his office by six.

BUT: He said that, *as you may already know,* he was planning to take early retirement. (Two commas are needed to set off an interrupting dependent clause. See also ¶131c.)

131 DEPENDENT CLAUSES ELSEWHERE IN THE SENTENCE

When a dependent clause follows the main clause or falls within the main clause, commas are used or omitted depending on whether the dependent clause is essential (restrictive) or non-essential (non-restrictive).

a. An *essential* clause is necessary to the meaning of the sentence. Because it *cannot be omitted*, it should not be set off by commas.

> The person *who used to be Nova's operations manager* is now doing the same job for Gucci Brothers. (Tells which person.)
>
> The Pennington bid arrived *after we had made our decision.* (Tells when.)
>
> Damato's suggestion *that we submit the issue to arbitration* may be the only sensible alternative. (Tells which of Damato's suggestions is meant.)
>
> Mrs. Foy said *that she would send us an advance program.* (Tells what was said.)

b. A non-essential clause provides additional descriptive or explanatory detail. Because it *can be omitted* without changing the meaning of the sentence, it should be set off by commas.

> George Pedersen, *who used to be Nova's operations manager,* is now doing the same job for Gucci Brothers. (The name indicates which person; the *who* clause simply gives additional information.)
>
> The Pennington bid arrived on Tuesday, *after we had made our decision.* (*Tuesday* tells when; the *after* clause simply adds information.)
>
> Damato's latest suggestion, *that we submit the issue to arbitration,* may be the only sensible alternative. (*Latest* tells which suggestion is meant; the *that* clause is not essential.)

c. A dependent clause not at the beginning of a sentence must always be set off by commas when it *interrupts* the flow of the sentence.

> We can review the wording of the announcement over lunch or, *if your time is short,* over the telephone.
>
> Please tell us when you plan to be in town and, *if possible,* where you will be staying. (The complete dependent clause is *if it is possible.*)
>
> Senator Jones, *when offered the chance to refute his opponent's charges,* said he would respond at a time of his own choosing.
>
> Mrs. Kourakis is the type of person who, *when you need help badly,* will be the first to volunteer.
>
> If, *when you have weighed the alternatives,* you choose one of the models that cost over $500, we can arrange special credit terms for you.
>
> **BUT:** He said that *if we choose one of the models that cost over $500,* his firm can arrange special credit terms for us. (See ¶130d for dependent clauses following *he said that, she knows that,* and similar expressions.)

132 The following list presents the words and phrases most commonly used to introduce dependent clauses. For most of these expressions, two sentences are given: one containing an essential clause and one a non-essential clause. In a few cases, only one type of clause is possible. If you cannot decide whether a clause is essential or non-essential (and therefore whether commas are required or not), compare it with the related sentences that follow.

> **After.** ESSENTIAL: His faxed response came *after you left last evening.* (Tells when.) NON-ESSENTIAL: His faxed response came this morning, *after the decision had been made.* (The phrase *this morning* clearly tells when; the *after* clause provides additional but non-essential information.)

(Continued on page 22.)

All of which. ALWAYS NON-ESSENTIAL: The rumours, *all of which were unfounded,* brought about his defeat in the last election.

Although, even though, and **though.** ALWAYS NON-ESSENTIAL: She has typed her letter of resignation, *although I do not believe she will submit it.*

As. ESSENTIAL: The results of the mailing are *as you predicted they would be.*
NON-ESSENTIAL: The results of the mailing are disappointing, *as you predicted they would be.* (See Section 11 for a usage note on *as.*)

As . . . as. ALWAYS ESSENTIAL: He talked *as* persuasively at the meeting *as* he did over the telephone. (See Section 11 for a usage note on *as . . . as.*)

As if and **as though.** ESSENTIAL: She drove *as if* (or *as though*) *the road were a minefield.* (The *as if* clause tells how she drove. See ¶1042.)
NON-ESSENTIAL: She drove cautiously, *as if* (or *as though*) *the road were a minefield.* (The adverb *cautiously* tells how she drove; the *as if* clause provides additional but non-essential information.)

As soon as. ESSENTIAL: We will fill your order *as soon as we receive new stock.*
NON-ESSENTIAL: We will fill your order next week, *as soon as we receive new stock.*

At, by, for, in, and **to which.** ESSENTIAL: I went to the floor *to which I had been directed.*
NON-ESSENTIAL: I went to the tenth floor, *to which I had been directed.*

Because. *Essential* or *non-essential,* depending on closeness of relation.
ESSENTIAL: She left *because she had another appointment.* (Here the reason expressed by the *because* clause is essential to complete the meaning.)
NON-ESSENTIAL: I need to have two copies of the final report by 5:30 tomorrow, *because I am leaving for Toronto on a 7:30 flight.* (Here the meaning of the main clause is complete; the reason expressed in the *because* clause offers additional but non-essential information.)

NOTE: See how the use or omission of a comma in the following sentences affects the meaning: I'm not taking that course of action, *because I distrust Harry's recommendations.* **BUT:** I'm not taking that course of action *because I distrust Harry's recommendations.* I based my decision on another reason altogether.

Before. ESSENTIAL: The shipment was sent *before your letter was received.*
NON-ESSENTIAL: The shipment was sent on Tuesday, *before your letter was received.* (*Tuesday* tells when the shipment was sent; the *before* clause provides additional but non-essential information.)

Even though. See *Although.*

For. ALWAYS NON-ESSENTIAL: Jim needs to raise money quickly, *for his tuition bill has to be paid by next Friday.* (A comma should always precede *for* as a conjunction to prevent misreading *for* as a preposition.)

If. ESSENTIAL: Let us hear from you *if you are interested.*
NON-ESSENTIAL: She promised to write from Toronto, *if I remember correctly.* (Clause added loosely.)

In order that. *Essential* or *non-essential,* depending on closeness of relation.
ESSENTIAL: Please notify your instructor promptly *in order that a make-up examination may be scheduled.*

NON-ESSENTIAL: Please notify your instructor if you will be unable to attend the examination on Friday, *in order that a make-up examination may be scheduled.*

No matter what (why, how, etc.). ALWAYS NON-ESSENTIAL: The order cannot be ready by Monday, *no matter what the store manager says.*

None of which. ALWAYS NON-ESSENTIAL: We received five boxes of samples, *none of which are in good condition.*

None of whom. ALWAYS NON-ESSENTIAL: We have interviewed ten applicants, *none of whom were satisfactory.*

Not so . . . as. ALWAYS ESSENTIAL: The second copy was *not so* clear *as* the first one. (See Section 11 for a usage note on *not so . . . as.*)

Since. ESSENTIAL: We have taken no applications *since we received your memo.* NON-ESSENTIAL: We are taking no more applications, *since our lists are now closed.* (Clause of reason.)

So that. *Essential* or *non-essential*, depending on closeness of relation. ESSENTIAL: Examine all shipments *so that any damage may be detected promptly.* NON-ESSENTIAL: Examine all shipments as soon as they arrive, *so that any damage may be detected promptly.*

So . . . that. ALWAYS ESSENTIAL: The costs ran *so* high *that we could not make a profit.*

Some of whom. ALWAYS NON-ESSENTIAL: The agency has sent us five applicants, *some of whom seem promising.*

Than. ALWAYS ESSENTIAL: The employees seem to be more disturbed by the rumour *than they care to admit.*

That. When used as a relative pronoun, *that* refers to things; it also refers to persons when a class or type is meant. ALWAYS ESSENTIAL: Here is a picture of the plane *that I own.* She is the candidate *that I prefer.* (See also ¶1062.) When used as a subordinating conjunction, *that* links the dependent clause it introduces with the main clause. ALWAYS ESSENTIAL: We know *that we will have to make concessions in the upcoming talks.* (See Section 11 for a usage note on *that.*)

Though. See *Although.*

Unless. ESSENTIAL: This product line will be discontinued *unless customers begin to show an interest in it.* NON-ESSENTIAL: I plan to work on the Delta proposal all through the weekend, *unless Cindy comes into town.* (Clause added loosely as an afterthought.)

Until. ALWAYS ESSENTIAL: I will continue to work *until my children are out of school.*

When. ESSENTIAL: The changeover will be made *when Mr. Ruiz returns from his vacation.* NON-ESSENTIAL: The changeover will be made next Monday, *when Mr. Ruiz returns from his vacation.* (*Monday* tells when; the *when* clause provides additional but non-essential information.)

(Continued on page 24.)

1

Where. ESSENTIAL: I plan to visit the town *where I used to live.*
NON-ESSENTIAL: I plan to stop off in London, *where I used to live.*

Whereas. ALWAYS NON-ESSENTIAL: The figures for last year cover urban areas only, *whereas those for this year include rural areas as well.* (Clause of contrast.)

Which. Use *which* (rather than *who*) when referring to animals, things, and ideas. Always use *which* (instead of *that*) to introduce non-essential clauses: The revised report, *which was done by Mark,* is very impressive. *Which* may also be used to introduce essential clauses. (See ¶1062c.)

While. ESSENTIAL: The union has decided not to strike *while negotiations are still going on.* (Here *while* means "during the time that.")
NON-ESSENTIAL: The workers at the Apex Company have struck, *while those at the Powers Company are still at work.* (Here *while* means "whereas.")

Who. ESSENTIAL: All students *who are members of the Backpackers Club* will be leaving for Banff on Friday.
NON-ESSENTIAL: John Behnke, *who is a member of the Backpackers Club,* will be leading a group on a weekend trip to Banff.

Whom. ESSENTIAL: This package is for the friend *whom I am visiting.*
NON-ESSENTIAL: This package is for my cousin Amy, *whom I am visiting.*

Whose. ESSENTIAL: The prize was awarded to the employee *whose suggestion yielded the greatest cost savings.*
NON-ESSENTIAL: The prize was awarded to Joyce Bruno, *whose suggestion yielded the greatest cost savings.*

With Clauses in Compound-Complex Sentences

133 A compound-complex sentence consists of two or more independent clauses (joined by *and, but, or,* or *nor,* and sometimes *for, so,* or *yet*) and one or more dependent clauses. To punctuate a sentence of this kind, first place a separating comma before the conjunction that joins the two main parts. Then consider each half of the sentence alone and provide additional punctuation as necessary.

> The computer terminals were not delivered until June 12, five weeks after the promised delivery date, and *when I wrote to complain to your sales manager,* it took another three weeks simply for him to acknowledge my letter. (No comma precedes *when* because the *when* clause is considered an introductory expression, not an interrupting expression. See also ¶127d.)

> Jeff Adler, the CEO of Marshfield & Duxbury, is eager to discuss a joint venture with my boss, *who is off on a six-week trip to the Far East,* but the earliest date I see open for such a meeting is Wednesday, October 30.

NOTE: If a misreading is likely or a stronger break is desired, use a semi-colon rather than a comma to separate the two main clauses. (See ¶177.)

134 a. When a sentence starts with a dependent clause or an introductory phrase that applies to both independent clauses that follow, do not use a comma to separate the independent clauses. (A comma would make the introductory dependent element seem to apply only to the first independent clause.)

Before you start to look for new capital, you need to prepare an analysis of the market *and* you must make a detailed set of financial projections. (The *before* clause applies equally to the two independent clauses that follow; hence no comma before *and*.)

BUT: Before you start to look for new capital, you need to prepare an analysis of the market, *but* don't think that's all there is to it. (The *before* clause applies only to the first independent clause; hence a comma is used before *but*.)

To get the best results, follow the directions exactly as shown *and* do not use any parts not provided by the manufacturer. (The introductory infinitive phrase applies equally to the two independent clauses that follow; hence there is no comma before *and*.)

b. When an introductory element is followed by two independent clauses that are rather long, omitting punctuation between the two clauses could reduce the clarity of the sentence. Insert a period or a semicolon after the first independent clause and introduce the second independent clause with a transitional expression.

To get the best results, follow the directions exactly as shown on the warranty and the bill of sale and do not use any parts not provided by the manufacturer.

BETTER: To get the best results, follow the directions exactly as shown on the warranty and the bill of sale. Moreover, do not use any parts not provided by the manufacturer.

With Participial, Infinitive, and Prepositional Phrases*

135 INTRODUCTORY PHRASES

a. Use a comma after an *introductory participial phrase.*

Seizing the opportunity, I presented an overview of our medium-range plans.

Established in 1905, our company takes great pride in its reputation for high-quality products and excellent service.

Having checked the statements myself, I feel confident that they are accurate.

NOTE: Watch out for phrases that look like introductory participial phrases but actually serve as the subject of the sentence or part of the predicate. Do not put a comma after these elements.

Looking for examples of good acknowledgement letters in our files has taken me longer than I had hoped. (Gerund phrase as subject.)

BUT: *Looking for examples of good acknowledgement letters in our files,* I found four that you can use. (Participial phrase used as an introductory element; the subject is *I*.)

Following Mrs. Forest's speech was a presentation by Ms. Paley. (With normal word order, the sentence would read, "A presentation by Ms. Paley was *following Mrs. Forest's speech."* The introductory phrase is actually part of the predicate; the subject is *a presentation by Ms. Paley.*)

BUT: *Following Mrs. Forest's speech,* Ms. Paley made her presentation. (Participial phrase used as an introductory element; the subject is *Ms. Paley.*)

(Continued on page 26.)

* See Section 19 for definitions of grammatical terms.

1

b. Use a comma after an *introductory infinitive phrase* unless the phrase is the subject of the sentence. (Infinitive phrases are introduced by *to*.)

To get the best results from your dishwasher, follow the printed directions. (The subject *you* is understood.)

To have displayed the goods more effectively, he should have consulted a lighting specialist. (The subject is *he*.)

BUT: *To have displayed the goods more effectively* would have required a lighting specialist. (Infinitive phrase used as subject.)

c. As a general rule, use a comma after all *introductory prepositional phrases*. A comma may be omitted after a *short* prepositional phrase if

- The phrase does not contain a verb.
- The phrase is not a transitional expression or an independent comment.
- There is no sacrifice in clarity or desired emphasis.

In response to the many requests of our customers, we are opening a branch in Hanover Square. (Comma required after a long phrase.)

In 2004 our entire inventory was destroyed by fire. (No comma required after a short phrase.)

BUT: *In 2004*, 384 cases of potential lung infections were reported. (Comma required to separate two numbers. See ¶456.)

In preparing your report, be sure to include last year's figures. (Comma required after a short phrase containing a verb.)

In addition, an 8 percent sales tax must be imposed. (Comma required after a short phrase used as a transitional expression. See ¶¶138a, 139.)

In my opinion, your ads are misleading as they now appear. (Comma required after short phrase used as an independent comment. See ¶¶138b, 139.)

In legal documents, amounts of money are often expressed both in words and in figures. (Comma used to give desired emphasis to the introductory phrase.)

CONFUSING: After all you have gone through a great deal.

CLEAR: *After all*, you have gone through a great deal. (Comma required after a short phrase to prevent misreading.)

NOTE: Omit the comma after an introductory prepositional phrase if the word order in the rest of the sentence is inverted.

Out of an initial investment of $5 000 came a stake that is worth over $2 500 000. (Normal word order: A stake that is worth over $2 500 000 came out of an initial investment of $5 000.)

In an article I read in <u>Maclean's</u> was an account of his trip. (Omit the comma after the introductory phrase when the verb in the main clause immediately follows.)

BUT: *In an article I read in* <u>Maclean's</u>, there was an account . . .

d. When a compound sentence starts with a phrase that applies to both independent clauses, do not use a comma to separate the two clauses if doing so would make the introductory phrase seem to apply only to the first clause. (See also ¶134.)

In response to the many requests of our customers, we are opening a branch in Hanover Square and we are extending our evening hours in all our stores.

136 PHRASES AT THE BEGINNING OF A CLAUSE

a. When a participial, infinitive, or prepositional phrase occurs *at the beginning of a clause within the sentence,* insert or omit the comma following, just as if the phrase were an introductory element at the beginning of the sentence. (See ¶135.)

I was invited to attend the monthly planning meeting last week, and *seizing the opportunity,* I presented an overview of our medium-range plans. (A separating comma follows the participial phrase just as if the sentence began with the word *Seizing.* No comma precedes the phrase because the phrase is considered introductory, not interrupting. See also ¶127d.)

The salesclerk explained that *to get the best results from your dishwasher,* you should follow the printed directions.

We would like to announce that *in response to the many requests by our customers,* we are opening a branch in the Bayview Centre.

Last year we had a number of thefts, and *in 2004* our entire inventory was destroyed by fire. (No comma is needed after a short introductory prepositional phrase.)

b. If the phrase interrupts the flow of the sentence, set it off with two commas.

Pamela is the type of person who, *in the midst of disaster,* will always find something to laugh about.

If, *in the attempt to push matters to a resolution,* you offer that group new terms, they will simply dig in their heels and refuse to bargain.

137 PHRASES ELSEWHERE IN THE SENTENCE

When a participial, infinitive, or prepositional phrase occurs *at some point other than the beginning of a sentence* (see ¶135) *or the beginning of a clause* (see ¶136), commas are omitted or used depending on whether the phrase is essential or non-essential.

a. An *essential* participial, infinitive, or prepositional phrase is necessary to the meaning of the sentence and cannot be omitted. Therefore, do not use commas to set it off.

The catalogue *scheduled for release in November* will have to be delayed until January. (Participial).

The decision *to expand our export activities* has proved sound. (Infinitive.)

The search *for a new general manager* is still going on. (Prepositional.)

b. A *non-essential* participial, infinitive, or prepositional phrase provides additional information and interrupts but is not needed to complete the meaning of the sentence. Set off such phrases with commas.

(Continued on page 28.)

This new collection of essays, *written in the last two years before his death*, represents his most distinguished work. (Participial.)

I'd rather not attend her reception, *to be frank about it.* (Infinitive.)

Morale appears to be much better, *on the whole.* (Prepositional.)

c. A phrase occurring within a sentence must always be set off by commas when it *interrupts* the flow of the sentence.

The commission, *after hearing arguments on the proposed new tax rate structure,* will consider amendments to the tax law.

The company, *in its attempt to place more women in high-level management positions,* is undertaking a special recruitment program.

The following rules (¶¶138–161) deal with the various uses of commas to set off non-essential expressions. See also ¶¶201–202 and ¶¶218–219 for the use of dashes and parentheses to set off these expressions.

With Transitional Expressions and Independent Comments

138 a. Use commas to set off *transitional expressions.* These non-essential words and phrases are called *transitional* because they help the reader mentally relate the preceding thought to the idea now being introduced. They express such notions as:

ADDITION:	additionally (see Section 11), also, besides, furthermore, in addition, moreover, too (see ¶143), what is more
CONSEQUENCE:	accordingly, as a result, consequently, hence (see ¶139b), otherwise, so (see ¶179), then (see ¶139b), therefore, thus (see ¶139b)
SUMMARIZING:	after all, all in all, all things considered, briefly, by and large, in any case, in any event, in brief, in conclusion, in short, in summary, in the final analysis, in the long run, on balance, on the whole, to sum up
GENERALIZING:	as a rule, as usual, for the most part, generally, generally speaking, in general, ordinarily, usually
RESTATEMENT:	in essence, in other words, namely, that is, that is to say
CONTRAST AND COMPARISON:	by contrast, by the same token, conversely, instead, likewise, on one hand, on the contrary, on the other hand, rather, similarly, yet (see ¶179)
CONCESSION:	anyway, at any rate, be that as it may, even so, however, in any case, in any event, nevertheless, still, this fact notwithstanding
SEQUENCE:	afterward, at first, at the same time, finally, first, first of all, for now, for the time being, in conclusion, in the first place, in time, in turn, later on, meanwhile, next, second, then (see ¶139b), to begin with
DIVERSION:	by the by, by the way, incidentally
ILLUSTRATION:	for example, for instance, for one thing

NOTE: The coordinating conjunctions *and, but, or,* or *nor* are sometimes used as transitional expressions at the beginning of a sentence. See ¶126b.

☞ *See ¶¶139–142 for the punctuation of transitional expressions depending on where they occur in a sentence.*

b. Use commas to set off *independent comments,* that is, non-essential words or phrases that express the writer's attitude toward the meaning of the sentence as a whole rather than a particular word within the sentence. By means of these independent comments, writers may give their wholehearted or lukewarm support, express personal views, present their honest positions, or arouse some emotion.

AGREEMENT:	by all means, indeed, of course, yes
DENIAL:	no
REGRET:	alas, unfortunately, regrettably
PLEASURE:	fortunately, happily
MODIFICATION OF A STATEMENT:	ideally, if necessary, if possible, literally, strictly speaking, theoretically, hopefully (see Section 11)
PERSONAL VIEW:	according to her, as I see it, in my opinion, personally
HONEST POSITION:	actually, frankly, in reality, to be honest, to say the least, to tell the truth
RESTATEMENT OF FACT:	as a matter of fact, as it happens, as you know, believe it or not, certainly, clearly, doubtless, in fact, naturally, needless to say, obviously, without doubt
WEAK SUPPORT:	apparently, perhaps, presumably, well

☞ *See ¶¶139–142 for the punctuation of independent comments depending on where they occur in a sentence.*

139 AT THE BEGINNING OF A SENTENCE

a. When the words and phrases listed in ¶138a–b appear at the beginning of a sentence, they should be followed by a comma unless they are used as essential elements.

NON-ESSENTIAL: *After all,* you have done more for him than he had any right to expect.
ESSENTIAL: *After all* you have done for him, he has no right to expect more.

NON-ESSENTIAL: *However,* you look at the letter yourself to see whether you interpret it as I do.
ESSENTIAL: *However* you look at the letter, there is only one interpretation.

NON-ESSENTIAL: *Obviously,* the guest of honour was quite moved by the welcome she received. (Here *obviously* modifies the meaning of the sentence as a whole.)

ESSENTIAL: *Obviously* moved by the welcome she received, the guest of honour spoke with an emotion-choked voice. (Here *obviously* modifies *moved.* In the preceding sentence, *obviously* modifies the meaning of the sentence as a whole.)

b. When *hence, then,* or *thus* occurs at the beginning of a sentence, the comma following is omitted unless the connective requires special emphasis or a non-essential element occurs at that point.

(Continued on page 30.)

Thus they thought it wise to get an outside consultant's opinion.

Then they decided to go back to their original plan.

BUT: *Then*, after they rejected the consultant's recommendation, they decided to go back to their original plan.

☞ *See also ¶142a note.*

c. When an introductory transitional expression or independent comment is incorporated into the flow of the sentence without any intervening pause, the comma may be omitted.

Of course I can handle it. *Perhaps* she was joking.
No doubt he meant well. *Indeed* she was not.

140 AT THE END OF A SENTENCE

Use one comma to set off a transitional expression or an independent comment at the end of a sentence. However, be sure to distinguish between non-essential and essential elements.

NON-ESSENTIAL: Philip goes to every employee reception, *of course*.
ESSENTIAL: Philip goes to every employee reception as a matter *of course*.

NON-ESSENTIAL: The deal is going to fall through, *in my opinion*.
ESSENTIAL: It doesn't rank very high *in my opinion*.

141 WITHIN THE SENTENCE

Use two commas to set off a transitional expression or an independent comment when it occurs as a non-essential element within the sentence.

I, *too*, was not expecting a six-month convalescence.

The doctors tell me, *however*, that I will regain full use of my left leg.

If, however, the expression is used as an essential element, leave the commas out.

NON-ESSENTIAL: Let me say, *to begin with*, that I have always thought highly of him.
ESSENTIAL: If you want to improve your English, you ought *to begin with* a good review of grammar.

NOTE: In many sentences the only way you can tell whether an expression is non-essential or essential is by the way you say it. If your voice tends to *drop* as you utter the expression, it is non-essential and should be set off by commas.

We concluded, *nevertheless*, that their offer was not serious.

Millie understands, *certainly*, that the reassignment is only temporary.

It is critical, *therefore*, that we recalculate all these cost estimates.

If your voice tends to *rise* as you utter the expression, it is essential and should not be set off by commas.

We *nevertheless* concluded that their offer was not serious.

Millie *certainly* understands that the reassignment is only temporary.

It is *therefore* critical that we recalculate all these cost estimates.

If commas are inserted in the last example above, the entire reading of the sentence will be changed. The voice will rise on the word *is* and drop on *therefore*. (If this is the inflection intended, then commas around *therefore* are appropriate.)

It is, *therefore*, critical that we recalculate all these cost estimates.

142 AT THE BEGINNING OF A CLAUSE

a. When a transitional expression or independent comment occurs *at the beginning of the second independent clause* in a compound sentence and is *preceded by a semicolon*, use one comma after the expression.

I would love to work in a side trip to Bali; *however*, I don't think I can pull it off.

My boss just approved the purchase order; *therefore*, let's confirm a delivery date.

In sentences like the two above, a period may be used in place of a semicolon. The words *however* and *therefore* would then be capitalized to mark the start of a new sentence, and they would be followed by a comma.

NOTE: When *hence, then*, or *thus* appears at the beginning of an independent clause, the comma following is omitted unless the connective requires special emphasis or a non-essential element occurs at that point. (See also ¶139b.)

Melt the butter over high heat; *then* add the egg.

BUT: Melt the butter over a high heat; *then*, when the foam begins to subside, add the egg.

☞ *For the use of a semicolon before a transitional expression, see ¶¶178–180.*

b. When the expression occurs *at the beginning of the second independent clause* in a compound sentence and is *preceded by a comma and a coordinating conjunction*, use one comma after the expression. (See also ¶127d.)

The location of the plant was not easy to reach, and *to be honest about it*, I wasn't very taken with the people who interviewed me.

The job seemed to have no future, and *to tell the truth*, the salary was pretty low.

In the first place, I think the budget for the project is unrealistic, and *in the second place*, the deadlines are almost impossible to meet.

NOTE: If the expression is a simple adverb like *therefore*, the comma following the expression is usually omitted. (See also ¶180.)

The matter must be resolved by Friday, and *therefore* our preliminary conference must be held no later than Thursday.

All the general managers have been summoned to a three-day meeting at the home office, and *consequently* I have had to reschedule all my meetings.

c. If the expression occurs *at the beginning of a dependent clause*, either treat the expression as non-essential (and set it off with two commas) or treat it as essential (and omit the commas).

(Continued on page 32.)

If, *moreover,* they do not meet the deadline, we can cancel the contract.

If *indeed* they want to settle the dispute, why don't they agree to arbitration?

He is a man who, *in my opinion,* will make a fine marketing director.

She is a woman who *no doubt* knows how to run a department smoothly and effectively.

The situation is so serious that, *strictly speaking,* bankruptcy is the only solution.

The situation is so serious that *perhaps* bankruptcy may be the only solution.

143 WITH THE ADVERB *TOO*

a. When the adverb *too* (in the sense of "also") occurs at the end of a clause or a sentence, the comma preceding is omitted.

If you feel that way *too,* why don't we just drop all further negotiation?

They are after a bigger share of the market *too.*

b. When *too* (in the sense of "also") occurs elsewhere in the sentence, particularly between subject and verb, set it off with two commas.

You, *too,* could be in the Caribbean right now.

Then, *too,* there are the additional taxes to be considered.

c. When *too* is used as an adverb meaning "excessively," it is never set off with commas.

The news is almost *too* good to be believed.

With Interruptions and Afterthoughts

144 Use commas to set off words, phrases, or clauses that interrupt the flow of a sentence or that are loosely added at the end as an afterthought.

Pam is being pursued, *so I've been told,* by three headhunters.

Bob spoke on state-of-the-art financial software, *if I remember correctly.*

Our order processing service, *you must admit,* leaves much to be desired.

His research work has been outstanding, *particularly in the field of ergonomics.*

☞ *See also* ¶¶*131c, 136b, 137c.*

CAUTION: When enclosing an interrupting expression with two commas, be sure the commas are inserted accurately.

WRONG: That is the best, *though not the cheapest way,* to proceed.
RIGHT: That is the best, *though not the cheapest,* way to proceed.

WRONG: This is better written, *though less exciting than,* her last book.
RIGHT: This book is better written, *though less exciting,* than her last book.

WRONG: Her work is as good, *if not better than,* that of the man she replaced.
RIGHT: Her work is as good as, *if not better than,* that of the man she replaced.

WRONG: Glen has a deep interest in, *as well as a great fondness,* for jazz.
RIGHT: Glen has a deep interest in, *as well as a great fondness for,* jazz.

With Direct Address

145 Names and titles used in direct address must be set off by commas.

> We agree, *Mrs. Connolly,* that your order was badly handled.
>
> No, *sir,* that is privileged information.
>
> I count on your support, *Bob.*

With Additional Considerations

146 **a.** When a phrase introduced by *as well as, in addition to, besides, along with, including, accompanied by, together with, plus,* or a similar expression falls between the subject and the verb, it is ordinarily set off by commas. Commas may be omitted, however, if the phrase fits smoothly into the flow of the sentence or is essential to the meaning.

> Everyone, *including the top corporate managers,* will be required to attend the in-house seminars on the ethical dimensions of business.
>
> The business plan *including strategies for the new market segments we hope to enter* is better than the other plans I have reviewed. (The *including* phrase is needed to distinguish this plan from the others; hence no commas.)
>
> One *plus one* doesn't always equal two, as we have seen in the Parker-Jackel merger. (The *plus* phrase is essential to the meaning; hence no commas.)
>
> Stephanie *as well as George* should be asked to attend the convention in Vancouver. (The *as well as* phrase flows smoothly in the sentence.)

☞ *For the effect these phrases have on the choice of a singular or a plural verb, see ¶1007. For a usage note on* as well as, *see Section 11.*

b. When the phrase occurs elsewhere in the sentence, commas may be omitted if the phrase is closely related to the preceding words.

> The refinancing terms have been approved by the trustees *as well as the creditors.*
>
> **BUT:** I attended the international monetary conference in Bermuda, *together with five associates from our Montreal office.*

With Contrasting Expressions

147 Use commas to set off contrasting expressions. (Such expressions often begin with *but, not,* or *rather than.*)

> The Sanchezes are willing to sell, *but only on their terms.*
>
> He had changed his methods, *not his objectives,* we noticed.
>
> Paula, *rather than Al,* has been chosen for the job.
>
> The CEO and not the president will make that decision. (See ¶1006b.)

NOTE: When such phrases fit smoothly into the flow of the sentence, no commas are required.

> It was a busy *but enjoyable* trip.   They have chosen Paula *rather than Al.*

☞ *For the punctuation of balancing expressions, see ¶172c.*

The following rules (¶¶148–153) deal with descriptive expressions that immediately follow the words to which they refer. When non-essential, these expressions are set off by commas.

With Appositives or Explanatory Expressions

148 Use commas to set off expressions that provide additional but non-essential information about a noun or pronoun immediately preceding. Such expressions serve to further identify or explain the word they refer to.

> Harriet McManus, *an independent real estate agent for the past ten years*, will be joining our agency on Tuesday, *October 1*. (Phrases such as those following *Harriet McManus* and *Tuesday* are appositives.)
>
> Acrophobia, *the fear of great heights*, can now be successfully treated.
>
> His first book, *written while he was still in graduate school*, launched a successful writing career.
>
> Our first thought, *to run to the nearest exit*, would have resulted in panic.
>
> Ms. Ballantine, *who has been a copywriter for six years*, will be our new copy chief.
>
> Everyone in our family likes outdoor sports, *such as tennis and swimming*. (See ¶149 note.)

NOTE: In some cases other punctuation may be preferable in place of commas.

> **CONFUSING:** Mr. Newcombe, *my boss*, and I will discuss this problem next week. (Does *my boss* refer to Mr. Newcombe, or are there three people involved?)
>
> **CLEAR:** Mr. Newcombe (my boss) and I will be discussing this problem next week. (Use parentheses or dashes instead of commas when an appositive expression could be misread as a separate item in a series.)
>
> There are two factors to be considered, *sales and collections*. (A colon or a dash could be used in place of the comma. See ¶¶189, 201.)

149 When the expression is *essential* to the completeness of the sentence, do not set it off. (In the following examples, the expression is needed to identify which particular item is meant. If the expression were omitted, the sentence would be incomplete.)

> The year *2007* marks the one hundredth anniversary of our company.
>
> The word *liaison* is often misspelled.
>
> The poet *Margaret Avison* gave a reading last week from a work in progress.
>
> The statement *"I don't remember"* was frequently heard in court yesterday.
>
> The impulse *to get away from it all* is very common.
>
> The notes *in green ink* were made by Mrs. Long.
>
> The person *who takes over as general manager* will need everyone's support.

NOTE: Compare the following examples:

> Her article *"Colour and Design"* was published in June. (The title is essential; it identifies *which* article.)
>
> Her latest article, *"Colour and Design,"* was published in June. (Non-essential; the word *latest* already indicates which article.)

Her latest article *on colour and design* was published in June. (Without commas, this means she had earlier articles on the same subject.)

Her latest article, *on colour and design*, was published in June. (With commas, this means her earlier articles were on other subjects.)

Everyone in our family likes such outdoor sports *as tennis and swimming*. (The phrase *as tennis and swimming* is essential; without it, the reader would not know which outdoor sports were meant.)

Everyone in our family likes outdoor sports, *such as tennis and swimming*. (The main clause, *Everyone in our family likes outdoor sports*, expresses a complete thought; the phrase *such as tennis and swimming* gives additional but non-essential information. Hence a comma is needed before *such as*.)

Words *such as peak, peek, and pique* can be readily confused. (The *such as* phrase indicates which words are meant.)

A number of Fortune 500 companies, *such as BCE, ATCO, and Shaw*, have introduced new programs to motivate their middle managers. (The *such as* phrase provides additional but non-essential information.)

150 A number of expressions are treated as essential simply because of a very close relationship with the preceding words. (If read aloud, the combined phrase sounds like one unit, without any intervening pause.)

After a while Gladys *herself* became disenchanted with the Vancouver scene.

We *legislators* must provide funds for retraining unemployed workers.

My wife Patricia has begun her own consulting business. (Strictly speaking, *Patricia* should be set off by commas, since the name is not needed to indicate *which* wife. However, commas are omitted in expressions like these because they are read as a unit.)

My brother Paul may join us as well.
BUT: My brother, *Paul Strand*, may join us.

The composer *Stephen Sondheim* has many broadway hits to his credit.
BUT: My favourite composer, *Stephen Sondheim*, has many Broadway hits . . .

The Story of English by Robert McCrum, William Cran, and Robert MacNeil has been made into a highly praised television series. (Since a book title and a *by* phrase are usually read as a unit, commas are usually omitted.)

151 When *or* introduces a word or a phrase that defines or explains the preceding word, set off the explanatory expression with commas.

Determine whether the clauses are coordinate *or of equal rank*. (The non-essential *or* phrase may also be set off by parentheses.)

However, if *or* introduces an alternative thought, the expression is essential and should not be set off by commas.

Determine whether or not the clauses are *coordinate*.

152 When a business letter or some other document is referred to by date, any related phrases or clauses that follow are usually non-essential.

Thank you for your letter of February 27, *in which you questioned the balance on your account*. (The date is sufficient to identify which letter is meant; the *in which* clause

(Continued on page 36.)

1

simply provides additional but non-essential information.) Of course, if one received more than one letter with the same date from the same person, the *in which* clause would be essential and the comma would be omitted.

However, no comma is needed after the date if the following phrase is short and closely related.

Thank you for your letter of February 27 *about the balance on your account.*

NOTE: Under certain circumstances—for example, around the end of the year—it is better to give the full date rather than the month and day alone. (See ¶409.)

Thank you for your letter of December 27, 2006, in which . . .

With Residence and Business Connections

153 Use commas to set off a *long phrase* denoting a person's residence or business connections.

Ken Gary, *of Hartco Enterprises in Anjou, Quebec,* will be visiting us next week.

Ken Gary *of Anjou, Quebec,* will be visiting us next week. (Omit the comma before *of* to avoid too many breaks in a short phrase. The provincial name must be set off by commas when it follows the name of a city. See also ¶160.)

Ken Gary *of Hartco Enterprises* will be visiting us next week. (Short phrase; no commas.)

Ken Gary *of Anjou* will be visiting us next week. (Short phrase; no commas.)

The following rules (¶¶154–161) deal with the treatment of certain non-essential elements in dates, personal names, company names, and addresses. However, the established tradition of setting them off with commas has in many cases begun to change.

In Dates

154 a. Use two commas to set off the year when it follows the month and day.

On July 1, *2009,* I plan to retire and open a bookshop in Moncton.

The August 28, *2006,* issue of *Legend* forecast that telecommunication carriers will continue to spend more in the critical area of bandwidth expansion.

b. When the month, day, and year are used as a non-essential expression, be sure to set the entire phrase off with commas.

The conference scheduled to begin on Monday, *November 27, 2006,* has now been rescheduled to start on *February 6, 2007.*

Payment of estimated income taxes for the fourth quarter of 2006 will be due no later than Wednesday, *January 15, 2007.*

155 a. Omit the commas when only the month and year are given.

In *May 2005* Ivan and I dissolved our partnership and went our separate ways.

Isn't it about time for *Consumer Reports* to update the evaluation of wireless telephones that appeared in the *November 2005* issue?

☞ *For additional examples involving dates, see ¶¶407–410.*

b. When the date is expressed in a day-month-year sequence (3 August 2007), do not use commas to set off the year unless the sentence needs a comma or some other mark of punctuation after the year.

With *Jr., Sr.,* Etc.

156 Do not use commas to set off *Jr., Sr.,* or Roman or Arabic numerals following a person's name unless you know that the person in question prefers to do so.

Kelsey R. Patterson *Jr.*   Benjamin Hart *2nd*
Christopher M. Gorman *Sr.* Anthony Jung *III*

NOTE: When a person prefers to use commas in his or her name, observe the following style:

Peter Passaro, *Jr.* (Use one comma when the name is displayed on a line by itself.)

Peter Passaro, *Jr.,* director of . . . (Use two commas when other copy follows.)

Peter Passaro, *Jr.'s* promotion . . . (Drop the second comma when a possessive ending is attached.)

157 Abbreviations like *Esq.* and those that stand for academic degrees or religious orders are set off by two commas when they follow a person's name.

Address the letter to Martin E. Prest, *Esq.,* in Winnipeg.

Roger Farrier, *LL.D.,* will address the Elizabethan Club on Wednesday.

Reverend James Hanley, *S.J.,* will serve as moderator of the panel.

158 When a personal name is given in inverted order, set off the inverted portion with commas.

McCaughan, James W., *Jr.*

With *Inc.* and *Ltd.*

159 Do not use commas to set off *Inc., Ltd.,* and similar expressions in a company name unless you know that a particular company prefers to do so. (See also ¶¶1326b–1326c.)

Time Inc. Field Hats, Ltd.

Time *Inc.* has expanded its operations beyond magazine publishing.

Field Hats, *Ltd.,* should be notified about this mistake.

NOTE: When commas are to be used in a company name, follow this style:

McGraw-Hill, Inc. (Use one comma when the name is displayed on a line by itself.)

McGraw-Hill, Inc., announces the publication of . . . (Use two commas when other words follow.)

McGraw-Hill, Inc.'s annual statement . . . (Drop the second comma after a possessive ending.)

☞ *For the use of commas with other parts of a company name, see ¶163.*

In Geographic References and Addresses

160 Use two commas to set off the name of a province, country, or the equivalent when it directly follows the name of a city or a county.

> Four years ago I was transferred from Calgary, *Alberta*, to Nairobi, *Kenya*.
>
> Could Parkview County, *Alberta*, become a haven for retired teachers?
>
> Our LaSalle, *Quebec*, office is the one nearest to you.
> **OR:** Our LaSalle (Quebec) office is the one nearest to you. (Parentheses are clearer than commas when a city-province expression serves as an adjective.)
>
> Victoria, *B.C.'s* transportation system has improved greatly since I was last there. (Omit the second comma after a possessive ending.)

NOTE: In sentences that mention one or more cities, omit the province or country names if the cities are well known and are clearly linked with only one province or country.

> We'll be holding meetings in Montreal, Toronto, and Vancouver.
>
> My agent has arranged for me to address delegates in Rome, Paris, and London.

161 When expressing complete addresses, follow this style:

> **IN SENTENCES:** During the month of August, you can send all documents directly to me at 402 Woodbury Road, Toronto, ON M3X 4B4, or you can ask my assistant to forward it. (Note that a comma follows the postal code but does not precede it.)
>
> **IN DISPLAYED BLOCKS:** 402 Woodbury Road
> Toronto, ON M3X 4B4

The following rules (¶¶162–175) deal with various uses of separating commas: to separate items in a series, to separate adjectives that precede a noun, and to clarify meaning in sentences with unusual word order or omitted words.

In a Series

162 When three or more items are listed in a series and the last item is preceded by *and, or,* or *nor,* place a comma before the conjunction as well as between the other items. (See also ¶126c.)

> Study the rules for the use of the comma, the semicolon, *and* the colon.
>
> The consensus is that your report is well written, that your facts are accurate, *and* that your conclusions are sound.
>
> The show will appeal equally to women and men, adults and children, *and* sophisticates and innocents. (See Section 11 for a usage note on *and*.)
>
> Only this software lets you fax, transfer files, exchange e-mail, access the Internet, *and* manage phone calls—all from one window on your computer.

NOTE: If a non-essential element follows the conjunction (*and, or,* or *nor*) in a series, omit the comma before the conjunction to avoid excessive punctuation.

> We invited Ben's business associates, his friends and, of course, his parents.
>
> (**RATHER THAN:** . . . his friends, and, of course, his parents.)

163 For a series in an organization's name, always follow the style preferred by that organization.

> Franklin, Templeton, Investments   McCarthy Tétrault LLP
> German Fong Albus Lam   Clay-Robinson Ltd.

If you do not have the company's letterhead or some other reliable resource at hand, follow the standard rule on commas in a series (see ¶162).

> Our primary supplier is *Ames, Koslow, Milke, and Company.*

NOTE: Do not use a comma before an ampersand (&) in an organization's name unless you know that a particular organization prefers to do so.

> Fric, Lowenstein & Co.

164 When an expression such as *and so on* or *etc.* closes a series, use a comma before and after the expression (unless the expression falls at the end of a sentence).

> Our sale of suits, coats, hats, *and so on*, starts tomorrow.
>
> Tomorrow morning we will start our sale of suits, coats, hats, *etc.*

☞ *For a usage note on* etc., *see Section 11.*

165 Do not insert a comma after the last item in a series unless the sentence structure demands a comma at that point.

> May 8, June 11, and July 14 are the dates for the next three hearings.
>
> May 8, June 11, and July 14, *2007*, are the dates for the next three hearings.
>
> (The comma after *2007* is one of a pair that sets off the year. See ¶154.)

166 When *and, or,* or *nor* is used to connect all the items in a series, do not separate the items by commas. (See also ¶123b.)

> Send copies to our employees *and* stockholders *and* major customers.

167 If a series consists of only two items, do not separate the items with a comma. (See also ¶125f.)

> We can send the samples to you *by regular mail* or *by one of the express services.*

NOTE: Use a comma, however, to separate two independent clauses joined by *and, but, or,* or *nor.* (See ¶¶123a, 126a.)

☞ *For the use of the semicolon in a series, see* ¶¶184–185.

With Adjectives

168 When two consecutive adjectives modify the same noun, separate the adjectives with a comma.

> Jean is a *generous, outgoing* person. (A person who is *generous and outgoing.*)

NOTE: Do *not* use a comma between the adjectives if they are connected by *and, or,* or *nor.*

> Jean is a *generous and outgoing* person.

169 When two adjectives precede a noun, the first adjective may modify the combined idea of the second adjective plus the noun. In such cases do not separate the adjectives by a comma.

> The estate is surrounded by an *old stone* wall. (A *stone* wall that is *old.*)

> Here is the *annual financial* statement. (A *financial* statement that is *annual.*)

TEST: To decide whether consecutive adjectives should be separated by a comma or not, try using them in a relative clause *after* the noun, with *and* inserted between them. If they read smoothly and sensibly in that position, they should be separated by a comma in their actual position.

> We need an *intelligent, enterprising* person for the job. (One can speak of "a person who is *intelligent* and *enterprising,*" so a comma is correct.)

> Throw out your *old winter* coat. (One cannot speak of "a coat that is *old* and *winter,*" so no comma should be used in the actual sentence.)

> You can purchase any of these printers with a *low down* payment. (In this case the adjective *low* modifies a compound noun, *down payment.*)

> To put it gently but plainly, I think Jason is a *low-down* scoundrel. (In this case *low-down* is a compound adjective and requires a hyphen to connect *low* and *down.* See ¶¶813–832 for a discussion of compound adjectives.)

170 When more than two adjectives precede a noun, insert a comma only between those adjectives where *and* could have been used.

> a relaxed, unruffled, confident manner (a relaxed *and* unruffled *and* confident manner)

> an experienced, efficient legal assistant (an experienced *and* efficient legal assistant)

> the established Canadian political system (*and* cannot be inserted between these three adjectives)

171 Do not use a comma between the final adjective in a series and the following noun.

> I put in a long, hard, *demanding day* on Monday.

> (**NOT:** I put in a long, hard, *demanding, day* on Monday.)

To Indicate Omitted Words

172 **a. Omission of Repetitive Wording.** Use a comma to indicate the omission of repetitive wording in a compound sentence. (This use of the comma usually occurs when clauses are separated by semicolons.)

> Employees aged 55 and over are eligible for a complete physical examination every year; those between 50 and 54, every two years; and those under 50, every three years.

> **NOTE:** If the omitted words are clearly understood from the context, simpler punctuation may be used.

> Employees aged 55 and over are eligible for a complete physical examination every year, those between 50 and 54 every two years, and those under 50 every three years.

b. Omission of *That*. In some sentences the omission of the conjunction *that* creates a definite break in the flow of the sentence. In such cases insert a comma to mark the break.

Remember, this offer is good only through May 31.

The problem is, not all of these assumptions may be correct.

The fact is, things are not working out as we had hoped.

Chances are, the deal will never come off.

c. In sentences that are introduced by expressions such as *he said, she thinks, we feel,* or *they know,* the conjunction *that* is often omitted after the introductory expression. In such cases no comma is necessary because there is no break in the flow of the sentence.

We know you can do it.   She said she would handle everything.

They think our price is too high.   We believe we offer the best service.

NOTE: Do not omit *that* if a misreading is possible.

CONFUSING: Researchers have found some medications, even though approved, carry unforeseen risks. (When *that* is omitted, you might initially mistake *some medications* for the object of *have found* whereas it is the subject of a relative clause.)

CLEAR: Researchers have found *that* some medications, even though approved, carry unforeseen risks.

d. Balancing Expressions. Use a comma to separate the two parts of a balancing expression from which many words have been omitted.

First come, first served.   The more we give, the more they take.

First in, last out.   Here a comma, there a comma.

Here today, gone tomorrow.   The less I see of him, the better I like it.

NOTE: The phrase *The sooner the better* usually appears without a separating comma.

To Indicate Unusual Word Order

173 In some colloquial sentences, clauses or phrases occur out of normal order and connective words may be omitted. Use a comma to mark the resulting break in the flow of the sentence.

You must not miss the play, it was that good.

(**NORMAL ORDER:** The play was so good that you must not miss it.)

Why he took the money, I'll never understand.

That the shipment would be late, we were prepared to accept; that you would ship the wrong goods, we did not expect.

NOTE: In formal writing, these sentences should be recast in normal word order.

☞ *See also ¶135c note.*

For Special Emphasis

174 Individual words may be set off by commas for special emphasis.

I have tried, *sincerely,* to understand your problems.

(Continued on page 42.)

1

They contend, *unrealistically*, that we can cut back on staff and still generate the same amount of output.

NOTE: The use of commas in the examples above forces the reader to dwell momentarily on the word that has been set off in each case. Without this treatment *sincerely* and *unrealistically* would not receive this emphasis.

For Clarity

175 a. Use a comma to prevent misreading.

> As you know, nothing came of the meeting.
>
> (**NOT:** As you know nothing came of the meeting.)
>
> To a skydiver like Marc, Garneau seems to be out in space.
>
> Soon after, the committee disbanded without accomplishing its goal.

b. Sometimes, for clarity, it is necessary to separate two verbs.

> All any insurance policy is, is a contract for services.

c. Use a comma to separate repeated words.

> It was a *long, long* time ago.
>
> That was a *very, very* old argument.
>
> *Well, well,* we'll find a way.
>
> *Now, now,* you don't expect me to believe that!

☞ *Commas with dashes: see ¶¶213, 215b.*
Commas in numbers: see ¶¶413b, 461–463.
Commas with questions within sentences: see ¶¶114–117.
Commas with parentheses: see ¶224a.
Commas inside closing quotation marks: see ¶247.
Commas at the end of quotations: see ¶¶253–255.
Commas preceding quotations: see ¶256.
Commas with quotations within a sentence: see ¶¶259–261.
Commas to set off interruptions in quoted matter: see ¶¶262–263.
Spacing with commas: see ¶298.

THE SEMICOLON

Between Independent Clauses—*And, But, Or,* or *Nor* Omitted

176 a. When a coordinating conjunction (*and, but, or,* or *nor,* and sometimes *for, so,* or *yet*) is omitted between two independent clauses, use a semicolon—not a comma—to separate the clauses. If you prefer, you can treat the second clause as a separate sentence. (See ¶187.)

> Most of the shareholders favoured the sale; management did not.
> **OR:** Most of the shareholders favoured the sale. Management did not.
> **NOT:** Most of the shareholders favoured the sale, management did not.
>
> Bob is going for his M.B.A.; Janet already has hers.

Notebooks aren't just smaller; they're cheaper.

NOT: Notebooks aren't just smaller, they're cheaper.

b. If the clauses are not closely related, treat them as separate sentences.

WEAK: Thank you for your letter of September 8; your question has already been passed on to the manager of mail-order sales, and you should be hearing from Ms. Livonia within three days.

BETTER: Thank you for your letter of September 8. Your question has already been passed on to the manager of mail-order sales, and you should be . . .

c. The omission of *but* between two independent clauses requires, strictly speaking, the use of a semicolon between the two clauses. However, when the clauses are short, a comma is commonly used to preserve the flow of the sentence.

Not only was the food bad, the portions were minuscule.

Between Independent Clauses—
And, But, Or, or Nor Included

177 A comma is normally used to separate two independent clauses joined by a coordinating conjunction. However, under certain circumstances a semicolon is appropriate before the coordinating conjunction.

a. Use a semicolon in order to achieve a stronger break between clauses than a comma provides.

NORMAL BREAK: Many people are convinced that they could personally solve the problem if given the authority to do so, but no one will come forward with a clear-cut plan that we can evaluate in advance.

STRONG BREAK: Many people are convinced that they could personally solve the problem if given the authority to do so; but no one will come forward with a clear-cut plan that we can evaluate in advance.

b. Use a semicolon when one or both clauses have internal commas, and a misreading might occur if a comma also separated the clauses.

CONFUSING: I sent you an order for copier paper, computer paper, and No. 10 envelopes, and shipping tags, cardboard cartons, stapler wire, and binding tape were sent to me instead.

CLEAR: I sent you an order for copier paper, computer paper, and No. 10 envelopes; and shipping tags, cardboard cartons, stapler wire, and binding tape were sent to me instead.

NOTE: To prevent misreading, you will usually find it better to reword the sentence than rely on stronger punctuation.

BETTER: I sent you an order for copier paper, computer paper, and No. 10 envelopes, and you sent me shipping tags, cardboard cartons, stapler wire, and binding tape instead.

(Continued on page 44.)

On June 8, 2006, I discussed this problem with your customer service manager, Betty Dugan; but your company has taken no further action.

All in all, we are satisfied with the job Chen Associates did; and in view of the tight deadlines they had to meet, we are pleased that they came through as well as they did.

☞ *For additional examples, see ¶133.*

With Transitional Expressions

178 When independent clauses are linked by transitional expressions (see a partial list below), use a semicolon between the clauses. (If the second clause is long or requires special emphasis, treat it as a separate sentence.)

accordingly	however	so (see ¶179)
besides	moreover	that is (see ¶181)
consequently	namely (see ¶181)	then
for example (see ¶181)	nevertheless	therefore
furthermore	on the contrary	thus
hence	otherwise	yet (see ¶179)

They have given us an oral okay to proceed; *however,* we are still waiting for written confirmation.

Our costs have started to level off; our sales, *moreover,* have continued to grow.

Let's give them another month; *then* we can pin them down on their progress.

NOTE: Use a comma after the transitional expression when it occurs at the start of the second clause. (See the first example above.) However, no comma is needed after *hence, then, thus, so,* and *yet* unless a pause is wanted at that point. (See the third example above.)

☞ *For the use of commas with transitional expressions, see ¶¶138–143.*

REMEMBER: A semicolon is needed to separate independent clauses, not so much because a transitional expression is present but because a coordinating conjunction is absent.

179 An independent clause introduced by *so* (in the sense of "therefore") or *yet* may be preceded by a comma or a semicolon. Use a comma if the two clauses are closely related and there is a smooth flow from the first clause to the second. Use a semicolon or period if the clauses are long and complicated or if the transition between clauses calls for a long pause or a strong break.

Sales have been good, *yet* profits are low.

This report explains why production has slowed down; *yet* it does not indicate how to avoid future glitches.

These sale-priced attaché cases are going fast, *so* don't delay if you want one.

We have been getting an excessive number of complaints during the last few months about our service; *so* I would like each of you to review the operations in your department and indicate what corrective measures you think ought to be taken. (**OR:** . . . about our service. *So* I would like . . .)

180 If both a coordinating conjunction and a transitional expression occur at the start of the second clause, use a comma before the conjunction.

> The site has a number of disadvantages, *and furthermore* the asking price is quite high. (See ¶142b and note.)

With *For Example, Namely, That Is,* Etc.

181 BEFORE AN INDEPENDENT CLAUSE

a. In general, when two independent clauses are linked by a transitional expression such as *for example (e.g.)*, *namely*, or *that is (i.e.)*, use a semicolon before the expression and a comma afterward.

> She is qualified for the job; *for example,* she has had ten years' experience.

> **NOTE:** You can replace the semicolon with a period and treat the second clause as a separate sentence.

> She is qualified for the job. *For example,* she has had . . .

b. If the first clause serves to anticipate the second clause and the full emphasis is to fall on the second clause, use a colon before the transitional expression.

> Your proposal covers all but one point: *namely,* who is going to foot the bill?

c. For a stronger but less formal break between clauses, the semicolon or the colon may be replaced by a dash.

> Hampton says he will help—*that is,* he will help if you ask him to.

> **NOTE:** Use the abbreviated forms *e.g.* and *i.e.* only in informal, technical, or expedient documents (such as business forms, catalogues, and routine memos, e-mails, and letters between business offices). (See ¶502.)

182 AT THE END OF A SENTENCE

When *for example, namely,* or *that is* introduces words, phrases, or a series of clauses *at the end of a sentence*, the punctuation preceding the expression may vary as follows:

a. If the first part of the sentence suggests that an important explanation or illustration will follow, use a colon before the transitional expression to throw emphasis on what *follows*.

> My assistant has three important duties: *namely,* attending all meetings, writing the minutes, and sending out notices. (The word *three* anticipates the enumeration following *namely*. The colon suggests that what follows is the main thought of the sentence.)

> **NOTE:** Use a comma before the transitional expression to throw emphasis on what *precedes*.

> I checked these figures with three people, *namely, Joan, Andy,* and *Jim.* (This punctuation emphasizes *three people* rather than the specific names.)

(Continued on page 46.)

1

b. If the expression introduces an appositive that explains a word or phrase immediately preceding, a comma should precede the transitional expression.

Most of the committee voted to reject the plan, *that is, several of the more influential members.* (Here again, a comma is used because what precedes the transitional expression is more important than what follows.)

c. The colon and the comma in the examples in ¶182a–b may be replaced by a dash or by parentheses. The dash provides a stronger but less formal break; the parentheses serve to subordinate the explanatory element. (See also ¶¶201–205, 219.)

183 WITHIN A SENTENCE

When *for example, namely,* or *that is* introduces words, phrases, or clauses *within a sentence,* treat the entire construction as non-essential and set it off with commas, dashes, or parentheses. Dashes will give emphasis to the interrupting construction; parentheses will make the construction appear less important than the rest of the words in the sentence.

Many of the components, *for example, the motor,* are manufactured in Barrie.

Many of the components—*for example, the motor*—are manufactured in Barrie.

Many of the components (*for example, the motor*) are manufactured in Barrie.

NOTE: Commas can be used to set off the non-essential element so long as it contains no internal punctuation (other than the comma after the introductory expression). If the non-essential element is internally punctuated with several commas, set it off with either dashes or parentheses.

Many of the components—*for example, the motor, the batteries, and the cooling unit*—are manufactured . . . (Use dashes for emphasis. See ¶201.)

OR: Many of the components (*for example, the motor, the batteries, and the cooling unit*) are manufactured . . . (Use parentheses for subordination. See ¶219b.)

In a Series

184 Use a semicolon to separate items in a series if any of the items already contain commas.

The company will be represented on the Yorkton Environmental Council by May Janowski, director of public affairs; Harris Madsen, vice-president of manufacturing; and Daniel St. Clair, director of environmental systems.

NOTE: As an alternative, use parentheses to enclose the title following each name. Then use commas to separate the items in the series.

The company will be represented on the Yorkton Environmental Council by May Janowski (director of public affairs), Harris Madsen (vice-president of manufacturing), and Daniel St. Clair (director of environmental systems).

185 Avoid starting a sentence with a series punctuated with semicolons. Try to recast the sentence so that the series comes at the end. (See ¶160 note.)

AWKWARD: New offices in Whitby, Ontario; Brandon, Manitoba; Red Deer, Alberta; and Laval, Quebec, will be opened next year.

IMPROVED: Next year we will open new offices in Whitby, Ontario; Brandon, Manitoba; Red Deer, Alberta; and Laval, Quebec.

With Dependent Clauses

186 Use semicolons to separate a series of parallel dependent clauses if they are long or contain internal commas.

They promised that they would review the specifications, costs, and estimates; that they would analyze Mark's alternative figures; and that they would prepare a comparison of the two proposals and submit their recommendations.

If you have tried special clearance sales but have not raised the necessary cash; if you have tried to borrow the money and have not been able to find a lender; if you have offered to sell part of the business but have not been able to find a partner, then your only course of action is to go out of business. (See ¶185.)

NOTE: A simple series of dependent clauses requires only commas, just like any other kind of series. (See also ¶162.)

Mrs. Mah said that all the budgets had to be redone by Monday, that she could not provide us with any extra help, and that we'd better cancel any weekend plans.

☞ *Semicolons with dashes: see ¶¶213, 215c.*
Semicolons with parentheses: see ¶224a.
Semicolons with quotation marks: see ¶248.
Spacing with semicolons: see ¶298.

THE COLON
Between Independent Clauses

187 **a.** Use a colon between two independent clauses when the second clause explains or illustrates the first clause and there is no coordinating conjunction or transitional expression linking the two clauses.

I have a special fondness for the Nova Scotia coast: it reminds me of the many happy summers we spent there before our children went off to college.

I have two major hurdles to clear before I get my Ph.D.: pass the oral exam and write a dissertation.

NOTE: The second clause that explains or illustrates the first clause may itself consist of more than one independent clause.

It has been said that a successful project goes through three stages: it won't work, it costs too much, and I always knew it was a good idea.

b. Note the different uses of the colon and the semicolon in the following sentences.

The job you have described sounds very attractive: the salary, the benefits, and the opportunities for training and advancement seem excellent. (Use a colon when the second clause explains the first.)

(Continued on page 48.)

The job you have described sounds very attractive; it is the kind of job I have been looking for. (Use a semicolon when the second clause does not explain the first.)

The job you have described sounds very attractive; for example, the salary and the benefits are good, and the opportunities for advancement seem excellent. (Ordinarily, use a semicolon when a transitional expression links the clauses.)

c. If you aren't sure whether to use a semicolon or a colon between two independent clauses, you can always make each clause a separate sentence and use a period at the end of each.

The job you have described sounds very attractive. For example, the salary and the benefits are good, and the opportunities for advancement seem excellent.

Before Lists and Enumerations

188 Place a colon before such expressions as *for example, namely,* and *that is* when they introduce words, phrases, or a series of clauses anticipated earlier in the sentence. (See ¶¶181–182.)

The company provides a number of benefits not commonly offered in this area: for example, free dental insurance, low-cost term insurance, and personal financial counselling services.

189 When a clause contains an anticipatory expression (such as *the following, as follows, thus,* and *these*) and directs attention to a series of explanatory words, phrases, or clauses, use a colon between the clause and the series.

These are some of the new features in this year's models: a fuel economy indicator, a new rear suspension, and a three-year limited warranty.

The following staff members have been selected to attend the national sales conference in Quebec City:

Frances Beaulieu
Bayda Grewal
Kelly Chow

190 Use a colon even if the anticipatory expression is only implied and not stated.

The house has attractive features: cross ventilation in every room, a two-storey living room, and two terraces.

Scientists have devised a most appropriate name for a physical property opposed to gravity: levity. (The colon may be used even when what follows is only a single word. See also ¶210.)

191 **a.** If the anticipatory expression occurs near the beginning of a long sentence, do not use a colon.

We have set *the following* restrictions on the return of merchandise, so please be aware of this new policy when dealing with customers. Goods cannot be returned after five days, and price tags must not be removed.

BUT: We have set *the following* restrictions on the return of merchandise: goods cannot be returned . . .

b. If the sentence containing the anticipatory expression is followed by another sentence, do not use a colon.

Campers will find that *the following* small items will add much to their enjoyment of the summer. These articles may be purchased from a store near the camp.

Flashlight	Hot-cold food bag
Camera	Fishing gear

c. If an explanatory series follows an incomplete introductory clause that ends with a verb or a preposition, do not use a colon.

RIGHT: This set of china includes 12 dinner plates, 12 salad plates, and 12 cups and saucers.

RIGHT: This set of china includes the following items: 12 dinner plates, 12 salad plates, and 12 cups and saucers.

WRONG: This set of china includes: 12 dinner plates, 12 salad plates, and 12 cups and saucers. (The list follows a verb.)

RIGHT: The panel consists of Ms. Seidel, Mrs. Kitay, and Mr. Haddad.

RIGHT: The panel consists of the following people: Ms. Seidel, Mrs. Kitay, and Mr. Haddad.

WRONG: The panel consists of: Ms. Seidel, Mrs. Kitay, and Mr. Haddad. (The list follows a preposition.)

RIGHT: Some of the questions that this book answers are these: How can you reduce your insurance expenses without sacrificing protection? How can you avoid being over- or under-insured? How can you file a claim correctly the first time around? (Here the introductory clause is complete; hence a colon is acceptable.)

RIGHT: Here are some of the questions that this book answers: How can you . . . ? (Here again the introductory clause is complete: hence a colon is acceptable.)

WRONG: Some of the questions that this book answers are: How can you . . . ? (Here the introductory clause is incomplete and it ends with a verb.)

EXCEPTION: A colon may be used after a verb or a preposition if the items in the series are enumerated or listed on separate lines.

This set of china includes:	The panel consists of:
12 dinner plates	Ms. Seidel
12 salad plates	Mrs. Kitay
12 cups and saucers	Mr. Haddad

In Expressions of Time and Proportions

192 When hours and minutes are expressed in figures, separate them with a colon, as in the expression *8:25*. (No space precedes or follows this colon. See also ¶¶298, 1625b.)

193 A colon is used to represent the word *to* in proportions, as in the ratio *2:1*. (No space precedes or follows this colon. See also ¶298.)

In Business Documents

194 a. If punctuation is to follow the salutation in business letters, use a colon (see also ¶1338a). In social-business letters, use a comma. (See also ¶1373b.)

(Continued on page 50.)

b. In business letters, a colon is often used with such elements as reference notations (see ¶1315), attention and subject lines (see ¶¶1337–1342), and closing notations required after the signature line (see ¶¶1354–1362).

c. In memos and other business documents, use a colon after displayed guide words. (See ¶1375.)

TO: FROM: DATE: SHIP TO: BILL TO: *Distribution:*

In References to Books or Other Publications

195   **a.** Use a colon to separate the title and the subtitle of a book, even if the colon does not appear on the title page of the book.

W. F. Garrett-Petts, in *Writing About Literature: A Guide for Students,* has provided practical advice for writing essays.

b. A colon may be used to separate volume number and page number in footnotes and similar references. (Leave no space before or after the colon. See also ¶298.)

8:763–766 (meaning *Volume 8, pages 763–766;* see also ¶1517 note.)

Capitalizing After a Colon

196 Do not capitalize after a colon if the material that follows cannot stand alone as a sentence.

All cash advances must be countersigned by me, with one exception: when the amount is less than $50. (Dependent clause following a colon.)

Two courses are required: algebra and English. (Words following a colon.)

EXCEPTION: Capitalize the first word after the colon if it is a proper noun, a proper adjective, or the pronoun *I.*

Two courses are required: English and algebra.

197 Do not capitalize the first word of an independent clause after a colon if the clause explains, illustrates, or amplifies the thought expressed in the first part of the sentence. (See ¶196, exception.)

Essential and non-essential elements require altogether different punctuation: the latter should be set off by commas; the former should not.

198 Capitalize the first word of an independent clause after a colon if it requires special emphasis or is presented as a formal rule. (In such cases the independent clause expresses the main thought; the first part of the sentence usually functions only as an introduction.)

Let me say this: If the company is to recover from its present difficulties, we must immediately devise an entirely new marketing strategy.

Here is the key principle: Non-essential elements must be set off by commas; essential elements should not.

199 Capitalize the first word after a colon under these circumstances:

a. When the material following the colon consists of two or more sentences.

There are several drawbacks to this proposal: First, it will tie up a good deal of capital for the next five years. Second, the likelihood of a significant return on the investment has not been shown.

b. When the material following the colon is a quotation.

Frederick Raine responded in this way: "We expect to win our case once all the facts are brought out in the trial." (See ¶256 for the use of a colon before a quoted sentence.)

c. When the material following the colon starts on a new line (for example, the body of a letter following the salutation or the individual items displayed on separate lines in a list).

Dear John:

I have read your latest draft, and I find it much improved. However, on page 4 I wish you would redo . . .

Capitalize the first word of:

a. Every sentence.
b. Direct quotations.
c. Salutations in letters.

d. When the material *preceding* the colon is a short introductory word such as *Note, Caution,* or *Wanted.*

Deadline: All expense reports must be submitted no later than Friday.

Remember: All equipment must be turned off before you leave.

e. When the material *preceding* the colon is the name of a speaker in the transcription of court testimony or in a script for a play. (See also ¶270.)

THOMAS: Why commit robbery in Toronto?

VAILLANCOURT: I came because the banks have more money in them.

☞ *Colons with dashes: see ¶¶213, 215c.*

Colons with parentheses: see ¶224a.

Colons with quotation marks: see ¶¶248, 256.

Spacing with colons: see ¶298.

See the Online Learning Centre at www.mcgrawhill.ca/college/gregg for related Web links.

SECTION **TWO**

Punctuation: Other Marks

MARKS FOR EMPHASIS (¶¶285–290)

REMAINING PUNCTUATION MARKS (¶¶291–297)

SPACING: WITH PUNCTUATION MARKS (¶298)

THE DASH

Although the dash has a few specific functions of its own, it most often serves in place of the comma, the semicolon, the colon, or parentheses. When used as an alternative to these other marks, it creates a much more emphatic separation of words within a sentence. Because of its versatility, some writers are tempted to use a dash to punctuate almost any break within a sentence. However, this indiscriminate use of the dash destroys the special forcefulness that it can convey. So use the dash sparingly— and then only for deliberate effect.

The dash used in ¶¶201–215 is known as the **one-em dash** and has the same width as a capital M. The remaining dashes are discussed in ¶216.

In Place of Commas

201 Use dashes in place of commas to set off a non-essential element that requires special emphasis.

(Continued on page 54.)

At this year's annual banquet, the speakers—and the food—were superb.

Of all the colour samples you sent me, there was only one I liked—taupe.

202 If a non-essential element already contains internal commas, use dashes in place of commas to set the element off. (If dashes provide too emphatic a break, use parentheses instead. See ¶¶183, 219.)

Our entire inventory of Oriental rugs—including a fine selection of Sarouks, Kashans, and Bokharas—will be offered for sale at a 40 percent discount.

203 To give special emphasis to the second independent clause in a compound sentence, use a dash rather than a comma before the coordinating conjunction.

The information I sent you is true—and you know it!

In Place of a Semicolon

204 For a stronger but less formal break, use a dash in place of a semicolon between closely related independent clauses. (See ¶¶176, 178.)

I do the work—he gets the credit!

The job needs to be done—moreover, it needs to be done well.

Wilson is totally unqualified for a promotion—for example, he still does not grasp the basic principles of good management.

In Place of a Colon

205 For a stronger but less formal break, use a dash in place of a colon to introduce explanatory words, phrases, or clauses. (See ¶¶187–189.)

I need only a few items for my meeting with Kaster—namely, a copy of his letter of May 18, a copy of the contract under dispute, and a bottle of Aspirin.

My arrangement with Gina is a simple one—she handles sales and I manage production.

In Place of Parentheses

206 Use dashes instead of parentheses when you want to give the non-essential element strong emphasis. (See ¶¶183, 219.)

Call Mike Habib—he's with Jax Electronics—and get his opinion.

To Indicate an Abrupt Break or an Afterthought

207 Use a dash to show an abrupt break in thought or to separate an afterthought from the main part of a sentence. When a sentence breaks off after a dash, leave a space or two before the next sentence. (See ¶208.)

I wish you would— Is there any point in telling you what I wish for you?

We offer the best service in town—and the fastest!

Geoff Parry's plane will be landing at Toronto—or did he say Hamilton?

208 If a *question* or an *exclamation* breaks off abruptly before it has been completed, use a dash followed by a question mark or an exclamation point as appropriate. If the sentence is a *statement*, however, use a dash alone.

> Do you want to tell him or—? Suppose I wait to hear from you.
>
> If only— Yet there's no point in talking about what might have been. (**NOT:** If only—. Yet there's no point in talking about what might have been.)

☞ *For the use of ellipsis marks to indicate a break in thought, see ¶292a.*

To Show Hesitation

209 Use a dash to indicate hesitation, faltering speech, or stammering.

> The work on the Patterson project was begun—oh, I should say—well, about May 1—certainly no later than May 15.

To Emphasize Single Words

210 Use dashes to set off single words that require special emphasis.

> Jogging—that's what he lives for.
>
> There is, of course, a secret ingredient in my pasta sauce—fennel.

With Repetitions, Restatements, and Summarizing Words

211 **a.** Use dashes to set off and emphasize words that repeat or restate a previous thought.

> Next week—on Thursday at 10 a.m.—we will be making an important announcement at a press conference.
>
> Don't miss this opportunity—the opportunity of a lifetime!

b. Use a dash before such words as *these, they*, and *all* when these words stand as subjects summarizing a preceding list of details.

> Network television, magazines, and newspapers—*these* will be the big gainers in advertising revenues next year.
>
> India, Korea, and Australia—*all* are important new markets for us.
>
> **BUT:** India, Korea, and Australia are all important new markets for us. (No dash is used when the summarizing word is not the subject.)

Before Attributions

212 When providing an attribution for a displayed quotation—that is, when identifying the author or the source of the quotation—use a dash before the name of the author or the title of the work.

> My idea of luck is that it is opportunity seized.
> —Roy Thomson

NOTE: The attribution usually appears on a separate line, aligned at the right with the longest line in the displayed quotation above. For additional examples, see ¶284b.

Punctuation Preceding an Opening Dash

213 Do not use a comma, a semicolon, or a colon before an opening dash. Moreover, do not use a period before an opening dash (except a period following an abbreviation).

> Quality circles boost productivity—and they pay off in higher profits too.
> (**NOT:** Quality circles boost productivity,—and they pay off in higher profits too.)

> The catalogue proofs arrived before 11 a.m.—just as you promised.

Punctuation Preceding a Closing Dash

214 **a.** When a *statement* or a *command* is set off by dashes within a sentence, do not use a period before the closing dash (except a period following an abbreviation).

> After she won last year's literary award—there was a $10 000 cash prize—she pursued her studies at Simon Fraser University.

> (**NOT:** After she won last year's literary award—there was a $10 000 cash prize.—she pursued her studies at Simon Fraser University.)

> Your proposal was late—it arrived at 6:15 p.m.—and could not be considered as the submission deadline had passed.

b. When a *question* or an *exclamation* is set off by dashes within a sentence, use a question mark or an exclamation point before the closing dash.

> The representative of the ABD Company—do you know her?—has called again.

> The new plans—I can't wait to show them to you!—should be ready by Friday.

c. When a complete sentence is set off by dashes, do not capitalize the first word unless it is a proper noun, a proper adjective, the pronoun *I*, or the first word of a quoted sentence.

Punctuation Following a Closing Dash

215 When the sentence construction requires some mark of punctuation after a closing dash, either keep the dash or use the sentence punctuation—but do not use both marks together.

a. When a closing dash falls at the end of a sentence, it should be replaced by the punctuation needed to end the sentence—a period, a question mark, or an exclamation point. (See ¶208 for exceptions.)

> Wheeler's Transport delivers the goods—on time!

> (**NOT:** Wheeler's Transport delivers the goods—on time—!)

b. When a closing dash occurs at a point where the sentence requires a comma, retain the closing dash and omit the comma.

> The situation has become critical—indeed dangerous—but no one seems to care. (Here the closing dash is retained, and the comma before the coordinating conjunction is omitted.)

> If you feel you are qualified for the job—and you may very well be—you ought to take the employment test. (Here the closing dash is retained, and the comma that separates a dependent clause from an independent clause is omitted.)

Brophy said—and you can check with him yourself—"This office must be vacated by Friday." (Here the closing dash is retained, and the comma before the quotation is omitted.)

NOTE: Do not put a phrase in dashes if the closing dash occurs at a point where a comma is needed after an item in a series. Put the phrase in parentheses instead.

CONFUSING: I plan to ask Spalding, Crawford—Betty, not Harold—Higgins, and Martin to investigate why sales have fallen off so sharply.

CLEAR: I plan to ask Spalding, Crawford (Betty, not Harold), Higgins, and Martin to investigate why sales have fallen off so sharply.

c. If a closing dash occurs at a point where the sentence requires a semicolon, a colon, or a closing parenthesis, drop the closing dash and use the required sentence punctuation.

Please try to get your sales projections to us by Wednesday—certainly by Friday at the latest; otherwise, they will be of no use to us in planning next year's budget.

Here is what Marsha had to say—or at least the gist of it: look for new opportunities in niche marketing, and move quickly to capitalize on them.

You need a volunteer (for example, someone like Louis Morales—he's always co-operative) to play the part of the customer.

Constructing Dashes

216 **a.** Dashes can be found in some special character sets in word processing software, but the em dash may be constructed by using two hyphens. There are no spaces before or after an em dash.

Don't believe him—ever!   **NOT:** Don't believe him — ever!

b. Never use a single hyphen to represent a dash.

Only one person can do this job—you!

NOT: Only one person can do this job - you!   **OR:** . . . this job-you!

c. A two-em dash is used to indicate that letters are missing from a word. (Type two consecutive em dashes or four consecutive hyphens.) If letters are missing from *within* a word, leave no space before or after. If the letters are missing *at the end* of a word, leave no space before but leave one space after unless a mark of punctuation is required at that point.

Mr. T——n was the one who lied.   **OR:** Mr. T----n was the one . . .

Mrs. J—— asked not to be identified.   **OR:** Mrs. J---- asked not to be identified.

d. A three-em dash is used to indicate that an entire word has been omitted or needs to be provided. (Type three consecutive em dashes or six consecutive hyphens.) Leave one space before and after unless a mark of punctuation is required at this point.

Our sales will reach —— by March 31.   **OR:** reach ------ by March 31.

(Continued on page 58.)

NOTE: A three-em dash is also used in bibliographies to represent an author's name. See ¶1548 and the illustration on page 449.

e. Use an en dash—half the length of an em dash but longer than a hyphen—to connect numbers in a range. (If you do not have access to an en dash, use a hyphen.) The en dash means "up to and including" in expressions like these:

open 10 a.m.–6 p.m., Monday–Friday	see Chapters 2–3, pages 86–116
planned for the week of March 2–8	during the years 2002–2007
a loan of $50 000–$75 000 for 5–10 years	plans for employees aged 55–62

☞ *For the use of an en dash in certain compound adjectives, see ¶819b, note, and ¶821b. For other examples showing the use of an en dash, see ¶¶459–460. For proofreaders' coding of the length of dashes, see ¶1205.*

217 Type a dash at the end of a line (rather than at the start of a new line).

He lives in the Gatineaux—	NOT: He lives in the Gatineaux
in Wakefield, I believe.	—in Wakefield, I believe.

PARENTHESES

Parentheses and dashes serve many of the same functions, but they differ in one significant respect: parentheses can set off only non-essential elements, whereas dashes can set off essential and non-essential elements. **Remember:** In setting off elements, of a sentence, dashes emphasize but parentheses de-emphasize.

With Explanatory Matter

218 Use parentheses to enclose explanatory material that is independent of the main thought of the sentence. The material in parentheses may be a single word, a phrase, a sentence, a number, or an abbreviation.

Canada's official national games are lacrosse (summer) and hockey (winter). (Single words.)

By Friday (and sooner if possible) I will have an answer for you. (A phrase.)

Our competitors (we underprice them) can't understand how we do it. (A sentence.)

This note for Five Thousand Dollars ($5000) is payable within ninety (90) days. (Numbers. See ¶¶420a, 436 note.)

Many corporations have created a new top-level job: chief information officer (CIO). (Abbreviations. See ¶504 note.)

NOTE: Be sure that the parentheses enclose only what is truly parenthetical.

WRONG: I merely said I was averse (not violently opposed *to*) your suggestion.

RIGHT: I merely said I was averse (not violently opposed) *to* your suggestion.

219 Use parentheses to set off a non-essential element when dashes would be too emphatic and commas might create confusion.

a. Parentheses are clearer than commas when a city-province expression occurs as an adjective.

Sales are down in our Moncton (New Brunswick) office.

BETTER THAN: Sales are down in our Moncton, New Brunswick, office.

b. Parentheses are clearer than commas when the non-essential element already contains commas. (See ¶¶183, 202.)

In three of our factories (Oshawa, Hull, and Chicoutimi) output is up.

With References

220 Use parentheses to set off references and directions.

When I last wrote to you (see my letter of July 8 attached), I enclosed photocopies of cheques that you had endorsed and deposited.

When a reference falls *at the end of a sentence*, it may be treated as part of the sentence or as a separate sentence. (See also ¶225b.)

This point is discussed at greater length in Chapter 7 (see pages 90–101).

OR: This point is discussed at greater length in Chapter 7. (See pages 90–101.)

☞ *For the use of parentheses in footnotes, endnotes, and textnotes, see Section 15.*

With Dates

221 Use parentheses to enclose dates that accompany a person's name, a publication, or an event.

He claims that he can trace his family back to Charlemagne (742–814).

The "Sin On" Bible (1716) got its name from an extraordinary typographical error: instead of counselling readers to "sin no more," it urged them to "sin on more."

With Enumerated Items

222 a. Within a Sentence. Use parentheses to enclose numbers or letters that accompany enumerated items within a sentence.

We need the following information to complete our record of Ms. Pavlick's experience: (1) the number of years she worked for your company, (2) a description of her duties, and (3) the number of promotions she received.

NOT: . . . our record of Ms. Pavlick's experience: 1) the number of years she worked for your company, 2) a description of her duties, and 3) the number of promotions she received. (The only acceptable use of a single closing parenthesis is in an outline. See ¶223.)

NOTE: Letters are used to enumerate items within a sentence when the sentence itself is part of a *numbered* sequence.

3. Please include these items on your expense report: (a) the cost of your hotel room, (b) the cost of meals, and (c) the amount spent on travel.

b. In a Displayed List. If the enumerated items appear on separate lines, the letters or numbers are usually followed only by periods. (See ¶107.)

223 Subdivisions in outlines are often enclosed in parentheses. It is sometimes necessary to use a single closing parenthesis to provide another level of subdivision.

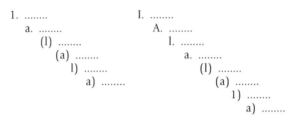

NOTE: At every level of an outline, there should be at least two items. If an item is labelled *A*, there must be at least one more item (labelled *B*) at the same level.

☞ *For guidelines on formatting outlines, see ¶¶1715–1719.*

Punctuation With Parenthetical Items

224 For punctuation either before or after a closing parenthesis, the following guidelines apply:

a. Make sure that any punctuation that comes after the item (such as a comma, a semicolon, a colon, or a dash) falls *outside* the closing parenthesis.

Unless I hear from you within five working days (by May 3), I will turn this matter over to my lawyer.

I tried to reach you last Monday (I called just before noon); however, no one in your office knew where you were.

For Jane there is only one goal right now (and you know it): getting that MBA.

I saw your picture in a newspaper last week (in the *Journal*, I think)—and how I laughed when I saw who was standing next to you!

NOTE: Do not insert a comma, a semicolon, a colon, or a dash *before* an opening parenthesis.

b. Do not use a period before the closing parenthesis except with an abbreviation.

RIGHT: Our office is open late on Thursdays (until 9 p.m.).

RIGHT: Our office is open late on Thursdays (we're here until nine).

WRONG: Our office is open late on Thursdays (We're here until nine.).

RIGHT: Plan to stay with us (we are only 15 minutes from the airport) whenever you come to Victoria.

WRONG: Plan to stay with us (We are only 15 minutes from the airport.) whenever you come to Victoria.

c. Do not use a question mark or an exclamation point before the closing parenthesis unless it applies solely to the parenthetical item *and* the sentence ends with a different mark of punctuation.

At the coming meeting (will you be able to make it on the 19th?), let's plan to discuss next year's budget. (Question mark used in parentheses because the sentence ends with a period.)

May I still get tickets to the show (and may I bring a friend), or is it too late? (Question mark omitted in parentheses because the sentence ends with a question mark.)

NOT: May I still get tickets to the show (and may I bring a friend?), or is it too late?

Do you know Ellen Smyth (or is it Smythe)?

NOT: Do you know Ellen Smyth (or is it Smythe?)?

I am through with this job (and I mean it)!

NOT: I am through with this job (and I mean it!)!

Capitalization of Parenthetical Items

225 **a.** Do not capitalize the first word of the item in parentheses, even if the item is a complete sentence. **EXCEPTIONS:** Proper nouns, proper adjectives, the pronoun *I*, and the first word of a quoted sentence. Note the examples below and those in ¶224.

Paul Melnick (Staple's new sales manager) wants to take you to lunch.

At last week's hearing (I had to leave at 4 p.m.) was the relocation proposed?

b. When a complete sentence occurs within parentheses at the end of another sentence, it may be incorporated into the sentence if it is short and closely related, as shown in some of the examples in ¶224 and ¶225; otherwise, make it a separate sentence (see ¶226).

Parenthetical Items as Separate Sentences

226 If the item in parentheses is to be made a *separate sentence:*

a. The preceding sentence should close with a punctuation mark of its own.

b. The item in parentheses should begin with a capital letter.

c. A period, a question mark, or an exclamation point should be placed *before* the closing parenthesis.

d. No other punctuation mark should follow the closing parenthesis. (See ¶298 for additional guidelines on spacing.)

Then Steven Pelletier made a motion to replace the existing board of directors. (He does this at every shareholders' meeting.) However, this year . . .

I was most impressed with the speech given by Helena Verdi. (Didn't you use to work with her?) She knew her subject and she knew her audience.

☞ *Parentheses around question marks: see ¶118.*
Parentheses around exclamation points: see ¶119c.

(Continued on page 62.)

Parentheses around confirming figures: see ¶420.
Parentheses around area codes in telephone numbers: see ¶454.
Parenthetical elements within parenthetical elements: see ¶297.
Plural endings in parentheses, see ¶626.

QUOTATION MARKS

Quotation marks have three main functions: to indicate the use of someone else's exact words (see ¶¶227–234), to set off words and phrases for special emphasis (see ¶¶235–241), and to display the titles of literary and artistic works (see ¶¶242–244).

To position punctuation marks in relation to the closing quotation mark—*inside* or *outside*—see ¶¶247–251.

For more specific guidance on when to use punctuation with quoted matter and which punctuation to use, refer to the following paragraphs:

☞ *Quotations standing alone: see ¶252.*
Quotations at the beginning of a sentence: see ¶¶253–255.
Quotations at the end of a sentence: see ¶¶256–258.
Quotations within a sentence: see ¶¶259–261.
Quotations with interrupting expressions: see ¶¶262–263.
Quotations within quotations: see ¶¶245–246.
Long quotations: see ¶264–265.
Quoted letters: see ¶266.
Quoted poetry: see ¶¶267–268.
Quoted dialogues and conversations: see ¶¶269–270.
Quotation marks as a symbol for inches: see ¶543.

With Direct Quotations

227 Use quotation marks to enclose a *direct quotation*, that is, the exact words of a speaker or a writer.

> Ferguson merely said, "Let's get out of here before someone reconsiders the verdict."

> When I asked Diana whether she liked the new format of the magazine, all she said was "No." (See ¶¶233, 256a.)

228 a. Do not use quotation marks for an *indirect quotation*, that is, a restatement or rearrangement of a person's exact words. (An indirect quotation is often introduced by *that* or *whether* and usually differs from a direct quotation in person, verb tense, or word order.)

> DIRECT QUOTATION: Mrs. Knudsen asked her supervisor, "Am I still being considered for the transfer?"
> INDIRECT QUOTATION: Mrs. Knudsen asked her supervisor whether she was still being considered for the transfer.

> DIRECT QUOTATION: Her supervisor said, "You're still in the running, but don't expect a quick decision."
> INDIRECT QUOTATION: Her supervisor said that she was still in the running but that she should not expect a quick decision.

NOTE: Sometimes *direct* quotations are introduced by *that*. See ¶¶256f and 272 note.

b. In some cases a person's exact words may be treated as either a direct or an indirect quotation, depending on the kind of emphasis desired.

> The chairman himself said, "The staff should be told at once that the rumours about a new building have no foundation." (The use of quotation marks emphasizes that these are the chairman's exact words.)

> The chairman himself said that the staff should be told at once that the rumours about a new building have no foundation. (Without quotation marks, the emphasis falls on the message itself. The fact that the chairman used these exact words is not important.)

229 Do not use quotation marks to set off a *direct question* at the end of a sentence unless it is also a *direct quotation* of someone's exact words.

> **DIRECT QUESTION:** The question is, Who will pay for restoring the landmark?

> **DIRECT QUOTATION:** Mrs. Burchall then asked, "Who will pay for restoring the landmark?" (See ¶¶247–249 for the order of punctuation marks.)

> **DIRECT QUOTATION:** Mrs. Burchall then replied, "The question is, Who will pay for restoring the landmark?" (See also ¶115.)

230 Quotation marks are not needed to set off interior thoughts or imagined dialogue. Treat this kind of material like a *direct question* (as shown in ¶229).

> After I left Joe's office, I thought, He has no business telling me what to do. I should have said, I can handle this situation—thank you very much!—without your help.

NOTE: In special cases quotation marks may help to preserve clarity or maintain stylistic consistency (for example, when imaginary dialogue is interspersed with actual dialogue).

231 **a.** When only a word or phrase is quoted from another source, be sure to place the quotation marks only around the words extracted from the original source and not around any rearrangement of those words.

> Tanya said she would need "more help" in order to finish your report by this Friday. (Tanya's exact words were, "How can he expect me to finish his report by this Friday without more help?")

b. When a quoted word or phrase comes at the end of a sentence, the period goes *inside* the closing quotation mark.

> Barbara described the plain white shift she wore to the masquerade party as a "Freudian slip." (See also ¶247a, particularly examples 2–4.)

c. Be particularly sure not to include such words as *a* and *the* at the beginning of the quotation or *etc.* at the end unless these words were actually part of the original material.

> Ben thought you did a "super" job on the packaging design. (Ben's exact words were, "Tell Bonnie I thought the job she did on the packaging design was super.")

> Explain the decision any way you want, but tell George I said, "I'm truly sorry about the way things turned out," etc., etc.

232   When quoting a series of words or phrases in the exact order in which they originally appeared, use quotation marks before and after the complete series. However, if the series of quoted words or phrases did not appear in this sequence in the original, use quotation marks around each word or phrase.

> According to Selma, the latest issue of the magazine looked "fresh, crisp, and appealing." (Selma's actual words were, "I think the new issue looks especially fresh, crisp, and appealing.")
>
> **OR:** Selma thinks the magazine looks "fresh" and "crisp."
> (**NOT:** Selma thinks the magazine looks "fresh and crisp.")

233   Do not quote the words *yes* and *no* unless you wish to emphasize that these were (or will be) the exact words spoken.

> Please answer the question yes or no.
>
> Don't say no until you have heard all the terms of the proposal.
>
> When asked if he would accept a reassignment, Nick thought for a moment; then, without any trace of emotion, he said "Yes." (The quotation marks imply that Nick said precisely this much and no more. See ¶256a note for the use or omission of a comma after *he said*.)

NOTE: When quoting the words *yes* and *no*, capitalize them if they represent a complete sentence.

> All she said was "No."
>
> I would have to answer that question by saying "Yes and no."
>
> **BUT:** That question requires something more than a yes-or-no answer.

234   Do not use quotation marks with well-known proverbs and sayings. They are not direct quotations.

> Sidney really believes that an apple a day keeps the doctor away.

For Special Emphasis

235   When using technical terms, business jargon, or coined words not likely to be familiar to your reader, enclose them in quotation marks when they are first used.

> Some software users become confused when directed to press any key. They complain that they cannot find the "any" key.
>
> Will you agree to a "desktop" approach for approving the trustee's accounts?

236   **a.**   Words used humorously or ironically may be enclosed in quotation marks. However, unless you are convinced your reader will otherwise miss the humour or the irony, omit the quotation marks.

> I was totally underwhelmed by Joe's proposal to centralize all purchasing.
> (**RATHER THAN:** I was totally "underwhelmed" by Joe's proposal . . .)
>
> HDL cholesterol is the good kind; it's LDL that's the bad kind.
> (**RATHER THAN:** . . . the "good" kind . . . the "bad" kind . . .)
>
> Nothing would please me more than looking at the slides of Mike's tour of Egypt. (One might reasonably conclude that the writer takes unalloyed pleasure at the prospect.)

BUT: "Nothing" would please me more than looking at the slides of Mike's tour of Egypt. (When *Nothing* is enclosed in quotation marks, the writer makes it clear that doing nothing would be preferable to looking at Mike's slides.)

b. A slang expression, the use of poor grammar, or a deliberate misspelling is enclosed in quotation marks to indicate that such usage is not part of the writer's normal way of speaking or writing.

Now that his kids have run off to Europe with the college tuition money, Bob has stopped boasting about his close-knit "nucular" family. (The writer is mimicking Bob's habitual mispronunciation of *nuclear*.)

As far as I'm concerned, Polly Harrington's version of what happened "ain't necessarily so."

c. Quotation marks are not needed for colloquial expressions.

She cares less about the salary than she does about the perks—you know, chauffeured limousine, stock options, and all the rest of it. (*Perks* is short for perquisites, meaning "special privileges.")

Pam is planning to temp until she's sure about staying in Sherbrooke. (*To temp* means "to do temporary work.")

237 a. Use quotation marks to enclose words and phrases that have been made to play an abnormal role in a sentence—for example, verb phrases made to function as adjectives.

We were all impressed by her "can do" attitude. (*Can do* is a verb phrase used here as an adjective modifying *attitude*.)

OR: We were all impressed by her can-do attitude. (A hyphen may also be used to hold together a phrase used as an adjective before a noun. See ¶828.)

NOT: We were all impressed by her "can-do" attitude. (Do not use both quotation marks and a hyphen for the same purpose.)

I'm selling my car on an "as is" (**OR** as-is) basis.

NOTE: When a verb like *must* or a preposition and adverb like *in* becomes established as a noun or an adjective (as indicated in the dictionary), use quotation marks only when confusion could otherwise result.

You have to read that book; it's a must.

BUT: You have to get that book; it's "must" reading.

Frank must have an in with their purchasing department.

BUT: I guess she thinks it's still the "in" thing to do.

b. Do not use quotation marks to enclose phrases that are taken from other parts of speech and are now well established as nouns. (See also ¶625.)

a helpful list of dos and don'ts.

all the whys and wherefores.

a lot of ifs, ands, or buts. (See also ¶285.)

238 When a word or an expression is being formally defined, it is usually italicized or underlined and the definition is usually put in quotation marks so that the

(Continued on page 66.)

two elements may be easily distinguished from one another. (See ¶¶285a, 289b.)

A mari usque ad maris, Canada's motto, is officially translated as "From sea to sea."

☞ *For guidelines on italics and underlining, see ¶288a, 289.*

239 **a.** Words and phrases introduced by such expressions as *marked, labelled, signed, titled,* and *entitled* are enclosed in quotation marks.

The carton was marked "Fragile."

He received a message signed "A Friend."

The article entitled "Write Your Chairman" was in that issue. (See ¶260.)

b. Titles of complete published works following the expression *entitled, titled,* or *called,* require italics or underlining rather than quotation marks. (See ¶287 and ¶289 for titles to be italicized or underlined; ¶¶242–244 for titles to be put in quotation marks.)

240 Words and phrases introduced by *so-called* do not require quotation marks, italics, or underlining. The expression *so-called* is sufficient to give special emphasis to the term that follows.

The so-called orientation session struck me as an exercise in brainwashing.

241 The translation of a foreign expression is enclosed in quotation marks; the foreign word itself is italicized or underlined. (See ¶¶285d, 289b.)

With Titles of Literary and Artistic Works

242 Use quotation marks around the titles of *part* of a complete published work—for example, the titles of chapters, lessons, topics, and sections in a book; the titles of articles and feature columns in newspapers and magazines; and the titles of essays, short poems, lectures, sermons, and conference themes. (Italicize or underline titles of *complete* published works. See ¶289.)

The heart of her argument can be found in Chapter 3, "The Failure of Traditional Therapy." You will especially want to read the section entitled "Does Father Know Best?"

An exciting article—"Can Cancer Now Be Cured?"—appears in the magazine I'm enclosing. (See ¶¶260–261 for the use of commas, dashes, and parentheses with titles in quotation marks.)

The theme of next month's workshop is "Imperatives for the Twenty-First Century—From the Ragged Edge to the Cutting Edge."

The title of my speech for next month's luncheon will be "Reforming Our Sales Tax Policy."

BUT: At next month's luncheon, I will be talking about reforming our sales tax policy. (Do not enclose the words in quotation marks when they describe the topic rather than signify the exact title.)

NOTE: The words *Preface, Contents, Appendix,* and *Index* are not put in quotation marks, even though they are parts of a book. They are often capitalized, however, for special emphasis.

All the supporting data is given in the Appendix. (Often capitalized when referring to another section of the same work.)

BUT: You'll find that the most interesting part of his book is contained in the appendix. (Capitalization is not required when reference is made to a section within another work.)

243 Use quotation marks around the titles of *complete but unpublished* works, such as manuscripts, dissertations, and reports.

I would like to get a copy of Sandor's study, "Criteria for Evaluating Staff Efficiency."

Thank you for giving us the chance to review "Working out of Your Home." I have given your manuscript to an editor with a good deal of personal experience in this field.

244 Use quotation marks around the titles of songs and other short musical compositions and around the titles of individual segments or programs that are part of a larger television or radio series. (Series titles are italicized or underlined.)

Just once I would like to get through a company party without having to hear Reggie sing "Danny Boy."

I understand that our company was briefly mentioned on the *Sunday Report* program entitled "Ottawa, Inc.," which was shown last Sunday night.

Quotations Within Quotations

245 A quotation within another quotation is enclosed in single quotation marks. Use the apostrophe for a single quotation mark.

Fowler then said, "We were all impressed by her 'can do' attitude."

246 If a quotation appears within the single-quoted material, revert to double quotation marks for the inner portion.

Mrs. DeVries then remarked, "I thought it a bit strange when Mr. Fowler said, 'Put these cheques in an envelope marked "Personal Funds," and set them aside for me.'" (When single and double quotation marks occur together, insert extra space between the two marks to keep them distinct.)

NOTE: For the positioning of punctuation in relation to a single quotation mark, see the following paragraphs:

☞ *For placement of periods and commas, see ¶247b.*

For placement of semicolons and colons, see ¶248b.

For placement of question marks and exclamation points, see ¶249d.

For placement of dashes, see ¶250b.

The following rules (¶¶247–251) indicate how to position punctuation marks in relation to the closing quotation mark—inside *or* outside.

With Periods and Commas

247 a. Periods and commas always go *inside* the closing quotation mark. This is the preferred North American style. (Some writers, however, follow the British style: Place the period *outside* when it punctuates the whole sentence, *inside*

(Continued on page 68.)

2

when it punctuates only the quoted matter. Place the comma *outside*, since it always punctuates the sentence, not the quoted matter.)

Before the conference began, Mr. Karras made a point of saying, "Let me do the talking."

He wants to change "on or about May 1" to read "no later than May 1."

The price tag on the leather couch was clearly marked "Sold."

Sign your name wherever you see an "X."

"Let's go over the details again," she said.

"The date stamp indicates that my copy arrived at 10:50 a.m.," he said.

Their latest article, "Scanning the Future," will appear in next month's issue of *Equinox* magazine.

"Witty," "clever," "amusing," and "hilarious" are only a few of the adjectives that are being applied to her new book.

The package was labelled "Fragile," but that meant nothing to your delivery crew.

b. Periods and commas also go *inside* the single closing quotation mark.

Mr. Poston said, "Please let me see all the orders marked 'Rush.'"

"All he would say was 'I don't remember,'" answered the witness.

NOTE: Do not confuse a single quotation mark with an apostrophe used to show possession. When a sentence requires the use of a comma or a period at the same point as an apostrophe showing possession, the comma or period *follows* the apostrophe.

I recently took over the management of the Murrays', the Boyarskys', and the Cabots' investment portfolios.

With Semicolons and Colons

248 a. Semicolons and colons always go *outside* the closing quotation mark.

Last Tuesday you said, "I will mail a cheque today"; it has not yet arrived.

Please send me the following items from the file labelled "In Process": the latest draft of the Berryman agreement and CJS Statement 33.

The memo I sent you yesterday said that the new workstations would cost "a nominal egg"; it should have said "an arm and a leg."

b. Semicolons and colons also go *outside* the single closing quotation mark.

Alice Arroyo called in from her country place to say, "Please send me the following items from the file labelled 'In Process': the latest draft of the Berryman agreement and CJS Statement 33."

With Question Marks and Exclamation Points

249 a. A question mark or an exclamation point goes *inside* the closing quotation mark when it applies only to the quoted material.

His first question was, "How long have you worked here?" (Quoted question at the end of a statement.)

Garland still ends every sales meeting by shouting, "Go get 'em!" (Quoted exclamation at the end of a statement.)

b. A question mark or an exclamation point goes *outside* the closing quotation mark when it applies to the entire sentence.

> When will she say, for a change, "You did a nice job on that"? (Quoted statement at the end of a question.)
>
> Stop saying "Don't worry"! (Quoted statement at the end of an exclamation.)

c. If the quoted material and the entire sentence each require the same mark of punctuation, use only one mark—the one that comes first. (See also ¶¶257–258.)

> Have you seen the advertisement that starts, "Why pay more?" (Quoted question at the end of a question.)
>
> Let's not panic and yell "Fire!" (Quoted exclamation at the end of an exclamation.)

d. These same principles govern the placement of a question mark or an exclamation point in relation to a single quotation mark.

> What prompted her to say, "Be careful in handling documents marked 'Confidential'"? (Quoted phrase within a quoted statement within a question.)
>
> Dr. Marks asked, "Was the cheque marked 'Insufficient Funds'?" (Quoted phrase within a quoted question within a statement.)
>
> Miss Parsons then said, "How did you answer him when he asked you, 'How do you know?'" (Quoted question within a quoted question within a statement.)

With Dashes

250 **a.** A dash goes *inside* the closing quotation mark to show that the speaker's or writer's words have broken off abruptly.

> It was tragic to hear Tom say, "If he had only listened—"

b. A dash goes *outside* the closing quotation mark when the sentence breaks off abruptly *after* the quotation.

> If I hear one more word about "boosting productivity"—
>
> **BUT:** Mrs. Halliday said, "If I hear one more word from the general manager about 'boosting productivity'—"

c. A closing dash goes *outside* the closing quotation mark when the quotation itself is part of a non-essential element being set off by a pair of dashes.

> Get the latest draft—it's the one with the notation "Let's go with this"—and take it to Gladys Pomeroy for her approval.

With Parentheses

251 **a.** The closing parenthesis goes *inside* the closing quotation mark when the parenthetical element is part of the quotation.

> Fox agreed to settle his account "by Friday (July 28)" when he last wrote us.

b. The closing parenthesis goes *outside* the closing quotation mark when the quotation is part of the parenthetical element.

> Joe Elliott (the one everyone calls "Harper's gofer") will probably get the job.

(Continued on page 70.)

The following rules (¶¶252–270) indicate what punctuation to use with various kinds of quoted matter.

Punctuating Quotations That Stand Alone

252 When a quoted sentence stands alone, put the mark of terminal punctuation—a period, a question mark, or an exclamation point—*inside* the closing quotation mark.

> "I think we should switch suppliers at once."
>
> "Can you send us your comments within two weeks?"
>
> "I won't accept that kind of response!"

Punctuating Quotations That Begin a Sentence

253 **a.** When a quoted *statement* occurs at the beginning of a sentence, omit the period before the closing quotation mark and use a comma instead.

> "I think we should switch suppliers at once," he said.
> (**NOT:** . . . at once.," he said.)

> **EXCEPTION:** Retain the period if it accompanies an abbreviation.

> "I'm still planning to go on for an LL.B.," she said.

b. Omit the comma after a quoted statement if it is smoothly woven into the flow of the sentence.

> "He hasn't a clue" is all Bert says when you ask how Joe is doing.
> (**NOT:** "He hasn't a clue," is all Bert says . . .)

254 When a quoted *question* or *exclamation* occurs at the beginning of a sentence, retain the question mark or the exclamation point before the closing quotation mark and do *not* insert a comma.

> "Can you send us your comments within two weeks?" she asked.
> (**NOT:** . . . within two weeks?," she asked.)

> "I won't accept that kind of response!" I told him.
> (**NOT:** . . . that kind of response!," I told him.)

255 When a quoted *word* or *phrase* occurs at the beginning of a sentence, no punctuation should accompany the closing quotation mark unless required by the overall construction of the sentence.

> "An utter bore" was the general reaction to yesterday's speaker.

> "Managing Your Portfolio," the second chapter in the Klingenstein book, sets forth some guidelines I have never seen anywhere else. (The comma that follows the chapter title is the first of a pair needed to set off a non-essential expression.)

Punctuating Quotations That End a Sentence

256 **a.** When a quoted *statement, question,* or *exclamation* comes at the end of a sentence and is introduced by an expression such as *he said* or *she said*, a comma usually precedes the opening quotation mark.

> Mr. Kelley said, "We'll close early on Friday."

> In her letter Diana said, "I plan to arrive on Thursday at 6 p.m."

NOTE: If the quotation is quite short or is woven into the flow of the sentence, omit the comma.

All she said was "No." **OR:** All she said was, "No." (The comma creates a slight pause and throws greater emphasis on the quotation.)

Why does he keep saying "It won't work"?

b. Use a colon in place of a comma if the introductory expression is an independent clause.

Jerry would say only this: "I'll send you my new address once I'm settled."

Here is the key statement in his letter: "If my loan is approved, the deal is on."

c. Use a colon in place of a comma if the quotation contains more than one sentence.

Mr. Bowles then said: "If the legislation is passed by Parliament, we have an excellent chance to compete effectively in international markets. However, if the legislation is held up in committee, our competitive position will worsen."

d. Use a colon in place of a comma if the quotation is set off on separate lines as an extract. (See also ¶265.)

Sheila's letter said in part:

> I have greatly valued your assistance. You have always
> acted as if you were actually part of our staff, with our best
> interests in mind.

e. Do not use either a comma or a colon before an indirect quotation.

Sheila said that she had always valued Bob's assistance on various projects.

f. Do not use either a comma or a colon when a direct quotation is introduced by *that* or is otherwise woven into the flow of the sentence.

In a previous letter to you, I noted that "you have always acted as if you were actually part of our staff, with our best interests in mind."

NOTE: The first word of the quotation is not capitalized in this case, even though it was capitalized in the original. Compare *you* here with *You* in the example in *d* above. (See ¶272 for the rule on capitalizing the first word of a quoted sentence.)

257 When a quoted *sentence* (a statement, a question, or an exclamation) falls at the end of a larger sentence, do not use double punctuation—that is, one mark to end the quotation and another to end the sentence. Choose the stronger mark. (**REMEMBER:** *A question mark is stronger than a period; an exclamation point is stronger than a period or a question mark.*) If the same mark of punctuation is required for both the quotation and the sentence as a whole, use the first mark that occurs—the one within quotation marks.

Quoted Sentences at the End of a Statement

Bob said, "I can't wait to get back to work." (**NOT** .".)

Mrs. Fahey asked, "How long have you been away?" (**NOT** ?".)

Mr. Auden shouted, "We can't operate a business this way!" (**NOT** !".)

(Continued on page 72.)

Quoted Sentences at the End of a Question

Did you say, "I'll help out"? (NOT ."?)

Why did Mary ask, "Will Joe be there?" (NOT ?"?)

Who yelled "Watch out!" (NOT !"?)

Quoted Sentences at the End of an Exclamation

How could you forget to follow up when you were specifically told, "Give this order special attention"! (NOT ."!)

Stop saying "How should I know"! (NOT ?"!)

How I'd like to walk into his office and say, "I quit!" (NOT !"!)

NOTE: When a quoted sentence ends with an abbreviation, retain the abbreviation period, even though a question mark or an exclamation point follows as the terminal mark of punctuation.

The reporter asked, "When did you first hear about the board's decision to sell Modem Inc.?"

Didn't Larry tell Meg, "I'll help you with the tuition for your M.D."?

However, if a period is required as the terminal mark of punctuation, use only one period to mark both the end of the abbreviation and the end of the sentence.

Gloria said, "You can call as early as 6:30 a.m." (NOT .".)

☞ *For placement of periods, see ¶247.*

For placement of question marks and exclamation points, see ¶249.

258 When a quoted *word* or *phrase* occurs at the end of a sentence, punctuate according to the appropriate pattern in the following examples. (NOTE: If the quoted word or phrase is a complete sentence, follow the patterns shown in ¶257.)

Quoted Words and Phrases at the End of a Statement

He says he is willing to meet "at your convenience." (NOT ".)

I thought her letter said she would arrive "at 10 p.m." (NOT .".)

I've been meaning to read "Who Pays the Bill?" (NOT ?".)

Critics have praised his latest article, "Freedom Now!" (NOT !".)

Quoted Words and Phrases at the End of a Question

Why is he so concerned about my "convenience"?

Didn't she clearly state she would arrive "at 10 p.m."?

Have you had a chance to read "Who Pays the Bill?" (NOT ?"?)

What did you think of the article "Freedom Now!"?

Quoted Words and Phrases at the End of an Exclamation

He couldn't care less about my "convenience"!

You are quite mistaken—she clearly said "at 10 a.m."!

Don't waste your time reading "Who Pays the Bill?"!

What a reaction he got with his article "Freedom Now!" (NOT !"!)

Punctuating Quotations Within a Sentence

259 Do not use a comma before or after a quotation when it is woven into the flow of the sentence.

> Don't say "I can't do it" without trying.
>
> No considerate person would say "Why should I care?" under such desperate circumstances.
>
> The audience shouted "Bravo!" and "Encore!" at the end of Ben Heppner's recital last night.

NOTE: In such cases do not use a period at the end of a quoted statement, but retain the question mark or the exclamation point at the end of a quoted question or exclamation (as illustrated in the examples above).

260 Do not use commas to set off a quotation that occurs within a sentence as an *essential* expression. (See ¶149.)

> It has been mistakenly claimed that the luxurious practice of booking passage between England and India on the basis of "Port Out, Starboard Home" (so as to get a cabin on the cooler side of the ship) is the origin of the word *posh*.
>
> The chapter entitled "Locating Sources of Venture Capital" will give you specific leads you can pursue.

261 **a.** When a quotation occurs within a sentence as a *non-essential* expression, use a comma before the opening quotation mark and before the closing quotation mark.

> His parting words, "I hardly know how to thank you," were sufficient.
>
> The next chapter, "The Role of Government," further clarifies the answer.

b. If the *non-essential* quoted matter requires a question mark or an exclamation point before the closing quotation mark, use a pair of dashes or parentheses (rather than commas) to set off the quoted matter.

> Your last question—"How can we improve communications between departments?"—can best be answered by you.
>
> **RATHER THAN:** Your last question, "How can we improve communications between departments?," can best be answered by you.

NOTE: When some or all of the quoted items in a series end with a question mark or an exclamation point, display them in a list to avoid the awkwardness of inserting commas before the quotation marks.

> Next month's issue will feature the following articles:
>
> > "What Is Your Investor Personality?"
> >
> > "Tax Law Changes—Again!"
> >
> > "Is It the Bay Connection?"
>
> **RATHER THAN:** Next month's issue will feature the following articles: "What Is Your Investor Personality?," "Tax Law Changes—Again!," and "Is It the Bay Connection?"

(Continued on page 74.)

c. If *essential* quoted matter ends with a question mark or an exclamation point and occurs within a sentence where a comma would ordinarily follow (for example, at the end of an introductory clause or phrase), omit the comma.

> Although we were all asked last week to read an article entitled "Can Our Manufacturers Prosper in Today's World Markets?" the topic was totally ignored in this week's seminar.

> **RATHER THAN:** . . . an article entitled "Can Our Manufacturers Prosper in Today's World Markets?," the topic was . . .

NOTE: If the omission of a comma at this point could lead to confusion, reword the sentence to avoid the problem.

> We were all asked last week to read an article entitled "Can Our Manufacturers Prosper in Today's World Markets?" Yet the topic was . . .

> **OR:** We were all asked last week to read an article entitled "Can Our Manufacturers Prosper in Today's World Markets?"; yet the topic was . . .

Punctuating Quoted Sentences With Interrupting Expressions

262 When a quoted sentence is *interrupted* by an expression such as *he asked* or *she said*, use a comma and a closing quotation mark before the interrupting expression and another comma after it. Then resume the quotation with an opening quotation mark. Put the first word in lower case letters unless it is a proper noun, a proper adjective, or the pronoun *I*.

> "During the past month," the memo said in part, "we have received some welcome news from our overseas branches."

263 If the interrupting expression ends the sentence and the quotation continues in a new sentence, put a period after the interrupting expression and start the new sentence with an opening quotation mark and a capital letter.

> "Perhaps we should decline the invitation," he said. "It would be better not to go than to arrive late."

Punctuating Long Quotations

264 If a quotation consists of more than one sentence without any interrupting elements, use quotation marks only at the beginning and at the end of the quotation. Do not put quotation marks around each sentence within the quotation.

> Here is the full text of the release he gave to the media: "I have decided to withdraw from the upcoming election. I wish to thank my supporters for their enormous help. I am sorry to disappoint them."

265 A long quotation that will make four or more lines may be handled in one of two ways:

a. The preferred style for displaying the quoted matter is to treat it as a single-spaced extract. (See ¶1425d for an illustration of an extract.)
- Indent the extract from each side margin 0.25" to 0.5", and leave one blank line above and below it.
- Do not enclose the quoted matter in quotation marks; the indention replaces them.

- Retain the quotation marks around any quoted material that appears within the extract.
- Leave a blank line between paragraphs if the extract consists of more than one paragraph.

b. Use the same length of line and spacing for the quoted matter as for other text on the page.
- If the quoted matter consists of one paragraph only, place quotation marks at the beginning and end of the paragraph. Use the normal paragraph indention.
- If the quoted matter consists of two or more paragraphs, put a quotation mark *at the beginning* of each paragraph but at the end of the last paragraph only.
- Change double quotation marks within the quoted matter to single quotation marks, and vice versa. (See ¶¶245–246.)

> "When you are writing a letter that grants a request, you can follow this pattern:
>
> "First, express appreciation for the writer's interest in the company's product or service.
>
> "Next, give the exact information requested and, if possible, additional information that may be of interest.
>
> "Finally, express willingness to 'be of further help.'"

Quoting Business Documents

266 For documents and letters that are to be quoted in their entirety, make a printout, a photocopy, or a scanned copy of the material. No quotation marks are needed. (See ¶1437 regarding copyright laws.)

Quoting Poetry

267 When quoting a complete poem (or an extended portion of one) in a letter or a report, key it line for line, single-spaced (except for stanza breaks). If the line length is shorter than that of the text above and below the poem, no quotation marks are needed; the poem will stand out sufficiently. If, however, quotation marks are needed to indicate the special nature of the poem, place quotation marks at the beginning of each stanza and at the end of only the last stanza.

NOTE: As a rule, follow the poet's layout of the poem. If the poet uses an irregular pattern of indention (instead of the customary practice of aligning all lines at the left), try to reproduce this layout.

268 A short extract from a poem is sometimes woven right into a sentence or a paragraph. In such cases use quotation marks at the beginning and end of the extract, and use a diagonal (with one space before and after) to show where each line breaks in the actual poem.

> In his poem entitled "Newfoundland," E. J. Pratt wrote, "And the story is told / Of human veins and pulses, / Of eternal pathways of fire, / Of dreams that survive the night, / Of doors held ajar in storms."

Quoting Dialogues and Conversations

269   When quoting dialogues and conversations, start the remarks of each speaker as a new paragraph, no matter how brief.

> "Do you have a college education?" she asked the applicant.
>
> "No, not at all."
>
> "Well then, I guess you'll have to use your brains."
>
> —J. Roby Kidd

270   In plays, court testimony, and transcripts of conversations, where the name of the speaker is indicated, quotation marks are not needed.

> Mr. Luney: Americans like to make money, he said.
>
> Ms. Beaver: Yes. That's certainly true, but we Canadians like to audit it.
>
> Mr. Luney: Well, if that's the case, I don't know of any other country where the accountant enjoys a higher social and moral status.
>
> —Nicholas Frye

The following rules (¶¶271–284) cover a number of stylistic matters, such as how to style quoted material (¶271), how to capitalize quoted material (¶¶272–273), how to handle omissions in quoted material (¶¶274–280), how to handle insertions in quoted material (¶¶281–283), and how to align quotation marks (¶284).

Style in Quoted Matter

271   In copying quoted matter, follow the style of the extract exactly in punctuation, spelling, hyphenation, and number style. (See ¶283 for the use of [*sic*] to indicate errors in the original.)

Capitalization in Quoted Matter

272   Ordinarily, capitalize the first word of every complete sentence in quotation marks.

> I overheard Chow mutter, "Only a fool would make such a claim."
>
> Here is the key sentence in her memo: "Despite the understaffing in the department, everyone is expected to meet the goals established for the coming year."

NOTE: If the quoted sentence is preceded by *that* or is otherwise incorporated into the flow of a larger sentence, do not capitalize the first word (unless it is a proper noun, a proper adjective, or the pronoun *I*).

> I overheard Chow mutter that "only a fool would make such a claim."
>
> In essence, she says that "despite the understaffing in the department, everyone is expected to meet the goals established for the coming year."

273   When quoting a word or phrase, do not capitalize the first word unless it meets *one* of these conditions:

a. The first word is a proper noun, a proper adjective, or the pronoun *I*.

No one is terribly impressed by his "Irish temper."

b. The first word was capitalized in its original use.

I watched her scrawl "Approved" and sign her name at the bottom of the proposal.

c. The quoted word or phrase is at the beginning of a sentence.

"Outrageous" was the publisher's reaction to Maxon's attempt to duck the questions of the reporters. (Even if the expression was not capitalized in the original material, it is capitalized here to mark the start of the sentence.)

d. The first word represents a complete sentence.

The Crawleys said "Perhaps"; the Calnans said "No way."

☞ *See ¶¶277–278 on capitalizing the first word of a quoted sentence fragment.*

Omissions in Quoted Matter

274 If one or more words are omitted *within a quoted sentence*, use ellipsis marks (three spaced periods, with one space before and after each period) to indicate the omission.

"During the past fifty years . . . we have been witnessing a change in buying habits, particularly with respect to food."

NOTE: Omit any marks of internal punctuation (a comma, a semicolon, a colon, or a dash) on either side of the ellipsis marks unless they are necessary for the sake of clarity.

ORIGINAL VERSION: "The objectives of the proposed bill are admirable, I will cheerfully concede; the tactics being used to gain support for the bill are not."

CONDENSED VERSION: "The objectives of the proposed bill are admirable . . . ; the tactics being used to gain support for the bill are not." (The comma preceding the omitted phrase is not needed; however, the semicolon following the omitted phrase must be retained for clarity.)

275 If one or more words are omitted *at the end of a quoted sentence*, use three spaced periods followed by the necessary terminal punctuation for the sentence as a whole.

"Can anyone explain why . . . ?" (The original question read, "Can anyone explain why this was so?")

"During the past fifty years, starting in the late 1950s, we have been witnessing a change in buying habits . . . . Consumers have become more concerned with what's in the package than with the package itself." (The first three periods represent the omitted words "particularly with respect to food"; the fourth period marks the end of the sentence. Two spaces follow before the next sentence.)

NOTE: If the quotation is intended to trail off, use only three spaced periods at the end of the sentence. (See also ¶292a.)

His reaction was, "If I had only known . . ."

276 If one or more sentences are omitted *between other sentences* within a long quotation, use three spaced periods *after* the terminal punctuation of the preceding sentence.

> "During the past fifty years, starting in the late 1950s, we have been witnessing a change in buying habits, particularly with respect to food. . . . How far this pattern of change will extend cannot be estimated."

NOTE: There is no space between *food* and the first period because that period marks the end of a sentence. The remaining three periods signify the omission of one or more complete sentences. Two spaces follow before the next sentence.

277 If only a fragment of a sentence is quoted within another sentence, it is not necessary to use ellipsis marks to signify that words before or after the fragment have been omitted.

> According to Robertson's report, there has been "a change in buying habits" during the past 50 years.

Moreover, if the fragment as given can be read as a complete sentence, capitalize the first word in the quoted fragment, even though this word was not capitalized in the original. (Compare *We* in the following example with *we* in the example in ¶276.)

> According to Robertson's report, "We have been witnessing a change in buying habits, particularly with respect to food."

278 If a displayed quotation starts in the middle of a sentence, use three spaced periods at the beginning of the quotation.

> According to Robertson's report, there has been
>
> > . . . a change in buying habits, particularly with respect to food. . . . How far this pattern of change will extend cannot be estimated.

If the fragment, however, can be read as a complete sentence, capitalize the first word of the fragment and omit the ellipsis marks. (Compare *Starting* in the following example with *starting* in the example in ¶276.)

> According to Robertson's report:
>
> > Starting in the late 1950s, we have been witnessing a change in buying habits, particularly with respect to food.

279 When a long quotation starts with a complete sentence and ends with a complete sentence, do not use three spaced periods at the beginning or at the end of the quotation unless you need to emphasize that the quotation has been extracted from a larger body of material.

280 If one or more paragraphs are omitted within a long quotation, indicate the omission by adding three spaced periods *after* the terminal punctuation that concludes the preceding paragraph.

Insertions in Quoted Matter

281 For clarity, it is sometimes necessary to insert explanatory words or phrases in quoted matter. Enclose such insertions in square brackets. (See also ¶¶296–297.)

> Miss Rawlings added, "At the time of the first lawsuit [2004], there was clear-cut evidence of an intent to defraud."

282 For special emphasis, you may wish to italicize words that were not so treated in the original. In such cases insert a phrase like *emphasis added* in square brackets at the end of the quotation or immediately after the italicized words.

> In the course of testifying, she stated, "I never met Mr. Norman in my life, *to the best of my recollection.* [Emphasis added.]"

283 When the original wording contains a misspelling, a grammatical error, or a confusing expression of thought, insert the term *sic* (meaning "so" or "this is the way it was") in square brackets to signify that the error existed in the original material.

> As he wrote in his letter, "I would sooner go to jail then [*sic*] have to pay your bill."

NOTE: Italicize the word *sic* when it is used in this way

☞ *For simple interruptions such as* he said *or* she said, *see ¶¶262–263.*

Aligning Quotation Marks

284 **a.** In a list, any opening quotation mark should align with the first letter of the other items.

> I urge you to read the following materials (which I am sending to you by courier tomorrow):
>
> > *Leading the Revolution* by Gary Hamel
> >
> > "The Bay Connection" by Bruce Thorson
> >
> > *The Money Machine* by Daniel Stoffman

b. In a poem, the opening quotation mark at the beginning of each stanza should clear the left margin so that the first letter of each line will align. (See also ¶267.)

> "The lonely sunsets flare forlorn
> Down valleys dreadly desolate;
> The lordly mountains soar in scorn
> As still as death, as stern as fate . . ."
>
> —Robert W. Service

MARKS FOR EMPHASIS

With word processing software, the typographical elements necessary to produce readable, attractive documents have become convenient and accessible. The application of these elements—boldface, different font sizes and styles, solid and small capitals, colour and shading—seem almost limitless.

(Continued on page 80.)

Italics

Italic type (the counterpart of underlining or underscoring) is the preferred means of giving emphasis to words, phrases, and the titles of literary and artistic works.

285 a. A word referred to as a word is usually italicized. (Some writers prefer to enclose the word in quotation marks.) A word referred to as a word is often introduced by the expression *the term* or *the word*.

> The term *muffin-choker* refers to a bizarre item in the morning newspaper that you read as you eat your breakfast.
>
> We use the word *eh?* too often, but it is only to include others in our conversation.
>
> If you used fewer compound sentences, you wouldn't have so many *and*s in your writing. (Only the root word is italicized, not the *s*.)
>
> **BUT:** She refused to sign the contract because she said it had too many ifs, ands, or buts. (No italics are needed for the phrase *ifs, ands, or buts* because the writer is not referring literally to these words as words. (The phrase means "too many conditions and qualifications.")

b. In a formal definition, the word to be defined is usually italicized and the definition put in quotation marks. In this way the two elements may be easily distinguished from one another.

> The verb *prevaricate* (a polite way of saying "to lie") comes from the Latin word *praevaricari*, which means "to go zigzag, to walk crookedly."

NOTE: An informal definition does not require any special punctuation.

> Voyageurs were canoemen employed by the early fur trading companies.
>
> The term *hat trick* refers to three hockey goals scored in one game by a single player. (Because the definition is informal, it does not have to be set off in quotation marks. However, *hat trick* is italicized, because the words are referred to as words.)

c. Italics are often used to emphasize a stressed word or key words, but be careful not to overuse them.

> Salary increases *must* be based on merit, not necessarily seniority.
>
> If you look back, you will find *someone* gaining on you.

d. Italicize foreign expressions that are not considered part of the English language. (Use quotation marks to set off translations of foreign expressions.)

> It's true, *n'est-ce pas?* (Meaning "isn't that so?")

NOTE: Once an expression of foreign origin becomes part of the English language, italics are no longer necessary. (Most dictionaries offer guidance on this point.) Here are some frequently used expressions that do not need italics or any other special display:

a priori	ad infinitum	alter ego	carte blanche
ad hoc	alma mater	bona fide	caveat emptor

de facto	hors d'oeuvre	per capita	raison d'être
de jure	in toto	per diem	repertoire
en mass	joie de vivre	prima facie	savoir faire
esprit de corps	laissez-faire	prix fixe	sine qua non
et al.	modus operandi	pro forma	status quo
ex officio	modus vivendi	pro rata	vis-à-vis
fait accompli	non sequitur	pro tem	vive
habeas corpus	par excellence	quid pro quo	voir dire

☞ *For the use of accents and other diacritical marks with foreign words, see ¶718.*

286 *Individual* names of ships, trains, airplanes, and spacecraft may be italicized for special display or written simply with initial caps.

The *St. Roch* braved the Northwest Passage route.   **OR:** The St. Roch . . .

BUT: Phil has just been cleared to fly a Cessna and the new Kodiak. (No special display is needed for the names *Cessna* and *Kodiak* because these are classes of aircraft and not the names of individual planes.)

With Titles of Literary and Artistic Works

287 **a.** Italicize titles of *complete* works that are published as separate items—for example, books, pamphlets, long poems, magazines, and newspapers. Also italicize titles of movies, plays, musicals, operas, video cassettes, CDs, DVDs, television and radio series, long musical pieces, paintings, and works of sculpture.

Our ads in *The Globe and Mail* have produced excellent results.

Next Friday we will hear *Der Rosenkavalier.*

The painting popularly referred to as *Whistler's Mother* is actually entitled *Arrangement in Gray and Black No. 1.*

b. Do not use italics or quotation marks for the titles of musical pieces that are identified by form (for example, *symphony, concerto, sonata*) or by key (for example, *A Major, B Flat Minor*). However, if a descriptive phrase accompanies this type of title, italicize this phrase if the work is long; quote this phrase if the work is short.

Beethoven's Sonata No. 18 in E Flat Minor, Op. 31, No. 3

Tchaikovsky's Symphony No. 6 in B Flat minor (the *Pathétique*)

Chopin's Etude No. 12 (the "Revolutionary" Etude)

c. In material that is being prepared for publication, titles of complete works must be italicized so that they will appear in italics in the final version.

Every executive will find *Right on Time!* a valuable guide.

d. In titles of magazines, do not italicize or capitalize the word *magazine* unless it is part of the actual title.

Chatelaine magazine   **BUT:** *The National Magazine*

(Continued on page 82.)

2

e. In some cases the name of the publishing company is the same as the name of the publication. Italicize the name when it refers to *the publication* but not when it refers to *the company.*

I saw her column in *Maclean's.*

BUT: I wrote to Maclean's about a job.

Joe used to be *Fortune's* management editor; now he works as a management consultant to half a dozen Fortune 500 companies.

f. Italicize a subtitle (but not an edition number) that accompanies the main title of a book.

If you're looking for a good overview of the subject, get hold of Kinnear and Taylor's *Marketing Research: An Applied Approach,* Fourth Edition.

g. Italicize the titles of books, newspapers, and magazines that are published in electronic form.

Britannica Online (the electronic version of the *Encyclopaedia Britannica*)

Globeandmail.com (the electronic version of *The Globe and Mail*)

Slate and *Feed* (electronic magazines, referred to as *Webzines*)

☞ *For the use of quotation marks with titles of literary and artistic works, see ¶¶242–244. For the treatment of titles of sacred works, see ¶350.*

Guidelines for Italics

288 Italicize as a unit whatever should be grasped as a unit—individual words, titles, phrases, or even whole sentences.

a. When you want to emphasize a unit consisting of two or more words, be sure to italicize the entire unit, including any punctuation that is part of the unit.

Ipso facto, sine qua non, and *pro forma:* these are the kinds of expressions you must be able to define. (**NOT:** *and pro forma:*)

b. Parentheses are italicized when the words they enclose begin *and* end with italicized words.

I do love all those French words *(j'aime les mots en français).*

Let's take the ferry (the new *Breeze*) from Toronto to Rochester. (Note that the first word is not italicized; therefore, the parentheses are not italicized.)

Is there some ice cream for the apple pie (*à la mode,* isn't it)? (In this case, the last word is not italicized.)

c. Do not italicize a possessive or plural ending that is added on to a word being emphasized.

too many *know-it-alls*   *Canadian Living's* article

d. Brackets are not usually italicized, even when they enclose italicized words; for example [*sic*].

UNDERLINING

289 Although italicizing is much preferred, underlining may also be used to empha-size words, phrases, and titles of literary and artistic works.

   a. Letters referred to as letters are often italicized or underlined if they are not capitalized. In such cases underlining may be preferable since an italic letter may not look sufficiently different to stand out.

     dotting your <u>i</u>'s (**OR** i's)   solving for <u>x</u> when <u>y</u> = 3 (**OR** for x when y)

     minding your <u>p</u>'s and <u>q</u>'s   **BUT:** three Bs and one C

   ☞ *For the plurals of letters such as i's and Rs, see ¶¶622–623.*

   b. When using **underlining** to give special emphasis to words or phrases in a series, underline only the terms themselves and not any punctuation that intervenes or follows.

     <u>Ipso facto</u>, <u>sine qua non</u>, and <u>pro forma</u>: these are the kinds of expressions . . .

     Have you ever read <u>Moby Dick</u> or <u>War and Peace</u>?

     EXCEPTION: This week the Confederation Theatre is presenting <u>Oklahoma!</u> (The exclamation point is underlined in this sentence because it is an integral part of the material to be emphasized.)

   c. Do not underline a possessive or plural ending that is added on to a word being emphasized.

     the <u>Times-Picayune</u>'s editorial   too many <u>and</u>s

   d. When giving special emphasis to an element that has to be divided at the end of a line, underline the dividing hyphen as well.

All Capitals

290 The use of all capitals is acceptable when titles of complete works occur fre-quently (as in the correspondence of a publishing house) or when the use of all-capital letters is intended to have an eye-catching effect. In e-mails, however, all capitals may be misconstrued by the reader as "screaming," so they should be used sparingly.

     It IS bad and they ARE out to get you.   RIGHT ON TIME! is the guide.

REMAINING PUNCTUATION MARKS
The Apostrophe (')

291 The use of the apostrophe is covered in the following paragraphs. (The font you select will determine the style of the apostrophe. If you wish, you can switch from the default style to an alternative one by accessing an extended character set. See ¶227.)

   ☞ *As a single quotation mark, see ¶¶245–246, 247b, 248b, 249d, 250b, 265b.*
     To indicate the omission of figures in dates, see ¶¶412, 439a.
     As a symbol for feet, see ¶¶432, 543.

(Continued on page 84.)

To form contractions, see ¶505.
To form plurals of figures, letters, etc., see ¶¶622–625.
To form possessives, see ¶¶247b, 627–651.
To form expressions derived from all-capital abbreviations, see ¶522d.

Ellipsis Marks (. . .)

292 Ellipsis marks are usually three spaced periods with one space before and after each period. However, to avoid an excess of white space when desktop software or line justification is used, no spaces are keyed with ellipsis marks.

a. As a general rule, do not use ellipsis marks in place of a period at the end of a sentence. However, ellipses may be used to indicate that a sentence trails off before the end. The three spaced periods create an effect of uncertainty or suggest an abrupt suspension of thought. (No terminal punctuation is used with ellipsis marks in this kind of construction.)

He could easily have saved the situation by . . . But why talk about it?

b. Ellipsis marks are often used in advertising to display individual items or to connect a series of loosely related phrases.

Where can you match these services?
. . . Free ticket delivery
. . . Flight insurance
. . . On-time departures

The Inn at the End of the Road . . . where you may enjoy the epicure's choicest offerings . . . by reservation only . . . closed Tuesdays.

☞ *For the use of ellipsis marks to indicate omissions in quoted matter, see ¶¶274–280.*

The Asterisk (*)

293 Although, strictly speaking, the asterisk is not a punctuation mark, it is closely related when used to refer the reader to footnotes or to replace unprintable words. (See ¶¶1502f, 1633c.)

a. When the asterisk and a mark of punctuation occur together within a sentence, the asterisk *follows* the punctuation mark, with no intervening space.

b. In the footnote itself, leave no space after the asterisk.

c. Asterisks are used to replace words that are considered unprintable.

If the TV cameras had been present when Finney called Schultz a ***** (and about 50 other names as well), tonight's newscast would have contained the longest bleep in television history.

The Diagonal (/)

294 The diagonal occurs (without space before or after) in certain abbreviations and expressions of time. (The diagonal is also called a *slash* or *solidus*.)

B/L	bill of lading	m/s	metres per second
w/	with	n/30	net amount due in 30 days
c/o	care of	/S/	signed (used before a copied signature)

The copy deadline for the fall '06/winter '07 catalogue is April 15.

Please check the figures for fiscal year 2006/07.

I'm concerned about their P/E ratio. (Referring to the price/earnings ratio of a company's stock.)

295 **a.** The diagonal is used to express alternatives.

a go/no-go decision	read/write files
input/output systems	meet on Monday and/or Tuesday
an AM/FM tuner	on/off switch

b. The diagonal may be used to indicate that a person has two functions or a thing has two components.

the owner/member	zoned for commercial/industrial activities
a client/server network	planning to elect a secretary/treasurer

NOTE: A hyphen may also be used in such expressions. (See ¶806.)

c. The diagonal is also used in writing fractions (4/5), code and serial numbers (2S/394), and Web site addresses (www.canoe.ca/macleans).

☞ *For the use of the diagonal when quoting poetry, see ¶268.*
For the use of the diagonal in telephone numbers, see ¶454.

Brackets ([], and <>)

296 **a.** Use square brackets ([ ]) to enclose a correction or an insertion in a quoted extract. (See also ¶¶281–283.)

His final request was this: "Please keep me appraised [*sic*] of any new developments." (See ¶283 note.)

The transcript contains this incredible statement: "I did not approach Officer Lali *at any time* [emphasis added] while my petition was being considered."

"Let us bring a new level of political leadership to this province. [Extended applause.] Please give me your support." (Note the capitalization of *Extended* and the use of a period before the closing bracket when the bracketed element is treated as a separate sentence. See also ¶¶226, 282.)

b. When a parenthetical element falls within another parenthetical element, enclose the smaller element in square brackets and enclose the larger element in parentheses.

Sihota said on television yesterday that prices would begin to fall sharply. (However, in an article published in the *Star* [May 12, 2006], he was quoted as saying that prices would remain steady for the foreseeable future.)

297 Use angle brackets (< >) to set off Web site and e-mail addresses when they appear in sentences or in bibliographical notes and citations. When an address is set off in this way, any punctuation that precedes or follows cannot be mistaken as part of the address. (See ¶1510c.)

> Please consult the publisher's Web site: <www.mcgrawhill.ca>.

SPACING: WITH PUNCTUATION MARKS

298 The following chart gives the *traditional* spacing used before and after punctuation marks and the asterisk symbol. Although it is generally accepted today that one space is sufficient after ending punctuation marks, there are some who still prefer the visual break that two spaces provide, especially when proportional fonts are used. However, if the justification feature is used to achieve even right margins, then one space only is necessary to avoid large areas of white space within a line of text.

Traditional Spacing

Punctuation	Space *Before*	Space *After*
Period (.)	none	one or two after the end of a sentence
		two after the period following an enumeration number or bullet [Software features will include an automatic tab which may be adjusted 0.25" to 0.5".]
		one after an abbreviation (See also ¶511.)
		none after a decimal point
		none when another punctuation mark follows (e.g., a closing quotation mark, parenthesis, dash; a comma, a semicolon, or a colon following an "abbreviation" period)
Question Mark (?) or Exclamation Mark (!)	none	one or two after the end of a sentence
		one if a question mark is within a sentence (See ¶¶116–117.)
		none if another punctuation mark follows (e.g., a closing quotation mark, parenthesis, or dash)
Comma (,)	none	one
		none if followed by closing quotation mark
		none if comma is in a number (e.g., 92,539)
Semicolon (;)	none	one
Colon (:)	none	two if it is within a sentence
	none *before* **or** *after* in expressions of time (8:20 p.m.) or in proportions (2:1)	

Punctuation	Space *Before*	Space *After*
En Dash (–) **Em Dash (—)**	none	none **EXCEPT** if the dash ends a statement that breaks off abruptly (See ¶¶207–208.)
Hyphen (-)	none	none
	one before *and* after if used in an address as follows: (e.g., 10964 - 125 Street, but 10964 Centre Street)	
Apostrophe (')	none	one if at the **end** of a word within a sentence
Asterisk (*)	none	one or two if at the end of a sentence one if within a sentence none if in a footnote (See ¶293.)
Diagonal (/)	none before *or* after (See ¶268 for exception in poetry.)	
Opening Parenthesis [(] **or Bracket ([)**	one if text is within a sentence one or two if text follows a sentence and is itself a separate sentence	none
Closing Parenthesis [)] **or Bracket (])**	none	one if text is within a sentence one or two if text is a complete sentence followed by another sentence (See ¶226.) none if another punctuation mark follows
Opening Quotation Mark (")	one or two if quoted text starts a new sentence or follows a colon none if a dash or opening parenthesis precedes one in all other cases	none
Closing Quotation Mark (")	none	one or two when quoted matter ends the sentence none when another mark of punctuation immediately follows (e.g., semicolon or colon) one in all other cases
Single Quotation Mark (')	Extra space between single and double quotation marks when they occur together (See ¶246.)	

Punctuation	Space *Before*	Space *After*
Ellipsis Marks (. . .) or (. . . .) includes the period at the end of a sentence	one space before and after each of the three periods within a sentence (See ¶¶274–275.)	
	none when preceded by a quotation mark	none when followed by a quotation mark (See last example in ¶275.)
		one or two after ellipses marks that follow a period, question mark, or exclamation point at the end of a sentence (See ¶276.)

☞ *See ¶543 for spacing required before and after symbols such as @, &, and =.*

See the Online Learning Centre at www.mcgrawhill.ca/college/gregg for related Web links.

Capitalization

BASIC RULES (¶¶301–310)
First Words (¶¶301–302)
Proper Nouns (¶¶303–306)
Common Nouns (¶¶307–310)

SPECIAL RULES (¶¶311–366)
Personal Names (¶311)
Titles With Personal Names (¶¶312–317)
Family and Religious Titles (¶¶318–319)
Names of Organizations (¶¶320–324)
Names of Government Bodies (¶¶325–330)
Names of Places (¶¶331–337)
Points of the Compass (¶¶338–341)
Days of the Week, Months, Holidays, Seasons, Events, Periods (¶¶342–345)
Acts, Laws, Bills, Treaties (¶346)
Programs, Movements, Concepts (¶347)
Races, Peoples, Languages (¶348)
Religious References (¶¶349–350)
Celestial Bodies (¶351)
Course Titles, Subjects, Academic Degrees (¶¶352–354)
Commercial Products (¶¶355–356)
Advertising Material (¶357)
Legal Documents (¶358)
Nouns With Numbers or Letters (¶359)
Titles of Literary and Artistic Works; Headings (¶¶360–362)
Hyphenated Words (¶363)
Awards and Medals (¶364)
Computer Terminology (¶365)
Intercaps (¶366)

The function of capitalization is to give distinction, importance, and emphasis to words. Thus the first word of a sentence is capitalized to indicate distinctively and emphatically that a new sentence has begun. Moreover, proper nouns like *Donald, Moncton, Scotiabank, the Paralympics, August,* and *Monday* are capitalized to signify the special importance of these words as the official names of particular persons, places, and things. A number of words, however, may function either as proper nouns or as common nouns—for example, terms like *the board of directors* or *the company*. For words like these, capitalization practices vary widely, but the variation merely reflects the relative importance each writer assigns to the word in question.

Despite disagreements among authorities on specific rules, there is a growing consensus against overusing capitalization in business writing. When too many words stand out, none stand out. The current trend, then, is to use capitalization more sparingly—to give importance, distinction, or emphasis only when and where it is warranted.

3 The following rules of capitalization are written with ordinary situations in mind. If you work in a specialized field, you may find it necessary to follow a different style.

BASIC RULES
First Words
301 Capitalize the first word of:

a. Every sentence. (See ¶302 for exceptions.)

Try to limit each of your e-mail messages to one screen.
Will you be able to pull everything together by then?
The deadline we have been given is absolutely impossible!

b. A word or phrase used as a sentence. (See also ¶¶102, 111, 119–120.)

Not likely.   Why bother?   Sweet!
All right.   How so?   Thank you!

c. A quoted sentence. (See also ¶¶272–273.)

Mrs. Eckstein herself said, "We surely have not heard the complete story."

d. An independent question within a sentence. (See also ¶¶115–117.)

The question is, Whose version of the argument shall we believe?
BUT: Have you approved the divisional sales forecasts? the expense projections? the requests for staff expansion? (See ¶117.)

e. Each item displayed in a list or an outline. (See also ¶¶107, 199c, 1344c, 1425e, 1719d.)

Here is a powerful problem-solving tool that will help you:
- Become an effective leader.
- Improve your relations with subordinates, peers, and superiors.
- Cope with stressful situations on the job.

f. Each line in a poem. (Always follow the style of the poem, however.)

And when those toils rewarding,
Broad lands at length they'll claim,
They'll call the new possession
By some familiar name.

—Agnes Strickland

g. The salutation and the complimentary closing of a letter. (See also ¶¶1338c, 1345b.)

> Dear Mrs. Pancetta   Sincerely yours

302 **a.** When a sentence is set off by *dashes* or *parentheses* within another sentence, do not capitalize the first word following the opening dash or parenthesis unless it is a proper noun, a proper adjective, the pronoun *I*, or the first word of a quoted sentence. (See ¶¶214, 224–225 for examples.)

b. Do not capitalize the first word of a sentence following a colon except under certain circumstances. (See ¶¶196–199.)

Proper Nouns

303 Capitalize every *proper noun*, that is, the official name of a particular person, place, or thing. Also capitalize the pronoun *I*.

Roberta Bondar Planetarium	Project Management 351
the Battle of Batouche	the Royal Ontario Museum
Canadian Living	Scotch Tape
the Internet (or the Net)	Stanley Cup
Kicking Horse Pass Ski Club	the Triassic Period
Kyoto Accord	the 2010 Winter Olympics
Louis Riel Public School	World Wide Web

NOTE: Prepositions (like *of*, *for*, and *in*) are not capitalized unless they have four or more letters (like *with* and *from*). (See also ¶¶360–361.) The articles *a* and *an* are not capitalized; the article *the* is capitalized only under special circumstances. (See ¶324.) Coordinating conjunctions (like *and* and *or*) are also not capitalized. However, follow the capitalization style used by the owner of the name: for example, *3-In-One oil, One-A-Day vitamins, Book-Of-The-Month Club, Fruit of the Loom*.

304 Capitalize adjectives derived from proper nouns.

Canada (n.), Canadian (adj.)	Liverpool (n.), Liverpudlian (adj.)
America (n.), American (adj.)	Halifax (n.), Haligonian (adj.)

EXCEPTIONS: Parliament, parliamentary; Senate, senatorial; Constitution, constitutional. (See also ¶306.)

305 Capitalize imaginative names and nicknames that designate particular persons, places, or things. (See ¶¶333–335 for imaginative place names; ¶344 for imaginative names of historical periods.)

Château Clique	Founding Fathers
Down Under	Group of Seven
the Dark Ages	Herring Chokers
the Establishment	Janey Canuck
the First Peoples	Twelve-Foot Davis
the Forty-Niners	Wheat City

306 Some words that were originally proper nouns or adjectives are now considered common nouns or adjectives and should not be capitalized. (See ¶309b.)

(Continued on page 92.)

| ampere | charley horse | fanny pack | jerry can |
| blue jeans | diesel | french fry | watt |

NOTE: Check an up-to-date dictionary to determine capitalization for words of this type.

Common Nouns

307 A *common noun* names a class of things (for example, *books*), or it may refer to one or more things within that class (*a book, several books*). Nouns used in this way are considered general terms of classification and are often modified by indefinite words such as *a, any, every,* or *some*. Do not capitalize nouns used as general terms of classification.

| a company | every board of directors |
| any corporation | some lawyers |

308 A common noun may also be used to name a *particular* person, place, or thing. Nouns used in this way are often modified (a) by *the, this, these, that,* or *those* or (b) by possessive words such as *my, your, his, her, our,* or *their*. Do not capitalize a general term of classification, even though it refers to a particular person, place, or thing.

| **COMMON NOUN:** our doctor | the hotel | the river |
| **PROPER NOUN:** Dr. Chow | the Frontenac Hotel | the Saguenay River |

309 **a.** Capitalize a common noun when it is part of a proper name but not when it is used alone in place of the full name. (For exceptions, see ¶310.)

Dean Thomas	**BUT:**	the dean
Hudson's Bay Company		the company
Neptune Theatre		the theatre

NOTE: Also capitalize the plural form of a common noun in expressions such as *the Red and Assiniboine Rivers, Yonge and Bloor Streets,* the *Rideau and Welland Canals,* and *the Bayshore and Riverside Malls.*

b. In a number of compound nouns, the first element is a proper noun or a proper adjective and the second element is a common noun. In such cases capitalize only the first element, since the compound as a whole is a common noun.

| Dutch door | Irish setter | Persian carpet | Swiss Army knife |
| Greek salad | Japanese lantern | Roman numerals | Turkish coffee |

NOTE: Check an up-to-date dictionary for words of this type. After extensive usage the proper noun or adjective may become a common noun and no longer require capitalization. (See ¶306.)

310 Some *short forms* (common-noun elements replacing the complete proper name) are capitalized when they are intended to carry the full significance of the complete proper name. It is in this area, however, that the danger of over-capitalizing most often occurs. Therefore, do not capitalize a short form unless it clearly warrants the importance, distinction, or emphasis that capitalization conveys. The following kinds of short forms are commonly capitalized:

PERSONAL TITLES: Capitalize titles replacing names of high-ranking international, national, and provincial officials (but not generally local officials or company officers). (See ¶313.)

ORGANIZATIONAL NAMES: Do not capitalize short forms of company names except in formal or legal writing. (See ¶321.)

GOVERNMENTAL NAMES: Capitalize short forms of names of international and national bodies (but not usually provincial or local bodies). (See ¶¶326–327, 334–335.)

PLACE NAMES: Capitalize only well-established short forms. (See ¶¶332, 335.)

NOTE: Do not use a short form to replace a full name unless the full name has been mentioned earlier or will be understood from the context.

SPECIAL RULES
Personal Names

311 **a.** Treat a person's name—in terms of capitalization, spelling, punctuation, and spacing—exactly as the person does.

Alice Mayer	Charles Burden Wilson
Rita Naser	L. Westcott Quinn
Steven J. Dougherty, Jr.	H. M. Nakagawa
Stephen J. Dockerty Jr.	Peter B. J. Hallman

☞ *For the treatment of initials, see ¶516.*
For the use or omission of commas with terms such as Jr., see ¶156.

b. Respect individual preferences in the spelling of personal names.

Ann Marie, Anne Marie, Anna Marie, Annemarie, Annamarie, Anne-Marie, AnnMarie

Macmillan, MacMillan, Mac Millan, Macmillen, MacMillen, MacMillin, McMillan, Mc Millan, McMillen, McMillin, McMillon

c. In names containing the prefix *O'*, always capitalize the *O* and the letter following the apostrophe; for example, *O'Brian* or *O'Brien*.

d. Watch for differences in capitalization and spacing in names containing prefixes like *d', da, de, del, della, di, du, l', la, le, van,* and *von.*

D'Amelio, d'Amelio, Damelio	deLaCruz, DeLacruz, Dela Cruz, DelaCruz
LaCoste, Lacoste, La Coste	VanDeVelde, Van DeVelde, vandeVelde

e. When a surname with an uncapitalized "particle" stands alone (that is, without a first name, a title, or initials preceding it), capitalize the particle to prevent a misreading.

Paul de Luca   Mr. de Luca   P. de Luca   **BUT:** Is De Luca leaving?

f. When names that contain prefixes are to be keyed in all-capital letters, follow these principles: If there is no space after the prefix, capitalize only the initial letter of the prefix. If a space follows the prefix, capitalize the entire prefix.

(Continued on page 94.)

NORMAL FORM:	MacDonald	Mac Donald
ALL-CAPITAL FORM:	MacDONALD	MAC DONALD

g. When a nickname or a descriptive expression precedes or replaces a person's first name, simply capitalize it. However, if the nickname or descriptive expression falls between a person's first and last names, enclose it either in quotation marks or in parentheses.

Rocket Richard	**BUT:**	Maurice "Rocket" Richard
	OR:	Maurice (Rocket) Richard

☞ *For the plurals of personal names, see ¶¶615–616.*

For the plurals of possessives of personal names, see ¶¶630–633.

Titles With Personal Names

312   a. Capitalize all official titles of honour and respect when they *precede* personal names.

PERSONAL TITLES:

Mrs. Norma Washburn (see ¶517)	Miss Yamulky
Ms. Terry Fiske	Mr. Benedict

EXECUTIVE TITLES:

President Julia McLeod	Vice-President Saulnier

PROFESSIONAL TITLES:

Professor Henry Pelligrino	Dr. Khalil (see ¶517)

POLITICAL TITLES:

Councillor Samuel O. Bolling	former Premier Bill Davis
Mayor-elect Louis K. Uhl (see ¶317)	ex-Senator Jones (see ¶317)

MILITARY TITLES:

Colonel Perry L. Forrester	Captain Comerford

RELIGIOUS TITLES:

the Reverend William F. Dowd	Rabbi Gelfand

b. Do not capitalize such titles when the personal name that follows is in apposition and is set off by commas.

Yesterday the *president*, Julia McLeod, revealed her plans to retire next June.

BUT: Yesterday *President* Julia McLeod revealed her plans to retire next June.

c. Do not capitalize an occupation (such as *author, surgeon, publisher,* and *lawyer*) preceding a name.

The reviews of *drama critic* Simon Ritchey have lost their bite.
(**NOT:** The reviews of *Drama Critic* Simon Ritchey have lost their bite.)

NOTE: Occupations can be distinguished from titles in that only titles can be used with a last name alone. Since one would not address a person as "Author Berton" or "Publisher Ward," these are not titles and should not be capitalized.

d. Do not confuse a true title preceding a name (such as *Judge*) with a generic expression (such as *federal judge*).

Judge Ann Bly **OR** federal judge Ann Bly (**NOT:** federal Judge Ann Bly)

President Julia McLeod **OR** company president Julia McLeod
(**NOT:** company President Julia McLeod)

313 **a.** In general, do not capitalize titles when they *follow* a personal name or are used *in place of* a personal name.

> Julia McLeod, *president* of McLeod Inc., has revealed her plans to retire next June. During her 16 years as *president*, the company grew . . .

However, exceptions are made for important officials and dignitaries, as indicated in the following paragraphs.

b. Capitalize titles of high-ranking national, provincial, and international officials when they *follow* or *replace* a specific personal name. Below are examples of titles that remain capitalized.

> **NATIONAL OFFICIALS:** the *Prime Minister*, Cabinet members (such as the *Secretary of State*, the *Speaker of the House of Commons,* and the *Attorney General*), the heads of government agencies and bureaus (such as the *Deputy Minister*, or the *Commissioner*), the *Chief Justice*, the *Ambassador*, the *Member of Parliament*.
>
> **PROVINCIAL OFFICIALS:** the *Premier*, the *Lieutenant-Governor*.
>
> **ROYAL DIGNITARIES:** the *Queen*, the *Duke*, the *Prince of Wales*.
>
> **INTERNATIONAL FIGURES:** the *Pope*, the *Secretary General of the United Nations*, the *President*.

c. Titles of local governmental officials and those of lesser federal and provincial officials are not usually capitalized when they follow or replace a personal name. However, these titles are sometimes capitalized in writing intended for a limited readership (for example, in a local newspaper, in internal communications within an organization, or in correspondence coming from or directed to the official's office), where the intended reader would consider the official to be of high rank.

> The *Mayor* promised only last fall to hold the property tax at its present level. (Excerpt from an editorial in a local newspaper.)
>
> **BUT:** Francis Fahey, *mayor* of Peterborough, Ontario, was interviewed at City Hall earlier today. The *mayor* spoke forcefully about the need to maintain aid to . . . (Excerpt from a national news service release.)
>
> I would like to request an appointment with the *Solicitor General*. (In a letter sent to the provincial solicitor general's office.)
>
> **BUT:** I have written for an appointment with the *solicitor general* and expect to hear from his office soon.

d. Titles of *company officials* (for example, the *president*, the *general manager*) should not be capitalized when they follow or replace a personal name. Exceptions are made in formal minutes of meetings (see page 488) and in rules and bylaws.

> The *president* will visit 13 countries in a tour of company installations abroad. (Normal style.)
>
> The *Secretary's* minutes were read and approved. (In formal minutes.)

(Continued on page 96.)

NOTE: Some companies choose to capitalize these titles in all their communications because of the great respect the officials command within the company. However, this practice confers excessive importance on people who are neither public officials nor eminent dignitaries, and it should be avoided.

e. In general, do not capitalize job titles when they stand alone. However, in procedures manuals and in company memos and announcements, job titles are sometimes capitalized for special emphasis.

Marion Conroy has been promoted to the position of *senior accountant* (**OR** *Senior Accountant*).

f. Titles *following* a personal name or *standing alone* are sometimes capitalized in formal citations and acknowledgements.

314 Do not capitalize titles used as general terms of classification. (See ¶307.)

a Canadian senator   every king
a provincial premier   any ambassador

EXCEPTION: Because of the special regard for the office of the Prime Minister of Canada, this title is often capitalized even when used as a general term of classification (for example, a *Prime Minister*, every *Prime Minister*).

315 Capitalize any title (even if not of high rank) when it is used in *direct address* (that is, quoted or unquoted speech made directly to another person).

DIRECT ADDRESS: Please tell me, *Doctor*, what risks are involved in this treatment.

INDIRECT ADDRESS: I asked the *doctor* what risks are involved in this treatment.

NOTE: In direct address, do not capitalize a term like *madam, miss,* or *sir* if it stands alone without a proper name following.

Isn't it true, *sir*, that the defendant offered you money for trade secrets?

316 In the *inside address* of a letter and in the *writer's name and title*, capitalize all titles whether they precede or follow the name. (See ¶¶1320–1324 and 1347–1353.)

317 Do not capitalize *former, late, ex-,* or *-elect* when used with titles. (See ¶363 for the style in headings.)

the late Premier Bennett   ex-Chairman Richards   mayor-elect Drever

Family and Religious Titles

318 Capitalize words such as *mother, father, sister, brother, aunt,* and *uncle* when they stand alone or are followed by a personal name.

Let me ask *Mother* and *Dad* if that date is open for them.

We'll be glad to put up *Aunt Peg* and *Uncle Fred* when they come to visit.

Music lessons are given by *Sister Sarah* at the convent.

Do you think *Grandmother Veinot* will be pleased when she hears the news?

319 Do not capitalize family titles when they are preceded by possessives (such as *my, your, his, her, our,* and *their*) and simply describe a family relationship.

> Let me ask my *mother* and *dad* if that date is open for them.

> Do you think your *brother* Bobby would like to meet my *sister* Fern?

NOTE: If the words *uncle, aunt,* or *cousin* form a unit when used together with a first name, capitalize these titles, even when they are preceded by a possessive.

> Frank wants us to meet his *Uncle John.* (Here *Uncle John* is a unit.)

> **BUT:** Frank wants us to meet his *uncle,* John Cunningham. (Here *uncle* simply describes a family relationship.)

> I hope you can meet my *Cousin May.* (The writer thinks of her as *Cousin May.*)

> **BUT:** I hope you can meet my *cousin* May. (Here the writer thinks of her as *May;* the word *cousin* merely indicates relationship.)

☞ *For family titles with a prefix* great, grand, in-law, *and* step, *see* ¶*839.*

Names of Organizations

320 Capitalize the names of companies, unions, associations, societies, independent committees and boards, schools, political parties, conventions, foundations, fraternities, sororities, clubs, and religious bodies.

Alzheimer Society	Montreal Alouettes
Amalgamated Transit Union	New Democratic Party
Alberta Cattle Commission	Prison Arts Foundation
Canadian Coaching Association	Northern Lights College
Canadian Wheat Board	Royal Bank of Canada
Central United Church	SIAST-Palliser Institute
Kiwanis Club of Moncton	Victorian Order of Nurses

NOTE: Try to follow the style established by the organization itself, as shown in the letterhead or some other written communication from the organization.

Talbots (Canada) Inc.	RE/MAX	Shoppers Drug Mart
Sears Canada Inc.	WAL-MART	Shopper's Optical

☞ *For the treatment of articles (like* the*), prepositions (like* of *or* for*), and conjunctions (like* and*), see* ¶*303 note.*

For the capitalization of abbreviations and acronyms used as organizational names, see ¶¶*520, 522.*

321 When the common-noun element is used in place of the full name (for example, *the company* in place of *the Antonia Leather Company*), do not capitalize the short form unless special emphasis or distinction is required (as in legal documents, minutes of meetings, bylaws, and other formal communications, where the short form is intended to invoke the full authority of the organization).

(Continued on page 98.)

In most cases, however, capitalization is unnecessary because the short form is used only as a general term of classification. (See ¶¶307–308.)

> The *company* has always made a conscientious effort to involve itself in community affairs. However, our *company* policy specifically prohibits our underwriting any activity in support of a candidate for public office. (As used here, *company* is a term of general classification.)
>
> **BUT:** On behalf of the *Company*, I am authorized to accept your bid. (Here the full authority of the company is implied; hence *Company* is spelled with a capital *C*.)
>
> Mr. Weinstock has just returned from a visit to Hillcrest College. He reports that the *college* is planning a new fund-raising campaign to finance the construction of the new media centre.
>
> **BUT:** The *College* hopes to raise an additional $10 million this year to finance the construction of the new media resource centre. (Announcement in the alumni bulletin.)

NOTE: Do not capitalize the short form if it is modified by a word other than *the*. In constructions such as *our company, this company,* and *every company,* the noun is clearly a general term of classification. (See also ¶308.)

322 Capitalize organizational terms within the writer's organization; for example, *advertising department, manufacturing division, finance committee,* and *board of directors*. These terms are not capitalized when they refer to an outside organization unless the writer has reason to give these terms special importance or distinction.

> The *Board of Directors* will meet next Thursday at 2:30. (From a company memo.)
>
> **BUT:** Julia Perez, senior vice-president of the Mulholland Bancorp, has been elected to the *board of directors* of the Kensington Trade Corporation. (From a news release intended for a general audience.)
>
> The *Finance Committee* will meet all week to review next year's budget. (Style used by insiders.)
>
> **BUT:** Gilligan says his company can give us no encouragement about the sponsorship of a new art centre until its *finance committee* has reviewed our proposal. (Style normally used by outsiders.)
>
> The *Advertising Department* will unveil the fall campaign this Friday. (Style used by insiders.)
>
> **BUT:** The *advertising department* of Black & London will unveil its fall campaign this Friday. (Style used by outsiders.)

NOTE: Constructions such as *this credit department, their credit department, every credit department,* and *your credit department* are terms of general classification and should not be capitalized. (See also ¶321 note.)

> Black & London seems to have a large turnover in *its advertising department*.
>
> We don't have as much turnover in *our advertising department* as you may think. (Some insiders prefer to write "our Advertising Department" because of the special importance they attach to their own organizational structure.)
>
> I would like to apply for the position of copywriter that is currently open in *your advertising department*. (Some outsiders might write "your Advertising Department" if they wanted to give special importance to the reader's organization.)

IMPORTANT: Companies' policies regarding capitalization of their organizational structures may vary from one business to another. Whatever style is dictated, it is important to maintain *consistency*.

> After visiting your business and receiving documents from Don Khu in *Corporate Law*, I returned to my office and gave the manager of *Corporate Affairs* the latest agreement between our two firms. (For consistency, the two departments have initial capitals.)

323 Capitalize such nouns as *marketing, advertising*, or *promotion* when they are used alone to designate a department within an organization.

> You should see *Personnel* about a move to the new assistant's position.
>
> All administrative clerks are employed in our *engineering* departments.
>
> Paul Havlicek in *Corporate Communications* is the person to talk with.
>
> I want to get a reaction from our people in *Marketing* first.
>
> **BUT:** I want to talk to our *marketing* people first. (Here *marketing* is simply a descriptive adjective.)

324 Capitalize the word *the* preceding the name of an organization only when it is part of the legal name of the organization.

> The Canadian Press   The House Doctor
> The Insurance Group   **BUT:** the Bay

a. Even when part of the organizational name, *the* is often uncapitalized except in legal or formal contexts where it is important to give the full legal name.

b. Do not capitalize *the* when the name is used as a modifier or is given in the form of an abbreviation.

> the Canadian Press report   the CP   works for the *Sun*

Names of Government Bodies

325 Capitalize the names of countries and international organizations as well as national, provincial, county, and city bodies and their subdivisions.

> Arctic Council Secretariat   Canada Council for the Arts
> the Crown Prosecutor's Office   Winnipeg Police Service
> the European Union   Summerside Board of Education
> International Olympic Committee   the Newfoundland House of Assembly
> Ontario Securities Commission   the World Health Organization
>
> **BUT:** the feds (referring to the federal government regulators)

☞ *For city and provincial names, see* ¶¶*334–335.*

326 Capitalize short forms of names of international and national bodies and their major divisions.

> the Commons or the House (referring to the House of Commons)
>
> the Agency (referring to the Canada Revenue Agency, Canada Border Services Agency, Parks Canada Agency, Atlantic Canada Opportunities Agency, etc.)

(Continued on page 100.)

the Department (referring to the Department of National Defence, the Department of Foreign Affairs and International Trade, Justice Canada, Industry Canada, etc.)

the Court (referring to the Supreme Court of Canada, the International Court of Justice, etc.)

Do not capitalize short forms of names of provincial or local governmental groups except when circumstances warrant emphasis or distinction. (See ¶327.)

327 Common terms such as *police service, board of education*, and *provincial court* need not be capitalized (even when referring to a specific body), since they are terms of general classification. However, such terms should be capitalized when the writer intends to refer to the organization in all of its official dignity.

The *Police Service* has announced the promotion of Robert Boyarsky to the rank of sergeant. (The short form is capitalized here because it is intended to have the full force of the complete name, the *Cornwall Police Service*.)

BUT: The *Cornwall police service* sponsors a youth athletic program that we could well copy. (No capitalization is used here because the writer is referring to the service in general terms and not by its official name.)

NOTE: Do not capitalize the short form if it is not actually derived from the complete name. For example, do not capitalize the short form *police service* if the full name is *Department of Public Safety*.

328 Capitalize *federal* only when it is part of the official name of a federal agency, a federal act, or some other proper noun. (The official name of the federal government is *Government of Canada*.)

the *Federal* Court of Canada   the *Federal*-Provincial Relations Office

BUT: . . . subject to federal, provincial, and local laws.

329 The terms *federal government* and *government* (referring specifically to the Canadian government) are now commonly written in small letters because they are considered terms of general classification. In government documents, however, and in other types of communications where these terms are intended to have the force of an official name, they are capitalized.

The *federal government* is questioning its corporate welfare policy—that is, *federal* subsidies to large corporations.

330 Capitalize such words as *union, commonwealth, republic*, and *kingdom* when they refer to a country or countries.

Argentine Republic; the Republic   Principality of Monaco; the Principality
Kingdom of Nepal; the Kingdom   State of Israel; the State

Names of Places

331 Capitalize the names of places, such as streets, buildings, parks, monuments, rivers, oceans, and mountains. Do not capitalize short forms used in place of the full name. (See ¶332 for a few exceptions.)

Hastings Street   **BUT:** the street
Niagara Falls   the falls

Peace Tower	the tower
Halifax Public Gardens	the gardens
Rockwood Park	the park
Athabasca River	the river
Champlain Bridge	the bridge
Lake Winnipeg	the lake
Queen Elizabeth Hotel	the hotel
Castle Mountain	the mountain
Pearson Airport	the airport
Vancouver Art Gallery	the gallery

☞ *For plural expressions like* the Atlantic and Pacific Oceans, *see ¶309a, note.*

For the treatment of prepositions and conjunctions in proper names, see ¶303 note.

332 A few short forms are capitalized because of clear association with one place

the Coast (the West Coast)	the Hill (Parliament Hill)
the Continent (Europe)	the Island (Prince Edward Island
the Channel (English Channel)	**OR** Vancouver Island)

333 **a.** Capitalize imaginative names that designate specific places or areas.

the Golden Horseshoe (southern Ontario)	Gateway to the North (Edmonton)
Gastown (Vancouver)	the Pacific Rim
Hogtown (Toronto)	the Breadbasket of Canada
the Big Nickel (Sudbury)	(the Prairies)
	the Rock (Newfoundland)
Wild Rose Country (Alberta)	the Cradle of Confederation (Charlottetown)
Gateway to the West (Winnipeg)	Land of the Midnight Sun (the Far North)

b. Some place names are used imaginatively to refer to types of businesses or institutions.

Wall Street (the U.S. financial industry)	Bay Street (brokerage firms in Toronto)

334 Capitalize the word *city* only when it is part of the corporate name of the city or part of an imaginative name.

Quebec City	the Stampede City (Calgary)
BUT: the city of Montreal	the Queen City (Regina **OR** Toronto)

335 **a.** Capitalize *province* only when it follows the name of a province or is part of an imaginative name.

Known as the Island, Prince Edward Island is the smallest *province*.

In 1949 the tenth *province*, Newfoundland, entered Confederation.

Victoria is the capital of the *province* of British Columbia.

New Brunswick is known as the Picture *Province*.

Next year we plan to visit the *States*. (Meaning the United States.)

(Continued on page 102.)

b. Do not capitalize *province* when used in place of the actual name.

He is an employee of the *province*. (People working for provincial governments, however, might write *Province*.)

336 According to Canadian dictionaries, the terms used to refer to the residents of provinces and territories are formed as follows:

A Resident of	Is Called a/an
Newfoundland and Labrador	Newfoundlander, Labradorian
Prince Edward Island	Prince Edward Islander
Nova Scotia	Nova Scotian
New Brunswick	New Brunswicker
Quebec	Quebecker or Québécois (m), Québécoise (f)
Ontario	Ontarian
Manitoba	Manitoban
Saskatchewan	Saskatchewanian or Saskatchewanite (informal)
Alberta	Albertan
British Columbia	British Columbian
Yukon	Yukoner
Nunavut	Nunavummiut
Northwest Territories	(None indicated)

337 **a.** Capitalize *the* only when it is part of the official name of a place.

The Pas   **BUT:** the Maritimes
The Hague   the Netherlands

b. Capitalize the words *upper* and *lower* only when they are part of an actual place name or a well-established imaginative name.

Upper Canada   Lower Fort Garry
Upper Chamber   Lower Town
Upper Arrow Lake   Lower Mainland

c. Capitalize the word *greater* when it precedes a city name and refers to the city together with the outlying suburbs: for example, *Greater Toronto Area*.

Points of the Compass

338 **a.** Capitalize *north, south, east, west,* and derivative words when they designate definite regions or are an integral part of a proper name.

in the North	the Far North	the North Pole
down South	the Deep South	the South Shore
out West	the Midwest	the West End
back East	the Near East	the Eastern Townships

b. Do not capitalize these words when they merely indicate direction or general location.

Many factories have relocated from the West Coast to the East. (Region.)

BUT: They maintain a villa in the *south* of France. (General location.)

OR: Go *north* on Highway 3 and then *east* on the Coquihalla. (Direction.)

John is coming back *East* after three years on the *West Coast*. (Region.)

BUT: The *west coast* of Canada borders on the Pacific. (Referring only to the shoreline, not the region.)

Most of our customers live in the *Far North*. (Definite locality.)

BUT: Most of our customers live on the *north side* of town. (General location.)

339 Capitalize such words as *Northerner, Southerner,* and *Westerner.*

340 Capitalize such words as *northern, southern, eastern,* and *western* when they refer to the people in a region or to their political, social, or cultural activities. Do not capitalize these words when they merely indicate general location or refer to the geography or climate of the region.

Eastern bankers	**BUT:** the eastern half of Ontario
Southern hospitality	southern temperatures
Western civilization	westerly winds
the Northern vote	a northern winter

The *Western* provinces did not vote as they were expected to. (Political activities.)

BUT: The drought is expected to continue in the *western* provinces. (Climate.)

My sales territory takes in most of the *eastern* provinces. (General location.)

NOTE: When terms like *western region* and *southern district* are used to name organizational units within a company, capitalize them.

The *Western Region* (referring to a part of the national sales staff) reports that sales are 12 percent over budget for the first six months this year.

341 When words like *northern, southern, eastern,* and *western* precede a place name, they are not ordinarily capitalized because they merely indicate general location within a region. However, when these words are actually part of the place name, they must be capitalized. (Check an atlas or the geographic listings in a dictionary when in doubt.)

Preceding a Place Name	Part of a Place Name
northern Alberta	**BUT:** Northern Peninsula
western Ontario	Western Australia

NOTE: Within certain regions it is not uncommon for many who live there to capitalize the adjective because of the special importance they attach to the regional designation. Thus people who live in southern Ontario may prefer to write *Southern Ontario*.

Days of the Week, Months, Holidays, Seasons, Events, Periods

342 Capitalize names of days, months, holidays, and religious days.

Tuesday	Father's Day	Good Friday
February	Remembrance Day	All Saints' Day
New Year's Eve	Victoria Day	Rosh Hashanah
April Fools' Day	Labour Day	Yom Kippur
Canada Day	Ramadan	**BUT:** election day

☞ *For the use of apostrophes in names of holidays, see ¶650.*

343 Do not capitalize the names of the seasons unless they are personified or used in promotional materials.

> We hold our regional sales conferences during the *fall* and *winter*, but our national conference always takes place early in the *spring*.

> We do not plan to announce our new line of software applications until our fall '06/winter '07 catalogue.

> **BUT:** The Winter speeds his fairies forth and mocks
> Poor bitten men with laughter icy cold.
>
> —Archibald Lampman

344 **a.** Capitalize the names of historical events and imaginative names given to historical periods.

the Riel Rebellion	the Renaissance
Second World War	the Counter-Reformation
the Holocaust	Confederation
Quebec's Quiet Revolution	the Great Depression

b. References to cultural *ages* are usually capitalized. However, contemporary references are not usually capitalized unless they appear together with a capitalized reference.

the Bronze Age	**BUT:** the space age
the Iron Age	the atomic age
the Middle Ages	the nuclear age

The course spans the development of civilization from the *Stone Age* to the *Space Age*.

c. References to cultural *eras* are usually capitalized, but references to cultural periods are usually not.

the Christian Era	**BUT:** the romantic period
the Edwardian Era	the colonial period

d. Capitalize the names of sporting events.

the Arctic Games	the Ironman Triathalon
the Commonwealth Games	the Scott Tournament of Hearts
the Grey Cup Game	the Special Olympic Games

345 Do not capitalize the names of decades and centuries.

during the sixties	in the twenty-first century
in the nineteen-nineties	during the nineteen hundreds

NOTE: Decades are capitalized, however, in special expressions.

the Networked Nineties	the Roaring Twenties

Acts, Laws, Bills, Treaties

346 **a.** Capitalize formal titles of acts, laws, bills, and treaties, but do not capitalize common-noun elements that stand alone in place of the full name.

the Public Safety Act   the act
Bill 178   the bill
the Treaty of Versailles   the treaty
the Canadian Constitution   **BUT:** the Constitution (see ¶304)

b. Do not capitalize generic or informal references to existing or pending legislation except for proper nouns and adjectives.

environmental protection laws   the Liberal tax proposals

c. "Laws" that make humorous or satirical observations about human and organizational behaviour are capitalized to suggest that they carry the same authority as an actual piece of legislation.

Parkinson's Law states that work expands to fill the time that has been allotted for its completion.

Murphy's Law holds that if something can go wrong, it will.

The *Peter Principle* maintains that people in an organization tend to be promoted until they reach their level of incompetence.

d. In the names of authentic scientific laws, capitalize only proper nouns and adjectives.

Gresham's law   Newton's first law of motion
Mendel's law   the first law of thermodynamics

Programs, Movements, Concepts

347   **a.** Do not capitalize the names of programs, movements, or concepts when used as general terms.

employment insurance benefits   the labour movement
BUT: the Employment Insurance Act   **BUT:** the Labour Program
equal opportunities   paternalism
BUT: Equal Opportunities Program   existentialism and rationalism

b. Capitalize proper nouns and adjectives that are part of such terms.

the Socratic method   Newtonian physics
Keynesian economics   Marxist-Leninist theories

c. Capitalize imaginative names given to programs and movements.

the New Deal   the New Frontier
the Just Society   the War on Terrorism

d. Capitalize terms like *liberal, socialist,* and *communist* when they signify formal membership in a political party but not when they merely signify belief in a certain philosophy.

a lifelong *Conservative* (refers to a   a lifelong *conservative* (refers to
   person who consistently votes for   a person who believes in the
   candidates of the Conservative Party)   principles of conservatism)
independent voters   leftists
the right wing   separatists

Races, Peoples, Languages

348   **a.**   Capitalize the names of races, peoples, bands, and languages.

Caucasians	Canadians	Kurds	the Blacks
East Indians	Hispanics	Afghani	Aboriginals
Anglophones	Francophones	First Nations	the Cree

NOTE: The majority of people who live in the North are called *Inuit*, meaning "the people." Therefore, they should never be referred to as *the* Inuit. The singular form of Inuit is *Inuk* and the language spoken by most inhabitants is *Inuktitut*.

b.   Do not hyphenate terms like *African Americans* or *French Canadians* when they are used as nouns, because the first word in each case modifies the second. However, hyphenate such terms when they are used as adjectives; for example, *African-American enterprises, French-Canadian voters*. Moreover, hyphenate such terms when the first element is a prefix; for example, *an Afro-American style, the Anglo-Saxons, the Indo-Chinese*.

Religious References

349   **a.**   Capitalize all references to a supreme being.

God	the Supreme Being	Allah
the Lord	the Messiah	Yahweh
the Holy Spirit	the Almighty	Jehovah

NOTE: The word *God* is capitalized in such compound expressions as *God-given* and *Godspeed* but not in such terms as *godforsaken* and *godless*.

b.   Capitalize personal pronouns referring to a supreme being when they stand alone, without an antecedent nearby.

Offer thanks unto *Him*.   **BUT:**   Ask the Lord for *his* blessing.

NOTE: Some writers capitalize these personal pronouns under all circumstances.

c.   Capitalize references to persons revered as holy.

the Prince of Peace	Buddha	John the Baptist
the Good Shepherd	Muhammad	Saint Peter (see ¶518e)
the Blessed Virgin	the Apostles	Luke the Evangelist

d.   Capitalize the names of religions, their members, and their buildings.

Reform Judaism	Mormons	First Assembly Church
Zen Buddhism	Methodists	Temple Beth Sholom

the Roman Catholic *Church* (meaning the institution as a whole)

BUT: the Roman Catholic *church* on Waverly Avenue (referring to a specific building)

e.   Capitalize references to religious events. (See also ¶342.)

the Creation	the Exodus	the Crucifixion
the Flood	the Second Coming	the Resurrection

f. In general, do not capitalize references to specific religious observances and services. However, if you are writing from the perspective of a particular religion, follow the capitalization style of that religion.

bar mitzvah	baptism	**BUT:** the Eucharist
seder	christening	the Mass

350 Capitalize (but do not quote, underscore, or italicize) references to works regarded as sacred.

the King James Bible	the Qur'an (Koran)	the Ten Commandments
BUT: biblical sources	the Talmud	the Sermon on the Mount
the Revised Standard Version	the Torah	Psalms 23 and 24
	the Our Father	Kaddish
the Old Testament	the Lord's Prayer	Hail Mary
the Book of Genesis	Hebrews 13:8	the Apostles' Creed

NOTE: Do not capitalize *bible* when the work it refers to is not sacred.

Celestial Bodies

351 Capitalize the names of planets (*Jupiter, Mars*), stars (*Polaris, the North Star*), and constellations (*the Big Dipper, the Milky Way*). However, do not capitalize the words *sun, moon,* and *earth* unless they are used in connection with the capitalized names of other planets or stars.

With the weather we've been having, we haven't seen much of the *sun*.

I have gone to the ends of the *earth* to assemble this collection of jewellery.

Compare the orbits of *Mars, Venus,* and *Earth.*

Course Titles, Subjects, Academic Degrees

352 Capitalize the names of specific courses. However, do not capitalize names of subjects or areas of study (except for any proper nouns or adjectives in such names).

Canadian History 201 meets on Tuesdays and Thursdays. (Course title.)

Harriet has decided to major in *Canadian history*. (Area of study.)

353 Do not capitalize academic degrees used as general terms of classification. However, capitalize a degree used after a person's name.

a bachelor of arts degree	received his bachelor's
a master of science degree	working for a master's
a doctor of laws degree	will soon receive her doctorate

BUT: Claire Hurwitz, Doctor of Philosophy

354 In references to academic years, do not capitalize the words *freshman* (or *first-year students*), *sophomore, junior,* and *senior*. In references to grade levels, capitalize the word *grade* when a number follows but not when a number precedes.

All *first-year students* must register by August 30.

Harriet spent her *senior* year in Germany.

Our oldest child is in *Grade 6*; our second child is in the *third grade*.

Commercial Products

355 Capitalize trademarks, brand names, proprietary names, names of commercial products, and market grades. The common noun following the name of a product should not ordinarily be capitalized; however, manufacturers and advertisers often capitalize such words in the names of their own products to give them special emphasis.

> Elmer's glue   **BUT:** Krazy Glue

NOTE: Be alert to the correct spelling of proper nouns.

> Macintosh computers   **BUT:** McIntosh apples

☞ *For the capitalization of short words in the names of products, see ¶303 note. For the use of intercaps, see ¶366.*

356 Capitalize all trademarks except those that have become clearly established as common nouns. To be safe, check an up-to-date Canadian dictionary or consult the Canadian Intellectual Property Office (CIPO); Industry Canada, 50 Victoria Street, Place du Portage I, Hull, QC K1A 0C9; or visit CIPO on the Web at http://www.cipo.gc.ca.

> Acrilan, Dacron, Lycra, Velcro   Crock-Pot, Pyrex, Plexiglas
> Band-Aid, Chap Stick, Kleenex   Dictaphone, Polaroid, Teflon
> Q-Tip, Tylenol, Dixie cup   Magic Marker, Post-it Notes
> Frisbee, Hula Hoop, Scrabble   Beaver Tail, Thermos bottle
> Trivial Pursuit, Monopoly   Astroturf, Walkman, Zamboni
> Rollerblades, Popsicle, Jacuzzi   but: epost, ping-pong

Advertising Material

357 Words ordinarily written in small letters may be capitalized in advertising copy for special emphasis. (This style is inappropriate in all other kinds of written communication.)

> Save money now during our *Year-End Clearance Sale*.
>
> It's the event *Luxury Lovers* have been waiting for . . . from Whitehall's!

Legal Documents

358 In legal documents many words that ordinarily would be written in small letters are written with initial capitals or all capitals—for example, references to parties, the name of the document, special provisions, and sometimes spelled-out amounts of money (see ¶420b).

> THIS AGREEMENT, made this 31st day of January, 2006
>
> . . . hereinafter called the SELLER . . .
>
> WHEREAS the Seller has this day agreed . . .
>
> WITNESS the signatures . . .

Nouns With Numbers or Letters

359 Capitalize a noun followed by a number or a letter that indicates sequence. EXCEPTIONS: Do not capitalize the nouns *line, note, page, paragraph, size, step,* and *verse.*

Account 66160	Cheque 181	Invoice 270487	Platform 3
Act 1	Class 4	Item 9859D	Policy 394857
Appendix A	Column 1	Lesson 20	Room 501
Article 2	Diagram 4	line 4	Rule 7
Book III	Exercise 8	Model B671-4	Section 1
Building 4	Exhibit A	note 1	size 10
Bulletin T-119	Extension 2174	Order J2462	step 3
Car 8171	Figure 9	page 158	Table 7
Channel 36	Flight 626	paragraph 2a	Unit 2
Chapter V	Highway 2	Part Three	verse 3
Chart 3	Illustration 19	Plate XV	Volume II

NOTE: It is often unnecessary to use *No.* before the number. (See ¶455.)

Purchase Order 4713 (**RATHER THAN:** Purchase Order *No.* 4713)

Titles of Literary and Artistic Works; Headings

360 **a.** In titles of literary and artistic works and in displayed headings, capitalize all words with *four or more* letters. Also capitalize words with fewer than four letters except:

ARTICLES: *the, a, an*

SHORT CONJUNCTIONS: *and, as, but, if, or, nor*

SHORT PREPOSITIONS: *at, by, for, in, of, off, on, out, to, up*

How to Succeed in Business Without Really Trying

b. Be sure to capitalize short verbs like *is* and *be.* However, do not capitalize *to* when it is part of an infinitive.

"Redevelopment Proposal Is Not Expected to Be Approved"

c. In magazine titles, capitalize the word *magazine* only if it part of the magazine name.

This Magazine   **BUT:** *Canadian Business* magazine

d. When citing titles in text, headings, source notes, or bibliographies, it is important to maintain a consistent capitalization style. It may be necessary to disregard the style used on a title page, in a heading, or in a catalogue listing. For reasons of sales appeal, such titles may appear in a variety of styles. With the exception of the all-cap style used for acronyms and initials (*OPEC, TSE*), impose a style that is consistent with ¶¶360–361.

361 Even articles, short conjunctions, and short prepositions should be capitalized under the following circumstances:

(Continued on page 110.)

a. Capitalize the first and last word of a title.

"A Home to Be Proud *Of*"

CAUTION: Do not capitalize *the* at the beginning of a title unless it is actually part of the title.

For further details check *the Encyclopaedia Britannica.*
This clipping is from *The Globe and Mail.*

b. Capitalize the first word following a dash or colon in a title.

Bob the Angry Flower: The Ultimate Book of Perfect Energy!
Lines on the Water—A Fisherman's Life on the Miramichi

c. Capitalize short words like *in, out, off,* and *up* in titles when they serve as adverbs rather than as prepositions. (These words may occur as adverbs in verb phrases or in hyphenated compounds derived from verb phrases. See ¶¶803, 1070.)

"AT&T Chalks *Up* Record Earnings for the Year"
"LeClaire Is Runner-*Up* in Election" (see also ¶363)
BUT: "Sailing *up* the St. Lawrence"
The Spy Who Came In From the Cold
"Foxworth Is Considered a Shoo-*In* for Premier"
BUT: "Pollster Project an Easy Win for Foxworth *in* Heavy Voter Turnout"

NOTE: Capitalize these short words when they are not prepositions.

Resolving the Conflict Is a Big *If*   Travelling With the *In* Crowd

d. Capitalize short prepositions like *on, for, in,* and *up* when used together with prepositions having four or more letters.

"Sailing *Up* and *Down* the St. Lawrence"
"Happenings *In* and *Around* Town"
"Mall Opening *On* or *About* May 1"

e. When a title or column heading is displayed on more than one line, do not capitalize the first word of any turnover line unless it needs to be capitalized on the basis of the preceding guidelines.

Should You Invest for the Long Pull   Millions   Income
or Should You Trade Continually?   *of* Dollars   *per* Capita

☞ *For the capitalization of* Preface, Contents, Appendix, *and* Index, *see ¶242 note. For the use of all capitals with titles, see ¶290.*

362 Do not capitalize a book title when it is incorporated into a sentence as a descriptive phrase.

In his book on *economics*, Samuelson points out that . . .
BUT: In his book *Economics*, Samuelson points out that . . .

Hyphenated Words

363 *Within a sentence*, capitalize only those elements of a hyphenated word that are proper nouns or proper adjectives. *At the beginning of a sentence*, capitalize the first element in the hyphenated word but no other elements unless they are proper nouns or adjectives. *In a heading or title*, capitalize all the elements except articles, short prepositions, and short conjunctions. (See ¶360.)

Within Sentences	Beginning Sentences	In Headings
up-to-date	Up-to-date	Up-to-Date
French-Canadian	French-Canadian	French-Canadian
English-speaking	English-speaking	English-Speaking
mid-September	Mid-September	Mid-September
ex-Premier Davies	Ex-Premier Davies	Ex-Premier Davies
Mayor-elect Smith	Mayor-elect Smith	Mayor-Elect Smith
self-confidence	Self-confidence	Self-Confidence
de-emphasize	De-emphasize	De-Emphasize
follow-up	Follow-up	Follow-Up (see ¶361c)
Thirty-ninth Parliament	Thirty-ninth Parliament	Thirty-Ninth Parliament
one-sixth	One-sixth	One-Sixth
post-World War II	Post-World War II	Post-World War II

Awards and Medals

364 Capitalize the names of awards and medals.

Dora Maver Moore Award	Lady Byng Trophy
the Grammy Awards	the Manning Awards
the Griffin Poetry Prize	Star of Military Valour

Computer Terminology

365 **a.** Use all-capital letters for the names of many programming languages. (See also ¶544.)

BASIC	HTML	**BUT:** Java

b. Use all-capital letters for the names of many operating systems.

DOS	UNIX	OS/2

Intercaps

366 The names of many organizations and products follow a special capitalization style known as *intercaps* or *Bicaps*. Follow the organization's style in each case.

a. The names of computer organizations and products commonly reflect an intercap style. For example:

AltaVista	PageMaker	TrueType
FrontPage	PowerPoint	VirusScan

(Continued on page 112.)

b. The use of intercaps appears in other areas of business as well. For example:

AquaFun Spas   KitchenAid appliances   Realemon juice
LiteTouch stereos   MasterCard purchases   Travelodge motels

Capitalization of questions within sentences: see ¶¶115, 117.
Capitalization after a colon: see ¶¶196–199.
Capitalization after an opening bracket: see ¶296.
Capitalization after an opening dash: see ¶214 note.
Capitalization with parenthetical items: see ¶¶224–226.
Capitalization after an opening quotation mark: see ¶¶272–273.
Capitalization of abbreviations: see ¶514.

See the Online Learning Centre at www.mcgrawhill.ca/college/gregg for related Web links.

SECTION **FOUR**

Numbers

BASIC RULES (¶¶401–406)
Figure Style (¶¶401–403)
Word Style (¶¶404–406)

SPECIAL RULES (¶¶407–471)
Dates (¶¶407–412)
Money (¶¶413–420)
At the Beginning of a Sentence (¶¶421–422)
Indefinite Numbers and Amounts (¶423)
Ordinal Numbers (¶¶424–426)
Fractions (¶¶427–428)
   Fractions Standing Alone (¶427)
   Fractions in Mixed Numbers (¶428)
Measurements (¶¶429–432)
Ages and Anniversaries (¶¶433–435)
Periods of Time (¶¶436–439)
Clock Time (¶¶440–442)
   With *a.m., p.m., Noon,* and *Midnight* (¶440)
   With *O'Clock* (¶441)
   Without *a.m., p.m.,* or *O'Clock* (¶442)
Decimal Fractions (¶¶443–446)
Percentages (¶¶447–449)
Ratios and Proportions (¶450)
Scores and Voting Results (¶451)
Numbers Referred to as Numbers (¶452)
Figures With Abbreviations and Symbols (¶453)
Telephone Numbers (¶454)
No. or # With Figures (¶455)
Adjacent Numbers (¶¶456–457)
Numbers in a Sequence (¶¶458–460)
Expressing Numbers in Figures (¶¶461–464)
Expressing Numbers in Words (¶¶465–467)
Roman Numerals (¶468)
Expressing Large Numbers in Abbreviated Form (¶469)
Numbers in Street Addresses (¶¶470–471)

There is a significant difference between using figures and using words to express numbers. Figures are big (like capital letters) and compact and informal (like abbreviations); when used in a sentence, they stand out clearly from the surrounding words. By contrast, numbers expressed in words are unemphatic and formal; they do not stand out in a sentence. It is this functional difference between figures and words that underlies all aspects of number style.

BASIC RULES

There are two sets of basic rules in wide use: the *figure style* (which uses figures for most numbers above 10) and the *word style* (which uses figures for most numbers above 100). Unless you deal with a very limited type of business correspondence, you should be prepared to use each as the situation demands.

In countries that follow the metric (SI) style, spaces are used to separate numbers. There is a trend, however, to return to the use of the comma. The main reason for this is to ensure readability of numbers, especially when smaller fonts are used. This is particularly true in legal and financial documents.

Figure Style

The figure style is most commonly used in ordinary business correspondence (dealing with sales, production, finance, advertising, and other routine commercial matters). It is also used in journalistic and technical material and in academic work of a technical or statistical nature. In writing of this kind, most numbers represent significant quantities or measurements that should stand out for emphasis or quick comprehension.

401 **a.** Spell out numbers from 1 to 10; use figures for numbers above 10. This rule applies to both exact and approximate numbers.

> I would like *ten* copies of this article, but I need only *two* or *three* right away.
>
> We expect about *30* to *35* employees to sign up for the graphic arts course.
>
> The advertising is deliberately pitched at the *40-plus* age group.
>
> My letter in last Sunday's paper provoked over *25* letters and *60-odd* phone calls.
>
> There has been a *sixfold* increase in the number of incidents. (See ¶817a.)
> **BUT**: There has been a *20-fold* increase in the number of incidents.
>
> One bookstore chain has already ordered *2500* copies. (See ¶461b on the omission of spaces.)
>
> We send out about *200 000* catalogues every month, but our year-end holiday catalogue is mailed to over *1 000 000* households. (See ¶403b.)

b. Use all figures (even for the numbers 1 to 10) in tables, statistical matter, and expressions like the following:

school marks:	86	dates:	May 3
ratios and proportions:	5-to-1 chance	money:	$6.75
highways:	Highway 2, 401	clock time:	4 p.m.
measurements:	parcels over 2 kg	percentages:	8 percent
abbreviations:	12 cm	symbols:	9°C

periods of time:	6-month loan	sports scores:	5 to 3
specific ages:	for all 6-year-olds	page numbers:	page 3
number as a number:	lucky number 7		

c. In isolated cases spell out a number above 10 in order to de-emphasize the number or make it seem indefinite.

Sanjay may give you *a thousand and one* reasons why he cannot go.

Thanks *a million* for all your help on the deposition.

I have *a hundred* things to do today. (In this context *100 things* would seem too precise, too exact.)

d. Use words for numbers at the beginning of a sentence, for most ordinals *(our twenty-fifth anniversary)*, for fractions *(one-third of our sales)*, and for non-technical or non-emphatic references to age *(my son just turned twelve)*, periods of time *(twenty years ago)*, and measurements *(I need to lose another thirty pounds)*.

☞ *For rules on how to express numbers in figures, see ¶¶461–464.*
For rules on how to express numbers in words, see ¶¶465–467.

402 Use the same style to express *related* numbers above and below 10. If any of the numbers are above 10, put them all in figures.

We used to have *two* dogs, *one* cat, and *one* rabbit.

BUT: We now have *5* dogs, *11* cats, and *1* rabbit.

Our *four* sons consumed a total of *18* hamburgers, *5* large bottles of diet Coke, *12* Mars Bars, and about *2000* cookies—all at *one* sitting. (Figures are used for all the related items of food; the other numbers—*four* and *one*—are spelled out, since they are not related and are not over 10.)

NOTE: In the names of companies and products, follow the organization's style.

a 7-Eleven store	3-In-One oil	9-Lives cat food
a can of 7UP	3M office products	V8 juice

403 **a.** For fast comprehension, numbers in the *millions* or higher may be expressed as follows:

21 million (in place of 21 000 000)

3 billion (in place of 3 000 000 000)

$14\frac{1}{2}$ million (in place of 14 500 000)

2.4 billion (in place of 2 400 000 000)

Bindel & Boggs is placing an order for *2.4 million* barrels of oil.

BUT: Bindel & Boggs is placing a *2.4-million-barrel* order. (See ¶817.)

NOTE: This style may be used only when the amount consists of a whole number with nothing more than a simple fraction or decimal following. A number

(Continued on page 116.)

such as 4 832 067 must be written all in figures. (However, if rounding numbers is permitted, this number could be rewritten as *4.8 million*.)

b. Treat related numbers alike.

Last year we sold *21 557 000* items; this year, nearly *23 000 000*.

(NOT: 21 557 000 . . . 23 million.)

☞ *For examples involving money, see ¶416.*

To prevent line-ending difficulties with larger numbers, see ¶919b.

Word Style

The word style of numbers is used in high-level executive correspondence (see ¶¶1374–1375) and in non-technical material, where the writing is more formal or literary and the use of figures would give numbers an undesired emphasis and obtrusiveness. See ¶¶404–406 for the basic word style rules.

404 Spell out all numbers, whether exact or approximate, that can be expressed in one or two words. (A hyphenated compound number like *twenty-one* or *twenty-nine* counts as one word.) In effect, spell out all numbers from 1 through 100 and all round numbers above 100 that require no more than two words (such as *sixty-two thousand* or *forty-five million*).

Mr. Ryan received *twenty-five* letters praising his talk last Wednesday at the Rotary Club.

Last year more than *twelve million* people attended the art exhibition our company sponsored.

Some *sixty-odd* people have called to volunteer their services.

Over *two hundred* people attended the reception for Helen and Frank Russo.

BUT: Over *250* people attended the reception. (Use figures when more than two words are required.)

NOTE: In very formal writing—proclamations, social invitations, and many legal documents—even a number that requires more than two words is spelled out. However, as a matter of practicality the word style ordinarily uses figures when more than two words are required.

☞ *For rules on how to express numbers in words, see ¶¶465–467.*

405 Express related numbers the same way, even though some are above 100 and some below. If any must be in figures, put all in figures.

We sent out *three hundred* invitations and have already received over *one hundred* acceptances.

BUT: We sent out *300 invitations and have already received 125* acceptances. (NOT: three hundred . . . 125.)

406 Numbers in the millions or higher *that require more than two words when spelled out* may be expressed as follows:

231 million (in place of 231 000 000)

$9\frac{3}{4}$ billion (in place of 9 750 000 000)

671.4 million (in place of 671 400 000)

Even a two-word number such as *sixty-two million* should be expressed as *62 million* when it is related to a number such as *231 million* (which cannot be spelled in two words). Moreover, it should be expressed as *62 000 000* when it is related to a number such as *231 163 520*.

SPECIAL RULES

The preceding rules on figure style and word style are basic guidelines. The following rules cover those situations that require special handling. In a number of cases where either figures or words are acceptable, the choice will depend on whether emphasis or formality is desired.

Dates

These rules apply to dates in sentences. See ¶1313 for date lines in business correspondence.

407 When the day *precedes* the month or *stands alone*, express it either in ordinal figures (*1st, 2nd, 3rd, 4th,* etc.) or in ordinal words (the *first*, the *twelfth*, the *twenty-eighth*). To avoid superscripts for ordinals in MS Word, be sure to turn off the default setting.

> **FOR EMPHASIS:** This year's international sales conference runs from Monday, the *2nd* of August, through Thursday, the *5th*.

> **FOR FORMALITY:** We leave for Europe on the *third* of June and do not return until the *twenty-fifth*.

NOTE: When the year is added to the day and month, the following forms should be avoided: the *sixth of March, 2007; 6th of March, 2007*.

408 When the day *follows* the month, use a cardinal figure (*1, 2, 3,* etc.).

> on March 6 (**NOT:** March *6th* **OR** March *sixth*)

> **NOTE:** Do not use the form *March 6th, 2007,* or *March sixth, 2007,* even though these versions reflect how the date is spoken.

409 **a.** Express complete dates in month-day-year sequence.

> March 6, 2007

> **NOTE:** In military correspondence and in letters from foreign countries, the complete date is expressed in day-month-year sequence.

> 6 March 2007

b. The form *3/6/07* or *03/06/07* indicating a *month*-day-year sequence is acceptable **only** on business forms and when instructed; but avoid this form if your reader could misinterpret it as a *day*-month-year sequence.

c. Descending order of magnitude in metric numeric dating expresses dates with 8 digits. March 8, 2007, is written as:

> 2007 03 08   2007-03-08   20070308

410 Note the use of commas and other punctuation with expressions of dates.

On *August 13, 2007,* my husband and I received the bank loan that permitted us to start our own restaurant. (Two commas set off the year following the month and day.)

We set a formal opening date of *November 15, 2006;* we actually opened on *March 18, 2007* (because of the flash fire that virtually destroyed the restaurant and forced us to start from scratch). (Note that the second comma is omitted *after 2006* and *2007* because in each case some other punctuation mark—a semicolon or an opening parenthesis—is required at that point.)

Sales for *February 2007* hit an all-time low. (Omit commas around the year when it follows the month alone.)

BUT: Once we introduced our new product line in *September 2007,* it was clear that we were finally on the road to a strong recovery. (The comma following *2007* is needed to separate an introductory dependent clause from the rest of the sentence, not because of the date.)

The *May 2006* issue of *Maclean's* carries an excerpt from Brenda's forthcoming book. (No commas are used when the month-year expression serves as an adjective.)

BUT: The *May 4, 2006,* issue of *Newsweek* broke the story. (Use two commas to set off the year when a complete date serves as an adjective. See ¶154.)

In *2006* we opened six branch offices in . . . (No comma follows the year in a short introductory phrase unless a non-essential element follows immediately.)

On *February 28* we will decide . . . (No comma follows the month and day in a short introductory phrase unless a non-essential element follows immediately.)

BUT: On *February 28,* the date of the next board meeting, we will decide . . . (Insert a comma when a non-essential element follows immediately.)

On *February 28,* 27 managers from the Oshawa plant will . . . (Insert a comma when another figure follows immediately. See ¶456.)

Yesterday, *April 3,* I spoke to a group of exporters in Calgary. On Tuesday, *April 11,* I will be speaking at an international trade fair in Singapore. (Set off a month-day expression when it serves as an appositive. See ¶148.)

☞ *For the use or omission of a comma when a date is followed by a related phrase or clause, see ¶152.*

411 In formal legal documents, formal invitations, and proclamations, spell out the day and the year. A number of styles may be used:

May twenty-first	two thousand and six
the twenty-first of May	in the year of our Lord two thousand
this twenty-first day of May	and six
executed on the 17th day of May, 2006	

412 **a.** Class graduation years and well-known years in history may appear in abbreviated form.

the class of '06   the winter of '05   the market crash of '29

b. Years also appear in abbreviated form in certain business expressions. (See also ¶294.)

fiscal year 2006/07 **or** FY 2006/07   the fall '07/08 catalogue

☞ *For the expression of centuries and decades, see ¶¶438–439.*
For dates in a sequence, see ¶¶458–460.

Money

413 **a.** Use figures to express exact or approximate amounts of money. There is no space between the dollar sign and the first number.

$7	about $1500	a $50 bill	less than $450
$13.50	nearly $50 000	$350 worth	over $10 000

b. When amounts of money from different countries are referred to in the same context, the unit of currency usually appears as an abbreviation or symbol (or both) directly preceding the numeral amount. (The use of commas rather than spaces is still preferred by many banking and legal institutions to prevent the addition of "bogus" figures.)

US$10 000	(10 000 U.S. dollars)
Mex$10 000	(10 000 Mexican pesos)
£10 000	(10 000 British pounds)
¥10 000	(10 000 Japanese yen)
€10 000	(10 000 euros)
Can$10 000	(10 000 Canadian dollars)

NOTE: Special character sets will print monetary symbols.

c. An isolated, non-emphatic reference to money may be spelled out.

two hundred dollars	half a million dollars
a twenty-dollar bill	five thousand dollars' worth (note
a million-dollar beach house	the apostrophe with *dollars*)

414 Spell out indefinite amounts of money.

a few million dollars   many thousands of dollars

415 It is not necessary to add a decimal point or zeros to a *whole* dollar amount when it occurs in a sentence.

I am enclosing a cheque for *$125*.

This model costs $12.50; that one costs *$10*.

In a column, however, if any amount contains cents, add a decimal point and two zeros to all *whole* dollar amounts to maintain a uniform appearance. (See also ¶1624.)

$150.50
 25.00
  8.05
$183.55

416 a. Money in round amounts of a million or more may be expressed partially in words. (The style given in the first column is preferred.)

$12 million	**OR**	12 million dollars			
$10½ million	**OR**	10½ million dollars			
$10.5 million	**OR**	10.5 million dollars			
$6¼ billion	**OR**	6¼ billion dollars	**OR**	$6250 million	
$6.25 billion	**OR**	6.25 billion dollars	**OR**	6250 million dollars	

b. This style may be used only when the amount consists of a whole number with nothing more than a simple fraction or decimal following:

10.5 million dollars   **BUT:** $10 235 000

c. Express related amounts the same way.

from $500 000 to $1 000 000 (**NOT:** from $500 000 to $1 million)

d. Repeat the word *million* (*billion*, etc.) with each figure to avoid misunderstanding.

$5 million to $10 million (**NOT:** $5 to $10 million)

417 Fractional expressions of large amounts of money should be either completely spelled out or converted to an all-figure style.

one-quarter of a million dollars **OR** $250 000
(**NOT:** ¼ of a million dollars **OR** $¼ million)

a half-billion dollars **OR** $500 000 000
(**NOT:** ½ billion dollars **OR** $½ billion)

418 a. For amounts under a dollar, ordinarily use figures and the word *cents*.

I am sure that customers will not pay more than *50 cents* for this item.

This machine can be fixed with *80 cents'* worth of parts. (Note the apostrophe with *cents*.)

These *25-cent* tokens can be used at all tollbooths.

NOTE: An isolated, non-emphatic reference to cents may be spelled out.

I wouldn't give *two cents* for that car.

b. Do not use the style *$.75* in sentences except when related amounts require a dollar sign.

It will cost you *$4.84* a copy to do the company manual: *$.86* for the paper, *$1.54* for the printing, and *$2.44* for the special binder.

c. The cent sign (¢) may be used in technical and statistical matter.

The price of lead, *34.5¢* a kilogram in 2003, is now *82¢* a kilogram; zinc, averaging *28¢* a kilogram in 2003, now sells for *98¢* a kilogram.

419 a. When using the dollar sign or the cent sign with a price range or a series of amounts, use the sign with each amount.

$5 000 to $10 000 $10 million to $20 million

10¢ to 20¢   (NOT: $10 to $20 million)

These three properties are valued at $832 900, $954 500, and $1 087 000 respectively.

b. If the term *dollars* or *cents* is to be spelled out, use it only with the final amount.

10 to 20 cents   10 million to 20 million dollars (see ¶416c)

420 a. In legal documents, amounts of money are often expressed first in words and then, within parentheses, in figures.

One Hundred Dollars ($100)   **OR**   One Hundred (100) Dollars
(NOT: One Hundred ($100) Dollars)

Three Thousand One Hundred and 50/100 Dollars ($3100.50)

b. When spelling out amounts of money, omit the *and* between hundreds and tens of dollars if *and* is used before the fraction representing cents.

Six hundred thirty-two and 75/100 Dollars
(NOT: Six hundred *and* thirty-two and 75/100 Dollars)

NOTE: In whole dollar amounts, the use of *and* between hundreds and tens of dollars is optional.

Six hundred and thirty-two dollars   **OR**   Six hundred thirty-two dollars

c. The capitalization of spelled-out amounts may vary. Sometimes the first letter of each main word is capitalized (as in the examples in ¶420a); sometimes only the first letter of the first word is capitalized (as in the examples in ¶420b); occasionally the entire amount is in all capital letters.

The following rules (¶¶421–428) cover situations in which numbers are usually spelled out: at the beginning of sentences and in expressions using indefinite numbers, ordinal numbers, and fractions.

At the Beginning of a Sentence

421 Spell out a number that begins a sentence, as well as any related numbers.

Thirty-four former students of Dr. Helen VanVleck came from all parts of the country to honour their professor on the occasion of her retirement.

Eight hundred people have already signed the recall petition.

Forty to *fifty* percent of the people were polled on different occasions.
(NOT: *Forty* to *50* percent . . .)

422 If the number requires more than two words when spelled out or if figures are preferable for emphasis or quick reference, reword the sentence.

You ought to consider a minimum of *456 MHz* if you want to boost your productivity.
(NOT: *456 MHz* are worth considering . . .)

The company sent out *298* copies of its consumer guidelines last month.
(NOT: *Two hundred and ninety-eight* copies of its consumer guidelines were sent out by the company last month.)

(Continued on page 122.)

We had a good year in *2005*.
(**NOT:** *Two thousand and five* [**OR** *2005*] was a good year for us.)

Our mines provide *60* to *70* percent of our revenues.
(**NOT:** *Sixty* to *seventy* percent of our revenues come from our mines.)

Indefinite Numbers and Amounts

423 Spell out indefinite numbers and amounts.

several hundred investors	thousands of readers
a few hundred kilometres	many millions of dollars
a man in his late forties	a roll of fifties and twenties

☞ *For approximate numbers, see ¶401 (figure style) and ¶404 (word style).*

Ordinal Numbers

424 In general, spell out all ordinal numbers (*first, second, third,* etc.) that can be expressed in one or two words. (A hyphenated number like *twenty-first* counts as one word.)

twentieth-century art (see ¶817)	the firm's one hundredth anniversary (**BUT:** the firm's 125th anniversary)
on the forty-eighth floor	the Thirty-ninth Parliament (in text)
my fifty-fifth birthday	the Thirty-Ninth Parliament (in
the Fourteenth Ward	headings and titles; see ¶363)
the two millionth visitor	the third quarter sales

NOTE: When a hyphenated term like *twenty-first* is the first element in a compound adjective (as in *twenty-first-century art*), the second hyphen may be changed to an en dash *(twenty-first–century art)*.

☞ *For the rule on how to express ordinal numbers in words, see ¶465.*
For the distinction between ordinals and fractions, see ¶427d.

425 Use figures for ordinals in certain expressions of dates (see ¶407), in numbered street names above 10 (see ¶1329b), and in situations calling for special emphasis.

In Advertising Copy

Come to our *25th* Anniversary Sale! (Figures for emphasis.)

Come to our *Twenty-fifth* Anniversary Sale! (Words for formality.)

In Ordinary Correspondence

Watkins & Glenn is having a *twenty-fifth* anniversary sale.

NOTE: Ordinal figures are expressed as follows: *1st, 2nd, 3rd,* or *4th, 5th, 6th,* etc. Do not use an abbreviation period after an ordinal figure. The superscript style should be used only in informal writing.

426 Ordinals that follow a person's name may be expressed in Arabic or Roman numerals. As a rule, use Arabic numerals unless you know that the person in question prefers Roman numerals.

James A. Wilson 3rd	**OR** James A. Wilson III
C. Roy Post 4th	C. Roy Post IV

☞ *For the use or omission of commas with numerals that follow a person's name, see ¶156.*

Fractions

427 FRACTIONS STANDING ALONE

a. Ordinarily, spell out a fraction that stands alone (that is, without a whole number preceding). Use figures, however, if the spelled-out form is long and awkward or if the fraction is used in some type of computation.

one-half the audience (see ¶427c)   three-fourths of the profits
a two-thirds majority   nine-tenths of a mile away
multiply by 13/32   a quarter box of pasta

He came back *a half hour* later (**or** *half an hour* later).

NOTE: Hyphenate *half dozen* or *half a dozen* when this phrase is used as a compound modifier before a noun. (See ¶817.)

I'll take *a half-dozen* eggs (**or** *half-a-dozen* eggs).

BUT: I'll take *a half dozen* (**or** *half a dozen*).

NOTE: In the metric system, numeric expressions in measurements show decimals in preference to mixed fractions. The decimal marker is placed as a point on the line.

73.6 kg   3.21 mm   7.5 m/s

b. When a fraction is spelled out, the numerator and the denominator should be connected by a hyphen unless either element already contains a hyphen.

five-eighths   thirteen thirty-seconds   twenty-seven sixty-fourths

c. In constructions involving the balanced phrases *one half . . . the other half*, do not hyphenate *one half*.

One half of the shipment was damaged beyond use; *the other half* was salvageable.

d. Distinguish between large spelled-out fractions (which are hyphenated) and large spelled-out ordinals (which are not).

The difference is less than *one-hundredth* of 5 percent. (Hyphenated fraction meaning *1/100*.)

BUT: This year the company will be celebrating the *one hundredth* anniversary of its founding. (Unhyphenated ordinal meaning *100th*.)

e. Fractions expressed in figures should not be followed by endings like *sts, nds, rds,* or *ths* or by an *of* phrase.

3/200 (**NOT:** 3/200ths)   9/64 (**NOT:** 9/64ths)

When an *of* phrase follows the fraction, spell the fraction out.

three-quarters of an hour (**NOT:** 3/4 of an hour)

428 FRACTIONS IN MIXED NUMBERS

a. Ordinarily use figures to express a mixed number (a whole number plus a fraction); for example, $3\frac{1}{4}$. Spell out a mixed number at the beginning of a sentence.

Our sales are not $4\frac{1}{2}$ times what they were in 2005.

Two and a quarter (**OR** *Two and one-quarter*) percent is too low. (Note the use of *and* between the whole number and the fraction.)

b. When constructing fractions that do not appear on the keyboard or in a special character set with word processing software, use the diagonal (/). Separate a whole number from a fraction by means of a space (not with a hyphen).

I can remember when an 8 5/8 percent mortgage seemed high.

(**NOT:** . . . an 8-5/8 percent mortgage.)

c. In the same sentence, do not mix ready-made fractions (such as $\frac{1}{2}$) with those that you construct yourself (7/8, 5/16).

The rate on prime commercial paper has dropped from 11 1/2 percent a year ago to 8 3/4 percent today.

(**NOT:** $11\frac{1}{2}$ . . . 8 3/4.)

NOTE: To simplify keying, convert constructed fractions (and simpler ones used in the same context) to a decimal form whenever feasible.

The rate on prime commercial paper has dropped from 11.5 percent a year ago to 8.75 percent today.

The following rules (¶¶429–442) deal with measurements and expressions of age and time (elements that often function as measurements). When these elements have technical or statistical significance, they are expressed in figures; otherwise, they are expressed in words.

Measurements

429 Most measurements have a technical significance and should be expressed in figures (even from 1 to 10) for emphasis or quick comprehension. However, spell out an isolated measurement that lacks technical significance.

A higher rate is charged on parcels over *2 kg*.
BUT: He weighed *two kilograms* too much for his weight class.

There is no charge for delivery within a *40-km* distance of Whitby.
BUT: It's only a *forty-kilometre* drive to our summer place.

NOTE: Dimensions, sizes, and actual temperature readings are always expressed in figures.

I'm looking for a *2- by 3-metre* Oriental rug for my reception room. (See also ¶432.)

Please send me a half-dozen blue oxford shirts, size $17\frac{1}{2}/33$.

The thermometer now stands at *22°C*, a drop of five degrees in the past two hours.

BUT: The temperature has been in the low *twenties* (**OR** *20s*) all week. (An indefinite reference to the temperature may be spelled out or expressed in figures.)

430 When an imperial measurement consists of several elements, do not use commas to separate the elements. They are considered a single unit.

Hal is *6 feet 8 inches* tall in his stocking feet.

NOTE: If this type of measurement is used as a compound modifier before a noun, use hyphens to connect all elements as a single unit. (See ¶817.)

a *6-foot-8-inch* man

431 In using a metric prefix, select the numerical value that lies between 0.1 and 1000; but when similar measurements are compared, it is better to use the same prefix for all items even though some values may fall outside that range.

12 000 g is better shown as *12 kg*; **BUT:** 321 mm is better than *0.003 21 m.*

The distance from Ottawa to Toronto is *400 km*; and from the North Pole to the Equator, it is *10 000 km.*

☞ *For the style of abbreviations for units of measure, see ¶¶535–538.*
For the use of figures with abbreviations and symbols, see ¶453.

432 Dimensions may be expressed as follows:

GENERAL USAGE:	a room 5 by 10 metres	a 5- by 10-metre room
TECHNICAL USAGE:	a room 5 m × 10 m	a 5-m × 10-m room
GENERAL USAGE:	15 feet 6 inches by 30 feet 9 inches	
TECHNICAL USAGE:	15 ft 6 in × 30 ft 9 in **OR** 15' 6" × 30' 9"	

Ages and Anniversaries

433 Express ages in figures (including 1 to 10) when they are used as significant statistics or as technical measurements.

The attached printout projects the amount of the monthly retirement benefit payable *at the age of 65.* (See the entry for *Age—aged—at the age of* in Section 11.)

A computer literacy program is being offered in the schools to all *8- and 9-year-olds.* (See ¶832.)

This insurance policy is specially tailored for people in the *50-plus* age group.

You cannot disregard the job application of a person *aged 58.* (**NOT:** age 58.)

NOTE: When age is expressed in years, months, and days, do not use commas to separate the elements; they make up a single unit.

On January 1 she will be *19 years 4 months and 17 days old.* (The *and* linking months and days may be omitted.)

434 Spell out ages in non-technical references and in formal writing.

My son is *three years old*, and my daughter is *two.*

Shirley is in her early *forties*; her husband is in his *mid-sixties.*

Have you ever tried keeping a group of *five-year-olds* happy?

435 Spell out ordinals in references to birthdays and anniversaries except where special emphasis or more than two words are required. (See also ¶¶424–425.)

on my thirtieth birthday   her forty-first class reunion
our twenty-fifth anniversary   the company's 135th anniversary

Periods of Time

436 Use figures (even from 1 to 10) to express periods of time when they are used as technical measurements or significant statistics (as in discounts, interest rates, and credit terms).

a 35-hour workweek   1 30-year mortgage   a note due in 6 months

NOTE: In legal documents, periods of time are often expressed twice: first in words and then in figures (enclosed in parentheses).

Payable in ninety (90) days   **NOT:** payable in ninety (90 days)

437 Spell out non-technical references to periods of time unless the number requires more than two words.

a twenty-minute wait   in twenty-four months   three hundred years ago
eight hours later   in the last thirty years **BUT:** 350 years ago
twelve days from now   forty-odd years ago   two thousand years ago

438 Centuries may be expressed as follows:

the 1900s   **OR**   the nineteen hundreds   **OR**   the twentieth century
the twenty-first century   twenty-first–century literature

439 **a.** Decades may be expressed as follows:

the 1990s **OR** the nineteen-nineties **OR** the nineties **OR** the '90s

the mid-1960s **OR** the mid-sixties **OR** the mid-'60s

in the 1980s and 1990s   **OR** in the '80s and '90s
NOT: in the 1980s and '90s   **OR** in the '80s and nineties

during the years 1999–2008 **OR** from 1999 to 2008 (see ¶459)

NOTE: Our present decade is best referred to as *the first decade of the twenty-first century.*

b. Decades are not capitalized except in special expressions such as *the Networked Nineties, the Roaring Twenties.*

Clock Time

440 WITH *A.M., P.M., NOON, AND MIDNIGHT*

a. Always use figures with *a.m.* or *p.m.*

We take off at *8:45 a.m.*   The bus is due at *2 p.m.*
By *8 p.m.*, CST, the first election returns should be in.

OR: By *8 p.m.* (CST) the first election returns should be in.

☞ *For abbreviations of time zones, see ¶534.*

b. In printed material, *a.m.* and *p.m.* sometimes appear in small capitals without an internal space (A.M., P.M.). In other material, *a.m.* and *p.m.* usually appear in small letters without internal space; however, you can use small capitals if you have that option. Avoid the use of all-capital letters.

c. For time "on the hour," zeros are not needed to denote minutes.

Our store is open from 9:30 a.m. to *6 p.m.* (**NOT:** 6:00 p.m.)

BUT: Our store is always open until 6:00. (See ¶442 for the use of zeros when *a.m.* or *p.m.* is omitted.)

We always close from *12 noon* to 1:30 p.m.

You can buy your tickets between *9* and *10 a.m.*

In tables, however, when some entries are given in hours and minutes, add a colon (no space before or after) and two zeros to exact hours to maintain a uniform appearance. (For more complex illustrations showing the alignment of clock times in columns, see ¶1625b.)

Arr.	Dep.
8:45	9:10
9:00	9:25
9:50	10:00

d. Do not use *a.m.* or *p.m.* unless figures are used.

this morning	tomorrow afternoon
(**NOT:** this a.m.)	(**NOT:** tomorrow p.m.)

e. Do not use *a.m.* or *p.m.* with *o'clock* or with the expressions *in the morning, in the afternoon, in the evening,* or *at night.* (See ¶441b.)

10 o'clock   **OR**   10 a.m.   **OR**   at ten in the morning
NOT: 10 a.m. o'clock   **NOT:** at 10 a.m. in the morning

NOTE: The expression *o'clock* is more formal than *a.m.* or *p.m.*

f. The times *noon* and *midnight* may be expressed in words alone. However, use the forms *12 noon* and *12 midnight* when these times are given with other times expressed in figures.

Dinner is served in the main dining room until *midnight.*

BUT: Dinner is served from *6 p.m.* until *12 midnight.*

441 WITH *O'CLOCK*

a. With *o'clock*, use figures for emphasis or words for formality.

3 o'clock (for emphasis)   three o'clock (for formality)
NOT: 3:00 o'clock

b. Expressions of time containing *o'clock* may be reinforced by such phrases as *in the morning* and *in the afternoon.*

10 o'clock at night   seven o'clock in the morning

For quick comprehension, the forms *10 p.m.* and *7 a.m.* are preferable.

442 WITHOUT *A.M.*, *P.M.*, OR *O'CLOCK*

When expressing time without *a.m.*, *p.m.*, or *o'clock*, either spell the time out (for quick comprehension) or convert the expression to an all-figure style. The 24-hour clock can also be used by adding 12 hours to the customary afternoon times.

arrive at eight	**OR**	8:00	**OR** 08 00 (**NOT:** at 8)
five after six	**OR**	6:05	**OR** 06 05 (18 05, if past noon)
a quarter past midnight	**OR**	12:15	**OR** 00 15
half past nine	**OR**	9:30	**OR** 09 30 (21 30, if past noon)
ten forty-two	**OR**	10:42	**OR** 10 42 (22 42, if past noon)

NOTE: A hyphen is used between hours and minutes (*seven-thirty*) but not if the minutes must be hyphenated (*seven thirty-five*).

4

The following rules (¶¶443–455) deal with situations in which numbers are always expressed in figures.

Decimal Fractions

443 Always write decimal fractions in figures.

165.318 436 8   58 919.237 85

☞ *For the metric style of writing decimal figures, see ¶461a.*

444 When a decimal fraction stands alone (without a whole number preceding the decimal point), insert a zero before the decimal point. (Reason: The zero keeps the reader from overlooking the decimal point and prevents a misreading of *0.5 percent* as the amount *5 percent.*

0.55   0.09

445 Ordinarily, drop the zero at the end of a decimal fraction (for example, write *2.78* rather than *2.780*). However, retain the zero (*a*) if you wish to emphasize that the decimal fraction is an exact number or (*b*) if the decimal has been rounded off from a longer figure. In a column of figures, add zeros to the end of a decimal expression in order to make the number as long as other numbers in the column. (For illustrations, see ¶¶1625, 1626, 1628.)

446 Do not begin a sentence with a decimal expression.

The temperature was 23.7. (**NOT:** 23.7 was the temperature.)

Percentages

447 Express percentages in figures, and spell out the word *percent*. (See ¶¶421–422 for percentages at the beginning of a sentence.)

When your mortgage rate goes from *6 percent* to *6.6 percent,* it may have increased by less than 1 percentage point, but you'll pay *10 percent* more in interest.

My client expected a *25 percent* discount. (**NOT:** a 25-percent discount. See ¶817.)

Our terms are *2 percent* 10 days, net 30 days. (These credit terms may be abbreviated as *2/10, n/30* on invoices and other business forms.)

NOTE: The % symbol may be used in tables, on business forms, and in statistical or technical matter.

448 **a.** Fractional percentages *under 1 percent* may be expressed as follows:

> one half of 1 percent **OR** 0.5 percent (See ¶444.)
> Workers were offered a *zero percent* wage package.

> **NOTE:** To avoid misreading, use *zero percent* unless it is shown with other percentages.

> Workers were offered a *0%, 0.5%,* and a *1%* increase.

b. Fractional percentages *over 1 percent* should be expressed in figures.

> $7\frac{1}{2}$ percent **OR** 7.5 percent $9\frac{1}{4}$ percent **OR** 9.25 percent

449 In a range or series of percentages, the word *percent* follows the last figure only. If the symbol % is used (see ¶447 note), it must follow each figure.

> Price reductions range from *20 to 50 percent.* (**OR:** from 20% to 50%.)
> We give discounts of *10, 20,* and *30 percent.* (**OR:** 10%, 20%, and 30%.)

☞ *For the use of % in a column of figures, see* ¶1627; *for the use of* percent *and* percentage, *see Section 11.*

Ratios and Proportions
450 As a rule, write ratios and proportions in figures.

> a proportion of 5 to 1 **OR** a 5-to-1 ratio **OR** a 5:1 ratio
> the odds are 100 to 1 **OR** a 100-to-1 shot

> **NOTE:** A non-technical reference may be spelled out.

> a *fifty-fifty* chance of success **OR** a *50-50* chance of success

Scores and Voting Results
451 Use figures (even for 1 to 10) to express scores and voting results.

> a score of 85 on the test   a vote of 17 to 6
> Montreal 8, Toronto 6   **BUT:** a 17-6 vote

Numbers Referred to as Numbers
452 Always use figures to express numbers referred to as numbers.

> pick a number from 1 to 10   divide by 16
> the number 7 is considered lucky   multiply by $\frac{7}{8}$

Figures With Abbreviations and Symbols
453 **a.** Always use figures with abbreviations and symbols.

$50	10:15 a.m.	43%	2 in **OR** 2"	FY2006 (see ¶1615c)
65¢	6 p.m.	No. 631	I-95	200 km (see ¶537)

b. If a symbol is used in a range of numbers, it should be repeated with each number. A full word or an abbreviation used in place of the symbol is given only with the last number.

(Continued on page 122.)

20°–30°C	**BUT:** 20 to 30 degrees Celsius (see ¶538c)
$8\frac{1}{2}" \times 11"$	$8\frac{1}{2}$ by 11 inches or $8\frac{1}{2} \times 11$ in
5 m × 8 m	5 by 8 metres
30%–40%	30 to 40 percent
50¢–60¢	50 to 60 cents
$70–$80	seventy to eighty dollars

NOTE: A symbol should be used with each number in a series.

discounts of 5%, 10%, and 15%   **BUT:** discounts of 5, 10, and 15 percent

Telephone Numbers

454   a. For a local telephone number of seven digits, it is usual to insert a hyphen after the first three digits; for example, *123-4567.* If a company chooses to express its number partially or entirely in words, follow the company's style; for example, *345-GIFT, 4-ANGIES, JOB-HUNT, CASH-NOW, GOFEDEX, PICK-UPS.*

  b. Once needed for long distance calls only, the great demand for telephones now has necessitated the inclusion of area codes as part of local telephone numbers. To write a telephone number with an area code, use hyphens, a diagonal, spaces, parentheses, periods, or a combination of these. When using hyphens, the diagonal, or periods, leave no space on either side of the elements. If using spaces, separate each element with one space only.

604-555-3998	604/555-3998	604.555.3998
604 555 3998	(604) 555-3998	

A style commonly seen is the area code placed inside parentheses. However, in text material when the area code and the telephone number as a unit have to be enclosed in parentheses, use one of the other four styles (as shown above). Using periods to separate the elements is relatively new to North Americans. This style is growing in popularity because these periods resemble dots in e-mail addresses.

You can always reach me by telephone (613-555-6939) between 8:30 and 11:30 a.m.

OR: . . . by telephone (613/555-6939) between 8:30 and 11:30 a.m.

NOT: . . . by telephone ((613) 555-6939) between 8:30 and 11:30 a.m.

  c. When an access code precedes the telephone number, use hyphens (or periods) to connect all the elements.

Use our toll-free telephone number: 1-866-555-6400 (1.866.555.6400)

  d. International telephone numbers often contain a series of special access codes. Hyphens (or periods) are used to connect all the elements.

011-64-9-555-1523
  └ international access code from Canada
      └ country access code
          └ city routing code

NOTE: Direct-dialed long distance calls within the United States, the Caribbean, and Canada do not require the use of international access codes.

e. When including a telephone extension along with the main number, use the following form: *244-4890, Ext. 6041.* (In formal correspondence, spell out *Extension.*)

No. or # With Figures

455 a. If the term *number* precedes a figure, express it as an abbreviation (singular: *No.*; plural: *Nos.*). At the beginning of a sentence, however, spell out *Number* to prevent misreading.

Our cheque covers the following invoices: *Nos.* 8592, 8653, and 8654.

Number 82175 has been assigned to your new policy. (**NOT:** No. 82175 . . .)

b. If an identifying noun precedes the figure (such as *Invoice, Cheque, Room, Box,* or the like), the abbreviation *No.* is usually unnecessary.

Our cheque covers *Invoices* 8592, 8653, and 8654.

EXCEPTIONS: Licence No. HLM 744; Social Insurance No. 604 356 289; Patent No. 953-461.

c. The symbol # may be used on business forms (such as invoices) and in technical matter.

☞ *For the capitalization of nouns preceding figures, see ¶359.*

The following rules (¶¶456–471) deal with two technical aspects of style: treating numbers that are adjacent or in a sequence and expressing numbers in figures, words, or Roman numerals.

Adjacent Numbers

456 When two numbers come together in a sentence and both are in figures or both are in words, separate them with a comma.

In *2007, 78* percent of our field representatives exceeded their sales goal.

Although the meeting was scheduled for *two, ten* of the participants did not show up until two-thirty.

On Account *53512, $125.40* is the balance outstanding.

NOTE: No comma is necessary when one number is in figures and the other is in words.

On May *9 seven* customers called to complain.

457 When two numbers come together in a compound adjective and one is part of a compound modifier, express one of the numbers in figures and the other in words. As a rule, spell out the first number unless the second number would make a significantly shorter word. (See ¶817.)

two 8-room houses	**BUT:** 500 four-page leaflets
sixty $5 bills	150 five-dollar bills

Numbers in a Sequence

458 Use commas to separate numbers that do not represent a continuous sequence.

on pages 18, 20, and 28   the years 2002, 2005, and 2008

459 **a.** Use an en dash to link two figures that represent a continuous sequence. The en dash means "up to and including" in the following expressions:

on pages 18–28   in Articles I–III
during the week of May 15–21   during the years 2001–2010

NOTE: Do not leave any space before or after the en dash or hyphen. (See ¶216.)

b. Do not use the en dash (or hyphen) if the sequence is introduced by the word *from* or *between*.

from 2003 to 2008   between 2001 and 2010
(**NOT:** from 2003–2008)   (**NOT:** between 2001–2010)

460 **a.** In a continuous sequence of figures connected by an en dash or a hyphen, the second figure may be expressed in abbreviated form. This style is used for sequences of page numbers or years when they occur quite frequently. (In isolated cases, do not abbreviate.)

1990–99 (**OR** 1990–1999)   pages 110–12 (**OR** pages 110–112)
2006–7 (**OR** 2006–2007)   pages 101–2 (**OR** pages 101–102)

b. Do not abbreviate the second number when the first number ends in two zeros.

2000–2009 (**NOT:** 2005–09)   pages 100–101 (**NOT:** pages 100–1)

c. Do not abbreviate the second number when it starts with different digits.

1999–2008 (**NOT:** 1999–08)   pages 999–1004 (**NOT:** pages 999–04)

d. Do not abbreviate the second number when it is under 100.

46–48 A.D. (See Section 11.)   pages 46–48

Expressing Numbers in Figures

461 **a.** When numbers run to five or more figures in the metric system, spaces (not commas) are left between groups of three figures to the left and right of the decimal point.

12 375 $411 275 478   4 300 000 000   0.594 31   70 670.372 48

b. When there are only four figures to the left or right of the decimal, the space is unnecessary unless these numbers occur together with larger numbers that require spaces.

5181 **OR** 5 181   0.3725 **OR** 0.372 5

☞ *For the use of commas with numbers, see ¶413b.*

462 Do not use commas in house or building numbers, postal or ZIP Code numbers, telephone numbers, page numbers, heat or temperature units, or years.

> 7351 Woodglen Drive   1-800-435-4321
> New York, New York   100221   2006

463 Serial numbers (for example, invoice, style, model, lot, licence, or card numbers) are usually written without commas. However, some serial numbers are written with hyphens, spaces, or other devices. In all cases follow the style of the source.

> Invoice 38162   Social Insurance No. 699 999 999
> Model G-43348   City Licence No. SO14.785.053

☞ *For the capitalization of nouns before numbers, see ¶359.*
For the use of No., *see ¶455.*

464 To form the plurals of figures, add *s* without an apostrophe. (See ¶624.)

> in the 1990s   '90s (decades)   in the 30s (temperature)

Expressing Numbers in Words

465 **a.** When expressing numbers in words, hyphenate all compound numbers between *21* and *99* (or *21st* and *99th*), whether they stand alone or are part of a number over 100.

> twenty-one   twenty-one hundred
> twenty-first   twenty-one hundredth
>
> seven hundred and twenty-five (*and* may be omitted)
>
> five thousand seven hundred and twenty-five (no commas)

b. Do not hyphenate other words in a spelled-out number over 99.

> one hundred   nineteen hundred
> two thousand   three hundred thousand
> four million   fifty-eight trillion

c. When a spelled-out number appears in a place name, follow the style shown in the *Postal Code Directory* or an authoritative atlas.

> Three Hills, AB   Seven Mile Lake, NB
> Trois-Rivières, QC   **BUT:** 100 Mile House, BC

☞ *For the capitalization of hyphenated numbers, see ¶363.*
For expressing numbers in street addresses, see ¶471.

466 When there are two ways to express a number in words, choose the simpler form. For example, use the form *fifteen hundred* rather than *one thousand five hundred*. (The longer form is rarely used except in formal expressions of dates. See ¶411 for examples.)

467 To form the plurals of spelled-out numbers, add *s* or *es*. (For numbers ending in *y*, change the *y* to *i* before *es*.)

ones	twos	threes	sixes	twenty-fives
thirds	sixths	eighths	twenties	thirty-seconds

☞ *For spelled-out dates, see ¶411.*

For spelled-out amounts of money, see ¶¶413c, 414, 417, 418, 420.

For spelled-out fractions, see ¶¶427–428.

Roman Numerals

468 **a.** Roman numerals are used chiefly for the important divisions of literary and legislative material, for main topics in outlines, for dates, and in proper names.

Chapter IX	World Wars I and II	MCMXCIX (1999)
Pentium IV	King George VI	MMVIII (2008)

NOTE: Pages in the front section of a book or a formal report (such as the preface and table of contents) are usually numbered in small Roman numerals: *iii, iv, v*, etc. Other pages are numbered in Arabic numerals: *1, 2, 3*, etc. (See ¶¶1429, 1633, 1719.)

b. To form Roman numerals, consult the table that follows. (A bar appearing over any Roman numeral indicates that the original value of the numeral is to be multiplied by 1000.)

1	I	13	XIII	60	LX	1100	MC
2	II	14	XIV	70	LXX	1400	MCD
3	III	15	XV	80	LXXX	1500	MD
4	IV	19	XIX	90	XC	1600	MDC
5	V	20	XX	100	C	1900	MCM
6	VI	21	XXI	200	CC	2000	MM
7	VII	24	XXIV	400	CD	5000	$\overline{V}$
8	VIII	25	XXV	500	D	10 000	$\overline{X}$
9	IX	29	XXIX	600	DC	50 000	$\overline{L}$
10	X	30	XXX	800	DCCC	100 000	$\overline{C}$
11	XI	40	XL	900	CM	500 000	$\overline{D}$
12	XII	50	L	1000	M	1 000 000	$\overline{M}$

Expressing Large Numbers in Abbreviated Form

469 In technical and informal contexts and in material where space is tight (for example, newspaper headlines and classified advertisements), numbers in the thousands, millions, or greater may be expressed as follows:

ROMAN STYLE: 38M (38 000); 6.3$\overline{\text{M}}$ (6 300 000)

METRIC STYLE: 31K (31 000); K stands for *kilo*, signifying thousands
5.2M (5 200 000); M stands for *mega*, signifying millions

8.76G (8 760 000 000); G stands for *giga*, signifying billions
2.9T (2 900 000 000 000); T stands for *tera*, signifying trillions

 For division of larger numbers at the end of a line: see ¶915.
For house, street, and postal code numbers: see ¶¶1329, 1332.

Numbers in Street Addresses

470 Use figures for house and building numbers. **EXCEPTION:** For clarity, use the word *One* instead of the figure *1* in a house or building number. (See ¶1329a.)

One Tulip Street   One Centre Avenue

471 Numbers used as street names are written as designated by the municipality. (See ¶1329b.)

209 Fifth Avenue   186 5th Street NW
209 – 5th Avenue   186 – 5 Street NW

See the Online Learning Centre at www.mcgrawhill.ca/college/gregg for related Web links.

SECTION **FIVE**

Abbreviations

Abbreviations are shortened forms of words or phrases used primarily to save space; they occur most often in technical writing, statistical matter, tables, and notes. Abbreviations that are pronounced letter by letter—for example, *RCMP, B.Sc., p.m.*—may be referred to as *initialisms*. Abbreviations pronounced as words—for example, *CUPE, NATO, modem*—are called *acronyms* (see ¶522).

BASIC RULES
When to Use Abbreviations

501 **a.** When using an abbreviation, do not follow it with a word that is part of the abbreviation (see ¶522f).

Marie has an enormous collection of *CD*s (**NOT**: CD discs).

502 In business writing, abbreviations are appropriate in documents where the emphasis is on communicating data in the briefest form, such as business forms, catalogues, routine e-mail messages, and memos. In other kinds of writing, where a more formal style is appropriate, use abbreviations sparingly. When in **doubt, spell it out.**

a. Some abbreviations are always acceptable, even in the most formal contexts: those that precede or follow personal names (such as *Mr., Ms., Mrs., Jr., Sr., Esq., Ph.D., S.J.*); those that are part of an organization's legal name (such as *Co., Inc., Ltd.*); those used in expressions of time (such as *a.m., p.m., CST, EDT*); and a few miscellaneous expressions (such as *A.D.* and *B.C.*).

b. Organizations with long names are now commonly identified by their initials in all but the most formal writing (for example, *YMCA, CDIC, IBM, CPI*).

c. Days of the week, names of the months, geographic names, and units of measure should be abbreviated only on business forms, in e-mails and memos, and in tables, lists, and narrow columns of text (for example, in a newsletter or brochure) where space is tight.

d. When an abbreviation is only one or two keystrokes shorter than the full word (for example, *Pt.* for *Part*), do not bother to abbreviate except to achieve consistency when similar terms are being abbreviated. (See also ¶532 for abbreviations of months.)

503 Consult a dictionary or an authoritative reference work for the acceptable forms of abbreviations. When a term may be abbreviated in several ways, choose the form that is shortest without sacrifice of clarity.

continued:	Use *cont.* rather than *contd.*
especially:	Use *esp.* rather than *espec.*
Enclosures 2:	Use *Enc. 2* rather than *Encs. 2* or *Encl. 2.*
24 hours:	Use *24 h* rather than *24 hrs.*
megabyte, kilobyte	Use *MB, KB* for clarity rather than *M, K.*

(Continued on page 138.)

NOTE: *The Canadian Oxford* Dictionary is the authority used for almost all spellings and abbreviations in this manual. Whenever two abbreviations are shown in the dictionary, the first form is the one given here. Punctuation is based on observations of actual practice and is consistent with the style recommended by other authorities.

504 Be consistent within the same material: do not abbreviate a term in some sentences and spell it out in other sentences. Moreover, having selected one form of an abbreviation (say, *c.o.d.*), do not use a different style (*COD*) elsewhere in the same material. (See ¶542.)

NOTE: When using an abbreviation that may not be familiar to the reader, spell out the full term along with the abbreviation when it is first used.

At the end of *fiscal year (FY) 2005*, we showed a profit of $1.2 million; at the end of *FY2006*, however, we showed a loss of $1.8 million.

OR: At the end of *FY2006 (fiscal year 2006)* . . .

505 **a.** Given a choice between an abbreviation and a contraction, choose the abbreviation. It not only looks better but is easier to key and to read.

acct. (**RATHER THAN:** acc't)	govt. (**RATHER THAN:** gov't)
dept. (**RATHER THAN:** dep't)	mfg. (**RATHER THAN:** m'f'g)

b. When a word or phrase is shortened as a contraction, an apostrophe is inserted at the exact point where letters are omitted and no period follows the contraction except at the end of a sentence.

let's	doesn't	you're
ma'am	o'clock	I'm

NOTE: Respect a company's preference when it uses a contraction in its corporate name or in the name of a product.

All N One	Subs N More	Wash 'n Dri
Dunkin' Donuts	Suds 'N Such	Winkin' Owl
Free Wheelin'	Toad N' Turtle	Wok N' Roll

c. As a rule, contractions are used only in informal writing or in tables where space is limited. However, contractions of verb phrases (such as *can't* for *cannot*) are commonly used in business letters where the writer is striving for an easy, conversational tone. In formal writing, contractions are not used (except for *o'clock*, which is considered a more formal way to express time than *a.m.* or *p.m.*).

d. Be sure to distinguish certain contractions from possessive pronouns that sound the same but do not use an apostrophe.

Ron has been pushing the Kirschner proposal for all *it's* worth. (In other words, for all *it is* worth.)

Let's get an outside consultant to analyze the Kirschner proposal and assess *its* worth. (Here *its* is a possessive pronoun; no apostrophe should be used.)

☞ *See ¶1056e for further examples and a test on how to determine the correct form.*

e. Note that certain contractions can have more than one meaning; for instance, the apostrophe plus *s* can represent *is, does, has, was,* or *us.*

What's her name? (What *is* her name?)

What's he do for a living? (What *does* he do for a living?)

What's been happening? (What *has* been happening?)

When's the last time you saw her? (When *was* the last time you saw her?)

Let's find out. (Let *us* find out.)

Punctuation and Spacing With Abbreviations

506 The abbreviation of a single word requires a period at the end.

ed.	Inc.	misc.	pkg.	Sat.
est.	lit.	Mr.	Sr.	Sep.

NOTE: Units of measurement are now commonly written without periods. (See ¶¶535a, 538a.)

507 Almost all lower-case abbreviations made up of single initials require a period after each initial but no space after each internal period.

a.m.	i.e.	f.o.b.	l.c.l.	**BUT:** dpi
p.m.	e.g.	e.o.m.	c.i.f.	km/h

☞ *For the omission of periods with abbreviations of units of measure, see ¶535a.*
For the definition of business abbreviations like f.o.b. *and* e.o.m., *see ¶541.*

508 All-capital abbreviations made up of single initials normally have no periods and no internal space.

CAA	CBA	CD	DNA	MRI
CAD	CBC	CB	ETA	POV

EXCEPTIONS: Use periods in abbreviations of geographic names (such as U.S.A.), academic degrees (B.A., M.Sc.), expressions (A.D., B.C.E., V.P.), and in the names of organizations and products (C.C.M. skates, S.O.S soap pads). (See ¶¶526–529.)

509 If an abbreviation stands for two or more words and consists of more than single initials, insert a period and a space after each element in the abbreviation.

at. no.	Co. Ltd.	Gov. Gen.	op. cit.	Rt. Hon.

EXCEPTIONS: Academic abbreviations like *Ph.D., B.Ed., LL.B.,* and *Litt.D.* are written with periods but no spaces. Units of measurement such as *sq ft* and *cu cm* are written with spaces but no periods.

510 A number of shortened forms of words are not abbreviations and should not be followed by a period.

(Continued on page 140.)

caps	exam	limo	prefab	specs
cell phone	expo	logo	prep	stereo
condo	fax	memo	promo	sync
co-op	high-tech	micros	repro	temp
deli	hype	perks	sales rep	typo
demo	lab	photo	sci-fi	before the 2nd

When you check the *repros* for *typos*, please watch out for the problems we had with *caps* in our last *promo* piece, and make sure our *logo* is not left off this time.

Also check everything against the original *specs*, and then *fax* me a copy.

511 *One space* should follow an abbreviation within a sentence unless another mark of punctuation follows immediately.

Dr. Watts works in Nanaimo, B.C., but his home is in Sidney. (See Note ¶526.)

Please call tomorrow afternoon (before 5:30 p.m.).

When Jonas asked, "When do you expect to finish your Ph.D.?" Fred looked embarrassed.

I'm waiting for some word on Harrison, Inc.'s stock repurchase plan. (See ¶¶638–639 for possessive forms of abbreviations.)

512 If the abbreviation ends with a period, that period also serves to mark the end of the sentence. However, if the abbreviation at the end of a sentence ends without a period, insert a period to mark the end of the sentence.

Helen will be returning to the office at 10 a.m. (Here the period applies to the end of the statement *and* the abbreviation.)

The correct postal abbreviation for the *Yukon Territory* is YT. (Here the period applies only to the end of the sentence.)

513 *No space* should follow an abbreviation at the end of a question or an exclamation. The question mark or the exclamation point should come directly after the abbreviation.

Did you see Shania Twain being interviewed last night on CBC?

Because of bad weather, our flight didn't get in until 4 a.m.!

Capitalization

514 Most abbreviations use the same capitalization as the words they stand for.

Mon.	Monday	PC	Personal Computer
Btu	British thermal unit	CFB	Canadian Forces Base
EXCEPTIONS: kW	kilowatt	A.D.	anno Domini

The following rules (¶¶515–546) offer guidance on how to treat specific types of abbreviations.

SPECIAL RULES
Personal Names and Initials

515 Use periods with abbreviations of first or middle names but not with nicknames.

Thos.	Jos.	Robt.	Benj.	Jas.	Wm.	Theo.	Edw.
Tom	Joe	Bob	Ben	Jim	Bill	Ted	Ed

NOTE: Do not abbreviate first and middle names unless (1) you are preparing a list or table where space is tight or (2) a person uses such abbreviations in his or her legal name. (See also ¶1320a.)

516 **a.** Each initial in a person's name should be followed by a period and one space.

John T. Noonan	Mr. L. Bradford Anders
J. T. Noonan & Co.	L. B. Anders Inc. (See also ¶159.)

NOTE: Respect the preference of the individual or of the company that uses a person's initials in its corporate name.

Lester B. Pearson	AMJ Campbell Van Lines
BFGoodrich	J.D. Edwards Canada Ltd.

b. When personal initials stand alone, it is preferable to key them without periods. If periods are used, omit the internal space.

JTN **OR** J.T.N.

c. For names with prefixes, initials are formed as follows:

JDM (for John D. MacDonald)   FGO (for Frances G. O'Brien)

NOTE: If you know that an individual prefers some other form (for example, *FGO'B* rather than *FGO*), respect that preference.

d. Do not use a period when the initial is only a letter used in place of a real name. (See also ¶109a.)

I have selected three case studies involving a Ms. A, a Mr. B, and a Miss C. (Here the letters are used in place of real names, but they are not abbreviations of those names.)

BUT: Call Mrs. G. when you get a chance. (Here *G.* is an initial representing an actual name like *Galanos*.)

e. The abbreviation *NMI* is sometimes used on forms and applications to mean that an individual has <u>n</u>o <u>m</u>iddle <u>i</u>nitial.

Abbreviations With Personal Names

517 **a.** Always abbreviate the following titles when they are used with personal names.

SINGULAR:	Mrs. (for Mistress) Mme. (for Madame)	Ms.		Mr.	Dr.
PLURAL:	Mmes. **OR** Mesdames	Mses. **OR** Mss.		Messrs.	Drs.

Mr. and *Mrs.* Pollo both speak highly of *Dr.* Fry.

Ms. Harriet Porter will serve as a consultant to the Finance Committee.

(Continued on page 142.)

NOTE: *Ms.* (**OR** *Ms*) is an imitation abbreviation made up to parallel *Mr.* and *Mrs.* Always respect the individual woman's preference for this title. It is used when

- A woman has indicated that she prefers this title.
- Her marital status is unknown.
- Her preference for the title is unknown. **BUT:** The title could be omitted altogether.

(See also ¶¶618, 1321b, 1351a.)

☞ *For the proper use of the singular and plural forms of these titles, see ¶618.*
For the use of Dr. *with degrees, see ¶519c.*

b. The titles *Miss* and *Misses* are not abbreviations and should not be followed by periods.

c. In general, spell out all other titles used with personal names.

Vice-President Howard Morse	Professor Zhang
Mayor Wilma Washington	Father Hennelly
Chairman William Rain	Dean Castaneda

d. Long military, religious, and honorary titles are spelled out in formal situations but may be abbreviated in informal situations as long as the surname is accompanied by a first name or initials.

Formal	Informal
Brigadier-General George Cook	Brig-Gen G. Cook
Lieutenant-Governor Marion Reid	Lt. Gov. Marion Reid

(**NOT:** Brig-Gen Cook, Lt. Gov. Reid)

NOTE: Do not abbreviate *Reverend* or *Honourable* when these words are preceded by *the*.

Formal	Informal
the Reverend William R. Bullock	Rev. W. R. Bullock
the Honourable Sarah T. McCormack	Hon. Sarah T. McCormack

☞ *For the treatment of titles in addresses, see ¶¶1320–1324.*
For the treatment of titles in salutations, see ¶¶1338–1340.

518 **a.** Always abbreviate *Jr.*, *Sr.*, and *Esq.* when these terms follow personal names.

b. The forms *Jr.* and *Sr.* should be used only with a full name or initials and not with a surname alone. A title like *Mr.* or *Dr.* may precede the name.

Mr. Henry J. Boardman *Jr.*   **OR**   Mr. H. J. Boardman *Jr.*

(**NOT:** Mr. Boardman *Jr.*)

☞ *For the use or omission of commas with* Jr. *and* Sr., *see ¶156.*

c. The form *Esq.* should also be used only with a full name or initials, and no title should precede the name. (See ¶157.)

George W. LaBarr, *Esq.*   **NOT:** Mr. George W. LaBarr, Esq.

NOTE: The formal title Esq. is now rarely used.

d. The terms *2nd* or *II* and *3rd* or *III* following personal names are not abbreviations and should not be used with periods.

e. When the word *Saint* is part of a person's name, follow that person's preference for abbreviating or spelling out the word.

Yves Saint-Laurent   Ruth St. Denis   Buffy Sainte-Marie

NOTE: When used with the name of a person revered as holy, the word *Saint* is usually spelled out, but it may be abbreviated in informal contexts and in lists and tables where space is tight.

Saint Martin   Saint Teresa   Saint Catherine

☞ *For the treatment of* Saint *in place names, see ¶529b.*

Academic Degrees, Religious Orders, Honours, Awards, and Professional Designations

519 a. These types of abbreviations require a period after each element in the abbreviation but no internal space.

B.Sc.	Ph.D.	D.D.S.	M.D.	S.J.
M.B.A.	LL.B.	B.Arch.	R.N.	O.C.

NOTE: The term *ABD* (without periods) is occasionally used to identify a graduate student who has completed all the requirements for a doctorate except the dissertation. (The initials stand for *all but dissertation.*)

So far we have received résumés from two *Ph.D.s* and seven *ABDs*. (See ¶622a for guidelines on forming the plurals of these abbreviations.)

b. The term *M.B.A.* is now commonly written without periods when it is used to signify an executive with a certain type of training rather than the degree itself.

We have just hired two *MBAs* from Western and one from McGill.

BUT: After I get my *M.B.A.*, I plan to get a second degree in law.

c. When academic degrees follow a person's full name, do not use such titles as *Dr., Mr., Ms., Miss,* or *Mrs.* before the name.

Dr. Helen Wadhera **OR** Helen Wadhera, M.D.

(**NOT:** Dr. Helen Wadhera, M.D.)

However, other titles may precede the name as long as they do not convey the same meaning as the degree that follows.

Professor Rex Ford, Ph.D.   the Reverend John Day, D.D.
President Jean Dill, M.Com.   **OR:** the Reverend Dr. John Day
Dean May Ito, Mus.D.   (**NOT:** the Reverend Dr. John Day, D.D.)

☞ *See also ¶¶1323c, 1349a.*

(Continued on page 144.)

d. When two or more academic degrees follow a person's name, list them in the order in which they were awarded. Honorary degrees (if any) should follow earned degrees.

Donalda Lewinsky, B.Sc., M.Ed., LL.D.

e. Academic degrees standing alone may be abbreviated except in very formal writing.

I am now completing my *Ph.D.* thesis.

She received her *M.A.* degree last year.

OR . . . her *master of arts* degree last year. (See also ¶353.)

f. Professional designations such as *CMA* (Certified Management Accountant), *CAP* (Certified Administrative Professional), *CFP* (Certified Financial Planner), *CLU* (Chartered Life Underwriter), and *FRCS* (Fellow of the Royal College of Surgeons) are listed after academic degrees and in no particular order. They are usually written *without periods* when they are used alone but with periods when they follow academic degrees.

Anthony Filippo, CMA **BUT:** Anthony Filippo, B.Sc., M.B.A., C.M.A.

Ruth L. Morris, CLU Ruth L. Morris, B.A., C.L.U.

NOTE: List professional designations after a person's name (for example, in the signature line in a letter) only in situations where one's professional qualifications are relevant to the topic under discussion.

Names of Organizations

520 Names of well-known business organizations, labour unions, societies, associations (trade, professional, charitable, and fraternal), and government agencies are often abbreviated except in the most formal writing. When these abbreviations consist of all-capital initials, they are keyed without periods or spaces.

CNIB	Canadian National Institute for the Blind
TSE	Toronto Stock Exchange
SPCA	Society for the Prevention of Cruelty to Animals
RCMP	Royal Canadian Mounted Police
YMCA	Young Men's Christian Association
IAAP	International Association of Administrative Professionals
CIBC	Canadian Imperial Bank of Commerce
CUPE	Canadian Union of Public Employees

521 The following terms are often abbreviated in the names of business organizations. However, follow the individual company's preference for abbreviating or spelling out.

Mfg.	Manufacturing	Co.	Company	Inc.	Incorporated
Mfrs.	Manufacturers	Corp.	Corporation	Ltd.	Limited

Acronyms

522 **a.** Acronyms, which are pronounced like words, are written in all capitals and without periods. Because they have been deliberately coined to replace the longer expressions they represent, acronyms are appropriate in most informal, expedient correspondence.

CIDA	Canadian International Development Agency
GATT	General Agreement on Tariffs and Trade
OPEC	Organization of Petroleum Exporting Countries
NAFTA	North American Free Trade Agreement
SARS	severe acute respiratory syndrome
SINK	single, independent, no kids
SOHO	small office, home office
WOMBAT	waste of money, brains, and time

b. In a few cases acronyms derived from initial letters are written entirely in small letters without periods.

scuba	self-contained underwater breathing apparatus
laser	light amplification by stimulated emission of radiation
yuppies	young urban professionals

c. Some coined names use more than the first letters of the words they represent.

modem	modulator and demodulator
canola (oil)	Canada, oil low acid
pixel	picture element
BUT: StatsCan	Statistics Canada
INTELPOST	International Electronic Postal Service
IMAX	I (eye) + Maximum (the most the eye can see)

d. In a few cases all-capital abbreviations such as *MC* (for *master of ceremonies*) or *DJ* (for *disc jockey*) may also be spelled out in an uncapitalized form (*emcee* and *deejay*). The spelled-out forms are preferable when such abbreviations are used as verbs.

Fran Zangwill *emceed* (**RATHER THAN:** MC'd) the fund-raiser kickoff dinner.

Who has been *okaying* (**RATHER THAN:** OK'ing) these bills? (See ¶545.)

e. Very long acronyms (with six or more letters) are sometimes written with only the initial letter capitalized to avoid the distracting appearance of too many capital letters.

UNESCO **OR** Unesco (the United Nations Educational, Scientific, and Cultural Organization)

INSTRAW **OR** Instraw (the International Research and Training Institute for the Advancement of Women)

f. Do not follow an acronym with a word that is part of that acronym. See the examples below using *PIN* (personal identification number) and *ATM* (automated teller machine).

(Continued on page 146.)

There are just too many PINs (**NOT** PIN numbers) to remember these days.

That ATM (**NOT** that ATM machine) has swallowed my card again.

Names of Broadcasting Stations and Systems

523 The names of radio and television broadcasting stations and the abbreviated names of broadcasting systems are written in capitals without periods and without spaces.

CBRT-FM	CFQR-FM	YTV	WTN
CIGV-FM	CKSO-TV	CBC	BVO

According to the *CBC* news reports, the fire blazed for two hours.

Names of Government and International Agencies

524 The names of well-known government and international agencies are often abbreviated. They are written without periods or spaces.

CMHC	Canada Mortgage and Housing Corporation
DND	Department of National Defence
EU	European Union
IOC	International Olympic Committee
NFB	National Film Board
OPEC	Organization of Petroleum Exporting Countries
WTO	World Trade Organization

525 The name *United States* is usually abbreviated when it is part of the name of a government agency. When used as an adjective, the name is often abbreviated, though not in formal usage. When used as a noun, the name is spelled out.

U.S. Air Force	**OR** USAF
the United States government	the U.S. government
United States foreign policy	U.S. foreign policy

We travelled throughout the United States (**NOT:** throughout the U.S.)

Geographic Names

526 Do not abbreviate geographic names except in tables, business forms, expedient documents (see ¶502), and when space is a factor in accommodating lengthy names. Use internal periods with no spaces for these abbreviations.

INFORMAL CONTEXT: Joe Mahal has been transferred from the P.E.I. office to our branch in B.C.

FORMAL CONTEXT: Joe Mahal has been transferred from the Prince Edward Island office to our branch in British Columbia.

527 When abbreviating the names of provinces and territories in addresses, use the following two-letter postal abbreviations, which are written without periods. (Additional postal abbreviations for street types are shown on the last page of the book.) These abbreviations are also used on many expedient business forms.

POSTAL ABBREVIATIONS FOR CANADA

Alberta	AB	Nova Scotia	NS
British Columbia	BC	Nunavut	NU
Manitoba	MB	Ontario	ON
New Brunswick	NB	Prince Edward	
Newfoundland and		Island	PE
Labrador	NL	Quebec	QC
Northwest		Saskatchewan	SK
Territories	NT	Yukon Territory	YT

☞ *For the two-letter postal abbreviations of American state names, see ¶1334.*

528 Geographic abbreviations made up of single initials require a period after each initial but **no space** after each internal period.

B.W.I.	British West Indies	U.K.	United Kingdom
N.A.	North America	C.I.S.	Commonwealth of Independent
S.A.	South Africa		States (formerly the U.S.S.R.)

529 **a.** In place names, do not abbreviate *Fort, Mount, Point,* or *Port* except in tables and lists where space is tight.

Fort Garry	Mount Logan	Pointe Claire	Port Elgin
Fort Henry	Mount Robson	Point McKay	Port Hardy

b. For place names involving *Saint,* follow the style shown in an authoritative dictionary or atlas.

St. Catharines, Ontario	Ste-Foy, Quebec
St. John's, Newfoundland	Sault Ste. Marie, Ontario
St. Lawrence River	Saint John, New Brunswick

☞ *For the abbreviation or the spelling out of names of streets, cities, and provinces, see the last page of the book and ¶¶1328–1330, 1333–1334.*

Compass Points

530 **a.** Spell out compass points used as ordinary nouns and adjectives.

The company has large landholdings in the *West.*

We purchased a lot at the *southwest* corner of Green and King Streets.

☞ *For the capitalization of compass points, see ¶¶338–341.*

b. Spell out compass points included in street names except in lists and tables where space is tight. (See also ¶1330a.)

143 South Mountain Avenue   1232 Franklin Street East

531 **a.** Abbreviate compass points without periods when they are used *following* a street name to indicate the section of the city.

1330 South Bay Boulevard SW   15 Varscona Drive NW

NOTE: Since postal regulations require no punctuation of any kind, compass points are not preceded by a comma. (See also ¶1330b.)

(Continued on page 148.)

b. In technical material (especially pertaining to real estate and legal or nautical matters), abbreviate compass points without periods.

N north   NE northeast   NNE north-northeast

Days and Months

532 Do not abbreviate names of days of the week and months of the year except in tables or lists where space is limited. In such cases the following abbreviations may be used:

Sun.	Thurs., Thu.	Jan.	May	Sep.
Mon.	Fri.	Feb.	Jun.	Oct.
Tues., Tue.	Sat.	Mar.	Jul.	Nov.
Wed.		Apr.	Aug.	Dec.

NOTE: When space is very tight, as in the column headings of some computer reports, the following one- and two-letter abbreviations may be used.

Su	M	Tu	W	Th/R	F	Sa				
Ja	F	Mr	Ap	My	Je	Jl	Au	S	O	N	D

Time and Time Zones

533 Use the abbreviations *a.m.* and *p.m.* in expressions of time. These abbreviations most commonly appear in small letters, but you may use small capitals (A.M., P.M.) too. (See ¶440.) For more formal expressions of time, use o'clock. (See ¶441.)

534 **a.** The time zones in Canada are abbreviated as follows:

Time Zones	Standard Time	Daylight Time	Alternate Abbrev.
Newfoundland	NST	NDT	NT
Atlantic	AST	ADT	AT
Eastern	EST	EDT	ET
Central	CST	CDT	CT
Mountain	MST	MDT	MT
Pacific	PST	PDT	PT

b. If it is 12 noon Pacific Standard Time, it is 1 p.m. Mountain Standard; 2 p.m. Central Standard; 3 p.m. Eastern Standard; 4 p.m. Atlantic Standard; but 4:30 p.m. Newfoundland Standard Time.

☞ *See ¶440a for examples.*

Imperial Measurements

535 Abbreviate imperial units of measure when they occur frequently on invoices, other business forms, and in tables.

a. Units of measure are now commonly abbreviated without periods. The abbreviations are the same for the singular and the plural.

yd (yard, yards)	oz (ounce, ounces)	rpm (revolutions per minute)
ft (foot, feet)	gal (gallon, gallons)	cpi (characters per inch)
mi (mile, miles)	lb (pound, pounds)	mph (miles per hour)

NOTE: The abbreviation *in* (for *inch* or *inches*) may be written without a period if it is not likely to be confused with the preposition *in*.

8 in   **OR**   8 in.   **BUT:** 8 sq in   8 ft 2 in

b. In a set of simple dimensions or a range of numbers, use an abbreviation only with the last number. Repeat a symbol with each number.

a room 10 × 15 ft   **BUT:** a room 10' × 15' (See ¶543b.)
35° to 45°F   **OR:** 35°–45°F (See ¶¶538c, 543b.)

NOTE: In a set of complex dimensions, where more than one unit of measure is involved, repeat the abbreviations with each number. (See ¶432.)

a room 10 ft 6 in × 19 ft 10 in   **OR:**   a room 10' 6" × 19' 10"

536   In non-technical writing, spell out units of measure.

a 20-gallon container $8\frac{1}{2}$ by 11 inches
a 150-acre estate   an $8\frac{1}{2}$- by 11-inch book (See ¶817.)

Metric Measurements

537   The rules of style followed in this manual are found in the *Metric Style Guide* published by the Council of Ministers of Education, Canada, 252 Bloor Street West, Toronto, Ontario M5S 1V5.

a. The most common metric units of measurement and their symbols are shown below.

Quantity	Unit	Symbol
Length	metre	m
Volume	litre	ℓ **OR** l **OR** L
Mass	gram	g
Time	second	s
Temperature	degree Celsius	°C

NOTE: There are two international symbols for the litre. Since the small *l* may be confused with the number one (1), the capital letter *L*, the full word *litre*, or the cursive ℓ should be used.

1 litre   **OR**   1 ℓ **OR**   1 L   **NOT:** 1 l

b. Prefixes, based on a decimal structure, are attached to units to give metric names.

kilo (k)	one thousand (1000)	deci (d)	one tenth
hecto (h)	one hundred (100)	centi (c)	one hundredth
deca (da)	ten (10)	milli (m)	one thousandth

NOTE: Units higher than a *kilo* are capitalized.

mega (M) one million (1 000 000)   giga (G) one billion (1 000 000 000)

The familiar everyday prefixes, *kilo, centi,* and *milli,* are used with metric units to form the following relationships:

(Continued on page 150.)

1 km = 1000 m	(One kilometre equals one thousand metres.)
1 kg = 1000 g	(One kilogram equals one thousand grams.)
1 m = 100 cm	(One metre equals one hundred centimetres.)
1 ℓ = 100 cℓ	(One litre equals one hundred centilitres.)
1 cm = 10 mm	(One centimetre equals ten millimetres.)

538 The symbols for metric units of measurement are always used with figures and should not be used to start a sentence.

a. Abbreviations of metric units of measurement are written without periods, except at the end of a sentence.

| 35-mm film | weighs 100 kg | a 100-km trip |
| an office 5 × 3 m | a 30-cm width | 50 to 75 kg |

NOTE: In abbreviations of expressions like *kilometres per hour*, a solidus (forward slash or diagonal) is used to express *per*.

an 80 km/h speed limit   an average run of 7 m/s

b. Metric abbreviations are the same for the singular and the plural.

1 kg (1 kilogram)   5 kg (5 kilograms)

c. When expressing temperatures, leave no space between the number and the degree symbol or between the degree symbol and the abbreviation for Celsius.

Water freezes at 0°C (**NOT** 0° C), and boils at 100°C.

d. Measurements for area and volume are expressed with superscript (raised) numbers.

m^2 square metre cm^3 cubic centimetre

Chemical and Mathematical Expressions

539 Do not use a period after the symbols that represent chemical elements and formulas.

K (potassium)   NaCl (sodium chloride—table salt)

The chemical notations H_2O and CO_2 stand for "dihydrogen oxide" (namely, water) and "carbon dioxide."

540 Do not use a period after such mathematical abbreviations as *log* (for *logarithm*) and *tan* (for *tangent*).

Common Business Expressions

541 The following abbreviations are commonly used on forms, in tables, in routine business correspondence, and in e-mails. Some common computer abbreviations and acronyms are also included; however, a more comprehensive list of these terms is found in Section 20.

acct.	account		cL	centilitre
addl.	additional		cm	centimetre
a.k.a.	also known as		CMA	certified management accountant (see ¶519f)
AI	artificial intelligence			
amt.	amount			
anon.	anonymous		Co.	company
AP	accounts payable		c/o	care of
approx.	approximately		c.o.d.	cash (or collect) on delivery (see ¶542)
appt.	appointment			
APR	annual percentage rate		COLA	cost of living adjustment
AR	accounts receivable		cont.	continued
ASAP	as soon as possible		COO	chief operating officer
Assn.	Association		Corp.	Corporation
Assoc.	Association; Associate		cpi	characters per inch
asst.	assistant		CPI	consumer price index
ATM	automated teller machine		CPS	certified professional secretary
att.	attachment		CPU	central processing unit
attn.	attention		Cr.	credit; creditor
AV	audiovisual		ctn.	carton
avg.	average		DAT	digital audio tape
bal.	balance		DBMS	database management system
bbl	barrel(s)			
bcc, bc	blind copy		dept.	department
bf	boldface type		dis.	discount
bit	binary digit		dist.	district
bps	bits per second		Div.	Division
BL	bill of lading		DIY	do-it-yourself
bldg.	building		DOS	disc operating system
bu	bushel(s)		doz.	dozen
c, cc	copy, copies, circulated or computer copy		dpi	dots per inch
			dr.	debit record
C	100; Celsius (see ¶538c)		DTP	desktop publishing
CA	chartered accountant		DVD	digital video (versatile) disc
CAD	computer-aided design			
CAI	computer-aided instruction		ea.	each
			enc.	enclosed (see ¶1355)
CAP	certified administrative professional (see ¶519f)		EOF	end of file
			e.o.m.	end of the month (see ¶542)
CB	citizens band (radio)		ETA	estimated time of arrival
CBA	Canadian Bar Association		exec.	executive
			F	Fahrenheit (temperature)
CD	compact disc			
CEO	chief executive officer		FAQ	frequently asked questions
CFO	chief financial officer			
cg	centigram		FIFO	first in, first out
chg.	charge		f.o.b.	free on board (see ¶542)
CGA	certified general accountant (see ¶519f); colour graphics adapter		ft	foot, feet
			fwd.	forward
			FY	fiscal year (see ¶504)
			FYI	for your information
c.i.f.	cost, insurance, and freight		g	gram(s) (see ¶537)

(Continued on page 152.)

GAAP	generally accepted accounting principles	mgt.	management
		mHz	megahertz
		mi	mile(s)
gal	gallon(s)	min	minute(s)
Gb	gigabyte (a billion bytes)	min.	minimum
		misc.	miscellaneous
GIC	guaranteed investment certificate	mL	millilitre(s)
		mm	millimetre(s)
GL	General Ledger	mo	month(s)
GM	general manager	MO	mail order, money order
GNP	gross national product	m/s	metres per second
GPA	grade point average	n/30	net in 30 days
gr. wt.	gross weight	n/a	not applicable; not available
GST	goods and services tax		
h	hour(s)	n.d.	no date
HO	head office	No., Nos.	number(s) (see ¶455)
h.p.	horsepower, high pressure	OAG	*Official Airline Guide*
		OCR	optical character reader or recognition
HQ	headquarters		
IC	integrated circuit	OJT	on-the-job training
in OR in.	inch(es) (see ¶535a)	OS	operating system; out of stock
Inc.	Incorporated		
incl.	including, include	OTC	over-the-counter
ins.	insurance	oz	ounce(s)
intl.	International	p., pp.	page, pages
inv.	invoice, investment	PA	public address
I/O	input/output	p.a.	per annum
ISP	Internet service provider	P & H	postage and handling
I-Way	Information Superhighway	P & L	profit and loss (statement)
JIT	just in time	pc	photocopy
kg	kilogram (s)	PC	personal computer, politically correct, postal code, police constable
KISS	keep it short and simple		
kL	kilolitre (s)		
km	kilometre (s)		
km/h	kilometres per hour	pd.	paid
km/L	kilometres per litre	p/e	price/earnings (ratio)
L	litre(s) (see ¶537a note)	PERT	program evaluation and review technique
l, ll	line, lines		
LAN	local area network	pkg.	package
lb	pound(s)	pl.	place, plate, plural
l.c.l.	less-than-carload lot	PO	post office, postal order, purchase order
Ltd.	Limited		
m	metre(s) (see ¶537)	pop.	population
M	thousand (Roman); mega (metric) (see ¶469)	POS	point of sale
		POV	point of view
		ppd.	postpaid, prepaid
max.	maximum	PR	public relations
Mb	megabyte (a million bytes)	pr.	pair
		PS	postscript
mdse.	merchandise	pt	pint(s)
mfg.	manufacturing	pt.	part; point; port
mfr.	manufacturer	Q&A	question and answer
mg	milligram(s)	QC	Queen's Counsel
Mgr.	Manager	qr.	quarter(s)

qt	quart(s)	t.b.a.	to be announced
qty.	quantity	TD	term deposit
®	registered trademark	TLC	tender, loving care
RAM	random access memory	™	trademark
R&D	research and develop-ment	24/7	store is open for 24 hours a day, 7 days a week
R&M	repairs and maintenance		
R&R	rest and recreation	UCE	unsolicited commercial e-mail
recd.	received		
reg.	registered; regular	UPC	Universal Product Code
ret.	retired; returned	UTC	Coordinated Universal Time (Universal Time Clock)
rev.	revised		
rm.	ream(s); room(s)		
ROM	read only memory	VAT	value-added tax
rpm	revolutions per minute	VCR	video cassette recorder
RRIF	registered retirement income fund	VIP	very important person
		V.P.	Vice-President
RSP	retirement savings plan	VM	voice mail
s	second(s)	WAN	wide area network
S&H	shipping and handling	w/o	without, week of
SASE	self-addressed, stamped envelope	W3C	World Wide Web Consortium
SOP	Standard Operating Procedure	yd	yard(s)
		yr.	year(s)
SRO	standing room only	YOB	year of birth
std.	standard	YTD	year to date

542 A few common business abbreviations listed in ¶541 are frequently keyed in lower case (with periods) when they occur within sentences but are capitalized (without periods) when they appear on business forms.

c.i.f. **OR** CIF	e.o.m. **OR** EOM	l.c.l. **OR** LCL
c.o.d. **OR** COD	f.o.b. **OR** FOB	p.o.e. **OR** POE

Symbols

543 A number of symbols are commonly used on business forms, in tables and statistical matter, and in informal business communications.

@	at	°	degree(s)		"	inches, ditto, second
&	and	=	equals		¶	paragraph
%	percent	#	number (before a figure)		§	section
$	dollar(s)	*	asterisk		×	by, multiplied by
¢	cent(s)	'	feet, minute			

a. Leave one space before and after the following symbols:

@	order 200 @ $49.95	=	if $a = 7$ and $b = 9$
&	Kaye & Elman Inc.	×	a room 4×6 m

NOTE: As a rule, do not leave a space before and after an ampersand (&) in all-capital abbreviations.

(Continued on page 154.)

AT&T pursues a wide range of R&D activities.

At the next shareholders' meeting, we need to anticipate some queries during the Q&A session about our M&A [merger and acquisition] plans.

b. Do not leave a space between a figure and any of the following symbols:

%	a 65% sales increase	°	reduce heat to 180°C
¢	about 30¢ a litre	"	an $8\frac{1}{2}$" × 11" page

c. Do not leave a space after these symbols when they are followed by a figure:

$	in the $250–$500 range	¶¶	as explained in ¶¶1218–1220
#	reorder #4659 and #4691	§	will be covered in §14.26

Foreign Expressions

544 Many foreign expressions contain or consist of short words, some of which are abbreviations and some of which are not. Use periods only with abbreviations.

ad hoc	meaning "for a particular purpose"
ad val.	*ad valorem,* meaning "according to the value"
c. **OR** ca	*circa,* meaning "approximately"
cf.	*confer,* meaning "compare"
Cie. **OR** cie.	*Compagnie,* meaning "Company"
C.V.	*curriculum vitae,* meaning "course of one's life"; a résumé
e.g.	*exempli gratia,* meaning "for example"
et al.	*et alii,* meaning "and other people"
etc.	*et cetera,* meaning "and other things," "and so forth"
ibid.	*ibidem,* meaning "in the same place"
idem	meaning "the same"
i.e.	*id est,* meaning "that is"
infra	meaning "below"
inst.	*instans,* meaning "the current month"
loc. cit.	*loco citato,* meaning "in the place cited"
M.O.	*modus operandi,* meaning "the way in which something is done"
N.B.	*nota bene,* meaning "note well"
nol. pros.	*nolle prosequi,* meaning "to be unwilling to prosecute"
non seq.	*non sequitur,* meaning "it does not follow"
op. cit.	*opere citato,* meaning "in the work cited"
p.a.	*per annum,* meaning "for each year"
p.d.	*per diem,* meaning "for each day"
pro tem.	*pro tempore,* meaning "for the time being"
Q.E.D.	*quod erat demonstrandum,* meaning "which was to be demonstrated"
q.v.	*quod vide,* meaning "which see"
re **OR** in re	meaning "in the matter of," "concerning"
R.S.V.P. **OR** r.s.v.p.	*Répondez s'il vous plaît,* meaning "please reply"
supra	meaning "above"
ult.	*ultimo,* meaning "in the last month"
via	way, meaning "by a route that passes through or along"

viz.	*videlicet*, meaning "namely"
vo.	*verso folio*, meaning "the left hand page or the reverse side of a sheet of paper"
v. **or** vs.	*versus*, meaning "against"

Miscellaneous Expressions

545 The abbreviation *OK* is written without periods. In sentences, the forms *okay, okayed,* and *okaying* look better than *OK, OK'd,* and *OK'ing,* but the latter forms may be used.

546 Some dictionaries recognize *x* as a verb; however, *cross out, crossed out,* and *crossing out* look better than *x out, x-ed out,* and *x-ing out.*

☞ *Plurals of abbreviations: see ¶¶619–624.*
Possessives of abbreviations: see ¶¶638–639.

 See the Online Learning Centre at www.mcgrawhill.ca/college/gregg for related Web links.

Plurals and Possessives

FORMING PLURALS (¶¶601–626)

FORMING POSSESSIVES (¶¶627–652)

FORMING PLURALS

When you are uncertain about the plural form of a word, consult a dictionary. *The Canadian Oxford Dictionary* is the authority used for virtually all words in this manual. If no plural is shown, form the plural according to the rules in ¶¶601–626.

Basic Rule

601　Plurals are regularly formed by adding *s* to the singular form.

alibi	alibis	menu	menus
committee	committees	quota	quotas
fabric	fabrics	rhythm	rhythms
freebie	freebies	suburb	suburbs
idea	ideas	taxi	taxis
length	lengths	yield	yields

NOTE: A few words have the same form in the plural as in the singular. (See ¶¶603, 1014, 1016, 1017.)

Nouns Ending in *S, X, CH, SH,* or *Z*

602　When the singular form ends in *s, x, ch, sh,* or *z,* the plural is formed by adding *es* to the singular.

bias	biases	sketch	sketches
summons	summonses	wish	wishes
virus	viruses	waltz	waltzes
fax	faxes	**BUT:** quiz	quizzes

NOTE: When *ch* at the end of a singular word has the sound of *k,* form the plural by simply adding *s.*

epoch	epochs	monarch	monarchs

603　Singular nouns ending in silent *s* do not change their forms in the plural. (However, the *s* ending is pronounced when the plural form is used.)

one corps	two corps	a faux pas　several faux pas

Nouns Ending in *Y*

604　When a singular noun ends in *y* preceded by a *consonant,* the plural is formed by changing the *y* to *i* and adding *es* to the singular.

copy	copies	liability	liabilities
policy	policies	proxy	proxies

605　When a singular noun ends in *y* preceded by a *vowel,* the plural is formed by adding *s* to the singular.

delay	delays	guy	guys
survey	surveys	**BUT:** soliloquy	soliloquies
boy	boys	colloquy	colloquies

NOTE: The regular plural of *money* is *moneys.* The plural form *monies* does not follow the rule, but it often appears in legal documents.

Nouns Ending in O

606 Singular nouns ending in *o* preceded by a *vowel* form their plurals by adding *s* to the singular.

ratio	ratios	shampoo	shampoos
portfolio	portfolios	tattoo	tattoos
scenario	scenarios	duo	duos

607 Singular nouns ending in *o* preceded by a *consonant* form their plurals in different ways.

a. Some nouns in this category simply add *s*.

ego	egos	photo	photos
fiasco	fiascos	proviso	provisos
logo	logos	typo	typos
memo	memos	zero	zeros

b. Some add *es*.

echo	echoes	potato	potatoes
embargo	embargoes	tomato	tomatoes
hero	heroes	volcano	volcanoes

c. Some have two plural forms. The preferred form is given first.

banjo	banjos, banjoes	memento	mementoes, mementos
cargo	cargoes, cargos	motto	mottoes, mottos
innuendo	innuendoes, innuendos	tuxedo	tuxedos, tuxedoes

d. Most singular musical terms ending in *o* form their plurals by simply adding *s*.

soprano	sopranos	piano	pianos
alto	altos	cello	cellos
basso	bassos	vibrato	vibratos

☞ *For foreign nouns ending in o, see* ¶614.

Nouns Ending in F, FE, or FF

608 **a.** Most singular nouns that end in *f, fe,* or *ff* form their plurals by adding *s* to the singular form.

belief	beliefs	safe	safes
proof	proofs	tariff	tariffs

b. Some commonly used nouns in this category form their plurals by changing the *f* or *fe* to *ve* and adding *s*.

half	halves	self	selves
wife	wives	shelf	shelves
leaf	leaves	knife	knives
thief	thieves	life	lives

c. A few of these nouns have two plural forms. (The preferred form is given first.)

scarf	scarves, scarfs	dwarf	dwarfs, dwarves

Nouns With Irregular Plurals

609 The plurals of some nouns are formed by a change of letters within.

woman	women	foot	feet
mouse	mice*	goose	geese

610 A few plurals end in *en* or *ren*.

ox	oxen	child	children
brother	brethren (*an alternative plural to* brothers)		

Compound Nouns

611 When a compound noun is a *solid* word, pluralize the final element in the compound as if it stood alone.

birth*day*	birth*days*	photo*copy*	photo*copies*
book*shelf*	book*shelves*	print*out*	print*outs*
eye*lash*	eye*lashes*	straw*berry*	straw*berries*
flash*back*	flash*backs*	tooth*brush*	tooth*brushes*
foot*hold*	foot*holds*	wine*glass*	wine*glasses*
fore*foot*	fore*feet*	**BUT:** *passer*by	*passers*by
grand*child*	grand*children*	*stand*by	*stand*bys
mouse*trap*	mouse*traps*	(**NOT:** *stand*bies)	

612 **a.** The plurals of *hyphenated* or *spaced* compounds are formed by pluralizing the chief element of the compound.

sister-in-law	*sisters*-in-law	*letter* of credit	*letters* of credit
court-martial	*courts*-martial	*leave* of absence	*leaves* of absence
runner-up	*runners*-up	*account* payable	*accounts* payable
notary public	*notaries* public	*chief* of staff	*chiefs* of staff
editor-in-chief	*editors*-in-chief	*coat* of arms	*coats* of arms
major-general	*major*-generals	*work* of art	*works* of art
BUT: time-*out*	time-*outs*	**BUT:** chaise *longue*	chaise *longues*

☞ *See ¶614 for the plurals of foreign compound words.*

b. When a hyphenated compound does not contain a noun as one of its elements, simply pluralize the final element.

go-*between*	go-*betweens*	two-by-*four*	two-by-*fours*
get-*together*	get-*togethers*	has-*been*	has-*beens*
hand-me-*down*	hand-me-*downs*	have-*not*	have-*nots*
tie-*in*	tie-*ins*	know-it-*all*	know-it-*alls*
fade-*out*	fade-*outs*	so-and-*so*	so-and-*sos*
show-*off*	show-*offs*	higher-*up*	higher-*ups*

c. Some of these compounds have two recognized plural forms. (The first plural form shown below is preferred because it adds the plural sign to the chief element of the compound.)

**Mice refers to computer devices as well as to rodents.

(Continued on page 160.)

auditor general	*auditors* general, auditor *generals*
attorney general	*attorneys* general, attorney *generals*

d. When the first element of a compound is a *possessive*, simply pluralize the final element.

traveller's cheque	traveller's cheques
rabbit's foot	rabbit's feet
proofreaders' mark	proofreaders' marks
rogues' gallery	rogues' galleries
finder's fee	finder's fees

NOTE: Do not convert a singular possessive form into a plural unless the context clearly requires it.

We issued 15 percent more *driver's licences* last year.

BUT: Over 200 *drivers' licences* have been revoked in the past four weeks.

☞ *See also ¶651.*

613 The plurals of compounds ending in *ful* are formed by adding *s*.

armful	armfuls	handful	handfuls
cupful	cupfuls	teaspoonful	teaspoonfuls

Compare the difference in meaning in these phrases:

six *cupfuls* of sugar (a quantity of sugar that would fill one cup six times)

six *cups full* of sugar (six separate cups, each filled with sugar)

Foreign Nouns

614 Many nouns of foreign origin retain their foreign plurals, others have been given English plurals, and still others have two plurals—an English and a foreign one. When two plural forms exist, one may be preferred to the other or there may be differences in meaning that govern the use of each. Consult your dictionary to be sure of the plural forms and the meanings attached to them.

☞ *For agreement of foreign-plural subjects with verbs, see ¶1018.*

WORDS ENDING IN *US*

Singular	English Plural	Foreign Plural
alumnus		alumni
apparatus		apparatus
cactus		cacti
corpus	corpuses	corpora*
focus	focuses*	foci
genus		genera
nucleus		nuclei
opus	opuses*	opera

*Preferred form.

radius	radiuses	radii*
stimulus		stimuli
syllabus	syllabuses*	syllabi
terminus	terminuses	termini*
BUT: census	censuses	
prospectus	prospectus	
status	status	

NOTE: The term *alumni* (the plural of *alumnus*) may be used to refer either to a group of male graduates or to a mixed group of male and female graduates. The term *alumnae* (the plural of *alumna*) is used to refer only to a group of female graduates.

WORDS ENDING IN *A*

Singular	English Plural	Foreign Plural
agenda	agendas	
alumna		alumnae
antenna	antennas (of radios)	antennae (of insects)
formula	formulas*	formulae
minutia		minutiae
schema	schemas	schemata*
stigma	stigmas*	stigmata
vertebra		vertebrae

WORDS ENDING IN *UM*

Singular	English Plural	Foreign Plural
addendum		addenda
auditorium	auditoriums*	auditoria
bacterium		bacteria
consortium	consortiums	consortia*
cranium	craniums*	crania
curriculum		curricula
datum		data (see ¶1018)
erratum		errata
gymnasium	gymnasiums*	gymnasia
maximum		maxima
medium	mediums (spiritualists or sizes)	media (mass communication)
memorandum		memoranda
millennium	millenniums*	millennia
minimum		minima
momentum		momenta
optimum	optimums	optima*
referendum	referendums*	referenda
stratum		strata
symposium	symposiums*	symposia
ultimatum	ultimatums*	ultimata

*Preferred form.

(*Continued on page 162.*)

WORDS ENDING IN *O*

Singular	English Plural	Foreign Plural
concerto	concertos*	concerti
graffito		graffiti
paparazzo		paparazzi
tempo	tempos*	tempi (in music)
virtuoso	virtuosos	virtuosi*

WORDS ENDING IN *ON*

Singular	English Plural	Foreign Plural
automaton	automatons	automata*
criterion		criteria
phenomenon		phenomena

WORDS ENDING IN *X*

Singular	English Plural	Foreign Plural
apex	apexes	apices*
appendix	appendixes	appendices*
codex		codices
crux	cruxes*	cruces
index	indexes*	indices
larynx		larynges
matrix	matrixes	matrices*
vertex	vertexes	vertices*
vortex	vortexes	vortices*

WORDS ENDING IN *IS*

Singular	English Plural	Foreign Plural
analysis		analyses
axis		axes
basis		bases
crisis		crises
diagnosis		diagnoses
ellipsis		ellipses
emphasis		emphases
hypothesis		hypotheses
parenthesis		parentheses
synopsis		synopses
synthesis		syntheses
thesis		theses

WORDS ENDING IN *EAU*

Singular	English Plural	Foreign Plural
beau	beaus	beaux*
bureau	bureaus*	bureaux
chateau		chateaux
plateau	plateaus*	plateaux
trousseau	trousseaus	trousseaux*

NOTE: The *x* ending for these foreign plurals is pronounced like *z*.

COMPOUND WORDS

Singular	English Plural	Foreign Plural
chargé d'affaires		chargés d'affaires
coup d'état		coups d'état
hors d'oeuvre		hors d'oeuvres
maître d'hôtel		maîtres d'hôtel
nouveau riche		nouveaux riches
table d'hôte		tables d'hôte

Names

615 **a.** Most *surnames* are pluralized by the addition of *s*, **NOT** with an apostrophe.

Mrs. and Mrs. Brinton	the Brintons
Mr. and Mrs. Romano	the Romanos
Mr. and Mrs. Yu	the Yus

b. When a surname ends in *s*, *x*, *ch*, *sh*, or *z*, add *es* to form the plural.

Mr. and Mrs. Banks	the Bankses
Mr. and Mrs. Van Ness	the Van Nesses
Mr. and Mrs. Maddox	the Maddoxes
Mr. and Mrs. March	the Marches
Mr. and Mrs. Welsh	the Welshes
Mr. and Mrs. Katz	the Katzes
Mr. and Mrs. Jones	the Joneses
Mr. and Mrs. James	the Jameses

NOTE: Omit the *es* ending if it makes the plural surname awkward to pronounce.

the Hodges (**NOT:** Hodgeses)   the Hastings (**NOT:** Hastingses)

c. Never change the original spelling of a surname when forming the plural. Simply add *s* or *es*, according to ¶615*a* and *b*.

Mr. and Mrs. McCarthy	the McCarthys (**NOT:** McCarthies)
Mr. and Mrs. Wolf	the Wolfs (**NOT:** Wolves)
Mr. and Mrs. Martino	the Martinos (**NOT:** Martinoes)
Mr. and Mrs. Goodman	the Goodmans (**NOT:** Goodmen)
Mr. and Mrs. Lightfoot	the Lightfoots (**NOT:** Lightfeet)

d. When a surname is followed by *Jr.*, *Sr.*, or a number like *2nd* or *II*, the plural can be formed two ways:

ORDINARY USAGE: the Roy Van Allen *Jrs.*   the Ellsworth Hadley *3rds*

FORMAL USAGE: the Roy Van *Allens* Jr.   the Ellsworth *Hadleys* 3rd

616 To form the plurals of *first names*, add *s* or *es* but do not change the original spellings.

Marie	Maries	Douglas	Douglases	Timothy	Timothys
Ralph	Ralphs	Dolores	Doloreses	Beatrix	Beatrixes
Waldo	Waldos	Gladys	Gladyses	Fritz	Fritzes

617 To form the plural of other proper names, add *s* or *es* but do not change the original spelling.

three Albertans
Winnipeggers
Februarys
the two Kansas Citys (**NOT:** Cities)

two Christmases ago
checked our Rolodexes
Marches (*es* after *ch* sound)
Czechs (*s* after *k* sound)

EXCEPTIONS:

the Gatineaux (for Gatineau Hills)

the Rockies (for Rocky Mountains)

NOTE: When forming the plural of an italicized or underlined proper name, do not italicize or underline the plural ending. (See ¶¶288c and 289c.)

Personal Titles

618 **a.** The plural of *Mr.* is *Messrs.*; the plural of *Ms.* is *Mses.* or *Mss.*; *the plural of Mrs. or Mme. is Mmes.* (for *Mesdames*); the plural of *Miss* is *Misses* (no period follows). However, the use of plural titles normally occurs only in formal situations. In ordinary usage, simply retain the singular form and repeat it with each name. (*Ms.* imitates *Mr.* and *Mrs.* as an abbreviation; hence the period. See ¶517.)

Formal Usage

Messrs. Rae and Tate
Mmes. (**OR** Mesdames) Byrd and Clyde
Misses Russo and Dupree
Mses. (**OR** Mss.) Lai and Cohen

Ordinary Usage

Mr. Rae and Mr. Tate
Mrs. Byrd and Mrs. Clyde
Miss Russo and Miss Dupree
Ms. Lai and Ms. Cohen

b. When personal titles apply to two or more people with the same surname, the plural may be formed in two ways: (1) pluralize only the title (formal usage); (2) pluralize only the surname (ordinary usage).

Formal Usage

the Messrs. Steele
the Mmes. (**OR** Mesdames) Bergeret
the Misses Conroy
the Mses. (**OR** Mss.) Purdy

Ordinary Usage

the Mr. Steeles
the Mrs. Bergerets
the Miss Conroys
the Ms. Purdys

Abbreviations, Letters, Numbers, and Words

619 Form the plurals of most abbreviations by adding *s* to the singular.

| bldg. | bldgs. | par. | pars. | No. | Nos. | Co. | Cos. |
| vol. | vols. | apt. | apts. | Dr. | Drs. | tsp. | tsps. |

620 **a.** The abbreviations of many imperial units of weight and measure, however, are the same in both the singular and plural.

oz (ounce **OR** ounces)
deg (degree **OR** degrees)
bbl (barrel **OR** barrels)

ft (foot **OR** feet)
in (inch **OR** inches)
mi (mile **OR** miles)

NOTE: For a number of these abbreviations, two plural forms have been widely used: for example, *lb* or *lbs* (meaning "pounds"), *yd* or *yds* (meaning "yards"), *qt* or *qts* (meaning "quarts"). However, the trend is toward using *lb*, *yd*, and *qt* to signify the plural.

b. The abbreviations of metric units of weight and measure are the same in both the singular and plural. (See also ¶¶537–538.)

km (kilometre **OR** kilometres)   cg (centigram **OR** centigrams)
mL (millilitre **OR** millilitres)   dam (dekametre **OR** dekametres)

☞ *For the omission of periods with abbreviations of measurements, see ¶¶535a, 538a. For the abbreviations of litre, see ¶537a.*

621 a. The plurals of a few single-letter abbreviations (such as *p.* for *page* and *c.* for *copy*) consist of the same letter doubled.

p. 64 (page 64)   l. 23 (line 23)
pp. 64–72 (pages 64 through 72)   ll. 23–24 (lines 23 to 24)
pp. 9 f. (page 9 and the following page) n. 3 (note 3)
pp. 9 ff. (page 9 and the following pages) nn. 3–4 (notes 3 and 4)

b. Plurals of certain symbols consist of the same symbol doubled.

¶ paragraph   ¶¶ paragraphs   § section   §§ sections

622 a. Capital letters and abbreviations ending with capital letters are pluralized by adding *s* alone.

three Rs   CEOs   VPs   M.D.s
four Cs   IQs   CPUs   LL.B.s
five VIPs   PTAs   MPs   Ph.D.s

b. Some authorities will sanction the use of an apostrophe before the *s* (for example, *four C's, PTA's*). However, the apostrophe is functionally unnecessary except where confusion might otherwise result.

three A's   too many I's   two U's   too many M's

BUT: His report card showed three As, two Bs, and one C. (When the context is clear, no apostrophes are necessary.)

623 For the sake of clarity, uncapitalized letters and uncapitalized abbreviations are pluralized by adding an apostrophe plus *s*. (See ¶¶285a, 288a, and 289.)

dotting the *i's*   *p's* and *q's*   four c.o.d.'s   n.p.'s

NOTE: When initials are spelled out in letters, the plurals are formed normally.

emcees   dejays   okays   Jaycees

624 Numbers expressed in figures are pluralized by the addition of *s* alone. (See, however, ¶622b.)

in the 1920s   sort the W2s   Catch-22s   file the T4s

(Continued on page 166.)

Numbers expressed in words are pluralized by the addition of *s* or *es*.

ones   twos   threes   sixes   twenties   twenty-fives

625 **a.** When words taken from other parts of speech are used as nouns, they are usually pluralized by the addition of *s* or *es*.

ifs, ands, or buts	the ins and outs	pros and cons	whereabouts
dos and don'ts	ups and downs	the haves and	whys and
yeses and noes	yeas and nays	the have-nots	wherefores

b. If the pluralized form is unfamiliar or is likely to be misread, use an apostrophe plus *s* to form the plural.

which's and that's   or's and nor's

c. If the singular form already contains an apostrophe, simply add *s* to form the plural.

ain'ts   mustn'ts   don'ts   ma'ams

☞ *For the use of italics or underlining with words referred to as words, see* ¶¶285a, 289.

Plural Endings in Parentheses

626 When referring to an item that could be either singular or plural, enclose the plural ending in parentheses.

Please send the appropriate form(s) to the appropriate *agency(ies)*.

FORMING POSSESSIVES
Possession Versus Description

627 A noun ending in the sound of *s* is usually in the possessive form if it is followed immediately by another noun. An apostrophe alone or an apostrophe plus *s* is the sign of the possessive. (See ¶¶630–640.) Note in the examples below that the possessive form expresses a variety of relationships.

the *company's* profits (meaning the profits *of the company*)

Hodgkins' product line (meaning the product line *of the Hodgkins Company*)

McTavish's property (meaning the property *belonging to McTavish*)

my *boss's* approval (meaning the approval of *my boss*)

Joe's nickname (meaning the nickname *given to* or *used by Joe*)

Atwood's novels (meaning the novels *written by Atwood*)

a two *weeks'* vacation (meaning a vacation *for* or *lasting two weeks*)

BUT: a *two-week* vacation (See Note ¶817b.)

NOTE: To be sure that the possessive form should be used, try substituting an *of* phrase or making a similar substitution as in the examples above. If the substitution works, the possessive form is correct.

628 Do not mistake a descriptive form ending in *s* for a possessive form.

sales effort (*sales* describes the kind of effort)

savings account (*savings* describes the kind of account)

news release (*news* describes the type of press release)

earnings record (*earnings* describes the type of record)

NOTE: Some cases can be difficult to distinguish. Is it *the girls basketball team* or *the girls' basketball team*? Try substituting an irregular plural like *women*. You wouldn't say *the women basketball team*; you would say *the women's basketball team*. By analogy, *the girls' basketball team* is correct.

☞ *For descriptive and possessive forms in organizational names, see ¶640.*

629 In a number of cases, only a slight difference in wording distinguishes a descriptive phrase from a possessive phrase.

Descriptive	Possessive
a six-month leave of absence	a six months' leave of absence
the Manitoba climate	Manitoba's climate
the Burgess account	Burgess's account
the Crosby children	the Crosbys' children
	OR: Mr. and Mrs. Crosby's children

Singular Nouns

630 **a.** To form the possessive of a singular noun *not* ending in an *s* sound, add an apostrophe plus *s* to the noun.

my lawyer's advice	Alberta's mountains
Gloria's career	Brantford's mayor
Mr. and Mrs. Goodwin's party	a child's game

b. When a singular noun ends in a silent *s*, add an apostrophe plus *s*.

The Pas's mayor	Trois-Rivières's historical sites
Sept-Îles's fort	Ville St-Georges's beach

631 To form the possessive of a singular noun that ends in an *s* sound, be guided by the way you pronounce the word.

a. If a new syllable is formed in the pronunciation of the possessive, add an apostrophe plus *s*.

your boss's approval	Hotel Ajax's lobby
the witness's reply	Mr. and Mrs. Morris's plane tickets
Rose's intention	Halifax's waterfront
Dundas's business district	Ms. Lopez's application

b. If the addition of an extra syllable would make a word ending in an *s* hard to pronounce, add the apostrophe only.

Mrs. Phillips' request	the Hayes' farm
Mr. Hastings' proposal	Delores' flight to Ottawa
the Burroughs' condominium	for goodness' sake (see ¶646)
the Laurentians' ski slopes	Achilles' heel
	BUT: Achilles tendon

NOTE: Individual differences in pronunciation will affect the way some of these possessives are written. For example, if you pronounce the possessive

(Continued on page 168.)

form of *Perkins* as two syllables, you will write *Mr. Perkins' kindness*; if you pronounce the possessive of *Perkins* as three syllables, you will write *Mr. Perkins's kindness*. The important thing is to listen to your own pronunciation. When you hear yourself pronounce the possessive of *boss* as two syllables (*boss's*) and the possessive of *witness* as *witness's*, you will not be tempted to write *your boss' approval* or *the witness' reply*. Naturally, tradition should take precedence over your ear. For example, High Commissioners to Great Britain are appointed to the *Court of St. James's* (not, as you might expect, *Court of St. James*).

c. When forming the possessive of any noun ending in *s* (for example, *Mr. Hodges*), always place the apostrophe at the end of the original word, never within it.

Robert's Rules of Order (**NOT:** *Roberts' Rules of Order*)
Brahms' symphonies (**NOT:** Brahm's symphonies)

Plural Nouns

632   a. For a *regular* plural noun (one that ends in *s* or *es*), add only an apostrophe to form the plural possessive. (See ¶¶639–640 for the use of the apostrophe in organizational names.)

investors' objectives	lawyers' fees
the witnesses' contradiction	the agencies' conflicting rules
the United States' policy	the Gaineses' legal residence

b. Since the singular and plural possessives for the same word usually sound exactly alike, pay particularly close attention to the meaning in order to determine whether the noun in question is singular or plural. To help determine whether the possessive is singular or plural (since they sound alike), you can isolate the phrase, turn it around, and look at the possessive to see if it ends in *s* or not.

I especially want to hear the last witness's testimony.
I especially want to hear the testimony of the last witness. (Singular)

I especially want to hear the last two witnesses' testimony.
I especially want to hear the testimony of the last two witnesses. (Plural)

633   For an *irregular* plural noun (one that does not end in *s*), add an apostrophe plus *s* to form the plural possessive.

women's blouses	men's shirts	the alumni's reunion
children's toys	**BUT:** menswear	the alumnae's contribution
	(originally, men's wear)	

IMPORTANT NOTE: To avoid mistakes in forming the possessive of plural nouns, form the plural first; then apply the rule in ¶632 or ¶633, whichever fits.

Singular	Plural	Plural Possessive
boy	boys (regular)	boys'
boss	bosses (regular)	bosses'
hero	heroes (regular)	heroes'

Mr. and Mrs. Fox	the Foxes (regular)	the Foxes'
child	children (irregular)	children's
mother-in-law	mothers-in-law (irregular)	mothers-in-law's
alumnus	alumni (irregular)	alumni's
alumna	alumnae (irregular)	alumnae's

Compound Nouns

634 To form the *singular* possessive of a compound noun (whether solid, spaced, or hyphenated), add an apostrophe plus *s* to the last element of the compound.

my son-in-law's job prospects	my stockbroker's advice
the secretary-treasurer's report	the notary public's seal
the owner-manager's policies	an eyewitness's account

635 To form the *plural* possessive of a compound noun, first form the plural.

a. If the plural form ends in *s*, add only an apostrophe.

Singular	Plural	Plural Possessive
shareholder	shareholders	shareholders'
vice-president	vice-presidents	vice-presidents'
do-it-yourselfer	do-it-yourselfers	do-it-yourselfers'
salesclerk	salesclerks	salesclerks'

b. If the plural form does not end in *s*, add an apostrophe plus *s*.

Singular	Plural	Plural Possessive
editor-in-chief	editors-in-chief	editors-in-chief's
brother-in-law	brothers-in-law	brothers-in-law's

NOTE: To avoid the awkwardness of a plural possessive such as *editors-in-chief's* or *brothers-in-law's*, rephrase the sentence.

AWKWARD: We may have to invite my three *sisters-in-law's* parents too.
BETTER: We may have to invite the parents of my three *sisters-in-law* too.

AWKWARD: Mr. Ahmed's statement agrees with both *attorneys general's* views.
BETTER: Mr. Ahmed's statement agrees with the views of both *attorneys general*.

Pronouns

636 The possessive forms of *personal pronouns* and of the relative pronoun *who* do not require the apostrophe. These pronouns have their own possessive forms.

I: my, mine	she: her, hers	they: their, theirs
you: your, yours	it: its	who: whose
he: his	we: our, ours	

My copy of the letter arrived last week, so she should have received *hers* by now. (**NOT:** her's.)

Each unit comes carefully packed in *its* own carton. (**NOT:** it's.)

The two products look so much alike that it's (it is) hard to tell *ours* from *theirs*. (**NOT:** our's from their's.)

CAUTION: Do not confuse personal possessive pronouns with similarly spelled contractions. (See ¶1056e for examples.)

637 Some *indefinite pronouns* have regular possessive forms.

one's choice	the other's claim	anybody's guess
anyone else's job	the others' claim	no one's responsibility
one another's time	each other's claim	someone's chance

For those indefinite pronouns that do not have possessive forms, use an *of* phrase.

Although the children in this group seem very much alike, the needs *of each* are different. (NOT: each's needs.)

Abbreviations

638 To form the singular possessive of an abbreviation, add an apostrophe plus *s*. To form the plural possessive, add an *s* plus an apostrophe to the singular form. (See also ¶639.)

Singular	**Plural**
Mr. C.'s opinion	the M.D.s' diagnoses
CBC's programming	the Ph.D.s' theses
the CA's audit	the CGAs' meeting

Personal, Organizational, and Product Names

639 To form the possessive of a personal or organizational name that ends with an abbreviation, a number, a mark of punctuation, or a prepositional phrase, add an apostrophe plus *s* at the end of the complete name.

the Winger Co.'s new plant	McGraw-Hill, Inc.'s dividends
Yahoo!'s Web site	Queen Elizabeth II's reign
Bank of Nova Scotia's loan rates	the G-7's proposal

NOTE: If *no* extra *s* sound is created when you pronounce the possessive form, add only an apostrophe.

the Gerald Curry Jrs.' yacht

☞ *For the treatment of possessive forms when terms like* Jr. *and* Inc. *are set off by commas, see* ¶¶156 *and* 159.

640 Many organizational names and products contain words that could be considered as either possessive or descriptive terms.

a. As a rule, use an apostrophe if the term is a singular possessive noun or an irregular plural noun.

Wendy's	Fanny's Fabrics	Women's Centre	Children's Hospital
McDonald's	Levi's jeans	Tony Roma's	Reese's Pieces

b. Do not use an apostrophe if the term is a regular plural.

Canadian Securities Institute	Hamilton Singles Society
Professional Marketers Association	Bankers Hall Club
Retail Merchants Association	Investors Group Inc.

c. In all cases follow the organization's preference or style as given.

Life Underwriters' Association	Ranchmen's Club
Consumer's Association of Canada	*Reader's Digest*

Grandma Lee's Bakery	Robin's Donuts
Western Stock Grower's Association	Fry's cocoa
Hudson's Bay Company	Planters peanuts
Campbell's soups	Tim Hortons Donuts

d. When adding the sign of the possessive to a phrase that must be italicized, do not italicize the possessive ending. (See also ¶288c.)

Jake and the Kid's story   *Remember*'s author   *Survivor*'s success

Nouns in Apposition

641 Sometimes a noun is followed by an *appositive*, a closely linked explanatory word or phrase. In such cases add the sign of the possessive to the appositive.

You will faint when you see Paul *the plumber*'s bill. (If the noun and the appositive are closely linked as a unit, even the first comma is omitted. See also ¶150.)

NOTE: To avoid an awkward construction, use an *of* phrase instead.

You will need to get the signature *of Mr. Bartel*, the executor.

(**BETTER THAN:** You will need to get Mr. Bartel, *the executor*'s signature.)

Separate and Joint Possession

642 **a.** To indicate separate possession, add the sign of the possessive to the name of each individual.

the buyer's and the seller's signatures   the Joneses' and the Browns' houses

NOTE: Repeating *the* with each name emphasizes that ownership is separate.

b. If one or both of the individuals' names are replaced by a possessive pronoun, watch out for awkwardness and reword if necessary.

AWKWARD: my and the seller's signatures
BETTER: the seller's and my signatures
OR: the seller's signature and mine

AWKWARD: their and our houses
BETTER: their house and ours

AWKWARD: your and your husband's passports
BETTER: your husband's and your passports

643 **a.** To indicate joint (or common) ownership, add the sign of the possessive to the *final* name alone.

the Barneses and Terrys' property line

NOTE: In organizational names, follow the company's preference.

Ben & Jerry's ice cream   Kroch's & Brentano's bookstores

b. If one of the owners is identified by a pronoun, make each name and pronoun possessive.

Karen's and my ski lodge   **BUT:** Karen and Brian's ski lodge

Possessives Standing Alone

644   Sometimes the noun that the possessive modifies is not expressed but merely understood.

> Fred is getting a *master's* [degree] in international economics.
>
> Ask for it at your *grocer's* [store].
>
> Wear your oldest shirt and *Levi's* [jeans]. (The trademark *Levi's* is a singular possessive form.)
>
> We have been invited to dinner at the *Furnesses'* [house].
>
> **BUT:** We always enjoy an evening with the *Furnesses*. (The people themselves are referred to; hence no possessive.)

NOTE: The possessive form must be used in the following construction in order to keep the comparison parallel.

> This year's product line is pulling better than *last year's* [product line].
>
> **NOT:** This year's product line is pulling better than *last year*. (Incorrectly compares *product line* with *last year*.)

Inanimate Possessives

645   As a rule, nouns referring to inanimate things should not be in the possessive. Use an *of* phrase instead.

> the bottom of the barrel (**NOT:** the barrel's bottom)
>
> the wording of the agreement (**NOT:** the agreement's wording)
>
> the lower level of the terminal (**NOT:** the terminal's lower level)

646   In many expressions referring to time and measurement and in phrases implying personification, the possessive form has come to be accepted usage. (See also ¶817a.)

one day's notice	a dollar's worth	a stone's throw
a nine days' wonder	several dollars' worth	in today's world
an hour's work	two cents' worth	for conscience' sake
two years' experience	at arm's length	(see ¶631b)
the company's assets	New Year's resolutions	the earth's atmosphere
the computer's memory	this morning's news	the next world's fair

NOTE: Be sure to distinguish possessive expressions like those above from similar wording where no possessive relation is involved.

> two weeks' salary   **BUT:** two weeks ago, two weeks later, two weeks overdue
>
> I bought *five dollars' worth* of chocolate truffles.
>
> **BUT:** I found *five dollars lying* on the sidewalk.

Possessives Preceding Verbal Nouns

647   **a.** When a noun or a pronoun modifies a *gerund* (the *ing* form of a verb used as a noun), the noun or pronoun should be in the possessive.

> What was the point of *our* asking any further questions? (**NOT:** of us asking.)

NOTE: The use of a possessive form before a gerund can produce a sentence that is grammatically correct but is awkward nonetheless. In such cases reword the sentence.

AWKWARD: He wanted to be reassured about his *children's* being given a ride home.

BETTER: He wanted to be reassured that his children would be given a ride home.

b. Not every noun or pronoun preceding the *ing* form of a verb should be in the possessive form. Compare the following pairs of examples:

I heard *you* singing at the party. (Here the emphasis is on *you*, the object of *heard*; *singing* is a participle that modifies *you*.)

I liked *your* singing at the party. (Here the emphasis is on *singing*, a gerund that is the object of *liked*; the pronoun *your* is in the possessive form because it modifies *singing*.)

Our success in this venture depends on *Allen* acting as the coordinator. (This suggests that the success depends on Allen himself rather than on the role he is playing. Even if Allen's role should change, success seems likely as long as he is associated with the project in some way.)

Our success in this venture depends on *Allen's* acting as the coordinator. (This puts the emphasis squarely on Allen's acting in a certain role. If he ceases to function as the co-ordinator, the venture may not succeed.)

Possessives in *Of* Phrases

648 **a.** The object of the preposition *of* should not ordinarily be in the possessive form, since the *of* phrase as a whole expresses possession. However, possessives are used in a few idiomatic expressions.

Tony and Fiona are good friends of *ours* as well as our *children's*.

Did you know that Polly and Fred are neighbours of the *Joneses'*?

Bobby Busoni is a business associate of *Gordon's*.

b. Note the difference in meaning in the following phrases:

a statue of Rodin (a statue showing the likeness of the sculptor Rodin)
a statue of Rodin's (a statue created by Rodin)

a controversial view of the Premier (a view held by someone else)
a controversial view of the Premier's (a view held by the Premier)

c. Avoid adding the sign of the possessive to an *of* phrase.

AWKWARD: A friend of mine's house burned down last night.

BETTER: The house of a friend of mine burned down last night.

AWKWARD: One of my friends' son plays hockey for the Calgary Flames.

BETTER: The son of one of my friends plays hockey for the Calgary Flames.

NOTE: Attaching the sign of the possessive to an *of* phrase can result in humorous confusion.

CONFUSING: Negotiate the purchase price with the owner of the horse's wife.

CLEAR: Negotiate the purchase price of the horse with the owner's wife.

Possessives Modifying Possessives

649 Avoid attaching a possessive form to another possessive. Change the wording if possible.

> **AWKWARD:** I have not yet seen the *utility company's lawyer's* petition.

> **BETTER:** I have not yet seen the petition of the *utility company's lawyer.*

Possessives in Holidays

650 Possessives in names of holidays are usually singular.

New Year's Eve	Valentine's Day	**BUT:** Robbie Burns' Day
Queen's Birthday	Saint Patrick's Day	April Fools' Day
Mother's Day	Orangeman's Day	National Bosses' Day

NOTE: Some holiday names contain a plural form rather than a plural possessive: for example, *United Nations Day.*

Possessives in Place Names

651 Place names that contain a possessive form do not usually have an apostrophe.

Baxters Corner, New Brunswick	Rogers Pass, British Columbia
Clarkes Beach, Nova Scotia	Smiths Falls, Ontario

Miscellaneous Expressions

652 A number of common expressions contain possessive forms.

driver's licence	journey's end
collector's item	visitor's permit
seller's market	lovers' lane
workers' compensation	writer's block
witches' brew	citizen's arrest
women's rights	teacher's pet
lion's share	monkey's uncle

☞ *For the plural forms of expressions like these, see ¶612d.*

See the Online Learning Centre at www.mcgrawhill.ca/college/gregg for related Web links.

SECTION **SEVEN**

Spelling

SPELLING GUIDES (¶¶701–718)

When a Final Consonant Is Doubled (¶¶701–702)
When a Final Consonant Is Not Doubled (¶¶703–706)
Final Silent *E* (¶¶707–709)
When Final *Y* Is Changed to *I* (¶¶710–711)
EI and *IE* Words (¶712)
Words Ending in *ABLE* and *IBLE* (¶713)
Words Ending in *ANT, ANCE, ENT,* and *ENCE* (¶714)
Words Ending in *IZE, ISE,* and *YZE* (¶715)
Words Ending in *CEDE, CEED,* and *SEDE* (¶716)
Words Ending in *C* (¶717)
Words With Diacritical Marks (¶718)

WORDS THAT SOUND ALIKE OR LOOK ALIKE (¶719)

TROUBLESOME WORDS (¶720)

COLOUR OR COLOR? (¶721)

The authority for the spelling of almost all the words used in this manual is *The Canadian Oxford Dictionary*. Whenever there are two spellings in the dictionary, only the first is given here.

Word processing spell checkers, especially those based on American dictionaries, may give different spellings for some words from those found in this manual. If a preferred spelling is not in your spell checker, expand its dictionary to reduce the number of replacement flags or "false alarms."

The use of a spell checker, unfortunately, is no guarantee that a correctly spelled word is the right word. Careful proofreading is always necessary. For example, if you write "Summer is our peek season," the spell checker will not question *peek* because it is spelled correctly. However, the correct spelling for the meaning of the sentence is *peak*. For more examples, see ¶1203.

SPELLING GUIDES
When a Final Consonant Is Doubled

701   When a word of one syllable ends in a single consonant (ba*g*) preceded by a single vowel (b*a*g), double the final consonant before a suffix beginning with a vowel (bagg*age*) or before the suffix *y* (bagg*y*). (See ¶703.)

rub	rub*bed*	swim	swim*mer*	slip	slip*page*
glad	glad*den*	skin	skin*ny*	star	star*ring*
beg	beg*gar*	clan	clan*nish*	bet	bet*tor*

EXCEPTIONS:

| yes | yeses | dew | dewy | fix | fixed |
| bus | buses | bow | bowed | tax | taxing |

NOTE: When a one-syllable word ends in *y* preceded by a single vowel, do not double the *y* before a suffix beginning with a vowel. (See ¶711.)

| pay | payee | joy | joyous | toy | toying |
| key | keyed | boy | boyish | buy | buyer |

702   When a word of more than one syllable ends in a single consonant (refe*r*) preceded by a single vowel (ref*e*r) and the accent falls on the last syllable of the root word (re*fer*), double the final consonant before a suffix beginning with a vowel (referr*ed*). (See ¶704.)

forbid	forbid*den*	begin	begin*ning*	infer	inferr*ed*
unclog	unclog*ged*	unzip	unzip*ped*	occur	occurr*ing*
control	control*ler*	concur	concur*rent*	regret	regret*table*

EXCEPTIONS (see ¶711):

| display | displaying | obey | obeyed | enjoy | enjoyable |

NOTE: When a suffix beginning with a vowel is added, do not double the final consonant if the accent *shifts* from the second syllable.

| refer | refer*red* | prefer | prefer*red* | transfer | transfer*red* |
| BUT: re*ference* | | BUT: p*referable* | | BUT: transfer*ee* | |

When a Final Consonant Is Not Doubled

703   When a word of one syllable ends in a single consonant (ba*d*) preceded by a single vowel (b*a*d), *do not* double the final consonant before a suffix beginning with a *consonant* (bad*ly*).

glad	glad*ness*	star	star*dom*	play	play*ful*
ten	ten*fold*	wit	wit*less*	joy	joy*fully*
ship	ship*ment*	flag	flag*ship*	boy	boy*hood*

704   When a word of more than one syllable ends in a single consonant (benefi*t*) preceded by a single vowel (benef*i*t) and the accent *does not* fall on the last syllable of the root word (*ben*efit), *do not* double the final consonant before a suffix beginning with a vowel (benefit*ed*).

benefit	benefited, benefiting	differ	differed, different
borrow	borrowed, borrowing	index	indexed, indexing
credit	credited, creditor	profit	profited, profiting

EXCEPTIONS:

cancel	cancelled, cancelling	handicap	handicapped, handicapping
format	formatted, formatting	program	programmed, programmer

705 When a word of one or more syllables ends in a single consonant (clou*d*, repea*t*) preceded by more than one vowel (cl*ou*d, rep*ea*t), *do not* double the final consonant before any suffix, whether it begins with a consonant (cloud*less*) or a vowel (repeat*ing*).

gain	gain*ful*	bias	bias*ed*	boil	boil*ed*
haul	haul*ing*	chief	chief*ly*	brief	brief*ly*
dream	dream*y*	riot	riot*ous*	loud	loud*ness*
cheer	cheer*y*	broad	broad*ly*	shout	shout*ing*
deceit	deceit*ful*	poet	poet*ic*	oil	oil*y*
feud	feud*al*	toil	toil*some*	buoy	buoy*ant*

EXCEPTIONS:

equip	equipped, equipping (**BUT:** equipment)	quit	quitting
quiz	quizzed, quizzing, quizzical	squat	squatter
equal	equalled, equalling	wool	woollen, woolly

706 When a word of one or more syllables ends with more than one consonant (wor*k*, deta*ch*), *do not* double the final consonant before any suffix (work*day*, detach*ed*).

comb	comb*ing*	back	back*ward*	shirr	shirr*ing*
hand	hand*y*	curl	curl*y*	mass	mass*ive*
self	self*ish*	warm	warm*ly*	slant	slant*wise*
swing	swing*ing*	return	return*ed*	jinx	jinx*ed*
wish	wish*ful*	harp	harp*ing*	blitz	blitz*ing*

NOTE: Words ending in *ll* usually retain both consonants before a suffix. However, when adding the suffix *ly*, drop one *l* from the root word. When adding the suffix *less* or *like*, insert a hyphen between the root and the suffix to avoid three *l*'s in a row.

full	fully	shell	shelly	hull	hull-less
skill	skilled	install	installed	bell	bell-like
(**BUT:** skilful)		(**BUT:** instalment)			

Final Silent E

707 **a.** Words ending in silent *e* usually *drop* the *e* before a suffix beginning with a vowel.

live	liv*able*	sense	sens*ible*	propose	propos*ition*
move	mov*able*	argue	argu*ing*	execute	execut*ive*
store	stor*age*	issue	issu*ing*	sincere	sincer*ity*
arrive	arriv*al*	blue	blu*ish*	desire	desir*ous*
accuse	accus*ation*	true	tru*ism*	use	us*ual*

EXCEPTIONS:

agree	agreeing	mile	mileage	dye	dyeing
see	seeing	acre	acreage	hoe	hoeing

(Continued on page 178.)

b. Words ending in silent *e* usually *drop* the *e* before the suffix *y.*

ease	easy	ice	icy	edge	edgy
chance	chancy	bounce	bouncy	range	rangy

EXCEPTIONS:

cage	cagey	dice	dicey	price	pricey

c. Words ending in *ce* or *ge* usually *retain* the *e* before a suffix beginning with *a* or *o* so as to preserve the soft sound of the *c* and *g.*

enforce	enforce*able*	advantage	advantag*eous*
notice	notice*able*	courage	courag*eous*
trace	trace*able*	knowledge	knowledge*able*
replace	replace*able*	manage	manage*able*
service	service*able*	outrage	outrag*eous*

EXCEPTIONS:

mortgage	mortgagor

NOTE: Before suffixes beginning with *i*, the *e* is usually dropped.

force	forc*ible*	college	colleg*ial*	rage	rag*ing*
reduce	reduc*ible*	finance	financ*ial*	enforce	enforc*ing*

EXCEPTIONS:

singe	singeing	tinge	tingeing	age	ageing

708 Words ending in silent *e* usually *retain* the *e* before a suffix beginning with a consonant.

hope	hope*ful*	flame	flame*proof*
care	care*less*	trouble	trouble*some*
sincere	sincere*ly*	nine	nine*ty*
manage	manage*ment*	subtle	subtle*ty*
like	like*ness*	edge	edge*wise*

EXCEPTIONS:

awe	awful	judge	judgment
true	truly	subtle	subtly
due	duly	nine	ninth
argue	argument	whole	wholly

709 Words ending in *ie* change the *ie* to *y* before *ing.*

die	dying	tie	tying	lie	lying

When Final Y Is Changed to I

710 Words ending in *y* preceded by a consonant change the *y* to *i* before any suffix except one beginning with *i.*

vary	vari*able*	accompany	accompani*ment*
custody	custodi*al*	happy	happi*ness*
Italy	Itali*an*	fallacy	fallaci*ous*
defy	defi*ant*	try	try*ing*
carry	carri*ed*	thirty	thirty*ish*

fly	fli*er*	lobby	lobby*ist*
easy	easi*er*	fancy	fanci*ful*
heavy	heavi*est*	likely	likeli*hood*
fifty	fifti*eth*	ordinary	ordinari*ly*

BUT:

sky	sky*ward*	shy	shy*ly*	country	country*side*
dry	dry*ly*	academy	academ*ic*	economy	econom*ist*

711 Words ending in *y* preceded by a vowel usually retain the *y* before any suffix.

okay	okay*ed*	convey	convey*ance*	employ	employ*able*
clay	clay*ey*	obey	obey*ing*	joy	joy*ful*
display	display*ing*	survey	survey*or*	buy	buy*er*

EXCEPTIONS:

pay	paid	day	daily	gay	gaily
lay	laid	say	said	slay	slain

EI and *IE* Words

712 According to the old rhyme:
Put *i* before *e*
Except after *c*
Or when sounded like *a*
As in *neighbour* and *weigh*.

I Before E

achieve	believe	anxiety	variety	**BUT:** either	neither
chief	relief	field	wield	height	seismic
friend	mien	niece	piece	seize	sheik
spiel	tier	patient	view	stein	weird

After C

deceive	receive	conceive	perceive	**BUT:** ancient	species
deceit	receipt	conceit	ceiling	science	financier

Sounded Like A

beige	feign	heir	rein	skein	vein
eight	freight	neigh	sleigh	veil	weight

Words Ending in *ABLE* and *IBLE*

713 **a.** The ending *able* is more commonly used.

admirable	dependable	likeable	probable	saleable
advisable	doable	movable	reasonable	transferable
changeable	knowledgeable	payable	receivable	valuable

☞ See ¶707 *on dropping or retaining silent* e *before the ending.*

b. However, a number of frequently used words end in *ible*.

compatible	eligible	irrepressible	possible	susceptible
convertible	feasible	irresistible	responsible	terrible
credible	flexible	legible	sensible	visible

Words Ending in *ANT, ANCE, ENT,* and *ENCE*

714 Words ending in *ant, ance, ent,* and *ence* follow no clear-cut pattern. Therefore, consult a dictionary when in doubt.

assist*ant*	exist*ent*	assur*ance*	defi*ance*	occurr*ence*
concord*ant*	immin*ent*	attend*ance*	inherit*ance*	persist*ence*
descend*ant*	insist*ent*	continu*ance*	intellig*ence*	prud*ence*

Words Ending in *IZE, ISE,* and *YZE*

715 **a.** Most words end in *ize.*

apologize	criticize	minimize	realize	summarize
authorize	economize	organize	recognize	vandalize
characterize	emphasize	prize	specialize	visualize

b. A number of common words end in *ise.*

advertise	compromise	enterprise	improvise	supervise
advise	devise	exercise	revise	televise

c. Only a few words end with *yze.*

analyze	paralyze	catalyze

Words Ending in *CEDE, CEED,* and *SEDE*

716 **a.** Only *one* word ends in *sede: supersede.*

b. Only *three* words end in *ceed: exceed, proceed, succeed.*

NOTE: Derivatives of these three words are spelled with only one *e:*

excess	process	success
excessive	procedure	succession

c. All other words ending with the sound of "seed" are spelled *cede: accede, concede, intercede, precede, recede, secede.*

Words Ending in *C*

717 Words ending in *c* usually take the letter *k* before a suffix so as to preserve the hard sound of the *c.*

mimic	mimicked, mimicking (**BUT:** mimicry)
panic	panicked, panicking, panicky
picnic	picnicked, picnicking, picnicker
shellac	shellacked, shellacking
traffic	trafficked, trafficking, trafficker
BUT: arc	arced, arcing

Words With Diacritical Marks

718 Many French words are now considered part of the English language and therefore do not require italics or underlining. (See ¶285d.) Nevertheless, some of these words retain diacritical marks from their original French form that can be accessed from special character sets.

a. Acute Accent. An acute accent (´) over the letter *e* (*é*) signifies that the letter is to be pronounced "ay" (as in *may*). Moreover, it signifies that at the end of a word the letter *é* is to be pronounced as a separate syllable.

attaché	crudités	glacé	purée
blasé	détente	habitué	risqué
café	éclair	ingénue	roué
canapé	éclat	macramé	sauté
chassé	élan	matinée	soirée
cliché	exposé	née	soufflé
communiqué	financé (m)	outré	touché
consommé	financée (f)	passé	toupée

A few words call for two acute accents:

protégé	Québécois	résumé	négligé

b. Grave Accent. A few expressions taken from the French retain a grave accent (`).

à la carte	crème de la crème	pied-à-terre	vis-à-vis
à la mode	derrière	tourtière	voilà

c. The Circumflex. A few phrases derived from the French still retain a circumflex (^).

tête-à-tête	crêpe suzette	papier-mâché	maître d'hôtel
château	raison d'être	pâté	table d'hôte

WORDS THAT SOUND ALIKE OR LOOK ALIKE

719 The following list contains two types of words: (a) words that are pronounced *exactly alike* though spelled differently; and (b) words that look and sound *somewhat alike*. Try reading aloud the words in this list and watch your pronunciation. (See Section 11 for more words that are frequently confused.)

accede to comply with; to give consent
exceed to surpass

accent stress in speech or writing
ascent act of rising
assent consent

accept to take; to receive
except (v.) to exclude; (prep.) excluding (see Section 11)

access admittance
excess surplus

ad short for *advertisement*
add to join

adapt to adjust
adept proficient
adopt to choose

addenda additional items
agenda list of things to be done

addition something added
edition one version of a printed work

adherence attachment
adherents followers

adverse hostile: unfavourable
averse disinclined

advice (n.) information; recommendation
advise (v.) to recommend; to give counsel

affect
effect (see Section 11)

aid (n.) a form of help; (v.) to help
aide an assistant

(Continued on page 182.)

ail to be in ill health
ale a drink much like beer

air atmosphere
err to make a mistake
heir one who inherits

aisle passage between rows
isle island

allot to assign or distribute a share of something (see Section 11)
a lot a great deal; **NOT:** alot

allowed permitted
aloud audibly

allusion an indirect reference
illusion an unreal vision; misapprehension
delusion a false belief
elusion adroit escape

altar part of a church
alter to change

alternate (n.) substitute; (v.) to take turns
alternative (n.) one of several things from which to choose

annual yearly
annul to cancel

ante- a prefix meaning "before"
anti- a prefix meaning "against"

antecedence priority
antecedents preceding things; ancestors

apportion to allot
portion a part

proportion a ratio of parts

appraise to set a value on
apprise to inform

arc something arched or curved
ark a ship; a place of protection and safety

area surface; extent
aria a song
arrears that which is due but unpaid

arrange to put in order
arraign to call into court

ascent (see *accent*)

assay to test, as an ore or a chemical
essay (n.) a treatise; (v.) to attempt

assistance help
assistants those who help

attain to gain; to achieve
attend to be present at

attendance presence
attendants escorts; followers; companions; associates

aught anything; all
ought should
naught nothing; zero

bail (n.) security; the handle of a pail; (v.) to dip water
bale a bundle

baited past tense of *bait*

bated restrained (as in *bated breath*)

bare (adj.) naked; empty; (v.) to expose
bear (n.) an animal; (v.) to carry; to endure; to produce

base (n.) foundation; (adj.) mean
bass a fish (rhymes with *mass*); lower notes in music (pronounced *base*)

bases plural of *base* and of *basis*
basis foundation

bazaar a place for selling goods
bizarre fantastic; extravagantly odd

beat (n.) throb; tempo; (v.) to strike, to win
beet a vegetable

berry a fruit
bury to submerge; to cover over

berth a bed
birth being born

better (adj.) greater than, more effective; (adv.) to a greater degree
bettor one who bets

bibliography list of writings pertaining to a given subject or author
biography written history of a person's life

billed charged
build to construct

blew past tense of *blow*

blue a colour

block (n.) a solid piece of material; (v.) to obstruct

bloc an interest group pursuing certain political or economic goals

board a piece of wood; an organized group; meals

bored penetrated; wearied

boarder one who pays for meals and often for lodging as well

border edge

bolder more daring

boulder a large rock

born brought into life

borne carried; endured

boy a male child

buoy a float

brake (n.) a retarding device; (v.) to retard

break (n.) an opening; a fracture; (v.) to shatter; to divide

bread food

bred brought up

breath respiration

breathe (v.) to inhale and exhale

breadth width

bridal concerning the bride or the wedding

bridle (n.) means of controlling a horse; (v.) to take offence

broach to open; to introduce

brooch ornamental clasp

bullion uncoined gold or silver

bouillon broth

cash ready money

cache a hiding place

cachet a mark of approval

calendar a record of time

calender a machine used in finishing paper and cloth

colander a strainer

callous (adj.) hardened

callus (n.) a hardened surface

cannot usual form (meaning "to be unable")

can not two words in the phrase *can not only* (where *can* means "to be able")

canvas (n.) a coarse cloth

canvass (v.) to solicit

capital (n.) city serving as the seat of government; a principal sum of money; a large-sized letter; (adj.) chief; foremost; punishable by death

capitol building in which a U.S. state legislative body meets

Capitol the building in which the U.S. Congress meets

caret a wedge-shaped mark (^)

carat a unit of weight for precious stones

karat a unit of quality for gold

carton a cardboard box

cartoon a caricature

casual incidental

causal causing

cease to stop

seize to grasp

cede to grant; to give up

seed that from which anything is grown

ceiling top of a room; any overhanging area

sealing closing

cell a small compartment

sell to transfer for a price

cellar an underground room

seller one who sells

censor (n.) an official authorized to suppress objectionable material; (v.) to make deletions or changes to material

sensor a device that detects a change in motion, light, heat, sound, or pressure

censure (n.) condemnation; (v.) to find fault with

(Continued on page 184.)

census statistics of population
senses mental faculties

cent penny
scent odour
sense meaning
sent did send

cereal any grain food
serial arranged in a series

cession a yielding up
session the sitting of a court or other body

choose to select
chose (past tense of *choose*)
chews masticates

chord combination of musical tones
cord string or rope

chute a slide
shoot to fire

cite (v.) to quote; to summon
sight a view; vision
site a place

click a slight, sharp noise
clique an exclusive group
cliché a trite phrase

climatic referring to climate
climactic referring to a climax

clothes garments
cloths fabrics
close (n.) the end; (v.) to shut

coarse rough; common
course direction; action; a way; part of a meal

collision a clashing
collusion a scheme to defraud

colonel military rank below general
kernel seed; essential part

coma an unconscious state
comma a mark of punctuation

command (n.) an order; (v.) to order
commend to praise; to entrust

commence (v.) to begin
comments (n.) remarks

complement something that completes
compliment (n.) a flattering remark; (v.) to praise

comprehensible understandable
comprehensive extensive

comptroller a manager of financial affairs
controller a person who directs, controls, or regulates

confidant a friend; an adviser (feminine form: *confidante*)
confident sure; positive

confidently certainty; positively
confidentially privately

conscience (n.) the sense of right or wrong
conscious (adj.) cognizant; sensible; aware

conservation preservation
conversation a talk

consul a foreign representative
council an assembly
counsel (n.) a lawyer, advice; (v.) to advise

consular (adj.) of a consul
councillor a member of a council
counsellor one who advises

continual occurring steadily but with occasional breaks
continuous uninterrupted; unbroken

co-operation working together
corporation a form of business organization

core the central part; the heart
corps a group of persons with a common activity

correspondence letters
correspondents those who write letters; journalists
corespondents certain parties in divorce suits

costume dress
custom habit

courtesy a favour; politeness
curtsy a gesture of respect

credible believable
creditable meritorious; deserving of praise
credulous ready to believe

critic one who makes judgments
criticize to judge negatively
critique (n.) a critical assessment; (v.) to judge; to criticize

cue a hint
queue a line of people

currant a berry
current (adj.) present time; (n.) a flow of water or electricity

curser one who curses
cursor a computer symbol used as a pointer

dairy source of milk products
diary daily record

deceased dead
diseased sick

decent proper; right
descent going down
dissent disagreement

decree a law
degree a grade; a step

deduce to infer
deduct to subtract

defer to put off
differ to disagree

deference respect; regard for another's wishes
difference dissimilarity; controversy

definite distinct, certain, unquestionable
definitive authoritative; providing a final answer

defuse to make less harmful; to make less tense
diffuse wordy, badly organized

deluded deceived
diluted watered down; thinned out

delusion (see *allusion*)

dependant (n.) one who relies on another
dependent (adj.) relying on another for help

deposition a formal written statement
disposition temper; disposal

depraved morally debased
deprived taken away from

deprecate to disapprove
depreciate to lessen in estimated value

desert (n.) barren land; (plural) a deserved reward; (v.) abandon
dessert the last course of a meal

desolate lonely; sad

dissolute loose in morals

detract to take away from
distract to divert the attention of

device (n.) a contrivance
devise (v.) to plan; to convey real estate by will

dew moisture
do to perform
due owing

die (n.) mould; (v.) to cease living
dye (n.) colouring matter; (v.) to become coloured; to change the colour of

disapprove to withhold approval
disprove to prove the falsity of

disassemble to take apart
dissemble to disguise; to feign

disburse to pay out
disperse to scatter

disc a flat surface; used with *laser, compact, optical*
disk a storage device; used with *drive, floppy, directory*

discreet prudent
discrete distinct; separate

disinterested unbiased; impartial
uninterested bored; unconcerned

(Continued on page 186.)

divers (adj.) various or sundry; (n.) plural of *diver*
diverse different

done finished
dun to demand payment

dose a measured quantity
doze to sleep lightly

dual double
duel a combat

ducked avoided
duct pipe or tube (as in *duct tape*)

dying near death
dyeing changing the colour of

edition (see *addition*)

effect (see *affect*)

elapse to pass
lapse to become void
relapse to slip back into a former condition

elicit to draw forth
illicit unlawful

eligible qualified
illegible unreadable

elusion (see *allusion*)

emanate to originate from; to come out of
eminent well known; prominent
immanent inherent; residing within
imminent threatening; impending

emerge to rise out of
immerge to plunge into

emigrate to go away from a country

immigrate to come into a country

en route (see *root*)

envelop (v.) to cover; to wrap
envelope (n.) a wrapper for a letter

equable even; tranquil
equitable just; right

erasable capable of being erased
irascible quick-tempered

especially to an exceptional degree
specially particularly, as opposed to generally

essay (see *assay*)

exalt to glorify
exult to be joyful

exceed (see *accede*)

excess (see *access*)

expand to increase in size
expend to spend

expansive capable of being extended
expensive costly

expatiate to enlarge on
expiate to atone for

explicit easily understood
implicit unquestioning

extant still existing
extent measure

facet aspect
faucet a tap

facetious witty
factitious artificial
fictitious imaginary

facilitate to make easy

felicitate to congratulate

facility ease
felicity joy

faint (adj.) dim; weak; (v.) to pass out
feint a trick; a deceptive move

fair (adj.) favourable; just; (n.) an exhibit
fare (n.) cost of travel; food; (v.) to go forth

faze to disturb
phase a stage in development

feet plural of *foot*
feat an act of skill or strength

finale the end
finally at the end
finely in a fine manner

fineness delicacy
finesse tact

fiscal financial
physical of the body

flack (n.) one who provides publicity; (v.) to provide publicity
flak criticism

flair aptitude
flare a light; a signal

flaunt to display showily
flout to treat with contempt

flew did fly
flue a chimney
flu short for *influenza*

flounder to move clumsily

founder to collapse; to sink; one who establishes something

flour ground meal
flower blossom

for a preposition
fore first; preceding; the front
four numeral

forbear to bear with
forebear an ancestor

forgo to relinquish; to let pass
forego to go before

formally in a formal manner
formerly before

fort a fortified place
forte (n.) area where one excels; (adv.) loudly (musical direction)

forth away; forward
fourth next after third

forward ahead
foreword preface

foul unfavourable; unclean
fowl a bird

gaff hook, ordeal, rough treatment
gaffe blunder

gage pledge, token of defiance
gauge measuring device

genius talent
genus a classification in botany or zoology

gibe (n.) a sarcastic remark; (v.) to scoff at
jibe to agree

gourmet a connoisseur of food and drink
gourmand a person who eats and drinks to excess

grate (n.) a frame of bars (as in a fireplace); (v.) to scrape; to irritate
great large; magnificent

guarantee an assurance of some kind
guaranty a promise to answer for another's debt

guessed past tense of *guess*
guest visitor

hail (n.) pellets of frozen rain; (v.) to call out to
hale (adj.) healthy (v.) to compel to go

hall a corridor
haul to drag

hangar a building relating to aircraft
hanger a device for hanging something

heal to cure
heel part of a foot or a shoe

hear to perceive by ear
here in this place

heard past tense of *hear*
herd a group of animals

heir (see *air*)

higher at a greater height
hire to employ; to use someone's services

hoard (n.) a hidden supply; (v) to hide a supply
horde a crowd or throng

hoarse harsh or rough in sound
horse a large animal

holy sacred
holey full of holes
wholly entirely
holly a tree

human pertaining to humanity
humane kindly

hypercritical overcritical
hypocritical pretending virtue

ideal a standard of perfection
idle unoccupied; without worth
idol object of worship
idyll a description of rural life

illegible (see *eligible*)

illicit (see *elicit*)

illusion (see *allusion*)

imitate to resemble; to mimic
intimate (adj.) innermost; familiar; (v.) to hint; to make known

immerge (see *emerge*)

immigrate (see *emigrate*)

(Continued on page 188.)

imminent (see *eminent*)

implicit (see *explicit*)

inane senseless
insane of unsound mind

incidence range of occurrence
incidents occurrences; happenings

incinerate to burn
insinuate to imply

incite (v.) to arouse
insight (n.) understanding

incredible unbelievable
incredulous skeptical

indict to charge with a crime
indite to compose; to write

indigenous native
indigent needy
indignant angry

inequity unfairness
iniquity wickedness; sin

ingenious clever
ingenuous naive

insoluble incapable of being dissolved
insolvable not explainable
insolvent unable to pay debts

instants short periods of time
instance an example

intelligent possessed of understanding
intelligible understandable

intense acute; strong
intents aims

interim intervening time; meanwhile
interment burial
internment confinement
internship a period of serving; a position

intermural between schools, colleges
intramural within one school or college

Internet globally linked computer networks
internet linked groups of local area networks
intranet organization's private network

irascible (see *erasable*)

isle (see *aisle*)

jibe (see *gibe*)

key a means of gaining entrance or understanding
quay a wharf (pronounced *key*)

knew understood
new fresh; novel

know to understand
no not any

lapse (see *elapse*)

lath a strip of wood
lathe a wood-turning machine

lead (n.) heavy metal (pronounced like *led*); (v.) to guide (pronounced *leed*)
led guided (past tense of *to lead*)

lean (adj.) thin; (v.) to incline
lien a legal claim

leased rented
least smallest

legislator a lawmaker
legislature a body of lawmakers

lend to allow the use of temporarily
loan (n.) something lent; (v.) to lend
lone solitary

lessee a tenant
lesser of smaller size
lessor one who gives a lease

lessen (v.) to make smaller
lesson (n.) an exercise assigned for study

levee embankment of a river
levy (n.) money raised by; authority; (v.) order to be paid

liable responsible
libel defamatory statement

licence (n.) card, plate, etc.; permission granted by law
license (v.) to authorize

lightening making lighter
lightning accompaniment of thunder
lighting illumination

load a burden to be carried
lode a mineral deposit; an abundant supply

loath (adj.) reluctant
loathe (v.) to detest

local (adj.) pertaining to a particular place
locale (n.) a particular place

loose (adj.) not bound; (v.) to release
lose (v.) to suffer the loss of; to part with unintentionally
loss something lost

made constructed
maid a servant

magnificent grand, stately
munificent unusually generous

mail correspondence
male masculine

main (adj.) chief; (n.) a conduit
mane long hair on the neck of certain animals

manner a way of acting
manor an estate

mantel a shelf above a fireplace
mantle a cloak

marital pertaining to marriage
martial military
marshal (n.) an official; (v.) to arrange

mean (adj.) unpleasant; (n.) the midpoint; (v.) to intend
mien appearance

meat flesh of animals
meet (v.) to join; (adj.) proper
mete to measure

medal badge of honour
meddle to interfere
metal a mineral
mettle courage; spirit

miner a worker in a mine
minor (adj.) lesser, as in size, extent, or importance; (n.) a person who is under legal age

missal a book of prayers
missile a rocket; a projectile

mist haze
missed failed to do

mite a tiny particle
might (n.) force; (v.) past tense of *may*

monogram a set of initials
monograph a short book; a pamphlet

mood disposition
mode fashion; method

moot debatable; disputed
mute unable to speak

moral virtuous
morale spirit

morality virtue
mortality death rate

morning before noon
mourning grief

naught (see *aught*)

new (see *knew*)

no (see *know*)

noisome offensive; smelly
noisy clamorous

oculist an ophthalmologist or an optometrist
ophthalmologist a doctor who treats eyes
optician one who makes or sells eyeglasses
optometrist one who measures vision

official authorized
officious overbold in offering services

one a single thing
won did win

ordinance a local law
ordnance arms; munitions

ought (see *aught*)

our (see *hour*)

overdo to do too much
overdue past due

packed crowded
pact an agreement

pail a bucket
pale (adj.) light-coloured; (n.) an enclosure

pain suffering
pane window glass

pair two of a kind
pare to peel
pear a fruit

(Continued on page 190.)

palate roof of the mouth; the sense of taste
palette an artist's board; a range of colours
pallet a bed; a mattress; a portable platform for stacking materials

parameter a quantity with an assigned value; a constant
perimeter the outer boundary

partition division
petition prayer; a formal written request

partly in part
partially to some degree

past (n.) time gone by; (adj., adv., or prep.) gone by
passed moved along; transferred (past tense of *pass*)

patience composure; endurance
patients sick persons

peace calmness
piece a portion

peak the top
peek to look slyly
pique (n.) resentment; (v.) to offend; to arouse
piqué cotton fabric

peal to ring out
peel (n.) the rind; (v.) to strip off

pedal (adj.) pertaining to the foot; (n.) a treadle

peddle to hawk; to sell

peer (n.) one of equal rank or age; (v.) to look steadily
pier a wharf

perfect without fault
prefect an official

perpetrate to be guilty of
perpetuate to make perpetual

perquisite privilege
prerequisite a preliminary requirement

persecute to oppress
prosecute to sue

personal private
personnel the staff

perspective a view in correct proportion
prospective anticipated

peruse to read
pursue to chase

phase (see *faze*)

physic a medicine
physics science dealing with matter and energy
psychic (adj.) of the soul or mind; (n.) a medium

physical (see *fiscal*)
psychical mental

plain (adj.) undecorated; (n.) prairie land
plane (n.) a level surface, an airplane; (v.) to make level

plaintiff party in a lawsuit
plaintive mournful

pleas plural of *plea*
please to be agreeable

pole a long, slender piece of wood or metal

poll (n.) a voting; survey; (v.) to register votes

poor (adj.) inadequate; (n.) the needy
pore to study intently; skin opening
pour to flow

populace the common people; the masses
populous thickly settled

portion (see *apportion*)
proportion (see *apportion*)

practicable workable; feasible
practical useful

practice (n.) exercise; custom; work or business of a professional
practise (v.) do again and again; do as a rule; to follow (a profession)

pray to beseech
prey a captured victim

precede to go before
proceed to advance

precedence priority
precedents established rules

preposition a part of speech
proposition an offer

prescribe to designate
proscribe to outlaw

presence bearing; being present
presents gifts

presentiment a foreboding
presentment a proposal

pretend to make believe
portend to foreshadow

principal (adj.) chief; main; (n.) main sum of money; chief official of a school
principle a general truth; a rule

profit gain
prophet one who forecasts

prophecy a prediction
prophesy to foretell

propose to suggest
purpose intention

quash to suppress (a legal motion)
squash (v) to press down; to flatten; (n.) a vegetable

quay (see *key*)

queue (see *cue*)

quiet calm; not noisy
quite entirely; wholly
quit to stop

rain falling water
rein part of a bridle; a curb
reign (n.) the term of a ruler's power; (v.) to rule

raise (n.) an increase; (v.) to lift

raze to destroy
rays beams

rap to knock
wrap (n.) a garment; (v.) to enclose

rapt engrossed
wrapped past tense of *wrap*

read to perform the act of reading
reed a plant; a musical instrument

real actual
reel (n.) a spool; a dance; (v.) to whirl

reality actuality
realty real estate

rebut to argue in opposition
refute to prove wrong

receipt an acknowledgement of a thing received
recipe a formula for mixing ingredients

recent (adj.) relating to a time not long past
resent (v.) to feel hurt by

reference that which refers to something
reverence profound respect

relapse (see *elapse*)

reprise a repeat performance
reprisal an act of revenge

residence a house
residents persons who reside in a place

respectably in a manner worthy of respect
respectfully in a courteous manner
respectively in the order indicated

rifle (v.) to ransack and steal
riffle to flip through (pages)

right (adj.) correct; (n.) a privilege
rite a ceremony
wright a worker; a maker (used as a combining form, as in *playwright*)
write to inscribe

role a part in a play
roll (n.) a list; a type of bread; (v.) to revolve

root (n.) underground part of a plant; (v.) to implant firmly
route (n.) an established course of travel; (v.) to send by a certain route
en route on or along the way
rout (n.) confused flight; (v.) to defeat

rote repetition
wrote did write

rye a grain to make bread; whiskey
wry ironically humorous

(Continued on page 192.)

sail (n.) part of a ship's rigging; (v.) to travel by water
sale the act of selling

scene a setting; an exhibition of strong feeling
seen past participle of *to see*

scent (see *cent*)

sealing (see *ceiling*)

seam a line of junction
seem to appear

seed (see *cede*)

seize (see *cease*)

sell (see *cell*)

seller (see *cellar*)

sense, sent (see *cent*)

senses (see *census*)

sensor (see *censor*)

serge a kind of cloth
surge (n.) a billow; (v.) to rise suddenly

serial (see *cereal*)

session (see *cession*)

sew to stitch
so therefore
sow to scatter seed

shear to cut; to trim
sheer transparent; steep; utter

shoot (see *chute*)

shown displayed; revealed; past participle of *show*
shone gave off light

sight, site (see *cite*)

simple uncomplicated

simplistic oversimplified

sleight dexterity, as in "sleight of hand"
slight (adj.) slender; scanty; (v.) to make light of

soar (see *sore*)

soared did fly
sword weapon

sole one and only
soul the immortal spirit

soluble having the ability to dissolve in a liquid
solvable capable of being solved or explained

sore painful
soar to fly

spacious having ample room
specious outwardly correct but inwardly false

specially (see *especially*)

staid grave; sedate
stayed past tense and past participle of *to stay*

stair a step
stare to look at

stake (n.) a pointed stick; the prize in a contest; (v.) to wager
steak a slice of meat or fish

stanch to stop the flow of something
staunch faithful, steadfast

stationary fixed
stationery writing materials

statue a carved figure
stature height
statute a law

steal to take unlawfully
steel a form of iron

storey a level or floor of a building
story a tale; account

straight not crooked; directly
strait a water passageway; (plural) a distressing situation; tight, narrow

succor (n.) something that provides relief; (v.) to relieve

sucker someone easily cheated

suit (n.) a legal action; clothing; (v.) to please
suite a group of things forming a unit
sweet having an agreeable taste; pleasing

superintendence management
superintendents supervisors

tack (n.) direction; (v.) to change direction
tact considerate way of behaving so as to avoid offending others

tail the end
tale a story

tare allowance for weight

tear (n.) a rent or rip (pronounced like *tare*); a secretion from the eye (pronounced like *tier*); (v.) to rip

tier a row or layer

taught did teach
taut tight; tense

team a group
teem to abound

tenant one who rents property
tenet a principle

their belonging to them (see ¶1056e)
there in that place
they're contraction of *they are*

theirs possessive form of *they*, used without a following noun (see ¶1056e)
there's contraction of *there is* or *there has*

therefor for that thing
therefore consequently

throes a painful struggle
throws hurls; flings

through by means of; from beginning to end; because of
threw did throw
thorough carried through to completion

to (prep.) toward
too (adv.) more than enough; also
two one plus one

tortuous winding; twisty; devious
torturous cruelly painful

track a trail
tract a treatise; a piece of land

trial examination; an experiment; hardship
trail a path

trooper a soldier
trouper a theatrical performer; one who endures hardships (as in a *real trouper*)

trustee a person to whom something is entrusted
trusty (n.) a convict who is considered trustworthy;

undo to open; to render ineffective
undue improper; excessive

uninterested (see *disinterested*)

urban pertaining to the city
urbane polished; suave

vain proud; conceited; futile
vane a weathercock
vein a blood vessel; a bed of mineral materials

vale a valley
veil a concealing cover or coth

vendee purchaser
vendor seller

veracious truthful
voracious greedy

veracity truthfulness
voracity ravenousness; greediness

vial a small flask for liquids
vile disgusting, despicable

vice wickedness; a prefix used with nouns to designate titles of office (see ¶808c)
vise a clamp

waist part of the body
waste (n.) needless destruction; useless consumption; (v.) to expend uselessly

wait to stay
weight heaviness

waive (v.) to give up
wave (n.) a billow; a gesture; (v.) to swing back and forth

waiver the giving up of a claim
waver to hesitate

want (n.) a need; (v.) to lack; to desire
wont a custom (pronounced like *want*)
won't contraction of *will not*

ware goods
wear to have on
were form of *to be*
where at the place in which

way direction; distance; manner
weigh to find the weight of

weak not strong
week period of seven days

wet (v.) to moisten
whet (v.) to sharpen

wholly (see *holy*)

whose possessive of *who*
who's contraction of *who is* (see ¶1063)

wilfully in a determined manner
willingly cheerfully; happily; with one's free will

whither to whatever place
wither to become dry; to lose freshness

won (see *one*)

wood lumber
would an auxiliary verb form (as in *they would like some*)

wrap (see *rap*)

wright, write (see *right*)

wrote (see *rote*)

yoke a crosspiece that holds two things together; an oppressive constraint
yolk the yellow part of an egg

yore of time long past
your belonging to *you* (see ¶1056e)
you're contraction of *you are*

TROUBLESOME WORDS

720   The following is a list of words that writers often misspell or puzzle over. In some cases the difficulty is the inability to apply an established rule; for such words, references are given. In other instances, however, errors result from the peculiar spelling of the words themselves; in these cases the only remedy is to master the correct spelling on an individual basis.

NOTE: For troublesome words that sound alike or look alike, see ¶719. For troublesome compound words, see Section 8. For alternative spellings such as *colour* or *color*, *centre* or *center*, *travelled* or *traveled*, see ¶721. For alternative words that have the same meaning, consult a thesaurus. Synonyms help create variety in your writing style.

abscess
absence
absorption
accessory
accidentally
accommodate
accompanying
accumulate
achievement
acknowledgement
acquaintance
acquire
acquisition
acquittal
adjacent
advantageous (see ¶707)
adviser
advisory
aegis

affidavit
affiliated
aggressive
aging
alignment
aluminum
amateur
amortize
analogous
analysis
anomalous
antecedent
appall
apparatus
apparent
appropriate
architect
argument (see ¶708)
assistance (see ¶714)

asterisk
asthma
attendance
attorney
auditor
autumn
auxiliary
bachelor
bankruptcy
basically
behaviour (see ¶721)
beautician
believe (see ¶712)
beneficiary
benefited (see ¶704)
benign
biased (see ¶705)
boundary
Brampton

Brantford
brilliant
brochure
buoyant
bureau
calendar
calibre (see ¶721)
campaign
cancelled (see ¶704)
candour (see ¶721)
Caribbean
carriage
catalogue
category
cemetery
census
changeable
Charlottetown
chronological
circuit
clientele
coincidence
collateral
collectable
colonel
colossal
column
comparative
competitor
concede (see ¶716)
conceive
condemn
connoisseur
conscience
conscientious
conscious
consensus
convenience
convertible (see ¶713b)
corduroy
correctable
correspondent
corroborate
courtesy
debt, debtor
deductible
de-emphasize
defence

defendant (see ¶714)
deficit
definitely
dependant (noun)
dependent (adj.)
descendant (see ¶714)
description
desirable
desperately
detrimental
development
dictionary
dietitian
dilemma
disastrous
disbursement
discrepancy
dissatisfied
dissimilar
dissipate
dossier
ecstasy
eighth
eligible (see ¶713b)
eliminate
embarrass
emphasize
endorsement
entrepreneur
enumerate
envelop (verb)
environment
erroneous
escrow
exaggerate
exceed (see ¶716)
excellent
exhaustible
exhibition
exhilarate
exonerate
exorbitant
extension
extraordinary
facsimile
fallacy
familiar
fascinating

fatigue
February
fiery
financier
flexible (see ¶713b)
fluctuation
fluorescent
foreign (see ¶712)
foresee
forfeit
forty
fourth
Fredericton (NB)
freight
fulfil (see ¶721)
gauge
gesture
glamour
government
grammar
grateful
gratuity
grievance
gruesome
guarantee
guardian
Guelph
harass
height (see ¶712)
hemorrhage
heterogeneous
hindrance
homogeneous
honourable
hors d'oeuvre
humorous
hygiene
hypocrisy
idiosyncrasy
illegible
impasse
impostor
inasmuch as
incidentally
indict
indispensable
innocuous
innuendo

(Continued on page 196.)

inoculate
insistent
instalment (see ¶721)
interim
intermediary
irrelevant
itinerary
jeopardy
jewellery
judgment (see ¶708)
judicial
knowledgeable
labelled
laboratory
leisure
liable
liaison
library
licence (noun)
license (verb)
lien
lieutenant
lightning
likeable (see ¶713a)
liquefy
maintenance
manoeuvre
marshal (see ¶721)
martyr
medieval
mediocre
memento
mileage
milieu
millennium
millionaire
miniature
minuscule
miscellaneous
mischievous
misspell
mnemonic
mortgage
necessary
negligence
negotiable
neighbour (see ¶721)
newsstand
nickel
niece (see ¶712)

ninety
ninth
noticeable (see ¶¶707c)
nuclear
obsolescent
occurrence (see ¶714)
offence
omission
oscillate
pamphlet
panicky (see ¶717)
paradigm
parallel
paralyze (see ¶715c)
parliament
part-time
pastime
patience
peaceable
permissible (see ¶713b)
perseverance
persistent
personnel
persuade
Peterborough
phase
phenomenal
Philippines
phony
physician
picnicking (see ¶717)
plagiarism
plausible (see ¶713b)
poinsettia
practice (noun)
practise (verb)
prairie
preceding (see ¶716c)
preferable (see ¶702)
preferred
prerogative
presumptuous
pretence (see ¶721)
privilege
procedure (see ¶716b)
proceed (see ¶716b)
programmed (see ¶704)
pronunciation
protégé
psalm

pseudonym
psychiatric
psychological
publicly
pursue
quantity
questionnaire
queue
rarefy
rarity
realize (see ¶715a)
receipt
receive (see ¶712)
recommend
reconnaissance
reinforce
relevant (see ¶714)
rendezvous
renowned
rescind
resistance
restaurant
rhetorical
rhyme
rhythm
sacrilegious
Saint John (NB)
Saskatchewan
satellite
Sault Ste. Marie
schedule
scissors
separate
sergeant
siege (see ¶712)
similar
simultaneous
sincerely (see ¶708)
skeptic
skilful
souvenir
specimen
sponsor
St. Catharines (ON)
St. John's (NL)
stratagem
strength
subpoena
subtlety
subtly

summary
superintendent
supersede (see ¶716a)
surgeon
surreptitious
surveillance
tangible
tariff
taxiing
technique
temperament
temperature
thoroughly
threshold
totalled (see ¶721)

tragedy
tranquillizer
truly (see ¶708)
unanimous
unctuous
unique
unmanageable
  (see ¶707c)
unwieldy (see ¶712)
usage (see ¶707a)
vaccinate
vacillate
vacuum
Vancouver

vicious
vinyl
volume
warrant
Wednesday
weird (see ¶712)
Westminster
wherever
Winnipeg
withhold
woeful
woollen (see ¶705)
worshipped (see ¶721)
yield (see ¶712)

COLOUR OR COLOR?

721 The following lists compare word variants according to *The Canadian Oxford Dictionary* with *Webster's New World Dictionary* (published in the United States). In all cases the first spelling given in a dictionary is the preferred spelling. Depending on your employer's preference, Canadianize your spell checker by adding the words in the first and third columns to your word processing default dictionary.

Canadian	**American**	**Canadian**	**American**

a. A single or double consonant when adding a suffix.

Canadian	American	Canadian	American
cancelled	canceled	councillor	councilor
counselling	counseling	diagrammed	diagramed
enrolment	enrollment	equalled	equaled
instalment	installment	jewellery	jewelry
labelled	labeled	programmed	programed
totalled	totaled	traveller	traveler
woollen	woolen	worshipped	worshiped

b. Words ending in *or* or *our*.

Canadian	American	Canadian	American
behaviour	behavior	candour	candor
colour	color	endeavour	endeavor
favourite	favorite	flavour	flavor
harbour	harbor	honour	honor
humour	humor	labour	labor
neighbour	neighbor	odour	odor
parlour	parlor	rumour	rumor
savour	savor	saviour	savior

c. Words ending in *er* or *re*.

Canadian	American	Canadian	American
calibre	caliber	centre	center
litre	liter	lustre	luster

(Continued on page 198.)

Canadian	American	Canadian	American
manoeuvre	maneuver	metre	meter
sabre	saber	theatre	theater

d. Other variants.

Canadian	American	Canadian	American
catalogue	catalog	cheque	check
defence	defense	offence	offense
licence (noun)	license (noun)	license (verb)	license (verb)
practice (noun)	practice (noun)	practise (verb)	practice (verb)
saleable	salable	likeable	likable
acknowledgement	acknowledgment		

 See the Online Learning Centre at www.mcgrawhill.ca/college/gregg for related Web links.

SECTION EIGHT

Compound Words

COMPOUND NOUNS (¶¶801–810)

COMPOUND VERBS (¶¶811–812)

COMPOUND ADJECTIVES (¶¶813–832)
Basic Rules (¶¶813–815)
Adjective + **Noun** (*as in* short-**term** *note:* ¶816)
Compound With Number or Letter (*as in* **40-hour** *week:* ¶817)
Compound With Noun (*as in* **high school** *graduate:* ¶818)
Proper Name (*as in* **Yonge Street** *agencies:* ¶819)
Noun + **Adjective** (*as in* tax-**free** *imports:* ¶820)
Noun + **Participle** (*as in* time-**consuming** *details:* ¶821)
Adjective + **Participle** (*as in* nice-**looking** *layout:* ¶822)
Adjective + **Noun + ED** (*as in* quick-**witted** *assistant:* ¶823)
Adverb + **Participle** (*as in* privately **owned** *stock* and *as in* well-**known** *facts:* ¶824)
Adverb + **Adjective** (*as in* very **exciting** *test results:* ¶825)
Participle + **Adverb** (*as in* warmed-**over** *ideas:* ¶826)
Adjective + **Adjective** (*as in* black **leather** *notebook:* ¶827)
Verb + **Verb** (*as in* stop-and-**go** *traffic:* ¶828)
Verb + **Adverb** (*as in* read-**only** *memory:* ¶829)
Verb + **Noun** (*as in* take-**home** *pay:* ¶830)
Phrasal Compound (*as in* **up-to-date** *accounts:* ¶831)
Suspending Hyphen (¶832)

PREFIXES AND SUFFIXES (¶¶833–846)

COMPOUND COMPUTER TERMS (¶847)

Some compound words are written as solid words, some are written as separate words, and some are hyphenated. However, the development of communication technology is so rapid that the rules affecting these words are continually changing. Dictionaries are not able to keep pace. Today the general tendency is for hyphenated forms to become either spaced or solid and for spaced forms to eventually become solid.

With a very few exceptions, the compound forms used in this section agree with those in *The Canadian Oxford Dictionary.*

COMPOUND NOUNS

801 Compound nouns follow no regular pattern. Some are written solid, some are spaced, and some are hyphenated.

a.

class action	classroom	class-consciousness
front office	frontperson	front-runner
knife block	knifepoint	knife-edge
pay envelope	payday	pay-TV
power bar	powerboat	power-broker
short list	shortfall	short-circuit
show home	showpiece	show-off
tie clip	tiebreaker	tie-line
time limit	timetable	time-share
work table	workstation	work-in-progress

b. To be sure of the spelling of a compound noun, consult a Canadian dictionary. If the noun is not listed, the traditional guideline is to treat the elements of the compound as separate words. As an alternative, you may treat the noun the same way that similar compounds appear in the dictionary.

c. For the spelling of compounds in a company name, check the letterhead. (Compare, for example, *On Line Hydro Services Inc., Online Business Systems,* and *On-Line Telecommunications Inc.*)

802 Some solid and hyphenated compound nouns closely resemble verb phrases. Be sure, however, to treat the elements in a verb phrase as separate words.

Nouns	Verb Phrases
protect data with regular *backups*	always *back up* the data in the file
a *breakdown* in communications	when communications *break down*
devise another plan as a *fallback*	we can always *fall back* on Plan B
a thorough *follow-up* of the report	to *follow up* on your recommendation
when they give us the *go-ahead*	we can *go ahead* with the project
they have the *know-how*	they *know how* to handle it
after you complete the *logon*	after you *log on* to the program
the *roundup* of local news	be sure to *round up* the crew
her *makeup* was applied with care	we will *make up* the time lost
work has come to a *slowdown*	must *slow down* to the speed limit
a *tie-in* with their business plans	policies *tie in* with their goals

803 **a.** *Up* **Words.** Compound nouns ending in *up* are either solid or hyphenated. For example:

checkup	blow-up	let-up	smash-up
cleanup	call-up	lock-up	start-up
getup	catch-up	mock-up	tie-up
hookup	close-up	paste-up	toss-up
lineup	crack-up	pull-up	tune-up
markup	cut-up	punch-up	walk-up
pickup	flare-up	run-up	warm-up
shakeup	freeze-up	set-up	wrap-up
windup	hang-up	slip-up	write-up

b. *Down* **Words.** Most compound nouns ending in *down* are solid. For example:

breakdown	playdown	slowdown	**BUT:** dressing-down
comedown	rundown	splashdown	knock-down
countdown	shakedown	touchdown	put-down
letdown	showdown	turndown	tie-down
lowdown	shutdown	writedown	wind-down

c. *In* **Words.** Compound nouns ending in *in* are usually hyphenated. For example:

call-in	fill-in	run-in	stand-in
check-in	lead-in	shoo-in	tie-in
cut-in	look-in	shut-in	walk-in
drive-in	phase-in	sit-in	write-in

d. *Out* **Words.** Compound nouns ending in *out* are either solid or hyphenated. For example:

blackout	holdout	shutout	call-out
burnout	layout	standout	carry-out
buyout	lockout	takeout	cut-out
checkout	lookout	turnout	fade-out
dropout	payout	walkout	fold-out
fallout	pullout	washout	get-out
hangout	printout	whiteout	phase-out
hideout	sellout	workout	put-out

e. *On* **Words.** Compound nouns ending in *on* are usually hyphenated. For example:

add-on	clip-on	hangers-on	slip-on
carry-on	come-on	lookers-on	turn-on
carryings-on	goings-on	put-on	walk-on

f. *Off* **Words.** Compound nouns ending in *off* are either solid or hyphenated. For example:

faceoff	playoff	brush-off	rip-off
kickoff	runoff	cast-off	set-off

(Continued on page 202.)

layoff	spinoff	cut-off	shut-off
liftoff	standoff	drop-off	trade-off
payoff	turnoff	knock-off	write-off

g. *Over* **Words.** Compound nouns ending in *over* are either solid or hyphenated. For example:

changeover	pullover	switchover	carry-over
crossover	pushover	takeover	going-over
handover	spillover	turnover	hold-over
layover	stopover	walkover	voice-over

h. *Back* **Words.** Compound nouns ending in *back* are usually solid. For example:

buyback	drawback	kickback	rollback
comeback	feedback	piggyback	setback
cutback	flashback	playback	throwback

i. *Away* **Words.** These compounds are usually solid. For example:

breakaway	getaway	layaway	stowaway
castaway	giveaway	rollaway	straightaway
cutaway	hideaway	runaway	throwaway

j. **Compounds Ending in** *About,* *Around,* **and** *By*. These compounds are usually solid. For example:

layabout	roustabout	turnaround	passerby
runabout	walkabout	wraparound	standby

804 **a.** Hyphenate a compound noun that has no noun as one of its elements.

a catch-all	the higher-ups	the so-and-sos
cut-and-paste	have a look-see	a whoop-de-do
a do-gooder	a meet-and-greet	**BUT:** hit and roll
the have-nots	smash-and-grab	touch and go

b. Words coined from repeated or rhyming syllables are usually hyphenated. Other coined words may be hyphenated, solid, or written as separate words.

hurly-burly	no-no	silly-billy
mucky-muck	palsy-walsy	tom-toms
mumbo-jumbo	phony-baloney	**BUT:** chick flick
nitty-gritty	razzle-dazzle	humdrum

c. Some compound nouns that end with a prepositional phrase are hyphenated.

aide-de-camp	heart-to-heart	**BUT:** bill of sale
barrister-at-law	play-by-play	line of credit
brother-in-law	stick-in-the-mud	play on words
sergeant-at-arms	stock-in-trade	seal of approval

805 Treat a compound noun like *problem solving* as two words unless your dictionary specifically shows it as solid or hyphenated. (Most words of this pattern are not shown in a dictionary. However, the solid and hyphenated examples below have been taken from *The Canadian Oxford Dictionary*.)

budget planning	headhunting	bean-counting
computer dating	nitpicking	fact-finding
digital archiving	peacekeeping	penny-pinching
rumour mongering	stonewalling	profit-taking
text messaging	wisecracking	sabre-rattling

☞ *For words like* fine tuning, *which are derived from hyphenated infinitives like fine-tune, see ¶812.*

806 Hyphenate two nouns when they signify that one person or one thing has two functions. (See also ¶295b.)

dinner-dance	owner-landlord	scanner-printer
editor-publisher	reader-writer	writer-producer

807 Compound nouns that have a single letter as their first element are usually hyphenated.

D-Day	T-ball	T-bill	U-boat	v-chip	V-shape
I-beam	T-bar	T-bone	U-joint	V-neck	X-ray

808 **a.** Do not hyphenate civil titles of two or more words.

a chief of police	City Commissioner	Registrar General
chief executive officer	Deputy Mayor	**BUT:** lieutenant-governor

b. Hyphenate military commissioned ranks in the Land and Air Command. With one exception, *Rear-Admiral*, Maritime Command ranks are not hyphenated.

Lieutenant-Colonel	Major-General	**BUT:** 2nd Lieutenant
Brigadier-General	Commander-in-Chief	Vice Admiral

c. Hyphenate compound titles containing *vice*, *ex*, and *elect*.

Vice-President	ex-Mayor White	Chairman-elect Lai
Vice-Chancellor	ex-President Mohtadi	Premier-elect Jarvis

NOTE: Also use a hyphen when *ex* is attached to a noun (for example, *ex-wife, ex-convict*), but omit the hyphen in Latin phrases (for example, *ex officio, ex cathedra, ex libris*).

☞ *For the capitalization of titles with ex and elect, see ¶¶317 and 363.*
For the correct usage of ex, *see the entry for* Ex—Former *in Section 11.*

809 **a.** The generic use of such compound nouns as *businessmen, manpower, man-hours, alderman, etc.*, is now unacceptable and should be avoided. The following list suggests alternatives.

In Place of the Generic Term	Use
layman	layperson
businessmen	business owners, business executives, business managers, business people

(Continued on page 204.)

alderman	city councillor, ward representative, alderperson
mankind	people, humanity, the human race, human beings, humankind
man-hours	worker-hours
manpower	work force, human resources, staff, personnel
salesmen	salespeople, sales representatives, salespersons, salesclerks, sales staff, sales force, sales associates
foremen	supervisors
policemen	police officers, the police, constables
mailmen	mail carriers, letter carriers, mailpersons
workmen	workers
a six-man team	a six-member team, a six-person team

b. Words like *chair, chairperson,* and *spokesperson* have been coined as a means of avoiding the generic use of masculine compound nouns. Personal taste or institutional policy will dictate whether to use these terms or not.

Who will be appointed as *head* of the committee? **OR** Who will be appointed to *chair* the committee? (**NOT:** . . . appointed *chairman* of the committee?)

c. Whenever possible, replace a word like *salesmanship* with an alternative expression (for example, *selling skills*). However, words such as *craftsmanship, workmanship, sportsmanship, horsemanship, brinkmanship,* and *one-upmanship* are still widely used because of the difficulty in devising alternative expressions.

☞ *See ¶840 for alternatives to words ending with feminine suffixes.*

810 Terms like *doctor, lawyer,* and *nurse* are generic—that is, they apply equally to women and men. Therefore, do not use compound nouns like *woman lawyer* and *male nurse* unless there is a legitimate reason for making a distinction according to gender.

There will be a meeting on Monday at 10 a.m. for male nurses only.

☞ *For capitalization of hyphenated compound nouns: see ¶363.*
For plurals of compound nouns: see ¶¶611–613.
For possessives of compound nouns: see ¶¶634–635.

COMPOUND VERBS

811 **a.** Compound verbs are usually hyphenated or solid.

to blue-pencil	to rubber-stamp	to download	to shortchange
to colour-code	to side-swipe	to downsize	to shortcut
to deep-freeze	to soft-pedal	to highlight	to waterproof
to double-cross	to spell-check	to pinpoint	to whitewash

NOTE: If you try to check the spelling of a compound verb in a dictionary and do not find the verb listed, *hyphenate the components.*

b. Do not hyphenate verb phrase combinations such as *make up, slow down, tie in.* (See ¶802 for examples.)

812 **a.** If the infinitive form of a compound verb has a hyphen, retain the hyphen in the other forms of the verb. (See ¶812b for one type of exception.)

Would you like to *fine-tune* the tactics for your renewal project?
This system has been *fine-tuned* for better sound effects.
We need *fine-tuning* experts to improve our recording systems

You need to *double space* all these reports.
Please *double space* this letter.
BUT: This should not be *double-spaced* material. (Hyphenate *double-spaced* when it is a compoud adjective.)

b. The gerund derived from a hyphenated compound verb requires no hyphen unless it is followed by an object. (See ¶135a.)

Deep frying is not the only way to cook potatoes.
BUT: *Deep-frying* green cheese is great!

Spell checking is necessary, but careful proofreading must follow.
BUT: *Spell-checking* this report will not be your last task.

COMPOUND ADJECTIVES

A compound adjective consists of two or more words that function as a unit and express a single thought. When such adjectives are shown hyphenated in the dictionary, you can assume only that the expressions are hyphenated when they occur directly *before* nouns. When the same words fall elsewhere in sentences, the omission of hyphens depends on how the words are used.

Basic Rules

813 Compound adjectives are one-thought modifiers, usually reduced to a few essential words. They take the place of adjective phrases and clauses, as shown in the following examples:

Adjective Phrase or Clause	Compound Adjective
terminals *installed at the point of sale*	*point-of-sale* terminals
a career *moving along a fast track*	a *fast-track* career
a woman *who speaks quietly*	a *quiet-spoken* woman
an actor *who is well known*	a *well-known* actor
a conference *held at a high level*	a *high-level* conference
a building *ten storeys high*	a *ten-storey* building
an article *that is as long as a book*	a *book-length* article
an environment *where people work under high pressure*	a *high-pressure* environment
a guarantee *to give you your money back*	a *money-back* guarantee
a PC *that delivers a high level of performance, carries a low cost, and is easy to use*	a *high-performance, low-cost, easy-to-use* PC

814 Hyphenate the elements of a compound adjective that occur *before* a noun. Hyphens are required to hold the words together. (A few expressions, such

(Continued on page 206.)

as *high school* and *income tax*, are readily understood as a unit and do not require hyphens. See ¶818.)

> *high-tech* equipment (equipment *that reflects a high level of technology*)
> a *worst-case* scenario (a scenario *based on the worst case that could occur*)
> a *$40 000-a-year* salary (a salary *of $40 000 a year*)
> *long-range* plans (plans *projected over a long range of time*)
> *machine-readable* copy (copy *readable by a machine*)
> an *eye-catching* display (a display *that catches the eye*)
> a *high-ranking* official (an official *who ranks high in the organization*)
> *same-day* service (service *completed the same day you bring the item in*)
> *bottom-line* results (the results *shown on the bottom line of a financial statement*)

815 **a.** When these expressions occur *elsewhere in the sentence*, drop the hyphen. They no longer function as compound adjectives but as individual words occurring in normal order and form.

Before the Noun	Elsewhere in Sentence
last-minute shopping	They go shopping up to the very *last minute.* (Object of preposition.)
an *up-to-date* report	Please bring the report *up to date.* (Prepositional phrase.)
a *follow-up* letter	Let's *follow up* at once with a letter. (Verb + adverb.)
a *high-level* decision	The decision must be made at a *high level.* (Object of preposition.)
a *never-to-be-forgotten book*	Your latest book is *never to be forgotten.* (Adverb + infinitive phrase.)
an *off-the-record* comment	The next comment is *off the record.* (Prepositional phrase.)
a *no-nonsense* attitude	Marion will tolerate *no nonsense* from you. (Object of verb.)
a *thank-you* note	We *thank you* for your contribution. (Object of verb.)
a *low-key* sales approach	Christopher pitches his sales approach in a *low key.* (Object of preposition.)
a *cause-and-effect* relationship	Is there a relationship of *cause and effect* in this case? (Object of preposition.)

b. When such an expression occurs elsewhere in the sentence *but is still used as an adjective*, use a hyphen. Compound adjectives like the following almost always need to be hyphenated.

Before the Noun	Elsewhere in Sentence
a *tax-exempt* purchase	The purchase was *tax-exempt.* (See ¶820.) **BUT:** The purchase was *exempt from taxes.*
government-owned lands	These lands are *government-owned.* (See ¶821.) **BUT:** These lands are *owned by the government.*

a *friendly-looking* salesclerk | That salesclerk is *friendly-looking*. (See ¶822.)
BUT: The salesclerk *looks friendly.*

high-priced cars | These cars are too *high-priced.* (See ¶823.)
BUT: The cars are listed at a *high price.*

Adjective + Noun (see also ¶¶817–819)

816 **a.** Hyphenate an adjective and a noun when these elements serve as a compound modifier *before* a noun. Do not hyphenate these elements when they play a normal role *elsewhere in the sentence* (for example, as the object of a preposition or of a verb). However, if the expression continues to function as a compound adjective, a hyphen is necessary.

Before the Noun	Elsewhere in Sentence
high-speed printers	These printers run at *high speed.* (Object of preposition.)
a *plain-paper* fax	Please be sure to order a fax that uses *plain paper.* (Object of verb.)
red-carpet treatment	They plan to roll out the *red carpet.* (Object of infinitive.)
a *closed-door* discussion	The discussion was held behind *closed doors.* (Object of preposition.)
an *all-day* seminar	The seminar will last *all day.* (Normal adverbial phrase.)
a *long-term* investment in bonds	This investment in bonds runs for a *long term.* (Object of preposition.)
	BUT: This investment in bonds is *long-term.* (Compound adjective.)
a *part-time* job	This job is *part-time.* (Compound adjective.)
	I work *part-time.* (Compound adverb.)
	I travel *part of the time.* (Normal adverbial phrase.)

b. Combinations involving comparative or superlative adjectives plus nouns follow the same pattern.

Before the Noun	Elsewhere in Sentence
a *larger-size* shirt	He wears a *larger size.* (Object of verb.)
the *finest-quality* goods	These goods are of the *finest quality.* (Object of preposition.)

c. A few compound adjectives in this category are now written solid—for example, *a commonplace event, a freshwater pond, a widespread belief.*

Compound With Number or Letter

817 **a.** When a number and a noun form a one-thought modifier *before* a noun (as in *six-storey building*), make the noun singular and hyphenate the expression. When the expression has a normal form and a normal function *elsewhere in the sentence*, do not hyphenate it.

(Continued on page 208.)

Before the Noun	Elsewhere in Sentence
a *one-way* street	a street that runs only *one way*
a *first-person* account	an account written in the *first person*
a *two-piece* suit	a suit consisting of *two pieces*
a *four-colour* illustration	an illustration printed in *four colours*
a *5-litre* container	a container that holds *5 litres*
an *8-foot* ceiling	a ceiling *8 feet* above the floor
a *20-year* mortgage	a mortgage running for *20 years*
an *$85-a-month* charge	a charge of *$85 a month*
a *100-metre* sprint	a sprint of *100 metres*
an *$8\frac{1}{2}$- by 11-inch* book (see ¶832)	a book *$8\frac{1}{2}$ by 11 inches*
an *80-kilometre-an-hour* speed limit	a speed limit of *80 kilometres an hour*
a *5-centimetre-thick* panel	a panel *5 centimetres thick*
24-hour-a-day service	service *24 hours a day*
600-dpi graphics	graphics composed of *600 dpi* (dots per inch)

EXCEPTIONS: a *15 percent* decline, a *$4 million* profit, a *twofold* increase (**BUT:** a *12-fold* increase).

☞ *For the hyphenation of fractional expressions serving as compound adjectives (like* half-dozen *or* 1/4-inch*), see* ¶427a.

b. A hyphenated compound adjective and an unhyphenated possessive expression often provide *alternative* ways of expressing the same thought. Do not use both styles together.

a *one-year* extension	a *two-week* vacation
OR: a *one year's* extension	**OR:** a *two weeks'* vacation
(**NOT:** a one-year's extension)	(**NOT:** a two-weeks' vacation)

c. Hyphenate compound adjectives involving a number and *odd* or *plus*.

The work cost me *500-odd* dollars.   I now give my age as *forty-plus* years.

d. Some compound expressions involving letters and numbers are expressed as follows:

the cost of *Class A* materials	in *A-one (A1)* condition
a call for blood group *AB*	a *B+* student
a *number-one (No. 1)* priority	a *1000-to-1* possibility
20/20 (**OR** *twenty-twenty*) vision	a *5-4* victory over the Canucks

☞ *See also* ¶¶450–451.

Compound With Noun

818 a. A number of adjective-noun combinations (such as *real estate* or *social studies*) and noun-noun combinations (such as *life insurance* or *money market*) are well-established compound nouns serving as adjectives. Unlike the examples in ¶816, these expressions refer to well-known concepts or institutions. Because they are easily grasped as a unit, they *do not* require a hyphen.

animal health controls	*fire insurance* premium	*money order* payment
branch factory reports	*hockey team* sponsor	*pension plan* annuity
brand name product	*human resources* officer	*retail store* merchant
consumer price index	*legal aid* proceedings	*second language* classes

EXCEPTION: a *mail-order* catalogue

b. When dictionaries do not list specific adjective-noun or noun-noun combinations, the decision to hyphenate or not will depend first on how familiar you think your reader is with the term in question; and second, on whether the expression is like a well-known compound, such as *real estate*, or whether it is more like *short-term*.

c. When a noun-noun combination involves two words of relatively equal rank, hyphenate the combination. (See also ¶¶295, 806.)

input-output device	the *space-time* continuum	an *air-sea* search
cost-benefit analyses	*labour-management* relations	a *sand-gravel* mixture

d. A compound like *French Canadian* is hyphenated when it is an adjective. (See ¶348 note.)

Proper Name

819 a. Do not hyphenate the elements in a proper name used as an adjective.

Parliament Hill landscape	*Deerfoot Trail* freeway
Canadian Idol contestants	*Celine Dion* perfumes

b. When two or more distinct names are combined to form a one-thought modifier, use a hyphen to connect the elements.

a *German-Canadian* restaurant	the cuisine is *German-Canadian*
the *Thunder Bay-Montreal-Quebec City* flight (no hyphens within *Thunder Bay* and *Quebec City*)	**BUT:** the flight to *Thunder Bay, Montreal,* and *Quebec City*
the *Borden-Carleton* span of the Confederation Bridge	

NOTE: If one of the elements already contains a hyphen, use an en dash to connect the two names.

Banff-Lake Louise–Jasper roadway   the *Ottawa–Whitby-Toronto* trip by rail

Noun + Adjective

820 a. Always hyphenate a compound adjective that consists of a noun followed by an adjective, regardless of whether it appears before or after the noun. (See ¶815b.)

(Continued on page 210.)

age-old	gender-neutral	road-weary	value-free
bone-dry	letter-perfect	rock-bottom	wafer-thin
cost-effective	pitch-black	snow-blind	weather-bound
fuel-efficient	reader-friendly	tone-deaf	year-long

Their inventory is absolutely *knee-deep* in *brand-new* cars.

These *soil-resistant* fabrics were imported *duty-free*.

The mall is *top-heavy* with executives who like *sky-high* prices.

b. Retain the hyphen in a noun + adjective combination when the expression functions as an adverb rather than as an adjective.

ADJECTIVE: Please call me on my *toll-free* number.
ADVERB: You can always call me *toll-free*.

ADJECTIVE: The information is encoded on *paper-thin* wafers.
ADVERB: The wafers have to be sliced *paper-thin*.

c. A few words in this category are now written solid. For example:

-proof   bulletproof, burglarproof, childproof, fireproof, leakproof, rain-proof, shatterproof, shockproof, waterproof, weatherproof

-sick   airsick, carsick, heartsick, homesick, lovesick

-wide   countrywide, nationwide, storewide, worldwide   **BUT:** city-wide

Noun + Participle

821 a. When a compound adjective consists of a noun plus a participle, hyphenate this combination whether it appears before or after the noun. (See ¶815b.)

blood-curdling	job-oriented	market-driven	tail-gating
decision-making	law-breaking	mind-blowing	time-saving
eye-opening	life-giving	smoke-filled	tongue-tied
home-cooked	load-bearing	snow-packed	Windows-based

Their *eye-catching* designs have now been *market-tested*.

Creating *attention-getting* letterheads is very *time-consuming*.

This *number-crunching* software uses *eye-popping* graphics.

b. When an open compound noun is combined with a participle to form a one-thought modifier, insert a hyphen only before the participle. For greater clarity use an en dash instead of a hyphen, as shown in the second column.

Giller Prize-winning book   *property tax–raising* concerns
high school-testing program   *senior citizens–retiring* packages
Saint John-based industry   *Wayne Gretzky–sponsored* game

Adjective + Participle (see also ¶824b)

822 a. When a compound adjective consists of an adjective plus a participle, hyphenate this combination whether it appears before or after the noun. (See ¶815b.)

clean-cut	high-ranking	ready-made
friendly-looking (see ¶824a)	long-standing	rough-hewn
hard-hitting	odd-sounding	sweet-smelling

EXCEPTIONS: *easygoing, hardworking*

I'm *half-tempted* to apply for the Singapore opening myself.

He is a *smooth-talking* operator who never delivers what he promises.

Betty was anything but *soft-spoken* in arguing against the new procedures.

b. Retain the hyphen even when a comparative or superlative adjective is combined with a participle—for example, *nicer-looking, best-looking, oddest-sounding, better-tasting.*

As the *highest-ranking* official present, Mrs. Egan took charge of the meeting.

This year's brochure is *better-looking* than last year's.

Why can't we attract the *best-qualified* people to our company?

Adjective + Noun + *ED*

823 a. When a compound adjective consists of an adjective plus a noun plus *ed,* hyphenate this combination whether it appears before or after the noun. (See ¶815b.)

bare-headed	good-natured	public-spirited
broad-based	hard-wired	quick-witted
deep-rooted	light-fingered	right-angled
double-sided	long-sleeved	sharp-eyed
empty-handed	loose-limbed	short-staffed
fair-minded	low-pitched	slow-footed
far-sighted	one-sided	smooth-faced
full-featured	open-ended	weak-kneed

His *good-humoured* interview can be seen on *closed-captioned* television.

Loose-limbed athletes are generally *quick-footed.*

This season our *full-fashioned* dresses will show the *long-waisted styles.*

b. Retain the hyphen in comparative or superlative forms—for example, *smaller-sized, highest-priced, best-natured.*

Our *higher-priced* articles sold well this year.
These goods are *higher-priced* than the samples you showed me.

Fred is the *longest-winded* speaker I ever heard.
Fred's speech was the *longest-winded* I ever heard.

c. Compound adjectives ending in *sized* (such as *pint-sized, pocket-sized, life-sized,* and *king-sized*) may also be written without the final *d.*

It was a *full-size (full-sized)* TV screen.
A *king-size (king-sized)* bed is about 200 cm long.

Adverb + Participle

824 **a.** Do not hyphenate an adverb-participle combination if the adverb ends in *ly*.

a *poorly constructed* house   a *wholly owned* corporation
a *highly valued* employee   a *newly formed* division
a *clearly defined* set of terms   an *extremely tiring* trip

NOTE: Unlike the adverb combination, the adjective ending in *ly* plus a participle is *hyphenated* and is easily distinguished from the adverb form because only the adjective makes sense when it stands alone with the noun. For example,

a *friendly-sounding* voice   is   a *friendly* voice
a *motherly-looking* lady   is   a *motherly* lady
a *poorly constructed* house   is not a *poorly* house

☞ *To distinguish between adjectives and adverbs ending in* ly, *see also* ¶1069.

b. Other adverb-participle compounds are hyphenated *before* a noun. When these same combinations occur in the predicate, drop the hyphen if the participle is part of the verb.

Before the Noun	Elsewhere in Sentence
a *well-known* consultant	This consultant *is* well *known*.
much-needed reforms	These reforms *were* much *needed*.
the *above-mentioned* facts	These facts *were mentioned* above.
a *long-remembered* tribute	Today's tribute *will be* long *remembered*.

However, if the participle does not become part of the verb and continues to function with the adverb as a one-thought modifier in the predicate, retain the hyphen.

Before the Noun	Elsewhere in Sentence
a *well-behaved* child	The child is *well-behaved*.
a *clear-cut* position	Their position was *clear-cut*.
a *well-intentioned* proposal	The proposal was *well-intentioned*.

NOTE: You couldn't say, "The child is behaved" or "Their position was cut" or "The proposal was intentioned." Since the participle is not part of the verb, it must be treated as part of a compound adjective. Compare the use of *fast-moving* in the following examples.

Before the Noun	Elsewhere in Sentence
a *fast-moving* narrative	The narrative is *fast-moving*.
	BUT: The narrative *is* fast *moving* toward a climax.

c. Hyphenated adverb-participle combinations like those in *b* retain the hyphen even when the adverb is in the comparative or superlative.

a *better-known* brand   the *hardest-working* assistant
the *best-behaved* child   a *faster-moving* stock clerk

Adverb + Adjective

825 **a.** A number of adverb-adjective combinations closely resemble the adverb-participle combinations described in ¶824. However, since an adverb normally modifies an adjective, do not use a hyphen to connect these words.

a *not too interesting* book   a *very moving* experience
a *rather irritating* noise   a *quite trying* day

NOTE: In these examples you can omit the adverb and speak of an *interesting* book, a *moving* experience, and a *trying* day; hence no hyphen is needed. However, in the second set of examples in ¶824b, you cannot speak of a *behaved* child or an *intentioned* proposal; for that reason, the adverb preceding *behaved* and *intentioned* must be linked by a hyphen.

b. Do not hyphenate comparative and superlative forms where the adverbs *more, most, less,* and *least* are combined with an adjective.

a *more determined* person   a *less complicated* transaction
the *most exciting* event   the *least interesting* lecture

Participle + Adverb

826 Hyphenate a participle-adverb combination *before* a noun but not when it occurs elsewhere in the sentence.

Before the Noun	Elsewhere in Sentence
a *cooling-off* period	Don't debate without *cooling off* first.
a *lived-in* appearance	The room appeared to have been *lived in.*
a *souped-up* engine	His motorcycle engine was *souped up.*
unheard-of bargains	These bargains were *unheard of.*
warmed-over ideas	His ideas were *warmed over* for the occasion.

☞ *See also the examples in ¶831.*

Adjective + Adjective

827 **a.** Do not hyphenate independent adjectives preceding a noun.

a *long* and *tiring* trip (*long* and *tiring* each modify *trip*)

a *warm, enthusiastic* reception (*warm* and *enthusiastic* each modify *reception;* a comma marks the omission of *and*)

a *distinguished public* orator (*public* modifies *orator; distinguished* modifies *public orator*)

☞ *For the use of commas with adjectives, see ¶¶168–171.*

b. In a few special cases, two adjectives joined by *and* are hyphenated because they function as one-thought modifiers. These, however, are rare exceptions to the rule stated in *a.*

a *cut-and-dried* answer   an *out-and-out* lie
an *in-and-out* operation   *rough-and-tumble* hijinks

(Continued on page 214.)

an *open-and-shut* case   an *up-and-coming* executive

Henry views the matter in overly simple or *black-and-white* terms. (A one-thought modifier.)

BUT: Why not pack your *black and white* dress? (Two independent adjectives.)

c. Hyphenate two adjectives that express the dual nature of the thing that they refer to. (See also ¶¶295b, 806.)

a *true-false* test   a *compound-complex* sentence
the *top-down* stages   **BUT:** a *bittersweet* ending

d. Hyphenate expressions such as *blue-black, green-grey, snow-white,* and *red-hot* before and after a noun. However, do not hyphenate expressions such as *bluish green, dark grey,* or *bright red* (where the first word clearly modifies the second).

The suit was a *greyish black.*   *Shocking-pink* is the rage this season.

Verb + Verb

828 a. Hyphenate a compound adjective consisting of two verbs (sometimes joined by *and* or *or*) when the adjective appears *before* a noun.

hunt-and-peck method   a *touch-and-go* situation
show-and-tell presentation   a *wait-and-see* attitude

b. Do not hyphenate these elements when they play a normal function *elsewhere in the sentence.* However, retain the hyphen if these expressions continue to function as a compound adjective.

They're never sure whether they'll *hit or miss* their marketing targets.

BUT: Their marketing strategy can best be described as *hit-or-miss.*

Verb + Adverb

829 a. Hyphenate a compound adjective consisting of a verb plus an adverb when the adjective appears *before* the noun.

our *break-even* point   a *run-on* sentence
a *drive-through* window   a *sit-down* dinner
a *live-in* nanny   a *walk-in* closet
a *pop-up* menu   a *zip-out* lining

b. Do not hyphenate these elements when they play a normal function *elsewhere in the sentence.*

At what point will we *break even?*   Does this lining *zip out?*

Verb + Noun

830 a. Hyphenate a compound adjective consisting of a verb plus a noun (or pronoun) when the adjective appears *before* the noun.

take-home pay	*make-work* programs
a *take-charge* kind of person	**BUT:** a *turnkey* computer system
a *thank-you* note	a *lacklustre* approach

b. Do not hyphenate these elements when they serve a normal function *elsewhere in the sentence*.

How much money do you *take home* each week?

Betsy is inclined to *take charge* of any situation.

Phrasal Compound

831 a. Hyphenate phrases used as compound adjectives *before* a noun. Do not hyphenate such phrases when they occur normally elsewhere in the sentence.

Before the Noun	Elsewhere in Sentence
down-to-earth projections	These projections appear to be *down to earth*.
on-the-job training	I got my training *on the job*.
a *well-thought-out* plan	Our plan was *well thought out*.
an *in-depth* analysis	Carpentier has analyzed the subject *in depth*.
an *out-of-the-way* location	Why is the shopping mall so far *out of the way*?
over-the-counter stocks	These stocks are sold only *over the counter*.
an *above-average* rating	Our unit's performance was rated *above average*.
below-the-line charges	These charges will show up *below the line*.
middle-of-the-road view	His view is not far from the *middle of the road*.
before-tax earnings	What were our earnings *before taxes*?
after-dinner speeches	Speeches *after dinner* ought to be prohibited.
around-the-clock service	We provide order service *around the clock*.
across-the-board cuts	The CEO wants budget cuts *across the board*.
behind-the-scenes talks	Contract talks are going on *behind the scenes*.
a *state-of-the-art* model	This model reflects the current *state of the art*.
a *change-of-address* form	Please show your *change of address*.
a *matter-of-fact* approach	Jan accepted the situation as a *matter of fact*.
made-to-order wall units	These wall units were *made to order*.
a *pay-as-you-go* tax plan	The new tax plan requires you to *pay as you go*.
a *would-be* expert	Roy hoped he *would be* accepted as an expert.
bumper-to-bumper traffic	The traffic stood *bumper to bumper*.
a *case-by-case* analysis	We must resolve these problems *case by case*.
a *by-invitation-only* seminar	Attendance at the seminar is *by invitation only*.
a *$150 000-a-year* fee	Our legal fees run about *$150 000 a year*.
a *nine-year-old* girl	Michelle is only *nine years old*.
BUT: a *$9\frac{1}{2}$-year-old* girl	Michelle is only *$9\frac{1}{2}$ years old*. (See ¶428a.)
(**NOT:** a nine-and-a-half-year-old girl)	

b. When two nouns joined by *and* or *to* are used as a compound adjective before a noun, hyphenate the phrase.

(Continued on page 216.)

back-to-back classes	*face-to-face* meeting
cat-and-mouse relationship	*foot-and-mouth* disease
day-to-day arrangement	*horse-and-buggy* days
eye-to-eye confrontation	*trial-and-error* approach

c. As a rule, do not hyphenate a foreign phrase used as an adjective before a noun. (See also ¶285d.)

an *ad hoc* committee	an *ex officio* member
an *à la carte* menu	a *pro rata* assessment
a *bona fide* transaction	a *per diem* fee

EXCEPTIONS: an *ad-lib* speech, a *laissez-faire* economic policy

d. When a compound modifier consists of two or more hyphenated phrases, separate the phrases with a comma.

a *first-come, first-served* policy	an *on-again, off-again* engagement
a *knock-down, drag-out* brawl	a *penny-wise, pound-foolish* spender

e. Hyphenate repeated or rhyming words used before a noun.

a *go-go* attitude	a *teeny-weeny* salary increase
a *hush-hush* plan	a *topsy-turvy* world

Suspending Hyphen

832 a. When a series of hyphenated adjectives has a common basic element and it is shown only with the last term, insert a suspending hyphen after each of the incomplete adjectives to indicate a relationship with the last term.

long- and short-term securities	*10- and 20-year* bonds
private- and public-sector partnerships	a *three- or four-colour* cover
single-, double-, or triple-spaced copy	*open- and closed-door* sessions

b. Use one space after each suspending hyphen unless a comma is required at that point.

a *six- to eight-week* delay	*3-, 5-, and 8-litre* buckets
a *10- to 12-hour* trip	*6-, 12-, and 24-month* terms

c. When two or more solid compound adjectives with a common element are used together (for example, *lightweight* and *heavyweight*) and the common element is shown only with the last term, use a suspending hyphen with the incomplete forms to indicate a relationship with the common element.

This product is available in *light-* and *heavyweight* versions.

Please provide *day-* and *nighttime* phone numbers.

NOTE: Repeat the common element with each word if the suspending hyphen looks odd or confusing; for example, *boyfriend or girlfriend* (rather than *boy- or girlfriend*).

☞ *See ¶833d–e for the use of a suspending hyphen with prefixes or suffixes.*

PREFIXES AND SUFFIXES

833 **a.** In general, do not use a hyphen to set off a prefix at the beginning of a word or a suffix at the end of a word. (See ¶808c for two exceptions: *ex-* and *-elect.*)

*after*taste	*multi*processing	book*let*
*ambi*dextrous	*off*beat	censor*ship*
*ante*date	*para*medical	change*able*
*anti*trust (see ¶834)	*poly*syllabic	child*like*
*audio*visual	*post*date	convert*ible*
*by*line	*pre*requisite	edge*wise*
*circum*locution	*pro*active	fifty*ish*
*counter*balance	*re*organize	fire*proof*
*de*centralize	*retro*active	free*dom*
*dis*appear	*sub*division	friend*ly*
*extra*marital	*super*natural	hand*some*
*fore*front	*supra*national	happi*ness*
*hyper*sensitive	*trans*continental	home*stead*
*il*legal	*ultra*sonic	induce*ment*
*im*material	*un*accustomed	meaning*ful*
*in*defensible	*under*current	misspell*ing*
*infra*structure	*up*shot	mono*gram*
*inter*provincial	**BUT:** *co*-author (see ¶835)	patron*age*
*intro*version	*de*-icer	photo*graph*
*micro*processor	*non*-essential	thank*less*
*mid*stream	*post*-operative	trust*worthy*
*mini*bus	*semi*-annual	upper*most*
*mis*spell	back*ward*	world*wide*
*mono*syllable		

b. Whenever necessary, use a hyphen to prevent one word from being mistaken for another. (See ¶837.)

lock the *coop*	*multiply* by 12	a *unionized* factory
join a *co-op*	a *multi-ply* fabric	an *un-ionized* substance

c. As a rule, when adding a prefix to a hyphenated or spaced compound word, use a hyphen after the prefix.

pre-high school texts	*non*-interest-bearing notes
post-bread-winning years	*non*-computer-literate adults
ex-attorney general	*non*-civil service position

EXCEPTIONS: unair-conditioned, unself-conscious

d. When two or more prefixes have a common element and this element is shown only with the final prefix, insert a suspending hyphen after each of the unattached prefixes to indicate a relationship with the common element.

pre- and *post*natal care	*maxi-, midi-,* and *mini*skirts
up- and *down*hill slopes	*inter-* and *intra*office networks
mono- and *duo*poly markets	*over-* and *under*qualified job applicants

(Continued on page 218.)

e. When two or more suffixes have a common element, it is possible to leave one of the suffixes unattached and insert a suspending hyphen to indicate the relationship with the common element. To avoid confusion or awkwardness, it is usually better to repeat the common element with each suffix.

AWKWARD: I thought Nancy's reaction was more *thoughtless* than *-ful.*
BETTER: I thought Nancy's reaction was more *thoughtless* than *thoughtful.*

AWKWARD: I would characterize his behaviour as *childlike* rather than *-ish.*
BETTER: I would characterize his behaviour as *childlike* rather than *childish.*

834 When the prefix ends with *a* or *i* and the base word begins with a vowel, use a hyphen after the prefix to prevent misreading.

anti-aircraft	intra-abdominal	semi-annual
anti-inflammatory	ultra-ambitious	semi-independent

835 **a.** When the prefix ends with *e* and the base word begins with *e,* the hyphen is usually added.

de-emphasize	pre-empt	re-educate	re-entry
de-escalate	pre-echo	re-elect	re-establish
pre-eminent	pre-existing	re-enact	re-examine

b. In most cases a hyphen follows *co.*

co-author	co-operate	**BUT:** coed	coexist
co-chair	co-pilot	coeducation	cohabit
co-edit	co-worker	coefficient	coordinate

836 **a.** Use a hyphen after *self* when it serves as a prefix.

self-addressed	self-evident	self-pity	self-supporting
self-confidence	self-help	self-serving	self-taught
self-educated	self-image	self-starter	self-worth

b. Omit the hyphen when *self* serves as the base word and is followed by a suffix.

selfish	selfhood	selfless	selfsame

837 As a rule, the prefix *re* (meaning "again") should not be followed by a hyphen. A few words require the hyphen so that they can be distinguished from other words with the same spelling but a different meaning.

to *re-collect* the slips	to *recollect* the mistake
to *re-cover* a chair	to *recover* from an illness
to *re-form* the class	to *reform* a sinner
she *re-marked* the ticket	as he *remarked* to me
to *re-press* the jacket	to *repress* one's emotions
to *re-sort* the cards	to *resort* to persuasion
to *re-sign* the contracts	to *resign* the position
to *re-treat* the cloth	to *retreat* to safer ground
a *re-creation* of the original sketches	a *recreation* program for employees

8

838 When a prefix is added to a word that begins with a capital, use a hyphen after the prefix.

anti-American mid-January non-Windows application
non-Asiatic trans-Canadian post-Second World War period

BUT: transatlantic, transpacific, the Midwest

839 Always hyphenate family terms involving the prefix *great* or the suffix *in-law*, but treat terms involving *step* and *grand* solid.

my great-grandfather my grandmother your brother-in-law
their great-aunt his grandchild my stepdaughter

840 Avoid feminine suffixes like *ess, ette,* and *trix.*

She has an established reputation as an *author* and a *poet.* (**NOT:** *authoress* and *poetess.*)

If you have any questions, ask your *flight attendant.* (**NOT:** *steward* or *stewardess.*)

NOTE: A few terms with feminine suffixes are still widely used; for example, *hostess, heroine, waitress,* and *fiancée.* In legal documents, the terms *executrix* and *testatrix* are increasingly being replaced by *executor* and *testator.*

841 Use a hyphen after *quasi* when an adjective follows.

quasi-independent **BUT:** quasi democracy
quasi-scientific quasi corporation

842 When *after* is used as a prefix, do not use a hyphen to set if off from the root word; but when *after* is used as a preposition in a compound adjective, insert a hyphen.

aftereffect aftershock **BUT:** an after-dinner speech
afterglow afterthought my after-tax income

843 When *in* is used as a prefix meaning "not," do not use a hyphen to set if off from the root word; but when it is a preposition in a compound adjective, insert a hyphen.

inaccessible incorrect **BUT:** an in-depth analysis
inappropriate infamous an in-house program

844 A hyphen normally follows *mid* in expressions involving numbers (see ¶439a) or capitalized words (see ¶838). When *mid* is used as a prefix, a hyphen is not ordinarily used.

the mid-'60s mid-sixties **BUT:** at midnight
mid-Atlantic mid-June a midway point

845 Words beginning with the prefix *off* are written solid or hyphenated.

offbeat offshoot **BUT:** off-centre
offhand offshore off-duty

846 If the addition of the suffix *less* or *like* causes three *l*'s to occur in succession, insert a hyphen before the suffix. (See also ¶706 note.)

shell-less   bell-like   hill-like

COMPOUND COMPUTER TERMS

847 The rapid growth of computer technology with its related compound terms presents a problem in establishing a hard-and-fast style that will last. At any given time a particular word may be in a state of unsettled transition and may appear hyphenated, spaced, and solid. The general trend is for hyphenated forms to give way to either spaced or solid forms and for the spaced forms to give way to solid forms.

Dictionaries show the more conservative spellings because they cannot keep pace with all the changes. However, a variety of reference sources, such as technology magazines, manuals, and style guides, provide updated versions of terms. One resource Web site, *dictionary.com*, compiles words from many recent publications. The following transitional computer terms are from that Web site, and the conservative terms were found in *The Canadian Oxford Dictionary.*

Transitional	Conservative	Transitional	Conservative
email	E-mail, e-mail	logout	log out, log-out
filename	file name	online	on-line
login	log in, log-in	wordwrap	word wrap
logoff	log off, log-off	website	Web site

☞ *Hyphens in spelled-out numbers: see ¶465.*
Hyphens in spelled-out dates: see ¶411.
Hyphens in spelled-out amounts of money: see ¶420.
Hyphens in spelled-out fractions: see ¶427.
Hyphens in numbers representing a continuous sequence: see ¶¶459–460.

See the Online Learning Centre at www.mcgrawhill.ca/college/gregg for related Web links.

SECTION NINE

Word Division

BASIC RULES (¶¶901–906)

PREFERRED PRACTICES (¶¶907–918)

BREAKS WITHIN WORD GROUPS (¶¶919–920)

GUIDES TO CORRECT SYLLABICATION (¶¶921–922)

A feature of word processing programs is automatic hyphenation. When turned on it will divide a word at the end of a line with a *soft hyphen* (a non-permanent hyphen). If the text changes and the divided word no longer falls at the end of a line, the soft hyphen will disappear. If you are typing an expression (such as a compound word) in which a hyphen must always appear, use a *regular hyphen*. When this expression crosses the end of a line, it will be divided after the hyphen. If you are typing a hyphenated expression (such as a telephone number) that should not be divided at the end of a line, use a *non-breaking hyphen*. In that way the complete expression will remain on the same line.

Automated hyphenation is best used after a document has been edited, when the non-breaking hyphen may be applied. However, in rare documents it is possible that all the features could be used, especially if a ragged right margin is particularly unattractive. If this is the case, always review the electronic word-division decisions and adjust if necessary.

It may be that the electronic dictionary disagrees with the authority for word divisions shown in this manual. Indeed, some of the word divisions may break the "unbreakable" rules in ¶¶901–906. The rules that should be followed whenever space permits a choice are given in ¶¶907–920.

NOTE: Professional typesetters often take liberties with rules of word division in order to fit copy within a limited amount of space.

BASIC RULES

901 Divide words only between syllables. Whenever you are unsure of the syllabication of a word, consult a dictionary. (See also ¶¶921–922 for some guides to correct syllabication.)

in-dividual   **OR** indi-vidual   **OR** individ-ual   **OR** individu-al

NOTE: Some syllable breaks shown in the dictionary are not acceptable as points of word division.

902 Do not divide one-syllable words. Even when *ed* is added to some words, they still remain one-syllable words and cannot be divided.

stressed	through	spring	strength
planned	thoughts	straight	breathe

903 Do not divide five-letter words. When dividing words of six letters or more, there must be a minimum of three characters, including the hyphen, at the beginning or at the end of a line.

ad- here	de- pend	un- even	in- cise
do- cile	re- turn	set- up,	happi- ly.

904 When keying a word like *e-business* or *e-commerce*, use a hard (non-breaking) hyphen to ensure that the word will remain as a single unit.

905 Do not divide abbreviations or acronyms.

Assoc.	abbrev.	UNESCO	UNICEF

NOTE: An abbreviation like *AFL-CIO* may be divided after the hyphen.

906 Do not divide contractions.

haven't	shouldn't	mustn't	doesn't

PREFERRED PRACTICES

It is often better to divide words at some points than at others in order to obtain a more intelligible grouping of syllables. The following rules indicate preferred practices whenever you have enough space in the line.

907 Divide a solid compound word between the elements of the compound.

eye- witness	time- table	photo- copy	trust- worthy

908 Divide a hyphenated compound word at the point of the hyphen.

self- confidence	father- in-law	cross- reference	mayor- elect

909 Divide a word *after* a prefix (rather than within the prefix).

circum- stances (**RATHER THAN:** cir- cumstances)
intro- duce (**RATHER THAN:** in- troduce)
inter- national (**RATHER THAN:** in- ternational)
super- sonic (**RATHER THAN:** su- personic)

Use divisions such as the following:

> am- bitious (**RATHER THAN:** ambi- tious)
> co- incide (**RATHER THAN:** coin- cide)
> ex- traneous (**RATHER THAN:** extra- neous)
> hy- perbole (**RATHER THAN:** hyper- bole)

910 Divide a word *before* a suffix (rather than within the suffix).

> appli- cable (**RATHER THAN:** applica- ble)
> comprehen- sible (**RATHER THAN:** comprehensi- ble)

911 When a word has both a prefix and a suffix or a suffix added to a suffix, choose the division point that groups the syllables more intelligibly and produces a better grouping.

> replace- ment (**RATHER THAN:** re- placement)
> helpless- ness (**RATHER THAN:** help- lessness)

912 Whenever you have a choice, divide after a prefix or before a suffix (rather than within the root word).

> over- active (**RATHER THAN:** overac- tive)
> success- ful (**RATHER THAN:** suc- cessful)
> co- defendant (**RATHER THAN:** code- fendant)
> re- ality (**RATHER THAN:** real- ity)
> re- arrange (**RATHER THAN:** rear- range)
> re- instate (**RATHER THAN:** rein- state)

913 When a one-letter syllable occurs within the root of a word, divide *after* it (rather than before it).

> apolo- gize   congratu- late   impera- tive   reme- dies

914 When two separately sounded vowels come together in a word, divide between them.

> cha- otic   courte- ous   patri- otic   influ- ential
> recre- ation   medi- ation   po- etry   ingenu- ity
> spontane- ity   experi- ence   situ- ated   continu- ous

NOTE: Do not divide between two or more vowels when they are used together to represent one sound.

> main- tained   treas- urer   en- croaching   pa- tience
> ac- quaint   es- teemed   amoe- ba   lieu- tenant
> guess- ing   per- ceive   ap- point   con- scious
> acquit- tal   sur- geon   ty- coon   opin- ion
> mis- quoted   neu- tral   pro- nounce   ma- noeuvre

915 *When absolutely necessary*, an extremely long number could be divided after a space or comma; for example, *24 358- 692 000*. Try to leave at least four digits on the line above and at least six digits on the line below, but always divide after a space or comma.

916 Try not to end more than two consecutive lines in hyphens.

917 Try not to divide at the end of the first line or at the end of the last full line in a paragraph.

918 Do not divide the last word on a page.

BREAKS WITHIN WORD GROUPS

919 **a.** Try to keep word groups together if they need to be read together—for example, page and number, month and day, month and year, title and first name or surname, surname and abbreviation (or number), number and abbreviation, or number and unit of measure.

page 203	September 2007	Paula Schein, J.D.	10:30 a.m.
April 29	Mrs. Connolly	Adam Hagerty Jr.	465 km

b. For elements of a word group that should not be broken at the end of a line, insert a **non-breaking (hard) space** or hyphen, whichever suits the situation. This will force the entire word group to move to the next line.

. . . . when
Mrs. Jean Yuen arrives . . . .

NOT: . . . . when Mrs.
Jean Yuen arrives . . . .

. . . . Purchase Order
259-6693 . . . .

NOT: . . . . Purchase Order 259-
6693 . . . .

920 When necessary, longer word groups may be broken as follows:

a. *Dates* may be broken between the day and year.

. . . . November 14,
2007 . . . .

NOT: . . . . November
14, 2007 . . . .

b. *Street addresses* may be broken between the name of the street and *Street, Avenue,* or the like. If the street name consists of two or more words, the break may come between words in the street name.

. . . . 1024 Westmount
Boulevard . . . .

NOT: 1024
Westmount Boulevard . . . .

. . . . 617 North
Fullerton Street . . . .

NOT: 617
North Fullerton Street . . . .

c. *Names of places in text* may be broken between the city and the province or between the province and the postal code. If either name consists of two or more words, the break may come between these words.

. . . . Kingston,
Ontario K7L 4T5 . . . .

OR: . . . . Kingston, Ontario
K7L 4T5 . . . .

. . . . Sault Ste.
Marie, Ontario P6C 1Y3 . . . .

OR: . . . . Summerside, Prince
Edward Island C1N 4S3 . . . .

d. *Names of persons* may be broken between the given name (including middle initial if given) and surname.

.... Mildred R. **NOT:** .... Mildred
Palumbo .... R. Palumbo ....

NOTE: If it is absolutely necessary, a person's name may be divided. Follow the same principles given for dividing ordinary words.

Diefen- baker   Spil- lane (See ¶922b.)   Kach- marski

e. *Names preceded by long titles* may be broken between the title and the name (preferably) or between words in the title.

.... Assistant Commissioner **OR:** .... Assistant
Roy N. Frawley .... Commissioner Roy N. Frawley ..

f. A *numbered or lettered enumeration* may be broken before (but not directly after) any number or letter.

.... these points: **NOT:** .... these points: (1)
(1) All cards should .... All cards should ....

g. A *sentence with a dash in it* may be broken after the dash.

.... Early next year— **NOT:** .... Early next year
say, in March—let's .... —say, in March—let's ....

h. A *sentence with ellipsis marks in it* may be broken after the ellipsis marks.

Tennis . . . health spa . . . golf . . . **NOT:** Tennis . . . health spa . . . golf
and more . . . make this a world-class . . . and more . . . make this a
resort. world-class resort.

GUIDES TO CORRECT SYLLABICATION

921 Syllabication is generally based on pronunciation rather than on roots and derivations. Careful pronunciation will often aid you in determining the correct syllabication of a word.

knowl- edge (**NOT:** know- ledge)   prod- uct (**NOT:** pro- duct)
chil- dren (**NOT:** child- ren)   ser- vice (**NOT:** serv- ice)

Note how syllabication changes as pronunciation changes.

Verbs	Nouns
pre- sent (to make a gift)	pres- ent (a gift)
re- cord (to make an official copy)	rec- ord (an official copy)
pro- ject (to throw forward)	proj- ect (an undertaking)

922 The following paragraphs offer some guides to syllabication when double letters occur in words.

a. If a final consonant of the base word is doubled *because* a suffix is added, you can safely divide *between* the double consonants (so long as the suffix creates an extra syllable).

ship- ping   omit- ted   begin- ner   drum- ming
BUT: shipped, drummed (which are one-syllable words; see ¶902)

(Continued on page 226.)

b. When double consonants appear elsewhere *within* the base word (but not as the final consonants), you can safely divide between them.

bub- bling	strug- gle	recom- mend	cur- rent
suc- cess	mil- lion	sup- pose	neces- sary

 See the Online Learning Centre at www.mcgrawhill.ca/college/gregg for related Web links.

SECTION **TEN**

Grammar

¶1002

10

☞ *For definitions of grammatical terms, see Section 19.*

Section 10 provides guidelines on how to make your sentences not only grammatically correct but correct for any occasion. Consider the person who will read what you are writing, and think about the effect your writing will have on that reader. Consider whether a formal approach is needed or whether it should be something more colloquial. In short, aim for sentences that are not only correct but also right for the occasion.

SUBJECTS AND VERBS
Basic Rule of Agreement
1001 a. A verb must agree with its subject in number and person.

I am eager to get back to work. (First person singular subject *I* with first person singular verb *am*.)

It *seems* odd that Farmer *has not followed up* on our report. (Third person singular subjects it and Farmer with third person singular verbs *seems* and *has not followed up*.)

He is coming to stay with us for a week. (Third person singular subject he with third person singular verb *is coming*.)

She does intend to call you this week. (Third person singular subject she with third person singular verb *does intend*.)

We were delighted to read about your promotion. (First person plural subject we with first person plural verb *were*.)

They are convinced that the Foys *are* worth millions. (Third person plural subjects they and Foys with third person plural verbs *are convinced* and *are*.)

Your *order* for six laptop computers *was shipped* last Friday. (Third person singular subject *order* with third person singular verb *was shipped*.)

Our *efforts* to save the business *have been* unsuccessful. (Third person plural subject *efforts* with third person plural verb *have been*.)

NOTE: A plural verb is always required after *you*, even when *you* is singular, referring to only one person.

You alone *have understood* the full dimensions of the problem. (Second person singular subject *you* with second person plural verb *have understood*.)

You both *have been* a great help to us. (Second person plural subject *you* with second person plural verb *have been*.)

b. Although *s* or *es* added to a *noun* indicates the plural form, *s* or *es* added to a verb indicates the third person singular. (See ¶1035.)

Singular	Plural
The price *seems* reasonable.	The prices *seem* reasonable.
The tax *applies* to everyone.	The taxes *apply* to everyone.

Subjects Joined by *And*
1002 a. Use a plural verb when the subject consists of two or more words that are connected by *and* or by *both . . . and*.

Ms. Rizzo and *Mr. Huynh have received* promotions.

Both the *collection* and the *delivery* of mail *are* to be curtailed as of July 1. (The repetition of *the* with the second subject emphasizes that two different items are meant.)

The *general managers* and the *controllers are attending* a seminar today.

The *director of marketing* and the *product managers are reviewing* their budgets.

10

(Continued on page 230.)

b. Use a singular verb when two or more subjects connected by *and* refer to the same person or thing. (See also ¶1028a, fourth example.)

Our *secretary and treasurer is* Frances Kernaghan. (One person.)

Corned beef and cabbage was his favourite dish. (One dish.)

Wear and tear has to be expected when you are renting. (One type of damage.)

c. Use a singular verb when two or more subjects connected by *and* are preceded by *each, every, many a,* or *many an.* (See also ¶1009b.)

Every computer, printer, and fax machine *is marked* for reduction.

Many a woman and man *has responded* to our plea for contributions.

Subjects Joined by *Or* or Similar Connectives

1003 If the subject consists of two or more *singular* words that are connected by *or, either . . . or, neither . . . nor,* or *not only . . . but also,* the subject is singular and requires a singular verb.

Either *July* or *August is* a good time for the sales conference.

Neither the *Credit Department* nor the *Accounting Department has* the file.

Not only a cost-profit *analysis* but also a marketing *plan needs* to be developed.

1004 If the subject consists of two or more *plural* words that are connected by *or, either . . . or, neither . . . nor,* or *not only . . . but also,* the subject is plural and requires a plural verb.

Neither the regional *managers* nor the *salesclerks have* the data you want.

Not only the *dealers* but also the *retailers are* unhappy about our new policy.

1005 If the subject is made up of both singular and plural words connected by *or, either . . . or, neither . . . nor,* or *not only . . . but also,* the verb agrees with the nearer part of the subject. Since sentences with singular and plural subjects usually sound better with plural verbs, try to locate the plural subject close to the verb whenever this can be done without sacrificing the emphasis desired.

Either *Miss Huva* or her *assistants have* copies of the new catalogue. (The verb *have* agrees with the nearer subject, *assistants.*)

Neither the *buyers* nor the *sales manager is* in favour of the system. (The verb *is* agrees with the nearer subject, *sales manager.*)

BETTER: Neither the *sales manager* nor the *buyers are* in favour of the system. (The sentence reads better with the plural verb *are.* The subjects *sales manager* and *buyers* have been rearranged without changing the emphasis.)

Not only the *teachers* but also the *superintendent is* in favour of the plan. (The verb *is* agrees with the nearer subject, *superintendent.* With the use of *not only . . . but also,* the emphasis falls on the subject following *but also.*)

Not only the *superintendent* but also the *teachers are* in favour of the plan. (When the sentence is rearranged, the nearer subject, *teachers,* requires the plural verb *are.* However, the emphasis has now changed.)

Not only my *colleagues* but I *am* in favour of the plan. (The first person verb *am* agrees with the nearer subject, *I.* Rearranging this sentence will change the emphasis.)

NOTE: When the subject consists of different grammatical persons (first, second, or third), the verb should agree in person as well as number with the nearer subject. If the result seems awkward, reword as necessary.

> **ACCEPTABLE:** Neither you nor *I am* in a position to pay Ben's legal fees.
> **BETTER:** Neither *one* of us *is* in a position to pay Ben's legal fees. (See ¶1009a.)

> **ACCEPTABLE:** Neither you nor *she has* the time to take on the Fuller case.
> **ACCEPTABLE:** Neither she nor *you have* the time to take on the Fuller case.
> **BETTER:** *You are* both too busy to take on the Fuller case.

> **AWKWARD:** If you or Gary *is coming* to the convention, please visit our booth.
> **BETTER:** If Gary or you *are coming* to the convention, please visit our booth.

☞ *For neither . . . nor constructions following* there is, there are, there were, *or* there was, *see the last four examples in* ¶1028a.

For examples of subject-verb-pronoun agreement in these constructions, see ¶1049c.

Intervening Phrases and Clauses

1006 a. When establishing agreement between subject and verb, disregard intervening phrases, clauses, and appositives. (See ¶148.)

> The *purchase order* for new diskettes *has not been found.* (Disregard *for new diskettes. Purchase order* is the subject and takes the singular verb *has not been found.*)

> The *prices* shown in our catalogue *do not include* sales tax.

> Only *one* of the items that I ordered *has been delivered.* (See also ¶1008.)

> A key *factor*, the company's assets, *is not being given* sufficient weight.

> **BUT:** The company's *assets*, a key factor, *are not being given* sufficient weight.

b. When a sentence has both a positive and a negative subject, make the verb agree with the positive subject. Set off the negative subject with commas unless it is preceded by *and* or *but*.

> *Profit* and not sales *is* the thing to keep your eye on. (The verb *is* agrees with the positive subject *profit*.)

> The *design* of the container, not the contents, *determines* what the consumer's initial reaction to the product will be.

> *It is* not the president but the *members* of the Executive Committee who *wield* the real power in the corporation. (In the main clause, the verb *is* agrees with the subject *it*; the verb *wield* in the *who* clause is plural to agree with the antecedent of *who*, the positive subject *members*. See ¶1062c.)

> **BUT:** It is the *president* and not the members of the Executive Committee who *wields* the real power in the corporation. (In this sentence the positive subject is *president*, a singular noun; therefore, the verb *wields* in the *who* clause must also be singular.)

1007 The number of the verb is not affected by the insertion between subject and verb of phrases with such expressions as:

along with	as well as	plus	except
together with	in addition to	besides	rather than
and not (see ¶1006b)	accompanied by	including	not even

(Continued on page 232.)

If the subject is singular, use a singular verb; if the subject is plural, use a plural verb.

> Mrs. *Swenson*, together with her husband and daughter, *is going* to Quebec.
>
> This *study*, along with many earlier reports, *shows* that the disease can be arrested.
>
> *No one*, not even the vice-president, *knows* when the CEO plans to resign. (See ¶1010.)
>
> The *divisional controllers*, not the director of finance, *are authorized* to approve unbudgeted expenditures over $500. (See ¶1006b.)

NOTE: When the construction of a sentence like those above requires a singular verb but a plural verb would sound more natural, reword the sentence to create a plural subject.

> **CORRECT:** The national sales *report*, as well as the regional breakdowns you requested plus the individual printouts, *was sent* to you last week.
>
> **BETTER:** The national sales *report*, the regional *breakdowns* you requested, and the individual *printouts were sent* to you last week. (The three subjects joined by *and*—*report*, *breakdowns*, and *printouts*—call for a plural verb.)

One of . . .

1008 a. Use a singular verb after a phrase beginning with *one of* or *one of the;* the singular verb agrees with the subject *one*. (Disregard any plural that follows *of* or *of the*.)

> *One* of my backup disks *has been lost*.
>
> *One* of the reasons for so many absences *is* poor motivation.
>
> *One* of us *has* to take over the responsibility for in-service training.
>
> *One* of you *is* to be nominated for the office.

b. Use a plural verb after the phrases *one of those who* and *one of the things that* because the verbs refer to *those* or *things* (rather than to *one*).

> She is one of *those* who *favour* increasing the staff. (In other words, of *those* who *favour* increasing the staff, she is one. Favour is plural to agree with *those*.)
>
> He is one of our *employees* who *are* never late. (Of our *employees* who *are* never late, he is one.)
>
> I ordered one of the new *copiers* that *were advertised* in Monday's paper. (Of the new *copiers* that *were advertised* in Monday's paper, I ordered one.)
>
> You are one of *those* rare individuals who *are* always honest with *themselves*. (Of those rare *individuals* who *are* always honest with *themselves*, you are one.)

EXCEPTION: When the words *the only* precede such phrases, the meaning is singular and a singular verb is required. Note that both words, *the* and *only*, are required to produce a singular meaning.

> John is *the only one* of the staff members who *is going* to be transferred. (Of the staff members, John is *the only one* who *is going* to be transferred. Here the singular verb *is going* is required to agree with *one*.)
>
> **BUT:** John is only one of the *staff members* who *are going* to be transferred. (Of the *staff members* who *are going* to be transferred, John is only one.)

Indefinite Pronouns That Are Always Singular

1009 a. The following words, when used as subjects or as adjectives modifying subjects, are **singular** and require singular verbs.

each   every   either   neither   one   another   much

Neither one of the applicants *is* eligible.   **OR** *Neither* applicant *is* eligible.

Much work *remains* to be done.   **OR** *Much remains* to be done.

Each has a clear-cut set of responsibilities.

Every employee *is* responsible for maintaining an orderly workstation.

One shipment *has* already gone out; *another is* to leave the warehouse tomorrow.

☞ *For the use of* either . . . or *and* neither . . . nor, *see* ¶¶*1003–1005.*

b. When *each, every, many a,* or *many an* precedes two or more subjects joined by *and,* the verb should be singular.

Every customer *and* supplier *has been notified.*

☞ *See* ¶1002c *for other examples.*

c. When *each* follows a plural subject, make the verb plural. In that position, *each* has no effect on the number of the verb. To test the correctness of such sentences, mentally omit *each.*

The *members* each *feel* their responsibility.

They each *have* high expectations.

1010 The following compound pronouns are always singular and require a singular verb:

anybody	everybody	somebody	nobody
anything	everything	something	nothing
anyone	everyone	someone	no one
OR any one	**OR** every one	**OR** some one	

Everyone is required to register in order to vote.

Something tells me I'm wrong.

NOTE: Spell *anyone, everyone,* and *someone* as two words when these pronouns are followed by an *of* phrase or are used to mean "one of a number of things."

Every one of us (each person in the group) *likes* to be appreciated.

BUT: *Everyone* (everybody) *likes* to be appreciated.

1011 Use a singular verb when two compound pronouns joined by *and* are used as subjects.

Anyone and *everyone is entitled* to a fair hearing.

Nobody and *nothing is going* to stop me.

Indefinite Pronouns That Are Always Plural

1012 The following words, when used as subjects or as adjectives modifying subjects, are **plural** and require plural verbs.

(Continued on page 234.)

10

both   few   many   others   several

Several members *were invited;* the *others were overlooked.*

Both books *are* out of print.

Many were asked, but *few were* able to answer.

Indefinite Pronouns That Are Singular or Plural

1013 a. The following words may be singular or plural, depending on the noun they refer to. (The noun often occurs in an *of* phrase that follows.)

all   any   more   most   none   some

All the manuscript *has been printed.*   *All* the books *have been printed.*

Is there *any* (money) left?   *Are* there *any* (bills) to be paid?

Most of the stock *has been sold.*   *More* of these stands *are* due.

Some of the software *was* acceptable.   *Some* of the tapes *were* acceptable.

Some was acceptable. (Meaning some of the software.)
Some were acceptable. (Meaning some of the tapes.)

Do any of you *know* Mas Fukumoto well? (*Any* is plural because it refers to the plural *you;* hence the plural verb *do know.*)
Does any one of you *know* Mas Fukumoto well? (*Any* is singular because it refers to the singular *one;* hence the singular verb *does know.*)

b. In formal usage, *none* is still considered a singular pronoun. In general usage, however, *none* is considered either singular or plural, depending on the number of the noun to which it refers. *No one* or *not one* is often used in place of *none* to stress the singular idea.

None of the merchandise *was stolen.*

None of the packages *were* properly *wrapped.*

None were injured. (Meaning none of the passengers.)

Not one of the associates *has* a good word to say about the managing partner.

Nouns Ending in S

1014 Some nouns appear to be plural but are actually singular. When used as subjects, these nouns require singular verbs.

news *(no plural)*   measles *(no plural)*
lens *(plural:* lenses)   summons *(plural:* summonses)

The *news* from overseas *is* discouraging.   The *lens has* to be reground.

1015 A number of nouns are always considered plural, even though they each refer to a single thing. As subjects, they require plural verbs.

assets	dues	grounds	proceeds	savings
belongings	earnings	odds	quarters	thanks
credentials	goods	premises	riches	winnings

The *premises are* available for viewing.   My *savings have* not increased.

NOTE: The following nouns are considered plural unless preceded by the term *a pair of*.

| glasses | scissors | jeans | pliers | trousers |

The *scissors need* sharpening. (**BUT:** A *pair* of scissors *needs sharpening*.)

1016 A few nouns (not all of which end in *s*) have the same form in the plural as in the singular. When used as subjects, these nouns take singular or plural verbs according to the meaning.

| series | means | chassis | headquarters | deer |
| species | gross | corps | sheep | moose |

The *series* of concerts planned for the spring *looks* very exciting. (One series.)
Three *series* of tickets *are going* to be issued. (Three series.)

One *means* of breaking the impasse *is* to offer more money.
Other *means* of solving the problem *have* not *come* to mind.

Headquarters is not pleased with the performance of the Eastern Region. (Referring to top management or central authority.)
Their *headquarters are located* at the corner of Seventh Street and Seventh Avenue. (Referring to the offices of top management.)

Nouns Ending in *ICS*

1017 Many nouns ending in *ics* (such as *acoustics, economics, ethics, politics,* and *statistics*) take singular or plural verbs, depending on how they are used. When they refer to a body of knowledge or a course of study, they are *singular*. When they refer to qualities or activities, they are *plural*.

Economics (a course of study) *is* a prerequisite for advanced business courses.
The *economics* (the economic aspects) of his plan *are* not very sound.

Statistics is the one course in which I needed my wife's help.
The *statistics indicate* that the market for this product line is shrinking.

Acoustics is not *listed* in next year's course offerings.
The *acoustics* in the new concert hall *are* remarkably good.

Nouns With Foreign Plurals

1018 a. Watch for nouns with foreign plural endings. (See ¶614.) Such plural nouns, when used as subjects, require plural verbs.

No *criteria have been established*.   **BUT:** No *criterion has been established*.

Parentheses set off expressions.   **BUT:** The closing *parenthesis was omitted*.

b. The noun *data*, which is plural in form, is commonly followed by a plural verb in technical and scientific usage. In general usage *data* in the sense of "information" is followed by a singular verb; in the sense of "distinct bits of information," it is followed by a plural verb.

The *data* obtained after two months of experimentation *is* now *being analyzed*. (Here *data* means "information.")

BUT: The *data* assembled by six researchers *are* now *being compared*. (Here *data* refers to several distinct bits of information.)

(Continued on page 236.)

10

c. The noun *media*, the plural form of *medium*, is now accepted as singular when it refers to all mass communication (reporters and broadcasters) acting collectively. The plural form is used when the communicators are not acting as a unified group. The singular word *medium* refers to various forms of mass communication, such as the press, radio, and television.

> The *media is* responsible for the effects of all this publicity.
> The *media are covering* all aspects of the election.
> The *medium* we find most effective *is* television.

Collective Nouns

1019 The following rules govern the form of verb to be used when the subject is a collective noun. (A *collective noun* is a word that is singular in form but represents a group of persons, animals, or things.)

Note the following examples:

army	committee	faculty	minority
audience	company	firm	public
board	corporation	group	school
cabinet	council	jury	society
class	department	majority	staff

a. If the group is acting as a unit, use a singular verb.

> The *Board of Directors meets* Friday.   The *firm is* one of the oldest in the city.
>
> The *committee has agreed* to submit *its* report on Monday. (The pronoun *its* is also singular to agree with *committee*.)

b. If the members of the group are acting separately, use a plural verb.

> A *group* of researchers *are coming* from all over the world for the symposium next month. (The members of the group are acting separately in the process of coming together from all over the world.)
>
> **BUT:** A *group* of researchers *is meeting* in Geneva next month. (The members of the group are acting as a unit in the process of meeting.)
>
> **NOTE:** The use of a collective noun with a plural verb often produces an awkward sentence. Whenever possible, recast the sentence by inserting a phrase like *the members of* before the collective noun.
>
> **AWKWARD:** The *Committee are* not in agreement on the action *they* should take. (The verb *are* and the pronoun *they* are plural to agree with the plural *committee*.)
>
> **BETTER:** The *members* of the committee *are* not in agreement . . .

c. In a number of constructions, the choice of a singular or plural verb often depends on whether you wish to emphasize the group as a unit or as a collection of individuals. However, once the choice has been made, treat the collective noun consistently within the same context. If the resulting sentence sounds awkward, recast it as necessary.

I hope your *family is* well. (Emphasizes the family as a whole.)
OR: I hope your *family* are all well. (Emphasizes the individuals in the family.)

SMOOTHER: I hope all the *members* of your family *are* well.
OR: I hope *everyone* in your family *is* well.

The *couple was married* (**OR** *were married*) last Saturday.
OR: *Bob and Pauline were married* last Saturday.

The *couple have moved* into *their* new house. (More idiomatic than: "The *couple has moved into its* new house.")
OR: The *Goodwins have moved* into *their* new house.

NOTE: The expression *a couple of* is usually plural in meaning.

A *couple of* customers *have already reported* the error in our ad.

A *couple of* orders *have been shipped* to the wrong address.

BUT: A *couple of days is* all I need to complete the report. (When the phrase refers to a period of time, an amount of money, or a quantity that represents a total amount, treat the phrase as singular. See also ¶1024.)

Organizational Names

1020 Organizational names may be treated as either singular or plural. Ordinarily, treat the name as singular unless you wish to emphasize the individuals who make up the organization; in that case, use the plural. Once a choice has been made, use the singular or plural form consistently within the same context.

Brooks & Rice *has lost its* lease. *It is* now *looking* for a new location.

OR: Brooks & Rice *have lost their* lease. *They are* now *looking* for . . .

(**BUT NOT:** Brooks & Rice *has lost its* lease. *They are* now *looking* for . . .)

NOTE: If the organization is referred to as *they* or *who,* use a plural verb with the company name. If the organization is referred to as *it* or *which,* use a singular verb. (See ¶1049a.)

Geographic Names

1021 Geographic names that are plural in form are treated as *singular* if they refer to only one thing.

The *Netherlands is* the first stop on my itinerary.

The *Queen Charlotte Islands consists* of two large islands (Graham and Moresby) and several smaller islands.

The *United States has undertaken* a new foreign aid program.

BUT: All the *United States are bound* together by a common heritage.

Names of Publications and Products

1022 The name of a publication or product is considered singular, even though it may be plural in form.

<u>*Physicians & Computers*</u> *is* the one magazine you should consider.

(Continued on page 238.)

Celestial Seasonings is a manufacturer of herbal teas.

Canadian Gardens is *offering* new subscribers a special rate for a limited time.

The Number; A Number

1023 The expression *the number* has a singular meaning and requires a singular verb; *a number* has a plural meaning and requires a plural verb.

The number of branch offices *has increased* in each of the last five years.

A number of our branch offices *are* now *located* in suburban malls.

Expressions of Time, Money, and Quantity

1024 When a subject expressing a period of time, an amount of money, or a quantity represents *a total amount*, use a singular verb. When the subject represents *a number of individual units*, use a plural verb.

Three months is too long a time to wait.
BUT: *Three months have passed* since our last exchange of letters.

That *$10 000 was* an inheritance from my uncle.
BUT: *Thousands* of dollars *have* already *been spent* on the project.

Ten hectares is considered a small piece of property in this area.
BUT: *Ten hectares were plowed* last spring.

Fractional Expressions

1025 When the subject is an expression such as *one-half of, two-thirds of, a part of, a majority of, a percentage of, a portion of,* or *the rest of*:

a. Use a *singular verb* if a singular noun follows *of* or is implied.

Three-fourths of the *mailing list has been checked.*

Part of our Windsor *operation is being closed down.*

A *majority of 2000 signifies* a landslide in this town. (The noun *2000* is considered singular because it is a total amount. See ¶1024.)

A large *percentage has* to be rekeyed. (Referring to a manuscript.)

b. Use a *plural verb* when a *plural noun* follows *of* or is implied.

One-third of our *clients live* downtown.   *Part* of the *walls are* to be papered.

A *majority* of our *employees have contributed* to the United Way.

A large *percentage work* part-time. (Referring to the students at a college.)

NOTE: When used as a subject, the word *percentage* preceded by *the* requires a singular verb.

The percentage of students who work part-time *is* quite large. (*The percentage* takes a singular verb, even though it is followed by a plural noun, *students.*)

c. Consider the word *half* as a condensed version of *one-half of.*

Half the *staff have signed up* for benefits. (A collective noun such as *staff*, though singular in form, takes a plural verb when it is plural in meaning. See ¶1019b.)

Phrases and Clauses as Subjects

1026 When the subject is a phrase or clause, the verb should be singular.

> *Reading e-mail is* the first item on my morning agenda.
>
> *How many brochures we print is* not my decision.
>
> *Whether the decision was right or not is* no longer important.
>
> *That they will accept the offer is* far from certain.

EXCEPTION: Clauses beginning with *what* may be singular or plural according to the meaning.

> What we need *is* a new *statement* of policy. (A *what* clause like this is always singular; hence the verb is singular.)
>
> What we need *is* some *guidelines* on personal time off. (Again, the verb is singular because the subject—the *what* clause—is singular. If a sentence like this seems awkward, it should be reworded: *What we need is a policy . . .; Some guidelines . . . are what we need.*)

Subjects in Inverted Sentences

1027 Whenever the verb precedes the subject, make sure they agree.

> *Attached are* two *copies* of the January mailing piece.
>
> What *were* your *reasons* for resigning?
>
> Where *is* this *strategy going* to take us?
>
> Where *are* the *reviews* of the Kelly book?
>
> There *appear* to be *problems* with your report.
>
> *Should a position become* available, we will let you know. (In this case, the helping verb *should* precedes the subject. If written in normal word order, this sentence would read: If a *position should become* available . . .)

1028 a. In a sentence beginning with *there is, there are, here is, here are,* or similar constructions, the real subject follows the verb. Use *is* when the real subject is singular, *are* when it is plural.

> There *are* a great many *angles* to this problem.
>
> Here *are* two *catalogues* and an *order blank.* (See ¶¶1002a, 1028b.)
> Here *is* an old *friend* and former *partner* of mine. (The subject, *friend and partner,* is singular because only one person is referred to. See ¶1002b.)
>
> There *is many an investor* who regrets not having bought bonds. (See ¶1002c.)
>
> There *is* a *branch office* or an *agency* representing us in every major city. (See ¶1003.)
>
> There *is* not only *GST* but *provincial tax* as well. (See ¶1003.)
>
> There *is* the *cost* of your own time in addition to the substantial outlay for materials that must be figured in the total. (See ¶1007.)
>
> There's (There *is*) *more* than one *way* to solve the problem. (See ¶1013a.)
>
> There *are more* than five *candidates* running for mayor.
>
> There *are a number* of problems to be resolved. (See also ¶1023.)
> Here *is the number* of orders received since Monday.

(Continued on page 241.)

Here *is $10* as a contribution. (See also ¶¶413, 1024.)
Here *are ten loonies* for your collection.

There *is* neither a *hospital* nor a *clinic* on the island. (See ¶1003 for two singular subjects joined by *neither . . . nor.*)

There *are* neither *motel rooms* nor *condominiums* available for rent this late in the season. (See ¶1004 for two plural subjects joined by *neither . . . nor.*)

There *were* neither *tennis courts* nor a *swimming pool* in the hotel where we finally found a room. (*Were* agrees with the nearer subject, *tennis courts.* See also ¶1005 for singular and plural subjects joined by *neither . . . nor.*)

There *was* neither central *air conditioning* nor *fans* for any of the rooms in the hotel. (*Was* agrees with the nearer subject, *air conditioning.* See also ¶1005.)

b. When the subject consists of a series of singular nouns—or a series of nouns, the first of which is singular—*there is* or *here is* usually sounds more idiomatic (despite the fact that the subject is plural) than *there are* or *here are.* If you do not feel comfortable with this idiomatic construction, change the wording as necessary.

In the higher-priced model there *is* a more powerful *processor*, a 19-inch *LCD panel*, and a 100-GB *hard drive.* (In this construction, *there is* is understood to be repeated before the second and third subjects.)

OR: In the higher-priced model there *are* the following features: a more powerful *processor*, a 19-inch *LCD panel*, and a 100-GB *hard drive.* (In this version, *are* agrees with the plural subject *features;* the three subjects in this sentence are now simply appositives modifying *features.*)

Within a kilometre of the airport, there *is* a full-service *hotel* and three *motels.*

OR: Within a kilometre of the airport, there *is* a full-service hotel *plus* (**OR** *in addition to* **OR** *as well as*) three motels. (By changing the connective from *and* to *plus* or something similar, you are left with a singular subject, *hotel*, that calls for the singular verb *is.*)

OR: Within a kilometre of the airport, there *are* three *motels* and a full-service *hotel.* (When the first subject in the series is plural, the verb *are* not only is grammatically correct but also sounds natural.)

Subjects and Predicate Complements

1029 a. Sentences containing a linking verb (such as *become* or some form of *to be*) sometimes have a plural subject and a singular complement or a singular subject and a plural complement. In such cases make sure that the verb agrees with the *subject* (and not with the complement).

Bicycles are the only product we make.   The key *issue is* higher wages.

One of the things we have to keep track of *is* entertainment expenses. (Use *is* to agree with *one*, the subject.)

It is they who are at fault. (Use *is* to agree with *it*, the subject.)

NOTE: Do not confuse the last two examples with the *inverted* sentences shown in ¶1028. In a sentence beginning with *here is* or *there is*, the subject *follows* the linking verb. In a sentence beginning with *it is* or *one . . . is*, the subject *precedes* the linking verb.

b. If sentences of this type seem awkward, try to rewrite them.

We *make* only one product: bicycles.   Higher wages *are* the key issue.

VERBS

This section deals with the correct use of verb tenses and other verb forms. For the rules on agreement of verbs with subjects, see ¶¶1001–1029.

Principal Parts

1030 The principal parts of a verb are the four simple forms upon which all tenses and other modifications of the verb are based.

a. For most verbs, the past and the past participle are formed simply by adding *d* or *ed* to the present form; the present participle is formed by adding *ing* to the present. (Some verbs require a minor change in the ending of the present form before *ed* or *ing* is added.)

Present	Past	Past Participle	Present Participle	
argue	argued	argued	arguing	(see ¶707)
die	died	died	dying	(see ¶709)
drop	dropped	dropped	dropping	(see ¶701)
fill	filled	filled	filling	(see ¶706)
need	needed	needed	needing	(see ¶705)
obey	obeyed	obeyed	obeying	(see ¶711)
occur	occurred	occurred	occurring	(see ¶702)
offer	offered	offered	offering	(see ¶704)
panic	panicked	panicked	panicking	(see ¶717)
try	tried	tried	trying	(see ¶710)
taxi	taxied	taxied	taxiing	(see ¶720)

b. Many frequently used verbs, however, have principal parts that are irregularly formed.

Present	Past	Past Participle	Present Participle	
am, is, are	was, were	been	being	(see pages 244–245)
begin	began	begun	beginning	(see ¶1032b)
choose	chose	chosen	choosing	
do	did	done	doing	
fly	flew	flown	flying	
get	got	got or gotten	getting	
give	gave	given	giving	
go	went	gone	going	
grow	grew	grown	growing	

(Continued on page 242.)

10

know	knew	known	knowing
lay (place)	laid	laid	laying
lie (recline)	lay	lain	lying
pay	paid	paid	paying
prove	proved	proved or proven	proving
ring	rang	rung	ringing
rise	rose	risen	rising
say	said	said	saying
set	set	set	setting
sit	sat	sat	sitting
speak	spoke	spoken	speaking
take	took	taken	taking
wear	wore	worn	wearing
write	wrote	written	writing

NOTE: Dictionaries typically show the principal parts for all *irregular* verbs. If you are in doubt about any form, consult your dictionary. If the principal parts are not shown, the verb is regular. (See ¶1030a.)

☞ *For the principal parts of verbs ending in* c (*for example,* to picnic), *see* ¶717.

c. The past participle and the present participle, if used as a part of a verb phrase, must *always* be used with one or more helping (auxiliary) verbs. The most common helping verbs are:

| is | was | can | do | has | have | might | shall | will |
| are | were | could | did | had | may | must | should | would |

Verb Tenses

1031 The first principal part of the verb (the *present tense*) is used:

a. To express *present time.*

We *fill* all orders promptly.   She *does* what is expected of her.

b. To make a statement that is *true at all times.*

There *is* an exception to every rule (including this one).

c. With *shall* or *will* to express *future time.*

We *will order* (OR *shall order*) new stock next week. (For the use of the helping verbs *shall* and *will* in the future tense, see Section 11.)

NOTE: For the third person singular form of the present tense, add s. (See ¶1035a)

1032 a. The second principal part of the verb (the *past tense*) is used to express *past time.* No helping verb is used with this form.

We *filled* the order yesterday.   She *did* what was expected of her.

b. Do not use a past participle to express the past tense.

He *drank* his coffee. (**NOT:** He *drunk* his coffee.)   I *saw* it. (**NOT:** I *seen* it.)

They *began* it together. (**NOT:** They *begun* it together.)

He was the one who *did* it. (**NOT:** He was the one who *done* it.)

I can't believe this sweater *shrank*. (**NOT:** . . . this sweater *shrunk*.)

Jill *brought* me up to date on the Cox project. (**NOT:** Jill *brung* me . . .)

Someone *sneaked* into my office last night. (**NOT:** Someone *snuck* . . .)

1033 The third principal part of the verb (the *past participle*) is used:

a. To form the *present perfect tense*. This tense indicates action that was started in the past and has recently been completed or is continuing up to the present time. It consists of the verb *have* or *has* plus the past participle.

We *have filled* the orders. (**NOT:** We *have filled* the orders yesterday.)

She *has* always *done* what we expect of her.

Consumers *have become* an articulate force in today's business world.

NOTE: Be careful not to use the past tense (the second principal part) in place of the past participle.

I have *broken* the racquet. (**NOT:** I have *broke* the racquet.)

The dress has *shrunk*. (**NOT:** The dress has *shrank*.)

Prices have *risen* again. (**NOT:** Prices have *rose* again.)

He has *worn* out his shoes. (**NOT:** He has *wore* out his shoes.)

b. To form the *past perfect tense*. This tense indicates action that was completed *before another past action*. It consists of the verb *had* plus the past participle.

We *had filled* the orders before we saw your letter.

She *had finished* the job before we arrived.

c. To form the *future perfect tense*. This tense indicates action that will be completed *before a certain time in the future*. It consists of the verb *shall have* or *will have* plus the past participle.

We *will have filled* the orders by that time. (See Section 11 for the use of *shall* and *will*.)

She *will have finished* the job by next Friday.

1034 The fourth principal part of the verb (the *present participle*) is used:

a. To form the *present progressive tense*. This tense indicates action still in progress. It consists of the verb *am, is,* or *are* plus the present participle.

We *are filling* all orders as fast as we can.

She *is doing* all that can be expected of her.

b. To form the *past progressive tense*. This tense indicates action in progress sometime in the past. It consists of the verb *was* or *were* plus the present participle.

We *were waiting* for new stock at the time your order came in.

She *was doing* a good job when I last checked her work.

(Continued on page 246.)

CONJUGATION OF THE VERBS *TO SEE, TO BE, TO HAVE*

PRESENT, PAST, AND FUTURE TENSES (¶¶1031–1032)

INFINITIVE	TO SEE		TO BE		TO HAVE	
PRESENT TENSE	I	see	I	*am*	I	have
First Principal Part	you	see	you	are	you	have
	he or she	*sees*	he or she	*is*	he or she	*has*
	we	see	we	are	we	have
	you	see	you	are	you	have
	they	see	they	are	they	have
PAST TENSE	I	saw	I	*was*	I	had
Second Principal Part	you	saw	you	were	you	had
	he or she	saw	he or she	*was*	he or she	had
	we	saw	we	were	we	had
	you	saw	you	were	you	had
	they	saw	they	were	they	had
FUTURE TENSE	I *shall*	see	I *shall*	be	I *shall*	have
Helping Verb (*shall* OR *will*)	you will	see	you will	be	you will	have
+	he or she will	see	he or she will	be	he or she will	have
Main Verb (first principal part)	we *shall*	see	we *shall*	be	we *shall*	have
	you will	see	you will	be	you will	have
	they will	see	they will	be	they will	have

PASSIVE TENSES (¶1036)

INFINITIVE	TO SEE	
PRESENT PASSIVE TENSE	I *am*	seen
Helping Verb (present tense of *be*)	you are	seen
+	he or she *is*	seen
Main Verb (past participle)	we are	seen
	you are	seen
	they are	seen
PAST PASSIVE TENSE	I *was*	seen
Helping Verb (past tense of *be*)	you were	seen
+	he or she *was*	seen
Main Verb (past participle)	we were	seen
	you were	seen
	they were	seen
FUTURE PASSIVE TENSE	I *shall* be	seen
Helping Verb (future tense of *be*)	you will be	seen
+	he or she will be	seen
Main Verb (past participle)	we *shall* be	seen
	you will be	seen
	they will be	seen

PROGRESSIVE TENSES (¶1034)

INFINITIVE	TO SEE	
PRESENT PROGRESSIVE TENSE	I *am*	seeing
Helping Verb (present tense of *be*)	you are	seeing
+	he or she *is*	seeing
Main Verb (present participle)	we are	seeing
	you are	seeing
	they are	seeing
PAST PROGRESSIVE TENSE	I *was*	seeing
Helping Verb (past tense of *be*)	you were	seeing
+	he or she *was*	seeing
Main Verb (present participle)	we were	seeing
	you were	seeing
	they were	seeing
FUTURE PROGRESSIVE TENSE	I *shall* be	seeing
Helping Verb (future tense of *be*)	you will be	seeing
+	he or she will be	seeing
Main Verb (present participle)	we *shall* be	seeing
	you will be	seeing
	they will be	seeing

10

PERFECT TENSES (¶1033)

INFINITIVE	TO SEE		TO BE	
PRESENT PERFECT TENSE	I have	seen	I have	been
Helping Verb (present tense of *have*)	you have	seen	you have	been
+	he or she *has*	seen	he or she *has*	been
Main Verb (past participle)	we have	seen	we have	been
	you have	seen	you have	been
	they have	seen	they have	been
PAST PERFECT TENSE	I had	seen	I had	been
Helping Verb (past tense of *have*)	you had	seen	you had	been
+	he or she had	seen	he or she had	been
Main Verb (past participle)	we had	seen	we had	been
	you had	seen	you had	been
	they had	seen	they had	been
FUTURE PERFECT TENSE	I *shall* have	seen	I *shall* have	been
Helping Verb (future tense of *have*)	you will have	seen	you will have	been
+	he or she will have	seen	he or she will have	been
Main Verb (past participle)	we *shall* have	seen	we *shall* have	been
	you will have	seen	you will have	been
	they will have	seen	they will have	been

PERFECT PASSIVE TENSES (¶1036)

INFINITIVE	TO SEE	
PRESENT PERFECT PASSIVE TENSE	I have been	seen
Helping Verb (present perfect tense of *be*)	you have been	seen
+	he or she *has* been	seen
Main Verb (past participle)	we have been	seen
	you have been	seen
	they have been	seen
PAST PERFECT PASSIVE TENSE	I had been	seen
Helping Verb (past perfect tense of *be*)	you had been	seen
+	he or she had been	seen
Main Verb (past participle)	we had been	seen
	you had been	seen
	they had been	seen
FUTURE PERFECT PASSIVE TENSE	I *shall* have been	seen
Helping Verb (future perfect tense of *be*)	you will have been	seen
+	he or she will have been	seen
Main Verb (past participle)	we *shall* have been	seen
	you will have been	seen
	they will have been	seen

PERFECT PROGRESSIVE TENSES (¶1034)

INFINITIVE	TO SEE	
PRESENT PERFECT PROGRESSIVE TENSE	I have been	seeing
Helping Verb (present perfect tense of *be*)	you have been	seeing
+	he or she *has* been	seeing
Main Verb (present participle)	we have been	seeing
	you have been	seeing
	they have been	seeing
PAST PERFECT PROGRESSIVE TENSE	I had been	seeing
Helping Verb (past perfect tense of *be*)	you had been	seeing
+	he or she had been	seeing
Main Verb (present participle)	we had been	seeing
	you had been	seeing
	they had been	seeing
FUTURE PERFECT PROGRESSIVE TENSE	I *shall* have been	seeing
Helping Verb (future perfect tense of *be*)	you will have been	seeing
+	he or she will have been	seeing
Main Verb (present participle)	we *shall* have been	seeing
	you will have been	seeing
	they will have been	seeing

10

c. To form the *future progressive tense*. This tense indicates action that will be in progress in the future. It consists of the verb *shall be* or *will be* plus the present participle.

We *will be working* overtime for the next two weeks. (See Section 11 for the use of *shall* and *will*.)

They *will be receiving* additional stock throughout the next two weeks.

d. To form the *present perfect progressive*, the *past perfect progressive*, and the *future perfect progressive tenses*. These tenses convey the same meaning as the simple perfect tenses except that the progressive element adds the sense of continuous action. (See ¶1033.) These tenses consist of the verbs *has been, have been, had been, shall have been*, and *will have been* plus the present participle. Compare the following examples with those in ¶1033.

We *have been filling* these orders with Model 212A instead of 212. (Present perfect progressive.)

We *had been filling* these orders with Model 212A until we saw your directive. (Past perfect progressive.)

By next Friday we *will have been working* overtime for two straight weeks. (Future perfect progressive.)

1035 The first principal part of the verb undergoes a change in form to express the third person singular in the present tense.

a. Most verbs simply add *s* in the third person singular.

he feels	**BUT:** I feel, you feel, we feel, they feel
she thinks	I think, you think, we think, they think
it looks	I look, you look, we look, they look

b. Verbs ending in *s, x, z, sh, ch,* or *o* add *es*. (See also ¶602.)

he misses	it buzzes	she watches
she fixes	he wishes	it goes

c. Verbs ending in a vowel plus *y* add *s*; those ending in a consonant plus *y* change *y* to *i* and add *es*. (See also ¶¶604–605.)

say: he says	employ: she employs	try: it tries
convey: she conveys	buy: he buys	apply: she applies

d. Verbs ending in *i* simply add *s*.

taxi: he taxis	ski: she skis

e. The verb *to be* is irregular since *be*, the first principal part, is not used in the present tense.

I am	he, she, it is	you are
you are	we are	they are

f. The present and past tenses of a few verbs remain unchanged in the third person singular.

he may	she can	it will
he might	she could	it would

☞ *See the entry for* Don't *in Section 11.*

Passive Forms

1036 The passive forms of a verb consist of the helping verb *to be* plus the past participle of the main verb.

> it is intended (present passive of *intend*)
>
> we were expected (past passive of *expect*)
>
> they will be audited (future passive of *audit*)
>
> she has been notified (present perfect passive of *notify*)
>
> you had been told (past perfect passive of *tell*)
>
> he will have been given (future perfect passive of *give*)

1037 While an *active* verb directs the action toward an object, a *passive* verb directs the action toward the subject.

> **ACTIVE:** Melanie *(subject)* will lead *(verb)* the discussion *(object).*
>
> **PASSIVE:** The discussion *(subject)* will be led *(verb)* by Melanie.

☞ *For additional examples, see the entry for* Voice *in Section 19.*

a. The passive form of a verb is appropriate (1) when you want to emphasize the *receiver* of the action (by making it the subject) or (2) when the *doer* of the action is not important or is deliberately not mentioned.

> I was seriously injured as a result of your negligence. (Emphasizes *I*, the receiver of the action. **RATHER THAN:** Your negligence seriously injured me.)
>
> The proposal is based on an analysis of all research studies. (Emphasizes the basis for the proposal; the person who drafted it is not important.)
>
> The decision was made without the knowledge of the board members. (Emphasizes how the decision was made and omits the name of the person responsible.)

b. The active form of a verb achieves a simpler and more vigorous style. Except in those circumstances cited in ¶1037a, passive verb forms typically produce awkward or stilted sentences.

> **WEAK PASSIVES:** It *has been decided* by the Human Resources Committee that full pay *should be given* to you for the period of your hospitalization.
>
> **STRONG ACTIVES:** The Human Resources Committee *has decided* that you *should receive* full pay for the period of your hospitalization.

c. Watch out for passive constructions that unintentionally point to the wrong *doer* of the action.

> **CONFUSING:** Two computer terminals were reported stolen over the weekend by the head of corporate security.

(Continued on page 248.)

10

CLEAR: The head of corporate security reported that two computer terminals were stolen over the weekend.

CONFUSING: One of our second-shift workers was found injured by a Good Samaritan outside the parking lot entrance last night.

CLEAR: Last night a Good Samaritan found one of our second-shift workers injured outside the parking lot entrance.

Verbs Following Clauses of Necessity, Demand, Etc.

1038 Sentences that express *necessity, demand, strong request, urging,* or *resolution* in the main clause require a *subjunctive* verb in the dependent clause that follows.

    a. If the verb in the dependent clause requires the use of the verb *to be,* use the form *be* with all three persons (not *am, is,* or *are*).

        NECESSITY: It is necessary (**OR** important **OR** essential) that these questions *be answered* at once. (**NOT:** are answered.)

        DEMAND: I insist that I *be allowed* to present a minority report at the next board meeting. (**NOT:** am allowed.)

        REQUEST: They have asked that you *be notified* at once if matters do not proceed according to plan. (**NOT:** are notified.)

        URGING: We urged (**OR** suggested) that he *be given* a second chance to prove himself in the job. (**NOT:** is given.)

        RESOLUTION: The committee has resolved (**OR** decided **OR** ruled) that the decision *be deferred* until the next meeting. (**NOT:** is deferred.)

    b. If the verb in the dependent clause is a verb other than *be,* use the ordinary *present tense* form for all three persons. However, do not add *s* (or otherwise change the form) for the third person singular.

        NECESSITY: It is essential that he *arrive* on time. (**NOT:** arrives.)

        DEMAND: They insist that he *do* the work over. (**NOT:** does.)

        REQUEST: They have asked that she *remain* on the committee until the end of the year. (**NOT:** remains.)

        URGING: I suggested that she *triple space* the material to allow room for some very heavy editing. (**NOT:** triple spaces.)

        RESOLUTION: They have resolved that Fred *represent* them. (**NOT:** represents.)

☞ *See the entry for* Mood, subjunctive *in Section 19.*

Verbs Following *Wish* Clauses

1039 Sentences that start with *I wish, she wishes,* and so on, require a subjunctive verb in the dependent clause that follows.

    a. To express *present* time in the dependent clause, put the verb in the *past tense.*

        I wish I *knew* how to proceed.   I wish I *could attend.*

        NOTE: If the verb is *to be,* use *were* for all three persons.

        I wish I *were going* to the reception. (**NOT:** was going.)

        I wish he *were going* with me.

b. To express *past* time in the dependent clause, put the verb in the *past perfect tense.*

I wish that she *had invited* me.   I wish that I *could have been* there.
Do you wish you *had been* there?   They wish they *had hired* you.

c. To express *future* time in the dependent clause, use the helping verb *would* instead of *will.*

I wish he *would arrive* on time.   I wish she *would make* an effort.

Verbs in *If* Clauses

1040 When an *if* clause states a condition that is *highly improbable, doubtful,* or *contrary to fact,* the verb in the *if* clause requires special treatment, like that described in ¶1039; *to express present time, use the past tense; to express past time, use the past perfect tense.* (In the following examples note the relationship of tenses between the dependent clause and the main clause.)

If I *knew* the answer (but I don't), I *would* not *ask* you.
If I *had known* the answer (but I didn't), I *would* not *have asked* you.

If I *were* you (but I am not), I *would take* the job.
If I *had been* in your shoes (but I wasn't), I *would have taken* the job.

If he *were invited* (but he isn't), he *would be* glad to go.
If he *had been invited* (but he wasn't), he *would have been* glad to go.

NOTE: Do not use *would have* for *had* in an *if* clause. See Section 11 for a usage note on *would have.*

1041 When an *if* clause states a condition that is *possible* or *likely,* the verb in the *if* clause requires no special treatment. *To express present time, use the present tense; to express past time, use the past tense.* Compare the following pairs of examples. Those labelled "Probable" reflect the verb forms described here in ¶1041. Those labelled "Improbable" reflect the verb forms described in ¶1040.

PROBABLE: If I *leave* this job (and I may do so), I *will take* a full-time teaching position.
IMPROBABLE: If I *left* this job (but I probably won't), I *would take* a full-time teaching position.

PROBABLE: If I *go* to Fredericton (and I may), I *will want* you to go with me.
IMPROBABLE: If I *were going* to Fredericton (but I probably won't), I *would want* you to go with me.

PROBABLE: If she *was* in yesterday (and she may have been), I *did* not *see* her.
IMPROBABLE: If she *had been* in yesterday (but she wasn't), I *would have seen* her.

Verbs in *As If* or *As Though* Clauses

1042 When an *as if* or *as though* clause expresses a condition *contrary to fact,* the verb in the clause requires special treatment, like that described in ¶1040.

She acts as if she *were* the only person who mattered. (But she isn't.)

He talks as if he *knew* the facts of the situation. (But he doesn't.)

You act as though you *hadn't* a care in the world. (But you have.)

10

1043 *As if* or *as though* clauses are now often used to express a condition that is *highly probable*. In such cases do not give the verb special treatment. *Use the present tense to express present time, the future tense to express future time, and the past tense to express past time.*

> It looks as if it *will* rain. (**OR:** It looks as if it *is going* to rain.)

> She acted as if she *planned* to look for another job.

Infinitives

1044 An infinitive is the form of the verb preceded by *to* (for example, *to write, to do, to be*). When two or more infinitives are used in a parallel construction, the word *to* may be omitted after the first infinitive unless special emphasis is desired.

> Ask Ruth Gregoire *to sign* both copies of the contract, *return* the original to us, and *keep* the other copy. (*Return* and *keep* are infinitives without *to*.)

> I would like you *to explain* the job to Harry, *to give* him help if he needs it, and *to see* that the job is done properly. (For emphasis, *to* is used with all three infinitives—*explain, give,* and *see*.)

NOTE: The word *to* is always dropped when the infinitive follows such verbs as *see, hear, feel,* and *let*; it is often dropped after *help* and *need*.

> Will you please help me *copy* the disk? (**RATHER THAN:** help me *to copy* . . .)

> You need not *return* the clipping. (**OR:** You do not need *to return* the clipping.)

1045 a. Infinitives have two main tense forms: present and perfect.

  (1) The perfect infinitive is used to express action that has been completed before the time of the main verb.

> I *am sorry to have caused* you so much trouble last week. (The act of causing trouble was completed before the act of expressing regret; therefore, the perfect infinitive is used.)

  (2) The present infinitive is used in all other cases.

> I planned *to leave* early. (**NOT:** *to have left.* The act of leaving could not have been completed before the act of planning; therefore, the present infinitive is used.)

  b. The passive form of the present infinitive consists of *to be* plus the past participle. Do not omit *to be* in such constructions. (See ¶1036.)

> This office needs *to be repainted.* (**NOT:** This office needs *repainted.*)

1046 *Splitting an infinitive* (that is, inserting an adverb between *to* and the verb) should be avoided when possible because (a) it often produces an awkward construction and (b) the adverb usually functions more effectively in another location.

> **WEAK:** It was impossible to *even* see a foot ahead.
> **BETTER:** It was impossible to see *even* a foot ahead.

> **WEAK:** He always tries to *carefully* do the work.
> **BETTER:** He always tries to do the work *carefully.*

However, split the infinitive when alternative locations of the adverb produce an awkward or poorly constructed sentence.

a. Before splitting an infinitive, first try to place the adverb *after the object* of the infinitive. In many instances the adverb functions most effectively in that location.

You ought *to review* these plans *thoroughly*.
(**BETTER THAN:** You ought to thoroughly review these plans.)

I need *to make* the decision *quickly*.
(**BETTER THAN:** I need to quickly make the decision.)

b. If step *a* does not produce an effective sentence, try putting the adverb directly *before* or directly *after* the infinitive. In some cases the adverb functions effectively in this position; in other cases the resulting sentence is awkward.

CONFUSING: I want you *to supervise* the work that is to be done *personally*. (When the object of the infinitive is long or involved, it is difficult to place the adverb after the object without creating confusion. Here *personally* seems to modify *to be done* when in fact it should modify *to supervise*.)

AWKWARD: I want you to supervise *personally* the work that is to be done.

GOOD: I want you *personally* to supervise the work that is to be done.

c. If steps *a* and *b* fail to produce an effective sentence, try splitting the infinitive. If a good sentence results, keep it; if not, try rewording the sentence.

CONFUSING: I want you *to consider* Jenkins' proposal to handle all our deliveries *carefully*. (When *carefully* is located after the complete object, it no longer clearly refers to *to consider*.)

AWKWARD: I want you *carefully* to consider Jenkins' proposal to handle all our deliveries.

AWKWARD: I want you to consider *carefully* Jenkins' proposal to handle all our deliveries.

GOOD: I want you to *carefully* consider Jenkins' proposal . . .

d. When an infinitive consists of *to be* plus a past or present participle of another verb, inserting an adverb before the participle is not considered splitting an infinitive. Nevertheless, in many such sentences it may be possible to locate the adverb to better advantage elsewhere in the sentence.

These plans need to be *thoroughly* reviewed.

Claude appears to be *continually* turning up with last-minute objections to any decision I make.

NOTE: By the same token, it is perfectly acceptable to position an adverb between a helping verb and a past or present participle. It is even acceptable to position an adverb *within* the elements of a helping verb.

This new technology has *already* been *effectively* applied in many industries.

I hear that Martha has been *seriously* considering early retirement.

☞ *For dangling infinitive phrases, see also ¶1086b.*

Sequence of Tenses

1047 When the verb in the main clause is in the past tense, the verb in a dependent *that* clause should also express past time. Consider the tenses in the following pairs of examples:

> She *says* (present) that she *is* now *working* (present) for CBC.
> She *said* (past) that she *was* now *working* (past) for CBC.
>
> He *says* (present) that he *has seen* (present perfect) your résumé.
> He *said* (past) that he *had seen* (past perfect) your résumé.
>
> I *think* (present) that he *will see* (future) you tomorrow.
> I *thought* (past) that he *would see* (past form of *will see*) you tomorrow.

EXCEPTION: The verb in the dependent clause should remain in the present tense if it expresses a general truth.

> Our legal adviser *pointed out* (past) that all persons under 18 *are* (present) legally considered minors. (General truth.)

Omitting Parts of Verbs

1048 When compound verbs in the same sentence share a common element, that element does not need to be repeated.

> We *have* received your letter and forwarded it to our Chatham office. (The helping verb *have* is shared by the two main verbs, *received* and *forwarded*.)
>
> We can and will *achieve* these goals. (The main verb *achieve* is shared by the two helping verbs *can* and *will*.)

However, do not omit any element when different parts of the main verb are required.

> **WRONG:** I never have and I never will forget what you have done for me.
> **RIGHT:** I never have *forgotten* and I never will *forget* . . .
>
> **WRONG:** We have and still are asking for an accounting of the assets.
> **RIGHT:** We have *asked* and still are *asking* for . . .

☞ *See individual entries listed alphabetically in Section 11 for troublesome verbs.*

PRONOUNS
Agreement With Antecedents: Basic Rules

1049 a. A pronoun must agree with its *antecedent* (that is, the word for which the pronoun stands) in number, gender, and person.

> *I* must stand by *my* client, just as *you* must stand by *yours*.
>
> *Frank* said that *he* could do the job alone.
>
> *Alice* wants to know whether *her* proposal has been approved.
>
> The *company* has not decided whether to change *its* policy on vacations. (See ¶¶1019–1020.)
>
> *We* plan to explain *our* shift in corporate strategy at the next shareholders' meeting.
>
> The company's *auditors* will issue *their* report tomorrow.
>
> The *Vanderveers* are giving a party at *their* house.

The *committee* has completed *its* investigation. (See ¶1019 for collective nouns.)

Why not have *each witness* write *his* or *her* version of the accident? (See ¶1053 for indefinite pronouns as antecedents.)

It is *I* who *am* at fault. (*Who* agrees in person and number with the antecedent *I*; the verb *am* also agrees with *I*.)

It is *she* who *is* willing to compromise.   It is *they* who *are* not.

It is *we*, the individual taxpayers, who *have* to make up for the loss of commercial property taxes.

It is *they* who *are* behind schedule.

It is *you* who *are* to blame. (*Who* refers to *you*; hence the verb *are* is plural to agree with *you*. (See also ¶1001a note.)

BUT: You are the *person* who *is* to blame. (Here *who* refers to *person*; hence the verb *is* is singular to agree with *person*.)

b. Use a plural pronoun when the antecedent consists of two nouns or pronouns joined by *and*.

Can *Mary* and *you* give us *your* decision by Monday?

Sonia and *Dave* say *they* will attend.

The *Montaignes* and the *Reillys* have sent *their* regrets.

Are *you* and *I* prepared to say that *we* can handle the assignment?

c. Use a singular pronoun when the antecedent consists of two *singular* nouns joined by *or* or *nor*. Use a plural pronoun when the antecedent consists of two *plural* nouns joined by *or* or *nor*. (See also ¶¶1003–1005.)

Either *Will* or *Ed* will have to give up *his* office. (**NOT:** their.)

Neither *Joan* nor *Helen* wants to do *her* share. (**NOT:** their.)

Either the *Kopecks* or the *Henleys* will bring *their* videocassette recorder.

NOTE: When *or* or *nor* joins a singular noun and a plural noun, a pronoun that refers to this construction should agree in number with the nearer noun. However, a strict application of this rule can lead to problems in sentence structure and meaning. Therefore, always try to make this kind of construction plural by locating the plural subject nearer the verb.

Neither Mr. Wing nor his *employees have* reached *their* goal. (The plural pronoun *their* is used to agree with the nearer noun, *employees*; the verb *have* is also in the plural.)

NOT: Neither the employees nor Mr. *Wing has* reached *his* goal. (The sentence follows the rule—*his* agrees with Mr. *Wing*, the nearer noun, and the verb *has* is singular; however, the meaning of the sentence has been distorted.)

d. Make sure that the pronouns you use agree in gender with their antecedents. To avoid confusion, reword as necessary.

The entire *staff* wishes to express *its* gratitude. (Third person singular.)

We (**OR** *All of us*) wish to express *our* gratitude. (First person plural).

(Continued on page 254.)

NOT: The entire *staff* wishes to express *our* gratitude. (Do not use a first person pronoun to refer to a third person antecedent.)

   e. Make sure that the pronouns you use refer to the antecedents you intend. To avoid confusion, reword as necessary.

Unrealistic deadlines, excessive pressures, and unsafe working conditions can be very damaging to your employees. You must do everything you can to eliminate these destructive conditions.

NOT: Unrealistic deadlines, excessive pressures, and unsafe working conditions can be very damaging to your employees. You must do everything you can to eliminate them. (The employees or the destructive conditions?)

Agreement With Common-Gender Antecedents

1050 Nouns that apply both to males and females have a *common* gender.

parent	doctor	assistant	writer
child	lawyer	supervisor	speaker
customer	professor	employee	listener
manager	instructor	student	consultant

When a singular noun of common gender serves as a *definite* antecedent (one that names a specific person whose gender is known), use the pronoun *he* or *she* as appropriate.

My *employer* (previously identified as Robert Hayes) prefers to open *his* own mail.

Ask your *doctor* (known to be a woman) to sign *her* name on the attached form.

1051 The masculine bias in the word *he* makes it unsuitable as a pronoun that applies equally to women and men. Moreover, the generic use of *she* serves to reinforce stereotyped notions about women's occupations or roles.

NOTE: A number of new words—without masculine or feminine connotations—have been proposed to take the place of the generic use of *he* or *she*. However, since none of these words have been accepted into common usage, consider the alternatives described in ¶1052.

1052 a. Use *he or she, his or her,* or *him or her.* This works well in isolated cases but can be clumsy if used frequently in the same context. (In any case, avoid the use of *he/she, s/he,* and similar constructions.)

An *instructor* should offer *his or her* students challenging projects.

(**RATHER THAN:** An instructor should offer *his* students . . .)

   b. Change the wording from singular to plural.

Parents of teenagers often *wonder* where *they* went wrong.

(**RATHER THAN:** The *parents* of a teenager often wonders where *he or she* went wrong.)

   c. Reword to avoid the generic pronoun.

When a customer calls, be sure to ask for a phone number.

(**RATHER THAN:** When a customer calls, ask *him or her* to leave *his or her* phone number.)

10

An assistant tries to anticipate the needs of the employer.

(**RATHER THAN:** An assistant tries to anticipate the needs of *his or her* employer.)

d. If the application of these various alternatives produces wordiness or an unacceptable shift in meaning or emphasis, then as a last resort use the generic *he* or the generic *she* as described in ¶1051. However, try to avoid doing so whenever possible.

Agreement With Indefinite-Pronoun Antecedents

1053 a. Use a singular pronoun when the antecedent is a singular indefinite pronoun. The following indefinite pronouns are always singular. (A few such as *each* and *every* are used as adjectives.)

anyone	everyone	someone	no one
anybody	everybody	somebody	nobody
anything	everything	something	nothing
each	every	either	one
each one	many a	neither	another

Every company has *its* own vacation policy. (**NOT:** their.)

Neither one of the campaigns did as well as *it* was supposed to. (**NOT:** they were.)

NOTE: These singular indefinite pronouns often call for the generic use of *he* or *she*. (See ¶¶1051–1052.) In the following sentences, alternative wording is shown to suggest how the generic *he* or *she* can be avoided.

Everyone should submit *his* expense report by Friday.
BETTER: All staff *members* should submit *their* expense reports by Friday.

If *anyone* should ask for me, tell *him* that I won't return until Monday.
BETTER: If anyone should ask for me, say that I won't return . . .

Does *every assistant* know how *she* is to handle *her employer's* calls?
BETTER: Do *all the assistants* know how *they* are to handle *their employers'* calls?

☞ *For agreement of these indefinite pronouns with verbs, see ¶¶1009–1011.*
For possessive forms of these pronouns, see ¶637.

b. Use a plural pronoun when the antecedent is a plural indefinite pronoun. The following indefinite pronouns are always plural:

many	few	several	others	both

Many customers prefer to help *themselves; others* usually like to have someone wait on *them.*

A *few* of the directors have not yet taken *their* vacations.

Several sales representatives made *their* annual goals in nine months.

Both managers have said that *they* want to be considered for Mr. Hall's job.

☞ *For agreement of these indefinite pronouns with verbs, see ¶1012.*

c. The following indefinite pronouns may be singular or plural, depending on the noun they refer to.

(Continued on page 256.)

| all | none | any | some | more | most |

When these words are used as antecedents, determine whether they are singular or plural. Then make the pronouns that refer to them agree in number.

Some of the employees have not yet had *their* annual physical checkup. (*Some* refers to *employees* and is plural; *some* is the antecedent of *their*.)

Some of the manuscript has been keyed, but *it* has not been proofread. (*Some* refers to *manuscript* and is singular; *some* is the antecedent of *it* in the second clause.)

☞ *For agreement of these indefinite pronouns with verbs, see ¶1013.*

d. Since indefinite pronouns are in the third person, pronouns referring to these antecedents should also be in the third person *(he, she, it, they).*

If *anyone* wants a vacation pay advance, *he* or *she* should apply for it in writing.

(**NOT:** If *anyone* wants a vacation pay advance, *you* should apply for it . . .)

If the indefinite pronoun is modified so that it strongly expresses the first or second person, the personal pronoun must also agree in number.

Most parents want *their* children to go to college. (Third person.)
Most of *us* want *our* children to go to college. (First person.)

A *few* have missed *their* deadlines. (Third person.)
A *few* of *you* have missed *your* deadlines. (Second person.)

Pronouns take different forms, not only to indicate a difference in person *(I, you, he)*, number *(he, they)*, and gender *(he, she)*, but also to indicate a difference in case *(nominative, possessive, objective)*. Although a pronoun must agree with its antecedent in person, number, and gender, it does *not* necessarily agree with its antecedent in case. The case of a pronoun depends on its own relation to the other words in the sentence. The rules in ¶¶1054–1064 indicate how to choose the right case for pronouns.

FORMATION OF PERSONAL PRONOUNS

	Subjective		Objective		Possessive		Reflexive	
	Singular	Plural	Singular	Plural	Singular	Plural	Singular	Plural
First person	I	we	me	us	my mine	our ours	myself	ourselves
Second person	you	you	you	you	your yours	your yours	yourself	yourselves
Third person	he she it	they	him her it	them	his hers its	their theirs	himself herself itself	themselves

Personal Pronouns
1054 NOMINATIVE FORMS OF PERSONAL PRONOUNS

Use *I, we, you, he, she, it, they*:

a. When the pronoun is the subject of a verb.

I wrote to Gemma Petrini, but *she* hasn't answered.

Debbie and *I* can handle the job ourselves.
(**NOT:** Debbie and me **OR:** me and Debbie.)

Either *he* or *I* can work late tonight. (**NOT:** him or me.)

NOTE: In sentences like the last two above, try each subject alone with the verb. You would not say "Me can handle the job" or "Him can work late tonight." Therefore, *I* and *he* must be used.

b. When the pronoun appears in the predicate after some form of the verb *to be* (*am, is, are, was, were*) or after a verb phrase containing some form of *to be* (see the list below). Pronouns that follow these verb forms should be in the nominative.

shall (**OR** will) be	have (**OR** has) been
should (**OR** would) be	had been
shall (**OR** will) have been	may (**OR** might) be
should (**OR** would) have been	may (**OR** might) have been
can (**OR** could) be	must (**OR** ought to) be
could have been	must have (**OR** ought to have) been

It could have been *they*.
It is *I*.

Was it *he* or *she* who phoned?
This is *she*.

NOTE: A sentence like *It could have been they*, while grammatically correct, would sound better if reworded in idiomatic English: *They could have been the ones.* When a telephone caller asks for you by name, you may respond correctly and naturally by saying *This is . . .* and then give your name, rather than by saying *This is he* or *This is she.*

☞ *For special rules governing pronouns with the infinitive* to be, *see* ¶1064.

1055 OBJECTIVE FORMS OF PERSONAL PRONOUNS

Use *me, us, you, him, her, it, them*:

a. When the pronoun is the direct or indirect object of a verb.

Larry gave Maris and *us* tickets for the opening.

They invited my husband and *me* for the weekend.

NOTE: When *my husband and* is mentally omitted, the objective form *me* is clearly the correct pronoun ("They invited *me* for the weekend").

b. When the pronoun is the object of a preposition.

This is for *you* and *her*.

No one knows except *you* and *me*. (**NOT:** except you and I.)

Between *you* and *me*, that decision is unfair. (**NOT:** between you and I.)

EXCEPTION: He is a friend of *mine* (*yours, his, hers, ours, theirs*). (See ¶648.)

c. When the pronoun is the subject or object of an infinitive. (See ¶1064.)

(Continued on page 258.)

The department head asked *him* to resign. (*Him* is the subject of *to resign.*)

Did you ask Janet to call *me*? (*Me* is the object of *to call.*)

NOTE: When the pronoun is the subject or complement of the infinitive *to be*, use a nominative form. (See ¶1064.)

I asked Russ *who* he wanted to be. (*Who* is the complement of *to be.*)

1056 POSSESSIVE FORMS OF PERSONAL PRONOUNS

a. Most personal pronouns have two possessive forms:

my	your	his	her	its	our	their
mine	yours	. . .	hers	. . .	ours	theirs

b. Use *my, your, his, her, its, our,* or *their* when the possessive pronoun immediately precedes the noun it modifies.

That is *my* book.   It was *their* choice.   George is *her* neighbour.

c. Use *mine, yours, his, hers, its, ours,* or *theirs* when the possessive pronoun stands apart from the noun it refers to.

That book is *mine*.   The choice was *theirs*.   George is a neighbour of *hers*.

NOTE: There is no apostrophe before the final *s* in possessive pronouns.

yours (**NOT:** your's)   ours (**NOT:** our's)
hers (**NOT:** her's)   theirs (**NOT:** their's)

d. A pronoun that modifies a *gerund* (a verbal noun ending in *ing*) should be in the possessive. (See ¶647.)

I appreciate *your shipping* the order so promptly.
(**NOT:** I appreciate *you shipping* the order so promptly.)

e. Do not confuse certain possessive pronouns with contractions and other phrases that have the same sound.

its (possessive)	it's (it is **OR** it has)
their (possessive)	they're (they are) **OR** there're (there are)
theirs (possessive)	there's (there is **OR** there has)
your (possessive)	you're (you are)

As a test for the correct form, try to substitute *it is, it has, they are, there are, there is, there has,* or *you are.* If the substitution does not make sense, use the corresponding possessive form.

The firm must protect *its* assets. ("Protect it is assets" makes no sense.)
BUT: *It's* time to take stock of our achievements.

How would you go about estimating *its* worth?
BUT: How much would you say *it's* worth?

Their investing in high-tech stocks was a shrewd idea.
BUT: *They're* investing in high-tech stocks.

Their complaints have proved to be unfounded.
BUT: *There are* complaints that have proved to be unfounded.

10

Theirs no longer works; that's why they borrow ours.
BUT: *There's* no use expecting him to change.

Your thinking is sound, but we lack the funds to underwrite your proposal.
BUT: *You're* thinking of applying for a transfer, I understand.

☞ *For other possessive pronouns, see also* ¶¶636–637.

1057 When a pronoun follows *than* or *as* in a comparison, determine the correct form of the pronoun by mentally supplying any missing words.

She writes better than *I*. (She writes better than *I* do.)

I like you better than *him*. (I like you better than *I like him*.)
BUT: I like you better than *he*. (I like you better than *he does*.)

Joe is not as talented as *she*. (Joe is not as talented as *she is*.)

1058 When a pronoun is used to identify a noun or another pronoun, it is either nominative or objective, depending on how the antecedent is used.

The committee has asked *us*, Ruth and *me*, to present the report. (Since *us* is objective, the identifying pronoun *me* is also objective.)

The explanation was for the *newcomers*, Marie and *me*. (Was for *me*.)

The exceptions were the *newcomers*, Marie and *I*. (Exception was *I*.)

Let's *you* and *me* schedule a brown-bag lunch. (*Let's* is a contraction for *let us*. Since *us* is the objective form, the pronouns *you* and *me* are also objective.)

NOTE: To determine the correct form in sentences like the following, mentally omit the noun *(employees)*.

The company wants *us* employees to work on Saturdays. (The company wants *us* to work on Saturdays.)

We employees need to confer. (*We* need to confer.)

1059 Some writers consistently use *we* instead of *I* to avoid a seeming overemphasis on themselves. However, it is preferable to use *we* only when you are speaking on behalf of an organization you represent and to use *I* when speaking for yourself alone.

We shall prepare the necessary forms as soon as you send *us* a signed release. (This writer is speaking on behalf of the firm.)

It is *my* opinion that this patient may be discharged at once. (This writer is speaking only for himself. Under these circumstances it would sound pompous to say, "It is *our* opinion.")

Compound Personal Pronouns

1060 The *self-* or *selves*-ending pronouns (*myself, yourself, himself, herself, itself, ourselves, yourselves, themselves*) should be used:

a. To direct the action expressed by the verb back to the subject.

She found *herself* the only one in favour of the move.

We have satisfied *ourselves* as to the wisdom of the action.

We think that *they* have insured *themselves* against a possible loss.

(Continued on page 260.)

b. To emphasize a noun or pronoun already expressed.

The *trainees themselves* arranged the program.

He will write to her *himself.*

I myself am bewildered. (**NOT:** *I myself* am *personally* bewildered. Using *myself* and *personally* in the same sentence creates redundancy, not emphasis.)

c. Place a compound personal pronoun carefully to prevent confusion or misreading.

CONFUSING: Now surgeons can have patients wheeled inside a new three-dimensional imaging machine; then they can step inside themselves to operate. (Are the surgeons stepping inside themselves or inside the machine?)
CLEAR: . . . then they themselves can step inside the machine to operate.

If necessary, reword the sentence without using a compound personal pronoun.

CONFUSING: Are you tired of cleaning yourself? Let us do it for you.
CLEAR: Are you tired of doing your own cleaning? Let us do it for you.

d. Use a compound personal pronoun only if the noun or pronoun it refers to is in the same sentence.

The tickets are for the Wrights and *me.* (**NOT:** myself.)

Henry and *I* can handle all the mail. (**NOT:** Henry and myself.)

Interrogative and Relative Pronouns
1061 *WHO* AND *WHOM; WHOEVER* AND *WHOMEVER*

a. These pronouns are both *interrogative* pronouns (used in asking questions) and *relative* pronouns (used to refer to a noun or pronoun in the main clause).

Who is going? (Interrogative.)

Mr. Sears is the one *who* is going. (Relative, referring to *one.*)

To *whom* shall I deliver the message? (Interrogative.)

Ms. DeAngelis, *whom* I have never met, is in charge of the program. (Relative, referring to *Ms. DeAngelis.*)

b. These pronouns may be either singular or plural in meaning.

Who is talking? (Singular.)   *Whom* do you prefer for this job? (Singular.)
Who are going? (Plural.)   *Whom* do you prefer for these jobs? (Plural.)

c. *Who* (or *whoever*) is the nominative form. Use *who* whenever *he, she, they, I,* or *we* could be substituted in the *who* clause. (If in doubt, mentally rearrange the clause as is done in parentheses after each of the following examples.)

Who is arranging the teleconference? (*She* is arranging the teleconference.)

Who shall I say is calling? (I shall say *he* is calling.)

Who did they say was chosen? (They did say *she* was chosen.)

Who could it have been? (It could have been *he*.)

The matter of <u>who should pay</u> was not decided. (*He* should pay.)

Everybody wants to know <u>who you think should be appointed</u>. (You think *she* should be appointed.)

<u>Whoever wins the nomination</u> will win the election. (*She* wins the nomination.)

We will select <u>whoever meets our minimum qualifications</u>. (*He* meets our minimum qualifications.)

I will speak to <u>whoever answers the phone</u>. (*He* answers the phone.)

Please write at once to <u>whoever you think can supply the information desired</u>. (You think *she* can supply the information desired.)

Gloria is the one <u>who can best do the job</u>. (*She* can best do the job.)

James is the one <u>who we expect will win</u>. (We expect *he* will win.)

Please vote for the member <u>who you believe has done the most for the firm</u>. (You believe *he* has done the most for the firm.)

We have referred your claim to our lawyer, <u>who we are sure will reply soon</u>. (We are sure *she* will reply soon.)

d. *Whom* (or *whomever*) is the objective form. Use *whom* whenever *him, her, them, me,* or *us* could be substituted as the object of the verb or as the object of a preposition in the *whom* clause.

Whom did you see today? (You did see *her* today.)

To *whom* were you talking? (You were talking to *him*.)

Whom did you say you wanted to see? (You did say you wanted to see *her*.)

It depends on <u>whom they mean</u>. (They mean *him*.)

The question of <u>whom we should charge</u> is at issue. (We should charge *her*.)

I will give the job to <u>whomever you think you can safely recommend</u>. (You think you can safely recommend *him*.)

BUT: I will give the job to <u>whoever you think can be safely recommended</u>. (You think *he* can be safely recommended.)

I need a cashier <u>whom I can trust</u>. (I can trust *her*.)

The man to <u>whom I was referring</u> is Ed Meissen. (I was referring to *him*.)

The person <u>whom I was thinking</u> of doesn't have all those qualifications. (I was thinking of *her*.)

The person <u>whom we invited to address the committee</u> cannot attend. (We invited *him* to address the committee.)

Jo Fry is the nominee <u>whom they plan to support</u>. (They plan to support *her*.)

1062 WHO, WHICH, AND THAT

a. *Who* and *that* are both used when referring to persons. Select *who* when the individual person or the individuality of a group is meant and *that* when a class or type is meant.

She is the only one of my managers *who* can speak Japanese fluently.

He is the kind of student *that* should take advanced math.

(Continued on page 262.)

10

b. *Which* and *that* are used when referring to places, objects, and animals. *Which* is always used to introduce non-essential clauses, and *that* is ordinarily used to introduce essential clauses.

Laura's report on employee benefits, *which* I sent you last week, should be of some help. (*Which* introduces a non-essential clause.)

The report *that* I sent you last week should be of some help. (*That* introduces an essential clause.)

c. Many writers use either *which* or *that* to introduce an essential clause. Indeed, *which* is preferred to *that* (1) when there are two or more parallel essential clauses in the same sentence, (2) when *that* has already been used in the sentence, or (3) when the essential clause is introduced by an expression such as *this . . . which, that . . . which, these . . . which,* or *those . . . which.*

Vivian is taking courses *which* will earn her a higher salary rating in her current job and *which* will qualify her for a number of higher-level jobs.

That is a movie *which* you must not miss.

We need to reinforce *those* ideas *which* were presented in earlier chapters.

d. The verb in a relative clause introduced by *who, which,* or *that* should agree in number with the subject of the relative clause.

The laser printer that *you have ordered* will be delivered in two weeks. (The subject of the relative clause is *you,* which requires a plural verb, *have ordered.*)

However, when the relative pronoun *who, which,* or *that* is itself the subject of the relative clause, the verb in the relative clause must agree with the antecedent of the relative pronoun.

The laser *printer* that *was ordered* on May 4 will be delivered in two weeks. (The relative pronoun *that* is the subject of the relative clause and refers to a singular antecedent, *printer.* Therefore, the verb in the relative clause—*was ordered*—must be singular.)

BUT: The laser *printers* that *were ordered* . . .

Sometimes it is difficult to determine the antecedent of the relative pronoun. In such cases mentally rearrange the wording, as is done in the following example.

Hyphenate the *elements* of a *compound adjective* that occur?/occurs? before a noun. (To determine whether the antecedent of *that* is the plural term *elements* or the singular term *compound adjective,* recast the sentence: "When a *compound adjective occurs* before a noun, hyphenate the elements." This makes it clear that in the original sentence *compound adjective* is the antecedent of *that*; thus the verb in the relative clause must be singular: *occurs.*)

Hyphenate the elements of a *compound adjective* that *occurs* before a noun.

e. *Which, that,* and *who* may be used to refer to organizations. When you are referring to the organization as a single entity (in other words, as *it*), then use *which* or *that* as indicated in ¶1062b. However, when you are thinking of the organization in terms of the individuals who make up the organization (in other words, when you think of the organization as *they*), you may use *who* or *that* as indicated in ¶1062a. (See also ¶1020.)

Whenever we run short of computer supplies, the Brown & Lebrun Company is the one *that* gives us the best service and the best prices.

We really like doing business with the people at the Brown & Lebrun Company. They are a customer-oriented group *who* give us the best service and the best prices. (*That* may also be used in this sentence in place of *who*.)

1063 WHOSE AND WHO'S

Do not confuse *whose* (the possessive form of *who*) with *who's* (a contraction meaning "who is" or "who has").

Whose house is it? (**NOT:** Who is house is it?)

Who's the owner of that house? (Who is the owner of that house?)

Who's had the most experience? (Who has had the most experience?)

Who's the most experienced person? (Who is the most experienced person?)

Whose experience is best? (**NOT:** Who is (has) experience is best?)

Pronouns With *To Be*

1064 a. If a pronoun is the subject of *to be*, use the *objective* form.

I want *her* to be successful.   I expected *them* to be late.

Whom do you consider to be the more expert driver? (You do consider *whom* to be the more expert driver?)

b. If *to be* has a subject and is followed by a pronoun, put that pronoun in the *objective* case.

They mistook the *visitors* to be *us*. (*Visitors*, the subject of *to be*, is in the objective; therefore, the predicate pronoun following *to be* is objective, *us*.)

They took *her* to be *me*.

Whom did you take *him* to be? (You did take *him* to be *whom*?)

c. If *to be* has *no* subject and is followed by a pronoun, put that pronoun in the *nominative* case.

The *caller* was thought to be *I*. (*I* agrees with the subject of the sentence, *caller*.)

The *Gaidhars* were thought to be *we*.

Who was *he* thought to be? (*He* was thought to be *who*?)

NOTE: The examples above are all grammatically correct, but they sound quite awkward. Whenever possible, use more idiomatic wording. For example, the three sentences above could be recast as follows:

They thought I was the one who called.

The Gaidhars were mistaken for us.

Who did they think he was?

☞ *See individual entries listed alphabetically in Section 11 for troublesome pronouns.*

ADJECTIVES AND ADVERBS

An adjective describes or modifies a noun or pronoun. An adverb modifies or qualifies the meaning of a verb, an adjective, or another adverb. (See Section 19.)

1065 Note that only an adverb can modify or expand the sense of an adjective.

> They will give you a *really* good buy on printers.
>
> (**NOT:** They will give you a *real* good buy on printers.)

1066 When a word in the predicate refers to the *action of the verb*, use an *adverb* (not an adjective).

> We guarantee *to ship* the portfolios *promptly.*
>
> They *were injured badly* in the accident.

TEST: If *in a . . . manner* can be substituted for the *ly*-ending word, choose the adverb.

> *Read* the directions *carefully* (in a careful manner).

1067 When a word in the predicate describes the *subject* of the sentence, use an *adjective* (not an adverb). Verbs of the *senses*, various forms of *linking* verbs, and a few other verbs are followed in most cases by adjectives.

Verbs of senses:	feel	look	smell	sound	taste
Linking verbs:	appear	be	become	seem	
Other verbs:	get	grow	keep	prove	remain	turn

> I feel *bad* (**NOT** badly). He has grown *tall.*
> She looked *happy.* The work proved *hard.*
> Your voice sounded *strong.* I got *lucky.*
> He seemed (**OR** appeared) *shy.* Let's all keep (**OR** remain) *calm.*
> They became *famous.* The weather has turned *cold.*

TEST: If *is, are, was, were,* or some other form of *be* can be substituted for the verb, choose the adjective.

> He *looks happy.* He *is happy.*

NOTE: In the following group of examples, verbs of the senses and linking verbs are used as verbs of action. (See ¶1066.) Since the modifier refers to the action of the verb (and does not describe the subject), the modifier must be an adverb.

> She *looked suspiciously* at the visitor in the reception room.
>
> He *felt carefully* along the ledge for the key.
>
> Our market share *has grown quickly.*
>
> He *appeared quietly* in the doorway.

1068 Several of the most frequently used adverbs have two forms.

close, closely	fair, fairly	loud, loudly	short, shortly
deep, deeply	hard, hardly	quick, quickly	slow, slowly
direct, directly	late, lately	right, rightly	wide, widely

a. In a number of cases the two forms have different meanings.

Ship the goods *direct*. (Meaning "straight," "without detour.")
They were *directly* responsible. (Meaning "without any intervention.")

They arrived *late*.   The truck stopped *short*.
I haven't seen her *lately*.   You will hear from us *shortly*.

You've been working too *hard*.   Turn *right* at the first traffic light.
I could *hardly* hear him.   I don't *rightly* remember.

b. In some cases the choice is largely a matter of idiom. Some verbs take the *ly* form; others take the short form.

dig deep	go slow	open wide	come close	play fair
wound deeply	proceed slowly	travel widely	watch closely	treat fairly

c. In still other cases the choice is simply one of formality. The *ly* forms are more formal.

sell cheap **OR** sell cheaply   talk loud **OR** talk loudly

1069 a. Although the *ly* ending usually signifies an adverb, a few adjectives also end in *ly*—for example, *costly, orderly, timely, motherly, fatherly, friendly, neighbourly, worldly, earthly, lively, lovely, lonely.*

Let's look for a less *costly* solution.

Her offer to help you was intended as a *friendly* gesture.

b. A few common *ly*-ending words are used both as adjectives and adverbs—for example, *early, only, daily, weekly, monthly, quarterly, yearly.*

I always try to leave for work at an *early* hour. (Adjective.)
The surge in sales began *early* last month. (Adverb.)

We issue our sales reports on a *quarterly* basis. (Adjective.)
We issue our sales reports *quarterly*. (Adverb.)

We are waiting for the *first-quarter* sales report. (Compound adjective.)
NOT: We are all waiting for the *first-quarterly* sales report.

c. The words *fast, long,* and *hard* are also used both as adjectives and as adverbs.

ADJECTIVES:	a *fast* talker	a *long, hard* winter
ADVERBS:	talks *fast*	thought *long* and *hard*

1070 Words such as *up, in, out, on,* and *off*—commonly recognized as prepositions—also function as adverbs, especially in verb phrases where these words are needed to complete the meaning of the verb. (See also ¶802.)

	Used as Adverbs	Used as Prepositions
up:	to look *up* the definition	to jog *up* the hill
down:	to take *down* your name	to walk *down* the street
in:	to trade *in* your old car	to see *in* the dark
out:	to phase *out* operations	to look *out* the window
on:	to put *on* a performance	to act *on* the stage
off:	to write *off* our losses	to drive *off* the road

(Continued on page 266.)

NOTE: When used in headings and titles as *adverbs*, these short words are capitalized; when used as *prepositions*, they are not. (See ¶361c–d.)

Forms of Comparison

1071 The various forms of an adjective or adverb indicate degrees in quality, quantity, or manner. The degrees are positive (simple form), comparative (a higher or lower degree of quality or manner), and the superlative (the highest or lowest degree).

a. Form the comparative degree of *one-syllable* adjectives or adverbs by adding *er* to the positive form. For *two-syllable* adjectives or adverbs add *er* or insert either *more* or *less* before the positive form. For *three or more syllables* insert *more* or *less*.

blue: bluer, more (**OR** less) blue	quick: quicker, more (**OR** less) quick
clever: cleverer, more (**OR** less) clever	often: oftener, more (**OR** less) often
competent: more competent	adventurous: less adventurous

b. Form the superlative degree of *one-syllable* adjectives or adverbs by adding *est* to the positive form. (For a few exceptions, see ¶1071e note.) For *two, three,* or more syllables add *est* or insert either *most* or *least* before the positive form.

high: highest	deep: deepest
happy: happiest, most (**OR** least) happy	likely: likeliest, most (**OR** least) likely
acceptable: most acceptable	carefully: least carefully

☞ *See ¶825b and Section 11 for a usage note on* more.

NOTE: If the positive form ends in a consonant plus *y* (for example, *happy, likely*), change the *y* to *i* before adding *er* or *est*. Some *ly*-ending words drop the *ly* in the comparative and superlative (for example, *highly, higher, highest; deeply, deeper, deepest*). (See also ¶710.)

c. In some cases the addition of *er* and *est* will create very awkward forms. Your ear will tell you when to avoid them.

more hopeful (**NOT:** hopefuller)	more hostile (**NOT:** hostiler)
most complex (**NOT:** complexest)	most troubled (**NOT:** troublest)

d. A few adjectives and adverbs have irregular comparisons. For example:

Positive	Comparative	Superlative
good or well (see Section 11)	better	best
bad or ill	worse	worst
far	farther, further (see Section 11)	farthest, furthest
late	later, latter (see Section 11)	latest, last
little	littler, less, lesser	littlest, least
many, much	more	most

10

e. When referring to *two* persons, places, or things, use the comparative form; when referring to *more than two*, use the superlative form.

That is the *finer* piece of linen. (Only two pieces are involved.)
This is the *finest* piece of linen I could find. (Many pieces are involved.)

Of the two positions open, you have chosen the *more* promising.
Of the three positions open, you have chosen the *most* promising.

That is the *more* efficient of the two methods.
This is the *most* efficient method that could be devised.

I like Evelyn's plan *better* than Joe's or Betty's. (Although three things are involved, they are being compared two at a time; hence the comparative.)

NOTE: In a few idiomatic expressions (such as *Put your best foot forward* and *May the best man win*), the superlative form is used, even though only two things are referred to.

f. When comparing a person or a thing *within* the group to which it belongs, use the superlative. When comparing a person or a thing with individual members of the group, use the comparative and the words *other* or *else*.

Susan is the *most* conscientious employee on the staff.
Susan is *more* conscientious than any *other* employee on the staff. (Without the word *other*, the sentence would imply that Susan is not on the staff.)

Toronto is the *largest* city in Ontario.
Toronto is *larger* than any *other* city in Ontario. (Without the word *other*, the sentence would imply that Toronto is not in Ontario.)

Bert's proposal was the *best* of all that were presented to the committee.
Bert's proposal was *better* than anyone *else's*. (**NOT:** anyone's.)

g. Be sure to compare like things. (See also Note ¶644.)

This year's output is lower than last year's. (In other words, "This year's *output* is lower than last year's *output*.")

NOT: This year's output is lower than last year. (Incorrectly compares *this year's output* with *last year*.)

h. Some adjectives and adverbs—for example, *square, round, unique, completely, universally, correct, perfect, always, never, dead*—do not logically permit comparison. A square cannot be any *squarer*; a circle cannot be the *roundest of all circles*. Nevertheless, a number of these words may be modified by *more, less, nearly, hardly, virtually*, and similar adverbs to suggest something less than absolute perfection in each case.

Next year we hope to do a *more complete* study.

He is looking for a *more universally* acceptable solution.

Handicraft of this calibre is *virtually unique* these days.

We *almost never* increase our prices more than once a year.

i. Avoid double comparisons.

cheaper (**NOT:** more cheaper)   unkindest (**NOT:** most unkindest)

1072 The adverbs *only, nearly, almost, ever, scarcely, merely, too,* and *also* should be placed as close as possible to the word modified—usually directly before it. Putting the adverb in the wrong position may change the entire meaning of the sentence.

> Our list of depositors numbers *almost* 50 000. (**NOT:** almost numbers.)
>
> *Only* the board can nominate the three new officers. (Cannot be nominated by anyone else.)
> The board can *only* nominate the three officers. (They cannot elect.)
> The board can nominate *only* the three officers. (They cannot nominate anyone else.)
>
> Maria and Dino Gados have been married for *not quite* two years.
> (**NOT:** Maria and Dino Gados have *not quite* been married for two years.)

1073 Do not use an adverb to express a meaning already contained in the verb.

> assemble (**NOT:** assemble together)   follow (**NOT:** follow after)
> begin (**NOT:** first begin)   refer (**NOT:** refer back)
> continue (**NOT:** continue on)   repeat (**NOT:** repeat again)
> convert (**NOT:** convert over)   return (**NOT:** return back)
> co-operate (**NOT:** co-operate together)   revert (**NOT:** revert back)

☞ *For troublesome adjectives and adverbs, see individual entries in Section 11.*

NEGATIVES

1074 To express a negative idea in a simple sentence, use only one negative expression in the sentence. (A *double negative*—two negative expressions in the same sentence—gives a *positive* meaning. Occasionally a double negative is used to emphasize a positive thought.)

> We can sit by and do *nothing*.
>
> We can*not* sit by and do *nothing*. (The *not* and *nothing* create a double negative; the sentence now has a positive meaning: "We ought to do something.")
>
> Jim is *un*aware of the facts. (Here the negative element is the prefix *un*.)
>
> Jim is *not un*aware of the facts. (With the double negative, the sentence means "Jim *is* aware of the facts.")

1075 A negative expression gives a negative meaning to the *clause* in which it appears. In a simple sentence, where there is only one clause, the negative expression affects the entire sentence. (See ¶1074.) In a sentence where there are two or more clauses, a negative expression affects only the clause in which it appears. Therefore, each clause may safely contain one negative expression. A double negative results when there are two negative expressions within the *same* clause.

> If Mr. Bogosian can*not* lower his price, there is *no* point in continuing the negotiations. (The *if* clause contains the negative *not*; the main clause contains the negative *no*. Each clause has its own negative meaning.)
>
> I have *not* met Hironaka, and I have *no* desire to meet him.
> **OR:** I have *not* met Hironaka, *nor* do I have *any* desire to meet him. (When the negative conjunction *nor* replaces *and*, the adjective *no* changes to *any* so as to avoid a double negative in the second clause.)
>
> We have *never* permitted, *nor* will we permit, any lowering of our standards. (Here the second clause interrupts the first clause. If written out in full, the sentence would read, "We have *never* permitted any lowering of our standards, *nor* will we permit any lowering of our standards.")

NOTE: A second negative expression may be used in a clause to repeat or intensify the first negative expression. This construction is not a double negative.

> *No,* I did *not* make that statement.
>
> He would *never, never* do a thing like that!   That's a *no-no*!

1076 To preserve the *negative* meaning of a clause, follow these basic principles:

a. If the clause has a *negative verb* (a verb modified by *not* or *never*), do not use an additional negative expression, such as *nor, neither . . . nor, no, none, no one,* or *nothing.* Instead, use the corresponding positive expression, such as *or, either . . . or, any, anyone,* or *anything.*

> I have *not* invited *anyone.* (**WRONG:** I have *not* invited *no one.*)
>
> She does *not* want *any.* (**WRONG:** She does *not* want *none.*)
>
> Mary did *not* have *anything* to do. (**WRONG:** Mary did *not* have *nothing* to do.)
>
> I *cannot* find *either* the letter *or* the envelope. (**WRONG:** I can*not* find *neither* the letter *nor* the envelope.)
>
> He did *not* say whether he would mail the money to us *or* whether he would bring it himself. (**WRONG:** He did *not* say whether he would mail the money to us *nor* whether he would bring it himself.)

b. If a clause contains any one of the following expressions—*no, no one, none, nothing,* or *neither . . . nor* (this counts as one expression)—make sure that the verb and all other words are *positive.*

> I see *nothing* wrong with *either* proposal. (**NOT:** neither proposal.)
>
> *Neither* Martha Gutowski *nor* Yvonne Christopher *can* attend. (**NOT:** cannot.)

c. The word *nor* may be used alone as a conjunction (see the second and third examples in ¶1075) or together with *neither.* Do not use *nor* in the same clause with any other negative; use *or* instead.

> There are *neither* diskettes *nor* printer cartridges in the stockroom.
> **BUT:** There are *no* diskettes *or* printer cartridges in the stockroom.
> (**NOT:** There are *no* diskettes *nor* printer cartridges.)
>
> There are *no* clear-cut rights *or* wrongs in the situation.
> (**NOT:** There are *no* clear-cut rights *nor* wrongs in the situation.)
>
> Francine has *not* called *or* written us for some time.
> (**NOT:** Francine has *not* called *nor* written us for some time.)

☞ *For* Hardly, Only, Scarcely, *and* Could Not Care Less *which have a negative meaning, see the appropriate entries in Section 11.*

PREPOSITIONS
Words Requiring Certain Prepositions

1077 Usage requires that certain words be followed by certain prepositions. Some frequently used combinations are given in the following list.

> **accompanied by** (a person): I was *accompanied by* my instructor.
> **accompanied with** (something): The speech was *accompanied with* gestures.

(Continued on page 270.)

account for something or someone: I find it hard to *account for* his behaviour.

account to someone: You will have to *account to* Anne Crump for the loss.

agree on or **upon** (reach an understanding): We cannot *agree on* the price.

agree to (to accept another person's plan): Will you *agree to* their terms?

agree with (concur with a person or an idea): I *agree with* your objectives.

angry at or **about** something: He was *angry about* the disorder.

angry with someone: You have every right to be *angry with* me.

apply for a position: You ought to *apply for* the job.

apply to someone or something: You must *apply* yourself *to* the job in order to master it. I am thinking of *applying to* that company.

argue about something: We *argued about* the terms of the contract.

argue with a person: It doesn't pay to *argue with* Bremer.

beneficial to: Exercise is *beneficial to* good health.

compare to (assert a likeness): She *compared* my writing *to* W. P. Kinsella's. (She said I wrote like W. P. Kinsella.)

compare with (analyze for similarities and differences): When she *compared* my writing *with* E. B. White's, she said that I had a similar kind of humour but that my sentences lacked the easy flow of words.

confer on or **upon** (give to): A medal was *conferred on* the brave soldier.

confer with (talk to): Tom *conferred with* his boss.

conform to (preferred to *with*): The drafts do not *conform to* the plans.

consists in (exists in): Happiness largely *consists in* wanting what you have, not having what you want.

consists of (is made up of): Their new formula for a wage settlement *consists of* the same old terms expressed in different language.

convenient for (suitable): What time will be most *convenient for* you?

convenient to (near at hand): Our plant is *convenient to* all facilities.

correspond to (agree with): The shipment does not *correspond to* the sample.

correspond with (exchange letters with): We must *correspond with* him today.

deal in (goods and services): The firm *deals in* heavy equipment.

deal with (a person): Judges *deal with* those who break the laws.

differ about (something): We *differed about* means but not about ends.

differ from (something else): This job *differs* very little *from* my previous one.

differ with (someone): I *differ with* you over the consequences of our plan.

different from: This product is *different from* the one I normally use.

different than: I view this matter in a *different* way *than* you do. (Although *from* is normally preferred, *than* is acceptable in order to avoid sentences like "I view the matter in a different way from the way in which you do.")

independent of (not *from*): He wants to be *independent of* his family.

interested in: We are *interested in* discussing the matter with you.

10

retroactive to (not *from*): This salary adjustment is *retroactive to* May 1.

speak to (tell something to): I will *speak to* the class about their test.

speak with (discuss with): It was good to *speak with* you yesterday.

Superfluous Prepositions

1078 Omit prepositions that add nothing to the meaning—as in the following examples. (See also Section 11 for a usage note on *all of*.)

Where is she [at]?

She could not help [from] laughing.

The chair is too near [to] the table.

Let's meet at [**OR** about] one o'clock.

We need to focus [in] on new ways.

Where did that paper go [to]?

His office is opposite [to] hers.

The strike is now over [with].

The box fell off [of] the truck.

Necessary Prepositions

1079 Conversely, do not omit essential prepositions.

I need to buy a couple *of* books. (**NOT:** I need to buy a couple books.)

We don't stock that type *of* filter. (**NOT:** We don't stock that type filter.)

He has a great interest *in*, as well as a respect *for*, fine antiques. (**NOT:** He has a great interest, as well as a respect *for*, fine antiques.)

She frequently appears in movies, *in* plays, and on television. (**NOT:** She frequently appears in movies, plays, and on television.)

NOTE: The preposition *of* is understood in expressions such as *what colour cloth* and *what size shoes*.

Prepositions at the End of Sentences

1080 a. Ending a sentence with a preposition is not incorrect. Whether you do so or not depends on the emphasis and effect you want to achieve. Moreover, trying to avoid ending a sentence with a preposition may lead to awkward results.

INFORMAL: I wish I knew which magazine her article appeared *in*.
FORMAL: I wish I knew *in which* magazine her article appeared.

STILTED: It is difficult to know *about* what you are thinking.
NATURAL: It is difficult to know what you are thinking *about*.

b. Short questions and statements frequently end with prepositions.

How many can I count *on*?

What is this made *of*?

Where did he come *from*?

He has nothing to worry *about*.

What is this good *for*?

We need tools to work *with*.

That's something we must look *into*.

There's a new computer I want to look *at*.

c. Some sentences end with words that seem to be prepositions but are really adverbs.

I'm sure another job will soon turn *up*.

After Yogita considers her alternatives, I'm sure she will come *around*.

(Continued on page 272.)

☞ *For troublesome prepositions, see individual entries listed alphabetically in Section 11.*

☞ *For the treatment of words that can be both prepositions and adverbs, see ¶1070. For the capitalization of such words, see ¶361c–d.*

WRITING MECHANICS
Word Use

Sentences can be made clear and effective by choosing verbs and concrete words and by avoiding "hidden verbs," unnecessary words, and out-of-date expressions.

1081 *Hidden verbs* in noun form tend to weaken a sentence and make it wordy.

> **WEAK:** Leonard *sent* Janet *an invitation* to dinner.
> **BETTER:** Leonard *invited* Janet to dinner.
>
> **WEAK:** Please *take into consideration* all the alternatives.
> **BETTER:** Please *consider* all the alternatives.

1082 *Redundancy* results from using words that are unnecessarily repetitive.

experience (**NOT:** past experience)	alike (**NOT:** both alike)
beginner (**NOT:** new beginner)	both (**NOT:** both together)
Yukon (**NOT:** territory of Yukon)	round (**NOT:** round in shape)
15 pages (**NOT:** 15 pages in length)	practice (**NOT:** usual practice)
weather (**NOT:** weather conditions)	emergency (**NOT:** emergency situation)

☞ *For additional examples, see ¶¶1073 and 1078.*

1083 *Out-of-date expressions* should be replaced by current, not slang, expressions. Remember that the use of generic nouns and masculine pronouns are not acceptable in most situations today. (See ¶¶809, 810, 1052, and 1053a.)

Out-of-Date	Current
advise, inform	say, tell, let us know
with reference to	about, regarding
enclosed please find	is/are enclosed
attached herewith	attached is/are
in the amount of	for
in the near future	on/by (give a date)
at the present time	now, currently
in the event that	if
due to the fact that	since, because, as
during the time that	when
under separate cover	will send, are sending separately
as per	as, according to
kindly	please
acknowledge receipt of	thank you for, we received
beg	ask, request
the fact of the matter is	the fact is

10

1084 *Concrete language* conveys a precise meaning to the reader.

> **WEAK:** Only a *few* employees went to the training program.
> **BETTER:** Only *15* employees went to the training program.

> **WEAK:** Conference Room A accommodates a *large group* of trainees.
> **BETTER:** Conference Room A accommodates *70* trainees.

Common Errors in Phrasing

Common phrasing errors to watch for are misplaced and dangling modifiers and a lack of parallel structure. Group words and phrases carefully because small differences in their placement can cause large differences in meaning.

1085 *Parallel structure* grammatically presents similar ideas.

a. Adjectives should be paralleled by adjectives, nouns by nouns, infinitives by infinitives, dependent clauses by dependent clauses, and so on.

> **WRONG:** Your training program was *stimulating* and a *challenge.* (Adjective and noun.)
> **RIGHT:** Your training program was *stimulating* and *challenging.* (Two adjectives.)

> **WRONG:** The sales representatives have already started *using the new techniques* and *to produce higher sales.* (Participial phrase and infinitive phrase.)
> **RIGHT:** The sales representatives have already started *using the new techniques* and *producing higher sales.* (Two participial phrases.)
> **RIGHT:** The sales representatives have already started *to use the new techniques* and *to produce higher sales.* (Two infinitive phrases.)

> **WRONG:** This scanner is *easy* to operate, *efficient,* and *it is relatively inexpensive.* (Two adjectives and a clause.)
> **RIGHT:** This scanner is *easy* to operate, *efficient,* and relatively *inexpensive.* (Three adjectives.)

> **NOTE:** Parallelism is especially important in displayed enumerations.

> **POOR:** This article will discuss:
> 1. How to deal with corporate politics.
> 2. Coping with stressful situations.
> 3. What the role of the manager should be in the community.

> **BETTER:** This article will discuss:
> 1. *Ways* to deal with corporate politics.
> 2. *Techniques* of coping with stressful situations.
> 3. The *role* of the manager in the community.

> **OR:** This article will tell managers how to:
> 1. *Deal* with corporate politics.
> 2. *Cope* with stressful situations.
> 3. *Function* in the community.

b. Be sure to check that all the essential words are used in modifiers, comparisons, verb phrases, and prepositional phrases. (See ¶¶1048 and 1079.)

> **WRONG:** She bought *a* coat, purse, and umbrella.
> **RIGHT:** She bought *a* coat, *a* purse, and *an* umbrella.

(Continued on page 274.)

10

> **WRONG:** Stephanie can create designs just *as well,* if not *better,* than Craig.
> **RIGHT:** Stephanie can create designs just as well *as, if not better than,* Craig.

c. Correlative conjunctions (*both . . . and, either . . . or, neither . . . nor, not only . . . but also, whether . . . or,* etc.) should be followed by elements in parallel form.

> **WRONG:** Kevin is not only *gifted as a painter* but also *as a sculptor.*
> **RIGHT:** Kevin is gifted not only *as a painter* but also *as a sculptor.*

> **WRONG:** We are flying both *to Toronto* and *Montreal.*
> **RIGHT:** We are flying to both *Toronto* and *Montreal.*
> **RIGHT:** We are flying both *to Toronto* and *to Montreal.*

> **WRONG:** He would neither *apologize* nor *would he promise to reform.*
> **RIGHT:** He would neither *apologize* nor *promise to reform.*
> **RIGHT:** He *would not apologize,* nor *would he promise to reform.*

1086 *Dangling constructions* occur mainly at the beginning and at the end of sentences. They include verbal constructions such as participial phrases, infinitive phrases, gerund phrases, or elliptical clauses (ones in which essential words are missing). Make sure that the phrase or clause logically agrees with the subject of the sentence; otherwise, the construction will "dangle." To correct this construction, make the subject of the sentence the doer of the action expressed by the opening phrase or clause. If that is not feasible, use an entirely different construction.

a. Participial Phrases

> **WRONG:** After coming out of a coma, the police officer asked the driver what caused the accident.
> **RIGHT:** After the driver came out of a coma, the police officer asked her what caused the accident.

> **WRONG:** Putting the issue of costs aside, the delays need to be discussed.
> **RIGHT:** Putting the issue of costs aside, we need to discuss the delays.

> **NOTE:** A few words ending in *ing* (such as *concerning, considering, pending,* and *regarding*) have now become established as prepositions. Therefore, when they introduce phrases at the start of a sentence, it is not essential that they refer to the subject of the sentence.

> *Considering* how long the lawsuit has dragged on, it might have been wiser not to sue.

b. Infinitive Phrases

> **WRONG:** To appreciate the full significance of Fox's latest letter, all the previous correspondence should be read.
> **RIGHT:** To appreciate the full significance of Fox's latest letter, you should read all the previous correspondence.

> **WRONG:** To obtain this free booklet, the enclosed coupon should be mailed at once.
> **RIGHT:** To obtain this free booklet, mail the enclosed coupon at once.

c. Prepositional-Gerund Phrases

> **WRONG:** By installing a control system, a saving in fuel costs was achieved.
> **RIGHT:** By installing a control system, we achieved a saving in fuel costs.

WRONG: In analyzing these specifications, several errors have been found.
RIGHT: In analyzing these specifications, I have found several errors.

d. Elliptical Clauses

WRONG: If ordered before May 1, a 5 percent discount will be allowed on these goods.
RIGHT: If ordered before May 1, these goods will be allowed a 5 . . .

WRONG: When four years old, my family moved to Oshawa.
RIGHT: When I was four years old, my family moved to Oshawa.

e. Absolute Phrases

Absolute phrases are not considered to "dangle," even though they come at the beginning of a sentence and do not refer to the subject.

All things considered, her plan may be the best way to proceed.

Weather permitting, the ceremonies will be held in the quadrangle.

Avoid using these phrases, however, when they produce awkward sentences.

WEAK: The speeches having been concluded, we proceeded to take a vote.

BETTER: After the speeches were concluded, we proceeded to take a vote.

1087 a. When verbal phrases and elliptical clauses fall elsewhere in the sentence, look out for illogical or confusing relationships. Adjust the wording as necessary.

WRONG: I saw two truck drivers get into a fistfight while jogging down the street.

RIGHT: While jogging down the street, I saw two truck drivers get into a fistfight.

b. A phrase will dangle at the beginning of a sentence if it leads the reader to expect a certain word as the subject and then another word is used instead.

WRONG: As head of the program committee, we think you should make immediate arrangements for another speaker. (The head of the committee is *you*, not *we*.)
RIGHT: We think that as head of the program committee, you should make immediate arrangements for another speaker.

WRONG: Having called in sick for the fifth straight day, Paula's colleagues began to worry about the state of her health. (This sentence suggests that Paula's colleagues are the ones who have been calling in sick.)
RIGHT: After Paula called in sick for the fifth straight day, her colleagues began to worry about the state of her health.

WRONG: As a young boy, the woman I was destined to marry did not appeal to me in any way. (That woman never was a "young boy.")
RIGHT: When I was a young boy, the woman I was destined to marry did not appeal to me in any way.

c. A verbal phrase will dangle at the end of a sentence if it refers to the meaning of the main clause as a whole rather than to the doer of the action.

WRONG: Our sales have been steadily declining for the past six months, thus creating a sharp drop in profits. (As worded, the sentence makes it appear that *our sales*, by themselves, have created the drop in profits. Actually, it is *the fact* that our sales have been declining which has created the drop in profits.)

(Continued on page 276.)

RIGHT: The steady decline in our sales for the past six months has created a sharp drop in profits.

RIGHT: Our sales have been steadily declining for the past six months. As a result, we have experienced a sharp drop in profits.

1088 *Misplaced modifiers* (either words or phrases) are modifiers that are placed in such a way that they can be misinterpreted.

a. Watch out for misplaced modifiers that may lead to unintended and even humorous interpretations.

WRONG: I suspect that my assistant accidentally dropped the report I had been drafting in the wastebasket. (What an uncomfortable location in which to draft a report!)
RIGHT: The report I had been drafting has disappeared. I suspect that my assistant accidentally dropped it in the wastebasket.

WRONG: Here are some helpful suggestions for protecting your valuables from our hotel security staff. (Can no one be trusted?)
RIGHT: Here are some helpful suggestions from our hotel security staff for protecting your valuables.

WRONG: One of our assistant vice-presidents has been referred to a personal finance counsellor with serious credit problems. (Would you consult such a counsellor?)
RIGHT: One of our assistant vice-presidents has serious credit problems and has been referred to a personal finance counsellor.

b. Watch out for adverbs such as *only* that must be positioned carefully to convey the intended meaning. (See ¶1072.)

Susan can only buy raffle tickets from me. (She can't sell them.)
Susan can buy only raffle tickets from me. (She can't buy anything else from me.)
Susan can buy raffle tickets only from me. (She can't buy from anyone else.)

c. The pronoun *which* often introduces a clause that modifies or explains another word in the sentence. If the antecedent of the *which clause* is unclear, the meaning can be ambiguous.

WRONG: Our store is featuring a book on the Group of Seven paintings, which you can purchase for the special price of $29.95.
RIGHT: Our store is featuring a book, which you can purchase for the special price of $29.95, on the Group of Seven paintings.

Planning and Organizing

10

Written communications are a key part of business activity, and as such they require careful planning and organization to accomplish their intended purpose.

1089 The following are suggestions for the initial planning of writing a business document.

a. Begin by analyzing your audience and determining the strategy to use (a direct or an indirect approach).

b. Consider the main reasons for the communication by answering the following questions:

- Why is the communication being written?
- What information must be conveyed?
- How can the message be conveyed effectively?

c. Gather all essential information to be conveyed in the message, arrange it in a logical order, and decide the most efficient way to present the information. When writing request letters,

- Enumerate or make a list of the information you need; then prepare short, specific questions written in parallel form. (See ¶1081.)
- Rephrase the questions to get more than a yes or a no answer, especially when detailed opinions or descriptions are wanted.
- Arrange the questions carefully, placing the easiest to answer first.

d. When writing response letters, a good rule is to answer the questions in the order they were asked and to supply additional information as required.

Sentence and Paragraph Construction

1090 A *simple* sentence is the easiest way to present a thought. However, if all the sentences in a document are short and simple, the writing will be dull and choppy. *Compound* and *complex* sentences will relieve the monotony. A compound sentence presents two *equal* ideas, while a complex sentence presents two *related* ideas by putting the main idea in the independent clause and the lesser idea in a dependent, subordinate clause.

☞ *See Section 19 for examples of the basic forms of sentences.*

a. A *run-on sentence* occurs when two independent clauses appear in the same sentence with only a comma to separate them. (See also ¶128.) To correct this error, use a stronger mark of punctuation (a semicolon, a colon, or a dash); insert a coordinating conjunction *(and, but, or nor)* after the comma; or make the two clauses into separate sentences.

WRONG: Steve is now at a meeting in Tokyo, he will be back early on Friday.

RIGHT: Steve is now at a meeting in Tokyo—he will be back early on Friday.

RIGHT: Steve is now at a meeting in Tokyo, *but* he will be back early on Friday.

RIGHT: Steve is now at a meeting in Tokyo. *He* will be back early on Friday.

b. A *sentence fragment* is a phrase or dependent clause that is incorrectly treated as a sentence. It should be incorporated with adjacent words to make a complete sentence. (See ¶132.)

WRONG: We failed to reach our quota. Although we made a determined effort.
RIGHT: We failed to reach our quota, although we made a determined effort.
RIGHT: Although we made a determined effort, we failed to reach our quota.

WRONG: In reference to the August 16 issue of *The Journal.* Please consider me a candidate for the position of marketing analyst.
RIGHT: In reference to the August 16 issue of *The Journal,* please consider me a candidate for the position of marketing analyst.

10

1091 The skilful use of transitional words and phrases can move the reader smoothly from one idea to another without a break in continuity. Transitional words act like a "bridge" to show how ideas are related in time (after, as soon as, meanwhile) and in relation to one another (for example, therefore, however). (See ¶138.)

1092 In general, choose the active voice of verbs because it is more effective and action-oriented. Since the active voice may be too forceful for negative messages, the passive voice is often used to soften the effect of bad news or to avoid assigning blame in sensitive situations. (See *Voice* in Section 19 and ¶1037.)

1093 The structure and length of a paragraph influences clarity because paragraphs divide material into manageable units of thought.

   a. Short, direct paragraphs are easier to read than long, involved ones.

   b. Generally four to eight lines of keyed material is a good length for each paragraph.

   c. The first and last sentences are the key emphasis positions for important ideas. Less important or negative ideas should be placed in the middle of the paragraph to de-emphasize them.

   d. Relationships between ideas should be coherent, presented logically, and connected by transitional words.

Tone in Writing

1094 A *considerate* tone in writing shows concern for and avoids blaming the reader. This can be achieved by referring specifically to the reader's request and by stressing what the reader wants to know. In cases of disagreement, avoid the word *you* and use impersonal expressions and passive verbs.

> **WEAK:** If you had paid your bill before the April 8 due date instead of on April 15, you would not have received the overdue notice.
> **BETTER:** Overdue notices were sent out for bills that were paid after the April 8 due date.

> **WEAK:** You didn't send us your cheque.
> **BETTER:** We have not received your cheque.

1095 A *courteous* tone in business writing means being polite and positive. *Please* should be used before a request, and *thank you* after a request has been granted.

> **WEAK:** I need the report on Monday, and I would like you to give it to me before noon.
> **BETTER:** Could you please complete the report and give it to me by noon on Monday.

> **WEAK:** Use the enclosed envelope to return your payment.
> **BETTER:** Please return your payment in the enclosed envelope.

1096 *Positive writing* can achieve far more than negative writing. In business situations, both positive and negative ideas have to be conveyed, but the *way* in which they are conveyed is crucial.

   • Avoid using words such as *claim, complaint, defective, failure, neglect,* and *regret.*

   • Change negative statements into positive ones.

- Focus on what can be done rather than on what cannot be done.
- Justify negative news by giving the reasons for the decision.

NEGATIVE: Because our next board meeting is not scheduled until May 19, we will not be able to consider your proposal until then.
POSITIVE: We will be pleased to consider your proposal at our next board meeting, on May 19.

NEGATIVE: The copy machine you sold us is defective so replace it with one that works.
POSITIVE: The copy machine you sold us required 12 service calls this month. Please replace it with one that provides better service.

NEGATIVE: Do not complete this form if you have not read all the directions carefully.
POSITIVE: Please complete this form after you have carefully read all the directions.

Business Writing Style

The mechanics of grammar and style should be applied to all business correspondence, especially to the writing of letters. The writing style follows the 5Cs of communication to ensure that the message is correct, concise, clear, coherent, and courteous. Generally, letters fall into two main categories: positive and negative.

1097 A positive letter transmits information, makes a request, or replies positively to a request. The following are suggestions for writing this kind of letter:

- State the main idea of the message, and give all the details necessary to support the main idea.
- Be specific by stating *what* is needed and *why* it is needed, but do not apologize for making the request.
- Answer questions definitely and courteously; assume the reader will respond favourably, but avoid using *if* (as it may remind readers that they have a choice).
- Close by using *appreciate* and *gratefully,* not *thank you* or *thank you in advance* (as these expressions are presumptuous); end pleasantly, generally looking forward to the future.

1098 A negative letter refuses a request, makes a complaint, or conveys some bad news.

- Avoid tactless, trite, and disappointing opening remarks like *We are sorry, We regret, We cannot;* do not thank the writer for the letter but say that the request is appreciated.
- Refer neutrally to the request; explain clearly and briefly the facts leading to the refusal (often called a *buffer*), and then state the refusal; but do not apologize for the decision or encourage further communication on the subject.
- Use longer sentences, longer paragraphs, and the passive voice of verbs.
- Be polite and positive in closing but do not repeat the details of the request that is being refused; instead, express a wish for success, offer possible solutions, or give constructive suggestions.
- Avoid stereotyped sentence closings that offer nothing, such as "If we can be of further assistance, please do not hesitate to contact us."

See the Online Learning Centre at www.mcgrawhill.ca/college/gregg for related Web links.

SECTION **ELEVEN**

Usage

A—An
A—Of
Above
Accidentally
A.D.–B.C.
Additionally
Affect—Effect
Age—Aged—At the Age of
All of
All Right
Allude—Refer
Almost—All Most
Already—All Ready
Altogether—All Together
Always—All Ways
Amount—Number
And
And Etc.
And/Or
Anxious—Eager
Anymore—Any More
Anyone—Any One
Anytime—Any Time
Anyway—Any Way
Appreciate
As
As . . . as—Not so . . . as
As Far As
As Well As
Awhile—A While
Bad—Badly
Balance
Because
Because of
Being That
Beside—Besides
Between—Among
Between You and Me
Biannual—Biennial—Semi-annual
Biweekly—Bimonthly
Both—Each

Both Alike—Equal—Together
Bring—Take
But . . . However
But What
Come—Go
Come and
Complementary—Complimentary
Comprise—Compose
Consist of—Include
Could Not Care Less
Data
Different—Differently
Different From—Different Than
Done
Don't (Do Not)
Doubt That—Doubt Whether
Due to—Because of—On Account of
Each Other—One Another
Ensure—Insure—Assure
Enthused Over
Equally as Good
Etc.—And so on—Such as
Everyday—Every Day
Everyone—Every One
Ex—Former
Except
Farther—Further
Fewer—Less
First—Firstly, etc.
Flammable—Inflammable
Former—First
From—Off
Good—Well
Graduated—Was Graduated
Hardly
Healthy—Healthful
Help
Historic—Historical
Hopefully
However

If—Whether
Imply—Infer
In—Into—In to
In Regard to
Incidentally
Indifferent—In Different
Indirect—In Direct
Individual—Party—Person—People
Irregardless
Is Where—Is When
Its—It's
Kind
Kind of—Sort of
Kind of a
Last—Latest
Latter—Last
Lay—Lie
Learn—Teach
Leave—Let
Like—As, As if
Literally
May—Can (Might—Could)
Maybe—May Be
Media
More
More Important—More Importantly
Most
Nobody—No Body
None—No One
Of—Have
Off
On—Onto—On to
On—Upon—Up on
Only
Opposite
Per—A
Percent—Percentage
Plus
Proved—Proven

Raise—Rise
Real—Really
Reason Is Because
Retroactive to
Said
Same
Scarcely
Serve—Service
Set—Sit
Shall—Will
Should—Would
Since
So—So That
Someday—Some Day
Someone—Some One
Sometime—Sometimes—Some Time
Supposed to
Sure—Surely
Sure and
Than—Then
That
That—That
That—Which—Who
This Here
This Sort—This Kind
Toward—Towards
Try and
Unique
Up
Used to
Very
Ways
Whatever—What Ever
Where—That
Who—Which—That
Who—Whom
Whoever—Who Ever
Wise
Would Have

☞ *See ¶719 for words frequently misused because they sound alike or look alike.*

1101 The following entries will help you avoid a number of errors in usage.

A—an. In choosing *a* or *an*, consider the sound (not the spelling) of the following word. Use the article *a* before all *consonant sounds*, including sounded *h*, long *u*, and *o* with the sound of *w* (as in *one*).

a day	a home	a unit	a youthful spirit	a one-week delay
a week	a house	a union	a euphoric feeling	a 60-day note
a year	a hotel	a uniform	a European trip	a CGA

(Continued on page 282.)

11

Use *an* before all *vowel sounds*.

an asset	an EOM inventory
an essay	an f.o.b. order
an input	an HQ command
an outcome	an LRT ticket
an upsurge	an M.B.A. degree
an hour	an NSF cheque
an honour	an ROI objective
an 8-hour-day	an SRO performance
an 11 a.m. meeting	an X-rated movie

NOTE: In speech, both *a historic occasion* and *an historic occasion* are correct, depending on whether the *h* is sounded or left silent. In writing, *a historic occasion* is more common.

A—of. Do not use *a* in place of *of*.

What sort *of* turnout did you have at your seminar?
(**NOT:** What sort *a* turnout did you have at your seminar?)

The weather has been kind *of* cool for this time of year.
(**NOT:** The weather has been *kinda* cool for this time of year.)

☞ *See* Kind of—sort of *and* Kind of a.

A—per. See *Per—a.*

Above. Avoid the use of **above** before a reference in a book or on a page.

In the graph *above* **OR** in the preceding graph   **NOT:** in the *above* graph

Accidentally. This word ends in *ally.* (*Accidently* is incorrect.)

A.D.–B.C. *A.D.* (Abbreviation of *Anno Domini*, Latin for "in the year of our Lord") and *B.C.* ("before Christ") are usually written all in caps or in small caps (A.D., B.C.), with a period after each letter and with no internal space. Do not use a comma to separate *B.C.* or *A.D.* from the year.

150 B.C.   first century B.C.   A.D. 465   **OR:**   465 A.D (in informal usage)

NOTE: In works of history and theology, the term *A.D.* is often replaced by the abbreviation *C.E.* (meaning "in the Common Era"); *B.C.* is replaced by *B.C.E.* (meaning "before the Common Era").

Additionally. Avoid the use of *additionally* as a transitional expression. Use *and, in addition, moreover, furthermore,* or *besides* instead. (See ¶138a.)

AWKWARD: *Additionally,* the new packaging will reduce costs by 20 percent.

BETTER: *Moreover,* the new packaging will reduce costs by 20 percent.

Affect—effect. *Affect* is normally used as a verb meaning "to influence, change, assume." *Effect* can be either a verb meaning "to bring about" or a noun meaning "result, impression."

The court's decision in this case will not *affect* (change) the legal precedent.

She *affects* (assumes) an unsophisticated manner.

It is essential that we *effect* (bring about) an immediate improvement in sales.

It will be months before we can assess the full *effect* (result) of the new law.

NOTE: In psychology, *affect* used as a noun means "emotion," and the related adjective *affective* means "emotional." Because of the limited contexts in which these terms are likely to be used, it should be easy to distinguish them from *effect* as a noun and the related adjective *effective*.

We need to analyze the *effects* (results) of this new marketing strategy.
We need to analyze the *affects* (emotions) produced by this conflict.

Which technique is *effective* (capable of producing the desired results)?
Let's deal with the *affective* (emotional) factors first.

Age—aged—at the age of.

I interviewed a man *aged* 52 for the job. (**NOT:** a man age 52.)

I don't plan to retire *at the age of 65*. (**NOT:** *at age 65*.)

NOTE: Elliptical references to age—for example, *at age 65*—should not be used except in technical writing such as human resources manuals.

All of. *Of* is not necessary after *all* unless the following word is a pronoun.

All of us belong to the softball team.

PREFERABLE: *All* the staff members belong to the softball team.
ACCEPTABLE: *All of* the staff members belong to the softball team.

All right. Like *all wrong*, the expression *all right* should be spelled as two words. (The spelling *alright* is not as yet generally accepted.)

Allude–refer. *Allude* means "to refer indirectly to something"; *refer* means "to make specific mention of."

The CEO merely *alluded* to a decline in sales, but he gave no specific details.

To divert the analysts' attention, he *referred* to last year's annual report.

Almost—all most. See also *Most*.

The plane was *almost* (nearly) three hours late.

We are *all most* pleased (all very much pleased) with the new schedule.

Already—all ready.

The order had *already* (previously) been shipped.

The order is *all ready* (all prepared) to be shipped.

Altogether—all together.

He is *altogether* (entirely) too lazy to be a success.

The papers are *all together* (all in a group) in the binder I sent you.

Always—all ways.

She has *always* (at all times) done good work.

We have tried in *all ways* (by all methods) to keep our employees satisfied.

11

Among—between. See *Between—among.*

Amount—number. Use *amount* for things in bulk, as in "a large amount of oil." Use *number* for individual items that can be counted, as in "a large number of tins."

And. Use *and* before the last item in a series, even though that last item consists of two words joined by *and.*

> We need to increase our expense budgets for advertising, staff training, *and* research and development.
>
> (**NOT:** We need to increase our expense budgets for advertising, staff training, research and development.)

Beginning a sentence with *and* or some other coordinating conjunction (*but, or,* or *nor*) can be an effective means—*if not overused*—of drawing special attention to the thought that follows the conjunction. No comma should follow the conjunction at the start of a new sentence unless a parenthetical element occurs at that point.

> Last Friday George promised to have the market analysis on my desk this Monday. *And* then he took off on a two-week vacation.
>
> Tell him to return to the office at once. *Or* else.
>
> **BUT:** George just called from his home to say that the report was undergoing some last-minute changes and would be on my desk at 11 a.m. *And,* to my delight, it was!

And etc. Never use *and* before *etc.* (See *Etc.*)

And/or. Try to avoid this legalistic term in ordinary writing. Usually either *and* or *or* is sufficient.

Anxious—eager. Both *anxious* and *eager* mean "desirous," but *anxious* also implies fear or concern.

> I'm *anxious* to hear whether we won the bid or not.
>
> I'm *eager* (**NOT** anxious) to hear about your new house.

Anymore—any more.

> We used to go to the club, but we don't go there *anymore* (any longer).
>
> Please call me if you have *any more* (any additional) suggestions.

Anyone—any one. See ¶1010 note.

Anytime—any time.

> Come see us *anytime* you are in town. (One word meaning "whenever.")
>
> Did you have dealings with Crosby at *any time* in the past? (Two words after a preposition such as *at.*)
>
> Can you spend *any time* (any amount of time) with Jill and me next week?

Anyway—any way. *Anyways* is never correct.

> *Anyway* (in any case), we can't spare him now.
>
> If we can help in *any way* (by any method), please phone.

Appreciate. When used with the meaning "to be thankful for," the verb *appreciate* requires an object.

NOT: We would appreciate if you could give us your decision by May 1.

BUT: We would appreciate *your* (**NOT** you) *giving us your decision by May 1.* (Noun clause as object. See ¶647b on the use of *your* before *giving.*)

OR: We would appreciate *it* if you could give us . . . (Pronoun as object.)

I will appreciate *whatever you can do for us.* (Noun clause as object.)

We will always appreciate the *help* you gave us. (Noun as object.)

As. Do not use for *that* or *whether.*

I do not know *whether* (**NOT** as) I can go.

Use *because, since,* or *for* rather than *as* in clauses of reason.

I cannot attend the meeting on Friday *because* (**NOT** as) I will be away that day.

As—as if. See *Like—as, as if.*

As . . . as—not so . . . as. The term *as . . . as* is now commonly used in both positive and negative comparisons. Some writers, however, prefer to use *not so . . . as* for negative comparisons.

Bob is every bit *as* bright *as* his older sister. (Positive comparison.)

It is *not as* important *as* you think. **OR:** . . . *not so* important *as* you think. (Negative comparison.)

NOTE: Do not replace the second *as* with *than.*

We spend twice *as* much money on entertainment *as* we do on food.

(**NOT:** We spend twice *as* much money on entertainment *than* we . . .)

As far as. *As far as* may be used as a preposition or as a subordinating conjunction.

I can drive you *as far as* Salmon Arm. (Used as a preposition.)

I would recommend this template *as far as* format is concerned. (Used as a subordinating conjunction.)

NOT: I would recommend this template *as far as* format. (Either create a clause following *as far as* or change *as far as* to *on the basis of* or a similar expression.)

As well as. When using *as well as,* be on guard against the possibility of misleading your reader.

CONFUSING: Ms. Paglia plans to meet with Mr. Pierce and Mrs. Hamer as well as Ms. Fieno. (Is Ms. Paglia planning to meet with three people, or are Ms. Paglia and Ms. Fieno both planning to meet with two people?)

CLEAR: Ms. Paglia plans to meet *with* Mr. Pierce and Mrs. Hamer as well as *with* Ms. Fieno. (Repeating the preposition *with* makes it clear that Ms. Paglia will meet with three people.)

CLEAR: Ms. Paglia *as well as* Ms. *Fieno* plans to meet with Mr. Pierce and Mrs. Hamer. (Rearranging the word order makes it clear that both Ms. Paglia and Ms. Fieno will meet with two people. Note that an *as well as* phrase following the subject, *Ms. Paglia,* does not affect the number of the verb. See ¶1007.)

Assure. See *Ensure—insure—assure.*

Awhile—a while. One word as an adverb; two words as a noun.

You may have to wait *awhile.* (Adverb.)

You may have to wait for *a while.* (Noun: object of the preposition *for.*)

Bad—badly. Use the adjective *bad* (not the adverb *badly*) after verbs like *feel, appear, seem,* or *look.* (See ¶1067.)

I feel *bad* (**NOT** badly) about the mistake. **BUT:** He was hurt *badly.*

NOTE: One way you can "feel badly" is to burn your fingertips!

Balance. Do not use *balance* to mean "rest" or "remainder" except in a financial or accounting sense.

I plan to use the *rest* of my vacation time next February.

(**NOT:** I plan to use the *balance* of my vacation time next February.)

BUT: The *balance* of the loan falls due at the end of this quarter.

Because. See *Reason is because.*

Because of. See *Due to—because of—on account of.*

Being that. Do not use for *since* or *because.*

Because I arrived late, I could not get a seat.

(**NOT:** *Being that* I arrived late, I could not get a seat.)

Beside—besides.

I sat *beside* (next to) Mr. Parrish's father at the meeting.

Besides (in addition), we need your support of the measure.

Between—among. Ordinarily, use *between* when referring to *two* persons or things and *among* when referring to *more than* two persons or things.

The territory is divided evenly *between* the two sales representatives.

The profits are to be evenly divided *among* the three partners.

Use *between* with more than two persons or things when they are being considered in pairs as well as in a group.

There are distinct differences *between* Montreal, Toronto, and Halifax.

In packing china, be sure to place paper *between* the plates.

The memo says something different when you read *between* the lines.

Between you and me (not *I*). See ¶1055b.

Biannual—biennial—semi-annual. *Biannual* and *semi-annual* both mean "occurring twice a year." *Biennial* means "occurring every two years." Because of the possible confusion between *biannual* and *biennial,* use *semi-annual* to describe something that occurs twice a year.

PREFERRED: our *semi-annual* sales conference

CLEARER THAN: our *biannual* sales conference

If you think that your reader could misinterpret *biennial*, avoid the term and use *every two years* instead.

> Each national sales conference is held semi-annually; an international sales conference is held *biennially* (**OR** *every two years*).

Biweekly—bimonthly. These two words do not mean the same thing. Moreover, *bimonthly* has two quite different meanings. Originally it meant *every two months*, but it is now more commonly used to mean *twice a month*. To avoid confusion, use *semi-monthly* or *twice a month* for one meaning and *every two months* for the other.

> If you are paid *biweekly* (every two weeks), you get 26 cheques a year.
>
> If you are paid *bimonthly* (twice a month), you get 24 cheques a year.
>
> **OR:** If you are paid *bimonthly* (every two months), you get only 6 cheques a year.

Both—each. *Both* means "the two considered together." *Each* refers to the individual members of a group considered separately.

> *Both* designs are acceptable.   The designs are *each* acceptable.
>
> *Each* boy wrote about the other.   **NOT:** *Both* boys wrote about the other.

Both alike—equal—together. *Both* is unnecessary when used with *alike*, *equal*, or *together*.

> These inkjet printers are *alike*. (**NOT:** both alike.)
>
> These tape systems are *equal* in cost. (**NOT:** both equal.)
>
> We will travel *together* to the Far East. (**NOT:** both travel together.)

Bring—take. *Bring* indicates motion toward the speaker. *Take* indicates motion away from the speaker.

> Please *bring* the research data with you when you next come to the office.
>
> Please *take* the enclosed letter to Farley when you go to see him.
>
> You may *take* my copy with you if you will *bring* it back by Friday.

☞ *See note under* Come—go.

But . . . however. Use one or the other.

> We had hoped to see the show, *but* we couldn't get tickets.
>
> **OR:** We had hoped to see the show; *however*, we couldn't get tickets.
>
> (**NOT:** . . . *but* we couldn't get tickets, *however*.)

But what. Use *that*.

> I do not doubt *that* (**NOT** but what) he will be elected.

Can—could. See *May—can (might—could)*.

Class. See *Kind*.

11

Come—go. The choice between verbs depends on the location of the speaker. *Come* indicates motion *toward; go,* motion *away from.* (See also *Bring—take.*)

> When Bellamy *comes* back, I will *go* to the airport to meet him.
>
> *A manager speaking over the phone to an outsider:* Will it be convenient for you to *come* to our office tomorrow?

NOTE: When discussing your travel plans with a person at your destination, adopt that person's point of view and use *come.*

> *An outsider speaking over the phone to a manager:* Will it be convenient for me to *come* to your office tomorrow?
>
> *Westerner to Nova Scotian:* I am *coming* to Nova Scotia during the week of the 11th. I will *bring* the plans with me if they are ready.

However, if you are discussing your travel plans with someone who is *not* at your destination, observe the regular distinction between *come* and *go.*

> *An outsider speaking to an outsider:* I hope it will be convenient for me to *go* to their office tomorrow.
>
> *Westerner to Westerner:* I am *going* to Nova Scotia during the week of the 11th. I will *take* the plans with me if they are ready.

Come and. In formal writing, use *come to* instead of the colloquial *come and.*

> Come *to* see me. (**NOT:** Come *and* see me.)

Complementary—complimentary. *Complementary* means "serving to complete" or "mutually supplying what each other lacks." *Complimentary* means "flattering" or "given free." (For the meanings of *complement* and *compliment,* see ¶719.)

> Our executives bring *complementary* skills and expertise to their jobs.
>
> May I get a *complimentary* copy of your new book?
>
> The practicum student received complimentary remarks on her report.

Comprise—compose. *Comprise* means "to include, contain, consist of"; *compose* means "to make up." The parts *compose* (make up) the whole; the whole *comprises* (includes) the parts; the whole *is composed of* (**NOT** is comprised of) the parts.

> The parent corporation *comprises* (consists of) three major divisions.
>
> Three major divisions *compose* (make up) the parent corporation.
>
> The parent corporation *is composed of* (is made up of) three major divisions.

Consists of—includes. Use *consists of* to introduce a complete list of items; use *includes* to introduce a partial list.

> This mailing list *consists of* all our active accounts.
>
> This mailing list *includes* the active accounts that were opened this year.

NOTE: Do not use *etc.* or *and so on* at the end of a list introduced by *includes,* since the verb makes it clear that the list is not complete.

Could not care less. To say that you "could not care less" means that you do not care at all. To say that you "could care less" means that you still have a long way to go before you reach the state of "no longer caring at all."

> If Val does not attend our reunion, I *could not care less.* (I don't care at all.)

Data. See ¶1018b.

Dependant—dependent. These words are now interchangeable as nouns; however, most writers use *dependant* only as a noun. *Dependent* is the adjective.

> The mother lives with her son as a *dependant.* (Used as a noun; she depends upon her son for support.)
>
> A good harvest is *dependent* on the weather. (Used as an adjective; the harvest is influenced by the weather.)

Different—differently. When the meaning is "in a different manner," use the adverb *differently.*

> I wish we had done it *differently.*   It came out *differently* than we expected.

After linking verbs and verbs of the senses, the adjective *different* is correct. (See ¶1067.)

> That music sounds completely *different.*
>
> He seems (appears) *different* since his promotion.
>
> Don't believe anything *different.* (Meaning "anything that is different.")

Different from—different than. See ¶1077.

Done. Do not say "I *done* it." Say "I *did* it." (See also ¶1032.)

Don't (do not). Do not use *don't* with *he, she,* or *it;* use *doesn't.*

> He *doesn't* talk easily.   **BUT:** I *don't* think so.
> She needs help, *doesn't* she?   They *don't* want any help.
> It *doesn't* seem right to penalize them.   We *don't* understand.

Doubt that—doubt whether. Use *doubt that* in negative statements and in questions. Use *doubt whether* in all other cases. (See also *If—whether.*)

> We do not *doubt that* she is capable. (Negative statement.)
>
> Does anyone *doubt that* the cheque was mailed? (Negative question.)
>
> I *doubt whether* I can go.

Due to—because of—on account of. *Due to* introduces an adjective phrase and should modify nouns. It is normally used only after some form of the verb *to be* (*is, are, was, were,* etc.).

> Her success is *due to* talent and hard work. (*Due to* modifies *success.*)

Because of and *on account of* introduce adverbial phrases and should modify verbs.

> He resigned *because of* ill health. (*Because of* modifies *resigned.*)
>
> (**NOT:** He resigned *due to* ill health.)

11

Each—both. See *Both—each*.

Each other—one another. Use *each other* to refer to two persons or things; *one another* for more than two.

> The two partners had greater respect for *each other's* abilities.
>
> The four winners congratulated *one another*.

Eager—anxious. See *Anxious—eager*.

Effect—affect. See *Affect—effect*.

Ensure—insure—assure. *Ensure* means "to make certain." *Insure* means "to protect against loss." *Assure* means "to give someone confidence"; the object of this verb should always refer to a person.

> I want to *ensure* (make certain) that nothing can go wrong tomorrow.
>
> I want to *insure* this necklace (protect it against loss) for $5000.
>
> I want to *assure* you (give you confidence) that nothing will go wrong.

Enthused over. Use *was* or *were enthusiastic about* instead.

> The sales staff *was enthusiastic about* (**NOT** enthused over) next year's styles.

Equal. See *Both alike—equal—together*.

Equally as good. Use either *equally good* or *just as good*. *Equally as good* is never correct.

> This model is newer, but that one is *equally good*. (**NOT:** equally as good.)
>
> Those are *just as good* as these. (**NOT:** equally as good.)

Etc.—and so on—such as. The abbreviation of *et cetera* means "and other things." Therefore, do not use *and* before it. A comma both precedes and follows *etc.* (See ¶164.) In formal writing, avoid the use of *etc.*; use a phrase such as *and the like* or *and so on*.

NOTE: Do not use *etc.* or an equivalent expression at the end of a series introduced by *such as*. The term *such as* implies that only a few selected examples will be given; therefore, it is unnecessary to add *etc.* or *and so on*, which suggests that further examples could be given.

> As part of its employee educational program, the company offers courses in report writing, business communication, grammar and style, *and so on*.
>
> **OR:** . . . the company offers courses *such as* report writing, business communication, and grammar and style.
>
> (**NOT:** . . . the company offers courses *such as* report writing, business communication, grammar and style, *and so on*.)

☞ *For the use or omission of a comma before* such as, *see* ¶¶148–149.

Everyday—every day. *Everyday* is an adjective followed by a noun. *Every day* is an adjective plus a noun.

> You'll soon master the *everyday* (ordinary or daily) routine of the job.
>
> He has called *every day* (each day) this week.

Everyone—every one. See ¶1010 note.

Ex—former. Use *ex-* with a title to designate the person who *immediately* preceded the current titleholder in that position; use *former* with a title to designate an earlier titleholder.

> Charles Fellows is the *ex-president* of the Hamilton Chamber of Commerce. (Held office immediately before the current president.)
>
> **BUT:** . . . is a *former* president of the Hamilton Chamber of Commerce. (Held office sometime before the current president and that person's immediate predecessor.)

Except. When *except* is a preposition, be sure to use the objective form of a pronoun that follows. (See also ¶1055b.)

> Everyone has been notified *except* Jean and *me*. (**NOT:** except Jean and I.)

Farther—further. *Farther* refers to actual distance; *further* refers to figurative distance and means "to a greater degree" or "to a greater extent."

> The drive from the airport was *farther* (in actual distance) than we expected.
>
> Let's plan to discuss the proposal *further* (to a greater extent).

Fewer—less. *Fewer* refers to number and is used with *plural* nouns. *Less* refers to degree or amount and is used with *singular* nouns.

> *Fewer* accidents (a smaller number) were reported than was expected.
>
> *Less* effort (a smaller degree) was put forth by the organizers, and thus *fewer* people (a smaller number) attended.

The expression *less than* (rather than *fewer than*) precedes plural nouns referring to periods of time, amounts of money, and quantities.

less than ten years ago	**FORMAL:** fewer than 60 people
less than $1 million	**COLLOQUIAL:** less than 60 people

The expression *or less* (rather than *or fewer*) is used after a reference to a number of items.

in words of 100 or less	in groups of six people or less

First—firstly, etc. In enumerations use the forms *first, second, third* (**NOT** firstly, secondly, thirdly).

Flammable—inflammable. Both terms mean "easily ignitable, highly combustible." However, since some readers may misinterpret *inflammable* to mean "*non*flammable," *flammable* is the clearer form.

Former—ex. See *Ex—former.*

Former—first. *Former* refers to the first of two persons or things. When more than two are mentioned, use *first.* (See also *Latter—last.*)

> This item is available in wool and in Dacron, but I prefer the *former.*
>
> This item is available in wool, in Dacron, and in Orlon, but I prefer the *first.*

11

From—off. Use *from* (**NOT** off) with persons.

I got the answer I needed *from* Margaret. (**NOT:** off Margaret.)

Go—come. See *Come—go*.

Good—well. *Good* is an adjective. *Well* is generally used as an adverb, but it may be used as an adjective to refer to the state of someone's health.

Marie got *good* grades in school. (Adjective.)

I will do the job as *well* as I can. (Adverb.)

He admits he does not feel *well* today. (Adjective.)

The security guards look *good* in their new uniforms. (Adjective.)

NOTE: *To feel well* means "to be in good health." *To feel good* means "to be in good spirits."

Graduated—was graduated. Both forms are acceptable, but the first is preferable. However, use *from* after either expression.

My son *graduated from* UBC last year. (**NOT:** My son *graduated* UBC last year.)

Hardly. *Hardly* is negative in meaning. To preserve the negative meeting, do not use another negative with it.

You *could hardly* (**NOT** couldn't hardly) expect him to agree.

Have—of. See *Of—have*.

Healthy—healthful. People are *healthy*; a climate or food is *healthful*.

You ought to move to a more *healthful* (**NOT** healthier) climate.

Help. Do not use *from* after the verb *help*. For example, "I couldn't *help* (**NOT** help from) telling her she was wrong."

Historic—historical. *Historic* means "important" or "momentous." *Historical* means "relating to the past."

July 1, 1867, is a *historic* date in Canadian history.

The following article provides a *historical* account of the War of 1812.

Hopefully. The use of *hopefully* at the beginning of a sentence should be avoided in formal writing. However, it is sometimes used as an independent comment functioning similarly to words such as *obviously, fortunately,* and *apparently*. (See ¶138b.) These adverbs express the writer's attitude toward what he or she is about to say.

Hopefully, the worst is over and we will soon see a strong upturn in sales.

However. *However,* as a transitional expression like *therefore* and *moreover,* connects the thought being introduced to the thoughts that went before. At the start of a sentence, *however* can have two meanings: "on the other hand" and "in whatever way." When it means "on the other hand," follow it with a comma to prevent a misreading.

However (meaning "on the other hand"), you decide what you want to say.

However (meaning "in whatever way") you decide to organize your presentation, I am sure it will be a success.

If—whether. *If* is often used colloquially for *whether* in such sentences as "He doesn't know *whether* he will be able to leave tomorrow." In written material, use *whether*, particularly in such expressions as *see whether, learn whether, know whether,* and *doubt whether.* Also use *whether* when the expression *or not* follows or is implied.

Find out *whether* (**NOT** if) this format is acceptable *or not.*

Imply—infer. *Imply* means "to suggest"; you imply something by *your own* words or actions.

Verna *implied* (suggested) that we would not be invited.

Infer means "to assume, to deduce, to arrive at a conclusion"; you infer something from *another person's* words or actions.

I *inferred* (assumed) from Verna's remarks that we would not be invited.

In—into—in to.

The correspondence is *in* the file. (*In* implies position within.)

He walked *into* the outer office. (*Into* implies entry or change of form.)

All sales reports are to be sent *in to* the sales manager. (*In* is an adverb in the verb phrase *are to be sent in; to* is a simple preposition.)

Mr. Boehme came *in to* see me. (*In* is part of the verb phrase *came in; to* is part of the infinitive *to see.*)

In regard to. Use *in regard to, with regard to, regarding,* or *as regards. In regards to* is never correct.

I am writing *in regard to* (**NOT** *in regards to*) your letter of May 1.

Incidentally. Note that this word ends in *ally.* Never spell it *incidently.*

Indifferent—in different.

She was *indifferent* (not caring one way or the other) to the offer.

He liked our idea, but he wanted it expressed *in different* (in other) words.

Indirect—in direct.

Indirect (not direct) lighting will enhance the appearance of this room.

This order is *in direct* (the preposition *in* plus the adjective *direct*) conflict with the policy of this company.

Individual—party—person—people. Use *individual* to refer to someone whom you wish to distinguish from a larger group of people.

We wish to honour those *individuals* who had the courage to speak out at a time when popular opinion was defending the status quo.

Use *party* only to refer to someone involved in a legal proceeding.

All the *parties* to the original agreement must sign the attached amendment.

(Continued on page 294.)

Use *person* to refer to a human being in all other contexts.

> Please tell me the name of the *person* in charge of your credit department.

If reference is made to more than one person, *people* usually sounds more natural than *persons*. In any event, always use *people* when referring to a large group.

> If you like, I can send you a list of all the *people* in our corporation who will be attending this year's national convention.

Inflammable—flammable. See *Flammable—inflammable.*

Insure. See *Ensure—insure—assure.*

Irregardless. The word *irregardless* is never correct. Use *regardless*.

Is where—is when. Do not use these phrases to introduce definitions.

> A dilemma is a situation in which you have to choose between equally unsatisfactory alternatives.

> (**NOT:** A dilemma *is where* you have to choose between equally unsatisfactory alternatives.)

However, these phrases may be correctly used in other situations.

> The Royal York *is where* the dinner-dance will be held this year.

> Two o'clock *is when* the meeting is scheduled to begin.

Its—it's. See ¶1056e.

Kind. *Kind* is singular; therefore, write *this kind, that kind, these kinds, those kinds* (**NOT** *these kind, those kind*). The same distinctions hold for *class, type,* and *sort*.

Kind of—sort of. These phrases are sometimes followed by an adjective (for example, *kind of sorry, sort of baffled*). Use this kind of expression only in informal writing. In more formal situations, use *rather* or *somewhat* (*rather sorry, somewhat baffled*).

> I was *somewhat* (**NOT** kind of, sort of) surprised.

> She seemed *rather* (**NOT** kind of, sort of) tired.

NOTE: When *kind of* or *sort of* is followed by a noun, the expression is appropriate in all kinds of situations.

> What *sort of business* is Vern Forbes in?

Kind of a. The *a* is unnecessary. For example, "That *kind of* (**NOT** kind of a) material is very expensive."

Last—latest. *Last* means "after all others"; *latest,* "most recent."

> Mr. Lin's *last* act before leaving was to recommend Ms. Roth's promotion.

> Attached is the *latest* report we have received from the Southern Region.

Latter—last. *Latter* refers to the second of two persons or things mentioned. When more than two are mentioned, use *last*. (See also *Former—first*.)

> July and August are good vacation months, but the *latter* is more popular.
>
> June, July, and August are good vacation months, but the *last* is the most popular.

Lay—lie. *Lay* (principal parts: *lay, laid, laid, laying*) means "to put" or "to place." This verb requires an object to complete its meaning.

> Please *lay* the *boxes* on the pallets with extreme care.
>
> I *laid* the *message* on your desk.
>
> I *had laid* two other *notes* there yesterday.
>
> He *is* always *laying* the *blame* on his assistants. (Putting the blame.)
>
> The dress *was laid* in the box. (A passive construction implying that someone *put* or *placed* the dress in the box.)

Lie (principal parts: *lie, lay, lain, lying*) means "to recline, rest, or stay" or "to take a position of rest." It refers to a person or thing as either assuming or being in a reclining position. This verb cannot take an object.

> Now he *lies* in bed most of the day.
>
> The mountains *lay* before us as we proceeded west.
>
> This letter *has lain* unanswered for two weeks.
>
> Today's mail *is lying* on the receptionist's desk.

TEST: To decide whether to use *lie* or *lay* in a sentence, substitute *place, placed*, or *placing* for the word in question. If the substitute fits, the corresponding form of *lay* is correct. If it does not, use the correct form of *lie*.

> I will (*lie* or *lay?*) down now. (You could not say, "I will *place* down now." Write "I will *lie* down now.")
>
> I (*laid* or *lay?*) the pad on his desk. ("I *placed* the pad on his desk" works. Write "I *laid* the pad.")
>
> I (*laid* or *lay?*) awake many nights. ("I *placed* awake" does not work. Write "I *lay* awake.")
>
> These files have (*laid* or *lain?*) untouched for some time. ("These files have *placed* untouched" does not work. Write "These files have *lain* untouched.")
>
> He has been (*laying* or *lying?*) down on the job. ("He has been *placing* down on the job" does not work. Write "He has been *lying* down.")

NOTE: When *lie* means "to tell a falsehood," it has regularly formed principal parts *(lie, lied, lied, lying)* and is seldom confused with the verbs just described.

Learn—teach. *Learn* (principal parts: *learn, learned, learned, learning*) means "to acquire knowledge." *Teach* (principal parts: *teach, taught, taught, teaching*) means "to impart knowledge to others."

(Continued on page 296.)

I *learned* from a master teacher.	A first-rate instructor *taught* me how.
(**NOT:** I *was learned* by a master teacher.)	I was *taught* by a first-rate instructor.

Leave—let. *Leave* (principal parts: *leave, left, left, leaving*) means "to move away, abandon, or depart." *Let* (principal parts: *let, let, let, letting*) means "to permit or allow." **TEST:** In deciding whether to use *let* or *leave*, substitute a suitable form of *permit*. If *permit* fits, use *let*; if not, use *leave*.

I now *leave* you to your own devices. (Abandon you.)

Mr. Morales *left* on the morning train. (Departed.)

Let me see the last page. (Permit me to see.)

Leave me alone. **OR:** *Let* me alone. (Either is acceptable.)

Less—fewer. See *Fewer—less.*

Like—as, as if. *Like* is correctly used as a preposition. Although *like* is also widely used as a conjunction in colloquial speech, use *as, as if,* or a similar expression in written material.

We need to hire another person *like* you.
Kate, *like* her predecessor, will have to cope with the problem.
As (**NOT** Like) I told you earlier, we will not reorder for six months.

It looks *like* snow.	It looks *as if* it will snow.
(**NOT:** It looks *like* it will snow.)	

Mary looks *like* her mother.	Mary looks *as* her mother did at the same age.
(**NOT:** Mary looks *like* her mother did at the same age.)	

Literally. This adverb means "actually, truly." Do not use it in the sense of "almost" to modify a reference to an exaggerated or unreal situation.

May—can (might—could). *May* and *might* imply permission or possibility; *can* and *could*, ability or power. *Might* is the past tense of *may; could* is the past tense of *can*. In expressing possibility *might* and *could* suggest more doubt than *may* or *can*.

You *may* send them a dozen cans of paint on trial. (Permission.)

The report *may* be true. (Possibility.)

Can he present a workable plan? (Has he the ability?)

Miss Kovacs said I *might* (permission) have the time off if I *could* (had the ability to) finish my work in time.

Call me if you think I *can* be of any help. (Emphasizes the ability to help.)

Call me if you think I *may* be of any help. (Emphasizes the possibility of helping.)

The CEO *could* change this policy if he wanted to. (Power.)

Maybe—may be. *Maybe* is an adverb; *may be* is a verb.

If we don't receive a letter from them today, *maybe* (an adverb meaning "perhaps") we should call.

Mr. Boston *may be* (a verb) out of town next week.

Media. (See ¶1018c.)

More. In some sentences it may not be clear whether *more* is being used to form the comparative degree of an adjective (for example, *more experienced*) or is being used as an adjective meaning "a greater number of." In such cases reword to avoid confusion.

> **CONFUSING:** We need to hire more experienced workers. (A greater number of experienced workers? Or workers who are more experienced than those now on staff?)

> **CLEAR:** We need to hire a greater number of experienced workers.

> **CLEAR:** We need to hire workers who are more experienced.

More important—more importantly. *More important* is often used as a short form for "what is more important," especially at the beginning of a sentence. *More importantly* means "in a more important manner."

> *More important*, we need to establish a line of credit very quickly. (What is more important.)

> The incident was treated *more importantly* than was necessary. (In a more important manner.)

Most. Do not use for *almost*.

> *Almost all* the money is gone. **OR:** *Most* of the money is gone.

> **BUT NOT:** *Most all* of the money is gone.

Nobody—no body.

> There was *nobody* (no person) at the information desk when I arrived.

> *No body* (no group) of employees is more co-operative than yours. (Spell *no body* as two words when it is followed by *of*. See also ¶1010.)

None—no one. See ¶1013.

Not so . . . as. See *As . . . as—not so . . . as*.

Number. See *Amount—number*.

Of—a. See *A—of*.

Of—have. Do not use *of* instead of *have*. The correct forms are *could have, would have, should have, might have, may have, must have, ought to have*, and so forth.

> What *could have* happened? (**NOT:** What could *of* happened?)

Off. Do not use *off of* or *off from* in place of *off*. (See also ¶1078.)

> The papers fell *off* the desk. (**NOT:** off of the desk.)

Off—from. See *From—off*.

On—onto—on to.

> It's dangerous to drive *on* the highway shoulder. (*On* is a preposition that implies position or movement over.)

> He lost control of the car and drove *onto* the sidewalk. (*Onto* is a preposition that implies movement toward and then over.)

(Continued on page 298.)

Let's go *on to* the next problem. (*On* is an adverb in the verb phrase *go on; to* is a preposition.)

On—upon—up on.

His statements were based *on* (**OR** *upon*) experimental data. (*On* and *upon* are interchangeable.)

Please follow *up on* the Underhill case. (*Up* is part of the verb phrase *follow up; on* is a preposition.)

On account of. See *Due to—because of—on account of.*

One another—each other. See *Each other—one another.*

Only. The adverb *only* is negative in meaning. Therefore, do not use another negative with it unless you want a positive meaning. (See ¶1072 for the placement of *only* in a sentence.)

I use this letterhead *only* for foreign correspondence. (I do not use this letterhead for anything else.)

BUT: I do not use this letterhead *only* for foreign correspondence. (I use it for a number of other things as well.)

Opposite. When used as a noun, *opposite* is followed by *of.*

Her opinion is the *opposite of* mine.

In other uses, *opposite* is followed by *to* or *from* or by no preposition at all.

Her opinion is *opposite to* (**OR** *from*) mine.

She lives *opposite* the school.

Party. See *Individual—party—person—people.*

Per—a. *Per,* a Latin word, means "by the" as in *80 kilometres per hour (80 km/h).* Whenever possible, replace with *a* or *an;* for example, *$8 an hour, 75 cents a dozen. Per* must be retained in Latin phrases; for example, *per diem* (by the day) or *per capita* (for each person).

NOTE: Do not use *per* to mean "according to" or "in accordance with."

We are sending you samples *as you requested.* (**NOT:** per your request.)

Percent—percentage. In ordinary usage, *percent* should always be accompanied by a number; for example, *20 percent, 0.5 percent.* In a table a column of percentage figures may be headed *Percent of Total* or something comparable. In all other cases, use the term *percentage.*

A large *percentage* of the calls we got yesterday came from customers who misread our ad. (**NOT:** A large *percent* of the calls . . .)

What *percentage* of our subscribers are in the 30–49 age group? (See ¶1025.)

NOTE: In the percentage formula (base × rate = amount), the rate is called a *percent* and the amount is called a *percentage.*

Plus. This word can be correctly used as a noun, an adjective, or a preposition. However, do not use it as a conjunction (with the sense of "and").

Your presence was a real *plus* for our cause. (*Plus* used correctly as a noun.)

The decision to offer a 10 percent discount on all orders received by June 1 was a *plus* factor in the campaign. (*Plus* used correctly as an adjective.)

Your willingness to innovate *plus* your patient perspective on profits has permitted this company to grow at an astonishing rate. (*Plus* used correctly as a preposition. Note that a *plus* phrase following the subject of a sentence does not affect the number of the verb. See ¶1007.)

NOT: You have always been willing to innovate, *plus* you have been patient about the profits to be derived from the innovations. (Do not use *plus* as a conjunction; use *and* instead.)

Proved–proven. Use *proven* only as a modifier before a noun. Otherwise, use *proved*.

> Here is a *proven* remedy for your condition.
>
> This remedy has *proved* to be extremely effective.

Raise—rise. *Raise* (principal parts: *raise, raised, raised, raising*) means "to cause to lift" or "to lift something." This verb requires an object to complete its meaning.

> Mr. Pon *raises* a good *question.*   Farmers *have raised* the *price* of grain.
>
> Our rent *has been raised.* (See ¶1036.)   We *are raising money* for the United Way.

Rise (principal parts: *rise, rose, risen, rising*) means "to ascend," "to move upward by itself," or "to get up." This verb cannot have an object.

> We will have to *rise* to the occasion.   The sun *rose* at 6:25 this morning.
>
> The river *has risen* to flood level.   The temperature *has been rising* all day.

TEST: Remember, you cannot "rise" anything.

Real—really. *Real* is an adjective; *really*, an adverb. Do not use *real* to modify another adjective; use *very* or *really*.

> One taste will tell you these cookies were made with *real* butter. (Adjective.)
>
> We were *really* expecting a lower price from you this year. (Adverb.)
>
> **BUT:** It was *very* nice (**NOT:** real nice) to see you and your family again.

Reason is because. Substitute *reason is that.*

> The *reason* for such low sales is *that* (**NOT:** *because*) prices are too high.

Retroactive to. After *retroactive* use *to* (**NOT:** *from*).

> These improvements in benefits under the company dental plan will be *retroactive to* July 1. (See also ¶1077.)

Said. The use of *said* in a phrase like "the *said* document" is appropriate only in legal writing. In normal usage write "the document referred to above."

Same. Do not use *same* to refer to a previously mentioned thing.

> We are now processing your order and will have *it* ready for you Monday.
>
> (**NOT:** We are now processing your order and will have *same* ready . . .)

11

Scarcely. The adverb *scarcely* is negative in meaning. To preserve the negative meaning, do not use another negative with it. (See ¶1072 for the placement of *scarcely*.)

> I *scarcely* recognized (**NOT** didn't scarcely recognize) you.

Semi-annual. See *Biannual—biennial—semi-annual*.

Serve—service. Things can be *serviced*, but people are *served*.

> We take great pride in the way we *serve* (**NOT** service) our clients.
>
> For a small additional charge we will *service* the equipment for a full year.

Set—sit. *Set* (principal parts: *set, set, set, setting*) means "to place something somewhere." In this sense, *set* must have an object to complete its meaning. **REMEMBER:** You cannot "sit" anything.

> It's important to *set* down your *recollections* while they are still fresh.
>
> I must have dropped my wallet when I *set* my *suitcase* down.
>
> I *have set* my *alarm* for six in the morning.
>
> The crew *was setting* the *stage* for the evening performance.
>
> The date *was set* some time ago. (A passive construction implying that someone *set* the date.)

NOTE: *Set* has a few other meanings in which the verb does *not* require an object, but these meanings are seldom confused with *sit*.

> He *set* out on a hiking trip.   The sun *set* at 5:34 p.m. Monday.
>
> Allow an hour for the sauce to *set*.   The bracelet is *set* with diamonds.

Sit (principal parts: *sit, sat, sat, sitting*) means "to be in a position of rest" or "to be seated." This verb cannot be used with an object.

> Here we *sit*, waiting for a decision.   They *had sat* on the plane for an hour.
>
> I *sat* next to Ebrahim at the meeting.   We *will be sitting* in the top balcony.

Shall—will. The helping verb *shall* has largely given way to the verb *will* in all but the most formal writing and speech. The following rules reflect both ordinary and formal usage:

a. To express simple future time:

   (1) In *ordinary* circumstances use *will* with all three persons.

> I (**OR** *we*) *will* be glad to help you plan the program.
>
> *You will* want to study these recommendations before the meeting.
>
> *He* (**OR** *she, it, they*) *will* arrive tomorrow morning.

   (2) In *formal* circumstances use *shall* with the first person (*I, we*) and *will* with the second and third persons (*you, he, she, it, they*).

> *I* (**OR** *we*) *shall* be glad to answer all inquiries promptly.
>
> *You will* meet the McGinnesses at the reception this evening.
>
> *They* (**OR** *he, she*) *will* not find the trip too tiring.

b. To indicate *determination, promise, desire, choice,* or *threat:*

(1) In *ordinary* circumstances use *will* with all three persons.

(2) In *formal* circumstances use *will* for the first person *(I, we)* and *shall* for the second and third persons *(you, he, she, it, they).*

In spite of the risk, *I will* go where I please. (Determination.)

They shall not interfere with my department. (Determination.)

I will send my cheque by the end of the week. (Promise.)

We will report you to the authorities if this is true. (Threat.)

You shall regret your answer. (Threat.)

He shall study or *he shall* leave college. (Threat.)

c. To indicate *willingness* (to be willing, to be agreeable to) in both *ordinary* and *formal* circumstances, use *will* with all persons.

Yes, I *will* meet you at six o'clock.

Should—would. *Should* and *would* follow the same rules as *shall* and *will* in expressions of future time, determination, and willingness. The distinctions concerning ordinary and formal usage also apply here.

ORDINARY: I *would* like to hear from you.
FORMAL: I *should* like to hear from you.

ORDINARY: We *would* be glad to see her.
FORMAL: We *should* be glad to see her.

ORDINARY: I *would* be pleased to serve on that committee.
FORMAL: I *should* be pleased to serve on that committee.

a. Always use *should* in all persons to indicate "ought to."

I *should* study tonight.   He *should* pay his debts.

You *should* report his dishonesty to the manager.

b. Always use *would* in all persons to indicate customary action.

Every day I *would* swim half a mile.   They *would* only say, "No comment."

c. Use *should* in all three persons to express a condition in an *if* clause.

If I *should* win the prize, I will share it with you.

If you *should* miss the train, please call me collect.

d. Use *would* in all three persons to express willingness in an *if* clause.

If he *would* apply himself, he could win top honours easily.

If you *would* delay your decision, I could offer you more attractive terms.

Since. *Since* has two meanings: it can refer to some point of time in the past, or it can mean "because."

Since (from the time that) we last met, I've found a better job.

Since (because) I will be travelling, please collect my mail.

So—so that. *So* as a conjunction means "therefore"; *so that* means "in order that."

(Continued on page 302.)

The work is now finished, *so* you can all go home. (See also ¶179.)

Please finish what you are doing *so that* we can all go home.

Someday—some day.

Please set up a meeting with Al and Jerry *someday* (on an unspecified day) next week.

BUT: Please set up a meeting with Al and Jerry *for some day* next week. (Two words when used as the object of a preposition such as *for*.)

Someone—some one. See ¶1010 note.

Sometime—sometimes—some time.

The order will be shipped *sometime* (at some unspecified time) next week.

Sometimes (now and then) reports are misleading.

It took me *some time* (a period of time) to complete the job.

I saw him *some time* ago (a long time ago).

NOTE: Spell *some time* as two words when the term follows a preposition.

We will be happy to reconsider your proposal *at some time* in the future.

I've been thinking about retiring *for some time*.

Sort. See *Kind*.

Sort of—kind of. See *Kind of—sort of*.

Such as . . . etc. See *Etc*.

Supposed to. Be sure to spell *supposed* with a *d*.

Under the circumstances what was I *supposed to* think? (**NOT:** suppose to.)

Sure—surely. *Sure* is an adjective, *surely* an adverb.

I am *sure* that I did not make that mistake. (Adjective.)

You can *surely* count on our help. (Adverb.)

Do not use *sure* as an adverb; use *surely*, *certainly*, or *very*.

I was *very* (**OR** *surely*) glad to be of help. (**NOT:** sure glad.)

Sure and. In formal writing use *sure to* in place of the colloquial *sure and*.

Be *sure to* give my best regards to the Nakanos.

(**NOT:** Be *sure and give* my best regards to the Nakanos.)

Take—bring. See *Bring—take*.

Teach—learn. See *Learn—teach*.

Than—then. *Than* is a conjunction introducing a dependent clause of comparison. *Then* is an adverb meaning "at that time" or "next."

They *then* asserted that they could handle the account better *than* we. (See ¶1057 for the case of pronouns following *than*.)

The compulsory retirement age is higher now *than* it was *then*.

NOTE: Remember that *then* (like *when*) refers to time.

11

That. As a subordinating conjunction, *that* links the dependent clause it introduces with the main clause. *That* is often omitted (but understood).

> We realize *that* our bargaining position is not a strong one.
>
> **OR:** We realize our bargaining position is not a strong one.

However, under certain circumstances *that* should not be omitted:

a. When the word or phrase following *that* could be misread as the object of the verb in the main clause.

> **NOT:** I heard your speech next Wednesday had to be rescheduled.
>
> **BUT:** I heard *that* your speech next Wednesday had to be rescheduled.

b. When *that* introduces two or more parallel clauses.

> **NOT:** Hilary said she had narrowed the applicants for the job down to three people and *that* she would announce her choice by this Friday.
>
> **BUT:** Hilary said *that* she had narrowed the applicants for the job down to three people and *that* she would announce her choice by this Friday.

c. When an introductory or interrupting element comes between *that* and the subject of the dependent clause.

> **NOT:** I think whenever possible, you should consult everyone involved before making your decision.
>
> **BUT:** I think *that* whenever possible, you should consult everyone involved before making your decision. (See ¶130d.)

NOTE: If you are in doubt, do not omit *that*.

That—that. Avoid unnecessary repetition of *that*.

> I think *that* the project should be finished.
>
> **NOT:** I think *that that* project should be finished.

That—where. See *Where—that*.

That—which—who. See ¶1062.

This here. Do not use for *this*; for example, "*this* (**NOT** this here) word processor."

This sort—this kind. The correct forms are *this* sort, *this* kind, these *sorts*, these *kinds*. (See Kind.)

Together. See *Both alike—equal—together*.

Toward—towards. *Toward* is more common, but both forms are correct.

Try and. In written material use *try to* rather than the colloquial *try and*. For example, "Please *try to* be here on time." (**NOT:** try and be here.)

Type. See *Kind*.

Unique. Do not use *unique* in the sense of "unusual." A unique thing is one of a kind. (See ¶1071h.)

11

Up. Many verbs (for example, *end, rest, lift, connect, join, hurry, settle, burn, drink, eat*) contain the idea of "up"; therefore, the adverb *up* is unnecessary. In the following sentences, *up* should be omitted.

You need to rest (up) for a bit.   Save $50 if you join (up) now.

Let's divide (up) the work load.   I will call him (up) tomorrow.

Upon—up on. See *On—upon—up on.*

Used to. Be sure to spell *used* with a *d* unless it follows *did*.

We *used* to use Foremost as our main supplier. (**NOT:** We *use* to use . . .)

BUT: Did you *use* to speak French at home? (**NOT:** Did you *used* . . .)

Very. This adverb can be used to modify an adjective, another adverb, a present participle, or a "descriptive" past participle.

We are *very happy* with the outcome. (Modifying an adjective.)

This finish dries *very quickly*. (Modifying an adverb.)

It was a *very disappointing* showing. (Modifying a present participle.)

I was *very pleased* with the pictures. (Modifying a descriptive past participle.)

When the past participle expresses action rather than description, insert an adverb like *much* after *very*.

They are *very much opposed* to your plan. (*Opposed* is part of the complete verb *are opposed* and expresses action rather than description.)

(**NOT:** They are *very opposed* to your plan.)

Ways. Do not use for *way* in referring to distance. For example, "I live a short *way* (**NOT** ways) from here."

Well—good. See *Good—well.*

Whatever—what ever.

You may write on *whatever* (any) topic you wish.

What ever made you think that was true? (*Ever* is an adverb here.)

Where—that. Do not use *where* in place of *that*.

I saw in the paper *that* Robinson's had changed its mind about closing its store.

(**NOT:** I saw in the paper *where* Robinson's had changed its mind about closing its store.)

Whether—if. See *If—whether.*

Who—which—that. See ¶1062.

Who—whom. See ¶1061.

Whoever—who ever.

Whoever (anyone who) made such a statement should be fired.

Who ever made such a statement? (*Ever* is an adverb.)

Will—shall. See *Shall—will.*

11

Wise. Avoid the temptation to coin new words by attaching the suffix *wise* to various nouns.

> **NOT:** *Costwise*, we're already 20 percent over budget.

> **BUT:** We're already 20 percent over budget on costs.

Would—should. See *Should—would*.

Would have. Note that the second word in this verb phrase is *have*. (The spelling *would of* is wrong.)

> I myself *would have* (**NOT** would of) taken a different tack.

In a clause beginning with *if*, do not use *would have* in place of *had*.

> If you *had* come early, you could have talked with Dr. Faqiryar yourself.

> **NOT:** If you would have come early, you could have talked with Dr. Faqiryar yourself.

See the Online Learning Centre at www.mcgrawhill.ca/college/gregg for related Web links.

P A R T

TWO

Techniques and Formats

SECTION **TWELVE**

Office Applications

Computers greatly affect the way documents are prepared today. More people not only compose and produce the final documents themselves, but they incorporate the skills of proofreading and editing as part of their overall writing process.

12 PROOFREADING AND EDITING

The Proofreading and Editing Process

1201 a. *Proofreading* is a mechanical process by which you compare the copy that you or some-one else has written and confirm that this version faithfully reproduces the original material in the intended form.

If the original material is complex or involved or contains figures, it is wise for two people to share the proofreading function: one (the *copyholder*) reads the text aloud and indicates the intended punctuation, paragraphing, capitalization, format, and details of style, while the other person (the *proofreader*) examines the copy closely to ensure that everything appears as it should.

b. *Editing* is an analytical and judgmental process that questions the material for accuracy, clarity, coherence, consistency, and effectiveness. If the material is yours, you may need to revise it several times. However, if it is someone else's writing, you may solve only those problems you are able and authorized to address.

Proofreading and Editing at the Computer

1202 Whether you are working on someone else's material or whether you are solely responsible for all phases of the writing process, proofreading and editing are necessary skills to practise and perfect.

a. One advantage computers bring to the production of documents is the ease with which changes can be made. Yet in this process of "cutting" and "pasting," new kinds of errors may be created:

- Accepting computerized spell checks too readily without checking for homonyms (see examples in ¶719) or errors in word use.
- Deleting only part of an old version
- Ignoring verb number when the subject changes from singular to plural
- Inserting new copy in the wrong place
- Reading on-screen for any length of time, which causes eyestrain and makes errors difficult to find

b. Run the text through spelling and grammar checkers; read the text on the screen for any obvious mistakes; and make the necessary corrections. Further proofreading and editing, however, will still be required.

c. It is imperative that copy be proofread from the printed page. Examine it carefully for all types of errors. After correcting the copy, review the text once more on the screen and then again on the final printout. Check to see that no new errors have been introduced. (See ¶1202a.)

What to Look for When Proofreading

1203 When *proofreading* a document, be especially watchful for the following types of mistakes:

a. Repeated words, especially at the end of one line and the beginning of the next. A spell checker may highlight some of these errors, but not all of them.

What are the chances of your
your coming to see us?

I can help you in the event
in the event you have more
work than you can handle.

I have been awaiting some indi-
indication of a compromise.

We are looking forward to the
to the reception you are planning for the Lockwoods.

b. Substitutions and omissions, especially those that change the meaning. Since nothing is misspelled, no spell checker will find them.

Original Material	Erroneous Copy
The courts have ruled that the contract is now legal.	The courts have ruled that the contract is not legal.
All Keng's actions reflect his upright character.	All Keng's actions reflect his uptight character.
In my opinion, there is no reason to suspect Fred.	In my opinion, there is reason to suspect Fred.
I hereby agree to pay you $87.50 in full settlement.	I hereby agree to pay you $8750 in full settlement.
I'll gladly give you the job if you'll do it in a week and if you'll reduce your price by $200.	I'll gladly give you the job if you'll reduce your price by $200.

c. Errors in copying key data.

	Original Material	Erroneous Copy
NAMES:	Katharine Ann Mar	Katherine Anne Mah
TITLES:	Ms. Margaret Peiris	Mrs. Margaret A. Peiris
INSIDE ADDRESSES:	519 Magnus Avenue Winnipeg, MB R2W 2C4	591 Magnus Avenue Winnipeg, MN R2W 2C4
DATES:	October 13, 2006	October 31, 2007
PHONE NOS.:	506-555-1551	306-555-1515
AMOUNTS OF MONEY:	$83 454 000 000	$38 454 000
DECIMALS:	sales fell 5.2 percent	sales fell 52 percent
CLOCK TIME:	arrive at 4:15 p.m.	arrive at 4:51 p.m.
PERIODS OF TIME:	boil for 2 minutes	boil for 20 minutes

d. Transpositions in letters, numbers, and words.

Original Material	Erroneous Copy
I'll buy two boats this May	I'll buy tow boats this May.
a process of trial and error	a process of trail and error

(Continued on page 312.)

Let's form a committee to review our pricing policy.	Let's from a committee to review our pricing policy.
We'll need 82 binders for the seminar beginning July 12.	We'll need 28 binders for the seminar beginning July 21.
How can we thank you all for your thoughtfulness?	How can we thank you for all your thoughtfulness?

e. Errors in spacing and inconsistencies in format (for example, indenting some paragraphs but not others, leaving too little or too much space between words or after punctuation, improperly aligning, or inappropriately placing hard returns in a line).

f. As a final step in proofreading, check the appearance of the document.

- Does each page as a whole look attractive?
- Is the style consistent in all headings? displayed extracts? lists?
- Is the vertical placement consistent throughout the document?
- Are there any widows or orphans?
- Are there too many large white spaces in a justified line?

What to Look for When Editing

1204 When *editing* a document at any stage in the writing process, consider the material in light of the following factors. (For an explanation of the proofreaders' marks used in the following examples, see pages 314–315.)

a. Use the spell checker first. Because it is not infallible, still check for errors in *spelling* (see Section 7) and particularly for words accepted by the spell checker that are not in the correct form for the word in context. Give special attention to *compound words* (see Section 8) and those with *plural and possessive endings* (see Section 6). Confirm the correctness of any *word divisions* (see Section 9).

> We had a similar break down when a high-level executive
> failed to inform us that the corporations attorneys had advised
> against it's proceeding with merger negotiations.

b. Make sure that every necessary mark of *punctuation* is correctly inserted. (See Sections 1 and 2.)

> How do you account for the fact that, whenever we are about to
> launch a new product, the company cuts our marketing dollars?

c. Inspect the material for possible errors in *capitalization, number,* and *abbreviation style.* (See Sections 3, 4, and 5.)

> Be sure to attend the Managers' meeting on june 4th at
> two p. m. There will be 5 or 6 announcements of special
> interest.

d. Correct any errors in *grammar* and *usage*. (See Sections 10 and 11.)

Every~~o~~ne of the sales representatives ~~have~~ **has** made ~~less~~ **fewer** calls in the past six months th~~e~~n ~~they did~~ in the previous period.

e. Be especially alert to wording that conveys a meaning you did not intend. If you are editing someone else's writing, resolve any problems that you can and refer the rest to the author.

> When I met with you, Harry Mills, ⟨and Paula Fierro⟩ on May 8, we agreed that . . . ⟨Ed: Wasn't Paula at the 5/8 meeting?⟩ I think that as a next move you ought to ⟨fill Paula Fierro in⟩ on what happened at our May 8 meeting.

f. Look for problems in *organization* and *writing style*. Grammar, style, and usage could still be correct yet contain unclear or repetitive wording, clumsy sentences, weak organization, or a tone that is not appropriate for the occasion. (See ¶¶1081–1099.)

g. Look at the document as a whole. Is it accomplishing its *objective*? Anticipate your readers' reactions before a misunderstanding arises.

NOTE: If you are editing material you yourself have written, consider all the points noted in ¶1204a–g. However, if you are editing material written by someone else, the extent of your editing will depend on your experience and your relationship with the writer. If you are on your first job, determine whether your employer has any special preferences with regard to matters of style, spelling, punctuation, etc.

Proofreaders' Marks

1205 Whether you are proofreading or editing, use the proofreaders' marks shown on pages 314 and 315 to show the corrections that need to be made. Minor variations in the way these marks are formed are unimportant as long as the marks clearly indicate what corrections have to be made.

DICTATING AND TRANSCRIBING

In dictating and transcribing both the dictator and transcriber have roles in how a document is to be produced.

The Dictating and Transcribing Process

1206 a. *Dictating* is composing and transmitting data with recording equipment. The first part of dictation is *instructional*, providing information on how a document is to be produced—detailing the length, copies required, and enclosures. The second part of dictation is the *delivery*.

- Speak in a conversational tone, grouping words evenly and naturally.

(Continued on page 314.)

12

PROOFREADERS' MARK	DRAFT	FINAL COPY
ss[Single-space	ss[I have heard / he is leaving.	I have heard he is leaving.
ds[Double-space	ds[When will you / have a decision?	When will you / have a decision?
+1ℓ#→ Insert 1 line space	**Percentage of Change** / +1ℓ# ⌐16.25	**Percentage of Change** / 16.25
−1ℓ#→ Delete (remove) 1 line space	Northeastern / −1ℓ#→ / regional sales	Northeastern regional sales
⌒ Delete space	to gether	together
# Insert space	It may be	It may not be
⌆ Move as shown	it is (not) true	it is true
∿ Transpose	belei vable	believable
	(is it) so	it is so
○ Spell out	②years ago	two years ago
	16 Elm (St.)	16 Elm Street
∧ Insert a word	How much it? is	How much is it?
✐ OR — Delete a word	it may not be true	it may be true
∧ OR ⋏ Insert a letter, space, or punctuation mark	temper a ture	temperature
℘ OR ⌄ Delete a letter and close up	commitment to buy	commitment to buy
∧ OR ⌒ Add on to a word	a real good day ly	a really good day
℘ OR / Change a letter	this superᵍedes	this supersedes
⌅ OR —Change a word	but / and if you won't can't	but if you can't
.... Stet (don't delete)	I was very glad	I was very glad
/ Lowercase a letter	⌿Federal ⌿Government	federal government
≡ Capitalize	Janet L. greyston	Janet L. Greyston

- Enunciate clearly, paying attention to the sounds of *p* and *b*, *m* and *n*, *f* and *v*, past tenses of verbs, and plural endings.
- Spell out proper names, technical terms, and foreign words. (Dictating capitalization, punctuation, and paragraphs is optional.)

b. *Transcribing* is placing the words of the dictator into print. Good listening skills are essential to produce good copy and to interpret the dictator's thoughts. The following techniques are suggested:

- Note instructions at the beginning of the dictation, listening carefully for references to dates and times, and adjust if necessary.
- Listen first to gain a sense of the dictation.

PROOFREADERS' MARK	DRAFT	FINAL COPY
∨ Raise above the line	in her new book∨	in her new book[*]
∧ Drop below the line	H2SO4	H_2SO_4
⊙ Insert a period	M Henry Grenada	Mr. Henry Grenada
�↗ Insert a comma	a large old house	a large, old house
⌄ Insert an apostrophe	my childrens car	my children's car
⌄⌄ Insert quotation marks	he wants a loan	he wants a "loan"
= Insert a hyphen	a first=rate job	a first-rate job
⊥/M Insert a one-em dash or change a hyphen to a one-em dash	Success at last! Here it is cash!	Success—at last! Here it is—cash!
⊥/N insert a one-en dash or change a hyphen to a one-en dash	Pages 15 to 18 / Pages 15–18	Pages 15–18 / Pages 15–18
ital Insert italics	Do it now, Bill!	Do it *now*, Bill!
no ital Delete italics	Do it now! no ital	Do it now!
〰 Change to boldface	CONFIDENTIAL	**CONFIDENTIAL**
Delete boldface	Ship by June 1 no bf	Ship by June 1
__ Insert underscore	an issue of Time	an issue of Time
Delete underscore	a very long day	a very long day
( ) Insert parentheses	left today(May 3)	left today (May 3)
⁋ Start a new paragraph	⁋ If that is so	If that is so
⊡ Indent 2 spaces	Net investment in ⊡ tangible assets	Net investment in tangible assets
½" Indent 0.5 inch	As a general rule leave a top margin	As a general rule leave a top margin
⊐ Move to the right	$38 367 000	$38 367 000
⊏ Move to the left	⊏ Anyone can win!	Anyone can win!
= Align horizontally	TO: / Bob Muller	TO: Bob Muller
‖ Align vertically	‖ Jon Peters Ellen March	Jon Peters Ellen March

12

- Listen again to recall a group of words or a phrase. Stop the recording and key the words, entering text as continuously as possible. (Voice changes and pauses are clues to punctuation and paragraphs.)
- Use the spell and grammar checkers before printing.
- Prepare draft copies if the text is complicated or technical in nature, or if the dictator makes frequent changes.
- Correct as many errors on the screen as you possibly can.
- Proofread and edit all copies, both draft and final.
- Show your first readable transcript to the dictator for changes or approval.

RULES FOR ALPHABETIC FILING

Regardless of what filing system a business follows (subject, numeric, or geographic) or what records it saves (correspondence or cards), the goal of records management is to establish a **consistent** method of sorting and storing so that everyone can retrieve documents quickly and easily.

Filing alphabetically is based on the principles of *indexing*, which is breaking down a name into units and arranging the units in a certain sequence. The units of one document are then compared to other documents for sorting into alphabetical order.

The basic principles of alphabetical filing by the indexing (unit-by-unit) method (see ¶¶1207–1209) and the more specific rules that follow (see ¶¶1210–1223) are those standardized by the Association of Records Managers and Administrators (ARMA). The specific needs of your office may require some modifications to these rules.

The following charts show the names with all capital letters in an indexed format (that is, arranged unit by unit in alphabetical order). This format ignores the size of letters, punctuation, and in some cases, a space or hyphen between parts of a name.

If you want to use a computer (1) to print names in alphabetical order and (2) to insert names in inside addresses as well as text, you may have to create two name fields—one in standard format (inside address format of a letter) and the other in indexed format.

☞ *For guidelines on how to create a computerized file name, see* ¶1382.

Basic Principles
1207 ALPHABETIZING UNIT BY UNIT

    a. Alphabetize names by comparing the first units letter by letter.

Name	Unit 1	Unit 2	Unit 3
Eagleton	EAGLETON		
Eaton	EATON		
Eberhardt	EBERHARDT		
Eberhart	EBERHART		
Eby Video	EBY	VIDEO	
ECO Lab Sales	ECO	LAB	SALES
Econo Holidays	ECONO	HOLIDAYS	

    b. Consider second units only when the first units are identical.

Name	Unit 1	Unit 2
Foley Enterprises	FOLEY	ENTERPRISES
Foley Industries	FOLEY	INDUSTRIES

c. Consider additional units only when the first two units are identical.

Name	Unit 1	Unit 2	Unit 3	Unit 4
Fox Hill Company	FOX	HILL	COMPANY	
Fox Hill Farm	FOX	HILL	FARM	
Fox Hill Farm Supplies	FOX	HILL	FARM	SUPPLIES

> **NOTE:** If two names are identical, they may be distinguished on the basis of geographical location. (See ¶1220.)

1208 NOTHING COMES BEFORE SOMETHING

A single letter comes before a name that begins with the same letter. For names consisting of initial identical filing units, each part of the name is considered a separate unit. Read from left to right until a point of comparison is reached.

Name	Unit 1	Unit 2	Unit 3	Unit 4
O	O			
Oasis	OASIS			
Oberon	OBERON			
Operations	OPERATIONS			
Operations Management Consultants	OPERATIONS	MANAGEMENT	CONSULTANTS	
Operations Technologies	OPERATIONS	TECHNOLOGIES		
Opus Creek	OPUS	CREEK		
Opus Creek Home Furnishings	OPUS	CREEK	HOME	FURNISHINGS
Opus Creek Homes	OPUS	CREEK	HOMES	

1209 DECIDING WHICH NAME TO USE

ARMA advocates filing "under the most commonly used name or title." This helpful principle provides the basis for choosing which name you should use for a person, persons, or an organization when other possible names exist. Select the name (the primary name for filing purposes) most likely to be used; prepare cross-reference sheets, folders, or cards for the alternative names; and place in the appropriate alphabetic sequence. Anyone who is searching for material under another name will then be referred directly to the primary name file. (See ¶¶1213c, 1215c, 1216a, note, and 1217a, note for specific applications of this principle.)

Personal Names

1210 RULE 1: NAMES OF PERSONS

    a. Treat each part of the name of a person as a separate unit, and consider the units in this order: last name, first name or initial, and any subsequent names or initials. Ignore any punctuation following or within an abbreviation.

Name	Unit 1	Unit 2	Unit 3	Unit 4
Jacobs	JACOBS			
L. Jacobs	JACOBS	L		
L. Mitchell Jacobs	JACOBS	L	MITCHELL	
Stephen Jacobson	JACOBSON	STEPHEN		
Steven O'K Jacobson	JACOBSON	STEVEN	OK	
B. T. Jacoby	JACOBY	B	T	
Bruce Jacoby	JACOBY	BRUCE		
C. Bruce Hay Jacoby	JACOBY	C	BRUCE	HAY

    b. When you cannot distinguish the last name from the first name, consider each part of the name in the order in which it is written. Whenever you can make the distinction, consider the last name first.

Name	Unit 1	Unit 2	Unit 3
Kwong Kow Ng	KWONG	KOW	NG
Ng Kwong Cheung	NG	KWONG	CHEUNG
Philip K. Ng	NG	PHILIP	K

    c. In a name like *Maria López y Quintana*, the last name consists of three separate words. For purposes of alphabetizing, treat these separate words as a single unit (for example, LOPEZYQUINTANA).

1211 RULE 2: PERSONAL NAMES WITH PREFIXES

Consider a prefix as part of the name, not as a separate unit. Ignore variations in spacing, capitalization, and punctuation (including the apostrophe). Treat all prefixes (for example, *d', D', Da, de, De, Del, De la, Des, Di, Du, El, Fitz, L', La, Las, Le, Les, Lo, Los, M', Mac, Mc, Saint, San, Santa, Santo, St., Ste., Ten, Ter, Van, Van de, Van der, Von,* and *Von Der*) exactly as they are spelled.

Name	Unit 1	Unit 2	Unit 3
A. Simon De laval	DELAVAL	A	SIMON
Anna C. de Laval	DELAVAL	ANNA	C
Michael B. DeLaval	DELAVAL	MICHAEL	B
Victor P. deLaval	DELAVAL	VICTOR	P
LaVerne P. De Lay	DELAY	LAVERNE	P
Angela G. Delaye	DELAYE	ANGELA	G
Irene J. MacKay	MACKAY	IRENE	J
Roy F. Mackay	MACKAY	ROY	F
Walter G. Mac Kay	MACKAY	WALTER	G
Agnes U. M'Cauley	MCAULEY	AGNES	U
Patrick J. McKay	MCKAY	PATRICK	J

Name	Unit 1	Unit 2	Unit 3
Andrew W. O'Hare	OHARE	ANDREW	W
Kyle N. Saint Clair	SAINTCLAIR	KYLE	N
Peter St. Clair	STCLAIR	PETER	
O. M. Ste. Marie	STEMARIE	O	M
D. E. van de Hoven	VANDEHOVEN	D	E
T. Van Den Hoven	VANDENHOVEN	T	

NOTE: If you are using a computer, insert a hard space between the parts of a name such as De Lay, Mac Kay, or Ste. Marie. The last name will be sorted as if it were keyed without spaces, but it will appear *with spaces* in the alphabetized list of names.

1212 RULE 3: HYPHENATED PERSONAL NAMES

Treat the hyphenated elements of a name as a single unit. Ignore the hyphen.

Name	Unit 1	Unit 2	Unit 3
S. T. Kelly-O'Brien	KELLYOBRIEN	S	T
Victor Olson-Jones	OLSONJONES	VICTOR	
Jean V. Vigneau	VIGNEAU	JEAN	V
Jean-Marie Vigneau	VIGNEAU	JEANMARIE	

1213 RULE 4: ABBREVIATED PERSONAL NAMES, NICKNAMES, AND PSEUDONYMS

a. Consider any abbreviated part of a name such as *Chas.* for *Charles* as if it were written in full. Initials standing for a first or middle name are not considered abbreviations. Names such as *Tony* and *Peggy* are considered only if they are the true name or if the true name is unknown.

Name	Unit 1	Unit 2	Unit 3
Chas. E. Kassily	KASSILY	CHARLES	E
Tony Leaden	LEADEN	TONY	
Peggy Sue Marker	MARKER	PEGGY	SUE
B. J. Purcell	PURCELL	B	J

b. If a person is known by a nickname alone (without a surname) or by a pseudonym, consider each word in the nickname or pseudonym as a separate unit. If the name begins with *The,* treat *The* as the last unit.

Name	Unit 1	Unit 2	Unit 3
Big Al	BIG	AL	
The Cookie Lady	COOKIE	LADY	THE
Handy Joe Bob	HANDY	JOE	BOB
Harry the Horse	HARRY	THE	HORSE
Heavy D	HEAVY	D	

(Continued on page 320.)

c. To decide whether file material under a person's formal name or under a nickname, pseudonym, or some abbreviated form, choose the form that you and others are most likely to look under. Prepare cross-references for the person's alternative names. For example, if *Big Al* is formally named Alan J. Sherman, the cross-reference entry in the file for *Sherman, Alan J.* would read: *See Big Al.* (See also ¶1209.)

1214 RULE 5: PERSONAL NAMES WITH TITLES AND SUFFIXES

a. A title (such as *Dr., Major, Mayor, Miss, Mr., Mrs.,* or *Ms.*) may be used as the *last* filing unit in order to distinguish two or more names that are otherwise identical. Treat any abbreviated titles as written.

Name	Unit 1	Unit 2	Unit 3	Unit 4
Dr. Leslie G. Mabry	MABRY	LESLIE	G	DR
Miss Leslie G. Mabry	MABRY	LESLIE	G	MISS
Mr. Leslie G. Mabry	MABRY	LESLIE	G	MR
Mrs. Leslie G. Mabry	MABRY	LESLIE	G	MRS
Ms. Leslie G. Mabry	MABRY	LESLIE	G	MS
Major Felix Novotny	NOVOTNY	FELIX	MAJOR	
Mayor Felix Novotny	NOVOTNY	FELIX	MAYOR	

b. When a title is used with only one part of a person's name, treat it as the *first* unit. (See ¶1209.)

Name	Unit 1	Unit 2
Dr. Ruth	DR	RUTH
Grandma Moses	GRANDMA	MOSES
King Abdullah	KING	ABDULLAH
Miss Manners	MISS	MANNERS
Mother Teresa	MOTHER	TERESA
Prince Andrew	PRINCE	ANDREW
Saint Elizabeth	SAINT*	ELIZABETH

*Note that *Saint* as a title is considered a separate unit, whereas *Saint* as a prefix in a personal name is considered only part of a unit. (See ¶1211 for examples of *Saint* as a prefix.)

c. Ordinarily, alphabetize a married woman's name on the basis of her own first name. However, consider the title *Mrs.* (as abbreviated) if a woman uses her husband's name and you do not know her first name.

Name	Unit 1	Unit 2	Unit 3	Unit 4
Mrs. June Y. Nearing	NEARING	JUNE	Y	
Mr. Peter J. Nearing	NEARING	PETER	J	
Mr. Harry L. Norton	NORTON	HARRY	L	MR
Mrs. Harry L. Norton	NORTON	HARRY	L	MRS

d. Consider a seniority term (such as *Jr., Sr., 2nd, 3rd, II,* or *III*), a professional or academic degree (such as *CMA, M.D.,* or *Ph.D.*), or any other designation following a person's name in order to distinguish names that are otherwise identical. Numeric designations precede alphabetic designations. Moreover, Arabic numerals precede Roman numerals, and each set of numbers is sequenced in numeric order. When dealing with ordinal numbers such as *3rd* or *4th*, ignore the endings.

Name	Unit 1	Unit 2	Unit 3	Unit 4
James R. Foster 2nd	FOSTER	JAMES	R	2
James R. Foster 3rd	FOSTER	JAMES	R	3
James R. Foster III	FOSTER	JAMES	R	III
James R. Foster IV	FOSTER	JAMES	R	IV
James R. Foster, D.D.	FOSTER	JAMES	R	DD
James R. Foster, M.D.	FOSTER	JAMES	R	MD
James R. Foster, Mr.	FOSTER	JAMES	R	MR
James R. Foster, Ph.D.	FOSTER	JAMES	R	PHD
James R. Foster, Sr.	FOSTER	JAMES	R	SR

NOTE: When inputting names on a computer, Arabic numerals will be sequenced in numeric order and will precede all names with a comparable unit composed of letters of the alphabet.

There is a problem, however, with Roman numerals since they are letters of the alphabet. A computer sequencing the names in the chart above would insert D.D. before the name ending with III. You will need to override the software and manually move the name with D.D. to the correct position after IV.

Organizational Names

1215 RULE 6: NAMES OF ORGANIZATIONS

a. Treat each word in the name of an organization as a separate unit, and consider the units in the same order as they are written on the company letterhead or some other authoritative document.

Name	Unit 1	Unit 2	Unit 3
Canadian Data Bank	CANADIAN	DATA	BANK
Canadian Data Express	CANADIAN	DATA	EXPRESS
I Deal Cards	I	DEAL	CARDS
Ideal Printers	IDEAL	PRINTERS	

b. When alphabetizing, ignore all punctuation—for example, periods, commas, hyphens, apostrophes, and diagonals. When words are joined by a hyphen or a diagonal, treat the phrase as a single unit.

(Continued on page 322.)

Name	Unit 1	Unit 2	Unit 3
Baskins' Artworks	BASKINS	ARTWORKS	
Baskin's Basket Shop	BASKINS	BASKET	SHOP
Baskin-Shaw Films	BASKINSHAW	FILMS	
Baskin/Shaw Foods	BASKINSHAW	FOODS	
Curtis Imports	CURTIS	IMPORTS	
Curtis's China Gallery	CURTISS	CHINA	GALLERY
Curtiss Couriers	CURTISS	COURIERS	
Oleander's Displays!	OLEANDERS	DISPLAYS	
O'Leary's Snap Shop	OLEARYS	SNAP	SHOP
What's New?	WHATS	NEW	

c. Treat prepositions (such as *of* and *in*), conjunctions (such as *and* and *or*), and articles (*the, a,* and *an*) as separate units. When *the, a,* or *an* is the first word in a name, treat it as the last unit.

Name	Unit 1	Unit 2	Unit 3	Unit 4
In-Plant Catering	INPLANT	CATERING		
Over the Rainbow Gifts	OVER	THE	RAINBOW	GIFTS
The Pen and Pencil	PEN	AND	PENCIL	THE
Photos in a Flash	PHOTOS	IN	A	FLASH
A Touch of Glass	TOUCH	OF	GLASS	A

d. When a compound expression is written as one word or hyphenated, treat it as a single unit. If the compound expression is written with spaces, treat each element as a separate unit.

Name	Unit 1	Unit 2	Unit 3
Aero Space Systems	AERO	SPACE	SYSTEMS
Aerospace Research	AEROSPACE	RESEARCH	
Aero-Space Unlimited	AEROSPACE	UNLIMITED	
South East Condos	SOUTH	EAST	CONDOS
Southeast Chemicals	SOUTHEAST	CHEMICALS	
South-East Dental Lab	SOUTHEAST	DENTAL	LAB

e. Although organizational names are usually considered in the same order in which they are written, there are exceptions to this rule. (See ¶1209.) For instance, if the name is *Hotel Plaza, Hotel* should be the first unit; but if you are more likely to look in the *P* section of the files, choose *Plaza* as the first unit and *Hotel* as the second. Be sure, when introducing exceptions to the basic rule for organizational names, that these exceptions are supported by cross-references. (See ¶1213c for an example of a cross-reference.)

1216 RULE 7: PERSONAL NAMES WITHIN ORGANIZATIONAL NAMES

a. When an organizational name includes a person's name, consider the parts of the personal name in the order in which they are written. Ignore any punctuation.

Name	Unit 1	Unit 2	Unit 3	Unit 4
Frank Balcom Construction Company	FRANK	BALCOM	CONSTRUCTION	COMPANY
Frank Balcom, Jr., Paving	FRANK	BALCOM	JR	PAVING
G. Ngan Optical Supplies	G	NGAN	OPTICAL	SUPPLIES
G. P. Ngan Autos	G	P	NGAN	AUTOS
Gai Ngan Interiors	GAI	NGAN	INTERIORS	
Gai P. Ngan Homes	GAI	P	NGAN	HOMES

NOTE: A more traditional rule that is still widely followed requires that a person's name within an organizational name be considered in the same way as if the person's name stood alone—namely, last name first. (See ¶1210.) On the other hand, the ARMA standard guidelines for personal names within organizational names require placing first names first. However, consider the way in which the name is most likely to be used and then supply cross-references between the alternative names and the primary name that has been selected. (See also ¶1209.)

b. If a prefix is used in a personal name that is part of an organizational name, do not treat the prefix as a separate unit. (See ¶1211.)

Name	Unit 1	Unit 2	Unit 3	Unit 4
A. de La Cruz Securities Company	A	DELACRUZ	SECURITIES	COMPANY
A. D'Elia Boat Sales	A	DELIA	BOAT	SALES
Peter Saint Clair Boatels	PETER	SAINTCLAIR	BOATELS	
Peter St. Clair Insurance Agency	PETER	STCLAIR	INSURANCE	AGENCY
R. Van Alstine Art Galleries	R	VANALSTINE	ART	GALLERIES

c. If a hyphenated personal name is part of an organizational name, treat the hyphenated elements as a single unit. (See ¶1212.)

Name	Unit 1	Unit 2	Unit 3	Unit 4
Mary Tom Packaging Consultants	MARY	TOM	PACKAGING	CONSULTANTS
Mary Tom-Katz Production Company	MARY	TOMKATZ	PRODUCTION	COMPANY

(Continued on page 324.)

d. Consider a title in an organization's name as a separate unit in the order in which it occurs. Treat abbreviated titles as they are written and ignore punctuation.

Name	Unit 1	Unit 2	Unit 3	Unit 4
Capt. Jack Seafood	CAPT	JACK	SEAFOOD	
Captain Ahab Tours	CAPTAIN	AHAB	TOURS	
Dr. Popper Vision Services	DR	POPPER	VISION	SERVICES
Ma Blake Food Shops	MA	BLAKE	FOOD	SHOPS
Miss Celeste Sportswear	MISS	CELESTE	SPORTSWEAR	
Mother Goose Nurseries	MOTHER	GOOSE	NURSERIES	
Mr. George Limousine Service	MR	GEORGE	LIMOUSINE	SERVICE
Mrs. Ellis Bakeries	MRS	ELLIS	BAKERIES	
Saint Margaret Thrift Shop	SAINT*	MARGARET	THRIFT	SHOP

*When *Saint* is used as a title rather than as a prefix in a personal name, it is considered a separate unit. (See ¶1214b.)

1217 RULE 8: ABBREVIATIONS, ACRONYMS, SYMBOLS, AND LETTERS IN ORGANIZATIONAL NAMES

a. Treat an abbreviation as a single unit. Consider it exactly as it is written, and ignore any punctuation.

Name	Unit 1	Unit 2	Unit 3	Unit 4
B. C. Data Sources	B	C	DATA	SOURCES
B C Datalink	B	C	DATALINK	
B.C. Data Files	BC	DATA	FILES	
BC Data Tracers	BC	DATA	TRACERS	
CBC	CBC			
CNIB	CNIB			
Union Grain Ltd.	UNION	GRAIN	LTD	
Unisource Canada Inc.	UNISOURCE	CANADA	INC	
Urban Business Corp.	URBAN	BUSINESS	CORP	
Ursis Data Systems Co.	URSIS	DATA	SYSTEMS	CO

NOTE: When organizations are better known by their abbreviated names (*CBC, CNIB, IBM*) or acronyms (*ACTRA, CARES, CUPE*) than by their formal names, use these short forms for filing purposes and provide cross-references as necessary. (See also ¶¶520, 522.)

b. Treat acronyms and the call letters of radio and TV stations as single units.

Name	Unit 1	Unit 2	Unit 3	Unit 4
ACTRA	ACTRA			
CARES	CARES			
CFRD Radio Station	CFRD	RADIO	STATION	
CUPE	CUPE			

c. When an ampersand (&) occurs in a name, consider it as if it were spelled out (that is, as *and*). If the ampersand is free-standing (that is, with space on either side), treat it as a separate filing unit.

Name	Unit 1	Unit 2	Unit 3	Unit 4
A & L Fabrics	A	AND	L	FABRICS
A&B Publications	AANDB	PUBLICATIONS		
Allen & Korn	ALLEN	AND	KORN	
AT&L Electrical Ltd.	ATANDL	ELECTRICAL	LTD	

d. Treat single letters as separate units. If two or more letters in a sequence are written solid or are connected by a hyphen or a diagonal, treat the sequence as a single unit.

Name	Unit 1	Unit 2	Unit 3	Unit 4
A D S Graphics	A	D	S	GRAPHICS
AAA	AAA			
ADS Reports	ADS	REPORTS		
A/V Resources	AV	RESOURCES		
A-Z Rental Corp.	AZ	RENTAL	CORP	
Triple A Realty Trust	TRIPLE	A	REALTY	TRUST
W Z Leasing Co.	W	Z	LEASING	CO
W. Z. Yee (person)	YEE	W	Z	

1218 RULE 9: GEOGRAPHIC NAMES WITHIN ORGANIZATIONAL NAMES

a. Treat each part of a geographic name as a separate unit. However, treat hyphenated parts of a geographic name as a single unit.

Name	Unit 1	Unit 2	Unit 3	Unit 4
Banff-Jasper Tours	BANFFJASPER	TOURS		
Golf PEI	GOLF	PEI		
Lake of the Woods Camping Store*	LAKE	OF	THE	WOODS
Niagara-on-the-Lake Tourist Centre	NIAGARAONTHELAKE	TOURIST	CENTRE	
Western Canada Importing	WESTERN	CANADA	IMPORTING	
Western Ontario Produce	WESTERN	ONTARIO	PRODUCE	

*The words *Camping* and *Store* are the fifth and sixth filing units in this name.

b. When a geographic name begins with a prefix followed by a space or hyphen, treat the prefix and the following word as a single unit. (See ¶1211 for a list of prefixes.)

(Continued on page 326.)

12

Name	Unit 1	Unit 2	Unit 3
La Baie Café	LABAIE	CAFÉ	
Le Gardeur Hardware	LEGARDEUR	HARDWARE	
Los Angeles Film Distributors	LOSANGELES	FILM	DISTRIBUTORS
Saint John Pharmacy	SAINTJOHN	PHARMACY	
Ste-Foy Inn	STEFOY	INN	
St. John's Lumber Mart	STJOHNS	LUMBER	MART

> **NOTE:** While a name like *St. Albert* is considered a single unit, *Sault Ste. Marie* or *Fort St. John* should be treated as three filing units (since the prefix *Ste.* or *St.* does not come at the beginning of the name).

1219 RULE 10: NUMBERS IN ORGANIZATIONAL NAMES

    a. Arabic numerals *(1, 3, 5)* and Roman numerals *(IV, XIX)* are considered separate units. Treat ordinal numbers such as *1st, 3rd,* and *5th* as if they were written *1, 3,* and *5.*

    b. The order of sequencing names with Arabic and Roman numbers and with letters of the alphabet is as follows:

      1. Arabic numbers arranged in numeric order.

      2. Roman numerals arranged in numeric order.

      3. Letters arranged in alphabetical order.

> **NOTE:** Computer programs will consider Arabic numerals from the left. Given the Arabic units in the following chart, a computer will place 1218 before 21 and 210. To avoid this outcome, add zeros to the left of 21 and 210 to make them the same length as 1218: 0021, 0210, 1218. The computer will then sequence these units in the correct order.

    ☞ *See ¶1214d, note, for an explanation in sequencing Roman numerals.*

Name	Unit 1	Unit 2	Unit 3
21st Century Travel	21	CENTURY	TRAVEL
210th St. Assn.	210	St	ASSN
1218 Corp.	1218	CORP	
III Brothers Outlets	III	BROTHERS	OUTLETS
VII Hills Lodge	VII	HILLS	LODGE
CUPE Local 3501	CUPE	LOCAL	3501
CUPE Local 4255	CUPE	LOCAL	4255
Sixth Street Fashions	SIXTH	STREET	FASHIONS

    c. Units containing numbers expressed in words are sequenced in alphabetic order. When a number is written with a hyphen *(Thirty-Six),* ignore the hyphen and treat the number as a single unit *(THIRTYSIX).*

Name	Unit 1	Unit 2	Unit 3	Unit 4
Twelve Sixteen Shoppe	TWELVE	SIXTEEN	SHOPPE	
Twentieth Century Press	TWENTIETH	CENTURY	PRESS	
Twenty-Eight Benbow Street Studios	TWENTYEIGHT	BENBOW	STREET	STUDIOS
The Warren 200 Colony	WARREN	200	COLONY	THE
Warren Sixty-Fourth Street Salon	WARREN	SIXTYFOURTH	STREET	SALON

d. When a phrase consists of a number (in figures or words) linked by a hyphen or a diagonal to a letter or word (for example, *1-A, A-1, 1-Hour, 4/Way, One-Stop*), ignore the punctuation and treat the phrase as a single unit.

e. When the phrase consists of a figure linked to another figure by means of a hyphen or a diagonal (for example, *80-20* or *50/50*), consider only the number that precedes the hyphen or diagonal.

NOTE: Most computer programs will consider the complete number and any punctuation.

f. When a phrase consists of a figure plus a letter or word (for example, *3M*) without any intervening space or punctuation, treat it as a single unit.

Name	Unit 1	Unit 2	Unit 3	Unit 4
1-A Physical Trainers	1A	PHYSICAL	TRAINERS	
3 Pro Corp.	3	PRO	CORP	
3M	3M			
4X Investment Group	4X	INVESTMENT	GROUP	
5-10 Household Wares	5	HOUSEHOLD	WARES	
5 Star Video Arcade	5	STAR	VIDEO	ARCADE
5-Corners Pasta Dishes	5CORNERS	PASTA	DISHES	
7-Eleven Food Store	7ELEVEN	FOOD	STORE	
20/20 Eye Care	20	EYE	CARE	
The 30-45 Singles Club	30	SINGLES	CLUB	THE
A-1 Autos Inc.	A1	AUTOS	INC	
Adam's 10-Minute Pizza	ADAMS	10MINUTE	PIZZA	

g. When a symbol appears with a number, treat the two elements as a single unit only if there is no space between the symbol and the number. Consider the symbol as if it were spelled out; for example, & *(and)*, ¢ *(cent or cents)*, $ *(dollar or dollars)*, # *(number)*, % *(percent)*, and + *(plus)*. When words or numbers are placed in parentheses, for example *(Canada)*, *(2000)*, ignore the parentheses and treat the items enclosed as separate units.

NOTE: Most computer programs will consider these symbols on the basis of where they occur in the sequence of character sets. If you convert the

(Continued on page 328.)

symbol to a spelled-out form, it will be sequenced in the correct alphabetic order.

Name	Unit 1	Unit 2	Unit 3	Unit 4
The $50 Dress Shop	50DOLLAR*	DRESS	SHOP	THE
50% Off Outlet	50PERCENT	OFF	OUTLET	
The 50+ Centre	50PLUS	CENTRE	THE	
The #1 Pizza Parlour	NUMBER1	PIZZA	PARLOUR	THE
The Original 5&10	ORIGINAL	5AND10	THE	
Plaza 5 & 10	PLAZA	5	AND	10
T&T (Canada) Inc.	TANDT	CANADA	INC	
Three-Hour Cleaners (1999) Ltd.	THREEHOUR	CLEANERS	1999	LTD

*When a $ sign precedes a number, consider the number and then the word DOLLAR (or DOLLARS) in that order.

1220 RULE 11: ALPHABETIZING BY ADDRESSES

When two organizational names are otherwise identical, alphabetize them according to address.

a. First alphabetize by city.

b. When filing units for city names are the same, consider the province. (For example, *St. Mary's, Newfoundland,* comes before *St. Marys, Ontario.*)

c. If both the city and the province are identical, alphabetize by street name.

Name	Unit 1	Unit 2	Unit 3	Unit 4
McDonald's Saint John New Brunswick	MCDONALDS	SAINTJOHN	NEW	BRUNSWICK
McDonald's St. Marys, Ontario	MCDONALDS	STMARYS	ONTARIO	
McDonald's Avenue Road Toronto, Ontario	MCDONALDS	TORONTO	AVENUE	ROAD
McDonald's 1414 Church St. Toronto, Ontario	MCDONALDS	TORONTO	CHURCH	STREET

d. If the street name is a number, treat it exactly as written. Numbered street names expressed *in figures* precede street names (numbered or otherwise) expressed *in words*. Numbered street names *in figures* are sequenced in numeric order. Numbered street names *in words* are sequenced (along with other street names in words) in alphabetic order.

e. If the street names are also the same, alphabetize by direction if it is part of the address (for example, *north, south, northeast, southwest*).

Name	Unit 1	Unit 2	Unit 3	Unit 4	Unit 5
McDonald's 2323 - 12 Ave. Toronto, Ontario	MCDONALDS	TORONTO	12	AVENUE	
McDonald's 3434 - 65 St. Toronto, Ontario	MCDONALDS	TORONTO	65	STREET	
McDonald's 4545 Fourth St. Toronto, Ontario	MCDONALDS	TORONTO	FOURTH	STREET	
McDonald's 5656 Queen St. E. Toronto, Ontario	MCDONALDS	TORONTO	QUEEN	STREET	EAST
McDonald's 6767 Queen St. W. Toronto, Ontario	MCDONALDS	TORONTO	QUEEN	STREET	WEST

f. If all the foregoing units are identical, consider the house or building numbers and sequence them in numeric order.

Name	Unit 1	Unit 2	Unit 3	Unit 4	Unit 5
McDonald's 170 Spadina Ave. Toronto, Ontario	MCDONALDS	TORONTO	SPADINA	AVENUE	170
McDonald's 2782 Spadina Ave. Toronto, Ontario	MCDONALDS	TORONTO	SPADINA	AVENUE	2782

Governmental Names

1221 RULE 12: FEDERAL GOVERNMENT NAMES

a. The first three filing units for any organization that is part of the federal government are *CANADA GOVERNMENT OF.*

b. The fourth filing unit for most departments is the name of its function—*Justice, Health, Industry,* etc. While the word *Canada* is added when referring to these departments (for instance, *Health Canada*), there is obviously no need to repeat *Canada* as it is the first filing unit. A few departments, however, use the words *Department of* in their titles. In such cases, transpose *Department of* and place at the end. (For example, treat *Department of National Defence* as four separate units: *NATIONAL DEFENCE DEPARTMENT OF.*)

c. Next consider the name of the office or bureau within the department. Transpose opening phrases such as *Office of* and *Bureau of* to the end. (For example, treat *Bureau of Pensions Advocates* as four separate units: *PENSIONS ADVOCATES BUREAU OF.*)

(Continued on page 330.)

Name	Unit 4*	Unit 5	Unit 6	Unit 7
Canada Customs and Revenue Agency	CUSTOMS	AND	REVENUE	AGENCY
Industry Canada Competition Bureau	INDUSTRY	COMPETITION	BUREAU	
National Film Board	NATIONAL	FILM	BOARD	
Statistics Canada Consumer Services	STATISTICS	CONSUMER	SERVICES	

*The first three units are *Canada Government of.*

1222 RULE 13: PROVINCIAL AND LOCAL GOVERNMENT NAMES

a. For any organization (except an educational institution) that is part of a province, county, city, or town government, first consider the distinctive place name (for example, *New Brunswick* or *Fredericton*).

b. Then consider the name of the department, bureau, or other subdivision, transposing elements (if necessary) as was done with federal departments and bureaus in ¶1221.

Name	Unit 1	Unit 2	Unit 3	Unit 4	Unit 5
Alberta Department of Education	ALBERTA	EDUCATION	DEPARTMENT	OF	
Manitoba Public Health Department	MANITOBA	PUBLIC	HEALTH	DEPARTMENT	
County of Parkland School District	PARKLAND	COUNTY	OF	SCHOOL	DISTRICT
Police Service, City of Victoria	VICTORIA	CITY	OF	POLICE	SERVICE

1223 RULE 14: FOREIGN GOVERNMENT NAMES

a. First consider the distinctive name of the country. (For example, select the distinctive name *Egypt* from the formal name *Arab Republic of Egypt.*)

b. Next, supply the appropriate term of classification—for example, *Republic, Commonwealth, Kingdom, State.*

c. Finally, consider the name of the department, bureau, or other subdivision.

Name	Unit 1	Unit 2
Commonwealth of Australia	AUSTRALIA	COMMONWEALTH
Republic of Austria	AUSTRIA	REPUBLIC
Kingdom of Belgium	BELGIUM	KINGDOM
State of Israel	ISRAEL	STATE

 See the Online Learning Centre at www.mcgrawhill.ca/college/gregg for related Web links.

SECTION THIRTEEN

Letters, Memos, and E-Mail

Section 13 provides guidelines for formatting letters and memos. These guidelines are not intended as inflexible rules. They can—and should—be modified to fit specific occasions as good sense and good taste dictate.

Most word processing software contains templates that may simplify your task of formatting documents. If the existing templates do not satisfy your needs, you can modify them to some extent or you can create your own.

The Professional letter template, one of three letter templates available in Microsoft Word, uses the default specification of Arial 10 point.

[Click **here** and type return address]

Company Name Here

[Current date will be inserted here]

[Click **here** and type recipient's address]

Dear Sir or Madam:

Type your letter here. For more details on customizing this letter template, double-click ✉.
To return to this letter, use the Window menu.

Sincerely,

[Click **here** and type your name]
[Click **here** and type job title]

The illustrations in this manual use the following system of notations to indicate how many blank lines to leave between the elements of a document.

↓2x	Press the Enter Key 2 times to create 1 blank line
↓3x	Press the Enter Key 3 times to create 2 blank lines
↓6x	Press the Enter Key 6 times to create 5 blank lines
↓2 or 3x	Choose to leave 1 **or** 2 blank lines when space is a consideration.

NOTE: Since most computer users prefer to use imperial (not metric) measurements, all formatting information in Sections 13 to 17 is presented in inches.

LETTERS
Parts of Letters

1301 A business letter has four parts with a variety of features:

	Standard	Optional
Heading:	Letterhead or return address (¶¶1310–1312)	Personal or confidential notation (¶1314)
	Date line (¶1313)	Reference notations (¶1315)
Opening:	Inside address or address block (¶¶1316–1336)	Attention line (¶1337)
	Salutation (¶¶1338–1341)	
Body:	Message (¶¶1343–1344)	Subject line (¶1342)
Closing:	Complimentary closing (¶1345)	Company signature (¶1346)
	Writer's signature block (¶¶1347–1353)	Enclosure notation (¶1355
	Reference initials (¶1354)	Delivery notation (¶1356)
		Confirmation notation (¶1357)
		Copy notation (¶¶1358–1361)
		Postscript (¶1362)
		File name notation (¶1363)

☞ *Each of these parts is illustrated in the model letters on pages 336–339.*

1302 A business letter is usually arranged in one of the following styles:

a. **Block (Full-Block) Style.** All lines begin at the left margin. Nothing is indented except displayed quotations, tables, and similar material. This is the style most commonly used. (See page 336.)

b. **Modified-Block (Semi-Block) Style—Standard Format.** The date line, the complimentary closing, and the writer's identification all begin at centre. All other lines begin at the left margin. (See page 338.)

c. **Modified-Block (Semi-Block) Style—With Paragraph Indentions.** This style is exactly the same as the standard format described in ¶1302b except for one additional feature: the first line of each paragraph is indented 0.25 to 0.5 inches (or more in special circumstances). This style is used most commonly in formal and in some legal correspondence. (See page 339.)

Stationery Sizes

1303 Standard-size stationery, $8\frac{1}{2}$" × 11", is the most commonly used, and computers and printers use this size as their default setting. For specific or social occasions, various other sizes may be preferred.

Letter Placement
1304 Top Margin

a. **First Page.** On printed letterhead stationery, the top margin is obviously preset and cannot be changed. When a *letterhead* is being created or when a *return address* is being used for a personal-business letter, the top margin varies.

- A *created letterhead* may have a top margin as small as 0.5 inch (depending on how deep the letterhead is).
- A *return address* is normally positioned 1.5 to 2 inches from the top of the page.

Any top margins that are created may be adjusted for better vertical placement if a letter is very long or very short. (See ¶1307.)

b. Continuation Pages. Use the header function in word processing software to create a continuous page header. Some computer programs default headers to a top margin of one inch, which is preferred. Always use unprinted stationery even if the first page is on printed letterhead. (See also ¶1364.)

1305 Side Margins

a. Word processing software includes default side margins: 1.25 inches for Word and 1 inch for WordPerfect. Generally either one of the defaults is adequate.

b. Under certain circumstances, wider or narrower side margins may be required, depending on the size of the stationery, the length of the document, or the size of the font.

Two common type sizes and typefaces are displayed below to show the variation in the number of characters in an inch. Review the typeface and type size options that are available to you, and select the one that best meets your needs. Serif fonts are preferred for letters because they are easier to read.

Common Type Sizes and Typefaces	Characters in 1 Inch
12 Point Times New Roman	Now is the time
10 Point Times New Roman	Now is the time for
12 Point Arial	Now is the tim
10 Point Arial	Now is the time f

c. If it is necessary or desirable to change the default side margins, maintain equal left and right measurements or settings. Generous white space makes a page more attractive and easier to read. Therefore, minimum side margins of 1 inch are preferred.

d. If you are using letterhead stationery with a column of printed copy running down the left side of the page, set the left margin 0.5 inch to the right of this copy and set the right margin at 1 inch from the right edge of the page.

e. If the printed letterhead goes across the page, set the right and left margins to match those of the letterhead.

1306 Bottom Margin

a. Most word processing software defaults to a 1-inch bottom margin.

(Continued on page 340.)

Block (Full-Block) Style

A **Compudata Systems Inc.**

34 Algonquin Avenue
Toronto, Ontario M6R 1K7
Telephone: 416-555-4605
Fax: 416-555-4602
Web site: www.compudatasystems.ca

2 inches from top of page **OR** ↓3x

B November 2, 2006 ↓4 to 6x   **HEADING**

C Ms. Susan W. Morales
2839 Carlyle Drive
London, ON N6V 4N8 ↓2x   **OPENING**

D Dear Ms. Morales: ↓2x

E We were pleased to receive your letter of application for a sales position with
Compudata Systems. ↓2x

At the moment we do not have an opening in the Lake Erie area, but we do need
a field representative who is based in North Bay and can cover the northern part
of the province. If you would like to be considered for this position, please
complete the enclosed application and return it to me. ↓2x   **BODY**

As it happens, I will be attending a convention in London next month. I would be
delighted to meet with you while I'm in town and describe the job that is available. ↓2x

When you return your completed application, please let me know whether you
would be free to meet me at 4 p.m. on Wednesday or Thursday of the first week
of January. I look forward to hearing from you. ↓2x

F Sincerely yours, ↓2x

G COMPUDATA SYSTEMS INC. ↓4 to 6x

Kenneth R. Willmott

H Kenneth R. Willmott
National Sales Manager ↓2x   **CLOSING**

I KRW/bjn
J Enclosure
K By Federal Express
L cc: A Rossi

M h:\gregg\illustration\willmott.sp3

A Letterhead. The company's name and address, along with other information (such as a telephone number, a fax number, and a Web address). (See ¶¶1310–1312.)

B Date Line. The date on which the letter is keyed, starts at the margin on the third line below the letterhead or 2 inches from the top of the page, whichever is lower. (See ¶1313.)

C Inside Address (Address Block). The name and address of the person to whom you are writing. (See ¶¶1316–1336.)

D Salutation. An opening greeting like *Dear Ms. Morales.* Do not use *Dear Susan Morales* or *Dear Ms. Susan Morales.* (See ¶¶1338–1341.)

E Message. The text of the letter; all paragraphs are keyed single-spaced with no indentions; leave 1 blank line between paragraphs. (See ¶¶1343–1344.)

F Complimentary Closing. A parting phrase like *Sincerely* or *Sincerely yours.* (See ¶¶1345.)

G Company Signature. An indication that the writer is acting on behalf of the company. (See ¶1346.)

H Writer's Signature Block. The writer's name and title. (See ¶¶1347–1353.)

I Reference Initials. The initials of the typist (see ¶1370a) and sometimes those of the writer as well. (See ¶1354.)

J Enclosure Notation. A reminder that the letter is accompanied by an enclosure. (See ¶1355.)

K Delivery Notation. An indication that the letter has been sent a special way. (See ¶1356 for alternative placement.)

L Copy Notation. The names of those who will receive copies of this letter. (See ¶¶1358–1361.)

M File Name Notation (Document ID). A coded notation that indicates where the document is stored in computer memory and usually placed in a footer in a smaller type size. (See ¶1363.)

The explanations below are illustrated on the following page.

N Confidential Notation. A note indicating that the letter should be read only by the person addressed. (See ¶1314.)

O International Address. The name of the country typed in all-capital letters on a line by itself. (See ¶1336.)

P Subject Line. A means of stating what the letter is about. (See ¶1342.)

Q Displayed Extract. Copy set off from the rest of the letter for emphasis; indented 0.5 inch from the left and right margins. (See ¶1344a.)

(Continued on page 339.)

Modified-Block (Semi-Block) Style—Standard Format

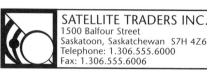

John P. Gage
President

SATELLITE TRADERS INC.
1500 Balfour Street
Saskatoon, Saskatchewan S7H 4Z6
Telephone: 1.306.555.6000
Fax: 1.306.555.6006

↓3 **OR** 2 inches from top of page

start at centre → 7 October, 2007 ↓2–3x

N   **CONFIDENTIAL** ↓2 or 3x   **HEADING**

Mr. Philip Wurlitzer Jr.
Executive Vice-President
Satellite Traders Inc.
Apartado Aero 11255
Bogota, D.E.   **OPENING**
O   COLOMBIA ↓2x

Dear Phil: ↓2x

P   **Subject: Your Request for Early Retirement** ↓2x

I presented your request to the Board of Directors last Friday. They were entirely
sympathetic to your reasons for wanting to take early retirement, but they did
express concern over the timing. Al Barnes, in particular, raised the following
points in a memo he sent me today: ↓2x

Q   Ask Phil to identify people in the Bogota office he considers   **BODY**
prospective candidates for his position. Please ask him to spell out
their present qualifications and estimate the time it would take to
groom any one of these people for his job. ↓2x

If you and I can identify at least one qualified candidate acceptable to Al and the
other directors, I know they will move quickly to honour your request. ↓2x

start at centre → Sincerely, ↓4 to 6x

John

John P. Gage ↓2x

                                                                                                                     CLOSING

npl
c A. J. Barnes
  C. L. Florio
  R. T. Eliuk
h:\gregg\illustration\gageconf.pw1

Modified-Block (Semi-Block) Style—With Paragraph Indentions

2 inches from top of page

R 1600 Fulton Road
Maple Ridge, BC V2X 7L4
November 25, 2006 ↓2x

S In reply to: Invoice 57389 ↓3x

HEADING

T Accounting Department
Byfield and Duff
Box 268
Vancouver, BC V7H 1V3 ↓2x

Dear Byfield and Duff: ↓2x

OPENING

U   Over two months ago I ordered a pair of hiking boots, size 5. You accepted
my order, informed me that you were temporarily out of stock, and told me I
could expect delivery within four weeks. ↓2x

      Today I received Invoice 57389, billing me for two log carriers which I did
not order and have not received. May I ask that you cancel this invoice. If the log
carriers arrive, I will refuse delivery and have them shipped back to you at once. ↓2

BODY

Sincerely, ↓4 to 6x

(Mrs.) Doris J. Hagerty

Doris T. Hagerty ↓2x

CLOSING

V   PS: I'm still eager to have those boots. When may I expect to receive them?

R Return Address. The arrangement that is used in a *personal-business letter* when an individual writes on blank stationery. Never include a writer's name in the return address. (For an alternative placement of the return address, see ¶1312; to replace the return address with professional-looking letterhead, see ¶1311.)

S Reference Notation. A filing code used by the writer or the addressee. (See ¶1315.)

T Attention Line. A means of directing the letter to a particular person or a specific department. Once positioned on a separate line below the inside address; often positioned as the first line of the inside address (without the word *Attention*) to reflect the recommended format for the envelope address. (See ¶1337.)

U Paragraph Indentation. Customarily 0.25 to 0.5 inches. (See ¶1343f.)

V Postscript. A note for capturing the reader's attention to express a final idea or an afterthought; it is not generally used in business letters. (See ¶1362.)

b. If the letter is longer than one page, the bottom margin on the first page may be adjusted to as much as 2 inches or to as little as 0.5 inch to accommodate *widow/orphan* and *block-protect* functions. (See ¶1364e.)

c. If you are using letterhead stationery with a band of printed copy running across the bottom of the page, leave a minimum margin of 0.5 inch between the last line of text and the band of printed copy.

☞ *For guidelines on carrying a letter over from one page to the next, see ¶1364.*

1307 Adjusting the Length of a Letter

a. Lengthening a Short Letter. For a more attractive appearance of a short letter (about 8 lines of text), use any combination of the following:

(1) Increase the side margins.

(2) Lower the date line by as many as 5 lines.

(3) Insert extra space above the inside address, the signature line, and the reference initials. (Do not use more than twice the recommended space in each case.)

(4) Place the writer's name and title on separate lines.

(5) Use 1.5 or double spacing in a 1- or 2-paragraph letter and triple space between the paragraphs.

(6) Use a modified-block style with paragraph indentions up to 1 inch.

(7) Increase the font size or select a font that yields fewer characters to an inch.

(8) Use the software command to centre the letter vertically. This adjusts the top and bottom margins.

b. Shortening a Long Letter. If only a few lines of a letter will print on a second page, it may be possible to retain readability and condense the text to fit on one page by using a software "shrink-to-fit" feature or by using any combination of the following techniques:

(1) Reduce the space between the date and the inside address to 2 or 3 blank lines (instead of the customary 3 to 5).

(2) Change the font size and/or the font style.

(3) Reduce the side margins and/or the top and bottom margins.

(4) In a modified style, put reference initials on the same line as the writer's identification.

(5) Avoid a letter style that has paragraph indentions.

(6) Reduce the space for the signature to a minimum of 3 blank lines.

☞ *See ¶1364 for formatting continuation pages.*

Punctuation Styles

1308 The message in a business letter is always punctuated with normal punctuation (see Sections 1 and 2). The other parts may be punctuated according to one of the following styles.

   a. Mixed (Standard, 2-point) Punctuation. A colon is used after the salutation and a comma after the complimentary closing.

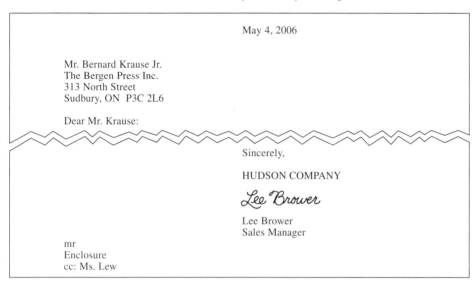

   b. Open Punctuation (No Point). No punctuation is used at the end of any line unless that line ends with an abbreviation.

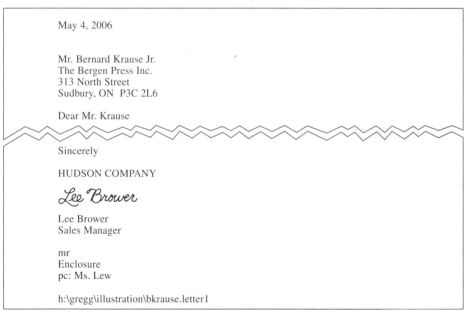

Spacing

1309 Ordinarily, type all letters single-spaced. Leave one blank line between paragraphs. (See ¶1307(5) for the use of double spacing in very short letters.)

Letterhead or Return Address
1310 Using a Printed Letterhead

a. The first page of a standard business letter is customarily written on stationery with a *printed letterhead* containing at least these elements: the organization's name, the street address or post office box number (or both), and the municipality, province, and postal code. Most letterheads also provide the following elements: a telephone number (with area code), a fax number, an e-mail address, a Web site URL, and a logo or some other graphic element. Some executives may have special letterheads showing their name and title. (See page 338 for an illustration.)

b. Avoid using abbreviations in a letterhead except those that are a part of an organization's legal name or that represent a provincial name. However, to achieve a more formal effect, spell out the provincial name.

c. Even if your organization uses a post office box number as its primary mailing address, show a street address as well. In that way, senders will know where to direct ordinary mail (to the post office) and where to direct express or courier mail (to the company's office). If the two addresses have different postal codes, be sure to provide this information.

COLE, STEELE & BACKUS

1880 Avenue Road   Hamilton, Ontario L9H 3V7
Telephone (416) 555-4345   www.colesteelebackus.ca
Fax (416) 555-4625   E-Mail CSB150@product.com

1311 Creating a Letterhead

In place of printed stationery, you can use templates and various fonts to create a professional-looking letterhead. The following illustrations show two such letterheads—one designed for a business and one for an individual working from home. An advantage to creating your own letterhead and printing it with the letter content enables changes to the letterhead (such as addressess and fax numbers) to be made easily and with minimum expense.

NOTE: Persons who want to make themselves available to clients and customers at all hours may insert additional elements in their letterheads beyond those listed in ¶1310—for example, home and business telephone numbers, cell phone, pager, and voice mail numbers.

↓ 0.5 " to 1"

ALBERS AND PARKER INC.

250 Murray Park Road
Winnipeg, MB R3Z 4B9
Telephone: 204-444-3600

Box 3291, Station B
Winnipeg, MB R2W 3P6
Fax: 204-444-3610

↓ 0.5 " to 1"

Merle C. Forrest

SECOND WIND • BISCAY ROAD • ST. CATHARINES, ONTARIO L2M 0C7 • 416-555-9097

13

1312 Using a Return Address

If you are using plain paper for a *personal-business letter*, key a *return address* or use your predesigned personal letterhead. (See ¶1311.)

a. As a rule, the return address appears 1.5 to 2 inches from the top of the page and shows the street address; the municipality, province, and postal code; perhaps the telephone number; and the date.

212 Westmount Drive, Apt. 2B
Cambridge, ON N1S 6J6
519-555-9097
January 24, 2006

OR Apartment 2B
212 Westmount Drive
Cambridge, ON N1S 6J6
519-555-9097
January 24, 2006

b. All lines are single spaced and each line is positioned as follows:

* Block (full-block) style letter, at the left margin
* Modified-block (semi-block) styles, at the centre of the page

Date Line

1313 a. The preferred date line style consists of the *name of the month* (written in full—never abbreviated), the *day* (written in figures and followed by a comma), and the *complete year* (using 4 digits).

December 28, 2006 (**NOT** Dec. 28, 2006 **OR** December 28th, 2006)

NOTE: Do not use the style *12/28/06* or *'06* in the date line of a business letter.

b. A dating system used for filing chronological documents is *numeric dating*. It is a system based on the 24-hour clock and records the date by means of 8 digits arranged in descending order—the *year* first, then the *month,* and the *day.* Hours and minutes may be added if required.

2006 10 08   2006-10-08   20061008   **ADD:** 2:30 p.m.: 2006 10 08 14 30

(Continued on page 344.)

13

c. Some writers write the date line in this order: day, month, year. This is the style used in military and overseas correspondence.

28 December 2006

d. When using letterhead stationery or a letter template, position the date line on the third line below the letterhead or 2 inches from the top of the page, whichever is lower. For the *block style,* start the date at the left margin. For the *modified-block styles,* position the date in one of the following ways:

- Start at the centre of the page (preferred style).
- Position it flush right.
- Place in a position that is relative to the letterhead design.

e. When using a return address at the top of the letter, position the date as shown in ¶1312a.

f. Be aware of the automatic update feature of your software, which will show the current date every time a document is opened. If a document is saved and the date does not update when the same document is opened, the automatic update feature must have been turned off before the document was saved.

☞ *See the illustrations on pages 336–339.*

Personal or Confidential Notation

1314 If the letter is of a personal or confidential nature, provide the appropriate notation on the second or third line below the date at the *left* margin. Bold the notation, preferably using all-capital letters. For greater emphasis change the font style and/or size.

       PERSONAL OR **Personal**   CONFIDENTIAL OR **Confidential**

Reference Notations

1315 a. Letterhead templates for law firms and large organizations sometimes contain a line that reads *When replying, refer to:* or something similar. When using this kind of letterhead, key the appropriate reference number or filing code after the colon.

b. If the guide words *When replying, refer to:* do not appear on the printed stationery but are desired, place them on the second line below the date (or on the second line below any notation that follows the date). Position the guide words at the same point as the date. (See page 339.)

      When replying, refer to: ALG-341

c. When you are replying to a letter that contains a reference number or when you want to emphasize the fact that your letter concerns an order, an employment competition, a policy, or a similar document, follow the guidelines as mentioned in ¶1315b above.

      In reply to: G214 782   Refer to: Competition No. 3642

d. When there are two reference notations to be given, place your own reference notation first (as indicated below). Then key the addressee's reference notation on the second line below. Align the notations with the date above.

Our reference: F-17865
Your reference: GAR-X-7

NOTE: Some writers, particularly in the field of law, prefer to give the addressee's reference notation in a subject line. (See ¶1342d.)

e. If you want the addressee of a letter to send a response by fax or e-mail, you may make this request in the body of the letter or in a reference notation.

When replying, send fax to: 780-555-9985
When replying, send e-mail message to: grewalk@aol.com

Inside Address or Address Block
1316 Letters to an Individual

Most businesses use their word processing software to format envelopes and labels. In the case of window envelopes, the inside address of the letter and the envelope is the same. When labels or envelopes are prepared separately, the standards set by Canada Post Corporation (CPC) should be followed to ensure the most efficient delivery. (See ¶1366 and ¶1367 for CPC address formats.) However, the traditional format for the inside address on the letter itself is preferable and more attractive than the CPC format.

The following examples show traditional styles, which are also acceptable on the mailing envelope.

a. The inside address should include the following information: (1) the name of the person to whom you are writing; (2) the apartment, unit, or suite number, the street address, the rural route number (or some other delivery indicator); and (3) the municipality, province, and postal code. The postal abbreviation for the province name is generally used, followed by 2 or 3 spaces before the postal code. Some writers prefer to spell out the province name and move the postal code to the line below.

b. Place an apartment number after the street address or, if it will not fit, on the line above. When the address line for the municipality and province is excessively long, the postal code could be placed on the line below.

Miss Shirley H. Eliasson   Mr. Albert W. Sung Jr.
313 Ash Street, Suite 23   Apartment 1415
Portage La Prairie, Manitoba   1533 De Monte-Carlo
R1A 1G1   Laval, QC H7K 1V9

☞ *For the placement of the inside address, see ¶1318a.*
For the use of the postal code, see ¶1332.

c. Use the postal abbreviations for delivery indicators such as *RR* (rural route), *SS* (suburban service), and *MR* (mobile route). If a street name is used with a mode of delivery, it should be placed on the line above.

(Continued on page 346.)

¶1317

Ms. Margaret James	Mrs. Yvonne Charlebois
114 Beaver Avenue	RR1, SS3, LCD 8
PO Box 99, Stn Main	Fort Saskatchewan, AB
Gander, NL A1V 1W7	T8L 4H2

1317 Letters to an Organization

a. The inside address should include the following information: (1) the name of the business or organization; (2) a street address or a post office box number; and (3) the municipality, province, and postal code. Whenever possible, address the letter to a specific person in the organization and include the person's job title and department (if known). If you do not have the name of a specific person, use a title instead (for example, *Director of Marketing* or *Advertising Manager*).

Mr. George J. O'Flanigan	Project Manager
Western Sales Manager	Holt Wholesalers, Inc.
National Carrier Services	4647 Manchester Road
415 Victoria Avenue	Okanagan Centre, BC
Brandon, MB R7A 4T8	V4J 8T2

b. When a room number or a suite number is included in the inside address, the following arrangements are acceptable:

Donald Campbell, M.D.	Miss Esther Karino
Suite 305	Milne & Walsh
401 Northumberland Street	141 Athol Street, Suite 201
Summerside, PE C1N 1M3	Regina, SK S4T 5J3

1318 a. Whether a letter is going to an individual's home or to an organization, start the inside address 4 to 6 lines below the date. If a notation falls between the date and the inside address (see ¶¶1314–1315), start the inside address 2 to 3 lines below the notation.

☞ *See the illustrations on pages 336–339.*

NOTE: You may need to modify these guidelines if you are planning to use a window envelope. (See ¶1366k.)

b. In a social-business letter (see ¶¶1372–1373), the inside address is placed at the bottom of the letter, aligned at the left margin and starting 4 to 6 lines below the writer's name or title (whichever comes last). In a purely personal letter, no inside address is required.

c. Single space the inside address and align each line at the left.

1319 a. If a letter is addressed to two or more people at the same address, list each name on a separate line. Do not show a position title for each person unless it is short and can go on the same line as the name. Omit the names of departments unless the persons are in the same department. In effect, key only those parts of the address that are common to the people named at the start. (On the respective envelopes for each individual, give the full address for that individual and omit all reference to others named in the inside address.)

Dr. Paul J. Rogers
Mr. James A. Dawes
Research Department
Sloan and Hewitt Advertising
700 North Heights Road
Toronto, ON M9B 4C2

b. If a letter is addressed to two or more people at different addresses, the individual address blocks may be placed one under the other (with 1 blank line between) or attractively positioned side by side.

Professor John W. Dean	Mr. Ivan Torstensen
Department of Mathematics	Economics Department
University of Winnipeg	Augustana University
515 Portage Avenue	4901 – 46 Avenue
Winnipeg, MB R3B 2E9	Camrose, AB T4V 2R3

c. If a letter is addressed to more than two people at different addresses, it is less cluttered if a customized version of the letter is prepared for each recipient. Include a *Distribution List* (see ¶1375e) after the last notation at the bottom of the letter. At the end of the file copy *only,* insert the address blocks for all recipients. If there is no room, use a separate sheet.

See the models in Section 18 for special forms of address used for individuals, couples, organizations, professional people, education and government officials, diplomats, military personnel, and religious dignitaries.

Name of Person and Title

1320 When writing the name of a person in an inside address or elsewhere in a letter, be sure to follow that person's preferences in the spelling, capitalization, punctuation, and spacing of the name. (See ¶311.)

a. Do not abbreviate or use initials unless the person to whom you are writing prefers that style. For example, do not write *Wm. B. Sachs* or *W. B. Sachs* if the person used *William B. Sachs* in his correspondence.

b. When writing to a married woman, follow her preference for first and last names if you know it. She may prefer to be addressed by her original name (for example, *Ms. Joan L. Conroy*). If you do know that she is using her husband's last name, use her own first name and middle initial (for example, *Mrs. Joan L. Noonan*). The form that uses her husband's first name as well (for example, *Mrs. James W. Noonan*) is acceptable only for social purposes. It should never be used (1) when addressing a business letter to a married woman, or (2) when a married woman becomes a widow unless she indicates that is her preference.

1321 In general, use a title before the name of a person in an inside address. (See ¶517 for appropriate abbreviations of such titles.)

a. If the person has no special title (such as *Dr., Professor,* or *The Honourable*), use the courtesy title *Mr., Miss, Mrs.,* or *Ms.* (See also ¶1801.)

(Continued on page 348.)

13

b. In selecting *Miss, Mrs.,* or *Ms.,* always respect the individual woman's preference. If her preference is unknown, use the title *Ms.* or omit the courtesy title altogether. (See also ¶1801b–c.) Follow the same practice in the salutation.

c. If you do not know whether the person addressed is a man or a woman, do not use any courtesy title. (See also ¶1801d.) Follow the same practice in the salutation.

NOTE: People who use initials in place of their first and middle names or who have ambiguous names (like *Pat, Dana, Laurie,* and *Cory*) should always use a courtesy title when they sign their letters so that others may be spared the confusion over which title to use. If they choose not to provide a title, they will have to accept the possibility that they may be inappropriately addressed. (See also ¶1351.)

d. Address teenage girls as *Miss* or *Ms.,* and respect the individual's preference if you know it. For girls younger than 13, *Miss* or *Ms.* may be used or omitted.

e. Address teenage boys as *Mr.* For boys younger than 13, omit the title. (*Master* is now rarely used except with the names of very young boys.)

1322 a. A letter to a husband and wife is traditionally addressed in this form:

Mr. and Mrs. Jamal S. Borhot (NOT: Mr. & Mrs.)

b. Some married couples prefer a style of address that uses the first names of the spouses and omits *Mr. and Mrs.* Those who use this style typically do so because it treats both spouses as equals and does not imply that the wife can only be identified by her husband's name. Respect such preferences when you are aware of them.

Janet and Allen Rossi OR Allen and Janet Rossi
(RATHER THAN: Mr. and Mrs. Allen Rossi)

☞ *For other forms of address to use for couples in special circumstances, see ¶1802.*

1323 a. When *Jr., Sr.,* or a Roman numeral such as *III* is written after a name, omit the comma before this element unless you know that the person being addressed prefers the use of a comma. (See also ¶156.)

Janet Rossi and Allen Rossi Jr. OR Allen Rossi Jr. and Janet Rossi
(NOT: Janet and Allen Rossi Jr.) OR Allen Jr. and Janet Rossi

b. Do not use a title before a name if the term *Esq.* follows the name. (See also ¶¶518c, 1804a.)

James A. Hira, Esq. (NOT: Mr. James A. Hira, Esq.)

NOTE: A comma separates the last name from the term *Esq.*

c. As a rule, do not use an academic degree with a person's name in an inside address. However, some doctors of medicine and divinity prefer the use of the degree after their names (rather than the title *Dr.* before). (See also ¶1804b.)

NOTE: If an academic degree follows the person's name, separate it from the last name with a comma. Also omit the titles *Dr., Miss, Mr., Mrs.,* and *Ms.* before the name. Another title (for example, *Professor, The Reverend, Captain, Dean*) may be used before the name as long as it does not convey the same meaning as the degree that follows. (See ¶519c.)

Reva C. Calhoun, M.D.   The Reverend Ernest G. Wyzanski, D.D.

d. Abbreviations of religious orders, such as *S.J.* and *O.S.A.*, are keyed after names and preceded by a comma. An appropriate title should precede the name, even though the abbreviation follows the name; for example, *The Reverend John DeMaio, O.P.* (See also ¶1813.)

1324 a. A title of position, such as *Vice-President* or *Sales Manager*, may be included in an inside address. Ordinarily, place it on the line following the name; if the title requires a second line, indent the turnover 2 or 3 spaces. Capitalize the first letter of every word in the title except (1) prepositions under four letters (like *of, for,* and *in*); (2) conjunctions under four letters (like *and*); and (3) the articles *the, a,* and *an* when they appear *within* the title.

Mrs. Martha Hansen Executive Vice-President	Mr. Ralph Nielsen Vice-President and (**NOT** &) General Manager
Mr. Harry F. Nguyen Chairman of the Board	Ms. Evangeline S. Sardau Director of In-Service Training

NOTE: In the last example above, *In* is capitalized because it is the first element in a compound adjective (rather than a pure preposition as in *Editor-in-Chief*). By the same token, in the title *Coordinator of On-the-Job Training, On* is capitalized as the first element in a compound adjective but *of* and *the* are not.

b. If the title is very short, it may be placed on the same line as the person's name or the person's department in order to balance the length of the lines in the address. (However, do not place a title on the same line as the name of an organization. See ¶1326.)

Mr. J. C. Lee, President National Appliance Ltd.	Mrs. Lucinda Hollingsworth Manager, Support Services The Hathaway Group
Mr. Armand F. Aristides Controller Dahl, Inc.	**NOT:** Mr. Armand F. Aristides Controller, Dahl, Inc.

In Care of . . .

1325 Sometimes a letter cannot be sent to the addressee's home or place of business; it must be directed instead to a third person who will see that the letter reaches the addressee. In such cases use an "in care of" notation as shown below.

Professor Eleanor Marschak   **OR** Professor Eleanor Marschak
In care of Henry Wardwell, Esq.   c/o Henry Wardwell, Esq.

Name of Organization

1326 a. A Place the organization's name on a line by itself. If the name of a division or a department is needed in the address, it should precede the name of the organization on a line by itself.

Ms. Lindsay Knight
Assistant Vice-President
Department of Corporate Planning
Hobday, Granger Co. Ltd.

b. When writing the name of an organization in an inside address, always follow the organization's style for spelling, punctuation, capitalization, spacing, and abbreviations. The letterhead on incoming correspondence is the best source for this information. Note the variations in style in these names.

Calgary Flames Hockey Club   Liberty Mutual Group
Colt Engineering Corporation   Lord's Lobsters Limited
Dynamic Flight Services Inc.   McLeod and Company LLP
Eagle Engineering Corp.   Sears Canada Ltd.
Keen Engineering Co. Ltd.   Stewart, Weir & Co. Ltd.

NOTE: If the name is long and takes more than one line, indent any turnover or runover line 2 or 3 spaces. (See ¶1326c(5) for examples.)

c. If you do not have some way of determining the official form of a company name, follow these rules:

(1) Spell out the word *and*. Do not use an ampersand (&).

Haber, Curtis, and Hall Inc.   Acme Lead and Tin Company

(2) Write *Inc.* for *Incorporated* and *Ltd.* for *Limited*. Do not use a comma before the abbreviation.

(3) As a rule, spell out *Company* or *Corporation*; if the name is extremely long, however, use the abbreviation *Co.* or *Corp.*

(4) Do not use the word *the* at the beginning of a name unless you are sure it is part of the official name; for example, *The Globe and Mail* (as illustrated in (5) below).

(5) Capitalize the first letter of every word except (1) prepositions under four letters (like *of, for,* and *in*); (2) conjunctions under four letters (like *and*); and (3) the articles *the, a,* and *an* when they appear *within* the organization's name.

Office of the Superintendent of   Get a Move On Moving
   Financial Institutions   Services Inc.
255 Albert Street   112 East 8th Street
Ottawa, ON K1A 0H2   Hamilton, ON L8M 1H1

NOTE: In the following example note that the article *the* is capitalized because it comes at the start of the organization's official name. Note also that the name of the newspaper is not italicized or underscored because it refers to the organization rather than to the actual newspaper. (See also ¶287e.)

The Globe and Mail
444 Front Street
Toronto, ON M5V 2S9

Name of Building; Number of Room, Suite, or Floor

1327 If the name of a building is included in the inside address, key it on a line by itself immediately above the street address. A room number, a suite number, or a floor number should follow the street address, but if it will not fit on that line, insert it before the building name on the line above.

Harbour Professional Building
515 Whipple Street, Room 212
Yarmouth, NS B5A 1V9

Suite 14, Medical Building
80 Hawthorne Avenue Extension
Saint John, NB E2L 9S6

☞ *For additional examples, see ¶1317b.*

Street Address

1328 a. Always key the street address on a line by itself, immediately preceding the municipality, province, and postal code. (See ¶¶1316–1317 for examples.)

  b. Use the word *and*, not an ampersand (&), in a street address; for example, *Tenth and Market Streets.* However, avoid the use of such "intersection" addresses if a house or building number plus a single street name is available (such as *304 Tenth Street*).

  c. Spell out such words as *Street* and *Avenue* in inside addresses. (**BUT:** Remember that Canada Post prefers abbreviations in envelope addresses. See ¶1389.)

☞ *For apartment, room, and floor numbers with street addresses, see ¶¶1316b, 1317b, 1327, and 1366.*

1329 a. Use figures for house and building numbers. Do not include the abbreviations *No.* or the symbol # before such numbers. **EXCEPTION:** For clarity, use the word *One* instead of the figure *1* in a house or building number; for example, *One Yonge Street.*

  NOTE: Some house numbers contain a hyphen or a fraction; for example, *220-03 - 46th Street, 234$\frac{1}{2}$ Elm Street.*

  b. Numbers used as street names should be written as assigned by the municipality and as shown in *Canada's Postal Code Directory.* If it appears as *3rd Avenue*, use that format. If it appears as *Third Avenue*, use that format.

  NOTE: Although some writers do not like it, the use of ordinals *st, nd, rd*, and *th* in street addresses is becoming more common and acceptable. Some software packages automatically print the ordinals as superscripts.

824 - 3rd Avenue   129 - 14th Street

1330 a. When a compass point (for example, *East, West, Southeast, Northwest*) appears *before* a street name, do not abbreviate it except in a very long street address when space is tight.

(Continued on page 352.)

330 West Hill Street   **BUT:** 3210 N. Christie Estates Terrace

b. When a compass point appears *after* a street name, follow these guidelines:

(1) Abbreviate compound directions *(NE, NW, SE, SW)* and omit any punctuation.

817 Peachtree Street NE   2320 Palliser Drive SW

(2) Spell out *North, South, East,* and *West* following a street name and omit the comma.

70 Hinton Avenue North   2049 Okanagan Avenue East

Box Number

1331 a. A post office box number should be used in place of the street address when it is listed as such in *Canada's Postal Code Directory.*

b. A station name, if needed, should follow the post office box number on the same line in both the inside address and on the envelope.

Post Office Box 101, Station M   PO Box 604, Stn. Victoria
Owen Sound, ON N4K 5P1   Montreal, QC H3Z 2S4

c. Some organizations show both a street address and a post office box number in their mailing address. When you are writing to an organization with two addresses, use the post office box number for ordinary mail and the street address for courier and express mail.

Henson Supply Corp.   **NOT:** Henson Supply Corp.
PO Box 181   315 South Shipyard Road
Rothesay, NB E0G 2W6   PO Box 181
          Rothesay, NB E0G 2W6

NOTE: Dual addressing as shown in the second example above should be avoided. Canada Post, in this case, would deliver the mail to the address immediately above the city-province-postal code line.

Municipality, Province, and Postal Code

1332 The municipality, province, and postal code must always be placed on the line following the street address, unless the name of the municipality is extremely long. (See ¶1316b.) Key the name of the municipality (followed by a comma and 1 space), the provincial postal abbreviation (followed by 2 or 3 spaces but no comma), and the postal code. The format of the alphanumeric postal code is *ANA NAN*, where *A* is an alpha character and *N* is a numeric one. There is one space between the first three and last three characters.

Edmonton, AB T5M 3N7   Vancouver, BC V6A 2T8

1333 When writing the name of a municipality (city, municipality, town, village, community, post office), use the one recognized as a valid mailing destination.

NOTE: The official name as recognized by the municipality must be used; for example, *Trois-Rivières* is correct, not *Three Rivers.*

a. Do not use an abbreviation (for example, *Mont'l* for *Montreal*, *P.A.* for *Prince Albert*, *TO* for *Toronto*).

b. Do not abbreviate the words *Fort*, *Mount*, *Point*, or *Port*. Write the name of the city or town in full; for example, *Fort McMurray*, *Mount Carmel*, *Point Edward*, *Port Elgin*.

c. Abbreviate the word *Saint* in the names of cities only if that is the correct postal designation; for example, *St. John's, NL*; *St. Catharines, ON*; *St. Paul, AB*. **EXCEPTIONS:** *Saint John, NB*; *Saint-Laurent, QC*.

1334 a. In an inside address, it may be considered more businesslike to spell out the name of the province. However, the CPC two-letter abbreviation is also acceptable. The abbreviated format should be keyed in capital letters with no spaces or punctuation. (See page 354 for Canadian and American postal abbreviations.)

b. When giving an address in a sentence, however, insert a comma after the street address and after the city or town. Leave 1 space between the province and the postal code. Insert a comma after the postal code unless a stronger mark of punctuation is required at that point. All the usual postal abbreviations may be omitted.

> My address next month will be Apt. 211, 2324 - 90th Avenue SW, Calgary, Alberta T2V 3X7, but mail sent to my office will reach me as well.

1335 Omit the name of the county or area (such as *York County*) in an address. However, the name of a community, subdivision, or real estate development may be included as long as it comes before the lines containing the mail delivery address.

Ms. Janet G. Arnold	**NOT:** Ms. Janet G. Arnold
Meadowland Park	39 Owen Street
39 Owen Street	Meadowland Park
Mill Village, NS B0J 2H0	Mill Village, NS B0J 2H0

1336 In foreign addresses, place the name of the country on a separate line in all-capital letters. Except for the United States of America, do not abbreviate the name of the country.

Rododendronplein 7B	4417 Brooks St NE
3053 ES Rotterdam	Washington DC 20019-4649
NETHERLANDS	USA

Attention Line

1337 When a letter is addressed directly to an organization, an attention line may be used to route the letter to a particular person (by name or title) or to a particular department. The attention line may be placed in one of two acceptable positions as noted in the following paragraphs.

a. The traditional placement of an attention line, if it is used at all, is on the second line below the inside address or address block. This format is used by a few businesses, particularly law firms.

(Continued on page 354.)

Alberta	AB	Nova Scotia	NS
British Columbia	BC	Nunavut	NU
Manitoba	MB	Ontario	ON
New Brunswick	NB	Prince Edward Island	PE
Newfoundland and		Quebec	QC
Labrador	NL	Saskatchewan	SK
Northwest Territories	NT	Yukon	YT
Alabama	AL	Missouri	MO
Alaska	AK	Montana	MT
American Samoa	AS	Nebraska	NE
Arizona	AZ	Nevada	NV
Arkansas	AR	New Hampshire	NH
California	CA	New Jersey	NJ
Colorado	CO	New Mexico	NM
Connecticut	CT	New York	NY
Delaware	DE	North Carolina	NC
District of Columbia	DC	North Dakota	ND
Federated States		Northern Mariana Islands	MP
of Micronesia	FM	Ohio	OH
Florida	FL	Oklahoma	OK
Georgia	GA	Oregon	OR
Guam	GU	Palau	PW
Hawaii	HI	Pennsylvania	PA
Idaho	ID	Puerto Rico	PR
Illinois	IL	Rhode Island	RI
Indiana	IN	South Carolina	SC
Iowa	IA	South Dakota	SD
Kansas	KS	Tennessee	TN
Kentucky	KY	Texas	TX
Louisiana	LA	Utah	UT
Maine	ME	Vermont	VT
Marshall Islands	MH	Virgin Islands	VI
Maryland	MD	Virginia	VA
Massachusetts	MA	Washington	WA
Michigan	MI	West Virginia	WV
Minnesota	MN	Wisconsin	WI
Mississippi	MS	Wyoming	WY

(1) The attention line may be keyed in initial capital and small letters or in all-capital letters and may be bolded. As well as these display features, some law firms may even add an underscore.

(2) Do not abbreviate *Attention* but follow it with a colon.

Ajax Construction Ltd.	Lincoln Silcox Labs
2530 Skymark Avenue	297 Progress Court
Hamilton ON L8W 3P6	Oakville ON L6L 4W7
Attention: Mr. James Berman	ATTENTION: SALES MANAGER

b. A more common practice today is to omit the attention line and use the individual's or the department name as the first line in the inside address.

  c. Another possible position for the attention line could be as the first line of the inside address.

    (1) In this position, window envelopes can be accommodated and mailing addresses can be computer generated by repeating the keyed inside address to envelopes or labels.

    (2) Canada Post Corporation prefers this first-line position for envelopes as it enables the OCR to read and sort faster. Any line above the organization's name is considered non-address data and not necessary for delivery purposes.

    (3) The word *Attention* is really immaterial and is not needed. However, its use or omission *does* affect the choice of a salutation. See ¶1341.

Mr. James Berman	Attention: Sales Manager
Ajax Construction Ltd.	Lincoln Silcox Labs
2530 Skymark Avenue	297 Progress Court
Hamilton ON L8W 3P6	Oakville ON L6L 4W7

☞ *For the treatment of an attention line on an envelope, see ¶1366m.*

Salutation

1338 a. Start the salutation at the left margin on the second line below the inside address or on the second line below the attention line (if used). Follow the salutation with a colon unless you are using open punctuation (see ¶1308) or you are keying a social-business letter. (See ¶1373b.)

  b. Abbreviate only the titles *Mr., Ms., Mrs., Messrs.,* and *Dr.* All other titles, such as *Professor* and *Father,* should be spelled out. (See Section 18 for titles used by officials, dignitaries, and military personnel.)

  c. Capitalize the first word as well as any nouns and titles in the salutation; for example, *Dear Sir, Dear Mrs. Brand.*

A complete list of commonly used forms of salutations with appropriate inside addresses for individuals, couples, organizations, officials, dignitaries, and military personnel is given in Section 18.

1339 a. Be sure that the spelling of the surname in the salutation matches the spelling in the inside address. If the person you are writing to has a hyphenated last name (for example, *Mrs. Hazel Merriman-Sparks),* the salutation should read *Dear Mrs. Merriman-Sparks.*

  b. When writing to someone you know well, use a first name or nickname in place of the more formal salutations shown above. However, once you start using an informal salutation, be sure that anyone who prepares your letters for you maintains that form of address. Otherwise, a person who is used to getting *Dear Mike* letters from you may one day receive a *Dear Mr. Romano* letter and waste a good deal of time brooding over what could have caused the sudden chill in your relationship. (See also ¶1345f.)

  c. When you are preparing a letter that may be sent or shown to a number of as yet undetermined individuals, use *Dear Sir or Madam* (rather than *To Whom It May Concern*).

(Continued on page 356.)

13

d. In salutations involving two or more people, use *and*, not &.

1340 a. Address a letter to the head of an organization rather than to the organization as a whole. Use the name and title if known; otherwise use the title alone. See ¶1324 for examples. The salutation should be one to an individual.

b. If a letter is addressed to an organization that is known to be composed of both men and women, the salutation is *Ladies and Gentlemen* or *Gentlemen and Ladies* (**NOT:** *Gentlemen*, and **NEVER:** *Dear Ladies and Gentlemen*).

c. In routine or informal letters when no specific information, as a last resort, use the name of the organization in the salutation, although many writers still prefer *Ladies and Gentlemen*. (See page 339 and ¶1803a.)

Dear Maritime Services Limited:

1341 a. When an attention line is used (see ¶1337), the letter is considered to be addressed to the organization rather than to the person named in the attention line. Therefore, use one of the organizational salutations shown in ¶¶1340 and 1803. (Whenever possible, omit the attention line and address the letter directly to an individual in the organization—either by name or by title.)

b. If the word *Attention* is dropped (as shown in ¶1337b) and the letter is addressed directly to an individual in the organization either by name or title, use one of the personal salutations shown in Section 18.

Subject Line

1342 a. The subject line (if used) appears between the salutation and the body of the letter, with 1 blank line above and below. (See the illustration on page 338.) The term *Subject:* or *Re:* usually precedes the actual subject line.

b. Ordinarily, the subject line starts at the left margin, but it may be centred for special emphasis. In a letter with indented paragraphs, the subject line may use the same tab setting as the paragraph.

c. Key the subject line either in capital and small letters or in all-capital letters. The subject line is usually keyed without italicizing or underlining, but for special emphasis the complete subject line is often bolded.

NOTE: A subject line should be short and clear. If it needs to be long, key it in two or more single-spaced lines of roughly equal length.

Subject: Introductory Offer to New   **SUBJECT: MORAN LEASE**
   Subscribers and Renewal
   Offer to Present Subscribers

d. When replying to a letter that carries a "refer to" notation, you may put the reference number or filing code either in a subject line or below the date line in a "refer to" line.

Subject: Policy 668485   Refer to: Policy 668485

Message

1343 a. Careful planning is required in writing your letters. Keeping the reader in mind, decide how formal or informal the letter should be and adjust the tone and wording of the message accordingly. (See ¶¶1089–1097.)

b. Try to organize the text of the letter in short paragraphs; long paragraphs are uninviting and harder to read. One-sentence paragraphs may be acceptable, but be aware that too many of them make the letter appear choppy and disconnected.

c. Begin the body (message) of the letter on the second line below the salutation or the subject line, if it is used.

d. If you are writing a reply to a letter, it is sometimes helpful to refer to that letter by date in the first sentence.

Thank you for your letter of May 9, 2006. (See ¶409.)

e. Use single spacing and leave 1 blank line between paragraphs. Very short letters may be keyed in 1.5 spacing or 2.0 (double) spacing or lengthened by means of other techniques. (See ¶1307.)

f. Align each line of the message at the left margin. However, for the *modified-block (semi-block) style with indented paragraphs* and the *modified-block (semi-block) style* with the body double-spaced, indent 0.25 to 0.5 inches. For special effect, some writers indent more than 0.5 inch.

g. The *full justification* setting can be used to make full lines of text not only begin but also end at the same point. Word processing software adds extra spaces between words to give this even appearance; however, it produces unwanted and unattractive "rivers" of white space running through the text. More important, text with a *ragged* (unjustified) right margin is easier to read. Some recipients of justified letters tend to regard them as form letters and do not take them seriously.

h. If you decide on a ragged right margin, try to avoid great variations in the length of adjacent lines. (See Section 9 for guidelines on word division to keep the lines of text roughly equal in length.)

i. If a letter takes two or more pages, do not divide a two- or three-lined paragraph at the bottom of the page. In order to leave at least two lines of the paragraph at the foot of one page and carry over at least two lines to the top of the next page, use the *widow/orphan* feature of your software program. (See ¶1364.)

1344 a. Quoted Material. If a quotation will make four or more lines, key it as a single-spaced extract. Indent the extract 0.5 inches from each side margin using the word processing *double indent* feature. Leave 1 blank line above and below the extract as illustrated on page 338. If the quoted matter represents the beginning of an indented paragraph in the original, tab the first word an additional 0.25 to 0.5 inches from the left margin.

☞ *For different ways of handling a long quotation, see ¶265.*

(Continued on page 358.)

b. Tables. When a table occurs in the text of a letter, centre it between the left and right margins. Try to indent the table at least 0.5 inches from each side margin. If the table is very wide, reduce the space between columns to a minimum of 2 spaces to prevent the table extending beyond the width of the text. Leave 1 to 3 blank lines above and below the table to set it off from the rest of the text. (See Section 16.)

c. Items in a List. Single space a list with short lines of text and add one blank line above and below the list as a whole. Either key the list on the full width of a letter that has no paragraph indentions (see the second illustration on this page) or use the word processing *indent* feature to indent the lines 0.5 inches from each side margin (see the illustration below). If *any* item in the list requires more than one line, align any turnovers or runovers with the first word in the line above. Leave a blank line after each item in the list to make each item clearly definable.

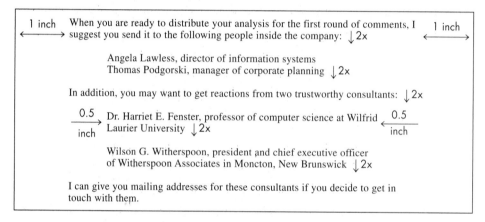

d. Enumerated Items in a List. If the items in a list each begin with a number or a letter, the *numbered list feature* of the word processing software will determine how the list will be presented. Depending on the software used and depending on the version of that software, the default settings could vary widely. The following sample text shows the preferred format.

When I review the situation as you described it in your letter of June 24, it seems to me that you have only two alternatives: ↓2x

1. Agree to pay the additional amount that Henning now demands before he will start construction. ↓2x

2. Drop Henning and start the search all over again to find a firm qualified to handle a project of this size and this complexity. ↓2x

---

In the preferred format shown above, note the following features:

- The items are single-spaced with a double space between the numbered items.

- The number (with a period) for the item is at the left margin.
- Each line of the item is indented 0.25 inch, which is acceptable for most font sizes.
- The list itself is separated from the body of text by a double space above and below it.

Word processing software users who are familiar with their program will be able to make adjustments in the default settings to achieve the desired format.

NOTE: An enumerated list may be keyed to the full width of the letter, or it may be indented 0.5 inches from each side margin. However, if the first line of each text paragraph is indented, indent the enumerations as well for a better appearance. If the software default is not the same as the paragraph indentions in the text, an adjustment may be made for the same indentions to give a more uniform and attractive look.

When I review the situation as you described it in your letter of June 24, it seems to me that you have only two alternatives:

1. Agree to pay the additional amount that Henning now demands before he will start construction.

2. Drop Henning and start the search all over again to find a firm qualified to handle a project of this size and this complexity.

As painful as it may be, you may find it easier to start looking for a new contractor than to have to deal with new demands from Henning once he is a quarter of the way through the job.

NOTE: The *numbered list* feature aligns numbers and letters at the left. If your list contains 10 or more items, it is possible to adjust the numbers to align at the right, but it is a time-consuming and frustrating task with certain word processing software. Some writers have abandoned the preferred right alignment for numbers, letting the software dictate the style.

e. **Bulleted Items in a List.** Instead of numbers or letters, you can use *bullets* before the items in a list. Software offers a choice from a variety of styles. Since the default position of a bullet varies with the software and the bullet type, the user may wish to adjust the left margins and indent settings. Some examples are shown below.

CHECK MARKS ✓✔✔   STARS ☆★☆   ARROWS ●▶➡→

When I review the situation as you described it in your letter of June 24, it seems to me that you have only two alternatives: ↓2x

- Agree to pay the additional amount that Henning now demands before he will start construction. ↓2x

- Drop Henning and start the search all over again to find a firm qualified to handle a project of this size and this complexity. ↓2x

---

Complimentary Closing

1345 a. Position the complimentary closing on the second line below the last line of the body of the letter. (See pages 336–339.) Placement rules include the following:

- Block (full-block) style letter, start the closing at the left margin
- Modified-block (semi-block) styles, start the closing at centre

NOTE: Word processing software allows you to use autotext for the complimentary closing and other elements that are frequently used in the closing of a letter.

b. Capitalize only the first word of a complimentary closing. Place a comma at the end of the line (except when open punctuation is used).

c. The following complimentary closings are commonly used:

PERSONAL IN TONE:	Sincerely,	Sincerely yours,
	Cordially,	Cordially yours,
MORE FORMAL IN TONE:	Very truly yours,	Very cordially yours,
	Very sincerely yours,	Respectfully yours,

d. An informal closing phrase may be inserted in place of one of the more conventional closings shown above. If the wording is an adverbial phrase (one that tells *how* or *in what manner*—for example, *With all best wishes* or *With warmest regards*), follow the closing with a comma. If the wording is a complete sentence (for example, *See you in Lake Louise*), follow the closing with a period. In each case the comma or the period may be replaced with stronger punctuation as appropriate—that is, a question mark, an exclamation point, or a dash.

e. If both a complimentary closing and an informal closing phrase are used, place the complimentary closing in its regular position, and (1) key the informal phrase at the end of the last paragraph or (2) treat it as the final paragraph with the correct terminal punctuation.

f. Once a pattern of personal or informal closings is begun, it should not be discontinued without good reason. Otherwise, the person who receives the letter may wonder what has happened to the relationship. (See ¶1339b.)

Company Signature

1346 A company signature is normally not required when letterhead stationery is used. In legal correspondence a company signature may be used to further emphasize the fact that a letter represents the views of the firm as a whole (and not merely those of the person who has written it). If included, the company signature should be in all-capital letters on the second line below the complimentary closing. Begin the company signature at the same point as the complimentary closing. (See the illustration on page 336.)

Very truly yours, ↓2x

HAGGET & SMITH ↓4 to 6x

John H. Smith, Q.C.

Writer's Signature Block

1347 a. Ordinarily place the writer's name on the fourth or fifth line below the complimentary closing or company signature, if used. (See the illustrations on pages 336–339.) Start keying at the same point as the complimentary closing.

☞ *For adjusting the length of a letter, see ¶1307.*

   b. Although some writers prefer to give only their title and department name in the signature block, a printed signature should also be included so that the unsigned copies will clearly show who sent the letter. If the writer prefers to omit his or her name from the signature block, then it should be spelled out in the reference initials. (See ¶1354d.)

   c. Top-level executives usually have special stationery with their name and title imprinted along with other elements of the letterhead. When using this type of stationery, key a signature line but omit the title.

1348 a. Arrange the writer's name, title, and department on two or more lines to achieve good visual balance. If a title takes more than one line, indent all turnovers 2 to 3 spaces from the word aligned above.

Janice Mahoney, Manager
Data Processing Division

Charles Saunders
Assistant Manager
Credit Department

Ernest L. Welhoelter
Head, Sales Department

Franklin Browning
Vice-President and
  General Manager

☞ *For guidance on capitalizing in signature blocks, see ¶1324a.*

   b. If an organization's letterhead stationery or computerized template does not easily accommodate the phone number and an e-mail address for each employee, this information can be included at the end of the signature block. The following arrangements are acceptable:

Charles Saunders
Assistant Manager
Credit Department
Phone: 403.555.5084   **OR**   tel   403-555-5084
Fax: 403.555.6594   fax 403-555-6594
e-mail: credit@benson.com   e-mail esaunders@benson.com

☞ *For telephone numbers with an area code, see ¶454.*

1349 For the use of a special title in a signature block, see the following guidelines:

(Continued on page 362.)

a. A person who wants to be addressed as *Dr.* should use an academic degree after his or her name (not *Dr.* before it).

Jane Bishop, M.D.   Nancy Buckwater, Ph.D.

b. A person who wishes to be addressed by a title of academic or military rank (*Dean, Professor, Major*) should put this title *after* the name or on the next line, not before it.

Helene C. Powell   Joseph F. Corey
Dean of Students   Major, Canadian Forces
(**NOT:** Dean Helene C. Powell)   (**NOT:** Major Joseph F. Corey)

c. When a title of address cannot be placed after a surname or cannot be inferred from the initials of an academic degree, then it may precede the name.

Rev. Joseph W. Dowd   Mother Ellen Marie O'Brien

1350 Ordinarily, a man should not include *Mr.* in his signature. However, if he has a name that could also be a woman's name (*Hilary, Lee, Lynn, Morgan*) or if he uses initials in place of a first and middle name (*J. G. Eberle*), he should use *Mr.* in either his handwritten or his printed signature when writing to people who do not know him.

Sincerely,   Sincerely,

(Mr.) Lynn Treadway   *Lynn Treadway*

Lynn Treadway   Mr. Lynn Treadway

NOTE: If the title is given in the handwritten signature, it is enclosed in parentheses; if given in the printed signature, it appears without parentheses.

1351 a. A woman should include a courtesy title (*Ms., Miss,* or *Mrs.*) or a special title in her signature. (See ¶1364.) If she gives her name without a title, someone writing to her may address her as *Ms.* or omit any title at all. If she uses initials or has a non-gender first name, she risks being addressed as *Mr.*

Sincerely,   Sincerely,

Joan Beaudoin   *(Mrs.) Lee Ellis*

Joan Beaudoin   Lee Ellis

b. A woman who wants to indicate her preference for *Ms.* should use this courtesy title in either her handwritten or typed signature (but not both).

Sincerely yours,   Sincerely yours,

(Ms.) Constance G. Booth   *Constance G. Booth*

Constance G. Booth   Ms. Constance G. Booth

c. A single woman who wants to indicate her preference for *Miss* should include this title in her handwritten or her typed signature (but not both).

Cordially,

(Miss) Margaret L. Galloway

Margaret L. Galloway

Cordially,

Margaret L. Galloway

Miss Margaret L. Galloway

d. A married woman who retains her original name for career purposes or who does not change her surname at all may use either *Ms.* or *Miss,* as illustrated in ¶1366b–c.

e. A married woman or a widow who prefers to be addressed as *Mrs.* has many variations to choose from. The following examples show some possible styles for a woman whose maiden name was Nancy O. Ross and whose husband's name is (or was) John A. Wells.

Cordially yours,

(Mrs.) Nancy O. Wells

Nancy O. Wells
Mrs. Nancy Ross Wells

Cordially yours,

Nancy Ross Wells

NOTE: Giving the husband's full name in the printed signature (as in the example below) is a style often used for social purposes. It should not be used in business, and it should not be used when a married woman becomes a widow unless she indicates that that is her preference.

Cordially yours,

Nancy O. Wells

Mrs. John A. Wells

f. A divorced woman who has resumed using her maiden name may use *Ms.* or *Miss* in any of the styles shown in ¶1366b–c. If she retains her ex-husband's surname, she may use *Ms.* or *Mrs.* in any of the styles shown in ¶1366b and e. (**EXCEPTION:** The style that uses the husband's full name in the printed signature is not appropriate for a divorced woman.)

1352 a. An assistant who signs a letter at the supervisor's request usually signs the supervisor's name and adds his or her own initials. However, if instructed to do so, the letter may be signed with the assistant's own name.

Sincerely yours,

Robert H. Benedict
DK

Robert H. Benedict
Production Manager

Sincerely yours,

Dorothy Kozinski

Ms. Dorothy Kozinski
Assistant to Robert H. Benedict

b. If a person other than the assistant signs for another, either of the following forms may be used:

Sincerely yours,

(Miss) Alice R. Brentano

For Robert H. Benedict
Production Manager

Sincerely yours,

Robert H. Benedict/
ARB

Robert H. Benedict
Production Manager

1353 When two people have to sign a letter, arrange the two signature blocks side by side or one beneath the other, depending on the amount of space available.

a. If they are placed side by side, start the first signature block at the left margin and the second block at centre. The complimentary closing should also begin at the left margin and is not repeated for the second signature block. This is correct for all letter styles.

b. If the signature blocks are positioned one beneath the other, align the second block on the fourth line below the first block. Both signature blocks begin at the left margin in a full-block style. Both blocks may align at a centre tab in a modified-block style. Do not repeat the complimentary closing for the second block.

Reference Initials

1354 a. When the writer's name is given in the signature block, the simplest and most unobtrusive way to provide the necessary information is to show the typist's initials alone in lower case letters. (See page 338.)

NOTE: Do not include reference initials in a personal-business letter (see page 339) or a social-business letter (see ¶¶1372–1373 and the illustration on page 377). Moreover, omit reference initials on letters you key yourself unless you need to distinguish them from letters prepared for you by someone else.

b. Place the initials of the typist at the left margin in lower case on the second line below the writer's name and title. If the writer prefers that his or her initials also be used, they should be keyed before those of the typist.

c. The preferred format for keying two sets of initials places the writer's initials in all capitals and the typist's in lower case. Some writers prefer to use the same case for both sets of initials. In either case, use a diagonal or a colon to separate them.

TYPIST ONLY:	mhs		
WRITER AND TYPIST:	CED/mhs	OR	CED:mhs
	CED/MHS	OR	ced:mhs

d. If the writer's name is not given in the signature block, key the initials and surname before those of the typist; for example, *CEDixon/mhs.*

e. When the letter is written by someone other than the person who signs it, this fact may be indicated by showing the writer's and the typist's initials (not the signer's and the typist's). See the illustration below.

Sincerely yours, ↓4 to 6x

Herbert Heymann

Herbert Heymann
President ↓2x

pbr/jbp

Enclosure Notation

1355 a. If one or more items are to be included in the envelope with the letter, indicate that fact by keying the word *Enclosure* (or a suitable alternative) at the left margin, on the line below the reference initials.

> **NOTE:** Before sending the letter, make sure that the number of enclosures shown in the enclosure notation agrees with (1) the number cited in the body of the letter and (2) the number of items actually enclosed.

b. The following styles are commonly used:

Enclosure	2 Enclosures	Enclosures:
Enc.	2 Enc.	1. Cheque for $500
1 Enclosure	Enclosures 2	2. Invoice A37512
Cheque enclosed	Enc. 2 (see ¶503)	

c. Some writers use the term *Attachment* or *Att.* when the material is actually attached to the cover letter rather than simply enclosed.

d. If material is to be sent separately instead of being enclosed with the letter, indicate this fact by keying *Separate cover* or *Under separate cover* on the line below the enclosure notation (if any) or on the line directly below the reference initials. The following styles may be used:

Separate cover 1	Under separate cover:
	1. Annual report
	2. Product catalogue
	3. Price list

Delivery Notation

1356 If a letter is to be delivered in a special way (other than by ordinary mail), key an appropriate notation below the reference initials as illustrated below and on page 336. To draw attention to this notation, a *preferable* format is to capitalize the notation a double space under the date and at the left margin. Leave 2 blank lines after the notation and before the inside address. Among the notations that could be used are *By e-mail, By registered mail, By Priority Post, By XPRESSPOST, By Federal Express (FedEx), By fax,* and *By courier.*

crj	HWM:FH	tpg/wwc
Enc. 2	By Federal Express	Enclosures 4
By e-mail	cc George Fox	By fax

> **NOTE:** If you send a letter by fax and want to record the fax number on your file copy, simply expand the delivery notation as follows: By fax (613-222-222).

Confirmation Notation

1357 When a letter is first faxed or e-mailed to the addressee and then a duplicate is sent by post, place a "confirmation" notation on the letter being mailed so that the addressee will realize that the document is not a new letter. Double space under the date of the letter *Confirmation of fax sent on* (or *e-mail transmitted on*) and then supply the date.

(Continued on page 366.)

NOTE: If a letter is first forwarded by e-mail, it should be forwarded as an attachment to preserve the integrity of the original format.

Copy Notation

1358 a. A copy notation lets the addressee know that one or more persons will also be sent a copy of a letter. The initials *cc* are still commonly used for this notation. Although the abbreviation originally stood for *carbon copies, cc* also means *circulated copies, computer copies,* or *courtesy copies.* Many e-mail and word processing memo templates continue to use the *cc* notation.

b. An alternative to *cc* is a single *c* or the phrase *Copies to* (or *Copy to*). Some writers prefer to use the abbreviation *pc* for *photocopies.*

c. Put the copy notation on the line directly under any previous notation (such as reference initials or an enclosure notation). If there is no previous notation, place the copy notation on the second line below the writer's name and title.

d. Type *cc* (in lower case) or other copy notation at the left margin. No punctuation is required, but if it is preferred, use a colon and leave 1 or 2 spaces after it.

e. If several persons are to receive copies, use the copy notation only with the first name. Set a tab to align all the other names with the start of the name above. List the names according to the rank of the persons or in alphabetic order.

AMH:HT	mfn	lbw/ncy
Enclosure	Enc. 4	copies to: Contract File
Registered	c Alice Chang	Toronto Office
cc Ms. J. Hope	Roy Flynn	Sales Department

f. When first names or initials are given along with last names, personal titles (*Mr., Miss, Mrs.,* and *Ms.*) may be omitted except in formal letters. Do not use personal titles if nicknames are given with last names.

c: James Dion	pc: J. Dion	cc Jim Dion
Kenneth Eustis	K. Eustis	Ken Eustis
Margaret Falmouth	M. Falmouth	Peggy Falmouth

1359 If you do not want the addressee to know that one or more persons are also being sent a copy of the letter, use a *blind copy notation.*

a. Print the original letter and any copies on which the regular copy notation is to appear. Then print the blind copies one at a time with a blind copy notation showing the name of the designated recipient. (Under certain circumstances, you may wish to let all recipients of blind copies know who the others are.)

b. Place the blind copy notation a double space under the date line (a triple space above the inside address) at the left margin so it is noticed immediately. As an alternative, key the blind copy notation on the line below the last item in the letter.

c. The form of a blind copy notation should follow the form of the copy notation. If you have used *cc* or *c* or *Copies to*, then use *bcc* or *bc* or *Blind copies to*.

d. The file copy should show all the blind copy notations, even though the individual copies do not. Whether the file copy is stored on disk or in hard-copy form, you may need to use the file copy later to make additional copies for distribution. Be sure that no blind copy notations appear on these new copies unless you want them to.

NOTE: In Alberta, the Freedom of Information and Protection of Privacy Act (FOIP) may change the use of blind copies.

1360 When a letter carries both an enclosure notation and a copy notation, it is assumed that the enclosures accompany only the original letter. If a copy of the enclosures is also to accompany a copy of the letter, this fact may be indicated as follows:

cc:	Mr. D. R. Leung	(will receive only the letter)
	Ms. N. A. Warren	(will receive only the letter)
cc/enc.:	Mr. J. Bitonti	(will receive the letter and the enclosures)
	Mrs. G. Conger	(will receive the letter and the enclosures)

1361 A copy is not usually signed unless the letter is addressed to several people, and the copy is intended for one of the people named in the salutation. However, a check mark next to the name or the name highlighted indicates for whom that copy is intended.

c: Ms. A. M. Starlight ✓	c: Ms. A. M. Starlight	c: Ms. A. M. Starlight
Mr. H. W. Fried	Mr. H. W. Fried ✓	Mr. H. W. Fried
Mrs. C. Quigley	Mrs. C. Quigley	Mrs. C. Quigley ✓

NOTE: When an unsigned copy is likely to strike the recipient as cold and impersonal, the writer may add a brief handwritten note at the bottom of the copy and sign or initial it.

Postscript

1362 a. A postscript can be effectively used to express an idea that has been deliberately withheld from the body of a letter; stating this idea at the very end gives it strong emphasis. A postscript may also be used to express an afterthought; however, if the afterthought contains something central to the meaning of the letter, the reader may conclude that the letter was badly organized.

b. When a postscript is used:

(1) Start the postscript on the second line below the copy notation (or whatever was keyed last). If the paragraphs are indented, indent the first line of the postscript (see page 338); otherwise, begin it at the left margin.

(2) Key *PS:* or *PS* before the first word of the postscript. Leave at least two spaces after the postscript to permit the alignment of turnover lines with the first word above.

(3) Use *PPS:* or *PPS* at the beginning of an additional postscript, and treat this postscript as a separate paragraph.

(Continued on page 368.)

> PS: Instead of dashing to the airport as soon as the meeting is over, why don't you have dinner and spend the night with us?
>
> PPS: Better yet, why don't you plan to stay the whole weekend?

(4) An alternative format is shown below.

> PS: Why don't you bring Joyce with you and plan to stay for the whole weekend?

File Name Notation

1363 Copies of letters, memos, and reports are normally saved on computer disks and printed as hard copies. Each document needs a unique file name so that it can be readily identified for retrieval from storage.

a. A file name or document ID has three components: a name, a period (called a *dot*) used as a separator, and an extension typically consisting of 1 to 3 characters. Current Windows programs allow a name preceding the dot of up to 255 characters. Some current programs permit more than 3 characters after the dot and allow the use of more than one extension. Users normally allow the word processing software to add its unique identifying extension automatically so documents can be found easily.

NOTE: Although 255 characters may be used in a file name, try to keep the name as short and as recognizable as possible.

b. In creating a file name or document ID, choose a name that is meaningful. Most often you can use the letters *a* to *z*, the figures *0* to *9*, spaces, and certain symbols. If an illegal symbol has been selected, a message will inform you that the file name is not accepted and needs to be changed. Refer to your software help file or your user's manual to confirm which symbols may or may not be used.

c. Establish whether a numeric or alphabetic filing system is suitable for your file names. Elements to help organize file names may include:

- an order number, a policy number, or some other specific identifying number added to the name of the recipient of the document.
- a date added to a recipient's name to identify one of several letters to the same person.
- a notation such as *draft 1, draft 2, final version* added to a file name to indicate a stage of revision.
- pre-assigned numbers added to the beginning of the file name to indicate a file folder number for documents relating to the same subject.

NOTE: Complex numbering systems to identify file folders and file names are often used by law firms.

d. Filing notations are usually placed in a footer. Most word processing software has an automatic file name insert function that guarantees that the file name notation placed on the document will include the entire path and file name. If the file name must be supplied manually, be sure that all parts of the path and file name are included. Use a small-size font (8- or 9-point).

C:\gregg reference manual\chapter 13.doc

NOTE: Many writers prefer to place the file name notation in a footer to appear on the last page only.

Continuation Pages

1364 a. Use plain paper of the same quality as the letterhead (but never a letterhead) for all but the first page of a long letter.

b. Use the same left and right margins that you used on the first page.

c. Use the header feature to set a continuation page heading. The header should contain the name of the addressee, the page number, and the date. A top margin of 1 inch is generally preferred. Some software defaults the header to a 0.5 inch top margin and a smaller font size. The first illustration below should be used for the block style letter while the second illustration is appropriate for the modified-block letter styles.

↓ 1"
Mrs. Laura R. Austin
Page 2
September 30, 2006 ↓ 3x

OR

↓ 1"
Mrs. Laura R. Austin – 2 – September 30, 2006 ↓ 3x

d. If the letter is addressed to *Dear Sir or Madam* or if it lacks the name of a particular recipient, use a brief phrase in the heading that clearly links the continuation page to the first page of the letter.

Recommendation for Karyn Hansen 2 September 30, 2006

e. Most software defaults or permits only one blank line after a continuation page heading. However, if you prefer to leave two blank lines below the page heading, a hard return added at the end of the header will allow the second blank line to be inserted.

f. Do not divide a short paragraph (with only two or three lines) at the bottom of a page. For a paragraph of four or more lines, always leave at least two lines of text at the bottom of the page and carry over at least two lines to the continuation page. This will be done automatically by most word processing software programs if the user ensures that the *Widow/Orphan* feature is turned on. (See also ¶1343i.)

g. Never divide a word at the end of a page.

h. Never use a continuation page just for the closing section of a business letter. (The complimentary closing should always be preceded by at least two lines of the message.)

i. Do not staple a document to be sent by mail in case the recipient wants to photocopy it.

ENVELOPES
1365 Envelope Sizes

a. Since most businesses use standard stationery ($8\frac{1}{2}"$ × 11"), the most common size of envelope is the No. 10 ($4\frac{1}{2}"$ × $9\frac{1}{2}"$). For stationery not of standard size, envelopes of different sizes are available. Contact Canada Post Corporation toll-free at 1-800-267-1133 or visit their Web site at www.canadapost.com for clarification on size, weight, and rates of letter-mail to Canada, to the United States, or to international destinations.

The maximum size, thickness, and weight of an envelope to qualify for automated processing and regular postage is

150 × 245 mm (size)   5.0 mm (thickness)   0.30 g (weight)

b. Using the envelope feature of a software program, you can select the envelope size you plan to use. The return address and the mailing address can be set with the default specifications, or you can modify them to suit your needs. Custom-size envelopes can also be accommodated (assuming your printer will support them).

1366 Inside-Address Style

You may choose from two possible formats when addressing envelopes: (1) the letter or inside-address style (¶¶1316–1336); and (2) the Canada Post Corporation (CPC) format, which contains all-capital letters, many abbreviations, and no punctuation (see ¶1367). The advantage of the letter style is that the computer will generate the same address information on both the letter and the envelope. Moreover, Canada Post's OCRs *(optical character readers)* are programmed to read both formats.

a. Always use single spacing and block each line at the left. Use a minimum of 3 lines. (See page 371 for an example.)

b. Follow the standard rules for capital letters in names, prepositions, and conjunctions in the address. (See ¶303.)

c. The preferred placement for the municipality, province, and postal code is the last line. If space makes it impossible for the postal code to fit on the same line, it may be keyed on the line directly below.

d. The province should be identified by the two-letter CPC abbreviation. (See page 354.)

e. Leave two or three spaces between the province abbreviation and the postal code.

f. The next-to-last line in the address block should contain a street address. If a municipal street address is not part of the address, include a postal service indicator such as a post office box number (PO Box), a rural route address (RR), a station designation (STN), or a general delivery notation (GD).

Mr. Christopher Scott
Colby Electronics Ltd.
PO Box, Stn. South
Brandon, MB R7B 3W9

Mr. and Mrs. A. Collard
Suite 202
9539 Old Millcreek Road
Shedden, ON N0L 2E0

g. When a room, suite, or apartment number is part of the address, insert it immediately after the street address on the same line. If the number does not fit on the same line, place it on the line above, never on the line below. (See the example above and in ¶1327.)

h. If the default settings for the envelope feature of a word processing program are being used, check that the address elements will be within the OCR reading area.

i. At present the POSTNET bar code feature in some software can be added only to envelopes addressed to the United States.

j. Adjustments may need to be made for window envelopes to ensure that the address block is clearly visible.

k. Some guidelines for formatting an envelope on a typewriter are as follows:

(1) Assuming a No. 10 envelope is being used, start the address 2.25 ($2\frac{1}{4}$) inches from the top and about 0.5 ($\frac{1}{2}$) inch left of centre. This will keep the address information within the OCR reading area.

(2) If there is no printed return address on the envelope, type one in the upper left corner. Begin approximately 0.5 ($\frac{1}{2}$) inch from the top edge and 0.75 ($\frac{3}{4}$) inch from the left edge.

(3) Follow the same mailing address format. Type the following on separate lines: the name of the writer; the company name; the street address or equivalent; and the municipality, province, and postal code.

Envelope With Non-Address Data Information

(Continued on page 372.)

l. Black ink on white envelopes is best for the OCRs. If white envelopes are not being used, make sure there is good contrast between the ink colour and the paper colour. Underlining, script fonts, or italics are not suitable attributes for the OCRs to read and should not be used.

m. Notations such as *Personal, Attention,* and *Hold for Arrival* are considered non-address data and could be placed on the first line of the address block or a triple space below the return address. (See the envelope illustration on page 371.)

☞ *For letters being sent to two or more people at the same address, see ¶1319b.*

1367 Canada Post (CPC) Style

The Canada Post style for addressing envelopes is an all-cap style, which is used on labels for mass mailing. This style was once the only style that could be read easily by the corporation's OCR. However, today all letter-size mail and postcards are processed just as easily by the OCR. This means that envelope addresses using the more attractive and readable inside-address format (see ¶¶1316–1319) can be just as easily processed as those using the all-cap style.

a. To use the Canada Post style, key all lines blocked at the left with
- All-capital letters
- Single spacing
- No punctuation

☞ *See the CPC Web site for street type abbreviations or visit www.mcrawhill.ca/college/sabin for this and more helpful information.*

b. For a U.S. address, your software may permit you to insert the United States Postal Service POSTNET bar code above or below the address block.

c. For the placement of all lines in the address block, follow the same rules in ¶1366a–m.

Envelope Showing a Mailing Label With the POSTNET Bar Code

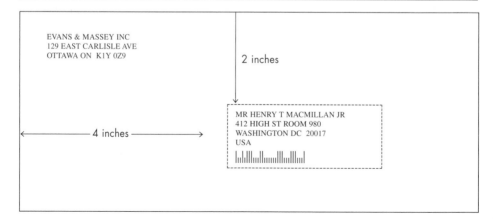

1368 Preparing an Envelope for a U.S.A. Address

a. USA (or U.S.A.) must appear alone on the last line of the address block.

b. The first part in the second last line of the address block is the full name of the municipality.

c. The two-character international state symbol follows the name of the municipality and is separated from it by a comma or one space, depending on the format used. (See the illustration below.) The use of the state symbol is preferred over the full name of the state.

d. The Zip Code is the last item in the second last line and is separated from the state symbol by two spaces. It may be either five or nine digits. If the nine-digit format is used, a hyphen will separate the fifth and sixth digits.

Inside-Address Format	CPC Format
Ms. Aileen O'Brien	MS AILEEN OBRIEN
398 North Michigan Avenue	398 N MICHIGAN AVE
Washington, DC 20019-4649	WASHINGTON DC 20019-4649
U.S.A.	USA

1369 Preparing an Envelope for an International Address

International mail as defined by CPC is mail addressed to countries other than Canada and the United States; it is sorted by country name only. Therefore, make sure the country name is correct; for example, do not use *England* for *Great Britain*.

The country name is placed alone on the last line of the address block.

MR THOMAS CLARK	KARL HAUSER GMBH
17 RUSSEL DR	LANDSTRASSE 15
LONDON W1P 6HQ	4100 DUISBURG 25
GREAT BRITAIN	GERMANY

Folding and Inserting Letters

1370 The following paragraphs describe methods for folding letters of standard size ($8\frac{1}{2}"\times 11"$) and inserting them into envelopes.

a. To fold a letter in thirds for a No. 10 envelope.

(1) (2) (3)

(1) Bring the bottom third of the letter up and make a crease.

(2) Fold the top of the letter down to within 0.25 inch of the crease you made in step 1. Then make the second crease.

(3) The creased edge made in step 2 goes into the envelope first.

(Continued on page 374.)

b. To fold a letter for insertion into a window envelope.

(1)   (2)   (3)

(1) Place the letter *face down* with the letterhead at the top, and fold the bottom third of the letter up.

(2) Fold the top third down so that the address shows.

(3) Insert the letter with the inside address toward the *front* of the envelope. The inside address should now be fully readable through the window. Preferably 0.25 inch white space should edge all four sides. (See ¶1366j.)

LABELS

1371 If you are using the label feature of word processing software, you can quickly prepare a wide variety of labels (for example, mailing labels, file folder labels, and cassette labels) by following these guidelines:

a. Use commercially prepared labels (packaged in rolls and sheets) that have been specifically designed for the purpose you have in mind and that are compatible with your printer.

b. Most software has a menu of label types and sizes. When you select the type and size you want to use, the program automatically sets up the label windows. All you need to do is type the necessary information in each window (as illustrated on page 375).

NOTE: You can also create your own specifications for a special type of label. See your software user's manual for the procedures to follow.

c. Before you begin to key text in each label window, consider the maximum number of characters you can fit on one line and the number of lines you can fit on one label. For example, if you are preparing mailing labels, you may very well find that some mailing addresses you formatted for an inside address are too wide to fit on the labels you are planning to use. In such cases use the all-cap style designed by Canada Post. The all-cap style, with its heavy reliance on abbreviations, was specifically created to take such limitations into account. (See ¶¶1366, 1367, and the illustration on page 375.)

d. When applying a label to a No. 10 envelope or a smaller envelope, follow the placement guidelines provided in ¶1366k. (For an illustration showing the correct placement of a mailing label on a No. 10 envelope, see page 372.) On envelopes larger than No. 10, position the label so that it appears visually centred horizontally and vertically.

Screen Shot Showing a Label Page

SOCIAL-BUSINESS CORRESPONDENCE

1372 The term *social-business correspondence* applies to the following types of letters:

a. Executive correspondence addressed to high-level executives, officials, and dignitaries. (Unlike ordinary business correspondence—which deals with sales, production, finance, advertising, and other routine commercial matters—these letters deal with such topics as corporate policy and issues of social responsibility, and they are written in a more formal style.)

b. Letters expressing praise, concern, or condolence to someone within or outside the organization. (The occasion that prompts the letter could be exceptional performance on the job or in the community, an employment anniversary, the death or serious illness of a family member, or an upcoming retirement. Such letters may be formal or informal, depending on the relationship between the writer and the person addressed.)

c. Letters to business associates within or outside the company on purely social matters.

1373 Social-business correspondence differs from ordinary business correspondence in several ways:

a. The inside address is placed at the bottom of the letter, aligned at the left margin, and keyed on the fourth to sixth line below the writer's signature or title (whichever comes last). The inside address would be typed without abbreviations for the street address and province, and a comma would be placed after the city name and before the name of the province.

b. The salutation is followed by a comma rather than a colon.

(Continued on page 376.)

13

c. Reference initials and notations pertaining to enclosures, copies, and mailing are usually omitted. (It would make good sense, however, to put such notations on the file copy in case this information is needed later.)

d. If the letter requires a *Personal* or *Confidential* notation, place the notation only on the envelope and the file copy, not on the letter itself. (For the placement of the notation on an envelope, see ¶1366m and the illustration on page 371.)

e. Social-business correspondence also differs by being *more* formal or *less* formal than ordinary business correspondence. For example, correspondence to high-level officials and dignitaries is customarily more formal. In such cases use the word style for numbers (see ¶¶404–406) and one of the special salutations listed in Section 18. However, in letters to business associates who are also close friends, the salutation and the complimentary closing may be very informal, and the writer's printed signature and title—and even the inside address—may be omitted. Moreover, when such letters are purely personal in nature, the writer may use plain stationery and omit the return address.

MEMOS

1374 The interoffice memo format was designed to simplify the exchange of information within an organization. Depending on the circumstances, a memo may be as terse as a telegram, as impersonal as a formal announcement, or as casual as a personal note. The printed memo form is now a thing of the past, but the memo format continues to be widely used for certain types of documents and is the template format for e-mail messaging. Most word processing software provides memo templates (see page 378 for an example), which may be used as is or altered to suit your purposes. Company names, company logos, graphics, and lines are often added to a company memo template.

1375 There is no one correct format for a memo. If you are formatting your own template, consider the following guidelines:

a. Use the default side, top, and bottom margins. Any of the margins may be adjusted to better suit your document. To prevent a memo from going onto a second page, adjust the side margins but keep them equal in size. None of the margins should be less than 0.5 inches.

b. All memo headings should include the following guide words:

> **To:** (The name(s) of the recipient or recipients)
> **From:** (The sender's name and, if applicable, a title)
> **Date:** (The current date)
> **Subject:** (A short subject description)
> NOTE: Some writers prefer to use *Re:*.

Guide words should stand out. Use bold, all-caps, or different-sized fonts. Place a colon after each guide word. Use a tab that leaves sufficient white space and aligns the input information. Normally, double

Avon Advisory Council

197 Avon Street   Stratford, Ontario   N5A 5N8

September 26, 2006 ↓6x

13

Dear Annie, ↓2x

You and I have worked together on the Advisory Council for nearly six years, and in that time we have gotten to know each other pretty well. So you'll understand why I was deeply pained to hear that you and your husband have sold your house and are planning to move to the North next month. ↓2x

We have not always seen eye to eye (I still think you were dead wrong to vote against the parking lot expansion), but there is no one who has given as much thought and imagination and caring service to this town as you have. ↓2x

All of us on the Advisory Council are going to miss you very much, both as a forceful participant and as a warm and generous friend, but we wish you and George the best of luck as you make new lives for yourselves. We envy your new neighbours, for they will be the beneficiaries of what we in Stratford have so long enjoyed—your vital presence. ↓2x

We won't forget you, Annie. ↓2x

Sincerely, ↓4x

Harlan

Harlan W. Estabrook
Chairman ↓6x

Mrs. Anne G. Wheatley
14 Avondale Avenue
Stratford, Ontario
N5A 6M4

space before each new guide word. If any input information takes more than one line, single space the input lines but double space before the next guide word.

Other words that may be used for further clarification or direction include the following: *Copies to, Department, Floor, Phone No., Fax No.,* etc.

(Continued on page 378.)

The MS Word Professional Memo Template (Using 10-Point Arial)

Memo

To:	[Click **here** and type name]
From:	[Click **here** and type name]
CC:	[Click **here** and type name]
Date:	[Current date will be inserted automatically]
Re:	[Click **here** and type subject]

How to Use This Memo Template

Select the text you would like to replace, and type your memo. Use styles such as Heading 1-3 and Body Text from the Styles and Formatting work pane from the Format menu. To save changes to this template for future use, choose Save As from the File menu. In the Save As type box, choose Document Template. Next time you want to use it, choose from New from the File menu, select General Templates from the work pane, and then double-click your template.

c. Company identification, such as company logos or slogans, may also be added.

d. Type the names of the addressee(s) and the name of the writer without personal titles. Depending on the formality or informality of the occasion, simply a first name or even initials may suffice. Add addtional information as required—phone number, department name, titles, etc.

John A. Mancuso (Ext. 8699) **OR** JAM **OR** Jack, Purchasing Dept.

e. If a memo is addressed to more than one person, choose one of the following formats:

(1) For two or three names, try to fit all the names on the same line, arranged in alphabetical order or in order of rank.

> **To:** Hal Parker, Meryl Crawford, Mike Najar

(2) For a few names that will not fit on one line, list the names, aligned in a single-spaced column after the guide word *To*.

> TO: Louise Letendre
>   Fred Mendoza
>   Jim Nakamura
>   Ruth O'Hare
>
> FROM: Neil Sundstrom

(3) For several names, use a *See Distribution Below* or a similar phrase after the guide word *To*. On the third line below the reference initials, the filing, or the enclosure notation (whichever comes last), key *Distribution:*. Use an initial capital letter and follow the word with a colon. Add italics, bold, underlining, or any combination of these for emphasis. (**Remember:** Italicize and bold a colon, but do not underline it.) Then leave 1 blank line and list by rank or by alphabetical order the names of those who are to receive a copy. Type the names blocked at the left margin. (See the illustration on page 380.) If space is tight, arrange the names in two or more columns.

f. Begin typing the body of the memo on the second or third line below the guide words. No salutation is required.

NOTE: If a numbered list appears within the body of a memo, the numbered items may be separated by 1 blank line for a more open look. If you use the numbered list feature of your word processing software and accept all the defaults, the list may be typed single-spaced.

g. Use single spacing and block the paragraphs. Leave 1 blank line between them.

h. Although memos do not require a signature line, some writers prefer to end their memos in this way. If this is the case, type the writer's name or initials on the *second* line below the last line of the message as shown on page 380. If the writer plans to insert a handwritten signature or initials above the signature line, type the signature line on the *fourth* line below to allow room for the handwriting. If the writer simply inserts handwritten initials next to the typed name in the heading, omit the signature line altogether.

NOTE: The position of the signature line may vary. A common placement is at the centre tab position, but it may also be placed at the left margin.

i. Key the reference initials at the left margin on the second line below the end of the message or the writer's typed name or initials, whichever comes last. (See ¶1354.)

j. Key an enclosure notation (if needed) on the line below the reference initials. Begin at the left margin. (See ¶1355.)

k. If a copy notation is needed and is not included in the heading, key it on the line below the enclosure notation or the reference initials, whichever comes last. Use the same style for the copy notation as in a letter. (See ¶¶1358–1361.) If the addressee of the memo is not to know that a copy of the memo is being sent to other persons, use a blind copy notation. (See ¶1359.)

l. Key a file name or document ID notation as a footer. (See ¶1363 and the illustration on page 336 .)

(Continued on page 380.)

¦13¦

Memorandum

1 to 2 inches

To:	See Distribution Below ↓2x
From:	Stanley W. Venner (Ext. 3835)
Date:	May 10, 2006
Subject:	Car Rentals ↓2 or 3x

We have just been informed that car rental rates will be increased by $1 to $2 a day effective July 1. A copy of the letter from Rentz is enclosed for your information. ↓2x

SWV ↓2x

jmb
Enclosure ↓2 or 3x

Distribution: ↓2x

G. Bonard
D. Catlin
S. Folger
V. Jellinek
E. Laliberte
P. Legrande

h:\miscellaneous\car rentals 05 2006

m. If the memo is confidential nature, key the word *CONFIDENTIAL* in bold capital letters. Centre the confidential notation on the second line below the last line of the memo heading.

↓2x
CONFIDENTIAL ↓2 or 3x

Begin typing the body of the memo on the second or third line below this notation.

n. If the memo continues beyond the first page, key a continuation heading on a fresh sheet of paper. (Use the same style as shown in ¶1364c for a letter.) Continue typing the message on the third line below the last line of the continuation-page heading. (See ¶1364d for additional details on continuing the message from one page to another.)

E-MAIL

E-mail (also referred to as an electronic memo) serves to overcome the problems associated with the delivery of regular mail (postal *snail mail*) and with the frustrations that result from playing telephone tag (leaving messages but never connecting). It allows communication to be precise, screens out cumbersome conversation, and expands personal contact.

The Nature of E-Mail

1376 a. Not everything transmitted by e-mail has to make use of an e-mail template. Letters or memos typed on a template, as well as reports, contracts, itineraries, and many other types of documents are often sent by e-mail. However, special precautions are required in order to preserve the original formatting of these documents (See ¶1384.)

b. Many people consider e-mail to be a very *informal* means of communication and therefore assume that e-mail messages do not have to comply with the normal standards of written English. This assumption is reflected all too often in hastily written messages that are badly organized and riddled with errors in spelling, grammar, usage, and style. If there were a motto for this style of e-mail composition, it would be "Anything Goes." This may be acceptable in one's personal e-mail messages, but business communications are business communications, no matter how they are sent—by e-mail, fax, or snail mail. Always remember that the e-mail messages you write in the course of doing your job belong to your organization and might one day be cited as part of a legal action.

1377 E-mail messages can be distributed through local and wide area networks, bulletin board systems, online services, and the Internet. Procedures for sending and receiving e-mail messages will therefore differ, depending on the system you use. Even the construction of mailing addresses will vary as a result.

a. An e-mail address is based on the Domain Name System (see ¶1509), which consists of a name or identifier, followed by @ (the symbol for *at*), and then followed by the domain name. Simply stated, it is *someone@somewhere*.

b. The address begins with a distinctive *user name*. How this part is written will depend on the e-mail system used, the Internet vendor, or the way that names are assigned on an organization's e-mail system.

      janiecanuck   janie.canuck   j_canuck   jcanuck463

An organization might use the name of a position, a department, or a function as a user name.

      info   customer service   applicants

(Continued on page 382.)

c. The user name is followed by the @ symbol and the domain name, which includes the name of the host computer, a "dot," and the type of domain (sometimes called the *zone*).

mcgrawhill.ca   cornell.edu   iaap-hq.org

☞ *For a more detailed discussion of the zones now being used, see ¶1508b.*

d. E-mail addresses may be typed in all-caps, in lowercase, or in some combination of the two. Never alter the spacing, the punctuation, or the symbols that appear as part of the e-mail address.

E-Mail Netiquette

1378 a. *Netiquette* is the name given to a code of behaviour for people who send and receive e-mail messages. Writers are encouraged to be considerate of the people written to, to protect e-mail address privacy, and to avoid burdening others with messages they do not need to see. Good netiquette can help you create messages that are more likely to achieve the results you want. Messages should be businesslike and free of bias. Often an impersonal approach is the best. To avoid complications resulting from errors in sending e-mails to the wrong person, confidential matters are often better communicated by other means. The privacy of e-mails cannot always be guaranteed.

b. Do not use e-mail to send unsolicited ads, chain letters, or other material that the recipient is likely to regard as junk mail or electronic garbage (known as *spam*). People who receive such material often take revenge by responding with *flames*, which are messages sent in anger.

c. Be sensitive to cultural differences. Remember: Time zone differences and other countries' holidays could delay responses.

d. If you want to criticize or reprimand someone, don't use e-mail. Remember: The privacy of e-mail messages cannot be guaranteed.

e. Respect the privacy of the messages you receive. Do not pass such messages on to others unless you are sure the sender will not object. Always delete names and e-mail addresses of people who were sent the original message.

E-Mail Format

1379 The format of an e-mail message is very much like that of a memo with guide words. The illustration on the following page shows copies of two e-mail messages—one, the original message, requests a meeting and the other is the reply received. The templates show the recipient's name and e-mail address, as well as the date, time, and subject of the message.

a. The most common guide words for a new message template are *To:*, *Cc:*, and *Subject.* If the entire heading shows, *Bcc:* may also appear as a guide word. If the message is sent to more than one person, use a comma or

(Continued on page 384.)

MS Outlook E-Mail—Original Message with Attachment Notation

Peggy Noble

From: 'Wendy Strashok'
Sent: Monday, November 29, 2004 4.57 PM
Subject: Ways and Means, Meeting

 Attachments: Fund raising strategies.doc (30 KB)

Peggy,

Could we get together on Monday at 2 p.m. to discuss our strategy for fund raising for the conference? We shouldn't need more than an hour. I have attached my initial thoughts for your review. If Monday is not convenient for you, could we arrange something for Tuesday or Wednesday?

Wendy

13

MS Outlook E-Mail—Original Message with Reply

Wendy Strashok

From: 'Peggy Noble'
Sent: Monday, November 29, 2004 4.57 PM
To: Wendy Strashok
Subject: Ways and Means, Meeting

Unfortunately, my meeting schedule is full for Monday. Let's meet Tuesday at 1 p.m. in the Ninth Floor Conference Room.

-----Original Message-----
From: **Wendy Strashok**
Sent: Monday, November 29, 2004 4.57 PM
To: Peggy Noble
Subject: Ways and Means, Meeting

Peggy,

Could we get together on Monday at 2 p.m. to discuss our strategy for fund raising for the conference? We shouldn't need more than an hour. I have attached my initial thoughts for your review. If Monday is not convenient for you, could we arrange something for Tuesday or Wednesday?

Wendy

a semicolon to separate the entries showing each recipient's name and e-mail address. If you have a contact list, only the persons' names will show, but the properties will display the entire e-mail address.

b. If you wish to send a message to several people who do not know each other and you do not wish to share e-mail addresses with each of them, use the *Bcc:* text box to "hide" the names. The *To:* text box will show "Undisclosed Recipient" or something similar. To display the names only of all recipients of a *Bcc:* e-mail, list the names at the end of the e-mail in a distribution list just as you would in a memo.

c. Always fill in the subject line. Provide a short distinct title, which will get the recipient's attention.

d. Many e-mail programs have a priority status symbol, which attracts special attention to a message. Specifying a high-priority status will add a symbol (for example, a red exclamation mark) to the e-mail address. It is visible in the recipient's **In Box** list.

The E-Mail Message

1380 Salutation

a. An e-mail, like a memo, does not require a salutation. If one is used for someone you know, one of the following formats could be used or the name incorporated in the opening line.

Hi Peggy,   Good morning, Peggy,   You're right, Peggy, the . . .

b. If the writer prefers to use a salutation for someone not known to the writer, use a more formal salutation.

Dear Ms. Squibb   Dear Pat Squibb

1381 Message

Keep in mind that some people may receive more than a hundred e-mails in one day. To avoid frustrating recipients of your e-mails, consider the following netiquette factors as you write.

a. Keep your message short and to the point. Try not to use more than one screen for the entire message.

b. Organize sentences in short, single-spaced paragraphs to make your message easier to read and understand. Use no indentions and leave a blank line between paragraphs.

c. Do not use all-capital letters. This is considered the e-mail equivalent to shouting. Follow the standard rules of capitalization. (See Section 3.)

d. Restrict each message to one subject. It is better to send separate messages than to cover all the topics in one message.

e. Consider how much background your reader needs to have in order to understand your message. It may be helpful to use the *Reply* feature in e-mail, which includes the original message as an easy and detailed point of reference for the originator.

f. Watch your tone in composing the message. Before you send it, read the message from the recipient's point of view to make sure that your words and your tone are not likely to be misconstrued.

g. Do not send a *flaming* message, for example, one that is angry, outrageous, or opinionated. Moreover, if you receive flames (angry messages), it is wiser to ignore them than to respond.

h. Do not put anything in an e-mail that you are not prepared to share with others. For example, do not provide credit card numbers or other confidential information that could end up in the wrong hands.

i. Edit and proofread each message carefully, and make the necessary corrections before sending the message. Because e-mail messages are composed on the computer, it is easy to make and overlook mistakes in grammar, usage, spelling, and style. (See ¶¶1203–1205.)

1382 Closing

a. A closing, if one is used, is placed on the second line below the message.

b. If there is no salutation, then there should be no closing.

c. Use a closing that corresponds to the familiarity of the salutation. If a first name only is used in the salutation, then a first name only is all that is required for a closing. In some cases, a surname is included to clearly identify one who shares the same first name with someone else in the same workplace.

d. An informal closing word or phrase, such as *Cheers* or *Best regards*, is often included.

1383 Writer's Signature Block

An electronic signature, an important part of business e-mails, adds the name of the writer, the writer's position, department, organization, telephone and fax numbers, e-mail address, website URL, and may also include the organization's address, or any other relevant information. By using the insert signature feature of the e-mail software, several kinds of signatures can be created, depending upon the destination of the e-mail—within or outside the business.

Some organizations require their employees to include a brief statement that describes the organization's mission. Other organizations require the automatic use of a confidential notation at the end of every e-mail message; for example:

> This e-mail may contain confidential material. If you were not an intended recipient, please notify the sender and delete all copies.

Sending Attachments

1384 a. One of the limitations of e-mail is that you cannot be sure how your message will appear on your recipient's computer. The font and the line length may be different from those on your computer, and any formatting you applied to your message may be lost or distorted in transmission. Whenever

(Continued on page 386.)

13

it is important to preserve the format of your original message, send it as an attachment to an e-mail message.

b. Some computer users do not open attachments out of fear of infection by computer viruses. Check with the recipient before you send an attachment.

c. Avoid sending large files that contain graphics or pictures. Such documents may take a long time to download and may prevent the recipient from using the computer while the downloading is taking place. Sometimes the downloading process can cause a computer to crash.

d. If an e-mail attachment doesn't work, you may have to resort to a faxed copy of the document. It will get there just as fast.

Responding to Messages

1385   To respond to a message, press *Reply*. The sender's name will automatically appear in the *To:* box. The sender's subject line will appear in the *Subject* box preceded by *Re:*. Type your message above (or below) the original message. Sometimes comments in a different size and colour of font are included in the midst of the original message where an answer or observation is required.

> NOTE: If the original message was sent to several people and you would like your response to go to all of them as well, click *Reply to All*. Otherwise, your response will go only to the sender.

Forwarding Messages

1386 a. Before you forward a message you have received, ask yourself whether the person who wrote it would like other people to read it. The message may contain confidential statements that were intended only for your eyes. If you are not completely sure that it is safe to proceed, do not forward the message—or at least don't do so without first consulting the writer.

b. Messages that have been forwarded several times typically display names and e-mail addresses of people who never intended to have their addresses publicized in this way. Be sure to delete all this material before you forward the original message to others.

c. If you *forward* an e-mail message that came with an attachment, the attachment will also be forwarded. If you *reply* to an e-mail message that came with an attachment, the recipient will not receive a copy of the attachment.

 See the Online Learning Centre at www.mcgrawhill.ca/college/gregg for related Web links.

SECTION FOURTEEN

Reports and Manuscripts

☞ *See Section 17 for Outlines.*

REPORTS

Reports serve all kinds of purposes. Some simply communicate information without any attempt to analyze or interpret the data. Others offer extensive analyses and make detailed recommendations for further action. As a result, reports come in all sizes and shapes. Some are done informally as memos or letters. Others consist of fill-ins on printed or computer-generated forms. Many, however, are done in a more formal style. There is a wide variation to be found in what is considered acceptable. Regardless of which guidelines you follow, be prepared to modify them to fit a specific situation.

"Contemporary" Report Template Provided by MS Word for Windows

---

14

FilmWatch Division Marketing Plan

Trey's Best Opportunity to Dominate
Market Research for the Film Industry

How To Use This Report Template

Change the information on the cover page to contain the information you would like. For the body of your report, use styles such as Heading 1-5, Body Text, Block Quotation, List Bullet, and List Number from the Styles box on the Formatting toolbar.

Using a Template

1401 Word processing software provides templates, similar to the one illustrated here, that you can use as is or modify to suit your preferences. A title page, table of contents, body, and back matter are usually included in the software, and features like fonts, margins, and headings are preselected.

Section 14 provides guidelines for creating your own formats (or templates) for formal and informal reports. There is a trend today to single space reports to save paper and electronic storage space. This section refers to both single- and double-spaced formats. Note the difference in the two formats when spacing vertically around headings. The following system of notation is used to indicate how many blank lines to leave between elements of a report.

↓2x: Space down 2 times to create 1 blank line.

↓3x: Space down 3 times to create 2 blank lines.

↓6x: Space down 6 times to create 5 blank lines. In the illustration below, this notation suggests that one should space down 6 times from the top default margin of 1 inch to create the appearance of a 2-inch top margin. (Some users prefer to set points "before or after" or to use a vertical advance feature for one-time settings.)

↓2 or 3x: Leave 1 or 2 blank lines at this point. The use of only 1 blank line provides a more condensed appearance and is useful when conserving space is an important consideration. The use of 2 blank lines creates a more open appearance and enhances readability.

The following models show how the first page of an informal report might appear if executed according to the guidelines. To create a more open look, the second model on page 390 is double-spaced and uses the two-blank line style (↓3x) after the title section and before the side headings. The first model (shown below) uses a single-spaced format to save space.

↓ 2" or ↓ 6x

NOTEBOOK COMPUTERS FOR THE FIELD SALES STAFF ↓2x

A Preliminary Assessment ↓2x

By Roger Khartoum ↓2x

November 14, 2006 ↓2x

0.25 to 0.5 inch

⟶ In mid-October the Sales Managers Committee asked me to evaluate notebook   1 inch
1 inch   computers now on the market in light of the need to improve the productivity of our ⟷
⟷ field sales staff. Here are my initial findings. ↓2 or 3x
(minimum)

SELECTION CRITERIA ↓2x

I propose the following criteria for determining which models we should evaluate before we decide which one to adopt.

Processor. The notebook computer we now use is much too slow. The models we consider must have a processor with a minimum processing speed of 1.5 gigahertz.

Memory. Since all the software is Windows-based, these models should

(Continued on page 390.)

In the figure:

2 inches or 6x

NOTEBOOK COMPUTERS FOR THE FIELD SALES STAFF ↓2x

A Preliminary Assessment ↓2x

By Roger Khartoum ↓2x

November 14, 2006 ↓2 or 3x

0.25 to 0.5 inch →

In mid-October the Sales Managers Committee asked me to evaluate notebook ↓2x

1 inch (minimum) → computers now on the market. Here are my initial findings. ↓2 or 3x

1 inch (minimum)

SELECTION CRITERIA ↓2x

Whatever models we select must meet the following specifications.

Processor. If we want to use an IBM-compatible notebook computer, it must

↓2 or 3x
MODELS TO BE CONSIDERED ↓2x

In identifying models that meet the foregoing criteria, we need to remember

that the market changes rapidly. Some of the models that I looked at only a month ago

1 inch

1

Establishing a Format

1402 If you are preparing a report at the request of someone else, always try to get some guidelines from that person on such matters as format, length, amount of detail desired, and distribution. Check the files for copies of similar reports done in the past. If guidelines or models are not provided or if you are doing the report on your own initiative, consider the following factors in choosing a format.

    a. *For whom are you writing the report?* If intended for your supervisor or a colleague on staff, the report could be done simply as a memo. If intended for top management or the board of directors, the report will often require a more formal approach. By the same token, an academic term paper will require a simpler format than a thesis for an advanced degree.

b. *What outcome do you hope to achieve?* If you are merely providing information without attempting to win someone over to your point of view, the simplest and clearest presentation of the information will suffice. If you are trying to persuade the reader to adopt your viewpoint and accept your recommendations, you may need to make a detailed argument and devise a more complex structure for your report.

c. *What is the existing attitude of your reader?* You may need to write a number of chapters, grouped by part. If you need to demonstrate that your argument is supported by much detailed research, you may have to quote from published sources and present an elaborate set of data in the form of tables and charts. If you know that your intended reader already supports your argument or simply wants your judgment on a certain matter, a shorter and simpler document will usually suffice.

Parts of a Formal Report

1403 A *formal* report typically has three parts: front matter, body, and back matter. Each of these parts, in turn, contains some (if not all) of the following elements in the sequence indicated.

a. Front Matter

TITLE PAGE	*In a business report:* gives the full title, the subtitle (if any), the writer's name, title, and department, and the date of submission; may also indicate for whom the report was written. *In an academic report:* gives the name of the writer, the instructor, and the course, along with the date of submission. (See ¶1413.)
LETTER OR MEMO OF TRANSMITTAL	May be done as a letter (for distribution outside the company) or as a memo (for inside distribution); may be clipped to the front of the report (or to the binder in which the report is inserted); may be inserted in the report itself as the page preceding the title page. (See ¶1414.)
TABLE OF CONTENTS	A list of all chapters (by number and title), along with the opening page number of each chapter. If chapters are grouped by part, the titles of the parts also appear in the table of contents. Sometimes main headings within the chapters are also given under each chapter title. Also list other sections not included in a chapter—such as a preface or an appendix. (See ¶¶1415–1416.)
LISTS OF TABLES AND ILLUSTRATIONS	Separate lists of tables and illustrations are included if they are numerous and likely to be frequently referred to by the reader. (See ¶¶1417–1418.)
FOREWORD	Written by someone other than the author of the report. May explain who commissioned the report, the reasons for doing so, and the qualifications of the writer to prepare the report. May also offer an evaluation of the report and may ask those who receive copies of the report to give their assessment or take some other action after they have read the report. (See ¶1419.)

(Continued on page 392.)

PREFACE	Written by the author of the report. Indicates for whom the report is written, the objectives and the scope of the report, and the methods used to assemble the material in the report. Acknowledgments of help received on the report are usually included here (placed at the end), but if special emphasis is desired, the acknowledgments can be treated as a separate element of the front matter, immediately following the preface. (See ¶1419.)
SUMMARY	Preferably limited to one page (two pages at most); designed to save the reader's time by presenting conclusions and recommendations right at the outset of the report. If there is no preface, the summary also includes some of the material that would have gone there. (See ¶1420.)

b. Body

INTRODUCTION	Sets forth (in greater detail than the preface) the objectives, the scope, and the methods, along with any other relevant background information. In a report with several chapters, the introduction may precede the first chapter of the text or be labelled as Chapter 1. (See ¶1422.)
MAIN DISCUSSION	Sets forth all the pertinent data, evidence, analyses, and interpretations needed to fulfil the purpose of the report. May consist of one long chapter that opens with an introduction and closes with conclusions and recommendations. May consist of several chapters; these may be grouped into *parts*, with a part-title page inserted to introduce each sequence of chapters. May use different levels of headings throughout the text to show what the discussion covers and how it is organized. (See ¶¶1423–1427.)
CONCLUSIONS	Summarizes the key points and the recommendations that the writer hopes the reader will be persuaded to accept. In a report with several chapters, this is the final chapter or the final part.

c. Back Matter

APPENDICES	A collection of tables, charts, or other data too specific or too lengthy to be included in the body of the report but provided here as supporting detail for the interested reader. (See ¶1429.)
ENDNOTES	A collection—all in one place at the end of the report—of what would otherwise appear as footnotes at the bottom of various pages in the report. (See ¶¶1501–1502, 1505–1506.)
BIBLIOGRAPHY	A list of all sources (1) that were consulted in the preparation of the report and (2) from which material was derived or directly quoted. (See ¶¶1545–1549.)
GLOSSARY	A list of terms (with definitions) that may not be readily understood when encountered in the body of the report. (See ¶1431.) May be treated as an appendix.

Parts of an Informal Report

1404 a. An *informal* report has no front matter. The information that would go on a separate title page appears at the top of the first page and is immediately followed by the body of the report. (See ¶¶1410–1412 for format guidelines.)

b. An informal report typically contains no back matter except possibly a list of *endnotes* (in place of separate footnotes throughout the body of the report) and a *bibliography*. (See ¶1505 for an illustration of endnotes and ¶1549 for an illustration of a bibliography.) Tables that cannot be easily incorporated in the body of the informal report may also be placed in an appendix in the back matter.

Margins
1405 Side Margins

a. Unbound Reports. If a report is to remain unbound or will simply be stapled in the upper left corner, use default side margins. (If the overall length of the report is not a problem, you can increase the side margins equally to give the report a more open look. See ¶1305b for guidelines on increasing margins.)

b. Bound Reports. Use a 1.5-inch left margin and a 1-inch right margin. (The extra half inch at the left will provide space for the binding.)

1406 Top and Bottom Margins of Opening Pages

The following guidelines apply to (1) the first page of each chapter, (2) the first page of each distinct element in the front matter and back matter, and (3) the

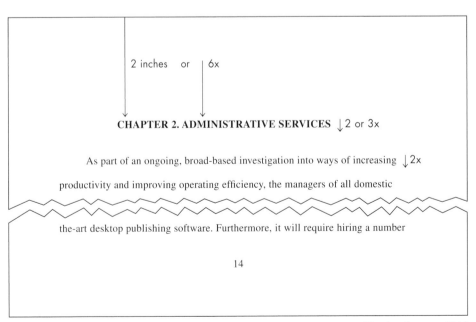

(Continued on page 394.)

first page of an informal report that consists of only one chapter (without any separate title page or other front matter). (See the illustration on page 390.)

a. On these opening pages, leave a top margin of 2 inches and use the default bottom margin (usually 1 inch). **EXCEPTION:** Title pages and part-title pages may be centred on the page by using the software page command to centre vertically.

b. Opening pages do not need page numbers. If showing a page is preferred, use the page numbering feature of the software to place the *page number only* at the bottom centre or the bottom right of the page.

c. Ordinarily, nothing is keyed in the space that represents the top margin. However, in informal academic reports, certain information is often keyed in the upper right or left corner. (See ¶1412.)

14

1407 Top and Bottom Margins of Other Pages

a. Use the default top and bottom margins of 1 inch.

b. For pages in the *body* and *back matter* of a report, use the page numbering feature of your word processing software and position the page number at the top centre or top right position. The word *Page* may also be used in the top right position only. Leave 1 or 2 blank lines before continuing the text. If you wish to provide additional information along with the page number (for example, the report or chapter title), use the header feature of your software rather than the page numbering feature. (See ¶1411c.)

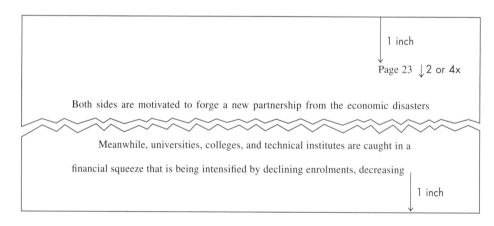

1 inch

Page 23 ↓2 or 4x

Both sides are motivated to forge a new partnership from the economic disasters

Meanwhile, universities, colleges, and technical institutes are caught in a

financial squeeze that is being intensified by declining enrolments, decreasing

1 inch

c. For pages in the *front matter* of a report, use the page numbering feature of your software to centre the page number at the bottom of the page. (See ¶1421.) Some software includes one blank line before the page number. If two blank lines are preferred before the page number line, make the necessary adjustments. If you wish to provide additional information along with the page number, use the footer feature of your software.

1 inch

Part Three will explore alternative recommendations for improving working

Part Six will analyze the advantages and disadvantages of constructing a

new, fully-automated facility for the manufacturing division as opposed to an

vii

14

1408 Handling Page Breaks

Your word processing software can help you avoid most page-ending problems as outlined in *a–d*. There are, however, page-ending situations in which you must use your own judgment as outlined in *e*.

a. The *page numbering feature* ensures that the bottom margin will always be 1 inch (or whatever margin setting you have selected). When your text reaches the bottom margin, the computer automatically inserts a page break, called a *soft page break*, to begin a new page (even if part of a sentence is carried to the top of the next page). Because a *soft page break* is defined by the computer program, it cannot be adjusted. If you do not like what the computer has done, you may insert a *hard page break*. (See ¶1408b.)

NOTE: The *preview* feature permits you to see an entire page on the screen before printing so that you can tell whether adjustments will be necessary. See ¶1408e–f below for page-ending situations that may require adjustments.

b. A *hard page break* permits you to end a page wherever you want and ensures that any copy that follows will appear at the top of the next page.

c. To prevent a single line of a paragraph from being left at the bottom of a page or carried over to the top of a new page, use the *widow/orphan* feature of your software. This will ensure that a minimum of two lines of a paragraph will stay together at a page ending or a page beginning. The widow/orphan feature should be turned on for any document that will be more than one page. In some software, it is on by default.

d. The *block protect* feature (or *keep lines together* or *keep with next*) ensures that a designated block of copy (such as a table, an enumerated list, or selected lines of text) will not be divided at the bottom of a page but will, if necessary, be carried over intact to the top of the next page. This feature should

(Continued on page 396.)

also be used to keep a heading with at least two lines of text together on the same page.

NOTE: If a list of items (see ¶1425e–f) has to be divided at the bottom of the page, try to **divide between items** (not within an item). Moreover, try to leave at least two items at the bottom of one page and carry over at least two items to the top of the next. If you do need to divide *within* an item, leave at least two lines at the bottom of one page and carry over at least two lines to the next.

e. If it is not possible to start a table at the desired point of reference and have it all fit on the same page, then insert a parenthetical note at the appropriate point in the text (referring the reader to the next page) and continue with the text to the bottom of the page. At the top of the next page, key the complete table, leave 1 to 3 blank lines, and resume keying the text. (See Section 16 for guidelines on the typing of tables.)

NOTE: If a table is so long that it will not fit on one page even when single-spaced, then look for a sensible division point in the body of the table and end the first page there. At the top of the next page, use software commands to repeat the complete title of the table and any column headings before continuing with the rest of the table. If there is any possibility that a reader could mistake the first part of the divided table as the complete table, key a continuation line (in parentheses or brackets) at the point where the table breaks off. (See ¶1635 for details.)

1409 Shortening a Long Report

When the cost of photocopying and distributing a large number of copies of a long report becomes prohibitive, consider the following devices for reducing the number of pages without having to cut the copy. (Note that these devices will also reduce the readability and the attractiveness of the report, so use them only in extreme circumstances.)

a. Use a smaller font size or choose a different font that yields more characters to an inch.

b. Reduce the standard top margin for all opening pages from 2 inches to 1.5 inches. (See ¶1406.)

c. Reduce side margins, top and bottom margins, or a combination of both for all other pages from 1 inch to as small as 0.5 inch.

NOTE: It may not be possible to reduce the top or bottom margin if the header, footer, or page numbering feature is placed in the margin area.

d. Single space the report (but always leave 1 blank line between paragraphs).

e. If the report has only one level of heading, use paragraph headings rather than side headings. (See ¶1426.)

f. Whenever the guidelines call for 2 blank lines between elements, use only 1.5 blank lines. Wherever 1 blank line is called for, reduce it to half a line.

Informal Business Reports

These guidelines apply to business reports that consist of only one chapter and have no separate title page or other front matter.

1410 If the first page is keyed on a *blank sheet of paper* (as in the illustration below):

a. Leave a top margin of 2 inches.

b. Set single spacing while executing the title, the subtitle, the writer's name, and the date, but leave one blank line between each element.

c. Key the title of the report centred in all-capital letters. If a subtitle is used, key it centred in capital and small letters on the second line below the main title. (If the title or subtitle is long, divide it into sensible phrases and arrange them on two or more single-spaced lines.)

NOTE: Use boldface for the title and subtitle (and for the writer's name and the date as well). The by-line and the date are optional and may be omitted.

d. If *By* and the writer's name are used, centre them in capital and small letters on the second line below the title and subtitle.

e. If a date is used, type the date on which the report is to be submitted on the second line, centred, below the writer's name.

NOTE: Additional details that appear on a title page (such as the writer's title and affiliation or the name and affiliation of the person or group for whom the report has been prepared) are omitted when the title starts on the same page as the body. If these elements are needed, you will have to prepare a separate title page. (See ¶1413.)

f. On the second or third line below the date, start the body of the report. (See ¶¶1425–1426.) At this point continue to use single spacing or switch to 1.5 or double spacing.

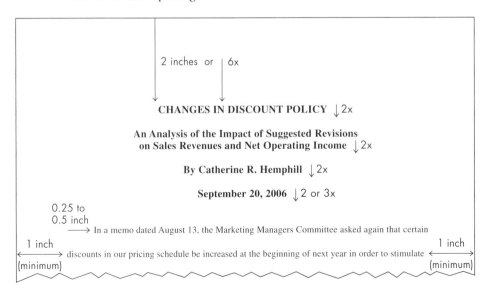

(Continued on page 398.)

NOTE: On the first page of an informal business report, a page number is not required. If the writer wishes to include a page number, it should be centred at the bottom of the page. Use the page numbering or footer feature of the software. (See ¶1407c.)

g. If the report requires more than one page, use the page numbering feature to automatically insert the page number at the top right margin of each continuation page. Leave 1 or 2 blank lines below the page number, and resume the text on the following line. (See also ¶1427g.)

> 1 inch
>
> Page 2 ↓2 or 3x
>
> we are expected to produce sales increases of over 20 percent in the first quarter of next year, 18 ↓2x
>
> percent in the second quarter, 15 percent in the third quarter, and 20 percent in the fourth quarter.

h. If the report has one or more elements of back matter—for example, endnotes or a bibliography—follow the style established for a formal report. (See ¶¶1501–1502, 1505–1506, 1545–1549.)

1411 If the first page of a report is prepared in *memo form*:

a. Give the report title (and subtitle, if any) as the *subject* of the memo. Supply all the other elements called for in the heading of the memo in the usual way. (See ¶¶1374–1375.)

b. Begin keying the body of the report on the second or third line below the last fill-in line in the heading. (See ¶¶1425–1426.)

c. If the report requires more than one page, use a blank sheet of paper for each continuation page. Key the same kind of continuation heading called for in

> ## MEMORANDUM
>
> **TO:**   Executive Committee ↓2x
>
> **FROM:**   Catherine R. Hemphill ↓2x
>
> **DATE:**   September 20, 2006 ↓2x
>
> **SUBJECT:** Changes in Discount Policy—An Analysis
> of the Impact of Suggested Revisions on
> Sales Revenues and Net Operating Income ↓2 or 3x
>
> In a memo dated August 13, the Marketing Managers Committee asked again that certain

any long memo. (See also ¶1375 note.) Leave 1 or 2 blank lines and resume the text on the following line.

1 inch

Executive Committee   2   September 20, 2006 ↓2 or 3x

OR:

1 inch

Executive Committee
Page 2
September 20, 2006 ↓2 or 3x

NOTE: If several names are included as recipients of a memo report, use an abbreviated subject line to identify page 2 or use the name of the first person in the list with a "See Distribution List" notation.

Jane Wong (See Distribution List)
Page 2
September 20, 2006

Informal Academic Reports

1412 An academic report that consists of only one chapter and has no separate title page or other front matter is keyed like an informal business report (see ¶¶1410–1411) except for the opening of the first page.

1 inch

Blake Trudeau
Mrs. Trenton
History 315
March 8, 2006 ↓2 or 3x

**ECONOMIC FACTORS CONTRIBUTING TO
THE WAR OF 1812** ↓2 or 3x

1 inch
→ INTRODUCTION ↓2x

While much emphasis has been placed on the political factors that led to the

start of the War of 1812, there has not been sufficient evidence to support the truth of

(Continued on page 400.)

a. Leave a default top margin of 1 inch. Type the following information on four separate lines, single-spaced, in the upper left or right corner of the first page: the writer's name, the instructor's name, the course title, and the date. If placed in the right corner, all lines should align at the left and the longest line should end at the right margin.

b. On the second or third line below the date, key the title and subtitle (if any) just as in an informal business report. (See ¶1410b and c.)

c. Start typing the body of the report on the second or third line below the preceding copy (the title or subtitle). At this point switch to double-spacing for the body text.

NOTE: Academic reports sometimes have to be formatted according to the styles of one of the following: the Modern Language Association (http://www.mla.org); the American Psychological Association (http://www.apa.org); or the *Chicago Manual of Style* (www.chicago-manualofstyle.org).

The Front Matter of Formal Reports

The following guidelines deal with the preparation of a title page, a letter or memo of transmittal, a table of contents, a list of tables, a list of illustrations, a preface or foreword, and a summary. For a formal report, only a separate title page is essential; all the other elements are optional.

1413 Title Page

There is no one correct arrangement for the elements on a title page.

- Horizontally centre each line of text leaving similar line spacing between sections.
- Double space between different parts of the same element.
- Use the centre page command to centre text vertically on the page.
  REMEMBER: Be careful not to have extra hard returns before the first line of text and after the last line of text.
- Enhance the title page with a combination of bold, italics, or a maximum of 2 different font sizes.

See the illustrations that follow for acceptable formats.

a. Three-Block Arrangement. Group the material into three blocks of type, and leave equal space above and below the middle block. Position the material as a whole so that it appears centred horizontally and vertically on the page. (See the illustration opposite.)

b. Two-Block Arrangement. Group the material into two blocks of type, and leave at least 5 blank lines between blocks. Centre the material as a whole horizontally and vertically on the page. (See the illustration opposite.)

NOTE: The two-block arrangement works well when the title page does not show the name of the person or group to whom the report is being submitted.

3-Block (Business Report Style)

TITLE TITLE TITLE
TITLE TITLE ↓2x

Subtitle Subtitle
Subtitle ↓6 to 12x

Prepared by ↓2x

Writer's Name
Writer's Title
Writer's Department ↓6 to 12x

Submitted to ↓2x

Name of Individual or Group
Organizational Affiliation ↓2x

Date

2-Block (Academic Report Style)

TITLE TITLE TITLE
TITLE TITLE ↓2x

Subtitle Subtitle
Subtitle ↓6 to 12x

Submitted by
Student's Name ↓2x

Instructor's Name
Course Title ↓2x

Date

14

c. **Margins.** Regardless of which arrangement you use, each line should be short and blocked as attractively as possible.

d. **Title.** Key the title in all-capital letters, using boldface. If the title is long, type it on two or more lines, single-spaced; try to divide the title into meaningful phrases.

e. **Subtitle.** Key the subtitle, if any, in capital and small letters, using boldface. If the subtitle requires more than one line, type it single-spaced. Leave 1 blank line between the main title and the subtitle.

f. **Writer's Identification.** Leave 1 to 2 inches above the writer's identification block. The writer's name may be preceded by the word *By* on the same line or by a phrase such as *Prepared by* or *Submitted by* (or simply *By*) keyed 2 lines above. If appropriate, the writer's name may be followed by a title on the next line and by an organizational affiliation on the following line.

↓6 to 12x

By Doris Eberle
Manager, Telemarketing
Circulation Department

↓6 to 12x

Prepared by ↓2x

Van Nguyen
Acting Director
Marketing Research Unit

(Continued on page 402.)

g. **Reader's Identification.** It is customary (but not essential) to name the individual or group for whom the report has been prepared. Leave 1 to 2 inches before keying *Submitted to* or *Prepared for* or a similar phrase. Then on the second line below, key the name of the individual or the group. On succeeding lines, supply a title, an organizational affiliation, or both.

6 to 12x	6 to 12x
Submitted to ↓2x	**Prepared for** ↓2x
Robert G. Paterno **General Manager** **Corporate Graphic Arts**	**The Finance Committee** **Davenport, Pierson,** **and Associates**

NOTE: As an alternative, provide the reader's identification in the form of a subtitle.

AN ANALYSIS OF COMPUTERIZED GRAPHICS EQUIPMENT ↓2x

A Report to Robert G. Paterno
General Manager, Corporate Graphic Arts

h. **Date.** Supply the date (month, day, and year) on which the report is being submitted. Key it on the second line below the reader's identification block (or, if none is given, on the second line below the writer's identification). (See the illustrations on page 401.)

i. **Graphic Elements.** You can use special display type and add an organizational logo or some other graphic element to enhance the appearance of a title page.

1414 Letter or Memo of Transmittal

a. A formal report is often accompanied by a letter or memo of transmittal. If you are sending the report to people outside the company, use the letter format (see the illustration opposite); if you are sending the report only to people within the company, use a memo transmittal either as a hard copy or an e-mail message.

b. The message usually covers the following points: (1) a brief description of what is being transmitted; (2) a brief reference to the circumstances that prompted the report; (3) if necessary, a brief indication of why the report is being sent to the addressee; and (4) a statement about what action the recipient is expected to take. (See the illustration opposite.)

c. The letter or memo of transmittal is typically clipped to the front of the report. If the report is in a binder, the transmittal document may be clipped to the front of the binder or inserted in the binder before the title page. If it is sent as e-mail, add the report as an attachment to the transmittal document.

ATLANTIC ENTERPRISES INCORPORATED

5280 Duke Street / Halifax, Nova Scotia / B3J 1P4 / 902-555-5166 Fax: 902-555-5167

↓2 inches from top of page or ↓2 or 3x

February 5, 2006 ↓4 to 6x

Mr. Frank M. Eggleston
Blockhouse Hill Road
Lunenburg, NS B0J 2C0 ↓2x

Dear Frank: ↓2x

1 inch Enclosed is a copy of the report, "Acquisition of Desktop Publishing Equipment," 1 inch
←——→ which I just completed for George Pendergast. Because of your expertise in this ←——→
(minimum) area, George has suggested that I send you the report with the hope that you (minimum)
might offer your comments and suggestions. ↓2x

Because we need to make a decision by April 1 on what equipment to buy, it
would help us greatly if we could hear from you by March 15. I know that given
your busy schedule, you may not be able to get back to us in writing that quickly.
If you would let George and me take you to lunch, we could talk about the report
then and spare you the need to put your thoughts in writing. ↓2x

I'll call you early next week so that we can decide what would be the best way to
proceed. ↓2x

Sincerely, ↓4 to 6x

Reta Nishikawa

Reta Nishikawa
Senior Systems Analyst
Office Systems Department ↓2x

ctl
Enclosure ↓2x

c:\wpwin\wpdocs\atlantic\transltr.wpd

14

1415 Table of Contents

Most word processing software has a feature that allows the creation of a table
of contents. Users scroll through the text and code (according to the level of
subordination) every part title, chapter title, main heading, and subheading
that should appear in the table of contents. If any titles or headings are subsequently added, deleted, or changed, the table of contents will reflect these
changes.

1416 If you do not like the default style for a table of contents that is provided by
your software, you may be able to modify that style or select a different style. If
you prefer to create your own format, the following guidelines may be helpful.

(Continued on page 404.)

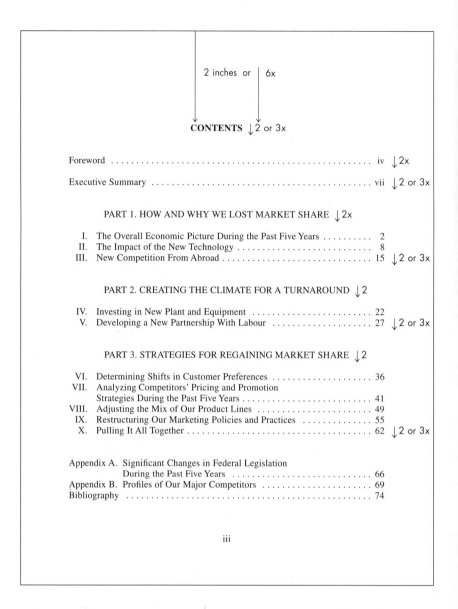

2 inches or │ 6x

CONTENTS ↓2 or 3x

iii

a. Type the table of contents on a new page. (See the illustration above.)

b. Start on line 2 inches. Type *CONTENTS* or *TABLE OF CONTENTS* in all-capital letters centred on the line. Bold the title to make it stand out.

c. On the second or third line below, begin keying the table of contents double-spaced. Use the same side and bottom margins as for the text pages in the body of the report. (See ¶¶1405–1407.)

d. In keying the body of the table of contents, list every separate element that *follows* the table of contents in order—whether in the front matter, the body of the report, or the back matter. In the illustration opposite, note the following aspects of the format:

- Individual entries pertaining to *front matter* and *back matter* begin at the left margin with the title keyed in capital and small letters or in all-capital letters. Set a right leader tab to include a line of leaders and to align the page number (Roman for front matter and Arabic for back matter) at the right margin. Leave 1 or 2 blank lines *after* the front matter entries and 1 or 2 blank lines *before* the back matter entries.

- Centre individual entries pertaining to *part titles* in all-capital letters. The part numbers that precede the titles may be in Arabic or Roman numerals or (for formality) may be spelled out. Leave 1 or 2 blank lines before each part title and 1 blank line after.

- Individual entries pertaining to *chapters* begin with a chapter number (Roman or Arabic), followed by a period, 1 or 2 spaces, and then the chapter title typed in capital and small letters or in all-capital letters. Set a right or decimal tab to align Roman chapter numbers at the right with the longest one positioned as close to the left margin as possible. After keying the chapter text, press the right tab key (as set in the first bulleted item above) to include the leaders before you type the page number. Leave 0 or 1 blank line after each chapter title in the listing.

- Some long titles should be keyed on two lines. Type the turnover line single-spaced and aligned with the first letter of the chapter title in the first line.

e. The *main headings* within each chapter may be included in the table of contents. One acceptable arrangement is to indent each heading 2 or 3 spaces from the start of the chapter title and key it in capital and small letters. Key the list of headings for each chapter as a single-spaced block, with 1 blank line above and below it. Page numbers may be provided with the headings if desired.

1417 List of Tables or Illustrations

Your word processing software may have a feature that allows the creation of a list of tables or illustrations and is similar to the feature used to create the table of contents. (See ¶1415 and ¶1416.)

1418 To create your own format, the following guidelines and illustrations may be helpful.

   a. Use a new page for each list. Leave a top margin of 2 inches.

   b. Centre the heading—*TABLES* (or *LIST OF TABLES*) or *ILLUSTRATIONS* (or *LIST OF ILLUSTRATIONS*)—in all-capital letters. Use boldface to make the title stand out.

   c. On the second or third line below the heading, type the first entry in the list. Use the same format as for chapter titles in a table of contents. (See ¶1416.) The tables or the illustrations may be numbered consecutively throughout the report or consecutively within each chapter. The latter technique uses the chapter number as a prefix in the numbering scheme. (See the illustration below.)

```
                          │
                          │ 2 inches  or │ 6x
                          ↓              ↓

                    TABLES  │2 or 3x


1-1.  Annual Sales, 2001–2005 . . . . . . . . . . . . . . . . . . . . . . . . . . . . . . . . .  6  │2x

1-2.  Projected Annual Sales, 2006–2010 . . . . . . . . . . . . . . . . . . . . . . . .  10

1-3.  Estimated Market Share, 2006–2010 . . . . . . . . . . . . . . . . . . . . . . .  13

2-1.  Marketing Costs as a Percentage of Sales . . . . . . . . . . . . . . . . . . . .  16
```

1419 Preface or Foreword

   a. If there is a preface (written by the author) or a foreword (written by someone else), then on a new page centre the appropriate title boldfaced in all-capital letters 2 inches from the top. Note that the correct spelling is *FOREWORD* (not *FORWARD*).

   NOTE: If both a preface and a foreword are to appear in the front matter, the foreword should precede the preface.

   b. Leave 1 or 2 blank lines below the heading and begin keying the actual text. Use the same side and bottom margins as for the text pages in the body of the report. (See ¶¶1405–1407.) Also follow the same guidelines for spacing, indentions, and headings as in the body of the report. (See ¶¶1425–1426.)

   c. The preface should cover the following points: (1) for whom the report is written, (2) what prompted the writing of the report, (3) what the report aims to accomplish, (4) what the report covers and what it does not try to deal with, (5) how the data and the conclusions were arrived at, and (6) acknowledgments of those individuals and organizations who helped the writer of the report.

NOTE: The acknowledgments may be treated as a separate element in the front matter, following the foreword and the preface (in that sequence if both are given) and using the same format.

d. The typical foreword deals with these topics: (1) who commissioned the report, (2) the reasons for doing so, (3) the writer's qualifications for undertaking the assignment, (4) an assessment of the job that the writer has done, and (5) a call for some follow-up action on the part of those who receive copies of the report.

1420 Summary

a. If there is to be a summary (frequently called an *executive summary*), follow the format guidelines for prefaces in ¶1419a–b.

b. Since this element is intended to be a time-saver, keep it short—ideally one page, at most two pages. The summary may be handled as a series of ordinary text paragraphs or as a series of paragraphs typed as items in a list. (See ¶1425e–g.)

1421 Numbering Front Matter Pages

a. On all pages of front matter except the title page, use the page numbering or footer feature of the software to place the page number in the bottom margin of the document.

b. Key the page number in small Roman numerals (*ii, iii, iv,* and so on).

c. Consider the title page as *page i,* even though no number appears on that page.

The Body of Formal Reports

1422 Introduction

a. If the body of a report contains several chapters and begins with a formal introduction, treat the introduction either as Chapter 1 or as a distinct element preceding Chapter 1.

- If you decide to treat it as Chapter 1, then consider *INTRODUCTION* to be the title of this chapter and handle it as you would any other title on a chapter-opening page. (See ¶1424.)
- If you decide to have the introduction precede Chapter 1, use a new page, leave a 2-inch top margin, and centre in all-capital letters *INTRODUCTION.* Use the boldface feature to make the heading stand out. On the second or third line below the heading begin the actual text.
- In either case treat the first page of the introduction as page 1 of the report. (See ¶1427.)

☞ *For guidelines on margins, see ¶¶1405–1407.*

For guidelines on spacing, indentions, and headings, see ¶¶1425–1426.

(Continued on page 408.)

b. If a report contains only one chapter and begins with an introductory section, treat the title *INTRODUCTION* as a first-level heading (see ¶1426) and key it on the second or third line below the block of copy (title, etc.) at the top of the page.

1423 Part-Title Pages

a. If the report contains several chapters organized in parts, insert a separate part-title page directly in front of the chapter that begins each part.

PART 3 ↓2 or 3x

STRATEGIES FOR
REGAINING MARKET SHARE

NOTE: If the body of the report begins with a formal introduction (see ¶1422a), then the part-title page for Part 1 should *follow* the introduction. (**REASON:** The introduction embraces the whole work and not simply Part 1.)

b. Key the word *PART* and the part number on one line. Underneath key the part title on one or more lines as appropriate. Use all-capital letters, boldface, and arrange the copy for maximum display effect. Centre the copy as a whole, horizontally and vertically.

1424 Chapter-Opening Pages

a. Use a new page for each opening page of a chapter. Leave a 2-inch top margin.

b. Centre and boldface the chapter number and title in all-capital letters.

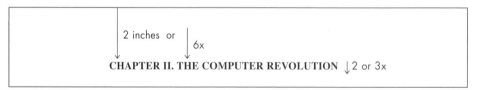

2 inches or
↓6x
CHAPTER II. THE COMPUTER REVOLUTION ↓2 or 3x

---

c. If the title is long, divide it into sensible phrases and arrange them on two or more single-spaced lines. Put the chapter number on a line by itself, and leave 1 blank line before starting the chapter title.

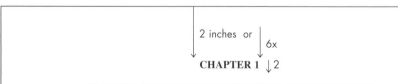

2 inches or
↓6x
CHAPTER 1 ↓2

**FACTORS CURRENTLY RESTRICTING OPPORTUNITIES
FOR INCREASED PRODUCTIVITY** ↓2 or 3x

---

d. Leave 1 or 2 blank lines and begin typing the first line of copy (whether text matter or a heading) on the second or third line below the title.

1425 Text Spacing and Indentions

a. **Text.** To enhance readability, double space all text matter. However, use single spacing or 1.5-line spacing when the report is short or when the costs of paper, photocopying, file space, and mailing are important considerations. Many writers include one blank line only before side headings when using this format. (See the illustration on page 391 and ¶1409 for a number of ways to shorten a long report.)

☞ *For guidelines on dividing words and word groups at the ends of lines and between one page and the next, see ¶¶901–920; for guidelines on the use of footnotes, endnotes, or textnotes, see Section 15; for guidelines on whether or not to justify the right margin, see ¶1343f–g.*

b. **Drafts.** Always double or triple space drafts that are to be submitted for editing or evaluation.

c. **Paragraphs.** Indent text paragraphs 0.25 inch to 0.5 inch. Leave 1 blank line between paragraphs, whether the text is typed in single-, double-, or 1.5-line spacing.

☞ *For guidelines on dividing short paragraphs at the bottom of a page, see ¶¶1408c.*

d. **Quoted Material.** If a quotation will make four or more lines, treat it as a single-spaced extract, leave 1 blank line above and below the extract, and use the word processing feature that will automatically indent *each side* margin by an additional 0.5 inch (sometimes called *double indent*). If the quoted matter represents the start of a paragraph in the original, indent the first word an additional 0.25 inch to 0.5 inch.

☞ *For another illustration, see page 338.*

e. **Items in a List.** Key the list single-spaced with 1 blank line above and below the list as a whole. (See ¶107.) Key the list on the full width of the text (as shown in ¶1425g); or for a more attractive format (especially when paragraph indentions are in the text), use the word processing double indent feature to indent the lines 0.5 inch from *each side* margin. (See ¶1425d above

(Continued on page 410.)

and the illustration below.) If any item in the list requires more than one line, leave a blank line after each item in the list.

NOTE: Sometimes a list of one-line items (with no turnovers) is double-spaced to enhance the readability.

☞ *For an example, see the illustration of an agenda in Section 17.*

14

f. **Enumerated Items in a List.** If each of the items begins with a number or a letter, you may use the numbered list feature of your word processing software. Each item will begin at the left margin, and turnovers will be indented to align with the first word in the line above. However, when the first line of each text paragraph is indented 0.5 inch (as is often done in reports), an enumerated list that falls within the text looks best when indented 0.5 inch from each margin. (See the illustration below.)

When you use the numbered list feature, the list will be typed single-spaced. Refer to your software for various ways to set this automatic function.

☞ *See ¶1344d note on the formatting of enumerated items in a list.*

g. **Bulleted Items in a List.** Instead of numbers or letters, you can use *bullets*, especially if there is no need to draw attention to a particular order of items. Choose from a variety of styles:

Circles: ○ ●   Triangles: ▷ ▶   Squares: □ ■   Other: > → *

> 0.5 inch $\longrightarrow$ In evaluating various companies as candidates for acquisition, we must address three basic questions: ↓2x
>
> 1 inch (minimum) $\longleftrightarrow$
>
> • What should be our criteria for identifying desirable candidates for acquisition? ↓2x
>
> • How much should we be prepared to pay? ↓2x
>
> • To what extent will each acquisition affect our overall financial performance? ↓2x
>
> 1 inch (minimum) $\longleftrightarrow$
>
>   Naturally, broad questions like these lead to a great number of other questions. We lack the internal resources to deal with the additional problems that

Most word processing software now sets bullets to default at 0.25 inches with text and turnover (runover) lines set to 0.5 inches. If you prefer, reset the bullets to begin at the left margin and reset the text indent to 0.25 inches. (See the illustration above.)

14

h. Tables. The table feature of your software should be used for the most efficient creation of tables. Establish one style of spacing for all tables within a given report.

☞ *See Section 16 for a full discussion on how to plan and execute tables and for numerous illustrations.*

1426 Text Headings

Headings let the reader see at a glance the scope of the writer's discussion and the way in which it is organized. Therefore, make sure that the headings used throughout the report properly reflect the coverage and the structure of the material. It is also essential that the headings be keyed in a way that clearly indicates different levels of importance or subordination.

Here are several techniques for achieving these objectives:

a. Try to limit yourself to three levels of text headings (not counting the chapter title). If you use more than three levels of text headings, it will be difficult for the reader to grasp the typographical distinction between one level and another. Moreover, the use of more than three levels of text headings suggests that you may be trying to cram too much into one chapter. Consider a different organization of the material to solve this problem.

NOTE: Carefully select typefaces, type sizes, attributes (such as boldface, italics, and so on), and heading style (centred, side, or paragraph headings) that clearly distinguish one level of text heading from another and the headings from the text.

b. Before preparing the final version of the report, make an outline of the heading structure as it then stands and analyze it for:

• *Comprehensiveness.* When the headings are viewed as a whole, do they cover all aspects of the discussion, or are some topics not properly represented?

(Continued on page 412.)

- *Balance.* Is one part of a chapter loaded with headings while a comparable part has only one or two?
- *Parallel structure.* Are the headings all worded in a similar way, or are some complete sentences and others simply phrases? (See ¶1085.)

On the basis of this analysis, revise the headings as necessary.

NOTE: Using the outline feature of your word processing software will greatly simplify the process of reviewing and improving the wording of the headings. You can use this feature to generate a complete list of the headings as they currently appear in the report. Any changes in wording that you make in the text will automatically be reflected in a newly generated outline.

c. Headings come in three styles:

- A *centred heading* is one centred on a line by itself, with 1 to 3 blank lines above (see ¶1426g) and 1 blank line below. Use boldface and all-capital letters. If the heading is too long to fit on one line, centre the turnover on the following line. (See ¶1426e–g for illustrations.)
- A *side heading* starts flush with the left margin, on a line by itself. For a double-spaced report, leave 2 blank lines above (see ¶1426g for an exception) and 1 blank line below. (See the illustrations in ¶1426d–g.) However, if a side heading comes directly below a centred heading (no intervening text), leave only 1 blank line above the side heading. (See the first illustration in ¶1426e.) Key every side heading in boldface, using all-capital letters or initial capitals and lowercase letters.
- A *paragraph heading* (also called a *run-in heading*) is one that begins a paragraph and is immediately followed by text matter on the same line. Like all new paragraphs, a paragraph that begins with a run-in heading should be preceded by 1 blank line (whether the text is keyed with single-, double-, or 1.5-line spacing). Indent a paragraph heading 0.25 or 0.5 inch from the left margin. Key it in initial capitals and lowercase letters, using any combination of boldface or italics. The paragraph heading should be followed by a period (unless some other mark of punctuation, such as a question mark, is required). The text then begins 1 to 2 spaces after the mark of punctuation. (See the illustrations in ¶1426e–f.)

☞ *For capitalization in headings, see ¶¶360, 363.*

d. In a report that calls for only *one* level of heading, choose a side heading and use one of the styles shown below.

XXXXXXXXXXXXXXXXXXXXXXXXXXXXXXXX
XXXXXXXXXXXXX. ↓2 or 3x

SIDE HEADING ↓2x

    Xxxxxxxxxxxxxxxxxxxxxxxxx
XXXXXXXXXXXXXXXXXXXXXXXXXXXXXXXX

XXXXXXXXXXXXXXXXXXXXXXXXXXXXXXXX
XXXXXXXXXXXXX. ↓2 or 3x

Side Heading ↓2x

    Xxxxxxxxxxxxxxxxxxxxxxxxx
XXXXXXXXXXXXXXXXXXXXXXXXXXXXXXXX

e. In a report that calls for *two* levels of headings, choose one of the styles shown below.

```
xxxxxxxxxxxxxxxxxxxxxxxxxxxxxxxxxxx          xxxxxxxxxxxxxxxxxxxxxxxxxxxxxxxxxxx
xxxxxxxxxxxxx. ↓2 or 3x                      xxxxxxxxxxxxx. ↓2 or 3x


        CENTRED HEADING ↓2x                  SIDE HEADING ↓2x

Side Heading ↓2x                                    Paragraph Heading.  Xxxxxxxx
                                            xxxxxxxxxxxxxxxxxxxxxxxxxxxxxxxxxxx
        Xxxxxxxxxxxxxxxxxxxxxxxxxxxxx        xxxxxxxxxxxxxxxxxxxxxxxxxxxxxxxxxxx
xxxxxxxxxxxxxxxxxxxxxxxxxxxxxxxxxxx          xxxxxxxxxxxxxxxxxxxxxxxxxxxxxxxxxxx
```

f. In a report with *three* levels of headings, choose one of the following styles.

```
xxxxxxxxxxxxxxxxxxxxxxxxxxxxxxxxxxx          xxxxxxxxxxxxxxxxxxxxxxxxxxxxxxxxxxx
xxxxxxxxxxxxx. ↓2 or 3x                      xxxxxxxxxxxxx. ↓2 or 3x


        CENTRED HEADING ↓2x                          CENTRED HEADING ↓2x


        Xxxxxxxxxxxxxxxxxxxxxxxxxxxx                 Xxxxxxxxxxxxxxxxxxxxxxxxxxxx
xxxxxxxxxxxxxxxxxxxxxxxxxxxxxxxxxxx↓2 or 3x   xxxxxxxxxxxxxxxxxxxxxxxxxxxxxxxxxxx↓2 or 3x


Side Heading ↓2x                             SIDE HEADING ↓2x

    Paragraph Heading.  Xxxxxxxx                Paragraph Heading.  Xxxxxxxxx
xxxxxxxxxxxxxxxxxxxxxxxxxxxxxxxxxxx          xxxxxxxxxxxxxxxxxxxxxxxxxxxxxxxxxxx
```

g. When showing double-spaced (body) text, the word processing software sometimes makes it difficult or awkward to leave 2 blank lines above centred and side headings. In this case, some writers choose one of the following styles. However, be consistent in your pattern of choices.

```
xxxxxxxxxxxxxxxxxxxxxxxxxxxxxxxxxxx          xxxxxxxxxxxxxxxxxxxxxxxxxxxxxxxxxxx
xxxxxxxxxxxxx. ↓4x                           xxxxxxxxxxxxxxxxxxxxxxxxxxxxxxxxxxx
                                            xxxxxxxxxxxxx. ↓2x

                                            Side Heading ↓2x

        CENTRED HEADING ↓2x                         Xxxxxxxxxxxxxxxxxxxxxxxxxxx
                                            xxxxxxxxxxxxxxxxxxxxxxxxxxxxxxxxxxx
        Xxxxxxxxxxxxxxxxxxxxxxxxxxx          xxxxxxxxxxxxxxxxxxxxxxxxxxxxxxxxxxx
xxxxxxxxxxxxxxxxxxxxxxxxxxxxxxxxxxx
```

1427 Numbering Text Pages

a. When the page numbering feature of your software is used, the page number will be properly positioned in the header or footer section on each page in the correct sequence. If you later add or delete copy in a way that changes the overall length of the report, the page numbering will be automatically adjusted. Some writers place all page numbers in a footer section.

NOTE: The page numbering feature will often leave only 1 blank line after a page number at the top of a page or before a page number at the bottom. However, for a better appearance, you can increase this space to 2 blank lines.

b. When the first page contains the title of the report and the body starts on the same page, count this as page 1. Generally, no page number is required on this page; but if one is desired, it must be set at the bottom of the page, regardless of the numbering format used for successive pages.

NOTE: With the page numbering feature, you can prevent or suppress a page number from being printed, yet still have the page counted in the overall numerical sequence.

c. When the report begins with a formal title page and one or more additional pages of front matter, give these pages a separate numbering sequence, using small *Roman* numerals. (See ¶1421.)

d. In a formal report, consider the first page *following* the front matter as page 1 in the *Arabic* numbering sequence.

e. If a part-title page is included in the report (see ¶1423), consider it in the numbering sequence for the body of the report. No page number is required on this page. However, if one is preferred, it must be at the bottom of the page, regardless of the numbering format followed for successive pages.

f. On the first page of each new element in the body or back matter of the report, use the page numbering or footer feature to centre the page number at the bottom of the page. Leave 2 blank lines above the page number.

g. On all other pages in the body or back matter of the report, place the page number in the same position on each page. Use the page numbering or the header/footer feature of your software program. Common placements include top-centred, top right-aligned, bottom-centred, and bottom right-aligned positions. At any right-aligned position, the word *Page* may be added. Adjust the header to include a top margin of 1 inch and 2 blank lines after the header. For a bottom-page placement, leave 2 blank lines above the page number.

h. If the final version of a report is to be printed on both sides of the paper (as in a book), the odd-numbered pages will appear on the front side of each sheet and the even-numbered pages on the back. If the report is bound, then on a spread of two facing pages, the even-numbered pages will appear on the left and the odd-numbered pages on the right. In such cases it is more

```
14 ↓2 or 3x                          ↓2 or 3x  15

xxxxxxxxxxxxxxxxxxxxxxxxxxxxxxxxxx    xxxxxxxxxxxxxxxxxxxxxxxxxxxxxxxxxx
xxxxxxxxxxxxxxxxxxxxxxxxxxxxxxxxxx    xxxxxxxxxxxxxxxxxxxxxxxxxxxxxxxxxx
```

convenient for the reader if the page numbers at the top or bottom of the page appear at the outside corners, as in the illustration above.

NOTE: You can direct the page numbering feature of a your word processing software to alternate the placement of these page numbers in the outside corners, depending on whether the page has an odd or even number.

i. In a long report with several chapters written by different authors under a tight deadline, it may be necessary to prepare the final version of the chapters out of order. In such cases, you may use a separate sequence of page numbers for each chapter, with the chapter number serving as a prefix. Thus, for example, the pages in Chapter 1 would be numbered 1-1, 1-2, 1-3, . . . ; those in Chapter 2 would be numbered 2-1, 2-2, 2-3, . . . ; and so on.

NOTE: If the authors submit their material on disk, it is possible to renumber the entire report at the last minute, using one continuous sequence of numbers throughout.

The Back Matter of Formal Reports

1428 Following the last page of the body of the report are those elements of back matter that may be needed: appendices, endnotes, bibliography, and glossary. Begin each of these elements on a new page. Use the same margins as for other pages in the report (see ¶¶1405–1407), and treat the numbering of these pages as discussed in ¶1427f–i.

1429 Appendices

a. If you plan to include more than one appendix, number or letter each one in order. (For an example of the treatment of two appendices, see the illustration of the table of contents on page 404.)

b. On a new page, start on line 2 inches. Centre and boldface in all-capital letters the word *APPENDIX* (plus a number or letter, if appropriate).

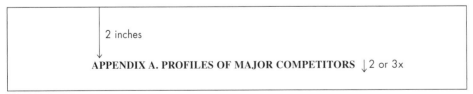

```
        2 inches
         ↓
    APPENDIX A. PROFILES OF MAJOR COMPETITORS  ↓2 or 3x
```

NOTE: If the title is long, key it in two or more centred lines, single-spaced. Leave 1 blank line before starting the appendix title.

(Continued on page 416.)

```
                    2 inches  or   6x

                    APPENDIX A   ↓2x

                SIGNIFICANT CHANGES IN
              FEDERAL LEGISLATION DURING
                THE PAST FIVE YEARS   ↓2 or 3x
```

    c. Leave 1 or 2 blank lines above the body of the appendix. Since this material may be a table, a chart, a list, or regular text, choose the format that displays this copy to the best effect.

1430 Endnotes and Bibliography

For detailed guidelines, see ¶¶1501–1502, 1505–1506, 1545–1549.

1431 Glossary

If you plan a glossary, then on a new page centre *GLOSSARY* or some other heading in boldface and all-capital letters. Leave a 2-inch top margin and begin the text on the second or third line below. There are a variety of ways to set up a glossary.

    a. Two Columns. In the left column, list the terms in alphabetic order, using boldface or italics. In the right column, put the corresponding definition. Begin the right column at least 2 to 3 spaces to the right of the longest term in the left column. Single space each definition, and align turnover lines flush with the left margin of the column. Leave 1 blank line between entries.

    NOTE: The table feature of your software can be used to create these columns.

```
Elliptical expression   A condensed expression from which key words are omitted.  ↓2x

Essential elements      Words, phrases, or clauses that are necessary to the com-
                        pleteness of the structure or the meaning of a sentence.
```

    b. Hanging Indention. Begin each term at the left margin, using boldface or italics. Follow with a colon, a dash, or some other device and then the definition. Key the definition single-spaced, and indent turnover lines 0.25 to 0.5 inch so that the term in the first line will stand out. Leave 1 blank line between entries. (Most software includes a hanging indent feature, which automatically indents the turnover lines.)

```
               elliptical expression: a condensed expression from which key words are
0.5 inch ⟶ omitted.  ↓2x

               essential elements: words, phrases, or clauses that are necessary to the
                   completeness of the structure or the meaning of a sentence.
```

c. **Paragraph Style.** Indent each term 0.25 to 0.5 inch from the left margin, using boldface or italics. Follow with a colon, a dash, or some other device and then the definition. Key the definition single-spaced, with turnover lines flush with the left margin. Leave 1 blank line between entries.

0.5 inch ———→ **Elliptical expression**—a condensed expression from which key words are omitted. ↓2×

        Essential elements—words, phrases, or clauses that are necessary to the completeness of the structure or the meaning of a sentence.

NOTE: Regardless of the format selected, the terms may be keyed with initial caps or all in small letters (except for proper nouns and adjectives). The definitions may also be styled either way; however, if they are written in sentence form, it is best to use initial caps for both the term and the definition. The use of periods at the end of definitions is optional unless, of course, the definitions are written as complete sentences. (See the illustration in ¶1431a for an example of the use of initial caps for both the term and the definition.)

14

MANUSCRIPTS

The preparation of manuscripts is subject to virtually the same considerations that apply to reports (¶¶1401–1431). However, manuscripts differ from reports in one fundamental way: They are written with the idea of publication in mind—as a book, magazine article, or bulletin or newsletter item. As a result, manuscripts require special formatting.

When you submit your manuscript to a publisher, the hard copy should be sent with a copy of your manuscript disk. It is possible that each copy may need to be formatted differently. Since the publisher will format the final text themselves, the disk be simply formatted with nothing more than double spacing and 1-inch side margins.

Preparing Manuscript for an Article

1432 If you have been invited to write an article for a specific publication, obtain as much format information as possible from the publisher. General instructions may be included in the publication itself, and the Web site is a good reference source.

1433 If it has been impossible to obtain format information from a publisher, follow a report style that shows headings clearly.

    a. Select a suitable font style and size.

    b. Choose a common paragraph indention for your copy.

    c. Leave one space after an ending punctuation mark. (See ¶298).

(Continued on page 418.)

d. Key your manuscript double-spaced to allow room for editing.

e. Print on one side of the paper only.

f. Be sure to keep the overall length of your manuscript within the range of the number of words typically used by the intended publication. There is little point in submitting a 2000-line manuscript to a publication that carries articles of no more than 500 lines.

NOTE: It is standard for editors and authors to use software that will count the number of characters, words, lines, paragraphs, etc. of a document.

Precautions for All Manuscripts

1434 When sending material to a publisher, always keep a duplicate of your hard copy and disk in case the material goes astray or the publisher calls to discuss the manuscript.

1435 Your unpublished manuscript is automatically protected by copyright law for the *written expression* of ideas and facts but not the ideas and facts themselves. If you fear possible infringement of your ideas or of not receiving credit or compensation for your work, you could place a note of copyright (© your name, date) on the front page of your book. It may be necessary, too, to consult a lawyer if you think you have an original publishing idea that could be misappropriated.

For information or an application for copyright registration, write to the Copyright Office, Canadian Intellectual Property Office (CIPO), Industry Canada, 50 Victoria Street, Place du Portage I, Hull, QC K1A 0C9, or visit CIPO on the Internet at http://cipo.gc.ca.

Some owners of copyrights belong to a not-for-profit licensing body that collects royalties on their behalf. *Access Copyright* (previously known as *CANCOPY*) grants permission to schools and industry to copy your work and collects the fee from them on your behalf. For information about photocopying of this kind, write to *Access Copyright*, The Canadian Copyright Licensing Agency, 1 Yonge Street, Suite 1900, Toronto, ON M5E 1E5, or refer to their Web site at www.accesscopyright.com.

See the Online Learning Centre at www.mcgrawhill.ca/college/gregg for related Web links.

Notes and Bibliographies

Report (¶1532)
Letter, Memo, or E-Mail Message (¶1533)
Independent Internet Document (¶1534)
Message Posted on Internet Forum, Newsgroup, or Listserv (¶1535)
Elements of Source Reference Notes (¶¶1536–1542)
Note Number (¶1536)
Names of Authors (¶1537)
Title of the Work (¶1538)
Publisher's Name (¶1539)
Place of Publication (¶1540)
Date of Publication (¶1541)
Page Numbers (¶1542)
Subsequent References (¶¶1543–1544)

BIBLIOGRAPHIES (¶¶1545–1549)

15 FOOTNOTES, ENDNOTES, AND TEXTNOTES
Functions of Notes

1501 a. In a report or manuscript, *notes* serve two functions: (1) they provide *comments* on the main text, conveying subordinate ideas that the writer feels might be distracting if incorporated within the main text; and (2) they serve as *source references*, identifying the origin of a statement quoted or cited in the text.

Comment

[1]The actual date on which Mayor Wade made this statement is uncertain, but there is no doubt that the statement is his.

Source Reference

[2]Patrick Watson, *The Canadians*, McArthur & Company, Toronto, 2000, p. 108.

b. When notes appear at the foot of a page, they are called *footnotes*. (See ¶¶1503–1504.)

---

sparking the cheer "I'll have Nunavut!" this frosty new baby of Canada became

a territory in 1999, and is the best place in the country to trip-out on Northern

Lights or eat a snow cone.[1]

---

[1]Kerry Colburn and Rob Sorensen, *So, You Want to Be Canadian?* Canadian edition, Raincoast Books, Vancouver, 2004, p. 17.

☞ *For a discussion on whether to type the note number as a superscript (as shown above) or on the line, see ¶1536b.*

c. When notes appear all together at the end of a complete report or manuscript (or sometimes at the end of each chapter), they are called *endnotes*. (See ¶¶1505–1506.)

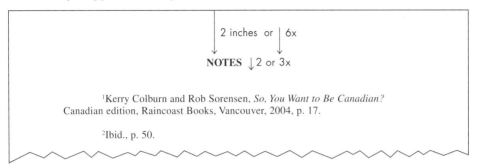

2 inches or │ 6x

NOTES ↓ 2 or 3x

[1]Kerry Colburn and Rob Sorensen, *So, You Want to Be Canadian?* Canadian edition, Raincoast Books, Vancouver, 2004, p. 17.

[2]Ibid., p. 50.

d. When source references appear parenthetically within the main text, they are called *textnotes*. (See ¶1507.)

and expectations. During your job search, it is important to keep in mind that

courtesy should always be your guideline. ↓ 2x

0.25 to 0.5 inch ⟶   Speaking rudely to the receptionist or telling her that her company is not high profile practically guarantees that your resume [sic] will go into the "no" pile . . . Don't underestimate the power of the company's front-line person. (Sharlene Massie, "Courtesy Vital in Job Search," *The Chronicle Herald*, November 2, 2003, Careers, p. 49, col. 6.)   ← 0.25 to 0.5 inch

e. Footnotes or endnotes are ordinarily keyed by an Arabic number to a word, phrase, or sentence in the text. Textnotes (which appear parenthetically at the desired point of reference right in the text itself) do not have to be keyed this way.

f. Endnotes are popular because they leave the text pages looking less cluttered and less complicated. They do present one drawback however: the reader does not know in each instance whether the endnote will contain a comment of substance (which is typically worth reading) or simply a source reference (which is usually of interest only in special cases).

g. Textnotes are also popular for the same reason: lack of clutter. While it is possible to provide in a textnote all the information that a source reference typically contains, writers more often use the textnote to provide an abbreviated reference in the text, with the understanding that the reader who wants complete information will be able to consult a bibliography at the back of the report or manuscript. (See ¶1507b for examples of these abbreviated references.)

h. To take advantage of the benefits and avoid the drawbacks of these three types of notes, some writers use a hybrid system: they treat *comments* as footnotes and *source references* as endnotes or textnotes. In this way comments of substance are conveniently at hand, whereas all or most of the information about sources is tucked out of sight but accessible when needed. (See ¶1502g.)

Text References to Footnotes or Endnotes

1502 a. To indicate the presence of a comment or a source reference at the bottom of the page or in a special section at the end of the report or manuscript, insert a superscript following the appropriate word, phrase, or sentence in the text. (See ¶1502b for examples.)

b. Do not leave any space between the superscript and the preceding word. If a punctuation mark follows the word, place the superscript immediately after the punctuation mark. (There is one exception: the superscript should precede, not follow, a dash.)

A research study published last month by a leading relocation consulting firm[1] provides the basis for the recommendations offered in Chapter 5.

The alternative approaches discussed in this report have been taken largely from an article entitled "Getting a Handle on Health Care Costs."[2]

An article entitled "Getting a Handle on Health Care Costs"[2]—written by an eminent authority in the field—was the source of the alternative approaches discussed in this report.

c. While the superscript should come as close as possible to the appropriate word or phrase, it is often better to place it at the end of the sentence so as to avoid distracting the reader in the midst of the sentence. Then leave 1 or 2 spaces before starting a new sentence.

PREFERABLE: Her latest article, "Automating the Small Legal Office," was published about three months ago.[1] I urge you to read it.

ACCEPTABLE: Her latest article, "Automating the Small Legal Office,"[1] was published about three months ago. I urge you to read it.

d. When a paragraph calls for two or more footnotes or endnotes, try to combine all the necessary information within one note if this can be done without any risk of confusing the reader. This approach will reduce the sense of irritation that large numbers of footnotes or endnotes tend to produce.

NOTE: When this approach is used, the superscript is typically placed after the last word in the sentence or paragraph, depending on how the text references are dispersed.

PREFERABLE: The following analysis draws heavily on recent studies undertaken by Andrew Bowen, Frances Kaplan, and Minetta Coleman.[1]

––––––––––––––––

[1]Andrew Bowen, . . . ; Frances Kaplan, . . . ; and Minetta Coleman, . . .

AVOID: The following analysis draws heavily on recent studies undertaken by Andrew Bowen,[1] Frances Kaplan,[2] and Minetta Coleman.[3]

––––––––––––––––

[1]Andrew Bowen, . . .

[2]Frances Kaplan, . . .

[3]Minetta Coleman, . . .

e. The numbering of footnotes or endnotes may run consecutively throughout or begin again with each new chapter.

f. Footnotes and endnotes are sometimes keyed by symbol rather than by number. This often occurs in tables with figures and in technical material with many formulas, where a raised figure—though intended to refer to a footnote or endnote—could be mistaken for part of the table text or the formula. When the use of symbols is appropriate, choose one of the following sequences: *, **, ***, etc.; *, †, ‡, §, ¶; or a, b, c, d, e, etc.

> These tests confirmed that there was a reduction over time of the consumption of natural gas by at least 2.3 m^3.***
>
> **NOT:** These tests confirmed that there was a reduction over time of the consumption of natural gas by at least 2.3 m^3.[3]

g. If you wish to treat *comments* as footnotes and *source references* as endnotes (as suggested in ¶1501h), use *symbols* for the notes containing comments (at the bottom of the page) and use *figures* for the notes containing source references (at the end of the report or manuscript).

Footnotes

1503 a. The footnote feature of a word processing program will automatically position your footnotes at the bottom of the page where the footnote reference appears in the text. The software will also (1) insert a horizontal line to separate the footnotes from the text above, (2) continue a footnote on the following page if it is too long to fit as a whole on the page where it started, and (3) automatically number your footnotes. If subsequent additions or deletions in the text cause the text reference to shift to another page, the related footnote will automatically shift as well. If a footnote is subsequently inserted or deleted, all the remaining footnotes (and their related text references) will be automatically renumbered from that point on.

b. The following illustration shows how your footnotes will look if you use the footnote feature of MS Word and if you accept all the defaults. Note the following default details: (1) the first line of each footnote begins at the left

MS Word Default Format for Footnotes

into the new century.[1] According to one source: ↓2x

0.25 to
0.5 inch ⟶

It is something many of us, in our day-to-day activities, are already actively engaged in . . . In the twenty-first century, it is *real* intelligence—not yet the random and raw data that spits out of a computer—that allow individuals, organizations, and countries to thrive.[2]

0.25 to
⟵ 0.5 inch

[1] For a more detailed analysis of these technological developments, see Chapter 2, pp. 29–38.
[2] Jennifer Welsh, *At Home in the World*, HarperCollins Publishers Ltd., Toronto, 2004, p. 239.

(Continued on page 424.)

Standard Format for Footnotes

into the new century.[1] According to one source: ↓2x

0.25 to
0.5 inch ⟶

It is something many of us, in our day-to-day activities, are already actively engaged in . . . In the twenty-first century, it is *real* intelligence—not yet the random and raw data that spits out of a computer—that allow individuals, organizations, and countries to thrive.[2]

0.25 to
⟵ 0.5 inch

↓2x
[1]For a more detailed analysis of these technological developments, see Chapter 2, pp. 29–38. ↓2x

[2]Jennifer Welsh, *At Home in the World*, HarperCollins Publishers Ltd., Toronto, 2004, p. 239.

margin; (2) no extra space is inserted between footnotes; (3) no extra space is inserted between the horizontal rule and the first footnote; and (4) one space is inserted after the superscript.

NOTE: Whether you are writing business or academic reports or developing a manuscript for a publisher, you will be expected in most cases to follow a definite style for footnotes. In situations where no format is prescribed but professional editorial standards must be met, follow the guidelines for the standard format in ¶1504.

1504 To create your own format for footnotes, consider the following guidelines. (See the illustration above.)

a. The line that separates footnote material from the main text above should be about 2 inches long.

NOTE: If the text runs short on a page (for instance, the last page of a chapter), any footnotes related to that text must still be positioned at the *foot* of the page.

b. Start the first footnote a double space below the separation line.

☞ *For guidelines on how to construct source reference footnotes, see ¶¶1513–1544.*

c. Single space the text within each footnote but double space *between* the footnotes.

d. Indent the first line of each footnote using the same paragraph tab that is used within the text material of the document, that is, 0.25 to 0.5 inch.

e. Type the footnote number as a superscript figure with no spaces after it. NOTE: An alternative format uses a number followed by a period placed normally on the line. The font style and size should match the font style and size of the body of the document. Leave one or two spaces after the period, and follow the same style for spacing after periods that is used in the body of the document.

Starting a Long Footnote

---

and computers should not be used to write thank-you notes.[2]

---

[2]Judith Martin (in *Miss Manners' Basic Training: Communications,* Crown, New York, 1998, p. 37) clearly supports this position: "Thank-you letters should be written by hand. Miss Manners . . . grants exemptions only to people with

---

    f. In some software, if a footnote is considered too long to fit on the same page as the actual reference, the software will automatically split the footnote text and place part of it on the next page. If at all possible, try to avoid this situation. You may have to reset some formatting (for example, the bottom margin) to accommodate this.

Continuing a Long Footnote on the Next Page

---

on which there still is a considerable difference of opinion.[3]

---

specific physical disabilities that prevent them from writing. Those who claim illegible handwriting should be home practicing their penmanship instead of bragging about it." ↓2x

    [3]Baldrige, p. 593.

    NOTE: If you have a number of long notes that may not easily fit on the page where they are first referred to, you have an excellent reason for abandoning the footnote format and using endnotes instead. (See ¶¶1505–1506.)

    ☞ *For the treatment of footnotes that pertain to a table, see ¶¶1631–1633.*

Endnotes

1505 **a.** The endnote feature of a software program will automatically position all endnotes at the end of the document. If you add or delete endnotes, all the remaining endnotes (and their related text references) will be automatically renumbered from that point on.

    b. The endnote feature will also automatically format the endnotes for you. Here is how your endnotes will look if you accept all the defaults of the endnote feature of MS Word. Note that the endnote section begins on the same page as the conclusion of the main text, separated by a short horizontal rule starting at the left margin but with no heading (such as *NOTES*) to introduce this section. Note also that each entry begins at the left margin with

(Continued on page 426.)

superscripts in small Roman numerals and a space after the superscript. There is no linespace between the notes.

MS Word Default Format for Endnotes

growth. Equipping your SOHO office with the right equipment is easy . . . The key is knowing which technological tools you need.[ii]

---

[i] Lisa Kanarek, "Wired for Business," *OfficePRO*, Vol. 61, No. 4, April 2001, p. 14.
[ii]Ibid.

1506 If you want to modify the default format shown above or if you prefer to create your own format for endnotes, consider the following guidelines. (See the illustration below.)

a. Endnotes should start on a new page. The title *NOTES* or *ENDNOTES* should be centred 2 inches from the top of the page and typed in all-capital letters and in boldface. Leave 1 or 2 linespaces after the title.

b. The preferred format for an endnote page is to have the first line of each endnote indented the equivalent to the tab stop that has been set for the body of the document, that is, 0.25 to 0.5 inch. For readability, place Arabic numbers on the line rather than using superscripts. (Although superscripts may appear, the on-the-line style is more common.) All turnover lines should return to the left margin.

c. Leave one or two spaces after the period. Follow the same format for spacing after punctuation that is used in the body of the document.

d. Single space the text within each endnote but double space *between* the endnotes.

☞ *For guidelines on how to construct source reference endnotes, see ¶¶1513–1535.*

Standard Format for Endnotes

2 inches

ENDNOTES ↓2 or 3x

0.25 to
0.5 inch ⟶ 1. Lisa Kanarek, "Wired for Business," *OfficePRO*, Vol. 61, No. 4, April 2001, p. 14. ↓2x

2. Ibid.

e. Use the same margins as for other pages in the body of the report or manuscript (see ¶¶1405–1407), and treat the numbering of these pages as shown in ¶1427f–g.

f. If the document consists of only one chapter, the endnotes may begin on the same page where the main text ends. In that case leave about 3 blank lines before the heading and 1 or 2 blank lines after it.

g. If the numbering of endnotes starts again with each new chapter or on each new page, insert an appropriate heading—*Chapter 1, Chapter 2*, etc., or *Page 1, Page 2*, etc.—over each sequence of endnotes in this section. Key the heading at the left margin in capital and small letters (using boldface or italics), and leave 2 blank lines above and 1 blank line below.

NOTE: If the numbering of endnotes is consecutive throughout, no headings are needed.

h. Insert this special section of endnotes in the back matter following any appendices. If no appendix is given, the endnotes begin the back matter. (See also ¶1428.)

NOTE: When individual chapters of a report or a manuscript are written by different people, it may be advantageous to have the endnotes that each author prepares inserted at the end of the respective chapter instead of redoing all the endnotes as one continuous section in the back matter. If this approach is used, expand the heading *NOTES* in each case to read *NOTES TO CHAPTER 1, NOTES TO CHAPTER 2*, and so on. The disadvantage of this approach is that the reader will have a bit more difficulty locating the notes for each chapter than when all the endnotes are presented in one section at the very end.

Textnotes

1507 a. In a report or manuscript with only a few source references and no bibliography at the end, the complete source data may be inserted within the text in the form of parenthetical textnotes. (See the illustration below.)

☞ *For guidelines on how to construct source reference textnotes, see ¶¶1513–1544.*

---

proper punctuation an endangered species. For those who get upset when it is

mishandled, here is what one authority has to say:

> It is sad to think people are no longer learning how to use the colon and semicolon, not least because, in this supreme QWERTY keyboard era, the little finger of the human right hand, deprived of its traditional function, may eventually dwindle down and drop off from disuse. (Lynne Truss, *Eats, Shoots and Leaves*, Penguin Group, Toronto, 2004, pp. 130–131.)

(Continued on page 428.)

NOTE: If some of the data called for in a source reference is already provided in the main text, there is no need to repeat it in the textnote.

---

proper punctuation an endangered species. For those who get upset when it is

mishandled, here is what Lynne Truss has to say:

> It is sad to think people are no longer learning how to use the colon and semicolon, not least because, in this supreme QWERTY keyboard era, the little finger of the human right hand, deprived of its traditional function, may eventually dwindle down and drop off from disuse. (*Eats, Shoots and Leaves*, Penguin Group, Toronto, 2004, pp. 130–131.)

---

b. In a report or manuscript that contains a number of source references *and* a complete bibliography, textnotes may be used as follows:

(1) At the appropriate point in the main text, supply the author's last name and the appropriate page number in parentheses. The reader who wants more complete information can consult the full entry in the bibliography.

As stated in her book about punctuation today (Truss, p. 142), interesting comments are presented.

NOTE: Some authorities omit *p.* and *pp.* as well as the comma between the name and the page number. For example:

. . . punctuation today (Truss 142), . . .

(2) If the author's name already appears in the main text, give only the page number in parentheses.

Lynne Truss, *Eats, Leaves and Shoots* (p. 142), says that . . .

(3) If the bibliography lists more than one publication by the same author, then in the textnote use an abbreviated title or the year of publication to indicate which publication is being referred to.

In her book about punctuation today (Truss, *Eats, Shoots and Leaves,* p. 142), . . .

OR: . . . about punctuation today (Truss, 2004, p. 142), . . .

(4) If the bibliography lists publications by two or more authors with the same surname, use each author's first name or initial along with the surname.

In her book about punctuation today (Lynne Truss, p. 142), . . .

(5) If the entries in the bibliography are numbered in sequence (see ¶1547c), then the textnote can simply list the appropriate "entry number" along with the page reference. Italicize or underline the entry number to distinguish it from the page number, especially if the abbreviation *p.* or *pp.* is omitted.

In her book about . . . (*18*, p. 142), . . . OR: (<u>18</u>, p. 142), . . .

NOTES BASED ON ONLINE SOURCES

Business and academic writers increasingly rely on the Internet as the source of information to be quoted, paraphrased, or summarized in the reports and manuscripts they prepare. Hence the critical need for guidelines on how to construct *online citations*—that is, footnotes, endnotes, and bibliographic entries that are based on online sources.

IMPORTANT: Users should be aware that information on the Internet is not always correct. Footnotes become very important as proof of information found. (See ¶1535.) Since much online material originally appeared in print (a much more stable medium), refer whenever possible to the printed source rather than the online source.

The feature that distinguishes an online citation from one based on printed material is the inclusion of an *online address*—an element that takes the place of information about the name and location of the publisher. There are two major types of online addresses: a URL (¶1508) and an e-mail address (¶1509).

URLs (Internet Addresses)

1508 Every unit of information on the Internet has its own unique address—a Uniform Resource Locator, commonly referred to as a URL. It represents not only the storage location of a particular document on the Internet but also the means by which a document can be retrieved. If a URL is not accurately presented in an online citation, it will be impossible to locate the material being cited.

A URL consists of at least two parts: (1) the *protocol* (the name of the system to be used in linking one computer with another on the Internet) and (2) the *host name* (the name of the host computer where the desired material is stored). Here, for example, is the URL for Yahoo!, a large directory of Web pages.

Protocol Host Name

http://www.yahoo.com

a. **Protocol.** There are a number of protocols that you can use to locate material stored on another computer on the Internet.

- **HTTP (HyperText Transfer Protocol).** The most widely used of all the protocols, HTTP permits you to surf the World Wide Web—that part of the Internet that provides access not only to text material but also to photographs, drawings, animations, and video and sound clips.

- **FTP (File Transfer Protocol).** FTP permits you to transfer text material from an *ftp server* (the host computer where the desired material is stored) to your own computer.

- **Usenet.** Usenet is a network consisting of thousands of newsgroups (discussion groups each focused on a particular topic of interest). A message posted to a particular newsgroup can be read and commented on by any interested member of that newsgroup, and those comments may prompt additional rounds of comments. The original message (known as an *article*) and the subsequent series of comments

(Continued on page 430.)

create what is known as a *thread*. Users doing research on Usenet have the option of citing only the article, one or more of the comments, or the entire thread.

When these protocols appear as the first part of a URL, they are represented as follows:

HTTP: http:// FTP: ftp:// Usenet: news://

The first part of a URL always ends with a colon and two forward slashes (://).

b. Host Name. The second part of a URL, the host name, consists of several elements separated by *dots* (never referred to as *periods*). Here are some representative host names as they appear in Web-based URLs:

	Protocol Host Name
eBay:	http://www.ebay.com
Bank of Nova Scotia	http://www.scotiabank.com
McGill University	http://www.mcgill.ca
United Nations	http://www.un.org
Sony	http://www.sony.biz

In the host names shown above, the first element—www—refers to the World Wide Web. The second and third elements—for example, *.ebay.com* (referred to as *dot-ebay-dot-com*)—represent the domain name. The second element often reflects some form of the organization's name. The third element is usually a two- or three-letter unit preceded by a dot; it is called a *top-level domain* (TLD) or a *zone*, and it indicates the country or type of organization that owns the host computer. For example:

.ca	Canada		.de	Germany
.cl	Chile		.it	Italy
.cn	China		.uk	United Kingdom
.com	commercial organization		.mil	military site
.edu	educational institution		.net	network organization
.gov	government body or agency		.org	non-profit, non-commercial organization
.int	international organization			

The following TLDs were established in 2000:

.aero	airline organization		.info	information services
.biz	business services		.pro	professional sevices
.coop	business co-operative		.name	personal Web site

c. File Name. A URL may also provide a file name as the final element. For example, the following URL directs a Web browser to retrieve a file named *iway.html* from a host computer named *www.cc.web.com* using the HyperText Transfer Protocol.

Protocol Host Name   File Name

http://www.cc.web.com/iway.html

NOTE: A *tilde* (~), also referred to as a *swung dash*, is sometimes used to introduce a file name. For example,

http://www.netaxs.com/~harrington

d. **Path.** A URL may also include one or more elements between the host name and the file name. These elements indicate the electronic path to be taken (after the host computer is reached) in order to locate the desired file. For example,

Protocol   Host Name   Path   File Name
http://www.yahoo.com/Computers/World_Wide_Web/HTML_Editors

e. URLs are usually typed in small letters, but when capital letters appear, follow the style of the particular URL exactly as shown. Also note that spaces between words in any part of a URL have to be signified by means of an underline (as in the example in *d* above) or some other mark of punctuation such as a hyphen (as in the example below).

http://www.vpl.vancouver.bc.ca/hypertext/faq/usenet/FAQ-List.html

NOTE: The URLs shown in ¶1508b–e end with a forward slash but others do not. Always follow the style of a URL exactly as shown.

f. When Web-based URLs are given in documents and publications aimed at computer professionals, the protocol *http://* is often omitted; the fact that the host name begins with *www* makes it clear to knowledgeable readers which protocol is to be used. When constructing your own citations, consider how much your readers will know. As a general rule, it is safer to insert the protocol at the start of a URL, even if it is omitted in your source.

E-Mail Addresses

1509 The following examples illustrate the elements of e-mail addresses.

jclarkson@shaw.ca   ipetrini@earthlink.net

The first part (*jclarkson* or *ipetrini*) is the user's name, which is followed by an *at* sign (@). The second part (*shaw* or *earthlink*) is the name of the host computer. The third part (*.ca* or *.net*) is the *top-level domain* (TLD) and is always preceded by a dot. TLDs indicate the country or the type of organization that owns the host computer. (See ¶1508b.)

☞ *For guidelines on the formatting of e-mail messages, see ¶¶1379.*

Guidelines for Online Citations

1510 Making use of online sources can pose special problems. After you have quoted or made reference to certain online materials in your report or your manuscript, the person who originally posted the material may later decide to change it or transfer it to a new location (with a new URL or e-mail address) or remove it from the Internet altogether. If any of these things should happen, readers who try to confirm the accuracy of your citations may very well draw unfair conclusions

(Continued on page 432.)

about your competence as a researcher and as a writer. To protect yourself against these potential problems, take the following precautions.

a. Save every cited online document as hard copy and as part of your backup files. If the document is very long, save at least enough of the document to establish the full context from which the cited material was taken. Then if the need arises, you can always show that you have not taken the material out of context or distorted its intended meaning.

NOTE: Since much online material originally appeared in print (a much more stable medium), refer whenever possible to the printed source rather than the online source.

b. Include not only the date on which the material was posted on the Internet but also the date on which you accessed the material you plan to cite. If the material is subsequently changed or removed, you will still be able to prove the accuracy of your citation if a hard copy of the cited material has been made.

c. When URLs or e-mail addresses appear in footnotes, endnotes, bibliographies, or in the main text, enclose each address in angle brackets (<>). The use of angle brackets makes it possible to insert sentence punctuation before and after a URL and not have the punctuation mistaken for part of the URL address. Moreover, when a long URL is divided at the end of a line, the closing angle bracket eliminates confusion by signalling where the URL ends.

d. Always present a URL or an e-mail address exactly as it is given. Never alter the capitalization, the internal spacing, or the symbols used. Failure to provide an accurate online address will usually make it impossible to locate the desired information.

NOTE: A URL or an e-mail address should never contain a blank space. If you want to show a blank space in your own address, insert an underline or a dot so that an unobtrusive mark will occupy that space.

Grace_Chung@primus.ca   OR: Grace.Chung@primus.ca

Division of Online Addresses

1511 a. URLs. Try to fit a URL on one line. If it becomes necessary to divide a URL at the end of a line, observe the following guidelines.

(1) Never insert a hyphen in an online address to signify an end-of-line break.

(2) You may break *after* the double (//) that marks the end of a protocol (but not within the protocol itself).

Acceptable Line Ending	Next Line
<http://	www.nowonder.com>
NOT <http:	NOT //www.nowonder.com>

(3) You may break *before* (but never after) a dot (.), a single slash (/), a hyphen (-), an underscore (_), or any other mark of punctuation.

Acceptable Line Ending	Next Line
<http://www	.pbs.org>
NOT <http://www.	NOT pbs.org>
<http://www/mcgraw	-hill.com>
NOT <http://www/mcgraw-	NOT hill.com>

b. E-mail Adddresses. Try to fit an e-mail address on one line. If it becomes necessary to divide it at the end of a line, observe the following:

(1) Never insert a hyphen within an e-mail address to signify an end-of-line-break.

(2) You may break *before* the *at* symbol (@) or *before* a dot.

Acceptable Line Ending	Next Line
<wryter6290	@aol.com>
NOT <wryter6290@	NOT aol.com>
<sines@home	.midcoast.com>
NOT <sines@home.	NOT midcoast.com>

Plagiarism

1512 Whether you are writing a business report, a school term paper, or a manuscript, take care to avoid the act of *plagiarism,* that is, taking and using the writings or ideas of others as your own without giving proper credit to the source. It is a serious offence, which can lead to dismissal from a job or expulsion from an academic institution.

Although some writers intentionally plagiarize the work of others, many writers are simply unaware of how or when to acknowledge the words and ideas they have taken from others. For example, it is generally acceptable to paraphrase someone else's words as long as an appropriate citation is made. If, however, the paraphrasing follows too closely to the original source or if you include exact words without (1) using quotation marks or (2) displaying the words as an extract, you may have committed plagiarism whether you intended to or not.

The guidelines on plagiarism apply not only to printed works but also to written and graphical material taken from a Web site, from TV and radio programs, and even from interviews and conversations. If you are uncertain about these guidelines, do an Internet search using *plagiarism* as your keyword. Detailed analyses and comparative examples that distinguish responsible research from accidental plagiarism can be found on many excellent Web sites.

CONSTRUCTION OF SOURCE REFERENCE NOTES

The following guidelines for constructing source reference notes deal with the situations that most commonly occur—whether in the form of footnotes, endnotes, or textnotes. There is no universal agreement among authorities on how these notes should be constructed. However, whichever style or pattern you choose to use, the

(Continued on page 434.)

goal of source reference notes is to make it easy for your readers to locate any of the sources that you cite. In fact, providing more information than a particular pattern calls for could only serve their best interests.

Of all the well-established conventions and variations of source reference notes, the one presented here, which is best suited for business use, is a style that employs the simplest punctuation and presentation of the necessary data without any sacrifice in clarity or completeness. Along with these basic patterns, there is an "academic" variation that you may need to use from time to time. However, certain professional organizations have established distinctive styles that sometimes show up in other fields. For example, the style recommended by the American Psychological Association (APA) is followed by some Canadian universities. Moreover, academic materials often use slightly different patterns, such as those featured in *The MLA [Modern Language Association] Style Manual* and *The Chicago Manual of Style*. The respective Internet addresses for these organizations are as follows: http://www.apa.org; http://www.mla.org; and www.chicagomanualofstyle.org.

Unless you are specifically directed to follow a particular style, the basic patterns in the following few pages should meet your needs in virtually every type of situation you encounter.

Patterns of Source Reference Notes

1513 Book Title: Basic Pattern

a. Business Style

[1]Author, *book title*, publisher, place of publication, year of publication, page number [if reference is being made to a specific page].

[1]Laurier L. LaPierre, *Quebec: A Tale of Love*, McClelland & Stewart, Toronto, 2001, p. 387.

OR:

1. Laurier L. LaPierre, *Quebec: A Tale of Love*, McClelland & Stewart, Toronto, 2001, p. 387.

---

in his recent book, *Quebec: A Tale of Love*, Laurier L. LaPierre reminds us of the

role of Quebec in shaping our nation.

0.25 to
0.5 inch ⟶ These people opened a continent to a civilization that has much
     nobility in it, and they introduced a new language to North America. . . .   0.25 to
0.25 to   These people have great courage and a zest for life that many try to ⟵ 0.5 inch
0.5 inch ⟶ emulate. They are a good people and sometimes a great people.[1]

-----

[1]McClelland & Stewart, Toronto, 2001, p. 387.

NOTE: If any of these elements have already been identified in the text (for example, the author's name and the book title), they need not be repeated in the note. Moreover, if reference is made to the book as a whole rather than to a particular page, omit the page number. In the following illustration, observe that the quoted material requires more than three lines. For that reason, it is indented 0.25 to 0.5 inch from each side margin. (See ¶1425d.)

☞ *For the guidelines on use of capitals in book titles, see ¶¶360–361.*

b. Academic Style

> [1]Author, *book title* (place of publication: publisher, year of publication), page number [if reference is being made to a specific page].

> [1]Laurier L. LaPierre, *Quebec: A Tale of Love* (Toronto: McClelland & Stewart, 2001), 387.

(In endnotes, the note number is shown on the line; in academic-style footnotes, the note number is typically shown as a superscript. See ¶1536b.)

While the patterns for books in ¶¶1514–1521 show only the business style, this style can be readily converted to the academic style by simply changing the treatment of publisher, place, and year of publication.

BUSINESS STYLE: . . . publisher, place of publication, year of publication . . .

ACADEMIC STYLE: . . . (place of publication: publisher, year of publication) . . .

☞ *For the academic style for entries in bibliographies, see ¶1549c.*

c. Online Books

(1) For the online version of a printed book, only two elements need to be added at the end of the basic pattern for books: the URL and the date on which you accessed this source.

> [1]Author, *book title*, publisher, place of publication, year of publication, page number (if needed), <URL>, **accessed on** date.

> [1]William Still, *The Underground Railroad*, Porter & Coates, Philadelphia, 1872, <http://invictus.quinnipiac.edu/ugrrmain.html>, accessed on May 28, 2007.

(2) For an unpublished book available only online, omit the publication details.

> [1]Author, *book title*, page number (if needed), date of posting, <URL>, **accessed on** date.

> [1]David Gettman, *The Twinkle Theory*, n.d., <http://www.onlineoriginals.com/freetitles/twinkle.prc>, accessed on April 10, 2007.

NOTE: If the date of posting cannot be determined, insert the abbreviation *n.d.* (no date).

1514 Book Title: With Edition

a. Edition Number

> [1]Author, *book title*, edition number [if not the first edition], publisher, place, year, page number.

> [1]Richard Organ, *Avro Arrow*, rev. ed., The Boston Mills Press, Erin, Ontario, 2004, p. 46.

(Continued on page 436.)

NOTE: Use an edition number only when the book is not the first edition in its country of origin. If included, the edition number follows the main title and any related elements, such as the subtitle or the volume number and title. The following abbreviated forms are commonly used: *2nd ed., 3rd ed., 4th ed.,* and *rev. ed.* (for "revised edition").

b. Edition Notation

[1]Author, *book title*, edition notation, publisher, place, year, page number.

[1]Catharine Parr Traill, *The Backwoods of Canada,* 1836 Charles Knight ed., Prospero Books, Toronto, 2003, pp. 191–202.

NOTE: Some books first published outside Canada, usually those from the United States and Great Britain, are edited for the Canadian market. The word *Canadian* is included in the title of the book or is used to note a particular edition. (See ¶1520.) Other descriptions, such as *International, Educational,* and *Special,* are sometimes indicated.

1515 Book Title: With Subtitle

[1]Author, *book title: subtitle*, edition number [if not the first edition], publisher, place, year, page number.

[1]Elizabeth McLachlan, *Gone but Not Forgotten: Tales of the Disappearing Grain Elevators,* NeWest Press, Edmonton, 2004, p. 44.

NOTE: Do not give the subtitle of a book unless it is significant in identifying the book or in explaining its basic nature. If a subtitle is to be shown, separate it from the main title with a colon (unless the title page shows some other mark such as a dash). Italicize the main title and the subtitle. Capitalize the first word of the subtitle, even if it is a short preposition like *for,* a short conjunction like *or,* or an article like *the* or *a.* (See ¶361b.)

[2]Roy MacGregor, *Escape: In Search of the National Soul of Canada,* McClelland & Stewart, Toronto, 2002, p. 87.

1516 Book Title: With Volume Number and Volume Title

[1]Author, *book title*, volume number, *volume title*, edition number [if not the first edition], publisher, place, year, page number.

[1]Doug Lennon, *Now You Know More,* Vol. 2, *The Book of Answers,* Dundurn Press, Toronto, 2004, p. 145.

NOTE: As a rule, do not show the volume title in a note unless it is significant in identifying the book. When the volume title is included, both the volume number and the volume title follow the book title (and subtitle, if any) but precede the edition number. The volume number is usually preceded by the abbreviation *Vol.* or by the word *Book* or *Part* (depending on the actual designation). The volume number may be Arabic or Roman depending on the style used in the actual book. Some writers prefer to use one style of volume number throughout the notes. (See also ¶1517.)

1517 Book Title: With Volume Number Alone

[1]Author, *book title*, edition number [if not the first edition], publisher, place, year, volume number, page number.

[1]Bob Dylan, *Chronicles*, Simon & Shuster, New York, 2004, Vol. One, p. 223.

NOTE: When the volume number is shown without the volume title, it follows the date of publication. When the volume number and page number occur one after the other, they may be styled as follows:

Style for Roman Volume Number	Style for Arabic Volume Number
Vol. III, p. 197 **OR** III, 197	Vol. 5, pp. 681–684 **OR** 5:681–684

[1]Bob Dylan, *Chronicles*, Simon & Schuster, New York, 2004, 1:223.

However, the form with figures alone may be difficult to follow.

1518 Book Title: With Chapter Reference

[1]Author, *book title*, publisher, place, year, chapter number, "chapter title" [if significant], page number.

[1]Gord Steinke, *Mobsters and Rumrunners of Canada: Crossing the Line*, Folklore Publishing, Edmonton, 2003, Legend Series 4, Chap. 6, "The Purple Gang," pp. 65–88.

NOTE: When a note refers primarily to the title of a book, the chapter number and the chapter title are not usually included. If they are considered significant, however, these details can be inserted just before the page numbers. The word *chapter* is usually abbreviated as *Chap.*, the chapter number is Arabic or Roman (depending on the original), and the chapter title is enclosed in quotation marks. Some writers prefer to use one style of chapter number throughout the notes.

1519 Selection From Collected Works of One Author

[1]Author, "title of selection," *book title*, publisher, place, year, page number.

[1]Carol Shields, "Segue," *The Collected Stories*, Random House Canada, Toronto, 2003, pp. 1–20.

1520 Selection in Anthology

[1]Author of selection, "title of selection," **in** editor of anthology (**ed.**), *book title*, publisher, place, year, page number.

[1]Lorna Crozier, "Seasons," in Paul Sonntag and Grant Loewen (eds.), *Moosemilk: The Best of Moosehead From 1977 to 1999*, DC Books, Montreal, 1999, p. 17.

[2]Hugh Graham, "That's All There Is," in Douglas Glover (ed.), *Best Canadian Stories*, Oberon Press, Ottawa, 2003, pp. 60–80.

[3]Farley Mowat, "Sea of Slaughter," in Nancy Pollak, Saeko Usukana, and Lucy Kenward (eds.), *Books of the Century*, Vancouver Public Library Edition, Douglas & McIntyre Ltd., Vancouver, 1999, p. 22.

1521 Article in Reference Work

[1]Author [if known], "article title," *name of reference work*, edition number [if not the first edition], publisher [usually omitted], place [usually omitted], year, volume [may be omitted], page number [may be omitted].

[1]Robert A. Cooke, "The Management Process," *Finance for Nonfinancial Managers*, 2nd ed., McGraw-Hill, New York, 2003, pp. 97–115.

[2]"Sentence Structure," *The Writer's Handbook*, 14th ed., Macmillan Publishers Ltd., 2002.

NOTE: It is not necessary to give the name of the publisher or the place of publication unless there is some possibility of confusion or the reference is not well known.

[3]"Canadian English: 250 Years in the Making," *The Canadian Oxford Dictionary*, 2001, pp. ix–x.

Moreover, if you are making reference to an article or an entry that appears in alphabetic order in the main portion of the work, even the page number may be omitted. If the reference work carries the name of an editor rather than an author, the editor's name is also usually omitted.

[4]"Legal Assistant," *Who's Hiring 2004*, 7th ed., Mediacorp Canada Inc., Toronto, 2004, p.338.

[5]"Malapropism," *The Penguin Concise Dictionary*, 2004.

1522 Article in Newspaper

[1]Author [if known], "article title," *name of newspaper*, date, section number, page number, column number.

[1]Pamela Klaffke, "Turning Over New Leaves," *Edmonton Journal*, August 28, 2004, Sec. E, p. 1, col. 2–5.
OR: . . . August 28, 2004, p. E1, col. 2–5.

For the online version of the newspaper rather than the printed one, use this pattern:

[1]Author (if provided), "article title," *name of newspaper*, date, <URL> **accessed on** date.

[2]Seth Schiesel, "In Frayed Networks, Common Threads," *The New York Times on the Web*, <http://www.nytimes.com/2003/08/21/technology/circuits/21nett.html?th>, accessed on April 7, 2004.

1523 Article in Magazine or Journal

a. Article in Magazine

[1]Author [if known], "article title," *name of magazine*, date, page number.

[1]Natalie Salat, "Multi-Tasking Mariners," *Legion Magazine*, September/October 2004, pp. 48–51.

[2]Andy Holloway, "Deconstructing Dell," *Canadian Business*, April 20, 2001, pp. 97–99.

NOTE: Omit the comma between the article title and the name of the periodical if the article title ends with a question mark or an exclamation point.

> [3]Ray Kurzweil, "Will My PC Be Smarter Than I Am?" *Time*, June 19, 2000, pp. 52–53.

> [4]Tracey Ho Lung, "Take It Outside?" *Chatelaine*, October 2004, p. 114.

For the online version of a printed magazine or for a non-print magazine (online format only), use this pattern:

> [1]Author (if known), "article title," *name of magazine*, date, <URL> **accessed on** date.

> [5]Irwin Jacobs, "Don't Scrimp on Tech," *BusinessWeek Online*, August 25, 2003, <http://www.businessweek.com/magazine/content/03_34/b3846645.htm> accessed on May 1, 2004.

b. Article in Professional Journal

> [1]Author, "article title," *title of journal* [frequently abbreviated], series number [if given], volume number, issue number [if given], date, page number.

> [1]Gracie Gibbs Franks, "Cooperative Education: A Principal's View," *The Delta Kappa Gamma Bulletin*, Vol. 70, No. 4, Summer 2004, p. 35.

NOTE: Titles of journals are often abbreviated in notes whenever these abbreviations are likely to be familiar to the intended readership or are clearly identified in a bibliography at the end.

> [1]Gracie Gibbs Franks, "Cooperative Education: A Principal's View," *DKG Bulletin*, Vol. 70, No. 4, Summer 2004, p. 35.

1524 Newsletter, Bulletin, Pamphlet, or Monograph

> [1]Author [if given], "article title" [if appropriate], *title of publication*, series title and series number [if appropriate], volume number and issue number [if appropriate], sponsoring organization, place [may be omitted], date, page number.

> [1]Judith Briles, "Plant Your Money Tree," *OfficePRO*, Vol. 61, No. 5, International Association of Administrative Professionals, May 2001, p. 11. (The name of the sponsoring organization is included since a reader may not know the initials *IAAP*.)

> [2]Barbara Wallraff, "The State of Our Art," *Copy Editor*, August-September 2003, pp. 1, 6–7.

For the online version of one of these works, add the URL to the basic pattern.

> [3]Barbara Wallraff, "The State of Our Art," *Copy Editor*, August-September 2003, pp.1, 6–7, <http://www.copyeditor.com/default.asp?id=3>.

NOTE: Because the pertinent data used to identify newsletters, bulletins, pamphlets, and monographs may vary widely, adapt the pattern shown above as necessary to fit each particular situation. For example, the name of the sponsoring organization may be omitted if it is in the title of the publication.

1525 Unpublished Dissertation or Thesis

[1]Author, "title of thesis," **doctoral dissertation OR master's thesis** [identifying phrase to be inserted], name of academic institution, place, date, page number.

[1]Colin Bryce Comfort, "Evaluating the Effectiveness of Parent Training for Preschoolers: A Meta-Analytical Review," doctoral dissertation, University of Calgary, 2002, p. 144.

For the online version of one of these works, add the URL to the basic pattern.

1526 Quotation From a Secondary Source

[1]Author, *book title*, publisher, place, date, page number, **quoted by or cited by** author, *book title*, publisher, place, date, page number.

[1]Lynne Truss, *Eats, Shoots and Leaves*, Penguin Group Inc., New York, 2004, pp. 112, quoted by Louis Menand, "Bad Comma," *The New Yorker*, June 28, 2004, p. 102.

[2]Pierre Elliott Trudeau, *Against the Current*, McClelland & Stewart, Toronto, 1944, cited in "The Ascetic in a Canoe," *Canadian Geographic*, November/December 2000, pp. 40–42.

NOTE: While it is always preferable to take the wording of a quotation from the original source, it is sometimes necessary to take it from a secondary source. In such cases construct the note in two parts: in the first part, give as much information as possible about the *original* source (derived, of course, from the reference note in the secondary source); in the second part, give the necessary information about the *secondary* source (which is at hand). Bridge the two parts of the note with a phrase such as *quoted by* (or *in*) or *cited by* (or *in*). The pattern shown above assumes that the quotation originally appeared in a book and that the secondary source for the quoted material was also a book. Naturally, if the original source or the secondary source is a work other than a book, use the pattern appropriate for that work.

1527 Quotation From a CD-ROM

[1]Author [if known], "article title" [if appropriate], *title of work* (**CD-ROM**), publisher [may be omitted], place of publication [may be omitted], year of publication, reference to location of quotation [if available].

[1]"Pronouns," *Glencoe Interactive Grammar* (CD-ROM), McGraw-Hill Companies Inc., Westerville, Ohio, 1999, Topic 4.

[2]"Sentence Structure," *Essential Business Communications* (CD-ROM), Pro One Software, Los Cruces, NM, 1996.

NOTE: When citing material taken from a CD-ROM, try to provide some specific guidance on how to access the quoted passage on the disk. For example, if the material is organized in numbered paragraphs or pages, give the paragraph or page number. If the quoted passage is taken from a work organized in alphabetical order like an encyclopedia or a dictionary, give the article title or key word used to identify the article or entry. Even without such assistance, however, a person can usually input a key phrase (or character string) from the quoted material and use the search feature of word processing software to locate the complete passage.

1528 Personal Interview or Conversation

When quoting or paraphrasing words or ideas derived from a face-to-face encounter or a telephone conversation, use the following pattern:

[1]Name of person interviewed (title or affiliation if appropriate), **personal interview OR telephone conversation**, date.

[1]W. G. Hart (IQON financial consultant), telephone conversation, June 7, 2004.

If you are relying on information acquired through an interview conducted by someone else, use the following pattern:

[2]Name of person interviewed (title or affiliation if appropriate), **interviewed by OR conversation with** name of interviewer, date of interview or conversation.

[2]W. G. Hart (IQON financial consultant), conversation with Abby Munro, June 7, 2004.

NOTE: If the person being interviewed is well known to your readers, you do not need to identify that person by title or organizational affiliation. Moreover, you can eliminate other elements from the citation by incorporating that information into the text itself.

1529 Television or Radio Interview

[1]Name of person interviewed, **interviewed by** name of interviewer, "program title," or *series title*, name of TV channel or radio station, date of broadcast.

[1]Daniel Igali, interviewed by Peter Mansbridge, *One on One*, CBC, July 24, 2004.

1530 Speech

[1]Name of speaker (title or affiliation if appropriate), "title of speech" (if known), **speech given at** type of meeting (conference, convention, seminar), place, date.

[1]Rod Sutherland (CanadaLife), "E-Mail Marketing and Privacy," speech given at the Canadian Life Underwriters Conference (**OR** CLU),Vancouver, October 10, 2005.

1531 Paper Read at Meeting

[1]Name of speaker, "title of paper," **paper presented at** type of meeting (conference, convention, seminar), place, date.

[1]Stephanie LeBlanc, "New Online Security Technology," paper presented at Quebec Consumers' Association Convention, Montreal, October 15, 2005.

1532 Report

[1]Name of author, "title of report," author's company or sponsoring organization, place, date, page number.

[1]Andrew Graham, "Marketing Strategy for Tomorrow," Atlantic Ventures Inc., Moncton, July 20, 2006, p. 5.

1533 Letter, Memo, or E-Mail Message

a. Letter or Memo

> [1]Name of author, "subject line" (if appropriate), type of document (letter or memo), date.

> [1]Laurie Stefaniuk, letter, November 22, 2006.

> [2]John Olsen, "Rethinking Our Mission," memo, August 15, 2004.

NOTE: Expand the basic pattern if the document you are citing was addressed to someone else.

> [2]Name of author, "subject line" (if appropriate), type of document (letter or memo), **addressed to** name of recipient, date.

> [3]Laurie Stefaniuk, letter, addressed to Kyle Keller, November 22, 2006.

b. E-Mail Message

> [1]Name of author (e-mail address of organization name only if appropriate), "subject line," **e-mail** message, date.

> [1]Helen Nguyen (nguyenh@aol.com), "Communications Made Simple," e-mail message, July 7, 2004.

NEVER GIVE OUT A PERSONAL E-MAIL ADDRESS without the owner's consent and then only if there is a compelling reason to do so.

1534 Independent Internet Document

To cite material in an independent Internet document—that is, one that does not appear within another online source (for example, an electronic newsletter)— use the following pattern.

> [1]Name of author (if known), "title of document," date of posting (if known), <URL>, **accessed on** date.

> [1]"Registration Inquiries," <http://www.unwt.edu/register/inq.htm>, accessed on June 5, 2004.

1535 Message Posted on Internet Forum, Newsgroup, or Listserv

> [1]Author's name, <e-mail address (if appropriate)>, "subject line," date of posting, <message URL or e-mail address (if appropriate)>, **accessed on** date.

> [1] M. J. Kristophersen, "Watch Out for Redundancy," January 30, 2005, <plain-language@yahoogroups.com>, accessed on March 5, 2005.

Elements of Source Reference Notes

1536 Note Number

a. Make sure that the number at the start of a footnote or an endnote corresponds to the correct reference number in the text.

b. Indent the note number 0.25 to 0.5 inch, and key it (1) on the line (like an ordinary number), followed by a period and 1 or 2 spaces, or (2) as a superscript without any space following it. The on-the-line style is more common in endnotes. (See ¶¶1505–1506.)

> 1. Pierre Berton, *Prisoners of the North*, Random House Canada, Toronto, 2004, p. 65.

OR:

> ¹Pierre Berton, *Prisoners of the North*, Random House Canada, Toronto, 2004, p. 65.

☞ *See ¶1502e on numbering notes; ¶1502f–g on the use of symbols in place of figures.*

1537 Names of Authors

a. Key an author's name (first name first) exactly as it appears on the title page of a book or in the heading of an article. (See ¶1508a note.)

> ¹Dr. Chris Bart, C.A., *A Tale of Two Employees*, Corporate Missions Inc., Surrey, B.C., 2003, p. 58.

> ²Eric W. Kierans with Walter Stewart, *Remembering*, Stoddart Publishing Co. Ltd., Toronto, 2001, p. 105.

> ³Maria Coffey and Dag Goering, *Sailing Back in Time*, rev. ed., Whitecap Books Ltd., North Vancouver, 2002, p. 45.

b. When two authors have the same surname, show the surname with each author's listing.

> ⁴Will Ferguson and Ian Ferguson, *How to Be a Canadian*, Douglas & McIntyre, Vancouver, 2001, p. 67.

c. When there are three or more authors, list only the first author's name followed by *et al.* (meaning "and others"). Do not italicize or underline *et al.*

> ⁵William A. Sabin et al., *The Gregg Reference Manual*, 7th Canadian Edition, McGraw-Hill Ryerson, Toronto, 2006, p. 443.

NOTE: The names of all the authors may be given, but once this style is used in a source reference note, it should be used consistently.

> ⁶William A. Sabin, Wilma K. Millar, Sharon L. Sine, G. Wendy Strashok, *The Gregg Reference Manual*, 7th Canadian Edition, McGraw-Hill Ryerson, Toronto, 2006, p. 443.

d. When an organization (rather than an individual) is the author, show the organization's name in the author's position.

> ⁷Southern Alberta Pioneers, *Pioneer Kitchens: Our Heritage From Many Lands*, Centax Books, Regina, 2001, p. 35.

However, if the organization is both the author and the publisher, show the organization's name only once—as the publisher.

> ⁸*Archives: Archeion*, Archives Association of Ontario, 2001, pp. 1–3.

e. When a work such as an anthology carries an editor's name rather than an author's name, list the editor's name in the author's position, followed by the abbreviation *ed.* in parentheses. (If the names of two or more editors are listed, use the abbreviation *eds.* in parentheses.)

(Continued on page 444.)

[9]Sam Solecki (ed.), *Yours, Al: The Collected Stories of Al Purdy*, Harbour Publishing, Madeira Park, B.C., 2004, pp. 67–84.

[10]Ross Freake and Don Plant (eds.), *Stories From the Firestorm*, M & S Publishing, Kelowna, 2004, pp. 135–146.

NOTE: If a reference work (such as an encyclopedia, a dictionary, or a directory) carries the name of an editor rather than an author, the editor's name is usually omitted. (See ¶1521 note.)

[11]*Oxford Thesaurus of Current English*, Oxford University Press, Oxford, 2003.

RATHER THAN:

[12]Allan Spooner (ed.), *Oxford Thesaurus of Current English*, Oxford University Press, Oxford, 2003.

f. If the author of a work is unknown, begin the note with the title of the work. Do not use *Anonymous* in place of the author's name.

1538 Title of the Work

a. In giving the title of the work, follow the title page of a book or the main heading of an article for wording, spelling, and punctuation. However, adjust the capitalization as necessary so that all titles cited in the notes conform to a standard style. For example, a book entitled *Assertiveness*, with a subtitle (*the right to be you*) shown entirely in small letters on the title page for graphic effect, would appear in a note as follows: Claire Walmsley, *Assertiveness: The Right to Be You.*

☞ *For the capitalization of titles, see ¶¶360–363.*

b. If a title and a subtitle are shown on separate lines in the original work without any intervening punctuation, use a colon to separate them in the source reference note. (See ¶1515 for an example.)

c. In general, use italics or underlining for titles of *complete* published works and quotation marks for titles that refer to *parts* of complete published works.

☞ *For the use of italics or underlining with titles, see ¶287; for the use of quotation marks with titles, see ¶¶242–243.*

1539 Publisher's Name

a. List the publisher's name as it appears on the title page (for example, *John Wiley & Sons*) or in a shortened form that is clearly recognizable (*Wiley*); use one form consistently throughout. If a division of the publishing company is also listed on the title page, it is not necessary to include this information in the footnote. Publishers, however, often do so in references to their own materials.

b. Omit the publisher's name from references to newspapers and other periodicals. The publisher's name is also usually omitted from references to dictionaries and similar works unless confusion might result or the work is not well known. (For examples, see ¶1521.)

1540 Place of Publication

a. As a rule, list only the city of publication (for example, *Vancouver, Winnipeg, Toronto, New York*). If the city is not well known to your intended audience or if it is likely to be confused with another city by the same name, add the country or the abbreviation for the province or state (for example, *Cambridge, England; Cambridge, ON; Cambridge, MA*). If the title page lists several cities in which the publisher has offices, use only the first city named.

b. Omit the place of publication from references to periodicals and well-known reference works.

c. Incorporate the city name in the name of a newspaper that might otherwise be unrecognized. For example, *The Sun* (a common newspaper name) should be referred to in notes as *The Vancouver Sun* or *The Calgary Sun*. (See ¶1522.)

1541 Date of Publication

a. For books show the year of publication. (Use the most recent year shown in the copyright notice.)

b. For monthly or seasonal periodicals show both the month or season and the year. (See ¶1523 for examples.)

c. For weekly or daily newspapers and other periodicals, show the month, day, and year. (See ¶1522 for examples.)

1542 Page Numbers

a. Page references in notes occur in the following forms:

p. 3   p. v

pp. 3–4   pp. v–vi

pp. 301 f. (meaning "page 301 and the following page")

pp. 301 ff. (meaning "page 301 and the following pages")

NOTE: Whenever possible, avoid using the indefinite abbreviations *f.* and *ff.*, and supply a specific range of page numbers instead.

b. In a range of page numbers, the second number is sometimes abbreviated; for example, *pp. 981–983* may be expressed as *pp. 981–83*. (See ¶460.)

c. There is a trend toward dropping *p.* and *pp.* when there is no risk of mistaking the numbers for anything but page numbers.

☞ *For the use of an en dash or a hyphen in a range of numbers, see ¶216e, 459a.*

Subsequent References

1543 a. When a note refers to a work that was fully identified in the note *immediately preceding*, it may be shortened by use of the abbreviation *ibid.* (meaning "in the same place"). *Ibid.* replaces all those elements that would otherwise be carried over intact from the previous note. Do not italicize or underline *ibid.*

(Continued on page 446.)

¹Chris Cobb, *Ego and Ink*, McLelland & Stewart, Toronto, 2004, pp. 36–48.

²Ibid., p. 57. (*Ibid.* represents all the elements in the previous note except the page number.)

³Ibid. (Here *ibid.* represents everything in the preceding note, including the same page number.)

b. If you plan to use *ibid.* in a *footnote*, make sure that the footnote "immediately preceding" is no more than a few pages back. Otherwise, the interested reader will have to riffle back through the pages in order to find the "immediately preceding" footnote. To spare your reader this inconvenience, use the forms suggested in ¶1544d.

c. Do not use *ibid.* in a *textnote* unless the one "immediately preceding" is on the same page and easy to spot; otherwise, your reader will have to search through lines and lines of text to find it. To spare your reader, construct these "subsequent reference" textnotes along the same lines as "first reference" textnotes. (See ¶1507b.)

NOTE: With *endnotes*, the use of *ibid.* will cause no inconvenience, since it refers to the note directly above.

1544 a. When a note refers to a work fully identified in an earlier note but *not the one immediately preceding*, it may be shortened as follows:

¹Author's surname, page number.

⁸Cobb, p. 101. (Referring to the work fully identified in an earlier note; see the first example in ¶1543a.)

NOTE: When short forms are used for subsequent references, it is desirable to provide a complete bibliography as well, so that the interested reader can quickly find the complete reference for each work in an alphabetic listing.

b. When previous reference has been made to different authors with the same surname, the use of a surname alone in a subsequent reference would be confusing. Therefore, the basic pattern in ¶1544a must be modified in the following way:

¹Author's initial(s) plus surname, page number.

OR: ²Author's full name, page number.

¹Matthew Jackson, *The Canada Chronicles*, Summit Studios, Calgary, p. 361.

²R. J. Jackson, *Politics in Canada*, Prentice Hall Canada, Toronto, 2002. pp. 113–145.

³R. J. Jackson, p. 167.

⁴Matthew Jackson, p. 442.

c. If previous reference has been made to different works by the same author, any subsequent reference should contain the title of the specific work now being referred to. This title may be shortened to a key word or phrase; the word or phrase should be sufficiently clear, however, so that the full title can be readily identified in the bibliography or in an earlier note.

¹Author's surname, *book title* [shortened if feasible], page number.

[1]Don Tapscott and David Ticoll, *Digital Capital: Harnessing the Power of Business*, McGraw-Hill, New York, 2000, p. 58.

[2]Don Tapscott, David Ticoll, and Alex Lowy, *Blueprint to the Digital Economy*, McGraw-Hill, New York, 1998, p. 89.

[3]Don Tapscott and David Ticoll, *The Naked Corporation*, Pearson Penguin Canada Inc., Toronto, 2003, p. 144.

[4]Tapscott, *Digital Capital*, p. 85.

[5]Tapscott, *Blueprint*, p. 89.

If referring to an article in a periodical, use the periodical title rather than the article title.

[2]Author's surname, *periodical title* [shortened if feasible], page number.

[6]Jacqueline Thompson, "Small Business: Tech Support," *IE: Money*, June 2001, p. 31.

[7]Arthur Siegel, . . .

[8]Thompson, *IE: Money*, p. 33. (Referring to the work identified in note 6 above.)

d. A more formal style in subsequent references uses the abbreviations *loc. cit.* ("in the place cited") and *op. cit.* ("in the work cited").

[1]Author's surname, **loc. cit.** (This pattern is used when reference is made to the *very same page* in the work previously identified.)

[2]Author's surname, **op. cit.**, page number. (This pattern is used when reference is made to a *different page* in the work previously identified.)

[1]Lloyd Axworthy, *Navigating a New World*, Random House Canada, Toronto, 2003, p. 101.

[2]Keith McArthur, *Air Monopoly*, McClelland & Stewart, Toronto, 2004, p. 85.

[3]Axworthy, op. cit., p. 167. (Referring to a different page in *Navigating*.)

[4]McArthur, loc. cit. (Referring to the same page in *Air Monopoly*.)

[5]Ibid. (Referring to exactly the same page as shown in note 4. *Ibid.* may be used only to refer to the note immediately preceding. See ¶1543.)

NOTE: Do not italicize or underline *loc. cit., op. cit.,* or *ibid.*

BIBLIOGRAPHIES

A bibliography at the end of a report or a manuscript typically lists all the works *consulted* in the preparation of the material as well as all the works that were actually *cited* in the notes. The format of a bibliography is also used for any list of titles, such as a list of recommended readings or a list of new publications.

1545 Word processing software may provide templates for bibliographies. Some special software, however, will format not only footnotes and endnotes but bibliographies as well. You create a database (also referred to as a *reference library*) in which you enter the necessary data for each title you plan to cite. Then you select one of the standard formats built into the software or a format that you

(Continued on page 448.)

have modified or created. In effect, once you have developed the reference library, you can extract the data in the form of footnotes, endnotes, or entries in a bibliography.

1546 Consider the following guidelines for formatting a bibliography. (See the illustration on page 450.)

a. On a new page key *BIBLIOGRAPHY* (or some other appropriate title, such as *REFERENCES*) in all-capital letters and in boldface. Centre this title 2 inches from the top and begin the text on the second or third line below.

b. Use the same margins as for other pages in the body of the report or manuscript (see ¶¶1405–1407), and treat the numbering of these pages as indicated in ¶1427f–g.

c. Bibliographical entries are usually not numbered. (See ¶1547c.) Use the *hanging indent* feature to start the first line of the entry at the left margin and to begin the turnover lines at the tab setting already established for the body of the document.

d. Leave 1 blank line between entries (whether they are single- or double-spaced).

1547 a. List the entries alphabetically by author's last name.

b. Entries lacking an author are alphabetized by title. Disregard the word *The* or *A* at the beginning of a title in determining alphabetic sequence. (For examples, see the fourth and eleventh entries in the illustration on page 450.) Note that the fourth entry is alphabetized on the basis of *Guide* following *Galbraith* and the eleventh entry is alphabetized on the basis of *Two* following *Tapscott*.

NOTE: When a publication lacks an author and the title begins with a figure (see the last entry in the illustration on page 450), alphabetize the title on the basis of how the figure would appear if spelled out. Thus when *2005* is converted to *Two Thousand Five*, the title is alphabetized on the basis of *Two*, following *Tapscott*.

c. If you plan to use the style of textnotes described in ¶1507b(5), then the bibliographical entries should be numbered. In that case begin each entry of the bibliography with a number keyed at the left margin, followed by a period and 1 or 2 spaces. Then key the rest of the entry in the customary way, but indent any turnover lines so that they begin under the first word in the line above. (In the parenthetical textnotes, you can then make reference to different works by their bibliographic "entry number" instead of by author.)

d. In a bibliography with numbered entries, align the numbers on the period.

9. Broadhead, Rick, *The Little Book of Canadian Political Wisdom*, Key Porter Books Ltd., Toronto, 2004.

10. Dubuc, Joey, *Neither Either nor Or*, Conundrum Press, Montreal, 2004.

11. Roberts, Andrew, *What Might Have Been*, McArthur & Company, Toronto, 2004.

NOTE: If you use the numbered list feature of your software program, the turnover lines will automatically be indented. The list will also be typed single-spaced. For a more open look, insert 1 blank line between entries (as shown in the illustration above). The numbered list feature also aligns single- and double-digit numbers on the left. However, you can make an adjustment so that the numbers align at the right (as in the examples ¶1547d). For additional details, see ¶1344d.

1548 When a bibliography contains more than one work by the same author, replace the author's name with a long dash (using 3 em dashes or 6 hyphens) in all the entries after the first. List the works alphabetically by title. (See the eighth and ninth entries in the illustration on page 451 for examples.) Note that these titles are alphabetized on the key words *Naked* and *Digital*. The tenth entry involves co-authors and therefore follows the works written by the first author alone.

NOTE: As an alternative, multiple entries by the same author may be listed according to the date of each publication.

☞ *For guidelines on three-em dashes, see ¶216d.*

1549 Entries in bibliographies contain the same elements and follow the same style as source reference notes except for two key differences.

a. Begin each entry with the name of the author listed in inverted order (last name first). When an entry includes two or more authors' names, invert only the first author's name and insert a comma after it. When an organization is listed as the author, do not invert the name.

> Deloite & Touche, *How to Reduce the Tax You Pay*, 15th ed., Key Porter Books, Toronto, 2002.
>
> Duncan, Jennifer, *Frontier Spirit: The Brave Women of the Klondike*, Random House Canada, Toronto, 2003.
>
> Fisk, Larry, and John Schellenberg, *Pattern of Conflict Paths to Peace*, Broadview Press, Peterborough, 2000.

b. Include page numbers in bibliographic entries only when the material being cited is part of a larger work. In such cases show the page number or numbers (for example, *pp. 215–232*) on which the material appears.

> Trudeau, Alexandre, "The Burden of the Past," *Maclean's*, October 25, 2004, pp. 42–44.

☞ *For the use of an en dash or a hyphen in a range of page numbers, see ¶216e, ¶459a.*

c. In academic material, bibliographic entries follow a slightly different style. In the examples below, note that a period follows each of the three main parts of the entry (author's name, the title, and the publishing information). Also note that the parentheses that normally enclose the publishing information in an academic-style footnote or endnote are omitted in the bibliographic entry. (See ¶1513b.)

(Continued on page 450.)

15

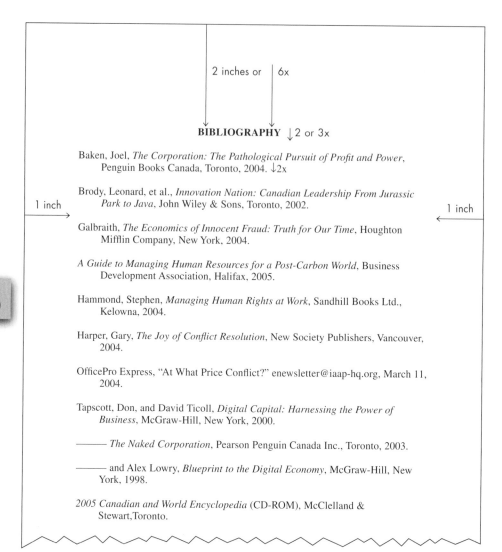

2 inches or | 6x

BIBLIOGRAPHY ↓2 or 3x

Baken, Joel, *The Corporation: The Pathological Pursuit of Profit and Power*, Penguin Books Canada, Toronto, 2004. ↓2x

Brody, Leonard, et al., *Innovation Nation: Canadian Leadership From Jurassic Park to Java*, John Wiley & Sons, Toronto, 2002.

1 inch →

Galbraith, *The Economics of Innocent Fraud: Truth for Our Time*, Houghton Mifflin Company, New York, 2004.

A Guide to Managing Human Resources for a Post-Carbon World, Business Development Association, Halifax, 2005.

Hammond, Stephen, *Managing Human Rights at Work*, Sandhill Books Ltd., Kelowna, 2004.

Harper, Gary, *The Joy of Conflict Resolution*, New Society Publishers, Vancouver, 2004.

OfficePro Express, "At What Price Conflict?" enewsletter@iaap-hq.org, March 11, 2004.

Tapscott, Don, and David Ticoll, *Digital Capital: Harnessing the Power of Business*, McGraw-Hill, New York, 2000.

———— *The Naked Corporation*, Pearson Penguin Canada Inc., Toronto, 2003.

———— and Alex Lowry, *Blueprint to the Digital Economy*, McGraw-Hill, New York, 1998.

2005 Canadian and World Encyclopedia (CD-ROM), McClelland & Stewart, Toronto.

← 1 inch

Brown, Chester. *Louis Riel.* Vancouver: Raincoast Books, 2003.

Murphy, Rex. *Points of View.* Toronto: McClelland & Stewart, 2003.

Trudeau, Alexandre. "The Burden of the Past." *Maclean's,* October 25, 2004, p. 42.

Reineberg Holt, Faye. *Prairie Twins.* Calgary: Detselig Enterprises Ltd., 2004.

 See the Online Learning Centre at www.mcgrawhill.ca/college/gregg for related Web links.

SECTION SIXTEEN

Tables

You can fit a good deal of material into a compact space when you present it in the form of a table—with items arranged in *rows* (to be read horizontally) and in *columns* (to be read vertically). However, in designing a table, you should aim for more than compactness. Your reader should be able to locate specific information more easily—and detect significant patterns or trends in the data more quickly—than if the same information were presented in the regular text.

The table feature of word processing programs is commonly used to display data that appears in a row and column format, including such documents as résumés, agendas, itineraries, etc. Most users who create tables with many calculations will use a spreadsheet program; they may import the table into a word processing document.

The following paragraphs provide detailed guidelines for creating a table with word processing software. Modify these guidelines as necessary to achieve results that are easy to understand, attractive to look at, and as simple as possible to execute.

Using the Software Table Feature

A table can be created with little advance planning. Corrections and format adjustments can be made with relative ease to give the appearance of a professionally typeset table.

<table>
<tr><td colspan="3">Table A-15

LIFE INSURANCE IN FORCE

($000 000 Omitted)</td></tr>
<tr><td>Year</td><td>Ordinary</td><td>Group</td></tr>
<tr><td>1910</td><td>11 783</td><td>—</td></tr>
<tr><td>1940</td><td>79 346</td><td>14 938</td></tr>
<tr><td>1950</td><td>149 116</td><td>47 793</td></tr>
<tr><td>1960</td><td>341 881</td><td>175 903</td></tr>
<tr><td>1970</td><td>734 730</td><td>551 357</td></tr>
<tr><td>1980</td><td>1 760 474</td><td>1 579 355</td></tr>
<tr><td>1990</td><td>5 366 982</td><td>3 753 506</td></tr>
<tr><td>2000</td><td>8 337 188</td><td>5 158 538</td></tr>
<tr><td colspan="3">Source: The Canadian World Almanac and Book of Facts: 2006, p. 837.</td></tr>
</table>

Note that within each column the column heading and the text are centred between vertical rules. Note also the use of extra space surrounding various elements of the table, which gives it an open look and makes it easier to read.

Paragraphs 1601–1606 show (1) the results you will achieve if you prepare this table with the MS Word table feature, accepting all the default specifications, and (2) the steps you need to take in order to achieve the look of a professionally typeset table.

IMPORTANT NOTE: When you use the table feature to execute a table, how far you go in modifying the default specifications will depend on a number of factors. If the table is intended for your eyes alone *and* speed rather than appearance is critical, you may want to limit modifying the default specifications. On the other hand, if the table will appear in a document to be presented to higher management or to people outside the organization, you will have to invest the extra time and effort needed to create a more professional-looking table.

1601 The default format of word processing software encloses the complete table (including any heading at the top and any notes at the bottom) in a grid of horizontal and vertical lines. Each "box" formed is called a cell.

- At the outset specify the number of columns and rows you may need to complete the table; this setting can be easily adjusted if more or fewer are required.

- In the absence of other instructions, the table grid will have the same width as the regular text. You may find it simpler to accept this dimension at the outset and adjust the width of the table later on.

- Tables will automatically be single-spaced.

1602 a. Begin by entering all the data for your table. Notice that everything defaults to a left alignment. For long lines of headings or titles, the text may not fit nicely into the table cell. This will be adjusted later. (See ¶¶1602c and 1603b.) Include the bold attribute for title(s) and column headings. Also use italics for the source reference referred to at the bottom of the table.

16

Table A-15 LIFE INSURANCE IN FORCE ($000 000 Omitted)		
Year	**Ordinary**	**Group**
1910	11 783	—
1940	79 346	14 938
1950	149 116	47 793
1960	341 881	175 903
1970	734 730	551 357
1980	1 760 474	1 579 355
1990	5 366 982	3 753 506
2000	8 337 188	5 158 538
Source: *The Canadian World Almanac and Book of Facts: 2006,* p. 837.		

(Continued on page 454.)

b. It is appropriate to use left alignment when the column text consists entirely of words or figures representing years as shown in the first column. However, when the column text consists of figures that have to be added or compared in some way, the figures should align at the right. The following illustration shows that the "align right" feature has been applied to the second and third columns.

c. In order to set up the titles and the source reference, refer to the illustration below to notice that the cells in the first row and the last row of the table have been joined (merged). To display these elements even more, centre align the titles and set the tab to 0.25 inch for the word *Source*.

16

Table A-15 LIFE INSURANCE IN FORCE ($000 000 Omitted)		
Year	Ordinary	Group
1910	11 783	—
1940	79 346	14 938
1950	149 116	47 793
1960	341 881	175 903
1970	734 730	551 357
1980	1 760 474	1 579 355
1990	5 366 982	3 753 506
2000	8 337 188	5 158 538
Source: *The Canadian World Almanac and Book of Facts: 2006*, p. 837.		

1603 a. The table, as it now stands, has excessively wide columns. To remedy the situation, adjust the column widths either manually or with an "adjust to fit" feature. Use the print preview feature (full page view) often to verify the most attractive horizontal position on the page.

NOTE: To centre a table exactly horizontally on a page, use the Table Properties feature to make the adjustment.

b. Once the table is sized, it will be obvious that the column headings need to be centred in each column. Use the centre align button.

Table A-15
LIFE INSURANCE IN FORCE
($000 000 Omitted)

Year	Ordinary	Group
1910	11 783	—
1940	79 346	14 938
1950	149 116	47 793
1960	341 881	175 903
1970	734 730	551 357
1980	1 760 474	1 579 355
1990	5 366 982	3 753 506
2000	8 337 188	5 158 538

Source: *The Canadian World Almanac and Book of Facts: 2006*, p. 837.

1604 To further improve the appearance of the table, consider making these adjustments.

a. Use *Enter* to insert 1 blank line space between the lines in the table heading and above and below the heading as a whole.

NOTE: If the table title or subtitle will not all fit on one line, break it into sensible phrases and single space the turnover. (See ¶1620 for illustrations of the ways in which the elements in the table heading may be arranged.)

b. Use *Enter* to insert 1 blank line space above and below the column headings.

c. Use *Enter* to insert 1 blank line space above and below the notes section at the bottom of the page.

d. If the footnotes each require no more than one full line, begin each note at the left margin. However, if any one of the notes turns over to a second line, indent the first line of each note 0.25 to 0.5 inch.

e. Add shading to portions of the table as desired to give special emphasis to certain elements and make the table more attractive as a whole.

NOTE: If all of these modifications are made, the table will then look like the following illustration.

(Continued on page 456.)

Table A-15

LIFE INSURANCE IN FORCE

($000 000 Omitted)

Year	Ordinary	Group
1910	11 783	—
1940	79 346	14 938
1950	149 116	47 793
1960	341 881	175 903
1970	734 730	551 357
1980	1 760 474	1 579 355
1990	5 366 982	3 753 506
2000	8 337 188	5 158 538

Source: *The Canadian World Almanac and Book of Facts: 2006*, p. 837.

16

1605 a. If you want to achieve a more open look, you can remove the borders and increase the space between rows as shown in the following illustration.

Table A-15

LIFE INSURANCE IN FORCE

($000 000 Omitted)

Year	Ordinary	Group
1910	11 783	—
1940	79 346	14 938
1950	149 116	47 793
1960	341 881	175 903
1970	734 730	551 357
1980	1 760 474	1 579 355
1990	5 366 982	3 753 506
2000	8 337 188	5 158 538

Source: *The Canadian World Almanac and Book of Facts: 2006*, p. 837.

b. As an alternative, you may simply eliminate all the vertical lines in the grid.

Table A-15

LIFE INSURANCE IN FORCE

($000 000 Omitted)

Year	Ordinary	Group
1910	11 783	—
1940	79 346	14 938
1950	149 116	47 793
1960	341 881	175 903
1970	734 730	551 357
1980	1 760 474	1 579 355
1990	5 366 982	3 753 506
2000	8 337 188	5 158 538

Source: *The Canadian World Almanac and Book of Facts: 2006*, p. 837.

16

1606 Word processing software provides a number of autoformats that can enhance the appearance of your tables. The following illustration is an example of a style offered by MS Word: Elegant.

TABLE A-15

LIFE INSURANCE IN FORCE

($000 000 OMITTED)

Year	Ordinary	Group
1910	11 783	—
1940	79 346	14 938
1950	149 116	47 793
1960	341 881	175 903
1970	734 730	551 357
1980	1 760 474	1 579 355
1990	5 366 982	3 753 506
2000	8 337 188	5 158 538

Source: *The Canadian World Almanac and Book of Facts: 2006*, p. 837.

(Continued on page 458.)

NOTE: When you create a table following the guidelines offered in ¶¶1601-1606, you will notice that the preceding illustration has "lost" the bold and italics attributes and some words in the heading have changed to all-capital letters. These changes are all attributes of the Elegant format. However, it is easy to reformat the fonts. Other autoformats enhance the appearance and readability of tables by shading every second line. Background and reverse font colours are also an option.

Locating Tables Within the Text

1607 a. Tables should be easy to refer to. Therefore, try to locate each table on the same page where the subject of the table is introduced in the text. In this way, the reader will have ready access to the table while reading the text commentary that may precede and follow.

b. Ideally, every table should fall immediately after the point in the text where it is first mentioned. However, if placing the table within a paragraph is likely to disrupt the reader's grasp of the material, then locate the table at the end of the paragraph or at the top or bottom of the page. (See ¶1609d.)

1608 a. Avoid breaking a table at the bottom of a page. If starting a table at the ideal point means that it will not all fit in the space remaining on the page, then place the complete table at the top of the next page. (At the point in the text where the table is first mentioned, insert an appropriate cross-reference in parentheses. See ¶1613.)

NOTE: Word processing software has a feature (*keep lines together*) that prevents a page break from occurring within a block of text. (See Section 20.)

b. If you have to fit a number of relatively short tables (half a page or less) in a document, single space the table text (MS Word default) to maximize your chances of locating each table in the ideal place. (See ¶1622.)

☞ *For other techniques to limit the length of a table to one page, see ¶1634. For guidelines on dealing with a table too long to fit on one page, see ¶1635.*

1609 If a table is to appear on a page that also carries regular text:

a. Centre the table horizontally within the established margins.

b. Try to indent the table at least 0.5 inch from each side margin. In any case, the width of the table should not exceed the width of the text. (See ¶1637.)

c. Use one blank line to set off a table from the text above and below it:

d. Use the table feature to insert the table copy at the desired location in the regular text. If you discover that the table will not all fit on the same page, you can move the table as a whole to the top or bottom of the page, make with prefixes indicating multiples or fractions of a unit. There are seven base units in the SI metric system. ↓2x

Quantity	Unit	Symbol
Length	metre	m
Mass	kilogram	kg
Time	second	s
Electric current	ampere	A
Thermodynamic temperature	kelvin	K
Amount of substance	mole	mol
Luminous intensity	candela	cd

↓2x

In addition, there are two supplementary units, the radian and the steradian.

other adjustments (as noted in ¶¶1634–1636), or place the table on a page by itself (see ¶¶1610–1613). If you use the *keep lines together* feature, the table will not be divided at the bottom of a page; instead the table as a whole will be moved to the top of the next page.

e. Be sure you can fit at least two full lines of regular text above or below the table. If the results look unattractive, devote the full page to the table (see ¶¶1610–1613) and resume the text on the following page.

Locating Tables on Separate Pages

1610 When a table occupies more than two-thirds of a page, it can often be difficult to fit it on the same page with regular text. In such cases type the table on a separate page and place it immediately after the text page on which the reference to the table is first made.

NOTE: Insert a hard page break before and after the table to ensure that the table will appear on a page by itself. (See ¶1636b.)

1611 If a document contains a number of tables, most of which will each require a separate page, then all the tables (short as well as long) may be executed as an appendix or as an attachment. This arrangement—which permits the reader to keep the full set of tables alongside the regular text (except in the case of bound reports)—can be very convenient, especially if some of the tables are repeatedly cited throughout the regular text. This arrangement also eliminates the problem of trying to fit long tables within the text.

1612 When a table is to appear on a page by itself, centre the table horizontally and vertically within the established margins of the page.

NOTE: If no margins have been established, leave a minimum margin of 1 inch on all four sides of the table.

1613 When a table must be placed on another page, provide a cross-reference in parentheses to the appropriate page.

(See Table 4 on page 18.)   **OR**   (See Table 2–2 on page 31.)

NOTE: These parenthetical cross-references may be treated as a separate sentence (as shown above) or as part of another sentence. (See ¶220.)

☞ *For the advisability of numbering tables to simplify the matter of cross-references, see ¶1616.*

Centring Tables

1614 a. The table feature of word processing software extends the table to the full width of the regular text. If you decide to reduce the overall width of the table, first type the table. Then *click and drag* the outside lines or use *autofit* to adjust the width of the columns. Choose the *centre alignment* setting to position the whole table horizontally.

b. If a table appears on a page by itself, centre the table vertically as well. (Use the *centre page* feature of your software.)

Table Identification

1615 Identify tables by *title* unless they are not very numerous and the significance of the material in the table is clear without some descriptive label. (See ¶1618a.)

1616 Also identify tables by *number* unless they are quite short, not very numerous, and referred to only on the page on which they fall. The use of table numbers simplifies the matter of cross-references, an important consideration if you expect that a number of tables will not fit on the page where they are first mentioned or if you know that certain tables will be referred to repeatedly throughout the regular text.

NOTE: Tables may be numbered consecutively throughout a document or consecutively within each chapter and each appendix. With the latter technique, the chapter number (or the appendix number or letter) is used as a prefix in the numbering scheme. For example, Table 3–2 would be the second table in Chapter 3, and Table A–5 would be the fifth table in Appendix A.

1617 The table title may be followed by a *subtitle*, which provides additional information about the significance of the table, the period of time it covers, or the manner in which the information is organized or presented. Since a subtitle should be held to one line if possible (two at the most), a lengthy comment on any of these points should be handled as a note to the table rather than as a subtitle. (See ¶¶1631–1633.)

1618 Type the elements of table identification as follows:

a. Table Title. Centre the table title, using all-capital letters in boldface. (See ¶1609c for spacing.)

b. Table Number. Type the word *Table* in capital and small letters, followed by the appropriate number. To give the table number special emphasis, centre it on the second line above the table title and use boldface. To hold down the length of the table, key the table number on the same line with the table title; in this case, insert a period after the table number and leave 1 or 2 spaces before keying the table title. (See the illustrations below.)

NOTE: Within a given document, treat all table numbers the same way.

c. Table Subtitle. Centre the subtitle on the second line below the title, using capital and small letters in boldface. The subtitle is usually enclosed in parentheses when it simply comments on the listing of data in some special order (for example, *In Descending Order by Sales Revenue*) or on the omission of zeros from figures given in the table (for example, *In Millions* or *000 Omitted*).

☞ *For examples of subtitles enclosed in parentheses, see the tables illustrated in* ¶¶1602–1606.

NOTE: If either the title or the subtitle requires more than one line, break it into sensible phrases; then single space and centre any turnover lines. If possible, try to hold the title and the subtitle to two lines each.

Column Headings

1619 a. Unless a table is very simple and the significance of the material is clear without headings, provide a heading for each column. (A heading may be omitted over the first column, also known as the *stub*. See, for example, the

```
            Table 5


      TITLE OF THE TABLE
   WITH ONE TURNOVER LINE

        Table Subtitle
```

```
   Table 3–4. TITLE OF THE TABLE
      WITH ONE TURNOVER LINE

           Table Subtitle
         With One Turnover Line
```

table in ¶1629c.)

b. Whenever possible, use singular forms in the column headings. Thus, for example, over a column listing a number of symbols, use the heading *Symbol* rather than *Symbols*. (See ¶1609.)

c. In order to hold down the length of column headings, use abbreviations and symbols as necessary. For example:

Acct. No.   Account number
% of Total   Percent of total

(Continued on page 462.)

FY2007 **OR** FY07	Fiscal year 2007 (also used to indicate that a company's *fiscal* year does not coincide with the *calendar* year)
1Q/2007 **OR** 1Q/07	First quarter of 2007 (also used with 2Q, 3Q, and 4Q to signify the other three quarters of the year)
2007A	Actual results in 2007
2008B	Budgeted results in 2008
2008E	Estimated results in 2008
2009F	Forecast of results in 2009

If your reader may not understand some of the abbreviations and symbols you use, explain the unfamiliar ones in a footnote to the table. For example:

> Note: A = actual; E = estimated; F = forecast. (See ¶1621c.)

NOTE: As an alternative to the use of abbreviations, select a smaller font size for the column headings.

d. Column headings should be single spaced and may be broken into as many as five lines. Column headings are normally centred on the column width, but under certain circumstances the lines that make up the column headings may all be blocked left or right on the column width. (See ¶1620.)

e. Capitalize the first letter of each word in a column heading except articles *(a, an, the)*, conjunctions under four letters (such as *and* and *or*), and prepositions under four letters (such as *of* and *in*). See ¶¶360–361, 363 for detailed guidance on capitalizing words in column headings.

f. Type all column headings in boldface.

g. If the column headings do not all take the same number of lines, align the column headings at the bottom. Choose the *cell bottom alignment* option for automatic alignment.

h. Leave 1 blank line above and below the tallest column heading.

i. When column headings are extremely long, consider using abbreviations in the column headings and explaining them (if necessary) in a table footnote. As an alternative, use a smaller font size. (See ¶1633.)

1620 a. When you use the table feature, the default alignment for all column headings is at the left. (See the illustration in ¶1602a.)

b. If you change the alignment of the column text from left to right (for example, with a column of figures), align the column heading at the right as well. (See the illustration in ¶1602c.)

c. When a very narrow column heading falls above a very wide column of text, the table may look more attractive if the column heading is centred over the column text.

Name	Name
A. Michael Ashworth	A. Michael Ashworth
Dwayne Gilpatrick Jr.	Dwayne Gilpatrick Jr.
Bradley M. Harrington	Bradley M. Harrington

Sales	Sales
95 517 833	95 517 833
1 039 875 742	1 039 875 742
874 320 199	874 320 199

d. When a very wide column heading falls above a very narrow column of text, you may produce some very odd-looking tables. To avoid this problem, centre the column text and heading as a block.

Applications Received	Applications Received
98	98
182	182
87	87

e. All column headings should be either blocked or centred. Do not mix styles within a table.

1621 BRACED COLUMN HEADINGS

a. Some complex tables contain *braced* column headings (headings that "embrace" two or more columns). They are also called *straddle* headings because they straddle two or more columns. (See the illustration on page 464.)

b. There are two ways to create a table with braced headings. You can create the table body—5 columns in the following illustration—and merge the cells that will be used for the braced headings. Or you can create a 3-column table, type the braced headings in the appropriate cells, and then split the cells below the braced headings to complete the table.

c. To achieve the best appearance, centre each braced column heading over the appropriate columns; centre the other column headings and the related column text between the vertical rules in each case.

Table Text

1622 SPACING

a. The table text may be typed with single, or one and a half, or double spacing. However, you may find it easier to accept the default spacing provided by your software. (MS Word uses single spacing.) Within the same document try to treat all tables alike.

b. Although double-spaced tables may be more readable, single spacing reduces the overall length of a document and maximizes your chances of locating each table on the page where it is first mentioned.

NOTE: You can make single-spaced tables more readable by retaining the horizontal rules between rows and by the use of shading. (See ¶1604.) A

(Continued on page 464.)

slight increase in spaces between rows can make single-spaced tables more readable. (See ¶1605a.)

c. As a rule, type the table with the same spacing (or less) used for the regular text. If regular text is single spaced, all the tables should also be single spaced. If regular text is double spaced, all tables may be typed with single or double spacing.

Table With Braced Column Headings

Table 12. CABLE DIVISION SALES AND NET OPERATING INCOME				
From 2007 to 2009				
	Sales		Net Operating Income	
Year	Thousands of Dollars	Percent of Increase	Thousands of Dollars	Percent of Increase
2007A	1429	—	252	—
2008E	1300	(13.3)	216	(9.2)
2009F	3000	130.8	480	122.2

Note: A = actual; E = estimated; F = forecast.

1623 ITEMS CONSISTING OF WORDS

If the table text consists of items expressed entirely in words:

a. Capitalize only the first word of each item in the table text plus any proper nouns and proper adjectives.

NOTE: In special cases, where it may be important to show whether terms are capitalized or written with small letters, the first word in each item need not be consistently capitalized. (See, for example, the second and third columns of the table in ¶1609c.)

b. Use abbreviations and symbols as necessary to hold down the length of individual items. (See ¶1619c for examples.)

c. Align each item at the left margin of the column. If any item requires more than one line, set a tab to indent the runover line 0.25 inch. However, if a column contains both main entries and subentries, begin the main entry at the left margin of the column text, set tabs to indent the first line of subentries 0.25 inch, and indent all turnover lines 0.5 inch.

Photographs, prints, and illustrations	Total weekly broad-
Scientific or technical drawings	cast hours
Commercial prints	General
Reproductions of works of art	programs
	Instructional
	programs

NOTE: You can avoid the need to indent turnovers (but not subentries) if you use horizontal rules or extra space to separate the entries. The table feature will automatically align turnovers at the left, and the horizontal rules or extra space will help to make each entry visually distinct.

Photographs, prints, and illustrations	Total weekly broadcast hours
Scientific or technical drawings	General programs
Commercial prints	Instructional programs
Reproductions of works of art	

16

d. If an item in the first column requires more than one line and all the other items in the same row require only one line, align all the items in that row at the bottom.

Chemical and allied products	151	201
Petroleum refining and related products	69	73
Paper and allied products	391	364

e. Do not use a period as terminal punctuation at the end of any item except in a column where all entries are in sentence form. Some writers prefer to retain the space or comma in four-digit numbers under all circumstances.

1624 Agendas, itineraries, and résumés are good examples of text that can be presented in table form. The following résumé shows a working screen copy of the student's printed résumé shown on page 490. Note that the lines and callout indicators disappear when the document is printed.

(Continued on page 466.)

¶1624

1. Create a two-column table.

2. Merge 2 cells.

TRACY FLEURY

¶ 66 Quidi Vidi Road St. John's, Newfoundland A1A 1C1 ¶	Telephone: 709.234.5641 E-mail: jlfleury@rogers.com Fax: 709.256.2921 ¶

3. This heading is centred in the merged cell.

4. Adjust default column widths.

SUMMARY OF QUALIFICATIONS¶

5. Split this cell into three cells (3 cols. 1 row).

• Typing: 65 wpm • WordPerfect 12 • Publisher MS	• MS Word Applications • Web Design • Project Management	• PowerPoint • Excel • AccPac

¶

EDUCATION¶

September 2006 to → March 2007	**Office Administration Diploma, Executive Program** College of the North Atlantic, St. John's, NL GPA 3.7¶ ¶ **Course Highlights** • Accounting→ • Office and Special Events Management • Business Law→ • Organizational Behaviour • Communications→ • Work Practicum ¶ **Awards and Activities** • Alumni Keyboarding Prize for attained speed and accuracy • Graduation Committee Treasurer • Participant in college curling and hockey leagues ¶
September 2005 to → April 2006	**Office Administration Certificate** College of the North Atlantic, St. John's, NL GPA 3.3¶

¶

EXPERIENCE¶

May 2006 to → August 2006	**Clerical Assistant:** Beazley General Insurance Co. Ltd., St. John's • Sorted mail, reorganized files, answered telephone, prepared claims • Developed self-reliance, yet appreciated the need for team work in an office¶
July 2005 to → August 2005	**Server:** Radisson Plaza Hotel Coffee Shop, St. John's • Served meals to customers, prepared bills, processed payments • Improved communication and organizational skills¶
2000 to 2005	**Babysitter:** Cared for a number of neighbourhood children

Note: Delete all borders (except the top border) for the printed copy.

1625 ITEMS CONSISTING OF FIGURES

a. If a column of table text consists of items expressed entirely in figures:

(1) Align columns of whole numbers at the right (right align).
(2) Align columns of decimal amounts on the decimal point (decimal tab).
(3) In a column that contains both whole numbers and decimals, add a decimal point and zeros to the whole numbers to maintain a consistent appearance.
(4) Omit spaces or commas in four-digit whole numbers unless they appear in the same column with larger numbers containing spaces or commas.

325	325	465.2137
1	1	1250.0004
152 657	152,657	1.0000
1 489	1,489	37.9898

b. If a column of table text consists entirely of "clock" times (as in a program or schedule):

(1) Align the figures in "on the hour" expressions at the right. Add 1 or 2 spaces before a single-digit number to maintain right alignment.

    11 a.m.
    12 noon
    1 p.m.
    12 midnight

(2) Align the figures in "hour and minute" expressions on the colon. (Add two zeros to exact times to maintain a uniform appearance.)

    8:15 a.m.
    10:30 a.m.
    1:45 p.m.
    12:00 midnight

(3) When the items in a column each consist of a starting and an ending time, either align them on the hyphen or en dash within the items or align all the items at the left.

Preferred	Acceptable	24-Hour Clock
8:30– 9:30	8:30–9:30	0830–0930
10:30–11:30	10:30–11:30	1030–1130
12:30– 1:30	12:30–1:30	1230–1330
2:30– 3:30	2:30–3:30	1430–1530
4:45– 6:00	4:45–6:00	1645–1800

NOTE: In the "24-hour" system of expressing clock time (in which midnight is 0000 and 11:59 p.m. is 2359), the alignment of clock times poses no problem since all times are expressed in four digits (with no colons and no reference to *a.m.* and *p.m.*).

1626 AMOUNTS OF MONEY

a. In a column containing dollar amounts, insert a dollar sign only before the first amount at the head of the column and before the total amount.

$ 45.00	**OR**	$ 165	**OR**	$43,376
2406.05		3 450		9,184
783.25		98 932		113,451
$3234.30		$102 547		$166,011

(Continued on page 468.)

16

b. The dollar signs at the head and foot of the column should align in the first space to the left of the longest amount in the column. (The total line is often the longest amount in the column.) If the item at the head of the column is shorter than the one at the foot, aligning the dollar signs can be troublesome. Choose one of the following approaches to deal with the problem:

(1) Avoid the problem altogether by incorporating the dollar sign in the column heading—for example *($000,000 Omitted)*. Then there is no need for dollar signs alongside the figures below.

(2) Type the dollar sign in the space before the first number. After the column is finished, insert spaces between the first dollar sign and the first digit to align the dollar signs (2 spaces for each digit, 1 space for each comma, if used).

c. Do not insert spaces or commas to set off thousands in four-digit numbers unless they appear in the same column with larger numbers. (See the examples in ¶1625a and ¶1626a.) Moreover, if all the amounts in a column are whole dollar amounts, omit the decimal and zeros (as in the second example in ¶1626a). However, if any amount in a column includes cents, use a decimal and zeros with any whole dollar amount in the same column (as in the first example in ¶1626a).

d. If the table text ends with a *total* line, a horizontal rule or border should separate the body of the table from the total line. Type the word *Total* or *Totals* in the first column, depending on the number of total amounts to be shown in this row. Use an initial capital or (for emphasis) all-capital letters. Start the word at the left margin of the column or indent it 0.5 inch.

2007 SALES REVENUES

Region	2007B	2007A	Percent of Difference
Eastern	$ 300 000	$ 345 108	15.0
Central	450 000	467 380	3.9
Southern	260 000	291 849	12.2
Western	240 000	241 005	0.4
Totals	$1 250 000	$1 345 342	7.6

1627 PERCENTAGES

a. If all the figures in a column represent percentages, type a percent sign (%) directly after each figure unless the column heading clearly indicates that these are percentages.

b. Percentages involving decimals should align on the decimal point. If necessary, add zeros after the decimal part of the number so that each figure will align at the right. If any percentage is less than 1 percent, add one zero to the left of the decimal point.

Increase	Percent of Increase	Increase (%)
55.48%	11.63	24
0.08%	4.00	37
2.09%	24.60	120
13.00%	0.40	8

1628 SPECIAL TREATMENT OF FIGURES IN TABLES

a. Columns of long figures can be reduced in width by omitting the digits representing thousands, millions, or billions and indicating this omission in parentheses. For example:

(In Thousands)	**OR**	(000 Omitted)
(In Millions)		(000 000 Omitted)
(In Billions)		(000 000 000 Omitted)

NOTE: The word forms on the left are easier to grasp.

b. If the parenthetical comment applies to all columns of figures in the table, insert it as a subtitle to the table. However, if the comment applies only to one column of figures, insert the parenthetical comment in the column heading.

NOTE: Sometimes because of space limitations a comment such as *(000 Omitted)* is reduced to *(000)*. The latter form is permissible if you are sure your reader will understand it.

c. If the parenthetical comment applies to columns of dollar amounts, this fact can also be noted within parentheses and the dollar sign can then be omitted from the column of figures.

($000 Omitted)   **OR**   (In Thousands of Dollars)   **OR**   ($000)

d. When omitting thousands, millions, or billions from a wide column of figures, you may use rounding or a shortened decimal (or both) to reflect the portion of the number that is being omitted. The following table illustrates metric number format.

Complete Version	Shortened Versions		
Sales Revenues	Sales Revenues ($000 Omitted)	Sales Revenues (In Millions)	Sales Revenues ($000 000)
$ 5 878 044	5 878	$ 5.9	6
29 023 994	29 024	29.0	29
14 229 683	14 230	14.2	14
$49 131 721	49 132	$49.1	49

(Continued on page 470.)

e. A negative figure in a column may be designated by enclosing the figure in parentheses or by inserting a minus sign (represented by a hyphen or an en dash) directly to the left of the negative figure.

$1642.38	28.2%	Sales in 2006 . . .	$264 238
-82.41	-14.5%	Sales in 2007 . . .	262 305
$1559.97	6.1%	Gain/(loss)	$ (1 933)

1629 LEADERS

a. If the items in the first column vary greatly in length, use leaders (rows of periods) to lead the eye across to the adjacent item in the next column. Every line of leaders should have at least three periods.

b. The *leader* feature in MS Word offers the choice of solid periods, solid hyphens, or solid underscores. Other programs may allow you to specify the character to be used and the space to be left between characters.

Table With Leaders

Table 3

NATIONAL INCOME BY SELECTED INDUSTRIES

(In Billions of Dollars)

	1980	1990	2000
Agriculture, forestry, and fisheries	61.4	97.1	105.3
Construction	126.6	234.4	228.0
Finance, insurance, and real estate	279.5	679.8	816.0
Government enterprises	321.8	657.9	765.3
Manufacturing	532.1	846.9	928.2
Services	341.0	948.3	1171.0

1630 ACCOUNTING FOR OMITTED ITEMS

When there is no entry to be keyed in a given row, you can simply leave a blank at that point. However, if doing so may raise a question in the mind of your reader, consider these alternatives:

a. Key the abbreviation *NA* (meaning "not available" or "not applicable") centred on the column width.

b. Key a row of periods or hyphens. Use as few as three (centred on the column width) or key the row to the full width of the column.

23 804	23 804	23 804
16 345	16 345	16 345
....	----	NA
38 442	38 442	38 442

NOTE: If any one of the columns in a table contains omitted items, you will not be able to use a formula to perform calculations.

Table Notes

1631 a. If a table requires any explanatory notes or an identification of the source from which the table was derived, place such material at the foot of the table. (Do not treat it as part of a sequence of notes related to the main text.)

   b. A horizontal rule should separate the body of the table from the table notes.

     (1) If the table displays horizontal rules, the separation will be automatically provided. (See ¶1604.)

     (2) If the table has been executed in an *open* style (without horizontal and vertical rules), leave 1 blank line below the last line of the table text and type a 1-inch line of underscores. (See ¶1605a.)

   c. Begin the first table note on the second line below the horizontal rule.

   d. If all the notes occupy no more than one full line each, begin each note at the left margin of the table text (for the sake of appearance) and single space the notes. However, if any of the notes turn over onto a second line, indent the first line of each note 0.25 to 0.5 inch, start all turnover lines at the left margin of the table text, and leave 1 blank line between each pair of notes.

1632 If the material in the table has been derived from another source, indicate this fact as follows:

   a. Type the word *Source* with an initial capital or in all-capital letters, followed by a colon, 1 or 2 spaces, and the identifying data. (See ¶¶1513–1544 for models to follow in presenting this bibliographic data.)

   b. A source note should precede any other table note. (See ¶1631.)

1633 a. If you use abbreviations or symbols that the reader may not understand, explain them in a note at the bottom of the table. This explanation should follow the source note (if any) and precede any other table note. If more than one abbreviation or symbol needs decoding, the explanation can be handled as a series of separate notes (each preceded by a superscript symbol or letter), or it may be done all in one note. (See ¶1621c, table.)

   b. Except for source notes and a single note explaining symbols and abbreviations (like the one shown on page 464), every table note should begin with a

(Continued on page 472.)

superscript symbol or letter that keys the note to the appropriate word or figure in the table text (or title or subtitle) above. Type the corresponding superscript symbol or letter immediately after the appropriate word or figure above, without any intervening space. (See ¶1633d, note.)

c. Use the following sequence of symbols: *, **, *** OR *, †, ‡, §, ¶. (See ¶1502f.)

d. Use superscript lower case letters (ᵃ, ᵇ, ᶜ, etc.) in place of symbols when there are more than five footnotes for a table.

NOTE: Avoid the use of superscript *figures* to identify table notes. They could be confusing if used in conjunction with figures in the table text. Moreover, if superscript figures are already used for notes pertaining to the main text, it is wise to use letters or symbols so as to distinguish notes that pertain to a specific table.

e. In assigning symbols or letters in sequence, go in order by row (horizontally), not by column (vertically).

Dealing With Long Tables

1634 To keep a table from extending beyond the page on which it starts, consider these techniques:

a. Put the table number (if any) on the same line as the table title rather than on the second line above. (See also ¶1618c.)

b. Use single spacing for the table text or group items within a cell.

c. Shorten the wording of the table title, subtitle, column headings, and items in the table text to reduce turnover lines. Use abbreviations and symbols to achieve this. (See also ¶1619c.) If necessary, provide a brief explanation in the table notes of any abbreviations and symbols that your reader may not immediately understand. (See also ¶1633.)

d. When there is a long item in the table text that is out of proportion to all the other items (or is to be entered in several places in the table text), try to convert the item into a table note, keyed by a symbol or letter appropriately placed in the table above.

e. If a table is both narrow and long, you can save space by repeating the same sequence of column headings on both the left and right sides of the table. The first half of the table text appears on the left side of the table, and the remaining table text appears on the right. Separate the two sections with a double vertical line.

FIRE LOSSES FROM 2000 TO 2007

Year	Total (000 000 Omitted)	Per Capita	Year	Total (000 000 Omitted)	Per Capita
2000	$5625	$24.50	2004	$7753	$32.47
2001	5894	25.42	2005	8488	35.21
2002	6320	26.98	2006	8634	35.44
2003	7602	32.15	2007	9626	39.12

f. Select a smaller size of font than the one you are using for other tables.

1635 If a table requires more than one page, follow this procedure:

a. At the bottom of the page where the table breaks, type a continuation line in parentheses—for example, *(Continued on page 14)*—unless it is quite obvious that the table continues on the next page. Merge the cells in the last row at the bottom of the page, then, using right alignment, type the continuation line.

TWENTIETH-CENTURY INVENTIONS

Invention	Date	Nation
Airship, rigid dirigible	1900	Germany
Washer, electric	1901	United States
Pen, ballpoint	1938	Hungary
Teflon	1938	United States
Airplane jet engine	1939	Germany
		(Continued on page 14)

b. At the top of the next page, before continuing with the table text, insert the table number (if used), title, and column headings by marking those rows as header rows. If your software will permit it, insert *Continued* in parentheses after the table number (if used) or after the table title.

(Continued on page 474.)

TWENTIETH-CENTURY INVENTIONS (Continued)

Invention	Date	Nation
CAT scan	1973	England
Microcomputer	1973	France
Disk player, compact	1979	Japan
Heart, artificial	1982	United States

If your software will not permit you to make insertions in the header rows, merge the cells in the first row beneath the column headings; then insert a continuation line in parentheses and align it at the left margin.

TWENTIETH-CENTURY INVENTIONS

Invention	Date	Nation
(Continued from page 13)		
CAT scan	1973	England
Microcomputer	1973	France
Disk player, compact	1979	Japan
Heart, artificial	1982	United States

c. Ordinarily, all table notes should appear only on the page on which the table ends. However, if certain notes will help the reader interpret the data in the table (for example, notes explaining certain abbreviations or symbols), repeat these notes on each page on which the table appears. (A source note would appear only on the page where the table ends.)

1636 a. Do not start a table at the bottom of one page and continue it on the top of the next page if the entire table will fit on one page (either by itself or with regular text). In such a case start the table at the top of the next page and insert a cross-reference in the text. (See ¶1613.)

b. If you use the *keep lines together* feature to keep a table from breaking at the bottom of a page, the table as a whole will appear at the top of the next page. However, the space previously occupied by the first part of the table will remain empty; the text that follows the table will not come forward to fill up this vacant space. If you want to avoid this result, do not use *keep lines together*. Use the following approach instead:

(1) Let the table break naturally and continue typing the rest of the document.

(2) When the document is completed in all other respects, select and cut the table; the text following the table will flow forward. Insert a hard page break at the bottom of the page where the table was removed, and paste the whole table at the top of the following page.

Dealing With Wide Tables

1637 To keep a wide table from extending beyond the margins established for the page, consider the following techniques:

a. Click and drag column borders or use the autofit feature to reduce the width of the columns.

b. Use abbreviations and symbols to hold down the length of lines in the column headings and the column text.

c. If only a few entries are disproportionately wide or are repeated in the table and make it difficult to fit the table in the space available, consider the possibility of converting these items to table footnotes. (See also ¶1634d.)

d. Select a smaller font size in order to make the table fit within the space available.

e. Whenever possible, a table should read horizontally *(portrait orientation)*, just like the regular text. However, when other alternatives do not work, create the table in *landscape orientation*, which places the table sideways on the page. This will allow two or more additional inches in width. Any other combination of the above considerations may also have to be used. If the finished document will be bound, leave a larger top margin (for instance, 1.5 inches) on a landscape table page to allow for the binding.

 See the Online Learning Centre at www.mcgrawhill.ca/college/gregg for related Web links.

SECTION SEVENTEEN

Other Business Documents

Section 17 provides models for a number of common business documents. The models reflect formats widely used, but they should not be regarded as rigid patterns. Modify these formats to fit your needs. As always, good sense and good taste should prevail.

IMPORTANT NOTE: Your software may have templates for many of the documents discussed in Section 17. If you decide to use a template provided by your software, you may find it helpful to examine the corresponding model in this section to see whether there are certain features or details that are worth adding to the basic template.

GENERAL FORMAT CONSIDERATIONS

Paragraphs 1701–1702 deal with the issues of formatting margins and headings and apply to all the documents discussed later in Section 17.

Margins

1701 a. Top Margin. Use a top margin of about 2 inches if you are using standard stationery. However, accept the default top margin of 1 inch in order to fit more copy on the page and avoid the need for a second page. If you are using letterhead for the first page, begin typing at least 0.5 inch below the letterhead. If the document requires more than one page, use plain paper for the continuation pages and leave a top margin of 1 inch.

  b. Side Margins. Leave the default settings as is for standard stationery. In some instances, it may be appropriate to set wider margins if you want to bring columns of text closer together for easier reading or you want to achieve a more open look or a more balanced copy arrangement.

  c. Bottom Margin. Leave a bottom margin of 1 inch but adjust if necessary.

  NOTE: Try to maintain consistency in white space around the document.

Headings

1702 a. Main Heading. The title of the document or the name of the organization ordinarily appears centred and bolded on the first line in all-capital letters. Additional details (such as a date or a location) appear in capital and small letters on separate lines, with 1 blank line between them. The use of boldface for these lines is optional. Leave 1 or 2 blank lines between the last line of the main heading and the body of the document. (See pages 482 and 483.)

  NOTE: If any item in the heading requires more than 1 line, type the turnover line single-spaced and centred on the line above.

  b. Continuation Heading. If a document requires more than one page, use the header feature to create and automatically position the continuation heading. (See ¶1364 for format details.)

EXECUTIVE DOCUMENTS

The following paragraphs (¶¶1703–1706) present formats for **agendas**, **minutes**, **itineraries**, and **fax cover sheets**.

Agendas

1703 An *agenda* is a list of items to be considered or acted upon. The format of an agenda varies with the circumstances. The agenda for an informal staff meeting may be done as a simple numbered list of topics in a memo addressed to the attendees. (See page 480.) The agenda for a formal meeting (for example, of a corporate board of directors) will typically call for a more structured list of

(Continued on page 478.)

topics. (See page 481.) The agenda for a formal program (for example, for a conference or a seminar) will be structured around a timetable, with specific time slots allotted to formal presentations by speakers and topical discussions in small groups. (See page 482.)

The illustrations that follow are intended only to suggest various ways in which an agenda can be formatted. The format you decide to use should be tailored to fit the needs of the meeting or program being planned.

Minutes

1704 *Minutes* are a record of what was discussed and decided upon at a meeting. The minutes of small committee meetings within an organization are usually done in an informal style. When the participants at a meeting come from a number of different organizations (for example, at meetings of professional associations), the minutes tend to be more formal.

Increasing government regulations and shareholders' lawsuits make it critically important that the minutes of a meeting of a corporation's board of directors be complete and accurate, since they may have to serve as legal evidence as to what the corporation's directors did or intended to do. When minutes may have to serve a legal use, they are typically done in a highly formal style.

☞ *Refer to* Robert's Rules of Order *for conducting meetings and recording minutes.*

Itineraries

1705 An itinerary should clearly set forth the travel arrangements and the appointment schedule of the person making the trip. If the itinerary is intended only for the use of the person travelling, it should be possible to eliminate certain items and abbreviate details that the person is quite familiar with. However, if the itinerary will be distributed to others (who may need to contact the person who is travelling), present the information as fully and as clearly as possible. (For an example, see the illustration on page 486.)

Fax Cover Sheets

1706 Most messages sent by fax (facsimile) equipment are accompanied by a fax cover sheet that indicates (1) the name and fax number of the person receiving the fax, (2) the name and fax number of the person sending the fax, (3) the number of pages being sent, and (4) the name and the telephone number of the person to be called in case the transmission is not satisfactorily completed. Rather than create your own cover sheet, you can use commercially prepared stick-on labels and stamps.

There are different ways to prepare a fax cover sheet. Your software may provide a fax template that you can use as is or modify to suit your preferences. If you are designing a fax cover sheet as a form to be filled in by hand, you will need to add fill-in lines. (See page 479.)

Fax Cover Sheet

BURNHAM & FRYE

226 High Ridge Road   Telephone: 519.555.5555
Stratford, ON N5A 4Y2   E-mail: burnfry@rogers.net

FAX TRANSMISSION

A

To: From:

Fax: Date:

B

Phone: Phone:

Re: **No. of Pages:** (Including this page)

☐ Urgent   ☐ Please Reply   ☐ For Review   ☐ For Your File

Message:

C   The contents of this fax transmission are confidential. If this transmission has been directed to the wrong office, please destroy the contents of this fax immediately and notify [name] and [phone number].

17

A Format Considerations. If you are using software to create a template for a fax cover sheet that only you will use, insert any information that will not change (such as your name and fax number) as a part of the template. However, if you are creating a form to be used by a number of people, provide headings to accommodate this variable information.

B Fill-in Lines. If you are designing a fax cover sheet as a form to be filled in by hand, arrange fill-in lines so that all entries can start at a common point.

C Confidentiality Statement. You may want to confirm that the recipient is standing by the receiving fax machine. Some cover sheet templates (particularly legal) include at the bottom of the page a confidentiality statement such as the one shown above.

Agenda—Informal (Memo) Style

A **TO:**   Marketing Managers' Committee ↓2x

     FROM: Dorothy Innie ↓2x *DI*

     DATE: July 10, 2007 ↓2x

     SUBJECT: Agenda for July 20 Meeting ↓2 or 3x

Our July 20 meeting will begin at 9:30 a.m. in the small conference room on the second floor. (The large conference room, where we normally meet, has been reserved by Mrs. Harper for an all-day meeting.) ↓2x

Please come prepared to discuss the following topics: ↓2x

B 1. Sales through June for each product line. ↓2x

    2. Year-end sales forecast vs. budget for each product line.

    3. Recommendations for changes in this year's marketing plans and requests for supplemental funding.

    4. Proposed changes in next year's marketing strategies.

C 5. Preliminary marketing budgets for next year. (Please put these in writing for me so that I can share them with Bill Carr, our friendly bean counter in the Finance Department.) ↓2x

ma ↓2 or 3x

Distribution: ↓2x

G. Albers
R. Fagan
K. Garcia-Lorca
F. Li

A **Memo Format.** For the format of a memo template, see ¶1374. For the format of a memo done on plain paper (as shown here), see ¶1375.

B **Numbered List.** The numbered list feature of your software may begin with each item at the left margin with turnovers indented to align with the first word above, and no space left between items. However, an agenda requires at least 1 blank line to make the list easier to read. (See ¶1344d.)

C **End Punctuation.** The items in an agenda typically require no end punctuation. However, if any item contains a complete sentence (as in item 5 in this illustration), place a period at the end of every item. For details on the use or omission of periods with items in a list, see ¶107.

Agenda—Formal Style

A

UNDERLOCK AND KEYE INC. ↓2x

Agenda ↓2x

Regular Meeting of Directors ↓2x

Wednesday, September 23, 2007—10 a.m. ↓2x

Boardroom, Fifth Floor ↓2 or 3x

B   1. Call to order

2. Approval of minutes

3. Report on August operation—G. A. Horne

4. Report on corporate financial matters—A. J. McGill

5. Report on corporate development matters—L. Soaries   C

6. Review of international operations—W. Burgos

7. Discussion of Real Estate Committee report

8. Overview of the performance of major competitors—T. Foy

9. New business

D   10. Adjournment

A Margins. Note the use of wide (1.75") side margins for the text. This agenda has a number of very short items. If default side margin settings were used, it would look unbalanced with a relatively small left margin and a very large right margin.

B Numbered List. The numbered list feature of your software may begin with each item at the left margin with no space left between items. Although single spacing is acceptable for items in a short list, an agenda requires the use of at least 1 blank line to make the list easier to read and work with during discussions. When the agenda lists ten or more items, try to align the single- and double-digit figures on the period, placing the double-digit figures at the left margin.

C End Punctuation. Note that no periods are needed at the end of the items in this illustration. (See also ¶107.)

D Formal Items. In a formal agenda it is customary to include such items as *Call to order, Approval of minutes, New business,* and *Adjournment* (or similar types of expressions).

Agenda—Program for a Conference or Seminar

A   SOFTWARE APPLICATIONS SEMINAR ↓2x

Saddle Brook Marriott ↓2x

July 13–14, 2007 ↓2 or 3x

B   Wednesday, July 13 ↓2x

	8:00– 9:00	Registration and Continental Breakfast **C**	Lobby
D	9:00– 9:40	Software Applications: A State-of-the-Art Overview Speaker: Joyce Stocker-Olsen	Salons A and B
	9:50–10:30	Word Processing and Communications Applications Speakers: Louis Serrano and Roy Pfaltz **E**	Salons A and B
	10:30–10:50	Coffee Break	Lobby
	10:50–11:30	Desktop Publishing and Graphics Applications Speakers: Sandra Scroggins and Ed Fox	Salons A and B
	11:40–12:20	Spreadsheet and Database Management Applications Speaker: Esther W. Benoit **E**	Salons A and B
	12:30– 1:45	Lunch	Ballroom
	1:45– 3:15	Concurrent Sessions	
D		Session 1: Microsoft Word—Updates and Shortcuts Speaker: Tony Muzaffar	Red Oak Suite

---

A **Headings.** Include the location and date(s) of the conference or seminar in the main heading unless the program is part of a larger document that features this information prominently in some other way.

B If the program lasts more than one day, insert an appropriate side heading above each day's listing of events.

C To create this three-column format, use the table feature.

D For the alignment of "clock" times, see ¶1625b(3).

E **Speaker Identification.** The speakers listed on the program may be further identified by title, organization, and/or place of residence. Use commas to separate these elements of identification and, if you wish, use parentheses to enclose these elements as a whole. For example:

Gary A. Grimes, software consultant,
Kanata, Ontario

Leola Leung, (vice-president
Solutions Canada Ltd.,
Oakville, Ontario)

Minutes—Informal Style

A   **UNDERLOCK AND KEYE INC.** ↓2x

Minutes ↓2x

Regular Meeting of Directors ↓2x

September 23, 2007 ↓2 or 3x

B   A regular meeting of the Board of Directors of Underlock and Keye Inc. was called to order at 71 Riverside Drive, Cambridge, Ontario, at 10 a.m.
C   pursuant to the notice sent to all directors in accordance with the by-laws. ↓2x

D   The following directors were present, constituting all the directors: Jared C. Allison II, Kenneth L. Calderone, Deborah Georgopoulos-Keye,

---

D   Also present by invitation were William Burgos, Thomas Foy, Gregory A. Horne, Angela J. McGill, and Lester Soaries.

       Jared C. Allison II, Chairman, presided and David K. Rust, Recording   J
Secretary, recorded the proceedings of the meeting.

       The minutes of the last meeting were approved.

       Mr. Allison introduced Gregory A. Horne, Executive Vice-President of   J
Operations, who reported on August operations.

17

E Minutes of Directors' Meeting   2   September 23, 2007 ↓2 or 3x

F   Henry Koyama reviewed the recommendations of the Real Estate Committee on the matter of building a new facility ↓2x

G   It was MOVED by Jared Allisson and SECONDED by Kenneth Calderone that the Corporation undertake the building of a new facility. The motion was CARRIED.

H   The next meeting of the Board will be held on November 24 at 10 a.m.

I   The meeting adjourned at 1:05 p.m. ↓3 or 4x

                                  Recording Secretary

A Heading. Use all-capital letters for the name of the company in the first line. Use capitals and lower case for the other lines. For the date line, use the date on which the meeting was held (not the date on which the minutes were prepared). Use bold-face for all the elements in the heading.

B Format Considerations. Use 1-inch side margins. Indent or block the first line of each paragraph 0.5 inch.

C Opening Content. Use the opening paragraph to indicate the name of the company; the time and the place where the meeting was "called to order" (the first item on the agenda shown on page 481); and whether it was a regular or special meeting.

D Attendance and Routine Content. Use the next paragraphs to indicate which directors were present (all were in this illustration); which were absent; which company officers and invited guests were present; who presided; and who recorded the proceedings and prepared the minutes.

E Continuation Page Heading. A heading for the second page of this document is required. (See ¶¶1364 and 1702b.)

F Record of Transactions. The body of the minutes should note in each paragraph what business was transacted and what actions were taken.

G Format for Motions. Treat motions as regular paragraph formats. Keywords such as *MOVED, MOTION, SECONDED, CARRIED, RESOLVED*, and *DEFEATED* are SHOWN in all capital letters. Some writers prefer to begin the exact wording of a motion with the word *THAT* capitalized.

H Next Meeting. Use the second last paragraph to indicate the date and time of the next meeting.

I Adjournment. Use the final paragraph to indicate the time of adjournment. This may be in the form of a motion, but if it is, a seconder is never required.

J Capitalization. Note that forms such as *Corporation* and *Board* are capitalized. As well, such titles as *Chairman, Recording Secretary,* and *Executive Vice-President of Operations* are capitalized when used after a person's name. (See ¶313d and note.)

Optional Format. A memo or e-mail format may also be used to record informal minutes. Items may be in a paragraph form or in an enumerated format. As in some memos, distribution lists may also be used. (See ¶¶1375e(3), 1344d.)

Minutes—Formal Style

North Vista Condominiums

BOARD OF MANAGERS MONTHLY MEETING

July 7, 2007

CALL TO ORDER   The regular meeting of the North Vista Condominiums
was held in Room 120 at 7:00 p.m. The meeting was
called to order by the Chairman, Kevin McLean. Phyllis
Bruneau was the Recording Secretary.

ATTENDANCE   All members were present with the exception of Pat
Olsen.

TREASURER'S REPORT   The treasurer reported that the balance as at June 30 was
$109,000. Two owners are delinquent with their monthly
condo fees and notices have been sent. The financial
statements were accepted as distributed and read.

OLD BUSINESS   Gary Mansbridge MOVED that a computer and printer
not to exceed a cost of $1500 be purchased for use in the
office. The motion was SECONDED by George Parker.
CARRIED.

NEW BUSINESS   Jim Eliuk MOVED that all residents each receive three
parking passes to be given to overnight guests, who will
place the passes on their dashboards. The motion was
seconded by Joy Tetreault. George Parker MOVED to
amend the motion by striking out "three" and inserting
"two." The members discussed the amendment and
voted. The amendment was carried. The AMENDED
MOTION that all residents each receive two parking
passes for their overnight guests to place on their dashboards was voted on and CARRIED.

NEXT MEETING   The next meeting will be held in Room 224 on
Wednesday, August 4.

ADJOURNMENT   Gary Mansbridge MOVED to adjourn the meeting at
8:30 p.m. The motion was CARRIED.

Itinerary

ITINERARY ↓2x

For Wallace F. Galloway ↓2x

April 12–14, 2007 ↓2 or 3x

A   Tuesday, April 12 ↓2x

5:30 a.m.	**B** Limo to airport: Town Taxi (454-1040) ↓2x	E
7:00 a.m.	Depart Ottawa. Air Canada Flight 113	
C 9:07 a.m.	Arrive Vancouver	
	D Limo to meeting: Arthur's Limo (604-348-5347) Driver will meet you at baggage carousel. Destination: Burnham & Frye Inc. 909 Burrard Street Vancouver, BC 604-555-1216	E
9:45 a.m.–2:00 p.m.	Meet with Ed Burnham and Norbert Pell. They will make lunch arrangements.	E
2:30 p.m.	BC Ferry to Victoria: Call Arthur's Limo if 2:30 pickup time has to be changed. Hotel: Empress Hotel 721 Government Street 604-384-8111 Conf. No. 8941HWXQ; late arrival guaranteed	
6:30 p.m.	Dinner with Doris and Jack Cuneen; meet at restaurant (Ocean Pointe, 45 Songhees Road, 667-4677). ↓2x	

A   Wednesday, April 13

9:00 a.m.–4:00 p.m.	Board meeting in headquarters building, 4th floor. Sam Hurley will drive you to the airport.	E

A Heading. If the intinerary is for two days or more, type each day as a side heading above the day's list of activities.

B Columnar Format. To create this two-column format, use the table feature.

C For the alignment of "clock" times in a column, see ¶1625b(3).

D Spacing. Leave 1 blank line between entries. Single space any turnovers.

E Content Considerations. List phone numbers for all hotels, restaurants, and transportation services in case plans change. Try to provide the first names (not titles or initials) of all people whom the traveller is planning to meet. Provide the names of airports only when there is more than one serving the city.

RÉSUMÉS

Planning a Résumé

1707 The purpose of a résumé is to get you an interview. Before writing your résumé, however, there must be careful yet creative planning in its preparation. The following guidelines should help you present your own high-quality résumé.

a. Make a list of your achievements and other information about yourself. Keep in mind your career or job objective, the type of job you are looking for, the strengths you can bring to the job, and what you think you can accomplish for the employer's benefit.

- Record your post-secondary education qualifications, listing the highest or most recent degree or completed program first. Indicate your academic standing or GPA (if above 3.00). Include high school education only if that is the highest level so far attained. (This is the most important area of a résumé for recent school or college graduates and should be placed before job experiences.)

- Note any job-related, continuing education courses you have taken to show that you are a person committed to learning new things.

- List both paid and non-paid experiences in reverse chronological order (the most recent item first). Focus on your achievements, capabilities, and activities rather than assigned duties. While this might appear to be a difficult task, especially for new entrants to the job market, reflect upon what you have learned from your limited job experiences or other related activities that could be relevant to the job you are seeking.

- Note any special skills, community service, professional affiliations, or special interests that could be job-related: for example, computer competencies, experience with certain equipment or machinery, mastery of spoken or written foreign languages, and honours or awards.

b. Review your list and consider how your background and accomplishments relate to specific areas of the job market. What can you offer to an employer with the experience you have acquired and the skills you have developed?

c. Prepare short, clear statements (not necessarily full sentences) that emphasize your achievements, skills, and results. Organize and focus your strengths in light of the employer's needs. Place your strongest statement first.

- Start each statement with an active, descriptive verb; for example, *organized, initiated, implemented, maintained, supervised.*

- Use numbers whenever possible—they are impressive. *How many people did you supervise? How much money did you raise?*

d. Avoid stating your age, marital status, sex, height or weight, social insurance number, religion, ethnic origin, etc., unless such personal details are clearly required for your suitability for the job.

e. Do not give references on the résumé. It is not even necessary to state that references are available upon request. Be prepared, however, to supply names, addresses, and phone numbers at the interview.

(Continued on page 488.)

f. Select a résumé format that places your qualifications in an effective, attractive, and professional way. If the employer you have in mind does not provide specific format guidelines, you will find the following Web sites helpful:

<http://ca.hotjobs.yahoo.com>   <http://www.jobsetc.ca>
<http://www.monster.ca>   <http://jobstar.org>

Choose a format that suits your own personal situation, but keep in mind how a specific employer will view it. The most common formats are:

- **Chronological.** Education and jobs are listed by date with the most recent date first. This is the format preferred by those on a consistent job-related path. Employers prefer this style because it shows career progression and job history. (See page 490.)
- **Functional.** Qualifications, skills, and achievements are emphasized in this format. Job history details may be omitted or, if included, may be listed in a separate section. This format is preferred by career-changers who want to avoid drawing attention to gaps of unemployment or who lack any direct experience. (See page 491.)
- **Combination.** This format combines the best features of the two styles already mentioned. (See page 493.)

g. Prepare a custom-tailored résumé that allows you to organize and focus your strengths to match a specific employer's needs rather than prepare a single résumé designed to fit a variety of job opportunities and a range of employers' needs.

h. While traditional résumés have not been replaced, the following electronic résumés may also attract the attention of prospective employers.

- **Web Résumé.** This résumé is posted on a public or a personal Web site, which allows for easy transmission of the URL (via links). Your résumé then appears on numerous search engines and is readily accessible to employers.
- **Scannable Résumé.** A popular method for screening job applicants is scanning a version of a résumé by an optical character reader (OCR) into a database, where keyword searches are used to select the best résumés. The more links between the keywords in a résumé and those in a job description, the more likely the applicant will be selected for further evaluation. (See page 495.)
- **E-mail Résumé.** This is a plain text document that can be sent by e-mail, but it should still look as professional as possible.
- **Flash Résumé.** This multimedia, animated, off-the-wall résumé is suitable to showcase a portfolio of creative computer skills.

  NOTE: Do not confuse a résumé, which should be as short as possible with a curriculum vitae, (CV), which should contain several pages. CVs are appropriate only for those in such professional fields as medicine, law, and media and would include lists of published works, special research projects, portfolios of roles played, etc.

Formatting a Résumé

1708 To present your résumé in a professional, readable format follow these suggestions:

a. Use the table format of your software to prepare your own custom-tailored résumé.

b. Select a serif font (such as Times New Roman) that is easy to read. However, if your résumé needs to be faxed or scanned, a sans serif font (such as Arial) may provide a more readable copy. A font size of 10 to 12 points is acceptable for either font style.

c. Keep stylistic embellishments to a minimum to yield a clean, uncluttered look. Use boldface for headings and bullets to separate items in the text sections. In the main body of your résumé, make consistent use of all-capitals, boldface, and italics—but use them sparingly.

d. Try to keep the résumé to one page, but no more than two pages. If a second page is used, key a proper continuation-page header.

NOTE: A one-page résumé is suitable for someone who is recently out of school and does not have much work experience. However, individuals with a great deal of work experience can also make effective use of a one-page format. In this case, the section dealing with educational achievements should *follow* the sections dealing with work experience and skills.

e. Edit continuously. Be sure to write résumé with two acute accents, especially if you are applying for a job that calls for good language skills and careful attention to detail.

f. Print your copy on best-quality paper, preferably in white, cream, or pale grey. Do not staple, paper-clip, or fold your résumé.

g. The envelope and stationery for the covering letter should be of the same quality and colour as your résumé. Place it on top of the résumé—also unstapled.

Résumé—Chronological Style (One Page)

TRACY FLEURY

A

66 Quidi Vidi Road
St. John's, Newfoundland
A1A 1C1

Telephone: 709.234.5641
E-mail: jlfleury@rogers.com
Fax: 709.256.2921

SUMMARY OF QUALIFICATIONS

- Typing: 65 wpm
- WordPerfect 12
- Publisher MS

- MS Word Applications
- Web Design
- Project Management

- PowerPoint
- Excel
- AccPac

EDUCATION

B

September 2006 to
March 2007

Office Administration Diploma, Executive Program
College of the North Atlantic, St. John's, NL
GPA 3.7

Course Highlights
- Accounting
- Business Law
- Communications

- Office and Special Events Management
- Organizational Behaviour
- Work Practicum

Awards and Activities
- Alumni Keyboarding Prize for attained speed and accuracy
- Graduation Committee Treasurer
- Participant in college curling and hockey leagues

September 2005 to
April 2006

Office Administration Certificate
College of the North Atlantic, St. John's, NL
GPA 3.3

EXPERIENCE

May 2006 to
August 2006

Clerical Assistant: Beazley General Insurance Co. Ltd., St. John's
- Sorted mail, reorganized files, answered telephone, prepared claims
- Developed self-reliance, yet appreciated the need for team work in an office

July 2005 to
August 2005

Server: Radisson Plaza Hotel Coffee Shop, St. John's
- Served meals to customers, prepared bills, processed payments
- Improved communication and organizational skills

2000 to 2005

Babysitter: Cared for a number of neighbourhood children

17

A Heading. The heading should give all the key data an employer needs to get in touch with you.

B Education. Provide the estimated date of graduation if you are currently enrolled in a program.

Résumé—Functional Style

ALICJA L. BEUGIN
Apartment 145
90 Wellesley Street East
Toronto, Ontario M4Y 1A3

Telephone: 416-555-7944
Fax: 416-555-8341
E-mail: beugin@rogers.ca

OBJECTIVE:

B A marketing management position in which marketing and administrative experience combined with strong writing and computer skills can be used to maximize sales and profitability.

A ACHIEVEMENTS:

MARKETING EXPERIENCE

B
- Participated in implementing market research studies to determine potential size of market for new product lines.
- Coordinated focus group sessions to determine customer attitudes.
- Analyzed field sales reports and wrote summaries highlighting problem areas and commented on the feasibility of changes to product design and customer service.
- Developed detailed market plans based on rough outlines provided by the marketing manager.

A

ADMINISTRATIVE EXPERIENCE

B
- Controlled budgeted expenses for advertising and promotion.
- Resolved customer complaints by taking direct action whenever possible or by routing complaint to the appropriate person.
- Established and maintained media contacts to obtain free publicity for new products.
- Supervised an assistant who handled all correspondence and clerical tasks.

A

WRITING SKILLS

B
- Wrote copy for mail campaigns and catalogues.
- Wrote summaries of field sales reports adding appropriate comments.
- Wrote copy for fund-raising brochures for art museum.

A Side Headings. The usual side heading *EXPERIENCE* in the left column has been replaced by *ACHIEVEMENTS* because the term *experience* has been used in two subsequent side headings in the right column. Note how the wording of the "objective" statement (*in which marketing and administrative experience combined with strong writing and computer skills*) leads into the wording for the four side headings.

B Wording of Entries. The entries under the side headings emphasize the applicant's strengths in each functional area independent of the job setting in which these strengths were developed.

ALICJA L. BEUGIN Page 2

A COMPUTER SKILLS

B • Initiated a software publishing program. Saved the company over $50 000 in the first year of operation.
• Designed space ads, catalogues, and fund-raising brochures.
• Created and managed a database to control budgeted expenses.
• Microsoft Office XP Pro, Corel WordPerfect Office 2002, CorelDRAW Graphics Suite11, Adobe PageMaker 7.0, Adobe Illustrator 10.0, Adobe Photoshop 7.0, QuarkXPress 5.01, Peachtree Accounting 2002 9.0, Microsoft Money 2003.

C EMPLOYMENT HISTORY:
• Administrative coordinator for director of marketing, Zimmer & Boyle Inc., York, Ontario, July 2003–Present.
• Administrative assistant to sales manager, Zimmer & Boyle Inc., York, Ontario, February 2001–June 2003.
• Secretary to marketing manager, Crouch and Cowar Incorporated, Toronto, Ontario, May 1999–January 2001.
• Assistant to director of public relations, the Royal Ontario Museum, Toronto, Ontario, January 1998–February 1999.

EDUCATION:
B.A. in marketing, 1997, minor in English.
University of Western Ontario, London, Ontario

• Wrote feature articles for *The Western Star* during second and third years.
• Created (with two partners) an on-campus birthday celebration service. Managed the service during third and fourth years. Tested various direct marketing techniques to solicit orders.

D CONTINUING EDUCATION:
Courses in copywriting, telemarketing techniques, niche marketing, and computer graphics, George Brown College, Toronto, Ontario, 2003–2005.

D COMMUNITY SERVICE:
Designed and wrote annual fund-raising brochures (since 2004) for the Toronto Shelter for Street Kids, using computer graphics.

C Employment History. Although this section would not appear in a purely "functional" résumé, an employment history provides prospective employers with a brief chronological listing of previous job titles, the name and location of previous employers, and employment dates. Including this section often serves to mollify employers who are more comfortable with résumés done completely in the chronological style.

D Optional Sections. As well as *Continuing Education* and *Community Service*, other optional job-related information provided could be *Professional Activities, Special Qualifications, Awards and Recognitions, Memberships,* and *Special Interests.*

Résumé—Combination Style (Emphasizing Job Titles)

ALICJA L. BEUGIN

AB Apartment 145
90 Wellesley Street East
Toronto, Ontario M4Y 1A3

Telephone: 416-555-7944
Fax: 416-555-8341
E-mail: beugin@rogers.ca

OBJECTIVE: A marketing management position in which marketing and administrative experience combined with strong writing and computer skills can be used to maximize sales and profitability.

EXPERIENCE:

A Administrative Coordinator for Director of Marketing

ZIMMER & BOYLE INC., York, Ontario, July 2003–Present

B Created and managed a database to control budgeted expenses. Participated in implementing market research studies to determine potential size of market for new product lines. Coordinated focus group sessions to determine customer attitudes. Initiated a software publishing program; saved the company over $50 000 in the first year of operation.

A Administrative Assistant to Sales Manager

ZIMMER & BOYLE INC., York, Ontario, February 2001–June 2003

B Analyzed field sales reports and wrote summaries highlighting problem areas and commented on the feasibility of changes to product design and customer service. Resolved customer complaints by taking direct

~~~~~~~~~~~~~~~~~~~~~~~~~~~~~~~~~~

17

COMMUNITY SERVICE: Designed and wrote annual fund-raising brochures (since 2004) for the Toronto Shelter for Street Kids, using computer graphics.

~~~~~~~~~~~~~~~~~~~~~~~~~~~~~~~~~~

A Experience. In this format, job titles (not dates) are featured in the left column. At the right the name and location of the organization plus the employment dates are given on one or two lines.

B Job Achievements. Arranging the specific achievements for each job in one paragraph is a common format, but it is not as readable as the bulleted formats found on pages 490, 491, and 492.

Planning a Scannable Résumé

1709 Compared to the traditional style of résumé writing, the scannable version is extremely plain. This is intentional because its design is to suit the needs of the OCR—not those of a human reader. Keep in mind that it is the number of keywords you write to match those of the job description in the database that is the important factor. Consider the following for maximizing the number of your keywords.

    a. Read help-wanted advertisements and job postings for the kind of job you want. Try to incorporate into your résumé as many keywords from those job descriptions as possible.

    b. Use industry jargon, current industry buzzwords, acronyms, and abbreviations. These are likely to be the kinds of keywords that the computer database will highlight. The first time an acronym or an abbreviation is used, however, the full name should be written immediately after and placed within parentheses.

    c. Increase the total number of keywords in your résumé by using synonyms whenever possible to avoid repeating the same keywords.

    d. Change the action verbs of your traditional résumé to keyword nouns.

Formatting a Scannable Résumé

1710 To be sure that your résumé is read by the OCR, the following guidelines are recommended:

    a. For the sharpest possible image, use the best-quality white paper and a laser printer with black ink.

    b. Select a standard font (Arial or Times New Roman) with 10- to 12-point size. Use no boldface, italics, underlines, script, bullets, logos, shading, horizontal or vertical lines, or any other graphic devices. If desired, asterisks may be used to introduce individual items in a list.

    c. Begin all lines in the body of the résumé at the left margin. Columnar formats are not used.

    d. Try to limit the résumé to one page. If more than one page is required, use a paper clip (not a staple) to keep the pages together. Use a continuation heading for the second page. (See pages 491–492.)

    e. Insert your completed résumé into a plastic sleeve to keep it clean and wrinkle-free. Do not fold or crease it in any way.

Scannable Résumé

A   ALICJA L. BEUGIN
Apartment 145
90 Wellesley Street East
Toronto, Ontario M4Y 1A3
Home: 416-555-7944
Fax: 416-555-8341
E-mail: beugin@rogers.ca

B OBJECTIVE

A marketing management position in which marketing and administrative experience combined with strong writing and computer skills can be used to maximize sales and profitability.

B MARKETING SKILLS

C Implementation of market research studies. Assessment of potential market size for new product lines. Coordination of focus group sessions. Assessment of customer attitudes toward product lines. Analysis of field sales reports. Prioritize problems for immediate action. Pinpoint the changes to product design and customer service. Development of detailed market plans based on input from marketing manager.

B ADMINISTRATIVE SKILLS

C Control of advertising and promotional expense budgets. Resolution of customer complaints. Contacts with newspapers, TV stations, and radio stations for free publicity. Supervised a clerical assistant.

B WRITING SKILLS

C Preparation of copy for mail campaigns and fund-raising brochures. Summaries of field sales reports.

B COMPUTER SKILLS

C Start-up of in-house software publishing program with first-year savings of $50 000. Design and layout of space ads, catalogues, and fund-raising brochures. Creation and management

A Heading. On separate single-spaced lines centred in a block, type your name (in all-capitals for this line only), address, telephone numbers, fax number and/or an e-mail address.

B Side Headings. Use all-capitals and leave 1 blank line above and below each heading. Remember: no embellishments.

C Skills. Under each side heading is one paragraph consisting of phrases, each ending with a period. The wording highlights keyword nouns rather than action verbs.

D Continuation Heading. Provide a heading that gives your name and the page number.

D ALICJA L. BEUGIN   Page 2

B EMPLOYMENT HISTORY

E * Administrative co-ordinator for director of marketing, Zimmer and Boyle Inc., York, Ontario, July 2003–Present.

G * Administrative assistant to sales manager, Zimmer and Boyle Inc., York, Ontario, February 1998–June 2003.
* Secretary to marketing manager, Crouch and Cowar Incorporated, Toronto, Ontario, May 1999–January 2001.
* Assistant to director of public relations, the Royal Ontario Museum, Toronto, Ontario, January 1998–February 1999.

B EDUCATION

F B.A. in marketing, 1997, minor in English, University of Western Ontario, London, Ontario

G Wrote feature articles for The Western Star during second and third years. Created (with two partners) an on-campus birthday celebration service. Managed the service during junior and senior years. Tested various direct marketing techniques to solicit orders.

B CONTINUING EDUCATION

F Courses in copywriting, telemarketing techniques, niche marketing, and computer graphics, George Brown College, Toronto, Ontario, 2000–2002.

B COMMUNITY SERVICE

F Designed and wrote annual fund-raising brochures (since 2004) for the Toronto Shelter for Street Kids, using computer graphics.

E Employment History. Start with the most recent job. If you wish, an asterisk may introduce each job listing. No other graphic device is scannable. There is no need to repeat the duties of each job as they have already been summarized in the Skills sections.

F Other Sections. The same sections found in a traditional résumé would certainly be included in a scannable one.

G Elimination of Graphic Elements. Because some OCRs cannot properly scan ampersands, note that the ampersand in *Zimmer & Boyle* has been replaced by *and*. For a similar reason, the title of the university newspaper, *The Western Star*, must appear in ordinary print and not in italics.

Résumé—Paragraph Style

JOSIE ST. PIERRE
144 Nahanni Road
Hay River, NT X0E 4R2
867-555-5555

OBJECTIVE: A		To gain experience as a bank teller as a first step toward a career in banking.
EDUCATION:		*Certificate in business management, 2006* *MacKenzie College, Hay River, NT*
		Courses in accounting, business communication, business management, finance, and office technology.
		Academic scholarhips, 2004–2006. Member of the intramural curling team, 2004–2005. Tutor in a school-sponsored literacy program. 2005–2006.
EXPERIENCE:		*Sales associate, Field's, Enterprise, NT, June 2006–Present*
	B	Processed cash and credit card transactions, using electronic cash register. Helped customers with produce selections and suggested tie-in purchases. Resolved customer problems. Assisted in taking inventory and restocking shelves. Suggested special promotions and helped design displays.
		Cashier, Tim Hortons, Hay River, NR, May 2001–August 2004
	B	Worked part-time after school and holidays. Handled cash transactions. Advised customers on menu selections. Set up seasonal displays and recommended special campaigns to boost sales.
SKILLS:	**B**	Strong number sense and mastery of electronic cash register and calculator. Proven ability to handle large amounts of money accurately. Outgoing personality with the ability to grasp and respond to customers' needs. Excellent communication skills in writing, over the telephone, and face to face. Mastery of MS Word Applications and Excel software. Facility in the use of e-mail and accessing information on the Web.

A The objective line is **optional** and used only when seeking a job in a particular field.

B Holding this résumé to one page is better in paragraph style for describing activities, experience, and skills rather than displaying bulleted items in a list. When the italics and boldface are eliminated, it is also suitable for scanning.

(Continued on page 498.)

OTHER EMPLOYMENT DOCUMENTS

As part of the job-seeking process, you will need to write three types of letters: letters of application, follow-up letters after an interview, and a letter of acceptance. Specific guidelines are provided in ¶¶1712–1714, but a few general guidelines (¶1711) apply to all employment communications.

1711 GENERAL GUIDELINES

a. Keep your letters short—less than one full page if possible.

b. Resist the temptation to copy sample letters word for word. Draw on these samples for ideas, but create your own letters—letters that communicate the distinctive flavour of your personality. Thank-you cards, with or without a printed or handwritten message, are never appropriate.

c. Edit and proofread your letters carefully. Simple typographical errors (not to mention more serious errors in grammar, style, and usage) will create a negative impression that damages your job-seeking campaign.

d. Always try to address your letters to a specific person, using that person's full name and title. If necessary, call the specific organization to obtain this information.

NOTE: The model letters on pages 501–503 are all written by Alicja Beugin, the fictitious person whose job qualifications are set forth in some of the résumés shown on pages 491–493. In these letters Ms. Beugin is trying to move up to a marketing management position.

☞ *See Section 13 for guidelines and illustrations of business letters.*

1712 APPLICATION LETTERS

Letters you write to apply for a job will vary to some extent, depending on whether you are (1) answering an advertisement, (2) writing "cold-call" letters to employment agencies or businesses, or (3) following suggestions after networking with acquaintances to explore job opportunities with an organization. Yet all the letters have the same three objectives: (1) to indicate what you have to offer the organization, (2) to transmit your résumé, and (3) to obtain an interview. Consider the following guidelines when you write an application letter.

a. Before you draft your letter, try to get as much information as you can about the organization you have in mind. For example, what products or services does it offer? What special strategy or philosophy governs the way the organization operates? Such information can help you focus your letter more effectively and will let the recipient of the letter know that you have taken the initiative to learn something about the organization.

NOTE: If you are responding to a blind advertisement (one that provides no organizational name and only a box number address), you will not be able to undertake this research. However, the advertisement will spell out the qualifications desired, something not usually available to you when you are simply exploring the possibility of job openings.

b. Begin your letter by indicating whether you are responding to an advertisement, following up on the suggestion of a mutual friend or acquaintance, or simply exploring what job opportunities currently exist.

c. Indicate what you have to offer the organization. If you are responding to an advertisement that states the qualifications desired, clearly indicate how your skills and experience relate to each of the qualifications listed. If you are simply exploring job openings, do not focus on specific tasks that you have performed in the past. Instead, highlight the things you have accomplished as a result of the way you applied your skills and experience. This approach will make it easier for someone to gauge how well you might fit the job available, even if you have not performed those exact tasks in the past.

NOTE: The recipient of your letter will probably be receiving many other application letters at the same time. It is important, therefore, that your letter and your résumé make you stand out from the others. In your letter you should aim to achieve—in much shorter form—the same things you are trying to achieve in your résumé.

d. The primary short-term objective of this letter is to arrange for an interview. When it is a "cold-call (unsolicited) application letter, indicate that you will call on a specific date to determine whether an interview can take place. In stating when you will call, allow enough time for your material to be delivered and looked at. Keep in mind that the recipient may be inundated with other matters or may be travelling and thus may not look at your letter and résumé as quickly as you would like.

NOTE: Keep a record of when you promised to call so that you follow through on time. Calling a day or two later could suggest that you are not a very good manager of your time.

☞ *For a model application letter written in response to an advertised opening, see following page.*

Application (Cover) Letter

A **ALICJA L. BEUGIN**

AB   Apartment 145
       90 Wellesley Street East
       Toronto, Ontario M4Y 1A3

Telephone: 416-555-7944
Fax: 416-555-8341
E-mail: beugin@rogers.ca

March 3, 2007

Mr. Oliver Digby
Director of Human Resources
Hunt and Ketcham Inc.
128 Euclid Street
Whitby, Ontario L1N 0K2

Dear Mr. Digby:

B   You advertised for a marketing manager in the March 2 *Plain Dealer*. As I have used many Hunt and Ketcham texts in my computer courses, I know that your company publishes high-quality books. As the following comparison shows, my experience and background would satisfy all the requirements stated in your advertisement.

Your Requirements	My Qualifications
College degree	B.A. in marketing plus continuing education courses in marketing and computer software applications.
Knowledge of technical market	Over six years' experience in sales and marketing publishing divisions of two educational publishing companies.
Field sales experience	Extensive contact with field sales reps and customers, resolving a wide range of sales support and customer service problems.

The enclosed résumé will provide additional information about my marketing experience.

I would appreciate an opportunity to meet with you and discuss the ways in which I can help Hunt and Ketcham achieve its marketing objectives. You can reach me at 555-7944.

Sincerely,

Alicja L. Beugin

Alicja L. Beugin

Enclosure

A Letterhead. The attractive letterhead design that Alicja Beugin has created will help make her application letter stand out. It is the same letterhead she used on the first page of her résumé.

B First Paragraph. Alicja uses her opening paragraph to say how she found out about the job, what she knows about the organization, and how her qualifications compare to the job requirements stated in the advertisement.

C Second Paragraph. Alicja refers to her résumé and shows how her qualifications compare with the job requirements stated in the advertisement.

D Final Paragraph. Alicja emphasizes her wish for an interview and provides her telephone number. At the same time she stresses her willingness to focus the interview on how she can help the organization achieve its goals and objectives.

1713 FOLLOW-UP LETTERS

After an interview, follow up within 48 hours with a letter that covers the following points:

a. Thank the interviewer for (1) taking the time to see you, (2) giving you better insight into the available job and the organization you would be working for, and (3) considering your qualifications in light of the available job.

b. Reinforce the positive impression you tried to make during the interview, and briefly restate why you think you would be an asset to the organization.

c. Offer additional information about your qualifications if they were not fully discussed during the interview. If you promised during the interview to supply additional information, do so now.

d. Address questions that arose during the interview that you were not fully prepared to answer at the time. If you know (or simply sense) that the interviewer had some doubts about your qualifications, use this opportunity to overcome such doubts if you can.

> **NOTE:** If the interviewer made it clear at the time that you were not right for the current job opening, send a follow-up letter nonetheless. Offer thanks for having been considered for this job, and express hope that you will be considered for other jobs that may open in the future. On the other hand, if *you* decide the job is not right for you, send a follow-up letter in which you thank the interviewer and ask not to be a candidate.

☞ *For an illustration of a follow-up letter, see page 502.*

1714 ACCEPTANCE LETTERS

Of all employment communications, this is the easiest—and the most pleasant—letter to write. Use this occasion to:

a. Formally accept the job.

b. Confirm the key details of your working arrangements (including starting date) that have been previously discussed. If any of these details are not clear, ask the person who hired you to spell them out.

c. Express your pleasure in coming to work for the organization and, more specifically, for the person who has offered you the job.

☞ *For an illustration of an acceptance letter, see page 503.*

Follow-Up Letter

ALICJA L. BEUGIN

AB Apartment 145
90 Wellesley Street East
Toronto, Ontario M4Y 1A3

Telephone: 416-555-7944
Fax: 416-555-8341
E-mail: beugin@rogers.ca

March 24, 2007

Mr. Oliver Digby
Director of Human Resources
Hunt and Ketcham Inc.
128 Euclid Street
Whitby, Ontario L1N 0K2

Dear Mr. Digby:

A Thank you for taking the time last Friday to explain why my lack of field sales experience in the technical publishing market would prevent me from being considered for the marketing manager's position at Hunt and Ketcham.

B Thank you also for arranging an interview that same day with your director of sales. Ms. Cantrell gave me a very detailed picture of a field representative's responsibilities. She also stated that in light of all my prior experience in educational publishing, I should make the transition to technical publishing very easily. I was also encouraged to learn that after a year or two of experience in the field, I would be a strong candidate for any marketing manager's position that might open at that time.

C Ms. Cantrell has indicated she will let me know within the next four weeks whether she is in a position to offer me a field representative's job. If she does, I very much look forward to seeing you again. In any event, thank you very much for all the help you have given me.

Sincerely,

Alicja L. Beugin

Alicja L. Beugin

A First Paragraph. Alicja thanks the interviewer for clarifying the demands of the job and pointing out where her qualifications fell short.
B Second Paragraph. Alicja thanks the interviewer for steering her to another opportunity in the organization and for setting up an interview that same day. (Alicja should also send a follow-up letter to the second person who interviewed her.) Note that she re-affirms her hope for a marketing management job in a year or two.
C Third Paragraph. Alicja ends on a warm note, thanking the first interviewer for all his help.

Acceptance Letter

ALICJA L. BEUGIN
AB Apartment 145
90 Wellesley Street East
Toronto, Ontario M4Y 1A3

Telephone: 416-555-7944
Fax: 416-555-8341
E-mail: beugin@rogers.ca

April 28, 2007

Ms. Jennifer Cantrell
Director of Sales
Hunt and Ketcham Inc.
128 Euclid Street
Whitby, Ontario L1N 0K2

Dear Jennifer:

A I am very pleased to accept the position of Field Service Representative with northeastern Ontario as my territory and to have the opportunity to work for Hunt and Ketcham.

B The materials that Oliver Digby sent me answered all my questions about compensation arrangements and company policies. I have now completed and returned the necessary paperwork. My understanding is that my starting date is June 2 in Whitby, where orientation and training will last for the month.

C If there is anything you think I should be reading or doing in the next month, please let me know. I would welcome the opportunity to prepare myself for the job before reporting for work on June 2.

Sincerely,

Alicja L. Beugin

Alicja L. Beugin

17

A First Paragraph. Alicja accepts the job with pleasure and acknowledges the opportunity to work for the company.

B Second Paragraph. Alicja uses this paragraph to deal with the technical details involved in starting a new job.

C Final Paragraph. Alicja shows initiative in offering to undertake advance preparation for the job before she officially starts work.

OUTLINES

1715 An outline can be used to *plan* the content and organization of any document. It identifies (1) the topics that are to be discussed and (2) the sequence in which they are to be introduced. An outline may consist of a simple list, or it may contain several levels of subtopics under each main topic (as in the illustrations on the following pages).

1716 After you have finished drafting a document, you can use an outline to *review* the document in terms of content and organization. An outline of this kind typically lists key words or phrases used as headings throughout the copy to identify topics and subtopics as they are each introduced. When you use an outline for reviewing purposes, you can more easily answer questions like these:

- Have all topics been included?
- Have all topics been fully developed?
- Does the sequence of headings provide a balanced representation of all aspects of the discussion, or do some parts of the text have many headings while others have very few?
- Are the headings worded in a similar way, or are some complete sentences and others simply phrases?

1717 If you are using software with an outline feature, you can create an outline by scrolling through the text and coding (according to a level of subordination) every heading in the text. If you revise the heading structure in the document, you can use the outline feature to generate a new outline to confirm that the document is now better organized.

1718 The use of numbers and letters with the items in an outline indicates the relative importance of these items to one another. The standard outline illustration on page 505 shows six levels of headings, but many outlines do not require that many and a few may require more.

> **NOTE:** Various combinations of letters and numerals can be used as level designators. The following examples show two common 9-level formats.

Level One Roman:	I. A. 1. a. (1) (a) i) a) 1)
Level One Arabic:	1. a. i. (1) (a) (i) 1) a) i)

At least two items are needed for each level used in an outline. If your outline shows a Roman I at the first level, it must also show a Roman II; if you use a capital A at the second level, you must also use a capital B, and so on.

1719 If you are devising your own format for an outline, consider the guidelines and refer to the outline illustration.

  a. **Margins.** Ordinarily, use default side and bottom margins. Leave a top margin of 1 to 2 inches. Try to keep the outline on one page. A one-page outline may be centred vertically on the page.

  b. **Heading.** Key the title in all-capital letters. Use capital and small letters for the other lines. If you wish, use boldface for the complete heading of the

Standard Outline Format

EQUIPMENT AND SOFTWARE ↓2×

Orientation for Department Staff ↓3×

   I.   INTRODUCTION ↓3×

  II. EQUIPMENT AND SOFTWARE ↓2×

       A.   Equipment
          1. Computer
             a) Drives
                (1) Types
                    (a)   Hard
                    (b)   Floppy
                (2) Capacity
                    (a)   Hard
                    (b)   Floppy
             b) RAM
          2. Monitor ↓3×

  III. OPERATION ↓2×

       A.   Startup
       B.   Start/Quit a Program

17

title only. Leave 1 blank line between the lines in the heading and 1 or 2 blank lines below the last line of the heading.

  c. Enumerations. The numbers or letters that identify the items at different levels in an outline should all be followed by a period or right parenthesis [)] and 1 or 2 spaces.

  d. Capitalization. Use all-capital letters for the first-level items (those preceded by Roman numerals). Use capital and small letters for items at all lower levels.

  e. Indentions. When using Roman numerals to identify first-level items, align the second level of items (those beginning with A and B) on the first word after the Roman I. Align the third level of items (those beginning with 1 and 2) on the first word after A in the second level; however, if there are more than nine items, align the longest number (Arabic or Roman) on the first word after the enumeration number in the previous level; then right align all the following numbers in the same level on the period.

 See the Online Learning Centre at www.mcgrawhill.ca/college/gregg for related Web links.

P A R T

THREE

References

SECTION **EIGHTEEN**

Forms of Address

INDIVIDUALS (¶1801)
Man With Courtesy Title (¶1801a)
Woman—Courtesy Title Known (¶1801b)
Woman—Courtesy Title Unknown (¶1801c)
Individual—Name Known, Gender Unknown (¶1801d)
Individual—Name Unknown, Gender Known (¶1801e)
Individual—Name and Gender Unknown (¶1801f)
Two Men (¶1801g)
Two Women (¶1801h)
Woman and Man—No Personal Relationship (¶1801i)

COUPLES (¶1802)
Married Couple With Same Surname—No Special Titles (¶1802a)
Married Couple With Same Surname—Husband Has Special Title (¶1802b)
Married Couple With Same Surname—Wife Has Special Title (¶1802c)
Married Couple With Same Surname—Both Have Special Titles (¶1802d)
Married Couple With Different Surnames (¶1802e)
Married Couple With Hyphenated Surname (¶1802f)
Unmarried Couple Living Together (¶1802g)

ORGANIZATIONS (¶1803)
Organization of Women and Men (¶1803a)
Organization of Women (¶1803b)
Organization of Men (¶1803c)

PROFESSIONALS (¶1804)
Lawyers (¶1804a)
Physicians and Others With Doctoral Degrees (¶1804b)

EDUCATION OFFICIALS (¶1805)
Chancellor of College or University (¶1805a)
President of College or University (¶1805b)
Dean of College or University (¶1805c)
Professor (¶1805d)
Superintendent of Schools (¶1805e)

Member of Board of Education (¶1805f)
Principal (¶1805g)
Teacher (¶1805h)

CANADIAN GOVERNMENT OFFICIALS (¶1806)

Governor General of Canada (¶1806a)
Prime Minister of Canada (¶1806b)
Cabinet Minister of Canada (¶1806c)
Member of the House of Commons (¶1806d)
Senator (¶1806e)
Chief Justice of Canada (¶1806f)
Judge of Federal, Provincial, County, or Territorial Court (¶1806g)
Lieutenant-Governor (¶1806h)
Premier (¶1806i)
Member, Provincial Cabinet (¶1806j)
Member, Legislative Assembly (¶1806k)
Mayor (¶1806l)
Member, Municipal Council (¶1806m)

AMERICAN GOVERNMENT OFFICIALS (¶1807)

President of the United States (¶1807a)
Cabinet Minister (¶1807b)
United States Senator (¶1807c)
United States Representative (¶1807d)
Governor (¶1807e)

THE ROYAL FAMILY (¶1808)

The Queen (¶1808a)
The Duke of Edinburgh (¶1808b)
The Prince of Wales (¶1808c)
The Duchess of Cornwall (¶1808d)
The Duke of York (¶1808e)
The Princess Royal (¶1808f)
The Earl and Countess of Wessex (¶1808g)

DIPLOMATS (¶1809)

Secretary-General of the United Nations (¶1809a)
Ambassador or High Commissioner of a Foreign Country to Canada (¶1809b)
Canadian Ambassador or High Commissioner Abroad (¶1809c)
American Ambassador to Canada (¶1809d)

INTERNATIONAL DIGNITARIES (¶1810)

An Emperor (¶1810a)
A King (¶1810b)
A Queen (¶1810c)

18

A Prince with the title *Royal* or *Serene Highness* (¶1810d)
A President of a Republic (¶1810e)
A Prime Minister (¶1810f)

MEMBERS OF THE CANADIAN ARMED FORCES (¶1811)
Officers (¶1811a)
Other Ranks (¶1811b)

NATIVE LEADERS (¶1812)
Indian Chiefs (¶1812a)
Band Councillors (¶1812b)

ROMAN CATHOLIC DIGNITARIES (¶1813)
Pope (¶1813a)
Cardinal (¶1813b)
Bishop (¶1813c)
Archbishop (¶1813d)
Monsignor (¶1813e)
Priest (¶1813f)
Sister (or Mother) Superior (¶1813g)
Sister (¶1813h)
Brother (¶1813i)

PROTESTANT DIGNITARIES (¶1814)
Anglican Primate (¶1814a)
Anglican Bishop (¶1814b)
Anglican Dean (¶1814c)
Moderator, United Church (¶1814d)
Minister With Doctor's Degree (¶1814e)
Minister Without Doctor's Degree (¶1814f)

JEWISH DIGNITARIES (¶1815)
Chief Rabbi (¶1815a)
Rabbi With Doctor's Degree (¶1815b)
Rabbi Without Doctor's Degree (¶1815c)

18

The following forms are correct for addressing letters to individuals, couples, organizations, professional people, education officials, government officials, diplomats, military personnel, and religious dignitaries.

In the salutations that follow the forms of address, the formal one is listed first. Unless otherwise indicated, the ellipses in the salutations stand for the surnames alone.

NOTE: Because of space limitations, only the masculine forms of address have been given in some illustrations. When an office or a position is held by a woman, make the following substitutions:

For *Sir*, use *Madam*.

For *Mr.* followed by a name (for example, *Mr. Wyatt*), use *Miss, Mrs.,* or *Ms.,* whichever is appropriate.

For *His*, use *Her*.

For *Mr.* followed by a title (for example, *Mr. President, Mr. Secretary, Mr. Mayor*), use *Madam*.

☞ *For further information on inside addresses, see* ¶¶1316–1336; *on salutation,.* ¶¶1338–1341; *and on placing addresses on envelopes,* ¶¶1365–1369.

For a discussion of Ms. *as a preferred courtesy title, see* ¶515a note.

1801 INDIVIDUALS

a. Man With Courtesy Title

Mr. . . . *(full name)*
Address

Dear Mr. . . . :

b. Woman—Courtesy Title Known

Ms. (**OR** Miss **OR** Mrs.) . . . *(full name)*
Address

Dear Ms. (**OR** Miss **OR** Mrs.) . . . :

c. Woman—Courtesy Title Unknown

Ms. . . . *(full name)*
Address

Dear Ms. . . . :

OR:

. . . *(full name with no title)*
Address

Dear . . . *(first name and surname)*:

d. Individual—Name Known, Gender Unknown

. . . *(full name with no title)*
Address

Dear . . . *(first name or initials plus surname)*:

e. Individual—Name Unknown, Gender Known

. . . *(title of individual)*
. . . *(name of organization)*
Address

Madam: **OR**   Sir:
Dear Madam: Dear Sir:

f. Individual—Name and Gender Unknown

. . . *(title of individual)*
. . . *(name of organization)*
Address

Sir or Madam: **OR**   Madam or Sir:
Dear Sir or   Dear Madam or
  Madam: Sir:

NOT: To Whom It May Concern:

g. Two Men

Mr. . . . *(full name)*
Mr. . . . *(full name)*
Address

Gentlemen:
Dear Messrs. . . . and . . . :
Dear Mr. . . . and Mr. . . . :

h. Two Women

Ms. . . . *(full name)*
Ms. . . . *(full name)*
Address

Dear Mses. (**OR** Mss.) . . . and . . . :
Dear Ms. . . . and Ms. . . . :

OR:

Mrs. . . . *(full name)*
Mrs. . . . *(full name)*
Address

Dear Mesdames . . . and . . . :
Dear Mrs. . . . and Mrs. . . . :

OR:

Miss . . . (*full name*)
Miss . . . (*full name*)
Address

Dear Misses . . . and . . . :
Dear Miss . . . and Miss . . . :

OR:

Ms. . . . (*full name*)
Mrs. . . . (*full name*)
Address

Dear Ms. . . . and Mrs. . . . :

OR:

Miss . . . (*full name*)
Ms. . . . (*full name*)
Address

Dear Miss . . . and Ms. . . . :

OR:

Mrs. . . . (*full name*)
Miss . . . (*full name*)
Address

Dear Mrs. . . . and Miss . . . :

i. Woman and Man—No Personal Relationship

Ms. (**OR** Mrs. **OR** Miss) . . . (*full name*)
Mr. . . . (*full name*)
Address

Dear Ms. (**OR** Mrs. **OR** Miss) . . .
and Mr. . . . :

OR:

Mr. . . . (*full name*)
Ms. (**OR** Mrs. **OR** Miss) . . . (*full name*)
Address

Dear Mr. . . . and Ms. (**OR** Mrs.
OR Miss) . . . :

☞ *For forms of address for teenagers and younger children, see ¶1321d–e.*

1802 COUPLES

a. Married Couple With Same Surname—No Special Titles

Mr. and Mrs. . . . (*husband's full name*)
(See ¶1322b.)
Address

Dear Mr. and Mrs. . . . (*husband's surname*):

b. Married Couple With Same Surname—Husband Has Special Title

Dr. and Mrs. . . . (*husband's full name*)
Address

Dear Dr. and Mrs. . . . (*husband's surname*):

c. Married Couple With Same Surname—Wife Has Special Title

Professor . . . (*wife's full name*)
Mr. . . . (*husband's full name*)
Address

Dear Professor and Mr. . . . (*husband's surname*):

d. Married Couple With Same Surname—Both Have Special Titles

Dr. . . . (*wife's full name*)
Dr. . . . (*husband's full name*)
Address

Dear Drs. . . . (*husband's surname*):

OR:

Captain . . . (*husband's full name*)
Professor . . . (*wife's full name*)
Address

Dear Captain and Professor . . .
(*husband's surname*):

e. Married Couple With Different Surnames

Ms. (**OR** Miss) . . . (*wife's full name*)
Mr. . . . (*husband's full name*)
Address

Dear Ms. (**OR** Miss) . . . (*wife's surname*)
and Mr. . . . (*husband's surname*):

OR:

Mr. . . . (*husband's full name*)
Ms. (**OR** Miss) . . . (*wife's full name*)
Address

Dear Mr. . . . (*husband's surname*) and
Ms. (**OR** Miss) . . . (*wife's surname*):

NOTE: If either spouse has a special title (like those shown in ¶1802b–d), use that special title here as well.

(Continued on page 514.)

18

f. Married Couple With Hyphenated Surname

> Mr. and Mrs. . . . (*husband's first name and middle initial, plus wife's original surname followed by hyphen and husband's surname*)
> Address
>
> Dear Mr. and Mrs. . . . (*wife's original surname followed by hyphen and husband's surname*):

g. Unmarried Couple Living Together

> Ms. (**OR** Miss) . . . (*full name*)
> Mr. . . . (*full name*)
> Address
>
> Dear Ms. (**OR** Miss) . . . and Mr. . . . :

OR:

> Mr. . . . (*full name*)
> Ms. (**OR** Miss) . . . (*full name*)
> Address
>
> Dear Mr. . . . and Ms. (**OR** Miss) . . . :

1803 ORGANIZATIONS

a. Organization of Women and Men

> . . . (*name of organization*)
> Address
>
> Ladies and Gentlemen:
> Gentlemen and Ladies:
> Dear . . . (*name of organization*):
>   (See ¶1340c.)

OR:

> Mr. . . . (*name or organization head*)*
> President (*or other appropriate title*)
> . . . (*name of organization*)
> Address
>
> Dear Mr. . . . :*

OR:

> Chief Executive Officer (*or other appropriate title*)
> . . . (*name of organization*)
> Address
>
> Sir or Madam: **OR**   Madam or Sir:
> Dear Sir or   Dear Madam or
>   Madam: Sir:
>
> **NOT:** Dear Ladies and Gentlemen:

*See the note on page 511.

b. Organization of Women

> . . . (*name of organization*)
> Address
>
> Mesdames: **OR**   Ladies:
>
> **NOT:** Dear Ladies:

c. Organization of Men

> . . . (*name of organization*)
> Address
>
> Gentlemen: **NOT:** Dear Gentlemen:

1804 PROFESSIONALS

a. Lawyers

> Mr. . . . (*full name*)*
> Barrister and Solicitor
> Address

OR:

> . . . (*full name*), Esq.
> Address
>
> Dear Mr. . . . :*

b. Physicians and Others With Doctoral Degrees

> Dr. . . . (*full name*)
> Address

OR:

> . . . (*full name*), M.D.
> Address
>
> Dear Dr. . . . :

> **NOTE:** When an abbreviation such as *Esq., M.D.,* or *Ph.D.* follows a name, do not use a courtesy title such as *Mr.* or *Dr.* before the name. (See also ¶¶518c, 519c.)

1805 EDUCATION OFFICIALS

a. Chancellor of College or University

> . . . (*full name, followed by comma and highest degree*)
> Chancellor, . . . (*name of college*)
> Address

OR:

> Dr. . . . (*full name*)
> Chancellor, . . . (*name of college*)

Address

Dear Chancellor . . . :

Dear Dr. . . . :

b. President of College or University

. . . (*full name, followed by comma and highest degree*)
President . . . (*name of college*)

OR:

Dr. . . . (*full name*)
President, . . . (*name of college*)

OR:

President . . . (*full name*)
. . . (*name of college*)
Address

Dear President . . . :

Dear Dr. . . . :

c. Dean of College or University

. . . (*full name, followed by comma and highest degree*)

OR:

Dr. . . . (*full name*)
Dean, . . . (*name of school or division*)
. . . (*name of college*)

OR:

Dean . . . (*full name*)
. . . (*name of school or division*)
. . . (*name of college*)
Address

Dear Dean . . . :

Dear Dr. . . . :

d. Professor

Professor . . . (*full name*)
Department of . . . (*subject*)
. . . (*name of college*)

OR:

. . . (*full name, followed by comma and highest degree*)
Department of (**OR:** Professor of) . . .
(*subject*)
. . . (*name of college*)
Address

*See the note on page 511.

OR:

Dr. (**OR** Mr.) . . . (*full name*)
Department of (**OR** Professor of) . . .
(*subject*)
. . . (*name of college*)
Address

Dear Professor (**OR** Dr.) . . . :

Dear Mr. . . . :*

e. Superintendent of Schools

Mr. (**OR** Dr.) . . . (*full name*)*
Superintendent, . . . (*name of city*) Board of Education
Address

Dear Mr. (**OR** Dr.) . . . :*

f. Member of Board of Education

Mr. . . . (*full name*)*
Member, . . . (*name of city*) Board of Education
Address

Dear Mr. . . . :*

g. Principal

Mr. (**OR** Dr.) . . . (*full name*)*
Principal, . . . (*name of school*)
Address

Dear Mr. (**OR** Dr.) . . . :*

h. Teacher

Mr. (**OR** Dr.) . . . (*full name*)*
. . . (*name of school*)
Address

Dear Mr. (**OR** Dr.) . . . :*

1806 CANADIAN GOVERNMENT OFFICIALS

a. Governor General of Canada

His Excellency the Right Honourable
(*full name*)* (Orders, decorations)
Governor General of Canada
Rideau Hall
One Sussex Drive
Ottawa, Ontario K1A 0A1

Excellency:

(*Continued on page 516.*)

b. Prime Minister of Canada

The Right Honourable . . . (*full name*),
   P.C., M.P.
Prime Minister of Canada
Langevin Block
Ottawa, Ontario K1A 0A2

Dear Prime Minister:

c. Cabinet Minister of Canada

The Honourable . . . (*full name*), P.C., M.P.
Minister of . . .
House of Commons
Ottawa, Ontario K1A 0A6

Dear Minister:

NOTE: The initials *P.C.* are for members of the Queen's Privy Council for Canada. *Honourable* is a life-time title.

d. Member of the House of Commons

Mr. . . . (*full name*), M.P.*
OR:
The Honourable . . . (*full name*),
   P.C., M.P.
House of Commons
Ottawa, Ontario K1A 0A6

Dear Mr. . . . (*surname*):*

NOTE: The initials *M.P.* follow the name of a Member of Parliament.

e. Senator

The Honourable . . . (*full name*), Senator
The Senate
Ottawa, Ontario K1A 0A1

Dear Senator . . . (*surname*):

f. Chief Justice of Canada

The Right Honourable . . . (*full name*),
   P.C.
Chief Justice of Canada
Supreme Court of Canada
Ottawa, Ontario K1A 0J1

Dear Chief Justice:

g. Judge of Federal, Provincial, County, or Territorial Court

The Honourable . . . (*full name*)
Judge of the . . . (*name of court*)

*See the note on page 511.

Address

Dear Mr. Justice . . . (*surname*):*

For Judges of Provincial or Territorial Courts:

Dear Chief Judge:
Dear Judge . . . (*surname*):

h. Lieutenant-Governor

His Honour the Honourable . . . (*full name*)*
Lieutenant-Governor of (*Province*)
Provincial Capital, Province
Postal Code

Your Honour:
My dear Lieutenant-Governor:

i. Premier

The Honourable . . . (*full name*)
Premier of (*Province*)
Provincial Capital, Province
Postal Code

Dear Premier:

j. Member, Provincial Cabinet

The Honourable . . . (*full name*), M.L.A.
   OR M.P.P. **OR** M.N.A. **OR** M.H.A.
Minister of . . .
Provincial Capital, Province
Postal Code

Dear Minister:

NOTE: In the two positions above, the title *Honourable* is only used while in office.

k. Member, Legislative Assembly

Mr. . . . (*full name*),* M.L.A. **OR** M.P.P.
   OR M.N.A. **OR** M.H.A.
Provincial Capital, Province
Postal Code

Dear Mr. . . . (*surname*):*

NOTE: M.L.A. is used by all provinces and territories, except Ontario, which uses *M.P.P.*; Quebec, *M.N.A.*; Newfoundland, *M.H.A.*

l. Mayor

His Worship . . . (*full name*)*

Mayor of . . . (*city or municipality*)
City (*or* Municipality) Hall
Municipality, Province
Postal Code

Dear Sir:*
Dear Mr. Mayor:*

m. Member, Municipal Council

Councillor . . . (*full name*)
OR:
Alderman . . . (*full name*)
City (*or* Municipality) Hall
Municipality, Province
Postal Code

Dear Councillor . . . (*surname*):
Dear Alderman . . . (*surname*):*

1807 AMERICAN GOVERNMENT OFFICIALS

a. President of the United States

The Honourable . . . (*full name*)
President of the United States
The White House
Washington, DC 20500

Mr. President:*
Dear Mr. President:*

b. Cabinet Minister

The Honourable . . . (*full name*)
Secretary of . . . (*department*)
Washington, DC Zip Code
U.S.A.

Dear Mr. Secretary:*

c. United States Senator

The Honourable . . . (*full name*)
United States Senate
Washington, DC 20510

Dear Senator:

d. United States Representative

The Honourable . . . (*full name*)
House of Representatives
Washington, DC 20515

Dear Representative . . . :
Dear Mr. . . . :*

e. Governor

The Honourable . . . (*full name*)
Governor of . . . (state)
State Capital, State Zip Code

Dear Governor . . . :

1808 THE ROYAL FAMILY

a. The Queen

Her Majesty The Queen
Buckingham Palace
London SW1A 1AA
United Kingdom

Your Majesty:

b. The Duke of Edinburgh

His Royal Highness The Prince Philip,
    Duke of Edinburgh
Buckingham Palace
London SW1A 1AA
United Kingdom

Your Royal Highness:

c. The Prince of Wales

His Royal Highness The Prince of Wales
Clarence House
London SW1A 1BA
United Kingdom

Your Royal Highness:

d. The Duchess of Cornwall

Her Royal Highness The Duchess of
    Cornwall
Clarence House
(*see address above*)

Your Royal Highness:

e. The Duke of York

His Royal Highness The Duke of York
Buckingham Palace
(*see address above*)

Your Royal Highness:

f. The Princess Royal

Her Royal Highness The Princess Royal
Buckingham Palace
(*see address above*)

Your Royal Highness:

18

*See the note on page 511.

(*Continued on page 518.*)

g. The Earl and Countess of Wessex

Their Royal Highnesses The Earl and
  Countess of Wessex
Bagshot Park
Bagshot, Surrey GU19 5PL

Your Royal Highnesses:

1809 DIPLOMATS

a. Secretary-General of the United Nations

His Excellency . . . (*full name*)*
Secretary-General of the United Nations
United Nations Plaza
New York, NY 10017

Excellency:
Dear Mr. Secretary-General:*
Dear Mr. . . . :*

b. Ambassador or High Commissioner of a Foreign Country to Canada

His Excellency . . . (*full name*)*
Ambassador of . . . (*country*)
OR:
High Commissioner for . . . (*country*)
Address

Dear Ambassador:
High Commissioner:

EXCEPTION: British High Commissioner,
not High Commissioner for Britain.

c. Canadian Ambassador or High Commissioner Abroad

Mr. . . . (*full name*)*
Ambassador of Canada to . . . (*country*)
OR:
High Commissioner for Canada to . . .
  (*country*)
Address

Dear Ambassador:
High Commissioner:

d. American Ambassador to Canada

The Honourable . . . (*full name*)
American Ambassador
(**OR** The Ambassador of the United
  States of America)

*See the note on page 511.

490 Sussex Drive
Ottawa, ON K1N 1G8
Sir:*
Dear Mr. Ambassador:*

1810 INTERNATIONAL DIGNITARIES

a. An Emperor

His Imperial Majesty . . . (*name*)*
Emperor of (*country*)
Address

Your dignified Majesty:

b. A King

His Majesty . . . (*name*)
King of . . . (*country*)
Address

Your Majesty: **OR:**   Sire:

c. A Queen

Her Majesty Queen . . . (*name*)
Queen of . . . (*country*)
Address

Your Majesty: **OR:**   Madame:

d. A Prince* with the title *Royal* or *Serene Highness*

His Royal Highness*
OR:
His Serene Highness*
The Prince of . . . (*country*)
Address

Your Royal (**OR:** Serene) Highness:

e. A President of a Republic

His Excellency . . . (*full name*)*
President of the Republic of . . .
  (*country*)
Address

Excellency:

f. A Prime Minister

His Excellency . . . (*full name*)*
Prime Minister of . . . (*country*)
Address

Dear Prime Minister:

1811 MEMBERS OF THE CANADIAN ARMED FORCES

The addresses of both officers and other ranks should include full rank, initials, last name, decorations, position title, and address. Honours and decorations, listed in sequence, are always included in the address. Below are two specific examples with appropriate salutations.

a. Officers

Brigadier-General (*initials, last name*), OMM, CD, Commandant
Address

Dear General:

NOTE: Use the salutation *Dear General*, whether the officer is a full general or only a lieutenant-general, a major-general, or a brigadier-general. Similarly, use *Dear Colonel* for a lieutenant-colonel and *Dear Lieutenant* for a 2nd Lieutenant. In the Maritime Command, use *Dear Admiral* for a vice admiral or a rear-admiral; *Dear Commander* for a lieutenant-commander; and *Dear Lieutenant* for a sub-lieutenant.

b. Other Ranks

Sergeant (*full name*), CD
Address

Dear Sergeant . . . :

OR:

Private . . . (*full name*)
Address

Dear Private (*surname*):

1812 NATIVE LEADERS

a. Indian Chiefs

Chief . . . (*full name*)
Chief of . . . (*name*)
Address

Dear Chief . . . (*surname*):

b. Band Councillors

Mr. . . . (*full name*)*
Address

Dear Mr. . . . (*surname*):*

*See the note on page 511.

1813 ROMAN CATHOLIC DIGNITARIES

a. Pope

His Holiness the Pope

OR:

His Holiness Pope . . . (*given name*)
Vatican City
00187 Rome
ITALY

Your Holiness:
Most Holy Father:

b. Cardinal

His Eminence . . . (*given name*) Cardinal
. . . (*surname*)
Archbishop of . . . (*place*)
Address

Your Eminence:
Dear Cardinal . . . :

c. Bishop

The Most Reverend . . . (*full name*), D.D.
Bishop of . . . (*place*)
Address

Your Excellency:
My Lord: (Only if local custom)

d. Archbishop

The Most Reverend . . . (*full name*), D.D.
Archbishop of . . . (*place*)
Address

Your Grace:

e. Monsignor

Right Reverend Monsignor . . . (*full name*)
Address

Right Reverend Monsignor . . . (*full name*)
Dear Monsignor . . .

f. Priest

Reverend **OR** Reverend Father . . . (*full name, followed by comma and initials of order*)
Address

Reverend Father:
Dear Father . . . :
Dear Father:

(Continued on page 520.)

g. Sister (OR Mother) Superior

Sister (OR Mother) Superior (name, followed by comma and initials of order)
Name of convent, abbey, etc.
Address

Sister (OR Mother) Superior
Dear Sister (OR Mother) . . . :
Dear Sister (OR Mother):

h. Sister

Sister . . . (name, followed by comma and initials of order)
Address

Dear Sister . . . :
Dear Sister:

i. Brother

Brother . . . (name, followed by comma and initials of order)
Address

Dear Brother . . . :
Dear Brother:

1814 PROTESTANT DIGNITARIES

a. Anglican Primate

The Most Reverend . . . (full name)
Address

Your Grace:

b. Anglican Bishop

The Right Reverend . . . (full name)
Bishop of . . . (place)
Address

Right Reverend Sir:*
Dear Bishop:

c. Anglican Dean

The Very Reverend . . . (full name)
Dean of . . . (place)
Address

Very Reverend Sir:*
Dear Dean:

*See the note on page 511.

d. Moderator, United Church

The Right Reverend . . . (full name)
Moderator of the United Church of Canada
Address

Right Reverend Sir:*
Dear Moderator:

e. Minister With Doctor's Degree

The Reverend Dr. . . . (full name)
Address

OR:

The Reverend . . . (full name), D.D.
Address

Reverend Sir:*
Dear Dr. . . . :

f. Minister Without Doctor's Degree

The Reverend . . . (full name)
Address

Reverend Sir:*
Dear Mr. . . . :*

1815 JEWISH DIGNITARIES

a. Chief Rabbi

The Very Reverend . . . (full name)
Chief Rabbi
Address

Dear Sir OR Rabbi:

b. Rabbi With Doctor's Degree

The Reverend Rabbi . . . (full name), D.D.
Address

Dear Rabbi OR Dr. . . . (full name):

c. Rabbi Without Doctor's Degree

Rabbi . . . (full name)
Address

Dear Rabbi . . . :

See the Online Learning Centre at www.mcgrawhill.ca/college/gregg for related Web links.

Glossary of Grammatical Terms

Active verb. See *Voice, active.*

Adjective. A word that answers the question *what kind* (*excellent* results), *how many* (*four* laptops), or *which one* (the *latest* data). An adjective may be a single word (a *wealthy* man), a phrase (a man of *great wealth*), or a clause (a man *who possesses great wealth*). An adjective modifies the meaning of a noun (*big* brother) or a pronoun (*unlucky* me, I was *wrong*).

Adverb. A word that answers the question *when, where, why, how, in what manner,* or *to what extent.* An adverb may be a single word (speak *clearly*), a phrase (speak *in a clear voice*), or a clause (speak *as clearly as you can*). An adverb modifies the meaning of a verb, an adjective, or another adverb. (See also *Adverbial clause.*)

> We closed the deal *quickly.* (Modifies the verb *closed.*)
> Caroline seemed *genuinely* pleased. (Modifies the adjective *pleased.*)
> My presentation went *surprisingly* well. (Modifies the adverb *well.*)

Adverbial conjunction (or **connective**). An adverb that connects the main clauses of a compound sentence; for example, *however, therefore, nevertheless, hence, moreover, otherwise, consequently.* Also referred to as a *conjunctive adverb* or a *transitional expression.* (See also ¶¶138a, 178.)

Antecedent. A noun or a noun phrase to which a pronoun refers.

> She is the *person who* wrote the letter. (*Person* is the antecedent of *who.*)
> *Owning a home* has *its* advantages. (*Owning a home* is the antecedent of *its.*)

Appositive. A noun or a noun phrase that identifies another noun or pronoun that immediately precedes it. (See ¶¶148–153.)

> Mr. Mancuso, *our chief financial officer,* would like to meet you.

Article. Considered an adjective. The *definite* article is *the*; the *indefinite, a* or *an.* (See *a—an* in Section 11 for a usage note.)

Case. The form of a noun or of a pronoun that indicates its relation to other words in the sentence. There are three cases: nominative, objective, and possessive. *Nouns* have the same form in the nominative and objective cases but a special ending for the possessive. The forms for *pronouns* are:

Nominative	Objective	Possessive
I	me	my, mine
you	you	your, yours

(Continued on page 522.)

Nominative	Objective	Possessive
he, she, it	him, her, it	his, hers, its
we	us	our, ours
they	them	their, theirs
who	whom	whose

Nominative case. Used for the subject or the complement of a verb.

> *She* publishes a newsletter. (Subject.)

> The person who called you was *I*. (Complement.)

Objective case. Used for (1) the object of a verb, (2) the object of a preposition, (3) the subject of an infinitive, (4) the object of an infinitive, or (5) the complement of the infinitive *to be*.

> Can you help *us* this weekend? (Object of the verb *help*.)

> Brenda has not written to *me*. (Object of the preposition *to*.)

> I encouraged *her* to enter the biathlon. (Subject of the infinitive *to enter*.)

> William promised to call *me* but he didn't. (Object of the infinitive *to call*.)

> They believed me to be *her*. (Complement of the infinitive *to be*.)

Possessive case. Used to show ownership and other relationships. (See ¶¶627–651, especially the examples in ¶627.)

> *Your* copy of the report contains a statistical analysis. *Mine* doesn't.

Clause. A group of related words containing a subject and a predicate. An *independent* clause (also known as a *main clause* or *principal clause*) expresses a complete thought and can stand alone as a sentence. A *dependent* clause (also known as a *subordinate clause*) does not express a complete thought and cannot stand alone as a sentence.

> I will go (independent clause) if I am invited (dependent clause).

Adjective clause. A dependent clause that modifies a noun or a pronoun in the main clause. Adjective clauses are joined to the main clause by relative pronouns *(which, that, who, whose, whom)*.

> Their bill, *which includes servicing,* seems reasonable. (Modifies *bill*.)

Adverbial clause. A dependent clause that functions as an adverb in its relation to the main clause. Adverbial clauses indicate time, place, manner, cause, purpose, condition, result, reason, or contrast.

> These orders can be filled *as soon as stock is received.* (Time.)

> I was advised to live *where the climate is dry.* (Place.)

> She worked *as though her life depended on it.* (Manner.)

> Please write me at once *if you have any suggestions.* (Condition.)

> *Because our plant is closed in August,* we cannot fill your order now. (Reason.)

Coordinate clauses. Clauses of the same rank—independent or dependent.

> *Carl will oversee the day-to-day operations,* and *Sheila will be responsible for the finances.* (Coordinate independent clauses.)

> *When you have read the user's manual* and *you have mastered all the basic operations,* try to deal with these special applications. (Coordinate dependent clauses.)

Elliptical clause. A clause from which key words have been omitted. (See ¶¶102, 111, 119, 130b, 1086d.)

> *Now, for the next topic.*   *Really?*   *If possible,* arrive at one.

Essential (restrictive) clause. A dependent clause that cannot be omitted without changing the meaning of the main (independent) clause. Essential clauses are *not* set off by commas.

> The magazine *that came yesterday* contains an evaluation of new software.

Non-essential (non-restrictive) clause. A dependent clause that adds descriptive information but could be omitted without changing the meaning of the main (independent) clause. Such clauses are separated or set off from the main clause by commas.

> Her latest book, *which deals with corporate finance,* has sold quite well.

> She has had a lot of success with her latest book, *which deals with finance.*

Noun clause. A dependent clause that functions as a noun in the main clause.

> *Whether the proposal will be accepted* remains to be seen. (Noun clause as subject.)

> They thought *that the plan was a failure.* (Noun clause as object.)

> Then he said, *"Who gave you that information?"* (Noun clause as object.)

Comparison. The forms of an adjective or adverb that indicate degrees in quality, quantity, or manner. The degrees are positive, comparative, and superlative. (See ¶1071.)

Positive. The simple form; for example, *new, efficient* (adjectives); *soon, quietly* (adverbs).

Comparative. Indicates a higher or lower degree of quality or manner than is expressed by the positive degree. The comparative is used when two things are compared and is regularly formed by adding *er* to the positive degree *(newer, sooner).* In longer words the comparative is formed by adding *more* or *less* to the positive *(more efficient, less efficient; more quietly, less quietly).*

Superlative. Denotes the highest or lowest degree of quality or manner and is used when more than two things are compared. The superlative is regularly formed by adding *est* to the positive degree *(newest, soonest).* In longer words the superlative is formed by adding *most* or *least (most efficient, least efficient; most quietly, least quietly).*

Complement. A word or phrase that completes the sense of the verb. It may be an object, a predicate noun, a predicate pronoun, or a predicate adjective.

Object. Follows a transitive verb. (See *Verb.*)

> I have already drafted the *contract.*

Predicate noun or pronoun. Follows a linking verb (such as *is, am, are, was, were, will be, has been, could be*). It explains the subject and is identical with it. (Also called a *predicate complement, subject complement,* and *predicate nominative.*)

> Miss Kwong is our new *accountant.* (*Accountant* refers to *Miss Kwong.*)

> The person responsible for the decision was *I.* (The pronoun *I* refers to *person.*)

(Continued on page 524.)

19

Predicate adjective. Completes the sense of a linking verb. (Also called a *predicate complement.*)

> These charges are *excessive.* (The adjective *excessive* refers to *charges.*)

Compound modifier. A phrase or clause that qualifies, limits, or restricts the meaning of a word. Also referred to as a *compound adjective.* (See also ¶¶813–832.)

Conjunction. A word or phrase that connects words, phrases, or clauses.

> **Coordinating conjunction.** Connects words, phrases, or clauses of equal rank. The coordinating conjunctions are *and, but, or,* and *nor* (sometimes *for, yet,* and *so*).
>
> **Correlative conjunctions.** Conjunctions consisting of two elements used in pairs; for example, *both . . . and, not only . . . but (also), either . . . or, neither . . . nor.*
>
> **Subordinating conjunction.** Used to join dependent clauses to main (independent) clauses; for example, *when, where, after, before, if.* (See ¶132.)

Connective. A word that joins words, phrases, or clauses. The chief types of connectives are conjunctions, adverbial conjunctives, prepositions, and relative pronouns.

Consonants. The letters *b, c, d, f, g, h, j, k, l, m, n, p, q, r, s, t, v, w, x, y, z.* The letter *y* sometimes serves as a vowel (as in *rhyme*).

Contraction. A shortened form of a word or phrase in which an apostrophe indicates the omitted letters or words; for example, *don't* for *do not.* (See ¶505b–e.)

Dangling modifier. A modifier that is attached either to no word in a sentence or to the wrong word. (See ¶¶1086–1088.)

Direct address. A construction in which a speaker or a writer addresses another person directly; for example, "What do you think, Sylvia?"

Elliptical expressions. Condensed expressions from which key words have been omitted; for example, *if necessary* (for *if it is necessary*). (See ¶¶102, 111, 119a; see also *Clause; Sentence.*)

Essential elements. Words, phrases, or clauses needed to complete the structure or meaning of a sentence. (See also *Clause; Phrase.*)

Gender. The characteristic of nouns and pronouns that indicates whether the thing named is *masculine (man, boy, he), feminine (woman, girl, she),* or *neuter (book, concept, it).* Nouns that refer to either males or females have *common* gender *(person, child).*

Gerund. A verb form ending in *ing* and used as a *noun.*

> *Selling* requires special skills. (Subject.)
>
> I enjoy *selling.* (Direct object of *enjoy.*)
>
> She is experienced in *selling.* (Object of preposition *in.*)

> **Dangling gerund.** A prepositional-gerund phrase that is attached either to no word in a sentence or to the wrong word. (See ¶1082c.)

Imperative. See *Mood.*

Indicative. See *Mood.*

Infinitive. The form of the verb usually introduced by *to* (see ¶¶1044–1046). An infinitive may be used as a noun, an adjective, or an adverb. (See *Phrase*.)

NOUN: *To find affordable housing* these days is not easy. (Subject.)
She is trying *to do a hatchet job on my proposal*. (Object.)

ADJECTIVE: I still have two more contracts *to draft*. (Modifies *contracts*.)

ADVERB: He resigned *to take another position*. (Modifies *resigned*.)

Interjection. A word that shows emotion; usually without grammatical connection to other parts of a sentence.

Oh, so that's what he meant.   *Wow!* What a weekend!

Modifier. A word, phrase, or clause that qualifies, limits, or restricts the meaning of a word. (See *Adjective; Adverb; Dangling modifier*.)

Mood (mode). The form of the verb that shows the manner of the action. There are three moods: indicative, imperative, and subjunctive.

Indicative. States a fact or asks a question.

Our lease has expired.   When does our lease expire?

Imperative. Expresses a command or makes a request.

Call me next week.   Please send me your latest catalogue.

Subjunctive. Used in dependent clauses following main (independent) clauses expressing necessity, demand, or wishing (see ¶¶1038–1039); also used in *if, as if,* and *as though* clauses that state conditions which are improbable, doubtful, or contrary to fact (see ¶¶1040–1043).

I demand that we *be* heard.   It is imperative that he *be* notified.

We urge that she *be* elected.   If he *were* appointed, I would quit.

I wish I *were* going.   If she *had* known, she would have come.

Nominative case. See *Case, nominative*.

Non-essential elements. Words, phrases, or clauses that are not needed to complete the structure or meaning of a sentence. (See also *Clause; Phrase*.)

Noun. The name of a person, place, object, idea, quality, or activity.

Abstract noun. The name of a quality or a general idea; for example, *courage, freedom.*

Collective noun. A noun that represents a group of persons, animals, or things; for example, *audience, company, flock.* (See ¶1019.)

Common noun. The name of a class of persons, places, or things; for example, *child, house.* (See ¶¶307–310.)

Predicate noun. See *Complement.*

Proper noun. The official name of a particular person, place, or thing; for example, *Ellen, Saskatoon, Wednesday.* Proper nouns are capitalized. (See ¶¶303–306.)

Number. The characteristic of a noun, pronoun, or verb that indicates whether one person or thing (singular) or more than one (plural) is meant.

> NOUN: beeper, beepers   PRONOUN: she, they   VERB: (she) works, (they) work

Object. The person or thing that receives the action of a transitive verb. An object may be a word, a phrase, or a clause. (See *Case, objective.*)

> I need a new laptop *computer.* (Word.)
>
> She prefers *to work with hard copy.* (Infinitive phrase.)
>
> We did not realize *that your deadline was so tight.* (Clause.)

Direct object. The person or thing that is directly affected by the action of the verb. (The object in each of the three sentences above is a *direct* object.)

Indirect object. The person or thing indirectly affected by the action of the verb. The indirect object can be made the object of the preposition *to* or *for.*

> Molly gave (to) *me* a hard time about my sales performance this quarter.

Ordinal number. The form of a number that indicates order or succession; for example, *first, second, twelfth* or *1st, 2nd, 12th.* (See ¶¶424–426.)

Parenthetical elements. Words, phrases, or clauses that are not necessary to the completeness of the structure or the meaning of a sentence.

> Gina Sala, *my wife's older sister,* is my accountant.

Participle. A word that may stand alone as an adjective or may be combined with helping (auxiliary) verbs to form different tenses (see ¶¶1033–1034). There are three forms: present, past, and perfect.

Present participle. Ends in *ing*; for example, *making, advertising.*

Past participle. Regularly ends in *ed* (as in *asked* or *filed*) but may be irregularly formed (as in *lost, seen,* and *written*). (See ¶1030a–b.)

Perfect participle. Consists of *having* plus the past participle; for example, *having asked, having lost.*

When a participle functions as an *adjective,* it modifies a noun or a pronoun.

> The *coming* year poses some new challenges. (Modifies *year.*)
>
> *Having retired* last year, I now do volunteer work. (Modifies *I.*)

Because a participle has many of the characteristics of a verb, it may take an object and be modified by an adverb. The participle and its object and modifiers make up a *participial phrase.*

> *Seizing the opportunity,* Orzo offered to buy the business. (*Opportunity* is the object of *seizing.*)
>
> *Moving aggressively,* we can control the market. (*Aggressively* modifies *moving.*)

Dangling participle. A participial phrase attached either to no word in a sentence or to the wrong word. (See *Phrase* and ¶1086a.)

Parts of speech. The eight classes into which words are grouped according to their uses in a sentence: verb, noun, pronoun, adjective, adverb, conjunction, preposition, and interjection.

19

Passive verb. See *Voice, passive.*

Person. The characteristic of a word that indicates whether a person is speaking *(first person)*, is spoken to *(second person)*, or is spoken about *(third person)*. Only personal pronouns and verbs change their forms to show person. All nouns are considered third person.

	Singular	Plural
FIRST PERSON:	*I* like this book.	*We* like this book.
SECOND PERSON:	*You* like this book.	*You* like this book.
THIRD PERSON:	*She* likes this book.	*They* like this book.

Phrase. A group of two or more words without a subject and a predicate; used as a noun, an adjective, or an adverb. (See *Predicate.*)

Noun phrase. A phrase that functions as a noun (such as a gerund phrase, an infinitive phrase, or a prepositional phrase.)

I like *running my own business.* (Gerund phrase as object.)

To provide the best possible service is our goal. (Infinitive phrase as subject.)

Before 9 a.m. is the best time to call me. (Prepositional phrase as subject.)

Adjective phrase. A phrase that functions as an adjective (such as an infinitive phrase, a participial phrase, or a prepositional phrase).

The time *to act* is now! (Infinitive phrase indicating what kind of time.)

Adverbial phrase. A phrase that functions as an adverb (such as an infinitive phrase or a prepositional phrase).

Let's plan to meet *after lunch.* (Prepositional phrase indicating when to meet.)

Gerund phrase. A gerund plus its object and modifiers; used as a noun.

Delaying payments to your suppliers will prove costly. (Gerund phrase as subject.)

Infinitive phrase. An infinitive plus its object and modifiers; may be used as a noun, an adjective, or an adverb. An infinitive phrase that is attached to either no word in a sentence or to the wrong word is called a *dangling* infinitive (see ¶1082b).

To get TF's okay on this purchase order took some doing. (As a noun; serves as subject of the verb *took.*)

The decision *to close the Belleville plant* was not made easily. (As an adjective; tells what kind of decision.)

Janice resigned *to open her own business.* (As an adverb; tells why Janice resigned.)

NOTE: An infinitive phrase, unlike other phrases, may sometimes have a subject. This subject precedes the infinitive and is in the objective case.

I have asked *her to review this draft for accuracy.* (*Her* is the subject of *to review.*)

Participial phrase. A participle and its object and modifiers; used as an adjective.

The committee *considering your proposal* should come to a decision this week.

I prefer the cover sample *printed in blue and yellow.*

19

(Continued on page 528.)

Prepositional phrase. A preposition and its object and modifiers; may be used as a noun, an adjective, or an adverb.

From Halifax to Tofino is about 6500 km. (As a noun; serves as subject of *is*.)

Profits *in the automobile industry* are up sharply this quarter. (As an adjective; indicates which type of profits.)

You handled Dr. Wenzlawe's objections *with great skill*. (As an adverb; indicates the manner in which the objections were handled.)

Prepositional-gerund phrase. A phrase that begins with a preposition and has a gerund as the object. (See *Gerund* and ¶1086c.)

By rechecking the material before it is set in type, you avoid expensive corrections later on. (*By* is the preposition; *rechecking*, a gerund, is the object of *by*.)

Essential (restrictive) phrase. A phrase that limits, defines, or identifies; cannot be omitted without changing the meaning of the sentence.

The study *analyzing our competitors' promotion activities* will be finished next week.

Non-essential (non-restrictive) phrase. A phrase that can be omitted without changing the meaning of the sentence.

Investors Group, *one of the country's largest financial organizations*, is expanding its advertising on the Internet.

Verb phrase. This term is often used to indicate the individual words that make up the verb in a sentence. Sometimes the verb phrase includes an adverb. A verb phrase can function only as a verb.

You *should work together* with Nora on the report. (The verb phrase consists of the verb form *should work* plus the adverb *together*.)

Positive degree. See *Comparison*.

Possessive case. See *Case, possessive*.

Predicate. That part of a sentence which tells what the subject does or what is done to the subject or what state of being the subject is in. (See also *Verb*.)

Complete predicate. The complete predicate consists of a verb and its complement or object along with any modifiers.

Barbara *has handled the job well*.

Simple predicate. The simple predicate is the verb alone, without regard for any complement, object, or modifiers that may accompany it.

Barbara *has handled* the job well.

Compound predicate. A predicate consisting of two or more predicates joined by conjunctions.

Barbara *has handled the job well* and *deserves a good deal of praise*.

Predicate adjective. See *Complement*.

Predicate nominative. See *Complement*.

Prefix. A letter, syllable, or word added to the beginning of a word to change its meaning; for example, *il*legal, *im*material, *under*nourished.

Preposition. A connective (such as *from, to, in, on, at, by, for, with*) that shows the relationship between a noun or pronoun and some other word in the sentence. The noun or pronoun following a preposition is in the objective case. (See ¶¶1077–1080.)

> Martin's work was reviewed *by Hedley and me.*

Principal parts. The forms of a verb from which all other forms are derived: the *present,* the *past,* the *past participle,* and the *present participle.* (See ¶¶1030–1035.)

Pronoun. A word used in place of a noun. (See ¶¶1049–1064.)

DEMONSTRATIVE:	*this, that, these, those*
INDEFINITE:	*each, either, any, anyone, someone, everyone, few, all,* etc.
INTENSIVE:	*myself, yourself, himself, herself, ourselves, themselves,* etc.
INTERROGATIVE:	*who, which, what,* etc.
PERSONAL:	*I, you, he, she, it, we, they,* etc.
RELATIVE:	*who, whose, whom, which, that,* and compounds such as *whoever*

Punctuation. Marks used to indicate relationships between words, phrases, and clauses.

Terminal (end) punctuation. The period, the question mark, and the exclamation point—the three marks that may indicate the end of a sentence.

NOTE: When a sentence breaks off abruptly, a dash may be used to mark the end of the sentence (see ¶207). When a sentence trails off without really ending, ellipses (three spaced periods) are used to mark the end of the sentence. (See ¶292a.)

Internal punctuation. *Commas, semicolons, colons, dashes, parentheses, quotation marks, apostrophes, ellipses, asterisks, diagonals,* and *brackets* are the most common marks of internal punctuation.

Question.

Direct question. A question in its original form, as spoken or written.

> He then asked me, "What is your opinion?"

Indirect question. A restatement of a question without the use of the exact words of the speaker.

> He then asked me what my opinion was.

Independent question. A question that represents a complete sentence but is incorporated in a larger sentence.

> The main question is, Who will translate this idea into a clear plan of action?

Quotation.

Direct quotation. A quotation of words exactly as spoken or written.

> I myself heard Ed say, "I will arrive in Brandon on Tuesday."

Indirect quotation. A restatement of a quotation without the use of the exact words of the speaker.

> I myself heard Ed say that he would arrive in Brandon on Tuesday.

19

Sentence. A group of words representing a complete thought and containing a subject and a predicate (a verb along with any complements and modifiers).

> **Simple sentence.** A sentence consisting of one independent clause.
>
> > I have no recollection of the meeting.
>
> **Compound sentence.** A sentence consisting of two or more independent clauses.
>
> > Our Regina office will be closed, and our Windsor office will be relocated.
>
> **Complex sentence.** A sentence consisting of one independent clause (also called the *main clause*) and one or more dependent clauses.
>
> > We will make an exception to the policy if circumstances warrant.
>
> **Compound-complex sentence.** A sentence consisting of two independent clauses and one or more dependent clauses.
>
> > I tried to handle the monthly report alone, but when I began to analyze the data, I realized that I needed your help.
>
> **Elliptical sentence.** A word or phrase treated as a complete sentence, even though the subject and verb are understood but not expressed.
>
> > Enough on that subject.   Why not?
>
> **Declarative sentence.** A sentence that makes a statement.
>
> > Our company is continually testing cutting-edge technologies.
>
> **Interrogative sentence.** A sentence that asks a question.
>
> > When will the conference begin?
>
> **Exclamatory sentence.** A sentence that expresses strong feeling.
>
> > Don't even think of smoking here!
>
> **Imperative sentence.** A sentence that expresses a command or a request. (The subject *you* is understood if it is not expressed.)
>
> > Send a cheque at once.   Please let us hear from you.

Sentence fragment. A phrase or clause that is incorrectly treated as a sentence. (See ¶102, note.)

Statement. A sentence that asserts a fact. (See also *Sentence.*)

Subject. A word, phrase, or clause that names the person, place, or thing about which something is said. (See *Case, nominative.*)

> *The law firm with the best reputation in town* is Barringer and Doyle.
>
> *Whoever applies for the job from within the department* will get special consideration.

> **Compound subject.** Two or more subjects joined by a conjunction.
>
> > *My wife and my three sons* are off on a white-water rafting trip.

Subjunctive. See *Mood.*

Suffix. A letter, syllable, or word added to the end of a word to modify its meaning; for example, trendy, friendly, countless, receivership, lonesome. (See ¶833a.)

Superlative degree. See *Comparison.*

Syllable. One or more letters that represent one sound.

Tense. The property of a verb that expresses *time.* (See ¶¶1031–1035.) The three *primary* tenses correspond to the three time divisions:

PRESENT:	they think
PAST:	they thought
FUTURE:	they will think

There are three *perfect* tenses, corresponding to the primary tenses:

PRESENT PERFECT:	they have thought
PAST PERFECT:	they had thought
FUTURE PERFECT:	they will have thought

There are six *progressive* tenses, corresponding to each of the primary and perfect tenses:

PRESENT PROGRESSIVE:	they are thinking
PAST PROGRESSIVE:	they were thinking
FUTURE PROGRESSIVE:	they will be thinking
PRESENT PERFECT PROGRESSIVE:	they have been thinking
PAST PERFECT PROGRESSIVE:	they had been thinking
FUTURE PERFECT PROGRESSIVE:	they will have been thinking

There are two *emphatic* tenses:

PRESENT EMPHATIC:	they do think
PAST EMPHATIC:	they did think

☞ *For an illustration of how these tenses are formed, see pages 244–245.*

Transitional expressions. Expressions that link independent clauses or sentences; for example, *as a result, therefore, on the other hand, nevertheless.* (See also ¶138a; *Adverbial conjunction.*)

Verb. A word or phrase used to express action or state of being. (See also *Mood.*)

Enniston *has boosted* its sales goals for the year. (Action.)

My son-in-law *was* originally a lawyer, but he *has* now *become* a computer-game designer. (State of being.)

Helping (auxiliary) verb. A verb that helps in the formation of another verb. (See ¶¶1030c, 1033–1034.) The chief helping verbs are *be, can, could, do, have, may, might, must, ought, shall, should, will, would.*

Transitive verb. A verb that requires an object to complete its meaning. (See also *Object.*)

Fusilli *has rejected* all offers to purchase his business.

(Continued on page 532.)

Intransitive verb. A verb that does not require an object to complete its meaning.

> As market growth *occurs* and customer interest *builds,* our sales expectations *are rising* and top management's excitement *has increased.*

Linking verb. A verb that connects a subject with a predicate adjective, noun, or pronoun. The various forms of *to be* are the most commonly used linking verbs. *Become, look, seem, appear,* and *grow* are also used as linking verbs. (See *Complement* and ¶1067.)

> Laura *seemed* willing to compromise, but Frank *became* obstinate in his demands.
>
> Was he afraid that any concession might make him *appear* a fool?

Principal parts of verbs. See *Principal parts.*

Verbal. A word that is derived from a verb but functions in some other way. (See *Gerund; Infinitive; Participle.*)

Voice. The property of a verb that indicates whether the subject acts or is acted upon.

Active voice. A verb is in the active voice when its subject is the doer of the action.

> About a dozen people *reviewed* the report in draft form.

Passive voice. A verb is in the passive voice when its subject is acted upon.

> The report *was reviewed* in draft form by about a dozen people.

Vowels. The letters *a, e, i, o,* and *u.* The letter *y* sometimes acts like a vowel (as in *cry*). (See also *Consonants.*)

 See the Online Learning Centre at www.mcgrawhill.ca/college/gregg for related Web links.

Glossary of Computer and Internet Terms

The following glossary provides brief and simple definitions of some key terms and concepts of computer and Internet terms. It should be noted that imperial measurements, not metric, are used with computer configurations and formats.*

NOTE: When boldface type is used to highlight a word or phrase within a definition, it signifies that the highlighted word or phrase is defined elsewhere in this glossary.

☞ *See ¶541 for a list of common computer abbreviations and acronyms.*

Access (also called *retrieve*). To call up information out of **storage**.

Active matrix display. A type of **monitor** typically used on **laptop** or portable **computers**; provides a brighter, more readable display than older **LCD** equipment.

Adapter. A **circuit** board that plugs into a **computer** and gives it additional capabilities.

Algorithm. A step-by-step procedure designed to solve a problem or achieve an objective.

Alphanumeric. Consisting of letters, numbers, and symbols.

Antivirus software. A **program** designed to look for and destroy a **virus** that may have infected a **computer's memory** or **files**.

Applet. A small **application**, that is, a **program** designed to perform a simple task. An applet is usually embedded within a larger program or **downloaded** from the **Internet**.

Application (also called *app*). A **program** designed to perform **information processing** tasks for a specific purpose or activity (for example, **desktop publishing** and **database management**).

Archie. A tool for finding a **file transfer protocol (FTP)** server.

Archive. A **file** compressed for more efficient use of storage space. The compression of files may be accomplished by means of such **programs** as WinZip.

Ascending sort. Sorting records from A to Z or 0 to 9. (See *Descending sort.*)

---

*To update this glossary in accordance with the 10th U.S.A. ed. of William A. Sabin's *The Gregg Reference Manual*, McGraw-Hill/Irwin, New York, 2005, the following works were consulted: *Webster's New World Computer Dictionary*, 10th ed., Wiley, New York, 2003; *Microsoft Computer Dictionary*, 5th ed., Redmond, Wash., 2002. For the most up-to-date vocabulary of computer technology, consult *Webopedia.com.*

ASCII (pronounced *as-kee*). An acronym derived from American Standard Code for Information Interchange. ASCII is a standard **8-bit** code that represents 256 **characters**. The use of this standard code permits **computers** made by different manufacturers to communicate with one another.

Background printing. The ability of a **computer** to print a **document** while other work is being done on the **keyboard** and the **display screen** at the same time.

Backup. Storage of duplicate **files** on **disks**, diskettes, or some other form of magnetic medium (such as tapes) as a safety measure in case the original medium is damaged or lost. (One word as a noun or an adjective: *backup* procedures; two words as a verb: *back up* your hard disk.)

Bandwidth. The volume of information that a network can handle (usually expressed in bits per second). The greater the bandwidth, the more quickly **data** can move from a **network** to a user's **computer**.

Binary Code. The language used by computers in which **data** and instructions are represented by a series of 1s and 0s.

BIOS (basic input/output system). A set of **programs** stored in **read-only memory (ROM)** on IBM-compatible **computers**. These programs control the **disk drives**, the keyboard, and the **display screen**; and they handle start-up operations.

Bit (b). An acronym derived from b̲inary dig̲it. The smallest unit of information that can be recognized by a **computer**. Bits are combined to represent **characters**. (See also *Byte*.)

Bitmap. A method of storing a graphic image as a set of **bits** in a computer's **memory**. To display the image on the screen, the **computer** converts the bits into **pixels**.

Bits per second (bps). A measurement that describes the speed of **data** transmission between two pieces of equipment.

Blackberry. A wireless **palmtop computer** that permits travellers to send and receive e-mail and view other documents that they have on file.

Block. A segment of **text** that is selected so that it can be moved or copied to another location or processed in some other way. (See *Copy; Delete; Cut and paste*.)

Block protect. A **command** to prevent a **page break** from occurring within a block of **text**. (See also *Keep lines together; Keep with next; Widow/orphan protection*.)

Blog. An online diary, which is created and maintained by a blogger.

Bluetooth. A **protocol** that permits a wireless exchange of information between **computers**, cell phones, and other electronic devices.

Boilerplate. Standard wording (for example, sentences or paragraphs in form letters or clauses) that is held in **storage**. When needed, it can be used as is, with minor modification, or in combination with new material to produce tailor-made documents. (See *Style sheet* and *Templates*.)

Bookmark list. A customized list of a user's favourite Web sites (also referred to as a *hot list*). A bookmark list permits the user to access a particular Web site with a single **command** (also referred to as *favourites* or *hot list*).

Boot (short for *bootstrap*). To start a **computer** and load the **operating system** to prepare the computer to **execute** an **application**.

Bozo filter. A **program** that screens out unwanted **e-mail** or other messages from individuals or organizations you no longer want to hear from.

bps. See *Bits per second*.

Broadband. A wide bank of electromagnetic frequencies, which can be divided and shared by multiple simultaneous signals (as for voice or **data** or video).

Browser. See *Web browser*.

Buffer. A holding area in **memory** that stores information temporarily. Also called *cache*.

Bug. A defect in the **software** or **hardware** that causes the **computer** to malfunction or cease to operate. (See also *Debugging; Glitch*.)

Bulletin board system (BBS). An electronic message centre serving specific interest **newsgroups**.

Bundled software. **Software** that is sold along with a **computer** system; several software **programs** packaged together (also called *software suites*).

Burn. To record information on a disc such as a **CD-R**, a **CD-RW**, a **DVD-R**, or a **DVD-RW**.

Bus. An internal pathway along which electronic signals travel between the components of a **computer** system.

Button bar. An on-screen element that offers a user instant **access** to commonly used **commands**. The commands are represented by **icons** on a row of buttons shown at the top of the screen. Also called a *tool bar*.

Byte (B). The sequence of **bits** that represents a **character**. Each byte has 8 bits.

Cache. See *Buffer*.

Cancelbot (from *cancel robot*). A **program** that detects **spamming** and automatically issues a cancel command.

Card. See *Circuit board*.

Carpal tunnel syndrome. A wrist or hand injury caused by using a keyboard or **mouse** for long periods of time. A type of repetitive strain injury (RSI). (See also *Mouse elbow*).

CD-R. Compact disc recordable.

CD-ROM. An acronym derived from compact disk—read-only memory. A form of optical **storage**. One compact **disk** can hold up to 250 000 **text** pages; it can also be used to store **graphics**, sound, and video. (See *DVD*.)

CD-RW. Compact disc rewritable.

Cell. A box or rectangle within a table or **spreadsheet** where a **column** and a **row** intersect; an area in which information can be entered in the form of **text** or figures.

Central processing unit (CPU). The brains of an **information processing** system; the processing component that controls the interpretation and execution of instructions. (See *Motherboard*.)

Character. A single letter, figure, punctuation mark, or symbol produced by a **keystroke** on a **computer**. Each character is represented by a **byte**.

Character set. The complete set of **characters**—alphabetic, numeric, and symbolic—displayed on a **computer**. (See *ASCII*.)

20

Character string. A specified sequence of keyed **characters**, usually representing a word or phrase. A character string is often used to locate a particular word or phrase wherever it appears in a **document** so that it can be automatically replaced with another word or phrase. If a person's name has been consistently misspelled or a date appears incorrectly in several places, the error can be easily corrected. (See also *Find and replace*.)

Characters per inch (cpi). The number of characters in a **monospace font** that will fit within 1 inch; for example, Courier style.

Characters per second (cps). The number of **characters** printed in one second; a measurement frequently used to describe the speed of a **printer**.

Chat. A method of communication in which people type text messages to each other, thereby holding a conversation over a **network** such as the **Internet**. (See also *newsgroup*.)

Check box. A small square box that appears on screen alongside each option displayed in a **dialog box**. When one or more options are selected, an X or a check mark appears inside the box. (See also *Option button, Radio button*.)

Chip. An **integrated circuit** used in **computers**.

Circuit board. A board or card that carries the necessary electronic components for a particular **computer** function (for example, **memory**). The circuit boards that come with the original equipment perform the standard functions identified with that type of equipment. Additional circuit boards expand the kinds of functions that the equipment can perform. (Also called a *board*, a *card*, or an *expansion board*.)

Client/server computing. A **network** of **computers** that consists of a **file server** (a computer that runs a **database management system**) and individual clients (computers that request and process **data** obtained from the file server).

Clipboard. A holding area in **memory** where information that has been copied or cut (**text**, **graphics**, sound, or video) can be stored until the information is inserted elsewhere. (See *Copy; Cut; Cut and paste*.)

Column. A vertical block of **cells** in a table or **spreadsheet**. (See also *Row*.)

Command. An instruction that causes a **program** or **computer** to perform a function. A command may be given by means of a special **keystroke** (or series of keystrokes), or the command may be chosen from a **menu**.

Compatibility. The ability of one type of **computer** to share information or to communicate with another computer. (See also *ASCII*.)

Computer. An electronic device that is capable of (1) accepting, storing, and logically manipulating **data** or **text** that is **input** and (2) processing and producing **output** (results or decisions) on the basis of stored **programs** of instructions. Some are also capable of processing **graphics**, video, and voice input. Computers include a **keyboard** for **text entry**, a **central processing unit**, one or more **disk drives**, a **display screen**, and a **printer**—components referred to as **hardware**.

Control menu. An on-screen Windows element that appears in a box in the upper right corner of a window. The control menu allows the user the option of adjusting the size of the window, closing or reopening the window, or switching to another window.

Cookie. A device that permits a **Web site** to identify and collect information about every user who visits that site.

Copy. To reproduce information elsewhere. The original information remains in place. (See *Cut.*)

cpi. See *Characters per inch.*

cps. See *Characters per second.*

CPU. See *Central processing unit.*

Cracker. The preferred term (rather than **hacker**) used to refer to a **computer** criminal who penetrates a computer to steal information or damage the program in some way.

Crash. A malfunction in **hardware** or **software** that keeps a **computer** from functioning. (See also *Bug; Glitch.*)

Cursor. A special **character** (usually a blinking underline, dot, or vertical line) that indicates where the next keyed character will appear on the **display screen**. Also refers to the **I-beam pointer** or **mouse** pointer (arrow). Microsoft Word refers to the cursor as the *insertion point.* (See also *Prompt.*)

Cursor positioning. The movement of the **cursor** or **I-beam pointer** on the display screen. Most computers have four keys to control up, down, left, and right movement. The **mouse** is also used to position the **cursor**.

Cut. To remove **text** from its original location and place it on a **clipboard**. (See *Paste; Copy.*)

Cut and paste. To move a **block** of **text** from one place to another.

Cyberspace. A realistic simulation of a three-dimensional world created by a **computer** system. Also referred to as *virtual reality.* Now commonly used to refer to the world of the **Internet** as a whole.

Data. Information consisting of letters, numbers, symbols, sounds, or images—in a form that can be processed by a **computer**.

Data compression. A procedure for reducing the volume of **data** so as to shorten the time needed to transfer the data.

Data mining. Database applications that look for hidden patterns or trends from groups of **data** that would predict future behaviour; that is, it could help retailers find customers with common interests, and could be used in scientific research, criminology, and other fields.

Database. A stored collection of information.

Database management system (DBMS). The **software** needed to establish and maintain a **database** and manage the stored information.

Debugging. Locating and eliminating defects in a **program**. (See also *Bug.*)

Decimal tab. A type of tab that aligns **columns** of figures on the decimal point.

Default settings. The pre-established settings (for margins, **font**, type size, tab stops, and so on) that a **program** will follow unless the user changes them.

Delete. A **command** to erase information in **storage**.

Denial of service (DoS) attack. A malicious act intended to shut down a **Web site** or a **network** by flooding it with too much information. Users who attempt to visit the site will be denied access.

20

Descending sort. Sorting records from Z to A or 9 to 0. (See *Ascending sort*.)

Desktop. The electronic work area on a **display screen**.

Desktop publishing (DTP). A system that processes **text** and **graphics** and, by means of page layout **software** and a **laser printer**, produces high-quality pages suitable for printing or in-house reproduction.

Dialog box. A message box on the screen that supplies information to—or requests information from—the user.

Dictionary. A **program** used to check the spelling of each word entered in the **computer**.

Directory. A list of **files** (**DOS** Application) stored on a **disk**. (See also *Folder*.)

Disk. A random-**access**, magnetically coated storage medium used to store and **retrieve** information. (See also *Flash Drive, CD-ROM*.)

Disk drive. The component of a **computer** into which a **disk** is inserted so that it can be read or written on.

Display screen. A device similar to a television screen and used on a **computer** to display **text** and **graphics**. Also called a *cathode-ray tube (CRT)*, a *video display terminal (VDT)*, or a *monitor*.

Distributed processing system. A form of a **local area network** in which each user has a fully functional **computer** but all users can share **data** and **application software**. The data and **software** are distributed among the linked computers and are not stored in one central computer.

Document. Any printed business communication—for example, a letter, memo, report, table, or form. (See *File*.)

Domain. Typically, a three-letter element in a Web address or an **e-mail** address. The domain (commonly referred to as the *zone*) indicates the type of organization that owns the **computer** being identified in the address. (See ¶1508b for list of common domains.)

Domain name. The second part of an **e-mail** address—what follows the @ symbol. The name of the **computer** intended to receive an e-mail message. In Web addresses (**URLs**) this element is referred to as the **host** name.

DOS. An acronym of disk operating system. It is a **program** that allows the **computer** to manage the **storage** of information on **disks** and controls other aspects of a computer's operation.

Dot. The period symbol used in **e-mail** addresses. Always referred to as a *dot* (never as a period).

Dot-com. An organization that sells its products or services on a **Web site** (with a URL ending in *.com*).

Download. To transfer information to the user's **computer** from another computer.

Drag-and-drop editing. A **software** feature that allows the user to (1) highlight **text** to be moved and (2) use a **mouse** to drag the text to a new location.

DRAM. Dynamic random access memory.

Duplexing. A procedure that permits two computers to transmit data to each other simultaneously.

20

DVD. An abbreviation for <u>d</u>igital <u>v</u>ideo/<u>v</u>ersatile <u>d</u>isc. As a recording medium, it is similar in application to a **CD-ROM**. It holds a minimum of 4.7 GB (**gigabytes**), enough for a full-length movie. DVDs can also be designated as **DVD-E** (erasable), **DVD-R** (recordable), **DVD-RW** (read/write), **DVD-RAM**, and DVD-ROM.

Easter egg. An unexpected image or message that pops up on the **display screen** when the user innocently enters a secret combination of **keystrokes**. Programmers playfully code Easter eggs into **software** and **operating systems** as a way of surprising and amusing users engaged in more serious tasks.

Editing. The process of changing information by inserting, deleting, replacing, rearranging, and reformatting. Also known as *changing* or *customizing*.

E-mail. Short for electronic mail. The term refers to the transfer of messages or **documents** between users connected by an electronic **network**.

Emoticon. An acronym for *emotion icon*, a small **icon** composed of punctuation characters that indicates how an **e-mail** message should be interpreted (that is, the writer's mood). For example, a :-) emoticon indicates that the message should not be taken seriously. Although some emoticons are quite witty, many people find them excessively cute. Therefore, do not use them unless you are sure they will be appreciated. An emoticon is also called a *smiley*.

Encryption. Coding confidential **data** so that only a user with the necessary **password** can read the data.

Enter. To **input data** into **memory**. (See *Type*.)

Ergonomics. The science of adopting working conditions and equipment to meet the physical needs of workers.

Escape key (Esc). Depending on the **software** used, usually cancels or aborts the current operation.

Ethernet. A type of **computer network**.

Ethernet card. A **circuit board** that allows a **computer** to be connected to a **network** by a cable.

Execute. To perform an action specified by the user of the **program**.

Expansion board. See *Circuit board*.

Export. To save information in a **format** that another program can read.

Extranet. A technology that permits users of one organization's **intranet** to enter portions of another organization's intranet in order to conduct business transactions or collaborate on joint projects.

E-zine. A magazine published in electronic format. Also called *Webzine*.

FAQ. <u>F</u>requently <u>a</u>sked <u>q</u>uestions. Pronounced as a word (to rhyme with *pack*) or as separate letters.

Favourites. See Bookmark list.

Fax. A shortened form of the word *facsimile*. A copy of a **document** transmitted electronically from one machine to another.

Fax modem. A device built into or attached to a **computer** that serves as a facsimile machine and a **modem**.

Field. A group of related **characters** treated as a unit (such as a name); also the area reserved for the entry of a specified piece of information.

File. A collection of information stored electronically and treated as a unit by a **computer**. Every file must have its own distinctive name.

File server. **Hardware** and **software** that together provide the handling of **files** and **storage** functions for multiple users on a **local area network**.

File transfer protocol (FTP). A set of guidelines or standards that establish the **format** in which **files** can be transmitted from one **computer** to another.

Find and replace. A **command** that directs the **program** to locate a **character string** or information (**text**, numbers, or symbols) wherever it occurs in a **document** and replace this material with new information.

Firewall. Software that prevents unauthorized persons from accessing certain parts of a **program**, **database**, or **network**.

Flame. A hostile message, often sent through e-mail or posted in a **newsgroup**, from an **Internet** user in reaction to a breach of **netiquette**.

Flash drive (jump drive). A small, portable flash-memory "stick" that plugs into a **computer's** USB **port**. It functions as a **hard drive** with up to 2-**GB storage** capacity. Because it has no moving parts, it is extremely durable.

Flat-panel display. A type of **desktop computer** monitor that consists of an **LCD** in a thin case. A flat-panel display has a smaller **footprint** than the traditional CRT (cathode ray tube).

Folder. A storage area (**Windows** application) on a **disk** used to organize files. (See also *Directory*.)

Font. A **typeface** of a certain size and style. Includes all letters of the alphabet, figures, symbols, and punctuation marks. (See *Monospace font; Proportional font*.)

Footer. Repetitive information that appears at the bottom (the foot) of every page of a **document**. A page number is a common footer. (See also *Header*.)

Footnote feature. The ability of a **program** to automatically position footnotes on the same page as the **text** they refer to. If the text is moved to another page, any related footnotes will also be transferred to that page.

Footprint. The amount of space a **computer** occupies on a flat surface.

Format. The physical specifications that affect the appearance and arrangement of a **document**—for example, margins, spacing, and **font**.

Forms mode. The ability of a **program** to store the **format** of a blank **document** or form so that it can later be viewed on the **display screen** and completed by the user. Once a fill-in has been entered, the **cursor** automatically advances to the beginning of the next area to be filled in. (See also *Style sheet; Template*.)

Forum. See *Newsgroup*.

Freenet. A local **network** that offers free (or low-cost) **access** to **host computers** located in libraries and to other public-interest groups in the community.

Freeware. Copyrighted **software** that is available for use without charge. (See also *Shareware*.)

Function keys. Keys on a **keyboard** (for example, F2) that give special **commands** to the **computer**—for example, to set margins or tabs.

20

Gateway. A machine that links two **networks** using different **protocols**.

Gigabyte (G or GB). A measurement of the **storage** capacity of a device. One gigabyte is equal to 1024 **megabytes**, or about one billion **bytes**.

Gigahertz (GHz). A measurement used to identify the speed of the **central processing unit**. One gigahertz is equal to 1 billion cycles per second.

Glitch. A **hardware** problem that causes a **computer** to malfunction or **crash**. (See *Bug*.)

Global. Describing any function that can be performed on an entire **document** without requiring individual **commands** for each use.

Graphics. Pictures or images presented or stored using a **computer**.

GUI. An acronym for graphical user interface. A **software** feature that permits the user to click on icons or select options from a **menu**.

Hacker. A dedicated **computer** programmer. (See also *Cracker*).

Handheld computer. A portable computer smaller than a **notebook computer**. Also called a **palmtop computer**.

Hard copy. **Text** or **graphics** printed on paper; also called a **printout**. (See also *Soft copy*.)

Hard disk. A rigid type of magnetic medium that can store large amounts of information.

Hard hyphen. See *Non-breaking hyphen*.

Hard page break. A page-ending code or **command** inserted by the user that must be changed by the user. A hard page break is often used (1) to prevent a table from being divided between two pages and (2) to signify that a particular section of a **document** has ended and the following **text** should start on a new page. (See also *Soft page break*.)

Hard return. A **command** used to end a paragraph, end a short line of **text**, or insert a blank line in the text. (See also *Soft return*.)

Hard space. See *Non-breaking space*.

Hardware. The physical components of a **computer**: the **central processing unit**, the **display screen**, the **keyboard**, the **disk drive**, and the **printer**. (See also *Software*.)

Hardwired. Describing any **computer** function that cannot be easily modified.

Header. Repetitive information that appears at the top (the head) of every page of a **document**. A page number is a common header. (See also *Footer*.)

Hit. A single request for information made by a client computer from a Web server. The popularity of a given **Web site** is measured by the number of hits it receives.

Home. The upper left corner of the **display screen**; the starting position of a page or **document**.

Home page. The main page for a **Web site** established by an organization or an individual; it usually serves as the entrance for a series of related pages.

Host computer. A computer that provides information or a service to other computers on the **Internet**. Every host computer has its own unique host name.

Hot key. A **keyboard** shortcut that allows quick access to a **command** or **menu** option.

20

HTML (hypertext markup language). The formatting language used to establish the appearance of a Web page.

HTTP (hypertext transfer protocol). The **protocol** used on the **World Wide Web** that permits Web clients (**Web browsers**) to communicate with Web servers. This protocol allows programmers to embed **hyperlinks** to Web documents, using **hypertext markup language**.

Hyperlink. A highlighted word or image on a Web page. When a user clicks on a word or image, the user is connected with another related Web page.

Hypermedia. An extension of **hypertext** that integrates audio, video, and **graphics** with **text**.

Hypertext. A technology that links **text** in one part of a **document** with related text in another part of the document or in other documents. A user can quickly find the related text by clicking on the appropriate keyword, key phrase, **icon**, or button.

Hyphenation. The ability of a **program** to automatically hyphenate and divide words that do not fit at the end of a line. If the **text** is later revised so that the divided word no longer begins at the right margin, the hyphen is automatically removed and the word prints solid. (See also *Soft hyphen.*)

I-beam pointer. A **mouse**-controlled **cursor** that looks like a capital *I*.

Icon. A symbol (such as a picture of a garbage can or a file folder) that represents a certain function. When the user **clicks** on the icon, the appropriate function is **executed**.

Import. To **retrieve** any **text** or other information created by one **program** (for example, images created by a **graphics** program) and transfer it to another program (for example, a **spreadsheet** program).

Indexing. The ability of a **program** to accumulate a list of key words or phrases that appear in a **document** or a **database** and to print or display the list in a selected order.

Information processing. The coordination of people, equipment, and procedures to handle information, including the **storage**, **retrieval**, distribution, and communication of information. The term *information processing* embraces the entire field of processing words, figures, **graphics**, video, and voice **input** by electronic means.

Ink-jet printer. A non-impact printer that forms **characters** by spraying tiny, electrically charged ink droplets on paper.

Input. To enter information into the computer by using a **hardware** component (such as a **mouse**, a **keyboard**, or a microphone).

Insert. To add information to a **file**.

Insertion point. See *Cursor.*

Instant messaging (IM). A **chat** program that lets people communicate over the **Internet** in real time.

Integrated circuit. Multiple electronic components combined on a tiny silicon **chip**. (See *Microprocessor.*)

Integrated software. Combines in one **program** a number of functions normally performed by separate programs.

Interface. The electrical connection that links two pieces of equipment so that they can communicate with each other. Also, the **software** that controls the interaction between the **hardware** and the user.

Internet (or Net). A system that links existing **computer networks** into a worldwide network. The Internet may be accessed by means of commercial online services and **Internet service providers**.

Internet Protocol (IP) address. A unique set of numbers that identifies a **computer** over a **network**.

Internet service provider (ISP). An organization that provides access to the **Internet** for a fee. These organizations may provide other services in addition to **Internet** access—for example, news, travel services, and financial and shopping information.

Intranet. A private **network** established by an organization for the exclusive use of its employees. **Firewalls** protect outsiders from gaining **access** to an organization's intranet. (See also *Extranet.*)

Java. A programming **language** designed for **programs** or **applets** used over the **Internet**.

jpeg. Joint Photographic Experts Group. A **format** for storing complex **graphics** in compressed form. The file extension *jpeg* or *jpg* indicates that a particular file uses this format.

Justification. Aligning lines of **text** at the left margin, the right margin, both margins, or the centre. Text aligned at both margins is considered *fully justified.* Text aligned only at the left margin is said to have a *ragged right margin.*

Keep lines together. A Microsoft Word feature that prevents a page break within a paragraph. (See *Block protect.*)

Keep with next. A Microsoft Word feature that prevents a page break between the selected paragraph and the following paragraph. (See *Block protect.*)

Kern. To make fine adjustments in the space between any two **characters**.

Keyword. A word or phrase that briefly identifies a **document**. Keywords serve as the basis for a variety of computer operations, such as an **online** search.

Kilobyte (K or KB). A measurement of the **storage** capacity of a device. One kilobyte equals 1024 bytes.

LAN. See *Network, Local area networks.*

Landscape orientation. The positioning of a page so that information is printed across the long dimension of the paper. (See *Portrait orientation.*)

Language. The **characters** and procedures used to write **programs** that a **computer** is designed to understand.

Laptop computer. A small portable **computer**; now more commonly called a **notebook computer**.

Laser printer. A non-impact high-resolution printer that uses a rotating **disk** to reflect laser beams onto the paper. (See also *ink-jet printer.*)

Line or paragraph numbering. The ability of a **program** to automatically number each line or paragraph sequentially in a **document**. The line or paragraph numbers can be deleted before the preparation of the final **printout**.

Line spacing. The ability of a **program** to automatically change vertical line spacing (for example, from double to single to double again.)

Linux. A type of **open source software**. When combined with other components, Linux serves as an increasingly popular **operating system** that competes with Microsoft Windows.

Liquid crystal display (LCD). A type of **monitor** typically used on **laptop computers** or portable computers. (See also *Active matrix display*.)

Listserv. Any **software** that manages a **mailing list**.

Load. To transfer information or **program** instructions into a **computer's memory**.

Log off. To exit or leave a **computer** system.

Log on. To **access** a **computer** system.

Macro. A time-saving feature (like telephone speed dialling) that allows the user to store in **memory** a set of keystrokes or **commands** that will accomplish a certain repetitious task.

Macro virus. A type of **virus** that attaches itself to **documents** or **word processing templates**.

Mail merge. The process of taking information from a **database** and inserting it into a form letter or other **document** in order to customize the document for an individual recipient. For example, mail merge can be used to create the inside address and the salutation for a form letter.

Mainframe. A large **computer** system.

MAN. See *Network, Metropolitan area network*

Maximize. A **command** used in a **graphical user interface (GUI)** that enlarges a **window** so that it fills a **desktop**.

Megabyte (M or MB). The **storage** capacity measurement of a device. One megabyte equals more than a million **bytes**.

Megahertz (MHz). Identifies the speed of the **CPU**. One megahertz is equal to 1 million cycles per second.

Memory. The part of a **computer** that stores information. (See also *Storage*.)

> **Random-access memory (RAM).** The temporary memory that allows information to be stored randomly and accessed quickly and directly (without the need to go through intervening **data**).

> **Read-only memory (ROM).** The permanent **memory** of a **computer**; a set of instructions that has been built into the computer by the manufacturer and cannot be accessed or changed by the user.

Menu. A list of choices shown on the **display screen**. For example, a **format** menu would include such options as the type style and the type size to be selected. A menu is often referred to as a *pull-down menu* or a *pop-up menu* because it appears on screen after the user **clicks** on the **menu bar** or on some other item on the screen.

Menu bar. The bar across the top of the screen or window that displays the names of available **menus**.

Merge. A **command** to create one **file** by combining information that is stored in two different locations. For example, a **computer** can merge the **text** in a form letter with a mailing list to produce a batch of letters with a different name, address, and salutation on each letter. (See also *Mail merge*.)

Meta tag. A special **HTML** tag that provides information about such things as the creator of a **web** page, the **keywords** that identify the content, and other descriptive details.

Microcomputer. A small and relatively inexpensive **computer**, commonly consisting of a **display screen**, a **keyboard**, a **central processing unit**, one or more **disk drives**, and a **printer**, with limited **storage** based upon a **microprocessor**. Also referred to as a **laptop computer**, **PC**, or desktop computer.

Microprocessor. An **integrated circuit** on a silicon **chip** that serves as the **central processing unit** of a **computer**.

Minimize. A **command** used in a **graphical user interface** that reduces a **window** to an **icon** or label, usually at the bottom of a **desktop**.

MIPS. An acronym derived from millions of instructions per second. Used to measure the speed of a **computer**.

Modem. An acronym derived from modulator/demodulator. A device that (1) converts digital signals into tones for transmission over telephone lines and (2) converts the tones back into digital signals at the receiving end.

Monitor. The **display screen** of a **computer**.

Monospace font. A **typeface** such as Courier in which each **character** has exactly the same width; commonly referred to as the *fixed-pitch* or *typewriter font*.

Morph (from *metamorphosis*). To change one image into another by means of digital technology.

Motherboard. The **computer's** main **circuit board**, which contains the **central processing unit**, the **memory**, and expansion slots for additional circuit boards (called *cards*).

Mouse. A hand-operated electronic device used to move a **cursor** or pointer on the **display screen**. Mostly used with **microcomputers**.

Mouse elbow. A repetitive strain injury (similar to tennis elbow) that is caused by repeatedly using a **mouse**. (See also *Carpal tunnel syndrome*.)

Mousetrapping. Blocking someone's exit from a **Web site**.

MS-DOS (pronounced *em-ess-doss*). Derived from <u>M</u>icro<u>s</u>oft <u>d</u>isk <u>o</u>perating <u>s</u>ystem used by IBM-compatible **microcomputers**. Newer operating systems do not rely on **DOS** to the same extent, and it is predicted by some sources that DOS will eventually disappear.

Multimedia. The use of several types of media (such as **text**, **graphics**, animation, sound, and video) in a **document** or an **application**.

Multitasking. The ability of a **computer** to **execute** more than one **program** at a time.

Net. See *Internet*.

Netiquette. A set of guidelines for formatting and composing **e-mail** messages.

Network. A system of interconnected computers.

> **Local area networks (LANs)** use cable to connect a number of **computers** within the same location or at most a 2-mile radius.

Metropolitan area networks (MANs). A **data network** designed for a town or a city.

Wide area networks (WANs) use telephone lines or other **telecommunication** devices to link **computers** in widely separated locations.

Internet is a system that links existing networks into a worldwide network.

Newsgroup (also called a *chat line* or a *forum*). An electronic discussion group tied into a **bulletin board system**. Each newsgroup is typically organized around a specific interest or matter of concern.

Newsreader. A **program** that permits users to read and respond to messages posted on **Usenet**.

Non-breaking hyphen (hard hyphen). A hyphen that is a permanent **character** in a word. A word that contains a non-breaking hyphen will not be divided at this point if the word comes at the end of a line. (See also *Soft hyphen*.)

Non-breaking space (hard space). A space inserted between words in a phrase that should remain together (for example, the word page and the number, month and day, number and unit of measure). The non-breaking space ensures that the phrase will not be broken at the end of a line.

Notebook computer. A portable **computer**. Also known as a *laptop computer*.

Number crunching. Processing large amounts of numerical **data**.

Object linking and embedding (OLE). A process that permits the user to take material (referred to as an *object*) from one source and **insert** *(embed)* it in another **document**. If the user subsequently makes changes in the original material, those changes will be automatically transferred to the second document as a result of the OLE linking process.

OCR. An acronym for <u>o</u>ptical <u>c</u>haracter <u>r</u>eader.

Off-line. Referring to the state in which a **computer** is temporarily or permanently unable to communicate with another computer (although it is turned on and capable of performing other functions).

Online. Referring to the state in which a **computer** is turned on and ready to communicate with other computers.

Onscreen. Refers to anything displayed on a **computer screen**.

Open. To transfer a **file** from a **disk** into a **computer's memory**.

Open Source Software. Software that makes the underlying source code available to all users at no charge. On a voluntary basis only, users may make changes and improvements. **Linux** is an example of this software.

Operating system (OS). Software that manages the internal functions and controls the operations of a **computer**.

Option button. An **onscreen** element that allows a user to select one option from a group of items. An empty circle precedes each option not selected. A dot appears in a circle to signify that the user has selected that option. Also referred to as a *radio button*.

Orphan protection. See *Widow/orphan protection*.

Outlining. The ability of a **program** to automatically number and letter items typed in an indented **format**.

Output. The results of a **computer** operation by a **hardware** component (such as a **monitor**, a **printer**, or a sound speaker) that delivers the results of the operations to the user.

Overwriting. Recording and storing information in a specific location on a **storage medium** that destroys whatever had been stored there previously.

Packet (datagram). Pieces of a message transmitted separately over a packet-switching **network** that upon arrival are recompiled into the original message. It is more efficient for **data** that can withstand some delays in transmission, i.e., not real-time data.

Page break. A **command** that tells the **printer** where to end one page and begin the next. (See *Hard page break; Soft page break.*)

Page numbering. The ability of a **program** to automatically print page numbers on the pages that make up an entire **document**. If the document is revised and the total number of pages changes, the page numbering is automatically adjusted.

Pagination. The ability of a **program** to take information and automatically divide it into pages with a specified number of lines per page. If the information is changed because of the addition, deletion, or rearrangement of copy, the material will be automatically repaged to maintain the proper page length. (See also *Soft page break.*)

Palmtop computer. A portable **computer** smaller than a **notebook computer**. Also called a **handheld computer** or a *personal digital assistant (PDA).*

Password. A user's secret identification code, required to **access** stored material. A procedure intended to prevent information from being accessed by unauthorized persons.

Paste. A **command** that transfers information from a **clipboard** and inserts it in another location. (See *Cut and paste.*)

Patch. A small program that improves an existing piece of **software** or corrects an error in it.

PC. The common name for a **personal computer**. It is a **microcomputer** for personal and office use.

Peripheral. A device that extends the capabilities of a **computer** (for example, a **printer**).

Personal digital assistant (PDA). A palm-sized, handheld **computer**.

Personal information manager (PIM). A **database management system** that permits a user to store and **retrieve** a wide range of personal information (for example, names, addresses, appointments).

Phishing (pronounced *fi-shing*)**.** A type of computer fraud that tries to trick users into revealing their passwords and other confidential information, which could be used for identity theft.

Piracy. The illegal copying of **software**.

Pixel. An acronym derived from p<u>i</u>ct<u>u</u>re <u>el</u>ement. The smallest element (a dot) on a **display screen**. Pixels are used to construct images on the screen.

Platform. The type of **microprocessor** and **operating system** on which a **computer** is based.

20

Plug-and-play. The ability to plug in a **peripheral** and have it work without difficulty.

Point. A measurement used to indicate the size of a **font**; 72 points equals 1 inch.

Pointer. An **onscreen** device that indicates the current position of the **mouse**.

Pop-up menu. A menu that appears in a **dialog box**; often activated by a click of the right-**mouse** button.

Port. A socket on a **computer** into which an external device (such as a printer cable) can be plugged.

Portable Document Format (PDF). A **format** that makes it possible (with Adobe Acrobat) to view documents that employ different **fonts**, various types of **graphics**, and complex layouts.

Portal (Web portal). A **Web site** or service that offers access to other services such as **e-mail**, forums, **search engines**, and on-line shopping; includes most traditional search engines.

Portrait orientation. Positioning paper so that information is printed across the short dimension of the paper. (See *Landscape orientation*.)

Posting. A message entered into a **network** (such as a **newsgroup**) or on a **Web site**.

Print preview. A **software** feature that reduces the pages of a **document** so that a full page, two facing pages, or several pages can be seen on the screen before printing. This feature permits the user to spot and correct problems in **format** and **page breaks**.

Printers. Output devices of various types that produce copy on paper. (See *Ink-jet printer*; *Laser printer*.)

Program. An established sequence of instructions that tells a **computer** what to do. The term *program* means the same as **software**.

Programming language. The rules, conventions, and specific **commands** used to write a **computer program**. Most programs must be converted into machine **language** or **binary code** so that the instructions can be performed on a specific computer **platform**.

Prompt. An on-screen symbol (for example, a **cursor**) that indicates where to **type** a **command**; a message that indicates what action is to be taken.

Proportional font. A **typeface** in which the width of each **character** varies (as in this sentence), so that the letter *I* takes much less space than the letter *M*. (See *Font*.)

Protocol. A set of standards for exchanging information between **computers**.

Pull technology. A process that allows a user to request **data** from another **program** or **computer**; the opposite to **push technology**. A page on the **World Wide Web** must be requested by a **browser**, i.e., pulled.

Push technology. A process that allows a user to obtain automatic delivery of specified information from the **Internet** to the user's **computer**—sport scores, weather forecasts, stock market quotes.

Radio button. See *Option button*.

RAM. See *Memory, random-access*.

Read. To transfer information from an external storage medium into internal storage. (See also *Storage, external* and *internal.*)

Record (n.). A collection of all the information **fields** pertaining to a particular subject.

Redline. A red line through **text** on a draft **document** shows material that may be deleted on a final copy of the document. In some legal applications, the redlining stays on the **file** document so all readers are made aware of the changes in wording. **Printers** that do not support this display will print the material in a shaded panel or in some other manner. (See also *Tracked changes.*)

ROM. See *Memory, read-only.*

Row. A horizontal block of **cells** in a table or **spreadsheet**. (See also *Column.*)

RSI. Repetitive strain injury. (See also *Carpal tunnel syndrome; Mouse elbow.*)

Ruler. A bar (displayed on the screen) that shows the width of the page, the margin settings, the paragraph indentions, and the tab stops.

Save. To store a **program** or **data** on a **storage** device such as a **disk**.

Scanner. An **input** device that can copy a printed page into a **computer's memory**, thus doing away with the need to **type** the copy. A scanner can also convert artwork and photographs into a digital **format** and **store** these in memory.

Screen shot (screen capture). A **printout** of what is displayed on the screen, created with the screen print function. (See ¶1371 for an illustration.)

Screen saver. A program that changes the screen display with a moving image. Without the use of a screen saver, a screen image that remains on display for any length of time can damage the screen.

Scroll. To move information horizontally or vertically on a **display screen** so that one can see parts of a **document** that is too wide or too deep to fit entirely on one screen.

Scroll bar. An on-screen element that allows a user to **scroll** by using a **mouse**.

Search and replace. See *Global; Find and replace.*

Search engine. A free program that helps Web users locate **data** by means of a key word or concept. Among the most popular search engines are Yahoo!, Excite, WebCrawler, Google, and AltaVista.

Server. A **computer** that delivers **data** to other computers (clients) linked on the same **network**.

Shareware. Software that usually may be **downloaded** and used initially without charge; the author may subsequently ask for some payment. (Compare with *Freeware.*)

Shouting. The use of all-capital letters in **e-mail**; considered a violation of **netiquette**.

Sig block. The signature block that automatically appears at the end of every outgoing **e-mail** message. Also referred to as a *.sigfile*.

Small computer system interface (SCSI). A type of **hardware** and **software** **interface** for connecting **peripherals** such as a **disk drive** or a **CD-ROM**.

Smiley. See *Emoticon.*

20

Soft copy. Information shown on the **display screen**. (See also *Hard copy.*)

Soft hyphen. A hyphen that divides a word at the end of a line; considered soft (non-permanent) because the hyphen will automatically be deleted if the word moves to another position as a result of a change in the **text**. (See *Hard hyphen; Hyphenation.*)

Soft page break. A line inserted by the **program** to show where a page will end. If copy is added or deleted, the original **page break** will be replaced with a new soft page break at the appropriate place. (By contrast, a **hard page break** will remain fixed, no matter what changes are made in the copy.) (See also *Pagination.*)

Soft return. A **software** feature that automatically breaks **text** between words at the right margin. The line ending is considered soft (non-permanent) because the line ending will change if the user adds or deletes **text**. (See *Hard return; Wordwrap.*)

Software. The instructions that a **computer** needs to perform various functions. The term *software* means the same as **program**. (See also *Hardware.*)

Sort. To arrange **fields**, **records**, or **files** in a predetermined sequence.

Spam. The electronic equivalent of junk mail; also called *unsolicited commercial e-mail* (UCE).

Spam guards. A filter (or a **program**) which can keep junk mail from coming into an **e-mail** box.

Spider. An automated **program** that searches the **Internet** for new **Web sites** and indexes their **URLs** and content descriptions in a **database** for examination by a **search engine** for matches.

Split screen. The ability of some **programs** to display information in two or more different areas on the screen at the same time. (See also *Windowing.*)

Spreadsheet. A **program** that provides a worksheet with **rows** and **columns** to be used for calculations and the preparation of reports.

Status line. A line of information on the **display screen** that indicates the position of the **cursor**, the page number, the **file** name, and any toggle keys in use (bold, typeover, capitals, etc.).

Storage. The **memory** of a **computer**.

> **External storage.** A **flash drive** or a **magnetic medium** such as a **disk**, diskette, tape, **CD**, or **DVD** used to store information; can be removed from the **computer**.

> **Internal storage.** An integral component of a **computer (hard drive)**; cannot be removed.

Store. To place information in **memory** for later use.

Streaming. The process of sending and temporarily storing large amounts of audio or video information in small pieces and playing them back on the **computer** so that there is a continuous flow.

Style sheet. A collection of the user's formatting decisions regarding **typeface**, font size, margins, **justification**, paragraph indentions, and the like.

Surfing the net. Browsing through various **Web sites** on the **Internet** in search of interesting things.

Surge protector. A device that protects **computer hardware** from being damaged by sudden increases in voltage.

Tablet. A computer that accepts handwritten notes entered on the display screen by means of an electronic pen. The notes are then converted into text.

Telecommunications. The process of sending and receiving information by means of telephones, satellites, and other devices.

Telecommuter. An employee who works away from the office (usually at home) and uses a **computer** (1) to **access** needed information on the organization's **intranet** and the **Internet** and (2) to communicate with other employees, suppliers, and customers or clients.

Teleconferencing. Conducting a conference by using **computers**, video, and **telecommunications** to share sound and images with others at remote sites.

Template. A pre-established **format** for a **document**, stored in a **computer**. The template determines the margins, the type style and size to be used for the **text**, placement instructions for various elements (such as the date line), and design specifications for certain items (such as a letterhead). A user can simply call up the appropriate template, **insert text** where needed, and then print a final document. The user can modify the original template or create a new template to satisfy personal preferences.

Terabyte. A measurement of the **storage** capacity of a device. One terabyte is equal to approximately 1 trillion **bytes**.

Terminal. Any device that can transmit or receive electronic information.

Text. The written material to be displayed on a screen or printed on paper.

TIFF (Tagged Image File Format). A widely supported file format for storing or transferring black and white or coloured **bitmap** images on **PC computers**. **File** names often show a .tif extension.

Tool bar. See *Button bar*.

Touchpad. The device on a laptop computer that takes the place of a **mouse**.

Touchscreen technology. The technology that permits a user to perform a function simply by touching the screen in an appropriate spot.

Trackball. An input device in which the user rolls a ball to move the **pointer**.

Tracked changes. A feature of some **software** which facilitates **online** review of **documents**. Users involved in creating the document can make and view all changes in the original draft. (See also *Redline*.)

Transfer Rate. The rate at which **data** is transmitted between two **computers** or other electronic equipment.

Transmission Control Protocol/Internet Protocol (TCP/IP). A collection of over 100 **protocols** that are used to connect **computers** and **networks**.

Typeover. See *Overwriting*.

Upload. To transfer information from a **client computer** to a **host** computer.

URL. The acronym of uniform resource locator. It is the specific **Internet** address for an individual or an organization. (See *World Wide Web*.)

20

Usenet (from Users' Network). A **bulletin board system** that hosts thousands of **newsgroups**.

User-friendly. A description for equipment or **application software** that is easy to use.

Userid (pronounced *user-eye-dee*). The name a person must use, along with a **password**, to gain **access** to restricted areas on a **network**.

Variable. Information in a standard **document** that changes each time the document is produced (for example, the name and address in a form letter).

Virtual reality. See *Cyberspace*.

Virus. A **program** designed as a prank or as a malicious act. When a virus invades another program, it can cause serious damage to **memory** or **disks**. (See *Denial of service attack, Antivirus software*.)

Voice over Internet Protocol (VoIP). The transmission of voice communications by means of the **Internet Protocol**. VoIP is an inexpensive alternative to long-distance telephone calls.

Web browser. Software that permits a user—with the click of a **mouse**—to locate, display, and download **text**, video, audio, and **graphics** stored in a **host computer** on the Web. Common Web browsers are Netscape Navigator and Microsoft Explorer.

Web site. One or more related pages created by an individual or an organization and posted on the **World Wide Web**. (See also *Home Page*.)

Webcam. A video camera that sends live images over the **Internet** to a **Web site**.

Webcaster. An **application** that can be custom-tailored to satisfy each user's need for constantly updated information in specific areas and will automatically deliver the needed information to the user's **computer**.

Webmaster. The person who maintains a specific **Web site** and is responsible for what appears there.

Wide-Area Information Server (WAIS). An **Internet** search system that will locate **documents** that contain **keywords** specified by the user.

Wide area network (WAN). See *Network, wide area networks*.

Widow/orphan protection. The ability of a **program** to avoid printing the first line of a paragraph as the last line of a page and to avoid printing the last line of a paragraph as the first line of the following page.

Wi-Fi. Wireless fidelity. A process that permits high-speed wireless transmission of data.

Wiki. A procedure that permits a **Web site** to be continually added to by those who visit the site.

Window. A frame that permits users to view messages they have received or **documents** they are working on.

Wizard. A feature of Microsoft Word **software** that helps a user create a customized **document**; it asks the user questions about formatting and content options and uses the answers to create the document. (In WordPerfect this feature is called an *expert*.)

Word processing. The electronic process of creating, formatting, **editing**, proof-reading, and printing **documents**. (See *Information processing*.)

Wordwrap. A **software** feature that detects when a word will extend beyond the right margin and automatically transfers it to the beginning of the next line.

Workstation. A **desktop computer** that runs **applications** and serves as an access point in a **local area network**. (See also *Network*.)

World Wide Web. The component of the **Internet** that combines audio, video, and **graphics** with **text**. Also called the *Web* or *WWW*.

Worm. A type of **computer virus** that runs a **program** to destroy **data** on a user's **hard drive**. Worms spread by sending copies of themselves to everyone in the user's **e-mail** address book.

 See the Online Learning Centre at www.mcgrawhill.ca/college/gregg for related Web links.

INDEX

To find individual words not listed in the index, please refer to ¶719, which is a 12-page guide to words that are often confused because they sound or look alike.

Grammatical terms are defined in the "Glossary of Grammatical Terms" (Section 19).

Computer terms are defined in the "Glossary of Computer and Internet Terms" (Section 20).

NOTE: **Boldface** numbers refer to paragraph numbers; lightface numbers refer to page numbers. Words referred to as words are *italicized*.

asterisk, **293**
 spacing with, **298**
as though clauses, **1042–1043**
as well as, 285
attributions
 dash before, **212**
awards, **364**, **519**
awhile, a while, 286

B
B.C. See A.D., 282
back matter of formal reports, **1428–1431**
bad, badly, 286
because. See reason is because
being that, 286
beside, besides, 286
between, among, 286
between you and me, **1055b**
biannual, biennial, semi-annual, 286
bibliographies, **1545–1549**
 academic, **1549c**
 alphabetizing, **1587a**
 author's name, **1547–1548**
 elements of, **1549**
 formatting, **1546–1548**
bills, **346**
bimonthly. See bimonthly
birthdays, **435**
biweekly, 287
blog, 534
both, both alike, both equal, both together, 287
brackets, **296–297** (*see also* parentheses)
 and italics, **288d**
brand names, **355–356**
breaks
 after dash, **920g**
 with ellipsis points, **920g**
breaks between words
 addresses, **920b**
 dates, **920a**
 in enumerations, **920f**
 names of persons, **920d**
 place names, **920c**
 titles of persons, **920e**
bring, take, 287
broadcasting systems, **523**
business correspondence
 writing style in, **1097–1098**
business documents, 476–505, **1701–1719**
 (*see also* agendas; e-mail; fax cover

sheets; itineraries; letters; manuscripts;
memos; minutes; outlines; reports)
 colon in, **194**
 formatting, **1701–1702**
business expressions
 abbreviations of, **541–542**
business names
 abbreviations, of, **520–521**
but . . . however, 287
but, omission of, **176**
but what, 287

C
Canadian Oxford Dictionary, 175, **503 note**
can, could. See may, can
capitalization, 89–112
 of abbreviations, **514**
 of academic degrees, **353**
 of academic years, **354**
 of acts, **346**
 of advertising material, **357**
 of amounts of money, **420c**
 of awards and medals, **364**
 basic rules, **301–310**
 of bills, **346**
 of brand names, **355–356**
 of celestial bodies, **351**
 of centuries, **345**
 of *city,* **334**
 after colon, **196–199**
 of commercial products, **355–356**
 of common nouns, **309**
 of computer terminology, **365**
 of courses, **352**
 of cultural eras, **344**
 of days, **342**
 of decades, **345**
 of displayed lists and outlines, **301e**
 of family and religious titles, **318–319**
 of *federal,* **328**
 of first words, **301**
 of government bodies, **325–330**
 of government programs, **347**
 of headings, **360–361**
 of historical events and periods, **344**
 of holidays, **342**
 of hyphenated words, **363**
 of languages, **348**
 of laws, **346**
 in legal documents, **358**

computer and Internet terms
definitions of, 533–553
computer terms
capitalization of, **365**
compound, **847**
confer on, confer upon, confer with, 275
confidential notation, **1314**
conjugation
of *to see, to be, to have*, 244–245
conjunctions
capitalization, **303**
correlative, **1085c**
in organizational names, **303 note**,
1215c
considerate tone in writing, **1094**
consist of, include, 288
consonants, 532
contractions, **505**
apostrophes in, **505**
not to be divided, **906**
contrasting expressions
commas with, **147**
conversations, quoted, 269–270
Copyright Office, **1435**
copyright protection, **1435**
correspondance. *See* letters
could not care less, 289
couples (forms of address)
married with different surnames, **1802e**
married with hyphenated surname, **1802f**
married with same surname
both with special titles, **1802d**
husband with special title, **1802b**
no special titles, **1802a**
wife with special title, **1802c**
unmarried, living together, **1802g**
courses, capitalization of, **352**
courteous tone in writing, **1095**
cultural eras, **344**
curriculum vitaes (CVs), **1707h note**

D

danglers, **1086** (*see also* misplaced
modifiers)
elliptical clauses as, **1086d**
gerundial phrases as, **1086c**
infinitive phrases as, **1086b**
participial phrases as, **1086a**
dash, **201–217**
before attributions, **212**

break after, **920g**
in place of colon, **205**
to emphasize words, **210–211**
how to construct, **216**
in place of comma, **201–203**
in place of parentheses, **206**
in place of semicolon, **204**
other punctuation with, **213–215**
position of in line, **217**
with quotation marks, **250**
to show abrupt break or hesitation,
207–209
spacing with, **298**
data, **1018b**
database, 537
dates, **401b, 407–412**
class graduation years, **412**
commas, **122, 154–155, 410**
complete, **409**
division of, **920a**
formal invitations, **411**
legal documents, **411**
numbers in, **407–412**
parentheses in, **221**
punctuation of, **122e, 154–155, 410**
in sentences, **407–412**
on title page, **1413h**
well-known historical years, **412**
days, **342**, 532
decades, **345, 439**
decimal fractions, **443–446**
period with, **105**
declarative sentences, 530
definitions
of computer and Internet terms,
533–553
formatting of, **238, 285b**
of grammatical terms, 521–532
degrees. *See* academic degrees
demand
clauses of, **1038**
departments, capitalization of, **323**
dependant, dependent, 289
dependent clauses
commas with, **131**
essential and non-essential, **131**
interruption of flow, **131c**
introductory
commas with, **130**
other than introductory, **131**

essential clauses, **131**
essential expressions, **260**, **261c**
  punctuation with, **149–151**
ess, as suffix, **840**
etc., and so on, such as, 290
etc., comma with, **164**
ette, as suffix, **840**
ever, **1072**
every, **1009a**
every- words, **1010**, **1011**, **1053a**
everyday, every day, 290
ex, **808**
ex, former, 291
ex-, with titles, **317**
except, 291
exclamation mark, **119–121**
  to express strong feeling, **119**
  after *oh* and *O*, **121**
  in parentheses, **119c**
  in place of question mark, **119b**
  with quotation marks, **249**
  after single word, **120a**
  spacing with, **298**
exclamations
  with comma or period, **120c**
explanatory expressions, **148–152**
  punctuation of, **148–152**
extranet, 539
e-zine, 539

F
family titles, **318–319**
farther, further, 291
fax cover sheets, **1706**
federal, capitalization of, **328**
federal government names, **1221**
fewer, less, 291
filing
  alphabetical, **1207–1223**
  basic principles, **1207–1209**
  by governmental name, **1221–1223**
    federal, **1221**
    local, **1222**
    provincial, **1222**
  by hyphenated name, **1212**
  by name with abbreviation or nickname, **1213**
  by name of person, **1210–1214**
  by name with prefix, **1211**
  by organizational address, **1220**
  by organizational name, **1215–1219**

    abbreviations in, **1217**
    acronyms in, **1217**
    compound words in, **1215d**
    conjunctions in, **1215c**
    geographic names in, **1218**
    letters in, **1217**
    numbers in, **1219**
    order of words in, **1215e**
    person's name within, **1216**
    prepositions in, **1215c**
    punctuation in, **1215b**
    symbols in, **1217**
  by person's name with title or suffix, **1214**
firewall, 540
first, firstly, 291
first, former, 291
flammable, inflammable, 291
follow-up letter, 502, **1713**
font. 540
footnotes, **1501** (*see also* endnotes; source notes; textnotes)
  format and position of, **1503–1504**
  MS Word default format for, 423
  standard format for, 424, 425
  text references to, **1502**
foreign expressions
  abbreviations, of, **544**
  italics, **285d**
foreign words, **285d**, 614
for example, **181–183**
former (see also *ex*)
  with titles, **317**
former, first, 291
formal report
  back matter, **1428–1431**
    appendixes, **1429**
    bibliography, **1430**
    endnotes, **1430**
    glossary, **1431**
  body, **1422–1427**
    bulleted items, **1425g**
    chapter-opening pages, **1424**
    drafts, **1425b**
    enumerated items, **1425f**
    indentations, **1425**
    introduction, **1422**
    lists, **1425e**
    page numbering, **1427**
    paragraphs, **1425c**

Q

quantity
  and subject-verb agreement, **1024**
quasi, **841**
question mark, **110–118**
  with direct questions, **110–113**
  to express doubt, **118**
  with requests, **103, 113**
  with questions within sentences, **114–117**
  with quotation marks, **249**
  spacing with, **298**
questions
  direct, **110–113**
    at beginning of sentence, **117**
    at end of sentence, **115**
  elliptical, **111, 117c**
  indirect, **115**
  rhetorical, **110b**
  within sentence
    capitalization of, **301d**
quotation marks, **227–284** (*see also*
    quotations; quoting)
  alignment of, **284**
  apostrophe as single quotation mark,
    245–246, 247b, 248b, 249d, 250b,
    265b
  with colloquial expressions, **236c**
  with colons and semicolons, **248, 256**
  with commas, **247, 253–255, 256,**
    259–261
  with dashes, **250**
  with definitions, **238**
  with dialogue, **269–270**
  with direct questions, **229**
  with direct quotations, **227–233**
  with foreign expressions, **241**
  for humour or irony, **236**
  with indirect quotations, **228**
  for interior thoughts, **230**
  with parentheses, **251**
  with periods, **247, 252, 253, 257–259**
  placement of, **232**
  with question marks and exclamation
    marks, **249, 252, 254, 257–259,**
    261b–c
  spacing with, **298**
  for special emphasis, **235**
  with technical or coined words, **235**
  with titles of literary and artistic works,
    242–244

  with translations, **241**
  when not to use, **228–230, 233, 234,**
    236c, 237b
  with words used abnormally, **237**
  with *yes* and *no*, **233**
quotations (*see also* quotation marks;
    quoting)
  at beginning of sentence, **253–255**
  in body of letter, **1344a**
  capitalization in, **272–273**
  capitalization of, **199b**
  direct, **227–233**
  at end of sentence, **256–258**
  in formal reports, **1425d**
  of fragment of sentence, **277**
  of fragment of sentence at beginning of
    displayed quotation, **278**
  indirect, **228**
  insertions in, **281–283**
  interrupted, **262**
  long, **264–265**
  omissions in, **274–280**
  as part of sentence, **259–261**
  preceded by *that*, **256f**
  punctuation of, **252**
  within quotation, **245–246**
  standing alone, **252**
  and style of original, **271**
quoting
  of business documents, **266**
  of dialogue and conversation, **269–270**
  of poetry, **267–268**

R

races, **348**
radio and television programs
  quotation marks with, **244**
radio and television stations, **523**
ragged right
  in letters, **1343h**
raise, rise, **299**
ratios, **401b, 450**
  colon in, **193**
re, as prefix, **837**
real, really, **299**
reason is because, **299**
redundancy, **1082**
references
  parentheses with, **220**
religious holidays and periods, **342**
religious orders, **519, 1323d**

and fractions, **1025**
and geographic names, **1021**
and indefinite pronouns
    plural, **1012–1013**
    singular, **1009–1011**, **1013**
in inverted sentences, **1027–1028**
and money, **1024**
and names
    of organizations, **1020**
    of publications and products, **1022**
and nouns ending in *ics*, **1017**
and nouns ending in *s*, **1014–1016**
and nouns with foreign plurals, **1018**
with phrase as subject, **1026**
and predicate complements, **1029**
subjects joined by *and*, **1002**
subjects joined by *or*, **1003–1005**
with *the (a) number*, **1023**
with *there is, there are*, **1028**
and time expressions, **1024**
subjunctive, **1038–1040**
subtitle
    comma before, **195**
such as. See *etc.*
suffixes, **487**, **833**, **840**, **846**
    feminine, **840**
    less, **846**
    like, **846**
    word division, **910–912**
superlative degree. *See* adjectives; adverbs
supposed to, 302
sure and, 302
sure, surely, 302
syllabication, **921–922**
symbols
    chemical, **539**
    common, **543**
    plural of, **621**

T
table feature, software, **452**, **1601–1606**
table of contents, **1403a**, **1415–1416**
tables, 451–475
    amounts of money in, **1626**
    centring, **1614**
    column headings in, 464, **1619–1621**
    items omitted from, **1630**
    leaders in, **1629**
    location in text, **1607–1609**
    long, **1634–1636**

made with software table feature, 452, **1601–1606**
name and number of, **1615–1618**
notes in, **1631–1633**
percentages in, **1627**
on separate pages, **1610–1613**
special treatment of figures in, **1628**
text of, **1622–1630**
    figures only, **1625**
    spacing of, **1622**
    words only, **1623**
used for résumé, **1624**
wide, **1637**
take. See *bring*
teach. See *learn*
telephone numbers, **454**
television stations, **523**
tenses. *See* verbs
tenses, sequence of, **1041**
textnotes, **1501**, **1507** (*see also* endnotes;
    footnotes; source notes)
    format for, 427–428
than, **1057**
than, then, 302
that, 303, **1062**
    before quotation, **256f**
that is, **181–183**
that, where. See *where, that*
the, capitalization of, **324**
therefore, **122c**, **138–142**, **178**
there is, there are
    and subject-verb agreement, **1028**
this here, 303
this sort, this kind, 303
time
    of day, **401b**, **440–442**
    expressions of
        colon in, **192**
        and subject-verb agreement, **1024**
    periods of, **436–439**
time zones, **533**
title page, **1403a**, **1413**
    date, **1413h**
titles of literary and artistic works, **239b**,
    360–362
    capitalization, **360–362**
    colon with, **195a**
    italicized, **287**
    and quotation marks, **242–244**
titles of persons, **1324a** (*see also* forms of